2nd Joint Conference on Lexical and Computational Semantics

(SEM 2013)

Held with SemEval 2013

Atlanta, Georgia, USA
13 – 14 June 2013

ISBN: 978-1-63439-626-4

Printed from e-media with permission by:

Curran Associates, Inc.
57 Morehouse Lane
Red Hook, NY 12571

Printed by Curran Associates, Inc. (2015)

For permission requests, please contact the Association for Computational Linguistics at the address below.

Association for Computational Linguistics
209 N. Eighth Street
Stroudsburg, Pennsylvania 18360

Phone: 1-570-476-8006
Fax: 1-570-476-0860

acl@aclweb.org

Additional copies of this publication are available from:

Curran Associates, Inc.
57 Morehouse Lane
Red Hook, NY 12571 USA
Phone: 845-758-0400
Fax: 845-758-2634
Email: curran@proceedings.com
Web: www.proceedings.com

Volume 1:

*SEM 2013: The Second Joint Conference on Lexical and Computational Semantics

Proceedings of the Main Conference and the Shared Task: Semantic Textual Similarity

June 13-14, 2013
Atlanta, Georgia, USA

Production and Manufacturing by
Omnipress, Inc.
2600 Anderson Street
Madison, WI 53707
USA

Sponsored in part by:
The US Defense Advanced Research Projects Agency (DARPA)

Organized and sponsored in part by:
The ACL Special Interest Group on the Lexicon (SIGLEX)
The ACL Special Interest Group on Computational Semantics (SIGSEM)

Introduction to *SEM 2013

Building on the momentum generated by the spectacular success of the Joint Conference on Lexical and Computational Semantics (*SEM) in 2012, bringing together the ACL SIGLEX and ACL SIGSEM communities, we are delighted to bring to you the second edition of the conference, as a top-tier showcase of the latest research in computational semantics. We accepted 14 papers (11 long and 3 short) for publication at the conference, out of a possible 45 submissions (a 31% acceptance rate). This is on par with some of the most competitive conferences in computational linguistics, and we are confident will set the stage for a scintillating conference.

This year, we started a tradition that we intend to maintain in all future iterations of the conference in integrating a shared task into the conference. The shared task was selected by an independent committee comprising members from SIGLEX and SIGSEM, based on an open call for proposals, and revolved around Semantic Textual Similarity (STS). The task turned out to be a huge success with 34 teams participating, submitting a total of 103 system runs.

*SEM 2013 features a number of highlight events:

Day One, June 13th:

- A timely and impressive panel on *Towards Deep Natural Language Understanding*, featuring the following panelists:
  - Kevin Knight (USC/Information Sciences Institute)
  - Chris Manning (Stanford University)
  - Martha Palmer (University of Colorado at Boulder)
  - Owen Rambow (Columbia University)
  - Dan Roth (University of Illinois at Urbana-Champaign)
- A Reception and Shared Task Poster Session in the evening, thanks to the generous sponsorship of the DARPA Deft program.

Day Two, June 14th:

- In the morning, a keynote address by David Forsyth from the Computer Science Department at the University of Illinois at Urbana Champagne on issues of Vision and Language. It promises to be an extremely stimulating speech, and is not to be missed.
- In the early afternoon, a panel on the relation between and future of *SEM, the *SEM Shared Task, SemEval and other events on computational semantics. In this panel, we will attempt to clarify and explain as well as devise plans for these different entities.
- Finally, at the end of the day, an award ceremony for the Best Long Paper and Best Short Paper.

As always, *SEM 2013 would not have been possible without the considerable efforts of our area chairs and an impressive assortment of reviewers, drawn from the ranks of SIGLEX and SIGSEM, and the computational semantics community at large. We would also like to acknowledge the generous support for the STS Task from the DARPA Deft Program.

We hope you enjoy *SEM 2013, and look forward to engaging with all of you,

Mona Diab (The George Washington University, General Chair)
Timothy Baldwin (The University of Mebourne, Program Committee Co-Chair)
Marco Baroni (University of Trento, Program Committee Co-Chair)

Introduction to SemEval

The Semantic Evaluation (SemEval) series of workshops focus on the evaluation and comparison of systems that can analyse diverse semantic phenomena in text with the aim of extending the current state-of-the-art in semantic analysis and creating high quality annotated datasets in a range of increasingly challenging problems in natural language semantics. SemEval provides an exciting forum for researchers to propose challenging research problems in semantics and to build systems/techniques to address such research problems.

SemEval-2013 is the seventh workshop in the series. The first three workshops, SensEval-1 (1998), SensEval-2 (2001), and SensEval-3 (2004), were focused on word sense disambiguation, each time growing in the number of languages offered in the tasks and in the number of participating teams. In 2007 the workshop was renamed SemEval and in the next three workshops SemEval-2007, SemEval-2010 and SemEval-2012 the nature of the tasks evolved to include semantic analysis tasks outside of word sense disambiguation. Starting in 2012 SemEval turned into a yearly event associated with *SEM.

This volume contains papers accepted for presentation at the SemEval-2013 International Workshop on Semantic Evaluation Exercises. SemEval-2013 is co-organized with the *SEM-2013 The Second Joint Conference on Lexical and Computational Semantics and co-located with The 2013 Conference of the North American Chapter of the Association for Computational Linguistics: Human Language Technologies (NAACL HLT).

SemEval-2013 included the following 12 tasks for evaluation:

- TempEval-3 Temporal Annotation
- Sentiment Analysis in Twitter
- Spatial Role Labeling
- Free Paraphrases of Noun Compounds
- Evaluating Phrasal Semantics
- The Joint Student Response Analysis and 8th Recognizing Textual Entailment Challenge
- Cross-lingual Textual Entailment for Content Synchronization
- Extraction of Drug-Drug Interactions from BioMedical Texts
- Cross-lingual Word Sense Disambiguation
- Evaluating Word Sense Induction & Disambiguation within An End-User Application
- Multilingual Word Sense Disambiguation
- Word Sense Induction for Graded and Non-Graded Senses

About 100 teams submitted more than 300 systems for the 12 tasks of SemEval-2013. This volume contains both Task Description papers that describe each of the above tasks and System Description papers that describe the systems that participated in the above tasks. A total of 12 task description papers and 101 system description papers are included in this volume.

We are indebted to all program committee members for their high quality, elaborate and thoughtful reviews. The papers in this proceedings have surely benefited from this feedback. We are grateful to *SEM 2013 and NAACL-HLT 2013 conference organizers for local organization and the forum. We most gratefully acknowledge the support of our sponsors, the ACL Special Interest Group on the Lexicon (SIGLEX) and the ACL Special Interest Group on Computational Semantics (SIGSEM).

Welcome to SemEval-2013!

Suresh Manandhar and Deniz Yuret

Organizers:

General Chair:

Mona Diab (George Washington University)

Program Committee Chairs:

Tim Baldwin (University of Melbourne)
Marco Baroni (University of Trento)

STS Shared Task Committee Chairs:

Anna Korhonen (University of Cambridge)
Malvina Nissim (University of Bologna)

SemEval Chairs:

Suresh Manandhar (University of York, UK)
Deniz Yuret (Koc University, Turkey)

Publications Chair:

Yuval Marton (Microsoft)

Sponsorship Chair:

Bernardo Magnini (Fondazione Bruno Kessler)

Panel organizer:

Martha Palmer (University of Colorado, Boulder)

Area Chairs:

Shane Bergsma (Johns Hopkins University)
Chris Biemann (TU Darmstadt)
Eduardo Blanco (Lymba Corporation)
Gemma Boleda (University of Texas, Austin)
Francis Bond (Nanyang Technological University)
Paul Cook (University of Melbourne)
Amaç Herdagdelen (Facebook)
Lauri Karttunen (Stanford University)
Diana McCarthy (University of Cambridge)
Roser Morante (University of Antwerp)
Smara Muresan (Rutgers University)
Preslav Nakov (Qatar Computing Research Institute)
Roberto Navigli (Sapienza University of Rome)
Hwee Tou Ng (National University of Singapore)
Becky Passonneau (Columbia University)
Laura Rimell (University of Cambridge)
Caroline Sporleder (University of Trier)
Fabio Massimo Zanzotto (University of Rome Tor Vergata)

Program Committee for Volume 1:

Nabil Abdullah (University of Windsor), Eneko Agirre (University of the Basque Country), Nicholas Asher (CNRS Institut de Recherche en Informatique de Toulouse), Eser Aygün, Timothy Baldwin (The University of Melbourne), Eva Banik (Computational Linguistics Ltd), Marco Baroni (University of Trento), Alberto Barrón-Cedeño (Universitat Politècnica de Catalunya), Roberto Basili (University of Roma, Tor Vergata), Miroslav Batchkarov (University of Sussex), Cosmin Bejan, Sabine Bergler (Concordia University), Shane Bergsma (Johns Hopkins University), Steven Bethard (University of Colorado Boulder), Ergun Bicici (Centre for Next Generation Localisation), Chris Biemann (TU Darmstadt), Eduardo Blanco (Lymba Corporation), Gemma Boleda (The University of Texas at Austin), Francis Bond (Nanyang Technological University), Paul Buitelaar (DERI, National University of Ireland, Galway), Razvan Bunescu (Ohio University), Harry Bunt (Tilburg University), Aljoscha Burchardt (DFKI), Davide Buscaldi (LIPN, Université Paris 13), Olivia Buzek (Johns Hopkins University), Nicoletta Calzolari (ILC-CNR), Annalina Caputo (Dept. Computer Science - Univ. of Bari Aldo Moro), Sandra Carberry (University of Delaware), Marine Carpuat (National Research Council), Irene Castellon (University of Barcelona), Julio Castillo (National University of Cordoba), Daniel Cer (Stanford University), Yee Seng Chan (Raytheon BBN Technologies), David Chen (Google), Colin Cherry (NRC), Jackie Chi Kit Cheung (University of Toronto), Christian Chiarcos, Sung-Pil Choi, Grzegorz Chrupała (Tilburg University), Philipp Cimiano (Univ. Bielefeld), Daoud Clarke, Bob Coecke (Oxford University), Paul Cook (The University of Melbourne), Bonaventura Coppola (IBM Research), Danilo Croce (University of Roma, Tor Vergata), Montse Cuadros (Vicomtech-IK4), Walter Daelemans (University of Antwerp, CLiPS), Ido Dagan (Bar-Ilan University), Avishek Dan (Indian Institute of Technology Bombay), Kareem Darwish (Qatar Computing Research Institute, Qatar Foundation), Dipanjan Das (Google Inc.), Marie-Catherine de Marneffe (The Ohio State University), Gerard de Melo (ICSI Berkeley), Pascal Denis, Mona Diab (GWU), Georgiana Dinu (University of Trento), Bill Dolan (Microsoft Research), Rebecca Dridan (University of Oslo), Kevin Duh (Nara Institute of Science and Technology), Micha Elsner (The Ohio State University), David Elson (Google), Stefan Evert (FAU Erlangen-Nürnberg), Dan Flickinger (Stanford), Anette Frank (Heidelberg Universiy), Andre Freitas (DERI, National University of Ireland, Galway), Claire Gardent (CNRS/LORIA, Nancy), Spandana Gella (University of Melbourne), Matthew Gerber (University of Virginia), Eugenie Giesbrecht (Karlsruhe Institute of Technology), Kevin Gimpel (Toyota Technological Institute at Chicago), Claudio Giuliano (FBK), Dan Goldwasser (University of Maryland), Edward Grefenstette (University of Oxford Department of Computer Science), Weiwei Guo (Columbia University), Iryna Gurevych (Ubiquitous Knowledge Processing (UKP) Lab), Yoan Gutiérrez (University of Matanzas), Nizar Habash (Columbia University), Bo Han (University of Melbourne), Lushan Han (University of Maryland, Baltimore County), Chikara Hashimoto (NICT), Mike Heilman (Educational Testing Service), Iris Hendrickx (Center for Language Studies, Radboud University Nijmegen), Verena Henrich (University of Tübingen), Aurelie Herbelot (Universität Potsdam), Amac Herdagdelen (Facebook), Veronique Hoste (Ghent University), Dirk Hovy (USC's Information Sciences Institute), Nancy Ide (Vassar College), Adrian Iftene (Al. I. Cuza University of Iasi), Diana Inkpen (University of Ottawa), Sambhav Jain (LTRC, IIIT Hyderabad), Sneha Jha, Sergio Jimenez (National University of Colombia), Richard Johansson (University of Gothenburg), David Jurgens (University of California, Los Angeles), Dimitri Kartsaklis (University of Oxford), Lauri Karttunen (Stanford University), Sophia Katrenko (Utrecht University), Bill Keller (The University of Sussex), Douwe Kiela (University of Cambridge Computer Laboratory), Su Nam Kim, Alexandre Klementiev (Saarland University), Valia Kordoni (Humboldt University Berlin), Ioannis Korkontzelos (National Centre for Text Mining, The University of Manchester), Zornitsa Kozareva (USC Information Sciences Institute), Ivana Kruijff-Korbayova, Man Lan (ECNU), Jey Han Lau (University of Melbourne), Yoong Keok Lee (MIT), Alessandro Lenci (University of Pisa), Maria Liakata (University of

Warwick), Ting Liu, Nitin Madnani (Educational Testing Service), Nikolaos Malandrakis (Signal Analysis and Interpretation Laboratory (SAIL), USC, Los Angeles, CA 90089, USA), Suresh Manandhar (University of York), Daniel Marcu (SDL), Erwin Marsi (Norwegian University of Science and Technology (NTNU)), Toni Marti (University of Barcelona), Diana McCarthy (University of Cambridge (DTAL)), John McCrae (University Bielefeld), Rada Mihalcea (University of North Texas), Shachar Mirkin (Xerox Research Centre Europe), Ray Mooney (University of Texas at Austin), Roser Morante (University of Antwerp), Paul Morarescu (Syracuse University), Mathieu Morey (Aix-Marseille Université), Alessandro Moschitti (DIS, University of Trento), Rutu Mulkar, Smaranda Muresan (Rutgers University), Preslav Nakov (Qatar Computing Research Institute, Qatar Foundation), Vivi Nastase (FBK), Roberto Navigli (Sapienza University of Rome), Ani Nenkova (University of Pennsylvania), Hwee Tou Ng (National University of Singapore), Shengjian Ni (College of Chinese Language and Literature,Wuhan University), John Niekrasz, malvina nissim (University of Bologna), Diarmuid Ó Séaghdha (University of Cambridge), Brendan O'Connor (Carnegie Mellon University), Kemal Oflazer (Carnegie Mellon University - Qatar), Akira Ohtani (Osaka Gakuin University), Manabu Okumura (Tokyo Institute of Technology), Lubomir Otrusina (Faculty of Information Technology, Brno University of Technology), Sebastian Pado (Heidelberg University), Alexis Palmer (Saarland University), Martha Palmer (University of Colorado), Rebecca J. Passonneau (Columbia University), Michael J. Paul (Johns Hopkins University), Anselmo Peñas (NLP & IR Group, UNED), Sasa Petrovic, Mohammad Taher Pilehvar (Sapienza University of Rome), Manfred Pinkal (Saarland University), Emily Pitler (University of Pennsylvania), Laura Plaza, Massimo Poesio (University of Essex), Tamara Polajnar (University of Cambridge), Simone Paolo Ponzetto (University of Mannheim), Hoifung Poon (Microsoft Research), octavian popescu (FBK-irst), Matt Post (Johns Hopkins University), Alexandros Potamianos (Technical University of Crete), Richard Power, Vinodkumar Prabhakaran (Columbia University), Stephen Pulman (Oxford University), Uwe Quasthoff, Carlos Ramisch (Université Joseph Fourier), Delip Rao (Johns Hopkins University), Reinhard Rapp (Aix-Marseille Université), Jonathon Read (University of Oslo), Marta Recasens (Stanford University), Siva Reddy (University of Edinburgh), Ines Rehbein (Potsdam University), Joseph Reisinger, Antonio Reyes (Laboratorio de Tecnologías Lingüísticas, Instituto Superior de Intérpretes y Traductores), Hannes Rieser, German Rigau (UPV/EHU), Ellen Riloff (University of Utah), Laura Rimell (University of Cambridge), Alan Ritter (University of Washington), Horacio Rodriguez (UPC), Carolyn Rose (Carnegie Mellon University), Andrew Rosenberg (CUNY Queens College), Paolo Rosso (Universitat Politècnica de València), Josef Ruppenhofer, patrick saint-dizier (IRIT-CNRS), Mark Sammons (University of Illinois at Urbana-Champaign), Fernando Sánchez-Vega (Laboratorio de Tecnologías del Lenguaje, Instituto Nacional de Astrofísica, Óptica y Electrónica, Puebla, Estado de México), Marina Santini, Christina Sauper, Roser Saurí (Barcelona Media), Hansen Andrew Schwartz (University of Pennsylvania), Aliaksei Severyn (University of Trento), Ehsan Shareghi (Concordia University - Master's Student), Eyal Shnarch (Bar Ilan University), Niraj Shrestha (KUL), Ekaterina Shutova (University of California at Berkeley), Ravi Sinha, Gabriel Skantze (KTH Speech Music and Hearing), Aitor Soroa (assistant lecturer), Caroline Sporleder (Trier University), Manfred Stede (University of Potsdam), Herman Stehouwer (Max Planck for Psycholinguistics), Benno Stein, Matthew Stone (Rutgers University), Veselin Stoyanov (Facebook), Michael Strube (HITS gGmbH), L V Subramaniam (IBM Research India), Md. Sultan (University of Colorado - Boulder), György Szarvas (Nuance Communications AG), Stefan Thater (Universität des Saarlandes), Kristina Toutanova (Microsoft Research), Yulia Tsvetkov (CMU), Tim Van de Cruys (IRIT & CNRS), Antal van den Bosch (Radboud University Nijmegen), Eva Vecchi (CIMeC - University of Trento), Paola Velardi, Erik Velldal, Noortje Venhuizen, Sriram Venkatapathy (Xerox Research Centre Europel), Yannick Versley (University of Tuebingen), Darnes Vilariño (Benemérita Universidad Autónoma de Puebla), Aline Villavicencio (Institute of Informatics, Federal University of Rio Grande do SUl), Veronika Vincze (University of Szeged), Vinod Vydiswaran (University of Illinois),

Ruibo WANG (Shanxi Univ. Wucheng Road 92, Taiyuan, Shanxi), Sai Wang (Shanxi University), Xinglong Wang, Yi-Chia Wang (Carnegie Mellon University), Bonnie Webber (University of Edinburgh), Julie Weeds (University of Sussex), Ben Wellner (The MITRE Corporation), Jan Wiebe (University of Pittsburgh), Michael Wiegand (Saarland University), Theresa Wilson (JHU HLTCOE), Kristian Woodsend (University of Edinburgh), Dekai Wu (HKUST), Stephen Wu (Mayo Clinic), Feiyu Xu (DFKI LT Lab), Jian Xu (The Hong Kong Polytechnic University), Eric Yeh (SRI International), Michael Yip (The Hong Kong Institute of Education), Deniz Yuret (Koc University), Roberto Zamparelli (Università di Trento), Fabio Massimo Zanzotto (University of Rome "Tor Vergata"), Luke Zettlemoyer (University of Washington), and Hermann Ziak (Know-Center GmbH).

Program Committee for Volume 2:

Ameeta Agrawal (York University), Itziar Aldabe (University of the Basque Country (UPV/EHU)), Marianna Apidianaki (LIMSI-CNRS), Pedro Balage Filho (University of São Paulo), Alexandra Balahur (European Commission Joint Research Centre), Timothy Baldwin (The University of Melbourne), Marco Baroni (University of Trento), Osman Baskaya (Koc University), Emanuele Bastianelli (University of Roma, Tor Vergata), Wesley Baugh (University of North Texas), Lee Becker (Avaya Labs), Satyabrata Behera (IIT Bombay), Luisa Bentivogli (Fondazione Bruno Kessler), Steven Bethard (University of Colorado Boulder), Ergun Bicici (Centre for Next Generation Localisation), Jari Björne (University of Turku), Tamara Bobic (Fraunhofer SCAI), Lorna Byrne (University College Dublin), Marine Carpuat (National Research Council), Giuseppe Castellucci (University of Roma, Tor Vergata), Tawunrat Chalothorn (University of Northumbria at Newcastle), Nate Chambers (US Naval Academy), Angel Chang (Stanford University), Karan Chawla (Indian Institute of Technology Bombay), Colin Cherry (NRC), Md. Faisal Mahbub Chowdhury (University of Trento, Italy and FBK-irst, Italy), Sam Clark (Swarthmore College), Kevin Cohen (Computational Bioscience Program, U. Colorado School of Medicine), Paul Cook (The University of Melbourne), Francisco M Couto (University of Lisbon), Leon Derczynski (University of Sheffield), Mohamed Dermouche (AMI Software R&D / Université de Lyon, ERIC (Lyon 2)), ALBERTO DIAZ (Universidad Complutense de Madrid), Myroslava Dzikovska (University of Edinburgh), Michele Filannino (University of Manchester), João Filgueiras (INESC-ID), Björn Gambäck (Norwegian University of Science and Technology), Martin Gleize (LIMSI-CNRS), Yvette Graham (The University of Melbourne, Centre for Next Generation Localisation), Tobias Günther (University of Gothenburg), Yoan Gutiérrez (University of Matanzas), Hussam Hamdan (AMU), Qi Han (IMS, University of Stuttgart), Viktor Hangya (University of Szeged), Mike Heilman (Educational Testing Service), David Hope (University of Sussex), Diana Inkpen (University of Ottawa), Harshit Jain (International Institute of Information Technology, Hyderabad), Sergio Jimenez (National University of Colombia), David Jurgens (University of California, Los Angeles), Ioannis Klapaftis, Nadin Kökciyan (Bogazici University), Oleksandr Kolomiyets (KU Leuven), Ioannis Korkontzelos (National Centre for Text Mining, The University of Manchester), Milen Kouylekov (CELI S.R.L.), Amitava Kundu (Jadavpur University), Man Lan (ECNU), Natsuda Laokulrat (The University of Tokyo), Alberto Lavelli (FBK-irst), Els Lefever (LT3, Hogeschool Gent), Clement Levallois (Erasmus University Rotterdam), Omer Levy (Bar-Ilan University), Nikolaos Malandrakis (Signal Analysis and Interpretation Laboratory (SAIL), USC, Los Angeles, CA 90089, USA), Suresh Manandhar (University of York), Morgane Marchand (CEA-LIST / CNRS-LIMSI), Eugenio Martínez-Cámara (University of Jaén), Saif Mohammad (National Research Council Canada), Preslav Nakov (Qatar Computing Research Institute, Qatar Foundation), Roberto Navigli (Sapienza University of Rome), Sapna Negi (University of Malta), Matteo Negri (Fondazione Bruno Kessler), Diarmuid Ó Séaghdha (University of Cambridge), IFEYINWA OKOYE (University of Colorado at Boulder), Reynier Ortega Bueno (CERPAMID, Cuba), Niels Ott (Eberhard Karls Universität Tübingen), Prabu palanisamy (Serendio), John Pavlopoulos (Athens

University of Economics and Business), Ted Pedersen (University of Minnesota, Duluth), David Pinto (Benemérita Universidad Autónoma de Puebla), Matt Post (Johns Hopkins University), Thomas Proisl (FAU Erlangen-Nürnberg), Majid Rastegar-Mojarad (University of Wisconsin-Milwaukee), Hilke Reckman (SAS Institute), Robert Remus (University of Leipzig), Tim Rocktäschel (Humboldt-Universität zu Berlin, Knowledge Management in Bioinformatics, Unter den Linden 6, Berlin, 10099), Carlos Rodriguez-Penagos (Barcelona Media Innovació), Sara Rosenthal (Columbia University), Alex Rudnick (Indiana University), Jose Saias (Departamento de Informatica - Universidade de Evora), Daniel Sanchez-Cisneros (Universidad Carlos III de Madrid), Didier Schwab (Univ. Grenoble Alpes), Isabel Segura-Bedmar (Carlos III University of Madrid), Reda Siblini (Concordia University), Amanda Stent (AT&T Labs - Research), Jannik Strötgen (Heidelberg University), Nitesh Surtani (IIIT-H), Liling Tan (Nanyang Technological University), Philippe Thomas (Humboldt-Universität zu Berlin, Knowledge Management in Bioinformatics, Unter den Linden 6, 10099 Berlin), Tim Van de Cruys (IRIT & CNRS), Maarten van Gompel (Radboud University Nijmegen), Daniele Vannella (Sapienza University of Rome), Yannick Versley (University of Tuebingen), Christian Wartena (Hochschule Hannover - University of Applied Sciences and Arts), Deniz Yuret (Koc University), Vanni Zavarella (Joint Research Center - European Commission), Zhemin Zhu (CTIT Database Group, EEMCS, University of Twente), and Hans-Peter Zorn (UKP Lab, Technische Universität Darmstadt).

Invited Speaker:

David Forsyth (University of Illinois, Urbana-Champaign)

Panelists for *SEM panel:

Kevin Knight (USC Information Sciences Institute)

Chris Manning (Stanford University)

Martha Palmer (University of Colorado at Boulder)

Owen Rambow (Columbia University)

Dan Roth (University of Illinois at Urbana-Champaign)

Panelists for Shared *SEM/SemEval panel:

*SEM and SemEval organizers

Table of Contents

This page intentionally left blank.

Conference Program Summary

	*SEM Main Conference and STS Shared Task (International D)	SemEval (starting on Day 2 below)
Day 1: Thursday June 13th 2013		
08:00--08:45	Registration	
08:45--10:30	Opening Remarks and *SEM Long Papers 1	*SEM1
10:30--11:00	Coffee Break	
11:00--12:30	STS Shared Task 1	ST1
12:30--2:00	Lunch	
2:00--3:30	STS Shared Task 2 and STS Poster boosters	ST2
3:30--4:00	Coffee Break	
4:00-4:25	*SEM Short Papers 1	*SEM2
4:30--6:00	*SEM Panel: Toward Deep Natural Language Understanding: Kevin Knight, Christopher Manning, Martha Palmer, Owen Rambow, and Dan Roth	*SEM2
6:30--8:30	*SEM Reception and STS Poster Session (PLN1)	

	*SEM Main Conference and STS Shared Task (International D)		SemEval (International E)	
Day 2: Friday June 14th 2013				
08:00--08:30	Registration			
08:30--09:30	*SEM Short Papers 2	*SEM3	SemEval Session 1	SE1
09:30--10:30	Keynote Address: David Forsyth (PLN2)			
10:30--11:00	Coffee Break			
11:00--12:30	*SEM Long Papers 2	*SEM4	SemEval Session 2	SE2
12:30--1:30	Lunch (ends earlier!)		Lunch + Poster Session 1 for Tasks 1, 5, 8	SP1
1:30--2:30	Joint Panel: Future of *SEM / STS Shared Task / SemEval (PLN3)			
2:30--3:30	*SEM Long Papers 3	*SEM5	SemEval Session 3	SE3
3:30--4:00	Coffee Break		Coffee + Poster Session 2 for Tasks 4, 10, 11, 12	SP2
4:00--4:30	*SEM Long Papers 4	*SEM6		
4:30--5:30			4:30--6:30 SemEval Session 4	SE4
5:30--6:00	Best Papers Awards & Closing remarks	*SEM7		
6:00--6:30				

			SemEval (International E)	
Day 3: Saturday June 15th 2013				
08:40--10:30			SemEval Session 5	SE5
10:30--11:00			Coffee Break	
11:00--1:10			SemEval Session 6	SE6
1:10-3:30			Lunch + Poster Session 3 for Tasks 2, 3, 7, 9, 13	SP3

Conference Program

Day 1: Thursday June 13th 2013

(08:00–08:45) Registration

Session *SEM1: (08:45–10:30) Opening Remarks and *SEM Long Papers (1)

09:00–09:30 *Towards a Formal Distributional Semantics: Simulating Logical Calculi with Tensors*
Edward Grefenstette

09:30–10:00 *Montague Meets Markov: Deep Semantics with Probabilistic Logical Form*
Islam Beltagy, Cuong Chau, Gemma Boleda, Dan Garrette, Katrin Erk and Raymond Mooney

10:00–10:30 *Coarse to Fine Grained Sense Disambiguation in Wikipedia*
Hui Shen, Razvan Bunescu and Rada Mihalcea

(10:30–11:00) Coffee Break

Session ST1: (11:00–12:30) STS Shared Task (1)

11:00–11:30 **SEM 2013 shared task: Semantic Textual Similarity*
Eneko Agirre, Daniel Cer, Mona Diab, Aitor Gonzalez-Agirre and Weiwei Guo

11:30–11:50 *UMBC_EBIQUITY-CORE: Semantic Textual Similarity Systems*
Lushan Han, Abhay L. Kashyap, Tim Finin, James Mayfield and Jonathan Weese

11:50–12:10 *iKernels-Core: Tree Kernel Learning for Textual Similarity*
Aliaksei Severyn, Massimo Nicosia and Alessandro Moschitti

12:10–12:30 *UNITOR-CORE_TYPED: Combining Text Similarity and Semantic Filters through SV Regression*
Danilo Croce, Valerio Storch and Roberto Basili

(12:30–2:00) Lunch

Session ST2a: (2:00–2:40) STS Shared Task (2)

2:00–2:20 *NTNU-CORE: Combining strong features for semantic similarity*
Erwin Marsi, Hans Moen, Lars Bungum, Gleb Sizov, Björn Gambäck and André Lynum

2:20–2:40 *SXUCFN-Core: STS Models Integrating FrameNet Parsing Information*
Sai Wang, Ru Li, Ruibo Wang, Zhiqiang Wang and Xia Zhang

Session ST2b: (2:40–3:30) STS Poster boosters

(3:30–4:00) Coffee Break

Session *SEM2a: (4:00–4:25) *SEM Short Papers (1)

4:00–4:25 *Distinguishing Common and Proper Nouns*
Judita Preiss and Mark Stevenson

Session *SEM2b: (4:30–6:00) *SEM Panel: Toward Deep Natural Language Understanding: Kevin Knight (USC/ISI), Christopher Manning (Stanford University), Martha Palmer (University of Colorado, Boulder), Owen Rambow (Columbia University), Dan Roth (University of Illinois Urbana Champagne)

Session PLN1: (6:30–8:30) *SEM Opening Reception and STS Poster Session

UCAM-CORE: Incorporating structured distributional similarity into STS
Tamara Polajnar, Laura Rimell and Douwe Kiela

PolyUCOMP-CORE_TYPED: Computing Semantic Textual Similarity using Overlapped Senses
Jian Xu and Qin Lu

HENRY-CORE: Domain Adaptation and Stacking for Text Similarity
Michael Heilman and Nitin Madnani

DeepPurple: Lexical, String and Affective Feature Fusion for Sentence-Level Semantic Similarity Estimation
Nikolaos Malandrakis, Elias Iosif, Vassiliki Prokopi, Alexandros Potamianos and Shrikanth Narayanan

UMCC_DLSI: Textual Similarity based on Lexical-Semantic features
Alexander Chávez, Héctor Dávila, Yoan Gutiérrez, Armando Collazo, José I. Abreu, Antonio Fernández Orquín, Andrés Montoyo and Rafael Muñoz

Day 1: Thursday June 13th 2013 (continued)

SOFTCARDINALIRY-CORE: Improving Text Overlap with Distributional Measures for Semantic Textual Similarity
Sergio Jimenez, Claudia Becerra and Alexander Gelbukh

CLaC-CORE: Exhaustive Feature Combination for Measuring Textual Similarity
Ehsan Shareghi and Sabine Bergler

UniMelb_NLP-CORE: Integrating predictions from multiple domains and feature sets for estimating semantic textual similarity
Spandana Gella, Bahar Salehi, Marco Lui, Karl Grieser, Paul Cook and Timothy Baldwin

CFILT-CORE: Semantic Textual Similarity using Universal Networking Language
Avishek Dan and Pushpak Bhattacharyya

CPN-CORE: A Text Semantic Similarity System Infused with Opinion Knowledge
Carmen Banea, Yoonjung Choi, Lingjia Deng, Samer Hassan, Michael Mohler, Bishan Yang, Claire Cardie, Rada Mihalcea and Jan Wiebe

INAOE_UPV-CORE: Extracting Word Associations from Document Corpora to estimate Semantic Textual Similarity
Fernando Sánchez-Vega, Manuel Montes-y-Gómez, Paolo Rosso and Luis Villaseñor-Pineda

CNGL-CORE: Referential Translation Machines for Measuring Semantic Similarity
Ergun Bicici and Josef Van Genabith

Day 2: Friday June 14th 2013

(08:00–08:30) Registration

Session *SEM3: (08:30–09:30) *SEM Short Papers (2)

08:30–08:55 *A Dataset of Syntactic-Ngrams over Time from a Very Large Corpus of English Books*
Yoav Goldberg and Jon Orwant

08:55–09:20 *Unsupervised Word Usage Similarity in Social Media Texts*
Spandana Gella, Paul Cook and Bo Han

9:20–9:30 Short break for re-organization

Day 2: Friday June 14th 2013 (continued)

Session PLN2: (09:30–10:30) Keynote address: David Forsyth (University of Illinois Urbana Champagne)

09:30–10:30 *More Words and Bigger Pictures*
David Forsyth

(10:30–11:00) Coffee Break

Session *SEM4: (11:00–12:30) *SEM Long Papers (2)

11:00–11:30 *Exploring Vector Space Models to Predict the Compositionality of German Noun-Noun Compounds*
Sabine Schulte im Walde, Stefan Müller and Stefan Roller

11:30–12:00 *Predicting the Compositionality of Multiword Expressions Using Translations in Multiple Languages*
Bahar Salehi and Paul Cook

12:00–12:30 *Metaphor Identification as Interpretation*
Ekaterina Shutova

(12:30–1:30) Lunch

Session PLN3: (1:30–2:30) *SEM / STS Shared Task / SemEval Panel

Session *SEM5: (2:30–3:30) *SEM Long Papers (3)

2:30–3:00 *Using the text to evaluate short answers for reading comprehension exercises*
Andrea Horbach, Alexis Palmer and Manfred Pinkal

3:00–3:30 *Choosing the Right Words: Characterizing and Reducing Error of the Word Count Approach*
Hansen Andrew Schwartz, Johannes Eichstaedt, Eduardo Blanco, Lukasz Dziurzyński, Margaret L. Kern, Stephanie Ramones, Martin Seligman and Lyle Ungar

Day 2: Friday June 14th 2013 (continued)

(3:30–4:00) Coffee Break

Session *SEM6: (4:00–5:30) *SEM Long Papers (4)

4:00–4:30 *Automatically Identifying Implicit Arguments to Improve Argument Linking and Coherence Modeling*
Michael Roth and Anette Frank

4:30–5:00 *Bootstrapping Semantic Role Labelers from Parallel Data*
Mikhail Kozhevnikov and Ivan Titov

5:00–5:30 *Semantic Parsing Freebase: Towards Open-domain Semantic Parsing*
Qingqing Cai and Alexander Yates

Session *SEM7: (5:30–6:00) Best Papers Awards and Closing Remarks

Towards a Formal Distributional Semantics: Simulating Logical Calculi with Tensors

Edward Grefenstette
University of Oxford
Department of Computer Science
Wolfson Building, Parks Road
Oxford OX1 3QD, UK
edward.grefenstette@cs.ox.ac.uk

Abstract

The development of compositional distributional models of semantics reconciling the empirical aspects of distributional semantics with the compositional aspects of formal semantics is a popular topic in the contemporary literature. This paper seeks to bring this reconciliation one step further by showing how the mathematical constructs commonly used in compositional distributional models, such as tensors and matrices, can be used to simulate different aspects of predicate logic.

This paper discusses how the canonical isomorphism between tensors and multilinear maps can be exploited to simulate a full-blown quantifier-free predicate calculus using tensors. It provides tensor interpretations of the set of logical connectives required to model propositional calculi. It suggests a variant of these tensor calculi capable of modelling quantifiers, using few non-linear operations. It finally discusses the relation between these variants, and how this relation should constitute the subject of future work.

1 Introduction

The topic of compositional distributional semantics has been growing in popularity over the past few years. This emerging sub-field of natural language semantic modelling seeks to combine two seemingly orthogonal approaches to modelling the meaning of words and sentences, namely *formal semantics* and *distributional semantics*.

These approaches, summarised in Section 2, differ in that formal semantics, on the one hand, provides a neatly compositional picture of natural language meaning, reducing sentences to logical representations; one the other hand, distributional semantics accounts for the ever-present ambiguity and polysemy of words of natural language, and provides tractable ways of learning and comparing word meanings based on corpus data.

Recent efforts, some of which are briefly reported below, have been made to unify both of these approaches to language modelling to produce *compositional distributional models of semantics*, leveraging the learning mechanisms of distributional semantics, and providing syntax-sensitive operations for the production of representations of sentence meaning obtained through combination of corpus-inferred word meanings. These efforts have been met with some success in evaluations such as phrase similarity tasks (Mitchell and Lapata, 2008; Mitchell and Lapata, 2009; Grefenstette and Sadrzadeh, 2011; Kartsaklis et al., 2012), sentiment prediction (Socher et al., 2012), and paraphrase detection (Blacoe and Lapata, 2012).

While these developments are promising with regard to the goal of obtaining learnable-yet-structured sentence-level representations of language meaning, part of the motivation for unifying formal and distributional models of semantics has been lost. The compositional aspects of formal semantics are combined with the corpus-based empirical aspects of distributional semantics in such models, yet the logical aspects are not. But it is these logical aspects which are so appealing in formal semantic models, and therefore it would be desirable to replicate the inferential powers of logic within

*Second Joint Conference on Lexical and Computational Semantics (*SEM), Volume 1: Proceedings of the Main Conference and the Shared Task*, pages 1–10, Atlanta, Georgia, June 13-14, 2013.

compositional distributional models of semantics.

In this paper, I make steps towards addressing this lost connection with logic in compositional distributional semantics. In Section 2, I provide a brief overview of formal and distributional semantic models of meaning. In Section 3, I give mathematical foundations for the rest of the paper by introducing tensors and tensor contraction as a way of modelling multilinear functions. In Section 4, I discuss how predicates, relations, and logical atoms of a quantifier-free predicate calculus can be modelled with tensors. In Section 5, I present tensorial representations of logical operations for a complete propositional calculus. In Section 6, I discuss a variant of the predicate calculus from Section 4 aimed at modelling quantifiers within such tensor-based logics, and the limits of compositional formalisms based only on multilinear maps. I conclude, in Section 7, by suggesting directions for further work based on the contents of this paper.

This paper does not seek to address the question of how to determine how words should be translated into predicates and relations in the first place, but rather shows how such predicates and relations can be modelled using multilinear algebra. As such, it can be seen as a general theoretical contribution which is independent from the approaches to compositional distributional semantics it can be applied to. It is directly compatible with the efforts of Coecke et al. (2010) and Grefenstette et al. (2013), discussed below, but is also relevant to any other approach making use of tensors or matrices to encode semantic relations.

2 Related work

Formal semantics, from the Montagovian school of thought (Montague, 1974; Dowty et al., 1981), treats natural languages as programming languages which compile down to some formal language such as a predicate calculus. The syntax of natural languages, in the form of a grammar, is augmented by semantic interpretations, in the form of expressions from a higher order logic such as the lambda-beta calculus. The parse of a sentence then determines the combinations of lambda-expressions, the reduction of which yields a well-formed formula of a predicate calculus, corresponding to the semantic representation of the sentence. A simple formal semantic model is illustrated in Figure 1.

Syntactic Analysis	Semantic Interpretation
S ⇒ NP VP	$[\![VP]\!]([\![NP]\!])$
NP ⇒ cats, milk, etc.	$[\![\text{cats}]\!]$, $[\![\text{milk}]\!]$, ...
VP ⇒ Vt NP	$[\![Vt]\!]([\![NP]\!])$
Vt ⇒ like, hug, etc.	$\lambda yx.[\![\text{like}]\!](x, y)$, ...

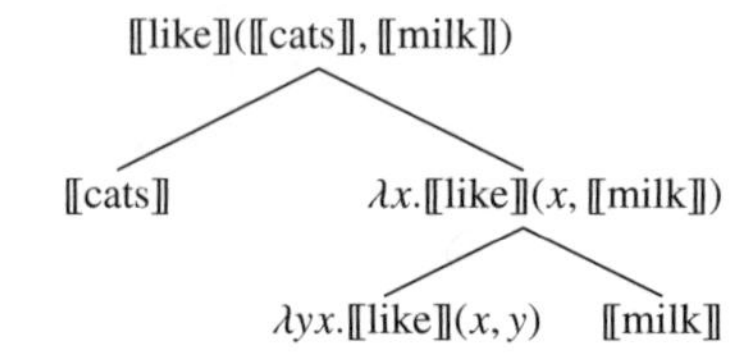

Figure 1: A simple formal semantic model.

Formal semantic models are incredibly powerful, in that the resulting logical representations of sentences can be fed to automated theorem provers to perform textual inference, consistency verification, question answering, and a host of other tasks which are well developed in the literature (e.g. see (Loveland, 1978) and (Fitting, 1996)). However, the sophistication of such formal semantic models comes at a cost: the complex set of rules allowing for the logical interpretation of text must either be provided *a priori*, or learned. Learning such representations is a complex task, the difficulty of which is compounded by issues of ambiguity and polysemy which are pervasive in natural languages.

In contrast, distributional semantic models, best summarised by the dictum of Firth (1957) that "You shall know a word by the company it keeps," provide an elegant and tractable way of learning semantic representations of words from text. Word meanings are modelled as high-dimensional vectors in large semantic vector spaces, the basis elements of which correspond to contextual features such as other words from a lexicon. Semantic vectors for words are built by counting how many time a target word occurs within a context (e.g. within k words of select words from the lexicon). These context counts are then normalised by a term frequency-inverse document frequency-like measure (e.g. TF-IDF, pointwise mutual information, ratio of probabilities), and are set as the basis weights of the vector representation of the word's meaning. Word vectors can then be compared using geometric distance

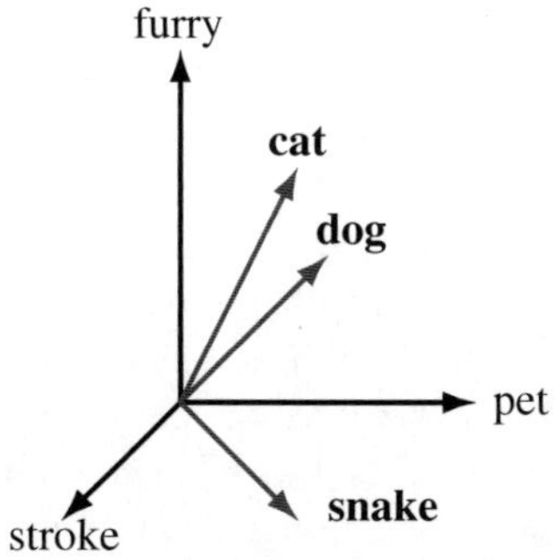

Figure 2: A simple distributional semantic model.

metrics such as cosine similarity, allowing us to determine the similarity of words, cluster semantically related words, and so on. Excellent overviews of distributional semantic models are provided by Curran (2004) and Mitchell (2011). A simple distributional semantic model showing the spacial representation of words 'dog', 'cat' and 'snake' within the context of feature words 'pet', 'furry', and 'stroke' is shown in Figure 2.

Distributional semantic models have been successfully applied to tasks such as word-sense discrimination (Schütze, 1998), thesaurus extraction (Grefenstette, 1994), and automated essay marking (Landauer and Dumais, 1997). However, while such models provide tractable ways of learning and comparing word meanings, they do not naturally scale beyond word length. As recently pointed out by Turney (2012), treating larger segments of texts as lexical units and learning their representations distributionally (the 'holistic approach') violates the principle of linguistic creativity, according to which we can formulate and understand phrases which we've never observed before, provided we know the meaning of their parts and how they are combined. As such, distributional semantics makes no effort to account for the compositional nature of language like formal semantics does, and ignores issues relating to syntactic and relational aspects of language.

Several proposals have been put forth over the last few years to provide vector composition functions for distributional models in order to introduce compositionality, thereby replicating some of the aspects of formal semantics while preserving learnability. Simple operations such as vector addition and multiplication, with or without scalar or matrix weights (to take word order or basic relational aspects into account), have been suggested (Zanzotto et al., 2010; Mitchell and Lapata, 2008; Mitchell and Lapata, 2009).

Smolensky (1990) suggests using the tensor product of word vectors to produce representations that grow with sentence complexity. Clark and Pulman (2006) extend this approach by including basis vectors standing for dependency relations into tensor product-based representations. Both of these tensor product-based approaches run into dimensionality problems as representations of sentence meaning for sentences of different lengths or grammatical structure do not live in the same space, and thus cannot directly be compared. Coecke et al. (2010) develop a framework using category theory, solving this dimensionality problem of tensor-based models by projecting tensored vectors for sentences into a unique vector space for sentences, using functions dynamically generated by the syntactic structure of the sentences. In presenting their framework, which partly inspired this paper, they describe how a verb can be treated as a logical relation using tensors in order to evaluate the truth value of a simple sentence, as well as how negation can be modelled using matrices.

A related approach, by Baroni and Zamparelli (2010), represents unary relations such as adjectives as matrices learned by linear regression from corpus data, and models adjective-noun composition as matrix-vector multiplication. Grefenstette et al. (2013) generalise this approach to relations of any arity and relate it to the framework of Coecke et al. (2010) using a tensor-based approach to formal semantic modelling similar to that presented in this paper.

Finally, Socher et al. (2012) apply deep learning techniques to model syntax-sensitive vector composition using non-linear operations, effectively turning parse trees into multi-stage neural networks. Socher shows that the non-linear activation function used in such a neural network can be tailored to replicate the behaviour of basic logical connectives such as conjunction and negation.

3 Tensors and multilinear maps

Tensors are the mathematical objects dealt with in multilinear algebra just as vectors and matrices are the objects dealt with in linear algebra. In fact, tensors can be seen as generalisations of vectors and matrices by introducing the notion of *tensor rank*. Let the rank of a tensor be the number of indices required to describe a vector/matrix-like object in sum notation. A vector $\mathbf{v}$ in a space V with basis $\{\mathbf{b}_i^V\}_i$ can be written as the weighted sum of the basis vectors:

$$\mathbf{v} = \sum_i c_i^v \mathbf{b}_i^V$$

where the c_i^v elements are the scalar basis weights of the vector. Being fully described with one index, vectors are rank 1 tensors. Similarly, a matrix $\mathbf{M}$ is an element of a space $V \otimes W$ with basis $\{(\mathbf{b}_i^V, \mathbf{b}_j^W)\}_{ij}$ (such pairs of basis vectors of V and W are commonly written as $\{\mathbf{b}_i^V \otimes \mathbf{b}_j^W\}_{ij}$ in multilinear algebra). Such matrices are rank 2 tensors, as they can be fully described using two indices (one for rows, one for columns):

$$\mathbf{M} = \sum_{ij} c_{ij}^M \mathbf{b}_i^V \otimes \mathbf{b}_j^W$$

where the scalar weights c_{ij}^M are just the ijth elements of the matrix.

A tensor $\mathbf{T}$ of rank k is just a geometric object with a higher rank. Let T be a member of $V_1 \otimes \ldots \otimes V_k$; we can express T as follows, using k indices $\alpha_1 \ldots \alpha_k$:

$$\mathbf{T} = \sum_{\alpha_1 \ldots \alpha_k} c_{\alpha_1 \ldots \alpha_k}^T \mathbf{b}_{\alpha_1}^{V_1} \otimes \ldots \otimes \mathbf{b}_{\alpha_k}^{V_k}$$

In this paper, we will be dealing with tensors of rank 1 (vectors), rank 2 (matrices) and rank 3, which can be pictured as cuboids (or a matrix of matrices).

Tensor contraction is an operation which allows us to take two tensors and produce a third. It is a generalisation of inner products and matrix multiplication to tensors of higher ranks. Let $\mathbf{T}$ be a tensor in $V_1 \otimes \ldots \otimes V_j \otimes V_k$ and $\mathbf{U}$ be a tensor in $V_k \otimes V_m \otimes \ldots \otimes V_n$. The contraction of these tensors, written $\mathbf{T} \times \mathbf{U}$, corresponds to the following calculation:

$$\mathbf{T} \times \mathbf{U} = \sum_{\alpha_1 \ldots \alpha_n} c_{\alpha_1 \ldots \alpha_k}^T c_{\alpha_k \ldots \alpha_n}^U \mathbf{b}_{\alpha_1}^{V_1} \otimes \ldots \otimes \mathbf{b}_{\alpha_j}^{V_j} \otimes \mathbf{b}_{\alpha_m}^{V_m} \otimes \ldots \otimes \mathbf{b}_{\alpha_n}^{V_n}$$

Tensor contraction takes a tensor of rank k and a tensor of rank $n - k + 1$ and produces a tensor of rank $n - 1$, corresponding to the sum of the ranks of the input tensors minus 2. The tensors must satisfy the following restriction: the left tensor must have a rightmost index spanning the same number of dimensions as the leftmost index of the right tensor. This is similar to the restriction that a m by n matrix can only be multiplied with a p by q matrix if $n = p$, i.e. if the index spanning the columns of the first matrix covers the same number of columns as the index spanning the rows of the second matrix covers rows. Similarly to how the columns of one matrix 'merge' with the rows of another to produce a third matrix, the part of the first tensor spanned by the index k merges with the part of the second tensor spanned by k by 'summing through' the shared basis elements $\mathbf{b}_{\alpha_k}^{V_k}$ of each tensor. Each tensor therefore loses a rank while being joined, explaining how the tensor produced by $\mathbf{T} \times \mathbf{U}$ is of rank $k + (n - k + 1) - 2 = n - 1$.

There exists an isomorphism between tensors and multilinear maps (Bourbaki, 1989; Lee, 1997), such that any curried multilinear map

$$f : V_1 \to \ldots \to V_j \to V_k$$

can be represented as a tensor $\mathbf{T}^f \in V_k \otimes V_j \otimes \ldots \otimes V_1$ (note the reversed order of the vector spaces), with tensor contraction acting as function application. This isomorphism guarantees that there exists such a tensor $\mathbf{T}^f$ for every f, such that the following equality holds for any $\mathbf{v}_1 \in V_1, \ldots, \mathbf{v}_j \in V_j$:

$$f \mathbf{v}_1 \ldots \mathbf{v}_j = \mathbf{v}_k = \mathbf{T}^f \times \mathbf{v}_1 \times \ldots \times \mathbf{v}_j$$

4 Tensor-based predicate calculi

In this section, I discuss how the isomorphism between multilinear maps and tensors described above can be used to model predicates, relations, and logical atoms of a predicate calculus. The four aspects of a predicate calculus we must replicate here using tensors are as follows: truth values, the logical domain and its elements (logical atoms), predicates, and relations. I will discuss logical connectives in the next section.

Both truth values and domain objects are the basic elements of a predicate calculus, and therefore it makes sense to model them as vectors rather than higher rank tensors, which I will reserve for relations. We first must consider the vector space used to model the boolean truth values of $\mathbb{B}$. Coecke et al. (2010) suggest, as boolean vector space, the space B with the basis $\{\top, \bot\}$, where $\top = [1\ 0]^\top$ is interpreted as 'true', and $\bot = [0\ 1]^\top$ as 'false'.

I assign to the domain $\mathcal{D}$, the set of objects in our logic, a vector space D on $\mathbb{R}^{|\mathcal{D}|}$ with basis vectors $\{\mathbf{d}_i\}_i$ which are in bijective correspondence with elements of $\mathcal{D}$. An element of $\mathcal{D}$ is therefore represented as a one-hot vector in D, the single non-null value of which is the weight for the basis vector mapped to that element of $\mathcal{D}$. Similarly, a subset of $\mathcal{D}$ is a vector of D where those elements of $\mathcal{D}$ in the subset have 1 as their corresponding basis weights in the vector, and those not in the subset have 0. Therefore there is a one-to-one correspondence between the vectors in D and the elements of the power set $\mathcal{P}(\mathcal{D})$, provided the basis weights of the vectors are restricted to one of 0 or 1.

Each unary predicate P in the logic is represented in the logical model as a set $M_P \subseteq \mathcal{D}$ containing the elements of the domain for which the predicate is true. Predicates can be viewed as a unary function $f_P : \mathcal{D} \to \mathbb{B}$ where

$$f_P(x) = \begin{cases} \top & \text{if } x \in M_P \\ \bot & \text{otherwise} \end{cases}$$

These predicate functions can be modelled as rank 2 tensors in $B \otimes D$, i.e. matrices. Such a matrix $\mathbf{M}^P$ is expressed in sum notation as follows:

$$\mathbf{M}^P = \left(\sum_i c_{1i}^{M^P} \top \otimes \mathbf{d}_i\right) + \left(\sum_i c_{2i}^{M^P} \bot \otimes \mathbf{d}_i\right)$$

The basis weights are defined in terms of the set M_P as follows: $c_{1i}^{M^P} = 1$ if the logical atom x_i associated with basis weight $\mathbf{d}_i$ is in M_P, and 0 otherwise; conversely, $c_{2i}^{M^P} = 1$ if the logical atom x_i associated with basis weight $\mathbf{d}_i$ is *not* in M_P, and 0 otherwise.

To give a simple example, let's consider a domain with three individuals, represented as the following one-hot vectors in D: $\mathbf{john} = [1\ 0\ 0]^\top$, $\mathbf{chris} = [0\ 1\ 0]^\top$, and $\mathbf{tom} = [0\ 0\ 1]^\top$. Let's imagine that Chris and John are mathematicians, but Tom is not. The predicate P for 'is a mathematician' therefore is represented model-theoretically as the set $M_P = \{chris, john\}$. Translating this into a matrix gives the following tensor for P:

$$\mathbf{M}^P = \begin{bmatrix} 1 & 1 & 0 \\ 0 & 0 & 1 \end{bmatrix}$$

To compute the truth value of 'John is a mathematician', we perform predicate-argument application as tensor contraction (matrix-vector multiplication, in this case):

$$\mathbf{M}^P \times \mathbf{john} = \begin{bmatrix} 1 & 1 & 0 \\ 0 & 0 & 1 \end{bmatrix} \begin{bmatrix} 0 \\ 1 \\ 0 \end{bmatrix} = \begin{bmatrix} 1 \\ 0 \end{bmatrix} = \top$$

Likewise for 'Tom is a mathematician':

$$\mathbf{M}^P \times \mathbf{tom} = \begin{bmatrix} 1 & 1 & 0 \\ 0 & 0 & 1 \end{bmatrix} \begin{bmatrix} 0 \\ 0 \\ 1 \end{bmatrix} = \begin{bmatrix} 0 \\ 1 \end{bmatrix} = \bot$$

Model theory for predicate calculus represents any n-ary relation R, such as a verb, as the set M_R of n-tuples of elements from $\mathcal{D}$ for which R holds. Therefore such relations can be viewed as functions $f_R : \mathcal{D}^n \to \mathbb{B}$ where:

$$f_R(x_1, \ldots, x_n) = \begin{cases} \top & \text{if } (x_1, \ldots, x_n) \in M_R \\ \bot & \text{otherwise} \end{cases}$$

We can represent the boolean function for such a relation R as a tensor $\mathbf{T}^R$ in $B \otimes \underbrace{D \otimes \ldots \otimes D}_{n}$:

$$\mathbf{T}^R = \left(\sum_{\alpha_1 \ldots \alpha_n} c_{1\alpha_1 \ldots \alpha_n}^{T^R} \top \otimes \mathbf{d}_{\alpha_1} \otimes \ldots \otimes \mathbf{d}_{\alpha_n}\right) + \left(\sum_{\alpha_1 \ldots \alpha_n} c_{2\alpha_1 \ldots \alpha_n}^{T^R} \bot \otimes \mathbf{d}_{\alpha_1} \otimes \ldots \otimes \mathbf{d}_{\alpha_n}\right)$$

As was the case for predicates, the weights for relational tensors are defined in terms of the set modelling the relation: $c_{1\alpha_1 \ldots \alpha_n}^{T^R}$ is 1 if the tuple $(x, \ldots, z)$ associated with the basis vectors $\mathbf{d}_{\alpha_n} \ldots \mathbf{d}_{\alpha_1}$ (again, note the reverse order) is in M_R and 0 otherwise; and $c_{2\alpha_1 \ldots \alpha_n}^{T^R}$ is 1 if the tuple $(x, \ldots, z)$ associated with the basis vectors $\mathbf{d}_{\alpha_n} \ldots \mathbf{d}_{\alpha_1}$ is *not* in M_R and 0 otherwise.

To give an example involving relations, let our domain be the individuals John (j) and Mary (m). Mary loves John and herself, but John only loves himself. The logical model for this scenario is as follows:

$$\mathcal{D} = \{j, m\} \qquad M_{\text{loves}} = \{(j, j), (m, m), (m, j)\}$$

Distributionally speaking, the elements of the domain will be mapped to the following one-hot vectors in some two-dimensional space D as follows:

$\mathbf{j} = [1\ 0]^\top$ and $\mathbf{m} = [0\ 1]^\top$. The tensor for 'loves' can be written as follows, ignoring basis elements with null-valued basis weights, and using the distributivity of the tensor product over addition:

$$\mathbf{T}^{\text{loves}} = \top \otimes ((\mathbf{d}_1 \otimes \mathbf{d}_1) + (\mathbf{d}_2 \otimes \mathbf{d}_2) + (\mathbf{d}_1 \otimes \mathbf{d}_2)) + (\bot \otimes \mathbf{d}_2 \otimes \mathbf{d}_1)$$

Computing "Mary loves John" would correspond to the following calculation:

$$(\mathbf{T}^{\text{loves}} \times \mathbf{m}) \times \mathbf{j} = ((\top \otimes \mathbf{d}_2) + (\top \otimes \mathbf{d}_1)) \times \mathbf{j} = \top$$

whereas "John loves Mary" would correspond to the following calculation:

$$(\mathbf{T}^{\text{loves}} \times \mathbf{j}) \times \mathbf{m} = ((\top \otimes \mathbf{d}_1) + (\bot \otimes \mathbf{d}_2)) \times \mathbf{m} = \bot$$

5 Logical connectives with tensors

In this section, I discuss how the boolean connectives of a propositional calculus can be modelled using tensors. Combined with the predicate and relation representations discussed above, these form a complete quantifier-free predicate calculus based on tensors and tensor contraction.

Negation has already been shown to be modelled in the boolean space described earlier by Coecke et al. (2010) as the swap matrix:

$$\mathbf{T}^{\neg} = \begin{bmatrix} 0 & 1 \\ 1 & 0 \end{bmatrix}$$

This can easily be verified:

$$\mathbf{T}^{\neg} \times \top = \begin{bmatrix} 0 & 1 \\ 1 & 0 \end{bmatrix} \begin{bmatrix} 1 \\ 0 \end{bmatrix} = \begin{bmatrix} 0 \\ 1 \end{bmatrix} = \bot$$

$$\mathbf{T}^{\neg} \times \bot = \begin{bmatrix} 0 & 1 \\ 1 & 0 \end{bmatrix} \begin{bmatrix} 0 \\ 1 \end{bmatrix} = \begin{bmatrix} 1 \\ 0 \end{bmatrix} = \top$$

All other logical operators are binary, and hence modelled as rank 3 tensors. To make talking about rank 3 tensors used to model binary operations easier, I will use the following block matrix notation for $2 \times 2 \times 2$ rank 3 tensors $\mathbf{T}$:

$$\mathbf{T} = \left[\begin{array}{cc|cc} a_1 & b_1 & a_2 & b_2 \\ c_1 & d_1 & c_2 & d_2 \end{array}\right]$$

which allows us to express tensor contractions as follows:

$$\mathbf{T} \times \mathbf{v} = \left[\begin{array}{cc|cc} a_1 & b_1 & a_2 & b_2 \\ c_1 & d_1 & c_2 & d_2 \end{array}\right] \begin{bmatrix} \alpha \\ \beta \end{bmatrix} = \begin{bmatrix} \alpha \cdot a_1 + \beta \cdot a_2 & \alpha \cdot b_1 + \beta \cdot b_2 \\ \alpha \cdot c_1 + \beta \cdot c_2 & \alpha \cdot d_1 + \beta \cdot d_2 \end{bmatrix}$$

or more concretely:

$$\mathbf{T} \times \top = \left[\begin{array}{cc|cc} a_1 & b_1 & a_2 & b_2 \\ c_1 & d_1 & c_2 & d_2 \end{array}\right] \begin{bmatrix} 1 \\ 0 \end{bmatrix} = \begin{bmatrix} a_1 & b_1 \\ c_1 & d_1 \end{bmatrix}$$

$$\mathbf{T} \times \bot = \left[\begin{array}{cc|cc} a_1 & b_1 & a_2 & b_2 \\ c_1 & d_1 & c_2 & d_2 \end{array}\right] \begin{bmatrix} 0 \\ 1 \end{bmatrix} = \begin{bmatrix} a_2 & b_2 \\ c_2 & d_2 \end{bmatrix}$$

Using this notation, we can define tensors for the following operations:

$$(\vee) \mapsto \mathbf{T}^{\vee} = \left[\begin{array}{cc|cc} 1 & 1 & 1 & 0 \\ 0 & 0 & 0 & 1 \end{array}\right]$$

$$(\wedge) \mapsto \mathbf{T}^{\wedge} = \left[\begin{array}{cc|cc} 1 & 0 & 0 & 0 \\ 0 & 1 & 1 & 1 \end{array}\right]$$

$$(\rightarrow) \mapsto \mathbf{T}^{\rightarrow} = \left[\begin{array}{cc|cc} 1 & 0 & 1 & 1 \\ 0 & 1 & 0 & 0 \end{array}\right]$$

I leave the trivial proof by exhaustion that these fit the bill to the reader.

It is worth noting here that these tensors preserve normalised probabilities of truth. Let us consider a model such at that described in Coecke et al. (2010) which, in lieu of boolean truth values, represents truth value vectors of the form $[\alpha\ \beta]^\top$ where $\alpha + \beta = 1$. Applying the above logical operations to such vectors produces vectors with the same normalisation property. This is due to the fact that the columns of the component matrices are all normalised (i.e. each column sums to 1). To give an example with conjunction, let $\mathbf{v} = [\alpha_1\ \beta_1]^\top$ and $\mathbf{w} = [\alpha_2\ \beta_2]^\top$ with $\alpha_1 + \beta_1 = \alpha_2 + \beta_2 = 1$. The conjunction of these vectors is calculated as follows:

$$(\mathbf{T}^{\wedge} \times \mathbf{v}) \times \mathbf{w} = \left[\begin{array}{cc|cc} 1 & 0 & 0 & 0 \\ 0 & 1 & 1 & 1 \end{array}\right] \begin{bmatrix} \alpha_1 \\ \beta_1 \end{bmatrix} \begin{bmatrix} \alpha_2 \\ \beta_2 \end{bmatrix} = \begin{bmatrix} \alpha_1 & 0 \\ \beta_1 & \alpha_1 + \beta_1 \end{bmatrix} \begin{bmatrix} \alpha_2 \\ \beta_2 \end{bmatrix} = \begin{bmatrix} \alpha_1 \alpha_2 \\ \beta_1 \alpha_2 + (\alpha_1 + \beta_1)\beta_2 \end{bmatrix}$$

To check that the probabilities are normalised we calculate:

$$\alpha_1\alpha_2 + \beta_1\alpha_2 + (\alpha_1 + \beta_1)\beta_2$$
$$= (\alpha_1 + \beta_1)\alpha_2 + (\alpha_1 + \beta_1)\beta_2$$
$$= (\alpha_1 + \beta_1)(\alpha_2 + \beta_2) = 1$$

We can observe that the resulting probability distribution for truth is still normalised. The same property can be verified for the other connectives, which I leave as an exercise for the reader.

6 Quantifiers and non-linearity

The predicate calculus described up until this point has repeatedly been qualified as 'quantifier-free', for the simple reason that quantification cannot be modelled if each application of a predicate or relation immediately yields a truth value. In performing such reductions, we throw away the information required for quantification, namely the information which indicates *which* elements of a domain the predicate holds true or false for. In this section, I present a variant of the predicate calculus developed earlier in this paper which allows us to model simple quantification (i.e. excluding embedded quantifiers) alongside a tensor-based approach to predicates. However, I will prove that this approach to quantifier modelling relies on non-linear functions, rendering them non-suitable for compositional distributional models relying solely on multilinear maps for composition (or alternatively, rendering such models unsuitable for the modelling of quantifiers by this method).

We saw, in Section 4, that vectors in the semantic space D standing for the logical domain could model logical atoms as well as *sets of atoms*. With this in mind, instead of modelling a predicate P as a truth-function, let us now view it as standing for some function $f_P : \mathcal{P}(\mathcal{D}) \to \mathcal{P}(\mathcal{D})$, defined as:

$$f_P(X) = X \cap M_P$$

where X is a set of domain objects, and M_P is the set modelling the predicate. The tensor form of such a function will be some $\mathbf{T}^{f_P}$ in $D \otimes D$. Let this square matrix be a diagonal matrix such that basis weights $c_{ii}^{T_{f_P}} = 1$ if the atom x corresponding to $\mathbf{d}_i$ is in M_P and 0 otherwise. Through tensor contraction, this tensor maps subsets of $\mathcal{D}$ (elements of D) to subsets of $\mathcal{D}$ containing only those objects of the original subset for which P holds (i.e. yielding another vector in D).

To give an example: let us consider a domain with two dogs (a and b) and a cat (c). One of the dogs (b) is brown, as is the cat. Let S be the set of dogs, and P the predicate "brown". I represent these statements in the model as follows:

$$\mathcal{D} = \{a, b, c\} \quad S = \{a, b\} \quad M_P = \{b, c\}$$

The set of dogs is represented as a vector $\mathbf{S} = [1\ 1\ 0]^\top$ and the predicate 'brown' as a tensor in $D \otimes D$:

$$\mathbf{T}^P = \begin{bmatrix} 0 & 0 & 0 \\ 0 & 1 & 0 \\ 0 & 0 & 1 \end{bmatrix}$$

The set of brown dogs is obtained by computing $f_B(S)$, which distributionally corresponds to applying the tensor $\mathbf{T}^P$ to the vector representation of S via tensor contraction, as follows:

$$\mathbf{T}^P \times \mathbf{S} = \begin{bmatrix} 0 & 0 & 0 \\ 0 & 1 & 0 \\ 0 & 0 & 1 \end{bmatrix} \begin{bmatrix} 1 \\ 1 \\ 0 \end{bmatrix} = \begin{bmatrix} 0 \\ 1 \\ 0 \end{bmatrix} = \mathbf{b}$$

The result of this computation shows that the set of brown dogs is the singleton set containing the only brown dog, b. As for how logical connectives fit into this picture, in both approaches discussed below, conjunction and disjunction are modelled using set-theoretic intersection and union, which are simply the component-wise *min* and *max* functions over vectors, respectively.

Using this new way of modelling predicates as tensors, I turn to the problem of modelling quantification. We begin by putting all predicates in vector form by replacing each instance of the bound variable with a vector **1** filled with ones, which extracts the diagonal from the predicate matrix.

An intuitive way of modelling universal quantification is as follows: expressions of the form "All Xs are Ys" are true if and only if $M_X = M_X \cap M_Y$, where M_X and M_Y are the set of Xs and the set of Ys, respectively. Using this, we can define the map *forall* for distributional universal quantification modelling expressions of the form "All Xs are Ys" as follows:

$$\mathit{forall}(\mathbf{X}, \mathbf{Y}) = \begin{cases} \top & \text{if } \mathbf{X} = \mathit{min}(\mathbf{X}, \mathbf{Y}) \\ \bot & \text{otherwise} \end{cases}$$

To give a short example, the sentence 'All Greeks are human' is verified by computing $\mathbf{X} = (\mathbf{M}^{\text{greek}} \times \mathbf{1})$, $\mathbf{Y} = (\mathbf{M}^{\text{human}} \times \mathbf{1})$, and verifying the equality $\mathbf{X} = \mathit{min}(\mathbf{X}, \mathbf{Y})$.

Existential statements of the form "There exists X" can be modelled using the function *exists*, which tests whether or not M_X is empty, and is defined as follows:

$$\mathit{exists}(\mathbf{X}) = \begin{cases} \top & \text{if } |\mathbf{X}| > 0 \\ \bot & \text{otherwise} \end{cases}$$

To give a short example, the sentence 'there exists a brown dog' is verified by computing $\mathbf{X} = (\mathbf{M}^{\text{brown}} \times \mathbf{1}) \cap (\mathbf{M}^{\text{dog}} \times \mathbf{1})$ and verifying whether or not $\mathbf{X}$ is of strictly positive length.

An important point to note here is that neither of these quantification functions are multi-linear maps, since a multilinear map must be linear in all arguments. A counter example for *forall* is to consider the case where M_X and M_Y are empty, and multiply their vector representations by non-zero scalar weights α and β.

$$\begin{aligned} &\alpha\mathbf{X} = \mathbf{X} \\ &\beta\mathbf{Y} = \mathbf{Y} \\ &\mathit{forall}(\alpha\mathbf{X}, \beta\mathbf{Y}) = \mathit{forall}(\mathbf{X}, \mathbf{Y}) = \top \\ &\mathit{forall}(\alpha\mathbf{X}, \beta\mathbf{Y}) \neq \alpha\beta\top \end{aligned}$$

I observe that the equations above demonstrate that *forall* is not a multilinear map.

The proof that *exists* is not a multilinear map is equally trivial. Assume M_X is an empty set and α is a non-zero scalar weight:

$$\begin{aligned} &\alpha\mathbf{X} = \mathbf{X} \\ &\mathit{exists}(\alpha\mathbf{X}) = \mathit{exists}(\mathbf{X}) = \bot \\ &\mathit{exists}(\alpha\mathbf{X}) \neq \alpha\bot \end{aligned}$$

It follows that *exists* is not a multi-linear function.

7 Conclusions and future work

In this paper, I set out to demonstrate that it was possible to replicate most aspects of predicate logic using tensor-based models. I showed that tensors can be constructed from logical models to represent predicates and relations, with vectors encoding elements or sets of elements from the logical domain. I discussed how tensor contraction allows for evaluation of logical expressions encoded as tensors, and that logical connectives can be defined as tensors to form a full quantifier-free predicate calculus. I exposed some of the limitations of this approach when dealing with variables under the scope of quantifiers, and proposed a variant for the tensor representation of predicates which allows us to deal with quantification. Further work on tensor-based modelling of quantifiers should ideally seek to reconcile this work with that of Barwise and Cooper (1981). In this section, I discuss how both of these approaches to predicate modelling can be put into relation, and suggest further work that might be done on this topic, and on the topic of integrating this work into compositional distributional models of semantics.

The first approach to predicate modelling treats predicates as truth functions represented as tensors, while the second treats them as functions from subsets of the domain to subsets of the domain. Yet both representations of predicates contain the same information. Let $\mathbf{M}^P$ and $\mathbf{M'}^P$ be the tensor representations of a predicate P under the first and second approach, respectively. The relation between these representations lies in the equality $\mathit{diag}(\mathbf{pM}^P) = \mathbf{M'^P}$, where $\mathbf{p}$ is the covector [1 0] (and hence $\mathbf{pM}^P$ yields the first row of $\mathbf{M}^P$). The second row of $\mathbf{M}^P$ being defined in terms of the first, one can also recover $\mathbf{M}^P$ from the diagonal of $\mathbf{M'}^P$.

Furthermore, both approaches deal with separate aspects of predicate logic, namely applying predicates to logical atoms, and applying them to bound variables. With this in mind, it is possible to see how both approaches can be used sequentially by noting that tensor contraction allows for partial application of relations to logical atoms. For example, applying a binary relation to its first argument under the first tensor-based model yields a predicate. Translating this predicate into the second model's form using the equality defined above then permits us to use it in quantified expressions. Using this, we can evaluate expressions of the form "There exists someone who John loves". Future work in this area should therefore focus on developing a version of this tensor calculus which permits seamless transition between both tensor formulations of logical predicates.

Finally, this paper aims to provide a starting point for the integration of logical aspects into compositional distributional semantic models. The work presented here serves to illustrate how tensors can simulate logical elements and operations, but does not address (or seek to address) the fact that the vectors and matrices in most compositional distributional semantic models do not cleanly represent elements of a logical domain. However, such distributional representations can arguably be seen as representing the properties objects of a logical domain hold in a corpus: for example the similar distributions of 'car' and 'automobile' could serve to indicate that these concepts are co-extensive. This suggests two directions research based on this paper could take. One could use the hypothesis that similar vectors indicate co-extensive concepts to infer a (probabilistic) logical domain and set of predicates, and use the methods described above without modification; alternatively one could use the form of the logical operations and predicate tensors described in this paper as a basis for a higher-dimensional predicate calculus, and investigate how such higher-dimensional 'logical' operations and elements could be defined or learned. Either way, the problem of reconciling the fuzzy 'messiness' of distributional models with the sharp 'cleanliness' of logic is a difficult problem, but I hope to have demonstrated in this paper that a small step has been made in the right direction.

Acknowledgments

Thanks to Ondřej Rypáček, Nal Kalchbrenner and Karl Moritz Hermann for their helpful comments during discussions surrounding this paper. This work is supported by EPSRC Project EP/I03808X/1.

References

M. Baroni and R. Zamparelli. Nouns are vectors, adjectives are matrices: Representing adjective-noun constructions in semantic space. In *Proceedings of the 2010 Conference on Empirical Methods in Natural Language Processing*, pages 1183–1193. Association for Computational Linguistics, 2010.

J. Barwise and R. Cooper Generalized quantifiers and natural language. *Linguistics and philosophy*, pages 159–219. Springer, 1981.

W. Blacoe and M. Lapata. A comparison of vector-based representations for semantic composition. *Proceedings of the 2012 Conference on Empirical Methods in Natural Language Processing*, 2012.

N. Bourbaki. *Commutative Algebra: Chapters 1-7*. Springer-Verlag (Berlin and New York), 1989.

S. Clark and S. Pulman. Combining symbolic and distributional models of meaning. In *AAAI Spring Symposium on Quantum Interaction*, 2006.

B. Coecke, M. Sadrzadeh, and S. Clark. Mathematical Foundations for a Compositional Distributional Model of Meaning. *Linguistic Analysis*, volume 36, pages 345–384. March 2010.

J. R. Curran. *From distributional to semantic similarity*. PhD thesis, 2004.

D. R. Dowty, R. E. Wall, and S. Peters. *Introduction to Montague Semantics*. Dordrecht, 1981.

J. R. Firth. A synopsis of linguistic theory 1930-1955. *Studies in linguistic analysis*, 1957.

M. Fitting. *First-order logic and automated theorem proving*. Springer Verlag, 1996.

E. Grefenstette, G. Dinu, Y. Zhang, M. Sadrzadeh, and M. Baroni. Multi-step regression learning for compositional distributional semantics. In *Proceedings of the Tenth International Conference on Computational Semantics*. Association for Computational Linguistics, 2013.

E. Grefenstette and M. Sadrzadeh. Experimental support for a categorical compositional distributional model of meaning. In *Proceedings of the 2011 Conference on Empirical Methods in Natural Language Processing*, 2011.

G. Grefenstette. *Explorations in automatic thesaurus discovery*. 1994.

D. Kartsaklis, and M. Sadrzadeh and S. Pulman. A Unified Sentence Space for Categorical Distributional-Compositional Semantics: Theory and Experiments. In *Proceedings of 24th International Conference on Computational Linguistics (COLING 2012): Posters*, 2012.

T. K. Landauer and S. T. Dumais. A solution to Plato's problem: The latent semantic analysis theory of acquisition, induction, and representation of knowledge. *Psychological review*, 1997.

J. Lee. *Riemannian manifolds: An introduction to curvature*, volume 176. Springer Verlag, 1997.

D. W. Loveland. *Automated theorem proving: A logical basis*. Elsevier North-Holland, 1978.

J. Mitchell and M. Lapata. Vector-based models of semantic composition. In *Proceedings of ACL*, volume 8, 2008.

J. Mitchell and M. Lapata. Language models based on semantic composition. In *Proceedings of the 2009 Conference on Empirical Methods in Natural Language Processing: Volume 1-Volume 1*, pages 430–439. Association for Computational Linguistics, 2009.

J. J. Mitchell. *Composition in distributional models of semantics*. PhD thesis, 2011.

R. Montague. English as a Formal Language. *Formal Semantics: The Essential Readings*, 1974.

H. Schütze. Automatic word sense discrimination. *Computational linguistics*, 24(1):97–123, 1998.

P. Smolensky. Tensor product variable binding and the representation of symbolic structures in connectionist systems. *Artificial intelligence*, 46(1-2):159–216, 1990.

R. Socher, B. Huval, C.D. Manning, and A.Y Ng. Semantic compositionality through recursive matrix-vector spaces. *Proceedings of the 2012 Conference on Empirical Methods in Natural Language Processing*, pages 1201–1211, 2012.

P. D. Turney. Domain and function: A dual-space model of semantic relations and compositions. *Journal of Artificial Intelligence Research*, 44:533–585, 2012.

F. M. Zanzotto, I. Korkontzelos, F. Fallucchi, and S. Manandhar. Estimating linear models for compositional distributional semantics. In *Proceedings of the 23rd International Conference on Computational Linguistics*, pages 1263–1271. Association for Computational Linguistics, 2010.

Montague Meets Markov: Deep Semantics with Probabilistic Logical Form

Islam Beltagy[§], Cuong Chau[§], Gemma Boleda[†], Dan Garrette[§], Katrin Erk[†], Raymond Mooney[§]
[§]Department of Computer Science
[†]Department of Linguistics
The University of Texas at Austin
Austin, Texas 78712
[§]{beltagy,ckcuong,dhg,mooney}@cs.utexas.edu
[†]gemma.boleda@utcompling.com, katrin.erk@mail.utexas.edu

Abstract

We combine logical and distributional representations of natural language meaning by transforming distributional similarity judgments into weighted inference rules using Markov Logic Networks (MLNs). We show that this framework supports both judging sentence similarity and recognizing textual entailment by appropriately adapting the MLN implementation of logical connectives. We also show that distributional phrase similarity, used as textual inference rules created on the fly, improves its performance.

1 Introduction

Tasks in natural language semantics are very diverse and pose different requirements on the underlying formalism for representing meaning. Some tasks require a detailed representation of the structure of complex sentences. Some tasks require the ability to recognize near-paraphrases or degrees of similarity between sentences. Some tasks require logical inference, either exact or approximate. Often it is necessary to handle ambiguity and vagueness in meaning. Finally, we frequently want to be able to learn relevant knowledge automatically from corpus data.

There is no single representation for natural language meaning at this time that fulfills all requirements. But there are representations that meet some of the criteria. Logic-based representations (Montague, 1970; Kamp and Reyle, 1993) provide an expressive and flexible formalism to express even complex propositions, and they come with standardized inference mechanisms. Distributional models (Turney and Pantel, 2010) use contextual similarity to predict semantic similarity of words and phrases (Landauer and Dumais, 1997; Mitchell and Lapata, 2010), and to model polysemy (Schütze, 1998; Erk and Padó, 2008; Thater et al., 2010). This suggests that distributional models and logic-based representations of natural language meaning are complementary in their strengths (Grefenstette and Sadrzadeh, 2011; Garrette et al., 2011), which encourages developing new techniques to combine them.

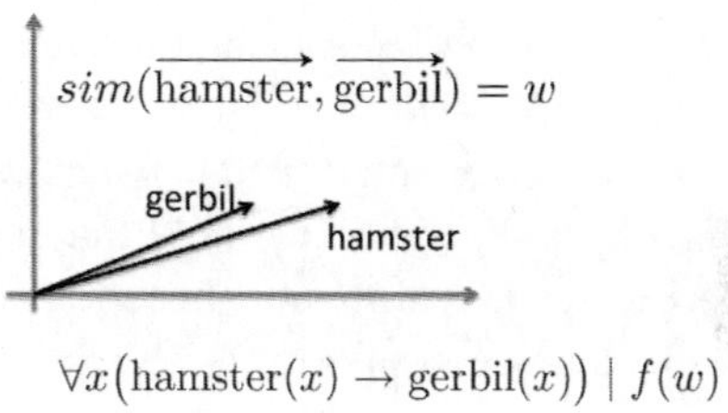

Figure 1: Turning distributional similarity into a weighted inference rule

Garrette et al. (2011; 2013) propose a framework for combining logic and distributional models in which logical form is the primary meaning representation. Distributional similarity between pairs of words is converted into weighted inference rules that are added to the logical form, as illustrated in Figure 1. Finally, Markov Logic Networks (Richardson and Domingos, 2006) (MLNs) are used to perform weighted inference on the resulting knowledge base. However, they only employed single-word distributional similarity rules, and only evaluated on a small

*Second Joint Conference on Lexical and Computational Semantics (*SEM), Volume 1: Proceedings of the Main Conference and the Shared Task*, pages 11–21, Atlanta, Georgia, June 13-14, 2013.

set of short, hand-crafted test sentences.

In this paper, we extend Garrette et al.'s approach and adapt it to handle two existing semantic tasks: recognizing textual entailment (RTE) and semantic textual similarity (STS). We show how this single semantic framework using probabilistic logical form in Markov logic can be adapted to support both of these important tasks. This is possible because MLNs constitute a flexible programming language based on probabilistic logic (Domingos and Lowd, 2009) that can be easily adapted to support multiple types of linguistically useful inference.

At the word and short phrase level, our approach model entailment through "distributional" similarity (Figure 1). If X and Y occur in similar contexts, we assume that they describe similar entities and thus there is some degree of entailment between them. At the sentence level, however, we hold that a stricter, logic-based view of entailment is beneficial, and we even model sentence similarity (in STS) as entailment.

There are two main innovations in the formalism that make it possible for us to work with naturally occurring corpus data. First, we use *more expressive distributional inference rules* based on the similarity of phrases rather than just individual words. In comparison to existing methods for creating textual inference rules (Lin and Pantel, 2001b; Szpektor and Dagan, 2008), these rules are computed on the fly as needed, rather than pre-compiled. Second, we use *more flexible probabilistic combinations of evidence* in order to compute degrees of sentence similarity for STS and to help compensate for parser errors. We replace deterministic conjunction by an average combiner, which encodes causal independence (Natarajan et al., 2010).

We show that our framework is able to handle both sentence similarity (STS) and textual entailment (RTE) by making some simple adaptations to the MLN when switching between tasks. The framework achieves reasonable results on both tasks. On STS, we obtain a correlation of $r = 0.66$ with full logic, $r = 0.73$ in a system with weakened variable binding, and $r = 0.85$ in an ensemble model. On RTE-1 we obtain an accuracy of 0.57. We show that the distributional inference rules benefit both tasks and that more flexible probabilistic combinations of evidence are crucial for STS. Although other approaches could be adapted to handle both RTE and STS, we do not know of any other methods that have been explicitly tested on both problems.

2 Related work

Distributional semantics Distributional models define the semantic relatedness of words as the similarity of vectors representing the contexts in which they occur (Landauer and Dumais, 1997; Lund and Burgess, 1996). Recently, such models have also been used to represent the meaning of larger phrases. The simplest models compute a phrase vector by adding the vectors for the individual words (Landauer and Dumais, 1997) or by a component-wise product of word vectors (Mitchell and Lapata, 2008; Mitchell and Lapata, 2010). Other approaches, in the emerging area of distributional compositional semantics, use more complex methods that compute phrase vectors from word vectors and tensors (Baroni and Zamparelli, 2010; Grefenstette and Sadrzadeh, 2011).

Wide-coverage logic-based semantics Boxer (Bos, 2008) is a software package for wide-coverage semantic analysis that produces logical forms using Discourse Representation Structures (Kamp and Reyle, 1993). It builds on the C&C CCG parser (Clark and Curran, 2004).

Markov Logic In order to combine logical and probabilistic information, we draw on existing work in Statistical Relational AI (Getoor and Taskar, 2007). Specifically, we utilize Markov Logic Networks (MLNs) (Domingos and Lowd, 2009), which employ weighted formulas in first-order logic to compactly encode complex undirected probabilistic graphical models. MLNs are well suited for our approach since they provide an elegant framework for assigning weights to first-order logical rules, combining a diverse set of inference rules and performing sound probabilistic inference.

An MLN consists of a set of weighted first-order clauses. It provides a way of softening first-order logic by allowing situations in which not all clauses are satisfied. More specifically, they provide a well-founded probability distribution across possible worlds by specifying that the probability of a world increases exponentially with the total weight of the logical clauses that it satisfies. While methods exist for learning MLN weights directly from training data, since the appropriate training data is lacking, our approach uses weights computed using distributional semantics. We use the open-source software package Alchemy (Kok et al., 2005) for MLN inference, which allows computing the probability of a query literal given a set of weighted clauses as background knowledge and evidence.

Tasks: RTE and STS Recognizing Textual Entailment (RTE) is the task of determining whether one natural language text, the *premise*, implies another, the *hypothesis*. Consider (1) below.

(1) *p:* Oracle had fought to keep the forms from being released
h: Oracle released a confidential document

Here, *h* is not entailed. RTE directly tests whether a system can construct semantic representations that allow it to draw correct inferences. Of existing RTE approaches, the closest to ours is by Bos and Markert (2005), who employ a purely logical approach that uses Boxer to convert both the premise and hypothesis into first-order logic and then checks for entailment using a theorem prover. By contrast, our approach uses Markov logic with probabilistic inference.

Semantic Textual Similarity (STS) is the task of judging the similarity of two sentences on a scale from 0 to 5 (Agirre et al., 2012). Gold standard scores are averaged over multiple human annotations. The best performer in 2012's competition was by Bär et al. (2012), an ensemble system that integrates many techniques including string similarity, n-gram overlap, WordNet similarity, vector space similarity and MT evaluation metrics.

Weighted inference, and combined structural-distributional representations One approach to weighted inference in NLP is that of Hobbs et al. (1993), who proposed viewing natural language interpretation as abductive inference. In this framework, problems like reference resolution and syntactic ambiguity resolution become inferences to best explanations that are associated with costs. However, this leaves open the question of how costs are assigned. Raina et al. (2005) use this framework for RTE, deriving inference costs from WordNet similarity and properties of the syntactic parse.

Garrette et al. (2011; 2013) proposed an approach to RTE that uses MLNs to combine traditional logical representations with distributional information in order to support probabilistic textual inference. This approach can be viewed as a bridge between Bos and Markert (2005)'s purely logical approach, which relies purely on hard logical rules and theorem proving, and distributional approaches, which support graded similarity between concepts but have no notion of logical operators or entailment.

There are also other methods that combine distributional and structured representations. Stern et al. (2011) conceptualize textual entailment as tree rewriting of syntactic graphs, where some rewriting rules are distributional inference rules. Socher et al. (2011) recognize paraphrases using a "tree of vectors," a phrase structure tree in which each constituent is associated with a vector, and overall sentence similarity is computed by a classifier that integrates all pairwise similarities. (This is in contrast to approaches like Baroni and Zamparelli (2010) and Grefenstette and Sadrzadeh (2011), who do not offer a proposal for using vectors at multiple levels in a syntactic tree simultaneously.)

3 MLN system

Our system extends that of Garrette et al. (2011; 2013) to support larger-scale evaluation on standard benchmarks for both RTE and STS. We conceptualize both tasks as probabilistic entailment in Markov logic, where STS is judged as the average degree of mutual entailment, i.e. we compute the probability of both $S_1 \models S_2$ and $S_2 \models S_1$ and average the results. Below are some sentence pairs that we use as examples in the discussion below:

(2) S_1: A man is slicing a cucumber.
S_2: A man is slicing a zucchini.

(3) S_1: A boy is riding a bicycle.
S_2: A little boy is riding a bike.

(4) S_1: A man is driving.
S_2: A man is driving a car.

System overview. To compute the probability of an entailment $S_1 \models S_2$, the system first constructs logical forms for each sentence using Boxer and then translates them into MLN clauses. In example (2) above, the logical form for S_1:

$$\exists x_0, e_1, x_2 \big(man(x_0) \land slice(e_1) \land Agent(e_1, x_0) \land cucumber(x_2) \land Patient(e_1, x_2)\big)$$

is used as evidence, and the logical form for S_2 is turned into the following formula (by default, variables are assumed to be universally quantified):

$$man(x) \land slice(e) \land Agent(e, x) \land zucchini(y) \land Patient(e, y) \rightarrow result()$$

where $result()$ is the query for which we have Alchemy compute the probability.

However, S_2 is not strictly entailed by S_1 because of the mismatch between "cucumber" and "zucchini", so with just the strict logical-form translations of S_1 and S_2, the probability of $result()$ will be zero. This is where we introduce distributional similarity, in this case the similarity of "cucumber" and "zucchini", $\cos(\overrightarrow{\text{cucumber}}, \overrightarrow{\text{zucchini}})$. We create inference rules from such similarities as a form of background knowledge. We then treat similarity as degree of entailment, a move that has a long tradition (e.g., (Lin and Pantel, 2001b; Raina et al., 2005; Szpektor and Dagan, 2008)). In general, given two words a and b, we transform their cosine similarity into an inference-rule weight $wt(a, b)$ using:

$$wt(a, b) = log\left(\frac{\cos(\vec{a}, \vec{b})}{1 - \cos(\vec{a}, \vec{b})}\right) - prior \qquad (5)$$

Where $prior$ is a negative weight used to initialize all predicates, so that by default facts are assumed to have very low probability. In our experiments, we use $prior = -3$. In the case of sentence pair (2), we generate the inference rule:

$$cucumber(x) \rightarrow zucchini(x) \mid wt(\text{cuc., zuc.})$$

Such inference rules are generated for all pairs of words (w_1, w_2) where $w_1 \in S_1$ and $w_2 \in S_2$.[1]

The distributional model we use contains all lemmas occurring at least 50 times in the Gigaword corpus (Graff et al., 2007) except a list of stop words. The dimensions are the 2,000 most frequent of these words, and cell values are weighted with point-wise mutual information. [2]

Phrase-based inference rules. Garrette et al. only considered distributional inference rules for pairs of individual words. We extend their approach to distributional inference rules for pairs of phrases in order to handle cases like (3). To properly estimate the similarity between S_1 and S_2 in (3), we not only need an inference rule linking "bike" to "bicycle", but also a rule estimating how similar "boy" is to "little boy". To do so, we make use of existing approaches that compute distributional representations for phrases. In particular, we compute the vector for a phrase from the vectors of the words in that phrase, using either vector addition (Landauer and Dumais, 1997) or component-wise multiplication (Mitchell and Lapata, 2008; Mitchell and Lapata, 2010). The inference-rule weight, $wt(p_1, p_2)$, for two phrases p_1 and p_2 is then determined using Eq. (5) in the same way as for words.

Existing approaches that derive phrasal inference rules from distributional similarity (Lin and Pantel, 2001a; Szpektor and Dagan, 2008; Berant et al., 2011) precompile large lists of inference rules. By comparison, distributional phrase similarity can be seen as a generator of inference rules "on the fly", as it is possible to compute distributional phrase vectors for arbitrary phrases on demand as they are needed for particular examples.

Inference rules are generated for all pairs of constituents (c_1, c_2) where $c_1 \in S_1$ and $c_2 \in S_2$, a constituent is a single word or a phrase. The logical form provides a handy way to extract phrases, as they are generally mapped to one of two logical constructs. Either we have multiple single-variable predicates operating on the same variable. For example the phrase "a little boy" has the logical form $boy(x) \land little(x)$. Or we have two unary predicates connected with a relation. For example, "pizza slice" and "slice of pizza" are both mapped to the

[1] We omit inference rules for words (a, b) where $\cos(a, b) < \theta$ for a threshold θ set to maximize performance on the training data. Low-similarity pairs usually indicate dissimilar words. This removes a sizeable number of rules for STS, while for RTE the tuned threshold was near zero.

[2] It is customary to transform raw counts in a way that captures association between target words and dimensions, for example through point-wise mutual information (Lowe, 2001).

logical form, $slice(x_0) \wedge of(x_0, x_1) \wedge pizza(x_1)$. We consider all binary predicates as relations.

Average Combiner to determine similarity in the presence of missing phrases. The logical forms for the sentences in (4): are

S_1: $\exists x_0, e_1 \big(man(x_0) \wedge agent(x_0, e_1) \wedge drive(e_1)\big)$

S_2: $\exists x_0, e_1, x_2 \big(man(x_0) \wedge agent(x_0, e_1) \wedge drive(e_1) \wedge patient(e_1, x_2) \wedge car(x_2)\big)$

If we try to prove $S_1 \models S_2$, the probability of the $result()$ will be zero: There is no evidence for a car, and the hypothesis predicates are conjoined using a deterministic AND. For RTE, this makes sense: If one of the hypothesis predicates is False, the probability of entailment should be zero. For the STS task, this should in principle be the same, at least if the omitted facts are vital, but it seems that annotators rated the data points in this task more for overall similarity than for degrees of entailment. So in STS, we want the similarity to be a function of the number of elements in the hypothesis that are inferable. Therefore, we need to replace the deterministic AND with a different way of combining evidence. We chose to use the average evidence combiner for MLNs introduced by Natarajan et al. (2010). To use the average combiner, the full logical form is divided into smaller clauses (which we call mini-clauses), then the combiner averages their probabilities. In case the formula is a list of conjuncted predicates, a mini-clause is a conjunction of a single-variable predicate with a relation predicate(as in the example below). In case the logical form contains a negated sub-formula, the negated sub-formula is also a mini-clause. The hypothesis above after dividing clauses for the average combiner looks like this:

$$man(x_0) \wedge agent(x_0, e_1) \rightarrow result(x_0, e_1, x_2) \mid w$$
$$drive(e_1) \wedge agent(x_0, e_1) \rightarrow result(x_0, e_1, x_2) \mid w$$
$$drive(e_1) \wedge patient(e_1, x_2) \rightarrow result(x_0, e_1, x_2) \mid w$$
$$car(x_2) \wedge patient(e_1, x_2) \rightarrow result(x_0, e_1, x_2) \mid w$$

where $result$ is again the query predicate. Here, $result$ has all of the variables in the clause as arguments in order to maintain the binding of variables across all of the mini-clauses. The weights w are the following function of n, the number of mini-clauses (4 in the above example):

$$w = \frac{1}{n} \times (log(\frac{p}{1-p}) - prior) \quad (6)$$

where p is a value close to 1 that is set to maximize performance on the training data, and $prior$ is the same negative weight as before. Setting w this way produces a probability of p for the $result()$ in cases that satisfy the antecedents of *all* mini-clauses. For the example above, the antecedents of the first two mini-clauses are satisfied, while the antecedents of the last two are not since the premise provides no evidence for an object of the verb $drive$. The similarity is then computed to be the maximum probability of any grounding of the $result$ predicate, which in this case is around $\frac{p}{2}$.[3]

An interesting variation of the average combiner is to omit variable bindings between the mini-clauses. In this case, the hypothesis clauses look like this for our example:

$$man(x) \wedge agent(x, e) \rightarrow result() \mid w$$
$$drive(e) \wedge agent(x, e) \rightarrow result() \mid w$$
$$drive(e) \wedge patient(e, x) \rightarrow result() \mid w$$
$$car(x) \wedge patient(e, x) \rightarrow result() \mid w$$

This implementation loses a lot of information, for example it does not differentiate between "A man is walking and a woman is driving" and "A man is driving and a woman is walking". In fact, logical form without variable binding degrades to a representation similar to a set of independent syntactic dependencies, [4] while the average combiner with variable binding retains all of the information in the original logical form. Still, omitting variable binding turns out to be useful for the STS task.

It is also worth commenting on the efficiency of the inference algorithm when run on the three different approaches to combining evidence. The average combiner without variable binding is the fastest and has the least memory requirements because all cliques in the ground network are of limited size (just 3 or 4 nodes). Deterministic AND is much slower than the average combiner without variable binding, because the maximum clique size depends on the sentence. The average combiner *with* variable binding is the most memory intensive since the

[3]One could also give mini-clauses different weights depending on their importance, but we have not experimented with this so far.

[4]However, it is not completely the same since we do not divide up formulas under negation into mini-clauses.

number of arguments of the $result()$ predicate can become large (there is an argument for each individual and event in the sentence). Consequently, the inference algorithm needs to consider a combinatorial number of possible groundings of the $result()$ predicate, making inference very slow.

Adaptation of the logical form. As discussed by Garrette et al. (2011), Boxer's output is mapped to logical form and augmented with additional information to handle a variety of semantic phenomena. However, we do not use their additional rules for handling implicatives and factives, as we wanted to test the system without background knowledge beyond that supplied by the vector space.

Unfortunately, current MLN inference algorithms are not able to efficiently handle complex formulas with nested quantifiers. For that reason, we replaced universal quantifiers in Boxer's output with existentials since they caused serious problems for Alchemy. Although this is a radical change to the semantics of the logical form, due to the nature of the STS and RTE data, it only effects about 5% of the sentences, and we found that most of the universal quantifiers in these cases were actually due to parsing errors. We are currently exploring more effective ways of dealing with this issue.

4 Task 1: Recognizing Textual Entailment

4.1 Dataset

In order to compare directly to the logic-based system of Bos and Markert (2005), we focus on the RTE-1 dataset (Dagan et al., 2005), which includes 567 Text-Hypothesis (T-H) pairs in the development set and 800 pairs in the test set. The data covers a wide range of issues in entailment, including lexical, syntactic, logical, world knowledge, and combinations of these at different levels of difficulty. In both development and test sets, 50% of sentence pairs are true entailments and 50% are not.

4.2 Method

We run our system for different configurations of inference rules and evidence combiners. For distributional inference rules (DIR), three different levels are tested: without inference rules (**no DIR**), inference rules for individual words (**word DIR**), and inference rules for words and phrases (**phrase DIR**). Phrase vectors were built using vector addition, as point-wise multiplication performed slightly worse. To combine evidence for the $result()$ query, three different options are available: without average combiner which is just using Deterministic AND (**Deterministic AND**), average combiner with variable binding (**AvgComb**) and average combiner without variable binding (**AvgComb w/o VarBind**). Different combinations of configurations are tested according to its suitability for the task; RTE and STS.

We also tested several "distributional only" systems. The first such system builds a vector representation for each sentence by adding its word vectors, then computes the cosine similarity between the sentence vectors for S_1 and S_2 (**VS-Add**). The second uses point-wise multiplication instead of vector addition (**VS-Mul**). The third scales pairwise words similarities to the sentence level using weighted average where weights are inverse document frequencies idf as suggested by Mihalcea et al. (2006) (**VS-Pairwise**).

For the RTE task, systems were evaluated using both *accuracy* and *confidence-weighted score* (*cws*) as used by Bos and Markert (2005) and the RTE-1 challenge (Dagan et al., 2005). In order to map a probability of entailment to a strict prediction of True or False, we determined a threshold that optimizes performance on the development set. The cws score rewards a system's ability to assign higher confidence scores to correct predictions than incorrect ones. For cws, a system's predictions are sorted in decreasing order of confidence and the score is computed as:

$$cws = \frac{1}{n}\sum_{i=1}^{n}\frac{\#\text{correct-up-to-rank-i}}{i}$$

where n is the number of the items in the test set, and i ranges over the sorted items. In our systems, we defined the confidence value for a T-H pair as the distance between the computed probability for the $result()$ predicate and the threshold.

4.3 Results

The results are shown in Table 1. They show that the distributional only baselines perform very poorly. In particular, they perform worse than strict

Method	acc	cws
Chance	0.50	0.50
Bos & Markert, strict	0.52	0.55
Best system in RTE-1 challenge (Bayer et al., 2005)	0.59	0.62
VS-Add	0.49	0.53
VS-Mul	0.51	0.52
VS-Pairwise	0.50	0.50
AvgComb w/o VarBind + phrase DIR	0.52	0.53
Deterministic AND + phrase DIR	0.57	0.57

Table 1: Results on the RTE-1 Test Set.

entailment from Bos and Markert (2005), a system that uses only logic. This illustrates the important role of logic-based representations for the entailment task. Due to intractable memory demands of Alchemy inference, our current system with deterministic AND fails to execute on 118 of the 800 test pairs, so, by default, the system classifies these cases as False (non-entailing) with very low confidence. Comparing the two configurations of our system, using deterministic AND vs. the average combiner without variable binding (last two lines in Table 1), we see that for RTE, it is essential to retain the full logical form.

Our system with deterministic AND obtains both an accuracy and cws of 0.57. The best result in the RTE-1 challenge by Bayer et al. (2005) obtained an accuracy of 0.59 and cws of 0.62. [5] In terms of both accuracy and cws, our system outperforms both "distributional only" systems and strict logical entailment, showing again that integrating both logical form and distributional inference rules using MLNs is beneficial. Interestingly, the strict entailment system of Bos and Markert incorporated generic knowledge, lexical knowledge (from WordNet) and geographical knowledge that we do not utilize. This demonstrates the advantage of using a model that operationalizes entailment between words and phrases as distributional similarity.

[5]On other RTE datasets there are higher previous results. Hickl (2008) achieves 0.89 accuracy and 0.88 cws on the combined RTE-2 and RTE-3 dataset.

5 Task 2: Semantic Textual Similarity

5.1 Dataset

The dataset we use in our experiments is the MSR Video Paraphrase Corpus (MSR-Vid) subset of the STS 2012 task, consisting of 1,500 sentence pairs. The corpus itself was built by asking annotators from Amazon Mechanical Turk to describe very short video fragments (Chen and Dolan, 2011). The organizers of the STS 2012 task (Agirre et al., 2012) sampled video descriptions and asked Turkers to assign similarity scores (ranging from 0 to 5) to pairs of sentences, without access to the video. The gold standard score is the average of the Turkers' annotations. In addition to the MSR Video Paraphrase Corpus subset, the STS 2012 task involved data from machine translation and sense descriptions. We do not use these because they do not consist of full grammatical sentences, which the parser does not handle well. In addition, the STS 2012 data included sentences from the MSR Paraphrase Corpus, which we also do not currently use because some sentences are long and create intractable MLN inference problems. This issue is discussed further in section 6. Following STS standards, our evaluation compares a system's similarity judgments to the gold standard scores using Pearson's correlation coefficient r.

5.2 Method

Our system can be tested for different configuration of inference rules and evidence combiners which are explained in section 4.2. The tested systems on the STS task are listed in table 2. Out experiments showed that using average combiner (**AvgComb**) is very memory intensive and MLN inference for 28 of the 1,500 pairs either ran out of memory or did not finish in reasonable time. In such cases, we back off to **AvgComb w/o VarBind**.

We compare to several baselines; our MLN system without distributional inference rules (**AvgComb + no DIR**), and distributional-only systems (**VS-Add**, **VS-Mul**, **VS-Pairwise**). These are the natural baselines for our system, since they use only one of the two types of information that we combine (i.e. logical form and distributional representations).

Finally, we built an ensemble that combines the output of multiple systems using regression trained

Method	r
AvgComb + no DIR	0.58
AvgComb + word DIR	0.60
AvgComb + phrase DIR	0.66
AvgComb w/o VarBind + no DIR	0.58
AvgComb w/o VarBind + word DIR	0.60
AvgComb w/o VarBind + phrase DIR	0.73
VS-Add	0.78
VS-Mul	0.58
VS-Pairwise	0.77
Ensemble (VS-Add + VS-Mul + VS-Pairwise)	0.83
Ensemble ([AvgComb + phrase DIR] + VS-Add + VS-Mul + VS-Pairwise)	0.85
Best MSR-Vid score in STS 2012 (Bär et al., 2012)	0.87

Table 2: Results on the STS video dataset.

on the training data. We then compare the performance of an ensemble with and without our system. This is the same technique used by Bär et al. (2012) except we used additive regression (Friedman, 2002) instead of linear regression since it gave better results.

5.3 Results

Table 2 summarizes the results of our experiments. They show that adding distributional information improves results, as expected, and also that adding phrase rules gives further improvement: Using only word distributional inference rules improves results from 0.58 to 0.6, and adding phrase inference rules further improves them to 0.66. As for variable binding, note that although it provides more precise information, the STS scores actually improve when it is dropped, from 0.66 to 0.73. We offer two explanations for this result: First, this information is very sensitive to parsing errors, and the C&C parser, on which Boxer is based, produces many errors on this dataset, even for simple sentences. When the C&C CCG parse is wrong, the resulting logical form is wrong, and the resulting similarity score is greatly affected. Dropping variable binding makes the systems more robust to parsing errors. Second, in contrast to RTE, the STS dataset does not really test the important role of syntax and logical form in determining meaning. This also explains why the "distributional only" baselines are actually doing better than the MLN systems.

Although the MLN system on its own does not perform better than the distributional compositional models, it does provide complementary information, as shown by the fact that ensembling it with the rest of the models improves performance (0.85 with the MLN system, compared to 0.83 without it). The performance of this ensemble is close to the current best result for this dataset (0.87).

6 Future Work

The approach presented in this paper constitutes a step towards achieving the challenging goal of effectively combining logical representations with distributional information automatically acquired from text. In this section, we discuss some of limitations of the current work and directions for future research.

As noted before, parse errors are currently a significant problem. We use Boxer to obtain a logical representation for a sentence, which in turn relies on the C&C parser. Unfortunately, C&C misparses many sentences, which leads to inaccurate logical forms. To reduce the impact of misparsing, we plan to use a version of C&C that can produce the top-n parses together with parse re-ranking (Ng and Curran, 2012). As an alternative to re-ranking, one could obtain logical forms for each of the top-n parses, and create an MLN that integrates all of them (together with their certainty) as an underspecified meaning representation that could then be used to directly support inferences such as STS and RTE.

We also plan to exploit a greater variety of distributional inference rules. First, we intend to incorporate logical form translations of existing distributional inference rule collections (e.g., (Berant et al., 2011; Chan et al., 2011)). Another issue is obtaining improved rule weights based on distributional phrase vectors. We plan to experiment with more sophisticated approaches to computing phrase vectors such as those recently presented by Baroni and Zamparelli (2010) and Grefenstette and Sadrzadeh (2011). Furthermore, we are currently deriving symmetric similarity ratings between word pairs or phrase pairs, when really what we need is directional similarity. We plan to incorporate directed similarity measures such as those of Kotlerman et al. (2010) and Clarke (2012).

A primary problem for our approach is the limitations of existing MLN inference algorithms, which do not effectively scale to large and complex MLNs. We plan to explore "coarser" logical representations such as Minimal Recursion Semantics (MRS) (Copestake et al., 2005). Another potential approach to this problem is to trade expressivity for efficiency. Domingos and Webb (2012) introduced a tractable subset of Markov Logic (TML) for which a future software release is planned. Formulating the inference problem in TML could potentially allow us to run our system on longer and more complex sentences.

7 Conclusion

In this paper we have used an approach that combines logic-based and distributional representations for natural language meaning. It uses logic as the primary representation, transforms distributional similarity judgments to weighted inference rules, and uses Markov Logic Networks to perform inferences over the weighted clauses. This approach views textual entailment and sentence similarity as degrees of "logical" entailment, while at the same time using distributional similarity as an indicator of entailment at the word and short phrase level. We have evaluated the framework on two different tasks, RTE and STS, finding that it is able to handle both tasks given that we adapt the way evidence is combined in the MLN. Even though other entailment models could be applied to STS, given that similarity can obviously be operationalized as a degree of mutual entailment, this has not been done before to our best knowledge. Our framework achieves reasonable results on both tasks. On RTE-1 we obtain an accuracy of 0.57. On STS, we obtain a correlation of $r = 0.66$ with full logic, $r = 0.73$ in a system with weakened variable binding, and $r = 0.85$ in an ensemble model. We find that distributional word and phrase similarity, used as textual inference rules on the fly, leads to sizeable improvements on both tasks. We also find that using more flexible probabilistic combinations of evidence is crucial for STS.

Acknowledgements

This research was supported in part by the NSF CAREER grant IIS 0845925, by the DARPA DEFT program under AFRL grant FA8750-13-2-0026, by MURI ARO grant W911NF-08-1-0242 and by an NDSEG grant. Any opinions, findings, and conclusions or recommendations expressed in this material are those of the author and do not necessarily reflect the view of DARPA, AFRL, ARO, DoD or the US government.

Some of our experiments were run on the Mastodon Cluster supported by NSF Grant EIA-0303609.

References

Eneko Agirre, Daniel Cer, Mona Diab, and Aitor Gonzalez-Agirre. 2012. Semeval-2012 task 6: A pilot on semantic textual similarity. In *Proceedings of SemEval*.

Daniel Bär, Chris Biemann, Iryna Gurevych, and Torsten Zesch. 2012. UKP: Computing semantic textual similarity by combining multiple content similarity measures. In *SemEval-2012*.

Marco Baroni and Roberto Zamparelli. 2010. Nouns are vectors, adjectives are matrices: Representing adjective-noun constructions in semantic space. In *Proceedings of the 2010 Conference on Empirical Methods in Natural Language Processing*, pages 1183–1193, Cambridge, MA, October. Association for Computational Linguistics.

Samuel Bayer, John Burger, Lisa Ferro, John Henderson, and Alexander Yeh. 2005. MITREs Submissions to the EU Pascal RTE Challenge. In *In Proceedings of the PASCAL Challenges Workshop on Recognising Textual Entailment*, pages 41–44.

Jonathan Berant, Ido Dagan, and Jacob Goldberger. 2011. Global learning of typed entailment rules. In *Proceedings of ACL*, Portland, OR.

Johan Bos and Katja Markert. 2005. Recognising textual entailment with logical inference. In *Proceedings of EMNLP 2005*, pages 628–635, Vancouver, B.C., Canada.

Johan Bos. 2008. Wide-coverage semantic analysis with boxer. In Johan Bos and Rodolfo Delmonte, editors, *Semantics in Text Processing. STEP 2008 Conference Proceedings*, Research in Computational Semantics, pages 277–286. College Publications.

Tsz Ping Chan, Chris Callison-Burch, and Benjamin Van Durme. 2011. Reranking bilingually extracted paraphrases using monolingual distributional similarity. In *Proceedings of the GEMS 2011 Workshop on GEometrical Models of Natural Language Semantics*, pages 33–42, Edinburgh, UK.

David L. Chen and William B. Dolan. 2011. Collecting highly parallel data for paraphrase evaluation. In *Proceedings of the 49th Annual Meeting of the Association for Computational Linguistics*, pages 190–200, Portland, Oregon, USA, June.

Stephen Clark and James R. Curran. 2004. Parsing the WSJ using CCG and log-linear models. In *Proceedings of ACL 2004*, pages 104–111, Barcelona, Spain.

Daoud Clarke. 2012. A context-theoretic framework for compositionality in distributional semantics. *Computational Linguistics*, 38(1).

Ann Copestake, Dan Flickinger, Carl Pollard, and Ivan A Sag. 2005. Minimal recursion semantics: An introduction. *Research on Language and Computation*, 3(2-3):281–332.

Ido Dagan, Oren Glickman, and Bernardo Magnini. 2005. The PASCAL Recognising Textual Entailment Challenge. In *In Proceedings of the PASCAL Challenges Workshop on Recognising Textual Entailment*, pages 1–8.

Pedro Domingos and Daniel Lowd. 2009. *Markov Logic: An Interface Layer for Artificial Intelligence*. Synthesis Lectures on Artificial Intelligence and Machine Learning. Morgan & Claypool Publishers.

Pedro Domingos and W Austin Webb. 2012. A tractable first-order probabilistic logic. In *Proceedings of the Twenty-Sixth National Conference on Artificial Intelligence*.

Katrin Erk and Sebastian Padó. 2008. A structured vector space model for word meaning in context. In *Proceedings of EMNLP 2008*, pages 897–906, Honolulu, HI.

Jerome H Friedman. 2002. Stochastic gradient boosting. *Computational Statistics & Data Analysis*, 38(4):367–378.

Dan Garrette, Katrin Erk, and Raymond Mooney. 2011. Integrating logical representations with probabilistic information using markov logic. In *Proceedings of IWCS*, Oxford, UK.

Dan Garrette, Katrin Erk, and Raymond Mooney. 2013. A formal approach to linking logical form and vector-space lexical semantics. In Harry Bunt, Johan Bos, and Stephen Pulman, editors, *Computing Meaning, Vol. 4*.

Lise Getoor and Ben Taskar, editors. 2007. *Introduction to Statistical Relational Learning*. MIT Press, Cambridge, MA.

David Graff, Junbo Kong, Ke Chen, and Kazuaki Maeda. 2007. English Gigaword Third Edition. `http://www.ldc.upenn.edu/Catalog/CatalogEntry.jsp?catalogId=LDC2007T07`.

Edward Grefenstette and Mehrnoosh Sadrzadeh. 2011. Experimental support for a categorical compositional distributional model of meaning. In *Proceedings of EMNLP*, Edinburgh, Scotland, UK.

Andrew Hickl. 2008. Using Discourse Commitments to Recognize Textual Entailment. In *Proceedings of COLING 2008*, pages 337–344.

Jerry R. Hobbs, Mark Stickel, Douglas Appelt, and Paul Martin. 1993. Interpretation as abduction. *Artificial Intelligence*, 63(1–2):69–142.

Hans Kamp and Uwe Reyle. 1993. *From Discourse to Logic; An Introduction to Modeltheoretic Semantics of Natural Language, Formal Logic and DRT*. Kluwer, Dordrecht.

Stanley Kok, Parag Singla, Matthew Richardson, and Pedro Domingos. 2005. The Alchemy system for statistical relational AI. Technical report, Department of Computer Science and Engineering, University of Washington. `http://www.cs.washington.edu/ai/alchemy`.

Lili Kotlerman, Ido Dagan, Idan Szpektor, and Maayan Zhitomirsky-Geffet. 2010. Directional distributional similarity for lexical inference. *Natural Language Engineering*, 16(04):359–389.

Thomas Landauer and Susan Dumais. 1997. A solution to Platos problem: the latent semantic analysis theory of acquisition, induction, and representation of knowledge. *Psychological Review*, 104(2):211–240.

Dekang Lin and Patrick Pantel. 2001a. DIRT - discovery of inference rules from text. In *In Proceedings of the ACM SIGKDD Conference on Knowledge Discovery and Data Mining*, pages 323–328.

Dekang Lin and Patrick Pantel. 2001b. Discovery of inference rules for question answering. *Natural Language Engineering*, 7(4):343–360.

Will Lowe. 2001. Towards a theory of semantic space. In *Proceedings of the Cognitive Science Society*, pages 576–581.

Kevin Lund and Curt Burgess. 1996. Producing high-dimensional semantic spaces from lexical co-occurrence. *Behavior Research Methods, Instruments, and Computers*, 28:203–208.

Rada Mihalcea, Courtney Corley, and Carlo Strapparava. 2006. Corpus-based and knowledge-based measures of text semantic similarity. In *Proceedings of the national conference on artificial intelligence*, volume 21, page 775. Menlo Park, CA; Cambridge, MA; London; AAAI Press; MIT Press; 1999.

Jeff Mitchell and Mirella Lapata. 2008. Vector-based models of semantic composition. In *Proceedings of ACL*, pages 236–244.

Jeff Mitchell and Mirella Lapata. 2010. Composition in distributional models of semantics. *Cognitive Science*, 34(8):1388–1429.

Richard Montague. 1970. Universal grammar. *Theoria*, 36:373–398. Reprinted in Thomason (1974), pp 7-27.

Sriraam Natarajan, Tushar Khot, Daniel Lowd, Prasad Tadepalli, Kristian Kersting, and Jude Shavlik. 2010. Exploiting causal independence in markov logic networks: Combining undirected and directed models. In *Proceedings of European Conference in Machine Learning (ECML)*, Barcelona, Spain.

Dominick Ng and James R Curran. 2012. Dependency hashing for n-best ccg parsing. In *In Proceedings of the 50th Annual Meeting of the Association for Computational Linguistics*.

Rajat Raina, Andrew Y. Ng, and Christopher D. Manning. 2005. Robust textual inference via learning and abductive reasoning. In *Proceedings of AAAI*.

Matthew Richardson and Pedro Domingos. 2006. Markov logic networks. *Machine Learning*, 62:107–136.

Hinrich Schütze. 1998. Automatic word sense discrimination. *Computational Linguistics*, 24(1).

Richard Socher, Eric Huang, Jeffrey Pennin, Andrew Ng, and Christopher Manning. 2011. Dynamic pooling and unfolding recursive autoencoders for paraphrase detection. In J. Shawe-Taylor, R.S. Zemel, P. Bartlett, F.C.N. Pereira, and K.Q. Weinberger, editors, *Proceedings of NIPS*.

Asher Stern, Amnon Lotan, Shachar Mirkin, Eyal Shnarch, Lili Kotlerman, Jonathan Berant, and Ido Dagan. 2011 Knowledge and tree-edits in learnable entailment proofs. In *TAC*, Gathersburg, MD.

Idan Szpektor and Ido Dagan. 2008. Learning entailment rules for unary templates. In *Proceedings of COLING*.

Stefan Thater, Hagen Fürstenau, and Manfred Pinkal. 2010. Contextualizing semantic representations using syntactically enriched vector models. In *Proceedings of ACL 2010*, pages 948–957, Uppsala, Sweden.

Richmond H. Thomason, editor. 1974. *Formal Philosophy. Selected Papers of Richard Montague*. Yale University Press, New Haven.

Peter Turney and Patrick Pantel. 2010. From frequency to meaning: Vector space models of semantics. *Journal of Artificial Intelligence Research*, 37:141–188.

Coarse to Fine Grained Sense Disambiguation in Wikipedia

Hui Shen
School of EECS
Ohio University
Athens, OH 45701, USA
hui.shen.1@ohio.edu

Razvan Bunescu
School of EECS
Ohio University
Athens, OH 45701, USA
bunescu@ohio.edu

Rada Mihalcea
Department of CSE
University of North Texas
Denton, TX 76203, USA
rada@cs.unt.edu

Abstract

Wikipedia articles are annotated by volunteer contributors with numerous links that connect words and phrases to relevant titles. Links to general senses of a word are used concurrently with links to more specific senses, without being distinguished explicitly. We present an approach to training coarse to fine grained sense disambiguation systems in the presence of such annotation inconsistencies. Experimental results show that accounting for annotation ambiguity in Wikipedia links leads to significant improvements in disambiguation.

1 Introduction and Motivation

The vast amount of world knowledge available in Wikipedia has been shown to benefit many types of text processing tasks, such as coreference resolution (Ponzetto and Strube, 2006; Haghighi and Klein, 2009; Bryl et al., 2010; Rahman and Ng, 2011), information retrieval (Milne, 2007; Li et al., 2007; Potthast et al., 2008; Cimiano et al., 2009), or question answering (Ahn et al., 2004; Kaisser, 2008; Ferrucci et al., 2010). In particular, the user contributed link structure of Wikipedia has been shown to provide useful supervision for training named entity disambiguation (Bunescu and Pasca, 2006; Cucerzan, 2007) and word sense disambiguation (Mihalcea, 2007; Ponzetto and Navigli, 2010) systems. Articles in Wikipedia often contain mentions of concepts or entities that already have a corresponding article. When contributing authors mention an existing Wikipedia entity inside an article, they are required to link at least its first mention to the corresponding article, by using *links* or *piped links*. Consider, for example, the following Wiki source annotations: *The [[capital city | capital]] of Georgia is [[Atlanta]].* The bracketed strings identify the title of the Wikipedia articles that describe the corresponding named entities. If the editor wants a different string displayed in the rendered text, then the alternative string is included in a piped link, after the title string. Based on these Wiki processing rules, the text that is rendered for the aforementioned example is: *The capital of Georgia is Atlanta.*

Since many words and names mentioned in Wikipedia articles are inherently ambiguous, their corresponding links can be seen as a useful source of supervision for training named entity and word sense disambiguation systems. For example, Wikipedia contains articles that describe possible senses of the word "capital", such as CAPITAL CITY, CAPITAL (ECONOMICS), FINANCIAL CAPITAL, or HUMAN CAPITAL, to name only a few. When disambiguating a word or a phrase in Wikipedia, a contributor uses the context to determine the appropriate Wikipedia title to include in the link. In the example above, the editor of the article determined that the word "capital" was mentioned with the political center meaning, consequently it was mapped to the article CAPITAL CITY through a piped link.

In order to use Wikipedia links for training a WSD system for a given word, one needs first to define a sense repository that specifies the possible meanings for that word, and then use the Wikipedia links to create training examples for each sense in the repository. This approach might be implemented using the following sequence of steps:

*Second Joint Conference on Lexical and Computational Semantics (*SEM), Volume 1: Proceedings of the Main Conference and the Shared Task*, pages 22–31, Atlanta, Georgia, June 13-14, 2013. ©2013 Association for Computational Linguistics

In global climate models, the state and properties of the [[atmosphere]] are specified at a number of discrete locations
General = **ATMOSPHERE**; *Specific* = ATMOSPHERE OF EARTH; *Label* = A → A(S) → AE

The principal natural phenomena that contribute gases to the [[Atmosphere of Earth|atmosphere]] are emissions from volcanoes
General = ATMOSPHERE; *Specific* = **ATMOSPHERE OF EARTH**; *Label* = A → A(S) → AE

An aerogravity assist is a spacecraft maneuver designed to change velocity when arriving at a body with an [[atmosphere]]
General = **ATMOSPHERE**; *Specific* = ATMOSPHERE ▷ *generic*; *Label* = A → A(G)

Assuming the planet's [[atmosphere]] is close to equilibrium, it is predicted that 55 Cancri d is covered with water clouds
General = **ATMOSPHERE**; *Specific* = ATMOSPHERE OF CANCRI ▷ *missing*; A → A(G)

Figure 1: Coarse and fine grained sense annotations in Wikipedia (**bold**). The proposed hierarchical *Label* (right). A(S) = ATMOSPHERE (S), A(G) = ATMOSPHERE (G), A = ATMOSPHERE, AE = ATMOSPHERE OF EARTH.

1. Collect all Wikipedia titles that are linked from the ambiguous anchor word.
2. Create a repository of senses from all titles that have sufficient support in Wikipedia i.e., titles that are referenced at least a predefined minimum number of times using the ambiguous word as anchor.
3. Use the links extracted for each sense in the repository as labeled examples for that sense and train a WSD model to distinguish between alternative senses of the ambiguous word.

Taking the word "atmosphere" as an example, the first step would result in a wide array of titles, ranging from the general ATMOSPHERE and its instantiations ATMOSPHERE OF EARTH or ATMOSPHERE OF MARS, to titles as diverse as ATMOSPHERE (UNIT), MOOD (PSYCHOLOGY), or ATMOSPHERE (MUSIC GROUP). In the second step, the most frequent titles for the anchor word "atmosphere" would be assembled into a repository $\mathcal{R}$ = {ATMOSPHERE, ATMOSPHERE OF EARTH, ATMOSPHERE OF MARS, ATMOSPHERE OF VENUS, STELLAR ATMOSPHERE, ATMOSPHERE (UNIT), ATMOSPHERE (MUSIC GROUP)}. The classifier trained in the third step would use features extracted from the context to discriminate between word senses.

This Wikipedia-based approach to creating training data for word sense disambiguation has a major shortcoming. Many of the training examples extracted for the title ATMOSPHERE could very well belong to more specific titles such as ATMOSPHERE OF EARTH or ATMOSPHERE OF MARS. Whenever the word "atmosphere" is used in a context with the sense of "a layer of gases that may surround a material body of sufficient mass, and that is held in place by the gravity of the body," the contributor has the option of adding a link either to the title ATMOSPHERE that describes this general sense of the word, or to the title of an article that describes the atmosphere of the actual celestial body that is referred in that particular context, as shown in the first 2 examples in Figure 1. As shown in bold in Figure 1, different occurrences of the same word may be tagged with either a general or a specific link, an ambiguity that is pervasive in Wikipedia for words like "atmosphere" that have general senses that subsume multiple, popular specific senses. There does not seem to be a clear, general rule underlying the decision to tag a word or a phrase with a general or specific sense link in Wikipedia. We hypothesize that, in some cases, editors may be unaware that an article exists in Wikipedia for the actual reference of a word or for a more specific sense of the word, and therefore they end up using a link to an article describing the general sense of the word. There is also the possibility that more specific articles are introduced only in newer versions of Wikipedia, and thus earlier annotations were not aware of these recent articles. Furthermore, since annotating words with the most specific sense available in Wikipedia may require substantial cognitive effort, editors may often choose to link to a general sense of the word, a choice that is still correct, yet less informative than the more specific sense.

2 Annotation Inconsistencies in Wikipedia

In order to get a sense of the potential magnitude of the general vs. specific sense annotation ambiguity, we extracted all Wikipedia link annotations for the words "atmosphere", "president", "game", "dollar", "diamond" and "Corinth", and created a special subset from those that were labeled by Wikipedia editors with the general sense links ATMOSPHERE, PRESIDENT, GAME, DOLLAR, DIAMOND, and CORINTH, respectively. Then, for each of the 7,079 links in this set, we used the context to manually determine the corresponding more specific title, whenever such a title exists in Wikipedia. The statistics in Tables 1 and 2 show a significant overlap between the general and specific sense categories. For example, out of the 932 links from "atmosphere" to ATMOSPHERE that were extracted in total, 518 were actually about the ATMOSPHERE OF EARTH, but the user linked them to the more general sense category ATMOSPHERE. On the other hand, there are 345 links to ATMOSPHERE OF EARTH that were explicitly made by the user. We manually assigned *general* links (G) whenever the word is used with a generic sense, or when the reference is not available in the repository of titles collected for that word because either the more specific title does not exist in Wikipedia or the specific title exists, but it does not have sufficient support – at least 20 linked anchors – in Wikipedia. We grouped the more specific links for any given sense into a special category suffixed with (S), to distinguish them from the general links (generic use, or missing reference) that were grouped into the category suffixed with (G).

For many ambiguous words, the annotation inconsistencies appear when the word has senses that are in a subsumption relationship: the ATMOSPHERE OF EARTH is an instance of ATMOSPHERE, whereas a STELLAR ATMOSPHERE is a particular type of ATMOSPHERE. Subsumed senses can be identified automatically using the category graph in Wikipedia. The word "Corinth" is an interesting case: the subsumption relationship between ANCIENT CORINTH and CORINTH appears because of a temporal constraint. Furthermore, in the case of the word "diamond", the annotation inconsistencies are not caused by a subsumption relation between senses. Instead of linking to the DIAMOND (GEMSTONE) sense, Wikipedia contributors often link to the related DIAMOND sense indicating the mineral used in the gemstone.

A supervised learning algorithm that uses the extracted links for training a WSD classification model

atmosphere	Size
ATMOSPHERE	932
Atmosphere (S)	*559*
Atmosphere of Earth	*518*
Atmosphere of Mars	*19*
Atmosphere of Venus	*9*
Stellar Atmosphere	*13*
Atmosphere (G)	*373*
ATMOSPHERE OF EARTH	345
ATMOSPHERE OF MARS	37
ATMOSPHERE OF VENUS	26
STELLAR ATMOSPHERE	29
ATMOSPHERE (UNIT)	96
ATMOSPHERE (MUSIC GROUP)	104
president	Size
PRESIDENT	3534
President (S)	*989*
Chancellor (education)	*326*
President of the United States	*534*
President of the Philippines	*42*
President of Pakistan	*27*
President of France	*22*
President of India	*21*
President of Russia	*17*
President (G)	*2545*
CHANCELLOR (EDUCATION)	210
PRESIDENT OF THE UNITED STATES	5941
PRESIDENT OF THE PHILIPPINES	549
PRESIDENT OF PAKISTAN	192
PRESIDENT OF FRANCE	151
PRESIDENT OF INDIA	86
PRESIDENT OF RUSSIA	101

Table 1: Wiki (CAPS) and manual (*italics*) annotations.

to distinguish between categories in the sense repository assumes implicitly that the categories, and hence their training examples, are mutually disjoint. This assumption is clearly violated for words like "atmosphere," consequently the learned model will have a poor performance on distinguishing between the overlapping categories. Alternatively, we can say that sense categories like ATMOSPHERE are ill defined, since their supporting dataset contains examples that could also belong to more specific sense categories such as ATMOSPHERE OF EARTH.

We see two possible solutions to the problem of inconsistent link annotations. In one solution, specific senses are grouped together with the subsuming general sense, such that all categories in the resulting repository become disjoint. For "atmosphere", the general category ATMOSPHERE would be augmented to contain all the links previously annotated

dollar	Size
DOLLAR	379
Dollar (S)	*231*
United States dollar	*228*
Canadian dollar	*3*
Australian dollar	*1*
Dollar (G)	*147*
UNITED STATES DOLLAR	3516
CANADIAN DOLLAR	420
AUSTRALIAN DOLLAR	124
DOLLAR SIGN	290
DOLLAR (BAND)	30
DOLLAR, CLACKMANNANSHIRE	30
game	Size
GAME	819
Game (S)	*99*
Video game	*55*
PC game	*44*
Game (G)	*720*
VIDEO GAME	312
PC GAME	24
GAME (FOOD)	232
GAME (RAPPER)	154
diamond	Size
DIAMOND	716
Diamond (S)	*221*
Diamond (gemstone)	*221*
Diamond (G)	*495*
DIAMOND (GEMSTONE)	71
BASEBALL FIELD	36
MUSIC RECORDING SALES CERT.	36
Corinth	Size
CORINTH	699
Corinth (S)	*409*
Ancient Corinth	*409*
Corinth (G)	*290*
ANCIENT CORINTH	92
CORINTH, MISSISSIPPI	72

Table 2: Wiki (CAPS) and manual (*italics*) annotations.

as ATMOSPHERE, ATMOSPHERE OF EARTH, ATMOSPHERE OF MARS, ATMOSPHERE OF VENUS, or STELLAR ATMOSPHERE. This solution is straightforward to implement, however it has the disadvantage that the resulting WSD model will never link words to more specific titles in Wikipedia like ATMOSPHERE OF MARS.

Another solution is to reorganize the original sense repository into a hierarchical classification scheme such that sense categories at each classification level become mutually disjoint. The resulting WSD system has the advantage that it can make fine grained sense distinctions for an ambiguous word, despite the annotation inconsistencies present in the training data. The rest of this paper describes a feasible implementation for this second solution that does not require any manual annotation beyond the links that are already provided by Wikipedia volunteers.

3 Learning for Coarse to Fine Grained Sense Disambiguation

Figure 2 shows our proposed hierarchical classification scheme for disambiguation, using "atmosphere" as the ambiguous word. Shaded leaf nodes show the final categories in the sense repository for each word, whereas the doted elliptical frames on the second level in the hierarchy denote artificial categories introduced to enable a finer grained classification into more specific senses. Thick dotted arrows illustrate the classification decisions that are made in order to obtain a fine grained disambiguation of the word. Thus, the word "atmosphere" is first classified to have the general sense ATMOSPHERE, i.e. "a layer of gases that may surround a material body of sufficient mass, and that is held in place by the gravity of the body". In the first solution, the disambiguation process would stop here and output the general sense ATMOSPHERE. In the second solution, the disambiguation process continues and further classifies the word to be a reference to ATMOSPHERE OF EARTH. To get to this final classification, the process passes through an intermediate binary classification level where it determines whether the word has a more specific sense covered in Wikipedia, corresponding to the artificial category ATMOSPHERE (S). If the answer is no, the system stops the disambiguation process and outputs the general sense category ATMOSPHERE. This basic sense hierarchy can be replicated depending on the existence of even finer sense distinctions in Wikipedia. For example, Wikipedia articles describing atmospheres of particular stars could be used to further refine STELLAR ATMOSPHERE with two additional levels of the type Level 2 and Level 3. Overall, the proposed disambiguation scheme could be used to relabel the ATMOSPHERE links in Wikipedia with more specific, and therefore more informative, senses such as ATMOSPHERE OF EARTH. In general, the Wikipedia category graph could be used to automatically create hierarchical structures for re-

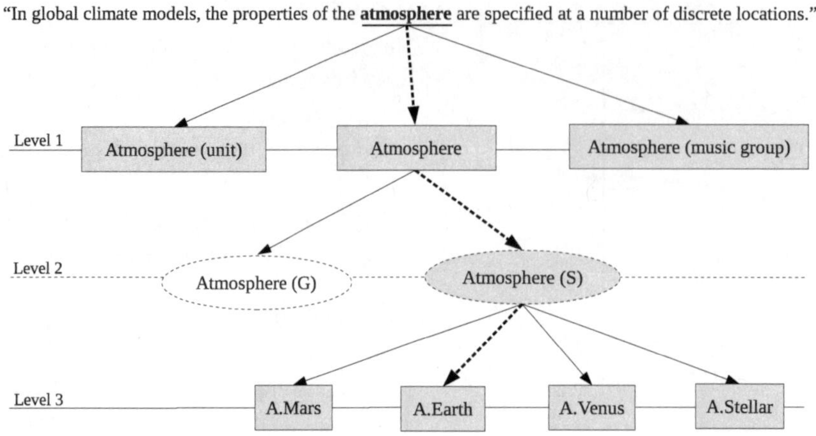

Figure 2: Hierarchical disambiguation scheme, from coarse to fine grained senses.

lated senses of the same word.

Training word sense classifiers for Levels 1 and 3 is straightforward. For Level 1, Wikipedia links that are annotated by users as ATMOSPHERE, ATMOSPHERE OF EARTH, ATMOSPHERE OF MARS, ATMOSPHERE OF VENUS, or STELLAR ATMOSPHERE are collected as training examples for the general sense category ATMOSPHERE. Similarly, links that are annotated as ATMOSPHERE (UNIT) and ATMOSPHERE (MUSIC GROUP) will be used as training examples for the two categories, respectively. A multiclass classifier is then trained to distinguish between the three categories at this level. For Level 3, a multiclass classifiers is trained on Wikipedia links collected for each of the 4 specific senses.

For the binary classifier at Level 2, we could use as training examples for the category ATMOSPHERE (G) all Wikipedia links that were annotated as ATMOSPHERE, whereas for the category ATMOSPHERE (S) we could use as training examples all Wikipedia links that were annotated specifically as ATMOSPHERE OF EARTH, ATMOSPHERE OF MARS, ATMOSPHERE OF VENUS, or STELLAR ATMOSPHERE. A traditional binary classification SVM could be trained on this dataset to distinguish between the two categories. We call this approach *Naive SVM*, since it does not account for the fact that a significant number of the links that are annotated by Wikipedia contributors as ATMOSPHERE should actually belong to the ATMOSPHERE (S) category – about 60% of them, according to Table 1. Instead, we propose treating all ATMOSPHERE links as unlabeled examples. If we consider the specific links in ATMOSPHERE (S) to be positive examples, then the problem becomes one of *learning with positive and unlabeled examples*.

3.1 Learning with positive and unlabeled examples

This general type of semi-supervised learning has been studied before in the context of tasks such as text classification and information retrieval (Lee and Liu, 2003; Liu et al., 2003), or bioinformatics (Elkan and Noto, 2008; Noto et al., 2008). In this setting, the training data consists of positive examples $x \in P$ and unlabeled examples $x \in U$. Following the notation of Elkan and Noto (2008), we define $s(x) = 1$ if the example is positive and $s(x) = -1$ if the example is unlabeled. The true label of an example is $y(x) = 1$ if the example is positive and $y(x) = -1$ if the example is negative. Thus, $x \in P \Rightarrow s(x) = y(x) = 1$ and $x \in U \Rightarrow s(x) = -1$ i.e., the true label $y(x)$ of an unlabeled example is unknown. For the experiments reported in this paper, we use our implementation of two state-of-the-art approaches to Learning with Positive and Unlabeled (LPU) examples: the *Biased SVM* formulation of Lee and Liu (2003) and the *Weighted Samples SVM* formulation of Elkan and Noto (2008). The original version of Biased SVM was designed to maximize the product between precision and recall. In the next section we describe a modification to the Biased SVM approach that can be used to maximize accuracy, a measure that is often used to evaluate WSD performance.

3.1.1 The Biased SVM

In the Biased SVM formulation (Lee and Liu, 2003; Liu et al., 2003), all unlabeled examples are considered to be negative and the decision function $f(x) = \mathbf{w}^T\phi(x) + b$ is learned using the standard soft-margin SVM formulation shown in Figure 3.

$$\text{minimize:} \quad \frac{1}{2}\|\mathbf{w}\|^2 + C_P \sum_{x \in P} \xi_x + C_U \sum_{x \in U} \xi_x$$

$$\text{subject to:} \quad s(x)\left(\mathbf{w}^T\phi(x) + b\right) \geq 1 - \xi_x$$
$$\xi_x \geq 0, \;\; \forall x \in P \cup U$$

Figure 3: Biased SVM optimization problem.

The capacity parameters C_P and C_U control how much we penalize errors on positive examples vs. errors on unlabeled examples. Since not all unlabeled examples are negative, one would want to select capacity parameters satisfying $C_P > C_U$, such that false negative errors are penalized more than false positive errors. In order to find the best capacity parameters to use during training, the Biased SVM approach runs a grid search on a separate development dataset. This search is aimed at finding values for the parameters C_P and C_U that maximize pr, the product between precision $p = p(y = 1|f = 1)$ and recall $r = p(f = 1|y = 1)$. Lee and Liu (2003) show that maximizing the pr criterion is equivalent with maximizing the objective $r^2/p(f = 1)$, where both $r = p(f = 1|y = 1)$ and $p(f = 1)$ can be estimated using the trained decision function $f(x)$ on the development dataset.

Maximizing the pr criterion in the original Biased SVM formulation was motivated by the need to optimize the F measure in information retrieval settings, where $F = 2pr(p+r)$. In the rest of this section we show that classification *accuracy* can be maximized using only positive and unlabeled examples, an important result for problems where classification accuracy is the target performance measure.

The accuracy of a binary decision function $f(x)$ is, by definition, $acc = p(f = 1|y = 1) + p(f = -1|y = -1)$. Since the recall is $r = p(f = 1|y = 1)$, the accuracy can be re-written as:

$$acc = r + 1 - p(f = 1|y = -1) \qquad (1)$$

Using Bayes' rule twice, the false positive term $p(f = 1|y = -1)$ can be re-written as:

$$\begin{aligned} p(f = 1|y = -1) &= \frac{p(f = 1)p(y = -1|f = 1)}{p(y = -1)} \\ &= \frac{p(f = 1)}{p(y = -1)} \times (1 - p(y = 1|f = 1)) \\ &= \frac{p(f = 1)}{p(y = -1)} - \frac{p(f = 1)}{p(y = -1)} \times \frac{p(y = 1)p(f = 1|y = 1)}{p(f = 1)} \\ &= \frac{p(f = 1) - p(y = 1) \times r}{p(y = -1)} \qquad (2) \end{aligned}$$

Plugging identity 2 in Equation 1 leads to:

$$\begin{aligned} acc &= 1 + r + \frac{r \times p(y = 1) - p(f = 1)}{p(y = -1)} \\ &= 1 + \frac{r - p(f = 1)}{p(y = -1)} \qquad (3) \end{aligned}$$

Since $p(y = -1)$ can be assimilated with a constant, Equation 3 implies that maximizing accuracy is equivalent with maximizing the criterion $r - p(f = 1)$, where both the recall r and $p(f = 1)$ can be estimated on the positive and unlabeled examples from a separate development dataset.

In conclusion, one can use the original Biased SVM formulation to maximize $r^2/p(f = 1)$, which has been shown by Lee and Liu (2003) to maximize pr, a criterion that has a similar behavior with the F-measure used in retrieval applications. Alternatively, if the target performance measure is accuracy, we can choose instead to maximize $r - p(f = 1)$, which we have shown above to correspond to accuracy maximization.

3.1.2 The Weighted Samples SVM

Elkan and Noto (2008) introduced two approaches for learning with positive and unlabeled data. Both approaches are based on the assumption that labeled examples $\{x|s(x) = 1\}$ are selected at random from the positive examples $\{x|y(x) = 1\}$ i.e., $p(s = 1|x, y = 1) = p(s = 1|y = 1)$. Their best performing approach uses the positive and unlabeled examples to train two distinct classifiers. First, the dataset $P \cup U$ is split into a training set and a validation set, and a classifier $g(x)$ is trained on the labeling s to approximate the label distribution i.e. $g(x) = p(s = 1|x)$. The validation set is then used to estimate $p(s = 1|y = 1)$ as follows:

$$p(s{=}1|y{=}1) = p(s{=}1|x, y{=}1) = \frac{1}{|P|}\sum_{x \in P} g(x) \quad (4)$$

The second and final classifier $f(x)$ is trained on a dataset of weighted examples that are sampled from the original training set as follows:

- Each positive example $x \in P$ is copied as a positive example in the new training set with weight $p(y = 1|x, s = 1) = 1$.
- Each unlabeled example $x \in U$ is duplicated into two training examples in the new dataset: a positive example with weight $p(y = 1|x, s = 0)$ and a negative example with weight $p(y = -1|x, s = 0) = 1 - p(y = 1|x, s = 0)$.

Elkan and Noto (2008) show that the weights above can be derived as:

$$p(y{=}1|x, s{=}0) = \frac{1{-}p(s{=}1|y{=}1)}{p(s{=}1|y{=}1)} \times \frac{p(s{=}1|x)}{1{-}p(s{=}1|x)} \quad (5)$$

The output of the first classifier $g(x)$ is used to approximate the probability $p(s = 1|x)$, whereas $p(s = 1|y = 1)$ is estimated using Equation 4.

The two classifiers g and f are trained using SVMs and a linear kernel. Platt scaling is used with the first classifier to obtain the probability estimates $g(x) = p(s = 1|x)$, which are then converted into weights following Equations 4 and 5, and used during the training of the second classifier.

4 Experimental Evaluation

We ran disambiguation experiments on the 6 ambiguous words *atmosphere*, *president*, *dollar*, *game*, *diamond* and *Corinth*. The corresponding Wikipedia sense repositories have been summarized in Tables 1 and 2. All WSD classifiers used the same set of standard WSD features (Ng and Lee, 1996; Stevenson and Wilks, 2001), such as words and their part-of-speech tags in a window of 3 words around the ambiguous keyword, the unigram and bigram content words that are within 2 sentences of the current sentence, the syntactic governor of the keyword, and its chains of syntactic dependencies of lengths up to two. Furthermore, for each example, a Wikipedia specific feature was computed as the cosine similarity between the context of the ambiguous word and the text of the article for the target sense or reference.

The Level_1 and Level_3 classifiers were trained using the SVM^{multi} component of the SVM^{light} package.[1] The WSD classifiers were evaluated in a 4-fold cross validation scenario in which 50% of the data was used for training, 25% for tuning the capacity parameter C, and 25% for testing. The final accuracy numbers, shown in Table 3, were computed by averaging the results over the 4 folds. Since the word *president* has only one sense on Level_1, no classifier needed to be trained for this case. Similarly, words *diamond* and *Corinth* have only one sense on Level_3.

	atmosphere	*president*	*dollar*
Level_1	93.1%	—	94.1%
Level_3	85.6%	82.2%	90.8%
	game	*diamond*	*Corinth*
Level_1	82.9%	95.5%	92.7%
Level_3	92.9%	—	—

Table 3: Disambiguation accuracy at Levels 1 & 3.

The evaluation of the binary classifiers at the second level follows the same 4-fold cross validation scheme that was used for Level_1 and Level_3. The manual labels for specific senses and references in the unlabeled datasets are always ignored during training and tuning and used only during testing.

We compare the Naive SVM, Biased SVM, and Weighted SVM in the two evaluation settings, using for all of them the same train/development/test splits of the data and the same features. We emphasize that our manual labels are used only for testing purposes – the manual labels are ignored during training and tuning, when the data is assumed to contain only positive and unlabeled examples. We implemented the Biased SVM approach on top of the binary SVM^{light} package. The C_P and C_U parameters of the Biased SVM were tuned through the c and j parameters of SVM^{light} ($c = C_U$ and $j = C_P/C_U$). Eventually, all three methods use the development data for tuning the c and j parameters of the SVM. However, whereas the Naive SVM tunes these parameters to optimize the accuracy with respect to the noisy label $s(x)$, the Biased SVM tunes the same parameters to maximize an estimate of the accuracy or

[1]http://svmlight.joachims.org

F-measure with respect to the true label $y(x)$. The Weighted SVM approach was implemented on top of the LibSVM[2] package. Even though the original Weighted SVM method of Elkan and Noto (2008) does not specify tuning any parameters, we noticed it gave better results when the capacity c and weight j parameters were tuned for the first classifier $g(x)$.

Table 4 shows the accuracy results of the three methods for Level_2, whereas Table 5 shows the F-measure results. The Biased SVM outperforms the Naive SVM on all the words, in terms of both accuracy and F-measure. The most dramatic increases are seen for the words *atmosphere*, *game*, *diamond*, and *Corinth*. For these words, the number of positive examples is significantly smaller compared to the total number of positive and unlabeled examples. Thus, the percentage of positive examples relative to the total number of positive and unlabeled examples is 31.9% for *atmosphere*, 29.1% for *game*, 9.0% for *diamond*, and 11.6% for *Corinth*. The positive to total ratio is however significantly larger for the other two words: 67.2% for *president* and 91.5% for *dollar*. When the number of positive examples is large, the false negative noise from the unlabeled dataset in the Naive SVM approach will be relatively small, hence the good performance of Naive SVM in these cases. To check whether this is the case, we have also run experiments where we used only half of the available positive examples for the word *president* and one tenth of the positive examples for the word *dollar*, such that the positive datasets became comparable in size with the unlabeled datasets. The results for these experiments are shown in Tables 4 and 5 in the rows labeled $president_S$ and $dollar_S$. As expected, the difference between the performance of Naive SVM and Biased SVM gets larger on these smaller datasets, especially for the word *dollar*.

The Weighted SVM outperforms the Naive SVM on five out of the six words, the exception being the word *president*. Comparatively, the Biased SVM has a more stable behavior and overall results in a more substantial improvement over the Naive SVM. Based on these initial results, we see the Biased SVM as the method of choice for learning with positive and unlabeled examples in the task of coarse to fine grained sense disambiguation in Wikipedia.

[2]http://www.csie.ntu.edu.tw/~cjlin/libsvm

Word	NaiveSVM	BiasedSVM	WeightedSVM
atmosphere	39.9%	**79.6%**	75.0%
president	91.9%	**92.5%**	89.5%
dollar	96.0%	**97.0%**	**97.1%**
game	83.8%	**87.1%**	84.6%
diamond	70.2%	74.5%	**75.1%**
Corinth	46.2%	**75.1%**	51.9%
$president_S$	88.1%	**90.6%**	87.4%
$dollar_S$	70.3%	**84.9%**	70.6%

Table 4: Disambiguation accuracy at Level_2.

Word	NaiveSVM	BiasedSVM	WeightedSVM
atmosphere	30.5%	**86.0%**	83.2%
president	94.4%	**95.0%**	92.8%
dollar	97.9%	**98.4%**	**98.5%**
game	75.1%	**81.8%**	77.5%
diamond	8.6%	**53.5%**	46.3%
Corinth	15.3%	**81.2%**	68.0%
$president_S$	90.0%	**92.4%**	89.5%
$dollar_S$	77.9%	**91.2%**	78.2%

Table 5: Disambiguation F-measure at Level_2.

In a final set of experiments, we compared the traditional flat classification approach and our proposed hierarchical classifier in terms of their overall disambiguation accuracy. In these experiments, the sense repository contains all the leaf nodes as distinct sense categories. For example, the word *atmosphere* would correspond to the sense repository $\mathcal{R}$ = {ATMOSPHERE (G), ATMOSPHERE OF EARTH, ATMOSPHERE OF MARS, ATMOSPHERE OF VENUS, STELLAR ATMOSPHERE, ATMOSPHERE (UNIT), ATMOSPHERE (MUSIC GROUP)}. The overall accuracy results are shown in Table 6 and confirm the utility of using the LPU framework in the hierarchical model, which outperforms the traditional flat model, especially on words with low ratio of positive to unlabeled examples.

	atmosphere	*president*	*dollar*
Flat	52.4%	89.4%	90.0%
Hierarchical	79.7%	91.0%	90.1%
	game	*diamond*	*Corinth*
Flat	83.6%	65.7%	42.6%
Hierarchical	87.2%	76.8%	72.1%

Table 6: Flat vs. Hierarchical disambiguation accuracy.

5 Future Work

Annotation inconsistencies in Wikipedia were circumvented by adapting two existing approaches that use only positive and unlabeled data to train binary classifiers. This binary classification constraint led to the introduction of the artificial specific (S) category on $Level_2$ in our disambiguation framework. In future work, we plan to investigate a direct extension of learning with positive and unlabeled data to the case of multiclass classification, which will reduce the number of classification levels from 3 to 2. We also plan to investigate the use of unsupervised techniques in order to incorporate less popular references of a word in the hierarchical classification.

Conclusion

We presented an approach to training coarse to fine grained sense disambiguation systems that treats annotation inconsistencies in Wikipedia under the framework of learning with positive and unlabeled examples. Furthermore, we showed that the true accuracy of a decision function can be optimized using only positive and unlabeled examples. For testing purposes, we manually annotated 7,079 links belonging to six ambiguous words [3]. Experimental results demonstrate that accounting for annotation ambiguity in Wikipedia links leads to consistent improvements in disambiguation accuracy. The manual annotations were only used for testing and were ignored during training and development. Consequently, the proposed framework of learning with positive and unlabeled examples for sense disambiguation could be applied on the entire Wikipedia without any manual annotations. By augmenting general sense links with links to more specific articles, such an application could have a significant impact on Wikipedia itself.

Acknowledgments

This work was supported in part by the National Science Foundation IIS awards #1018613 and #1018590, and an allocation of computing time from the Ohio Supercomputer Center.

[3] Data and code will be made publicly available.

References

D. Ahn, V. Jijkoun, G. Mishne, K. Muller, M. de Rijke, and S. Schlobach. 2004. Using Wikipedia at the TREC QA track. In *Proceedings of the 13th Text Retrieval Conference (TREC 2004)*.

Volha Bryl, Claudio Giuliano, Luciano Serafini, and Kateryna Tymoshenko. 2010. Using background knowledge to support coreference resolution. In *Proceedings of the 2010 conference on ECAI 2010: 19th European Conference on Artificial Intelligence*, pages 759–764, Amsterdam, The Netherlands.

Razvan Bunescu and Marius Pasca. 2006. Using encyclopedic knowledge for named entity disambiguation. In *Proceesings of the 11th Conference of the European Chapter of the Association for Computational Linguistics (EACL-06)*, pages 9–16, Trento, Italy.

Philipp Cimiano, Antje Schultz, Sergej Sizov, Philipp Sorg, and Steffen Staab. 2009. Explicit versus latent concept models for cross-language information retrieval. In *International Joint Conference on Artificial Intelligence (IJCAI-09*, pages 1513–1518, Pasadena, CA, july.

S. Cucerzan. 2007. Large-scale named entity disambiguation based on Wikipedia data. In *Proceedings of the Conference on Empirical Methods in Natural Language Processing*, pages 708–716.

Charles Elkan and Keith Noto. 2008. Learning classifiers from only positive and unlabeled data. In *Proceedings of the 14th ACM SIGKDD international conference on Knowledge discovery and data mining*, KDD '08, pages 213–220.

David A. Ferrucci, Eric W. Brown, Jennifer Chu-Carroll, James Fan, David Gondek, Aditya Kalyanpur, Adam Lally, J. William Murdock, Eric Nyberg, John M. Prager, Nico Schlaefer, and Christopher A. Welty. 2010. Building watson: An overview of the deepqa project. *AI Magazine*, 31(3):59–79.

Aria Haghighi and Dan Klein. 2009. Simple coreference resolution with rich syntactic and semantic features. In *Proceedings of the 2009 Conference on Empirical Methods in Natural Language Processing*, pages 1152–1161, Singapore, August.

M. Kaisser. 2008. The QuALiM question answering demo: Supplementing answers with paragraphs drawn from Wikipedia. In *Proceedings of the ACL-08 Human Language Technology Demo Session*, pages 32–35, Columbus, Ohio.

Wee Sun Lee and Bing Liu. 2003. Learning with positive and unlabeled examples using weighted logistic regression. In *Proceedings of the Twentieth International Conference on Machine Learning (ICML*, pages 448–455, Washington, DC, August.

Y. Li, R. Luk, E. Ho, and K. Chung. 2007. Improving weak ad-hoc queries using Wikipedia as external corpus. In *Proceedings of the 30th Annual International ACM SIGIR Conference on Research and Development in Information Retrieval*, pages 797–798, Amsterdam, Netherlands.

Bing Liu, Yang Dai, Xiaoli Li, Wee Sun Lee, and Philip S. Yu. 2003. Building text classifiers using positive and unlabeled examples. In *Proceedings of the Third IEEE International Conference on Data Mining*, ICDM '03, pages 179–186, Washington, DC, USA.

R. Mihalcea. 2007. Using Wikipedia for automatic word sense disambiguation. In *Human Language Technologies 2007: The Conference of the North American Chapter of the Association for Computational Linguistics*, pages 196–203, Rochester, New York, April.

D. Milne. 2007. Computing semantic relatedness using Wikipedia link structure. In *Proceedings of the New Zealand Computer Science Research Student Conference*, Hamilton, New Zealand.

Hwee Tou Ng and H. B. Lee. 1996. Integrating multiple knowledge sources to disambiguate word sense: An exemplar-based approach. In *Proceedings of the 34th Annual Meeting of the Association for Computational Linguistics (ACL-96)*, pages 40–47, Santa Cruz, CA.

Keith Noto, Milton H. Saier, Jr., and Charles Elkan. 2008. Learning to find relevant biological articles without negative training examples. In *Proceedings of the 21st Australasian Joint Conference on Artificial Intelligence: Advances in Artificial Intelligence*, AI '08, pages 202–213.

Simone Paolo Ponzetto and Roberto Navigli. 2010. Knowledge-rich word sense disambiguation rivaling supervised systems. In *Proceedings of the 48th Annual Meeting of the Association for Computational Linguistics*, pages 1522–1531, Stroudsburg, PA, USA. Association for Computational Linguistics.

Simone Paolo Ponzetto and Michael Strube. 2006. Exploiting semantic role labeling, wordnet and wikipedia for coreference resolution. In *Proceedings of the Human Language Technology Conference of the North American Chapter of the Association of Computational Linguistics*, pages 192–199.

M. Potthast, B. Stein, and M. A. Anderka. 2008. Wikipedia-based multilingual retrieval model. In *Proceedings of the 30th European Conference on IR Research*, Glasgow.

Altaf Rahman and Vincent Ng. 2011. Coreference resolution with world knowledge. In *Proceedings of the 49th Annual Meeting of the Association for Computational Linguistics: Human Language Technologies - Volume 1*, pages 814–824, Stroudsburg, PA, USA. Association for Computational Linguistics.

Mark Stevenson and Yorick Wilks. 2001. The interaction of knowledge sources in word sense disambiguation. *Computational Linguistics*, 27(3):321–349, September.

*SEM 2013 shared task: Semantic Textual Similarity

Eneko Agirre
University of the Basque Country
e.agirre@ehu.es

Daniel Cer
Stanford University
danielcer@stanford.edu

Mona Diab
George Washington University
mtdiab@gwu.edu

Aitor Gonzalez-Agirre
University of the Basque Country
agonzalez278@ikasle.ehu.es

Weiwei Guo
Columbia University
weiwei@cs.columbia.edu

Abstract

In Semantic Textual Similarity (STS), systems rate the degree of semantic equivalence, on a graded scale from 0 to 5, with 5 being the most similar. This year we set up two tasks: (i) a core task (CORE), and (ii) a typed-similarity task (TYPED). CORE is similar in set up to SemEval STS 2012 task with pairs of sentences from sources related to those of 2012, yet different in genre from the 2012 set, namely, this year we included newswire headlines, machine translation evaluation datasets and multiple lexical resource glossed sets. TYPED, on the other hand, is novel and tries to characterize why two items are deemed similar, using cultural heritage items which are described with metadata such as title, author or description. Several types of similarity have been defined, including similar author, similar time period or similar location. The annotation for both tasks leverages crowdsourcing, with relative high inter-annotator correlation, ranging from 62% to 87%. The CORE task attracted 34 participants with 89 runs, and the TYPED task attracted 6 teams with 14 runs.

1 Introduction

Given two snippets of text, Semantic Textual Similarity (STS) captures the notion that some texts are more similar than others, measuring the degree of semantic equivalence. Textual similarity can range from exact semantic equivalence to complete unrelatedness, corresponding to quantified values between 5 and 0. The graded similarity intuitively captures the notion of intermediate shades of similarity such as pairs of text differ only in some minor nuanced aspects of meaning only, to relatively important differences in meaning, to sharing only some details, or to simply being related to the same topic, as shown in Figure 1.

One of the goals of the STS task is to create a unified framework for combining several semantic components that otherwise have historically tended to be evaluated independently and without characterization of impact on NLP applications. By providing such a framework, STS will allow for an extrinsic evaluation for these modules. Moreover, this STS framework itself could in turn be evaluated intrinsically and extrinsically as a grey/black box within various NLP applications such as Machine Translation (MT), Summarization, Generation, Question Answering (QA), etc.

STS is related to both Textual Entailment (TE) and Paraphrasing, but differs in a number of ways and it is more directly applicable to a number of NLP tasks. STS is different from TE inasmuch as it assumes bidirectional graded equivalence between the pair of textual snippets. In the case of TE the equivalence is directional, e.g. a car is a vehicle, but a vehicle is not necessarily a car. STS also differs from both TE and Paraphrasing (in as far as both tasks have been defined to date in the literature) in that, rather than being a binary yes/no decision (e.g. *a vehicle is not a car*), we define STS to be a graded similarity notion (e.g. *a vehicle* and *a car* are more similar than *a wave* and *a car*). A quantifiable graded bidirectional notion of textual similarity is useful for a myriad of NLP tasks such as MT evaluation, information extraction, question answering, summarization, etc.

*Second Joint Conference on Lexical and Computational Semantics (*SEM), Volume 1: Proceedings of the Main Conference and the Shared Task*, pages 32–43, Atlanta, Georgia, June 13-14, 2013.

- (5) The two sentences are completely equivalent, as they mean the same thing.
  The bird is bathing in the sink.
  Birdie is washing itself in the water basin.
- (4) The two sentences are mostly equivalent, but some unimportant details differ.
  In May 2010, the troops attempted to invade Kabul.
  The US army invaded Kabul on May 7th last year, 2010.
- (3) The two sentences are roughly equivalent, but some important information differs/missing.
  John said he is considered a witness but not a suspect.
  "He is not a suspect anymore." John said.
- (2) The two sentences are not equivalent, but share some details.
  They flew out of the nest in groups.
  They flew into the nest together.
- (1) The two sentences are not equivalent, but are on the same topic.
  The woman is playing the violin.
  The young lady enjoys listening to the guitar.
- (0) The two sentences are on different topics.
  John went horse back riding at dawn with a whole group of friends.
  Sunrise at dawn is a magnificent view to take in if you wake up early enough for it.

Figure 1: Annotation values with explanations and examples for the core STS task.

In 2012 we held the first pilot task at SemEval 2012, as part of the *SEM 2012 conference, with great success: 35 teams participated with 88 system runs (Agirre et al., 2012). In addition, we held a DARPA sponsored workshop at Columbia University[1]. In 2013, STS was selected as the official Shared Task of the *SEM 2013 conference. Accordingly, in STS 2013, we set up two tasks: The core task **CORE**, which is similar to the 2012 task; and a pilot task on typed-similarity **TYPED** between semi-structured records.

For CORE, we provided all the STS 2012 data as training data, and the test data was drawn from related but different datasets. This is in contrast to the STS 2012 task where the train/test data were drawn from the same datasets. The 2012 datasets comprised the following: pairs of sentences from paraphrase datasets from news and video elicitation (MSRpar and MSRvid), machine translation evaluation data (SMTeuroparl, SMTnews) and pairs of glosses (OnWN). The current STS 2013 dataset comprises the following: pairs of news headlines, SMT evaluation sentences (SMT) and pairs of glosses (OnWN and FNWN).

The typed-similarity pilot task TYPED attempts to characterize, for the first time, the *reason* and/or *type* of similarity. STS reduces the problem of judging similarity to a single number, but, in some applications, it is important to characterize why and how two items are deemed similar, hence the added nuance. The dataset comprises pairs of Cultural Heritage items from Europeana,[2] a single access point to millions of books, paintings, films, museum objects and archival records that have been digitized throughout Europe. It is an authoritative source of information coming from European cultural and scientific institutions. Typically, the items comprise meta-data describing a cultural heritage item and, sometimes, a thumbnail of the item itself.

Participating systems in the TYPED task need to compute the similarity between items, using the textual meta-data. In addition to general similarity, participants need to score specific kinds of similarity, like similar author, similar time period, etc. (cf. Figure 3).

The paper is structured as follows. Section 2 reports the sources of the texts used in the two tasks. Section 3 details the annotation procedure. Section 4 presents the evaluation of the systems, followed by the results of CORE and TYPED tasks. Section 6 draws on some conclusions and forward projections.

[1] `http://www.cs.columbia.edu/~weiwei/workshop/`

[2] `http://www.europeana.eu/`

Compare the Meaning of Two Statements (v.2.5)

Instructions Hide

Two statements can mean the same thing even if they use very different words and phrases. Conversely, two statements that are superficially very similar in their word choice, phrasing and overall composition can have very different meanings.

Your job is to compare two statements and decide the type of relationship that holds between their underlying meanings or messages (i.e., what they say about or refer to in the world).

To do this task successfully, **picture** what is being described and contrast **exactly** what is conveyed by one statement versus what is being conveyed by the other.

Do the statements refer to the exact same person, action, event, idea or thing? Or, are they similar but differ according to either large or small details?

Tips:

- Be **precise** in your assignments and **try to avoid overusing any one of the category labels** (e.g., don't just label most of the pairs as "mostly equivalent" or "roughly equivalent").
- Be careful of **subtle differences** between the pairs that have an important impact on what is being said or described.
- Ignore grammatical errors and awkward wordings within the statements as long as they do not obscure what a statement is suppose to convey.

Figure 2: Annotation instructions for CORE task

year	dataset	pairs	source
2012	MSRpar	1500	news
2012	MSRvid	1500	videos
2012	OnWN	750	glosses
2012	SMTnews	750	MT eval.
2012	SMTeuroparl	750	MT eval.
2013	HDL	750	news
2013	FNWN	189	glosses
2013	OnWN	561	glosses
2013	SMT	750	MT eval.
2013	TYPED	1500	Cultural Heritage items

Table 1: Summary of STS 2012 and 2013 datasets.

2 Source Datasets

Table 1 summarizes the 2012 and 2013 datasets.

2.1 CORE task

The CORE dataset comprises pairs of news headlines (HDL), MT evaluation sentences (SMT) and pairs of glosses (OnWN and FNWN).

For HDL, we used naturally occurring news headlines gathered by the Europe Media Monitor (EMM) engine (Best et al., 2005) from several different news sources. EMM clusters together related news. Our goal was to generate a balanced data set across the different similarity ranges, hence we built two sets of headline pairs: (i) a set where the pairs come from the same EMM cluster, (ii) and another set where the headlines come from a different EMM cluster, then we computed the string similarity between those pairs. Accordingly, we sampled 375 headline pairs of headlines that occur in the same EMM cluster, aiming for pairs equally distributed between minimal and maximal similarity using simple string similarity. We sample another 375 pairs from the different EMM cluster in the same manner.

The SMT dataset comprises pairs of sentences used in machine translation evaluation. We have two different sets based on the evaluation metric used: an HTER set, and a HYTER set. Both metrics use the TER metric (Snover et al., 2006) to measure the similarity of pairs. HTER typically relies on several (1-4) reference translations. HYTER, on the other hand, leverages millions of translations. The HTER set comprises 150 pairs, where one sentence is machine translation output and the corresponding sentence is a human post-edited translation. We sample the data from the dataset used in the DARPA GALE project with an HTER score ranging from 0 to 120. The HYTER set has 600 pairs from 3 subsets (each subset contains 200 pairs): a. reference

Estimate the Similarity between Cultural Heritage Items

Instructions

Hide

The aim of this survey is to collect information about how people judge the relatedness of cultural heritage items in an online collection. You will be presented with pairs of cultural heritage items, including an image and additional textual information, and asked to judge how similar you think they are on the following scale:

5 - Identical
4 - Strongly Related
3 - Related
2 - Somewhat Related
1 - Unrelated
0 - Completely Unrelated

For each pair you will be asked to provide a general similarity score, plus an additional score for each of the types of similarity considered, as follows:

- similar author
(e.g. two items with the same creator should be rated 5 while two items with similar creators should be rated 4-3, etc)
- similar people involved
(e.g. two items showing the same people should be rated 5, two items showing children should be rated 4, showing similar people 4-3, etc.)
- similar time period
(e.g. two items from 1914 should be rated 5, from the World War II should be rated 4, etc.)
- similar location
(e.g. two items that showing scenes of the same street should be rated 5, of London should be rated 4, etc.)
- similar event or action involved
(e.g. two items showing weddings or people eating an ice-cream should be rated 5, etc.)
- similar subject
(e.g. two items about cars or cats should be rated 5, etc.)
- similar description (e.g. two items with identical description should be rated 5, etc.)

Note that if you think that a particular similarity type is not relevant to a pair of items then you should select the "Not Applicable" choice. For example, this would be the correct option for the "Author Similarity" if there is no information about the items' authors or creators.

Figure 3: Annotation instructions for TYPED task

vs. machine translation. b. reference vs. Finite State Transducer (FST) generated translation (Dreyer and Marcu, 2012). c. machine translation vs. FST generated translation. The HYTER data set is used in (Dreyer and Marcu, 2012).

The OnWN/FnWN dataset contains gloss pairs from two sources: OntoNotes-WordNet (OnWN) and FrameNet-WordNet (FnWN). These pairs are sampled based on the string similarity ranging from 0.4 to 0.9. String similarity is used to measure the similarity between a pair of glosses. The OnWN subset comprises 561 gloss pairs from OntoNotes 4.0 (Hovy et al., 2006) and WordNet 3.0 (Fellbaum, 1998). 370 out of the 561 pairs are sampled from the 110K sense-mapped pairs as made available from the authors. The rest, 291 pairs, are sampled from unmapped sense pairs with a string similarity ranging from 0.5 to 0.9. The FnWN subset has 189 manually mapped pairs of senses from FrameNet 1.5 (Baker et al., 1998) to WordNet 3.1. They are randomly selected from 426 mapped pairs. In combination, both datasets comprise 750 pairs of glosses.

2.2 Typed-similarity TYPED task

This task is devised in the context of the PATHS project,[3] which aims to assist users in accessing digital libraries looking for items. The project tests methods that offer suggestions about items that might be useful to recommend, to assist in the interpretation of the items, and to support the user in the discovery and exploration of the collections. Hence the task is about comparing pairs of items. The pairs are generated in the Europeana project.

A study in the PATHS project suggested that users would be interested in knowing why the system is suggesting related items. The study suggested seven similarity types: similar author or creator, similar people involved, similar time period, similar loca-

[3]http://www.paths-project.eu

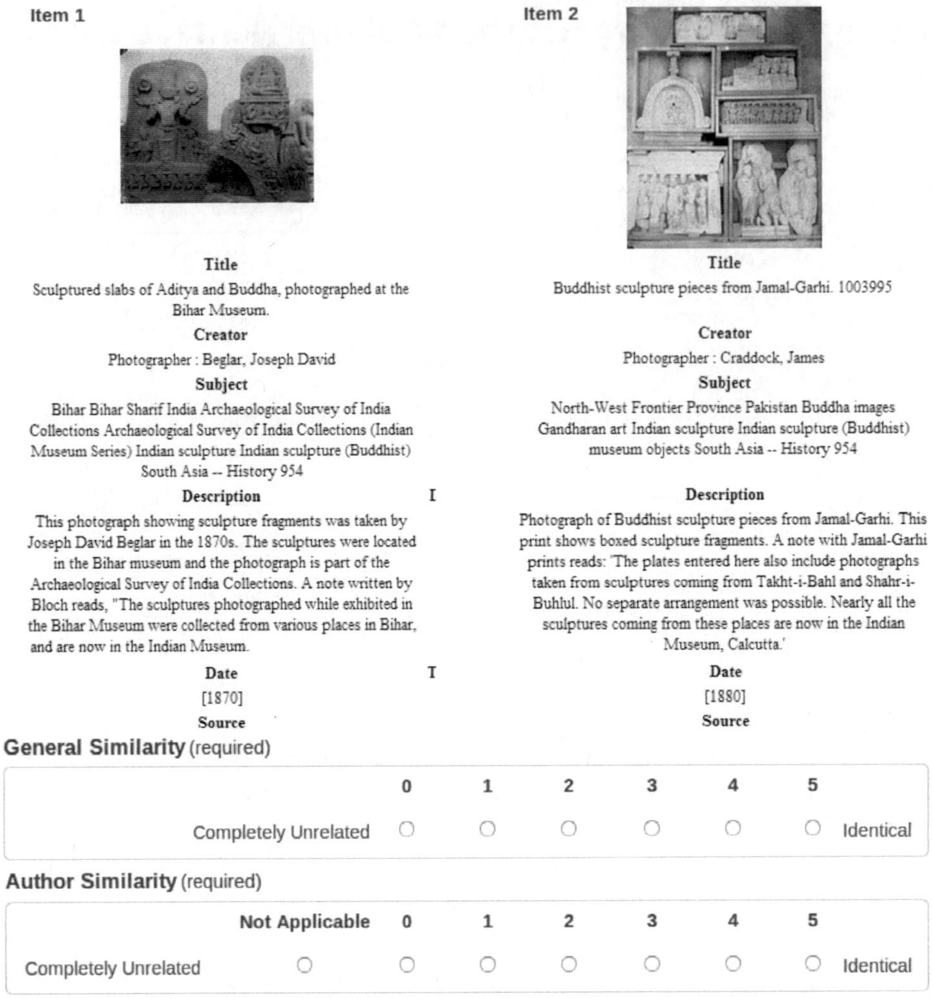

Figure 4: TYPED pair on our survey. Only *general* and *author* similarity types are shown.

tion, similar event or action, similar subject and similar description. In addition, we also include *general* similarity. Figure 3 shows the definition of each similarity type as provided to the annotators.

The dataset is generated in semi-automatically. First, members of the project manually select 25 pairs of items for each of the 7 similarity types (excluding general similarity), totalling 175 manually selected pairs. After removing duplicates and cleaning the dataset, we got 163 pairs. Second, we use these manually selected pairs as seeds to automatically select new pairs as follows: Starting from those seeds, we use the Europeana API to get similar items, and we repeat this process 5 times in order to diverge from the original items (we stored the visited items to avoid looping). Once removed from the seed set, we select the new pairs following two approaches:

- Distance 1: Current item and similar item.
- Distance 2: Current item and an item that is similar to a similar item (twice removed distance wise)

This yields 892 pairs for Distance 1 and 445 of Distance 2. We then divide the data into train and test, preserving the ratios. The train data contains 82 manually selected pairs, 446 pairs with similarity distance 1 and 222 pairs with similarity distance 2. The test data follows a similar distribution.

Europeana items cannot be redistributed, so we provide their urls and a script which uses the official

Europeana API to access and extract the corresponding metadata in JSON format and a thumbnail. In addition, the textual fields which are relevant for the task are made accessible in text files, as follows:

- dcTitle: title of the item
- dcSubject: list of subject terms (from some vocabulary)
- dcDescription: textual description of the item
- dcCreator: creator(s) of the item
- dcDate: date(s) of the item
- dcSource: source of the item

3 Annotation

3.1 CORE task

Figure 1 shows the explanations and values for each score between 5 and 0. We use the CrowdFlower crowd-sourcing service to annotate the CORE dataset. Annotators are presented with the detailed instructions given in Figure 2 and are asked to label each STS sentence pair on our 6 point scale using a dropdown box. Five sentence pairs at a time are presented to annotators. Annotators are paid 0.20 cents per set of 5 annotations and we collect 5 separate annotations per sentence pair. Annotators are restricted to people from the following countries: Australia, Canada, India, New Zealand, UK, and US.

To obtain high quality annotations, we create a representative gold dataset of 105 pairs that are manually annotated by the task organizers. During annotation, one gold pair is included in each set of 5 sentence pairs. Crowd annotators are required to rate 4 of the gold pairs correct to qualify to work on the task. Gold pairs are not distinguished in any way from the non-gold pairs. If the gold pairs are annotated incorrectly, annotators are told what the correct annotation is and they are given an explanation of why. CrowdFlower automatically stops low performing annotators – those with too many incorrectly labeled gold pairs – from working on the task.

The distribution of scores in the headlines HDL dataset is uniform, as in FNWN and OnWN, although the scores are slightly lower in FNWN and slightly higher in OnWN. The scores for SMT are not uniform, with most of the scores uniformly distributed between 3.5 and 5, a few pairs between 2 and 3.5, and nearly no pairs with values below 2.

3.2 TYPED task

The dataset is annotated using crowdsourcing. The survey contains the 1500 pairs of the dataset (750 for train and 750 for test), plus 20 gold pairs for quality control. Each participant is shown 4 training gold questions at the beginning, and then one gold every 2 or 4 questions depending on the accuracy. If accuracy dropped to less than 66.7% percent the survey is stopped and the answers from that particular annotator are discarded. Each annotator is allowed to rate a maximum of 20 pairs to avoid getting answers from people that are either tired or bored. To ensure a good comprehension of the items, the task is restricted to only accept annotators from some English speaking countries: UK, USA, Australia, Canada and New Zealand.

Participants are asked to rate the similarity between pairs of cultural heritage items from ranging from 5 to 0, following the instructions shown in Figure 3. We also add a "Not Applicable" choice for cases in which annotators are not sure or didn't know. For those cases, we calculate the similarity score using the values of the rest of the annotators (if none, we convert it to 0). The instructions given to the annotators are the ones shown in Figure 3. Figure 4 shows a pair from the dataset, as presented to annotators.

The similarity scores for the pairs follow a similar distribution in all types. Most of the pairs have a score between 4 and 5, which can amount to as much as 50% of all pairs in some types.

3.3 Quality of annotation

In order to assess the annotation quality, we measure the correlation of each annotator with the average of the rest of the annotators. We then averaged all the correlations. This method to estimate the quality is identical to the method used for evaluation (see Section 4.1) and it can be thus used as the upper bound for the systems. The inter-tagger correlation in the CORE dataset for each of dataset is as follows:

- HDL: 85.0%
- FNWN: 69.9%
- OnWN: 87.2%
- SMT: 65.8%

For the TYPED dataset, the inter-tagger correlation values for each type of similarity is as follows:

- General: 77.0%

- Author: 73.1%
- People Involved: 62.5%
- Time period: 72.0%
- Location: 74.3%
- Event or Action: 63.9%
- Subject: 74.5%
- Description: 74.9%

In both datasets, the correlation figures are high, confirming that the task is well designed. The weakest correlations in the CORE task are SMT and FNWN. The first might reflect the fact that some automatically produced translations are confusing or difficult to understand, and the second could be caused by the special style used to gloss FrameNet concepts. In the TYPED task the weakest correlations are for the *People Involved* and *Event or Action* types, as they might be the most difficult to spot.

4 Systems Evaluation

4.1 Evaluation metrics

Evaluation of STS is still an open issue. STS experiments have traditionally used Pearson product-moment correlation, or, alternatively, Spearman rank order correlation. In addition, we also need a method to aggregate the results from each dataset into an overall score. The analysis performed in (Agirre and Amigó, In prep) shows that Pearson and averaging across datasets are the best suited combination in general. In particular, Pearson is more informative than Spearman, in that Spearman only takes the rank differences into account, while Pearson does account for value differences as well. The study also showed that other alternatives need to be considered, depending on the requirements of the target application.

We leave application-dependent evaluations for future work, and focus on average weighted Pearson correlation. When averaging, we weight each individual correlation by the size of the dataset. In addition, participants in the CORE task are allowed to provide a confidence score between 1 and 100 for each of their scores. The evaluation script down-weights the pairs with low confidence, following weighted Pearson.[4] In order to compute statistical significance among system results, we use a one-tailed parametric test based on Fisher's z-transformation (Press et al., 2002, equation 14.5.10).

4.2 The Baseline Systems

For the CORE dataset, we produce scores using a simple word overlap baseline system. We tokenize the input sentences splitting at white spaces, and then represent each sentence as a vector in the multidimensional token space. Each dimension has 1 if the token is present in the sentence, 0 otherwise. Vector similarity is computed using the cosine similarity metric. We also run two freely available systems, DKPro (Bar et al., 2012) and TakeLab (Šarić et al., 2012) from STS 2012,[5] and evaluate them on the CORE dataset. They serve as two strong contenders since they ranked 1st (DKPro) and 2nd (TakeLab) in last year's STS task.

For the TYPED dataset, we first produce XML files for each of the items, using the fields as provided to participants. Then we run named entity recognition and classification (NERC) and date detection using Stanford CoreNLP. This is followed by calculating the similarity score for each of the types as follows.

- General: cosine similarity of TF-IDF vectors of tokens from all fields.
- Author: cosine similarity of TF-IDF vectors for dc:Creator field.
- People involved, time period and location: cosine similarity of TF-IDF vectors of location/date/people recognized by NERC in all fields.
- Events: cosine similarity of TF-IDF vectors of verbs in all fields.
- Subject and description: cosine similarity of TF-IDF vectors of respective fields.

IDF values are calculated from a subset of the Europeana collection (Culture Grid collection). We also run a random baseline several times, yielding close to 0 correlations in all datasets, as expected.

4.3 Participation

Participants could send a maximum of three system runs. After downloading the test datasets, they had a maximum of 120 hours to upload the results. 34 teams participated in the CORE task, submitting 89

[4] http://en.wikipedia.org/wiki/Pearson_product-moment_correlation_coefficient#Calculating_a_weighted_correlation

[5] Code is available at http://www-nlp.stanford.edu/wiki/STS

Team and run	Head.	OnWN	FNWN	SMT	Mean	#
baseline-tokencos	.5399	.2828	.2146	.2861	.3639	73
DKPro	.7347	.7345	.3405	.3256	.5652	-
TakeLab-best	.6559	.6334	.4052	.3389	.5221	-
TakeLab-sts12	.4858	.6334	.2693	.2787	.4340	-
aolney-w3c3	.5248	.4701	.1777	.2744	.3986	67
BGU-1	.5075	.3252	.0768	.1843	.3181	81
BGU-2	.3608	.3777	-.0173	.0698	.2363	88
BGU-3	.3591	.3360	.0072	.2122	.2748	85
BUAP-RUN1	.5005	.2579	.1766	.2322	.3234	78
BUAP-RUN2	.4860	.2872	.2082	.2117	.3216	79
BUAP-RUN3	.4817	.2711	.2511	.1990	.3156	82
CFILT-1	.5336	.2381	.2261	.2906	.3531	75
CLaC-RUN1	.6774	.7667	.3793	.3068	.5511	10
CLaC-RUN2	.6921	.7366	.3793	.3375	.5587	7
CLaC-RUN3	.5276	.6495	.4158	.3082	.4755	47
CNGL-LPSSVR	.6510	.6971	.1180	.2861	.4961	36
CNGL-LPSSVRTL	.6385	.6756	.1823	.3098	.4998	33
CNGL-LSSVR	.6552	.6943	.2016	.3005	.5086	30
CPN-combined.RandSubSpace	.6771	.5135	.3314	.3369	.4939	39
CPN-combined.SVM	.6685	.5096	.3621	.3408	.4939	38
CPN-individual.RandSubSpace	.6771	.5484	.3314	.2769	.4826	45
DeepPurple-length	.6542	.5105	.2507	.2803	.4598	56
DeepPurple-linear	.6878	.5105	.2693	.2787	.4721	50
DeepPurple-lineara	.6227	.5105	.3265	.2952	.4607	55
deft-baseline	.6532	**.8431**	.5083	.3265	.5795	3
deft-baseline2	.5706	.8111	.5503	.3325	.5495	13
DLS@CU-char	.3867	.2386	.3726	.3337	.3309	76
DLS@CU-charSemantic	.4669	.4165	.3859	.3411	.4056	64
DLS@CU-charWordSemantic	.4921	.3769	.4647	.3492	.4135	63
ECNUCS-Run1	.5656	.2083	.1725	.2949	.3533	74
ECNUCS-Run2	.7120	.5388	.2013	.2504	.4720	51
ECNUCS-Run3	.6799	.5284	.2203	.3595	.4967	35
HENRY-run1	.7601	.4631	.3516	.2801	.4917	41
HENRY-run2	.7645	.4631	.3905	.3593	.5229	26
HENRY-run3	.7103	.3934	.3364	.3308	.4734	48
IBM_EG-run2	.7217	.6110	.3364	.3460	.5365	19
IBM_EG-run5	.7410	.5987	.4133	.3426	.5452	15
IBM_EG-run6	.7447	.6257	.4381	.3275	.5502	11
ikernels-sys1	.7352	.5432	.3842	.3180	.5188	28
ikernels-sys2	.7465	.5572	.3875	.3409	.5339	21
ikernels-sys3	.7395	.4228	.3596	.3294	.4919	40
INAOE-UPV-run1	.6392	.3249	.2711	.3491	.4332	59
INAOE-UPV-run2	.6390	.3260	.2662	.3457	.4319	60
INAOE-UPV-run3	.6468	.6295	.4090	.3047	.5085	31
KLUE-approach_1	.6521	.6507	.3996	.3367	.5254	25
KLUE-approach_2	.6510	.6869	.4189	.3360	.5355	20

Team and run	Head.	OnWN	FNWN	SMT	Mean	#
KnCe2013-all	.3475	.3505	.1073	.1551	.2639	86
KnCe2013-diff	.4028	.3537	.1284	.1804	.2934	84
KnCe2013-set	.0462	-.1526	.0376	-.0605	-.0397	90
LCL_Sapienza-ADW1	.6943	.4661	.3571	.3311	.4880	43
LCL_Sapienza-ADW2	.6520	.5280	.3598	.3681	.5019	32
LCL_Sapienza-ADW3	.6205	.5108	.4462	.3838	.4996	34
LIPN-tAll	.7063	.6937	.4037	.3005	.5425	16
LIPN-tSp	.5791	.7199	.3522	.3721	.5261	24
MayoClinicNLP-r1wtCDT	.6584	.7775	.3735	.3605	.5649	6
MayoClinicNLP-r2CDT	.6827	.6612	.3960	.3946	.5572	8
MayoClinicNLP-r3wtCD	.6440	.8295	.3202	.3561	.5671	5
NTNU-RUN1	.7279	.5952	.3215	.4015	.5519	9
NTNU-RUN2	.5909	.1634	.3650	.3786	.3946	68
NTNU-RUN3	.7274	.5882	.3115	**.4035**	.5498	12
PolyUCOMP-RUN1	.5176	.1517	.2496	.2914	.3284	77
SOFTCARDINALITY-run1	.6410	.7360	.3442	.3035	.5273	23
SOFTCARDINALITY-run2	.6713	.7412	.3838	.2981	.5402	18
SOFTCARDINALITY-run3	.6603	.7401	.3347	.2900	.5294	22
sriubc-System1†	.6083	.2915	.2790	.3065	.4011	66
sriubc-System2†	.6359	.3664	.2713	.3476	.4420	57
sriubc-System3†	.5443	.2843	.2705	.3275	.3842	70
SXUCFN-run1	.6806	.5355	.3181	.3980	.5198	27
SXUCFN-run2	.4881	.6146	.4237	.3844	.4797	46
SXUCFN-run3	.6761	.6481	.3025	.4003	.5458	14
SXULLL-1	.4840	.7146	.0415	.1543	.3944	69
UCam-A	.5510	.3099	.2385	.1171	.3200	80
UCam-B	.6399	.4440	.3995	.3400	.4709	53
UCam-C	.4962	.5639	.1724	.3006	.4207	62
UCSP-NC‡	.1736	.0853	.1151	.1658	.1441	89
UMBC_EBIQUITY-galactus	.7428	.7053	.5444	.3705	.5927	2
UMBC_EBIQUITY-ParingWords	.7642	.7529	**.5818**	.3804	**.6181**	**1**
UMBC_EBIQUITY-saiyan	**.7838**	.5593	.5815	.3563	.5683	4
UMCC_DLSI-1	.5841	.4847	.2917	.2855	.4352	58
UMCC_DLSI-2	.6168	.5557	.3045	.3407	.4833	44
UMCC_DLSI-3	.3846	.1342	-.0065	.2736	.2523	87
UNIBA-2STEPSML	.4255	.4801	.1832	.2710	.3673	71
UNIBA-DSM_PERM	.6319	.4910	.2717	.3155	.4610	54
UNIBA-STACKING	.6275	.4658	.2111	.2588	.4293	61
Unimelb_NLP-bahar	.7119	.3490	.3813	.3507	.4733	49
Unimelb_NLP-concat	.7085	.6790	.3374	.3230	.5415	17
Unimelb_NLP-stacking	.7064	.6140	.1865	.3144	.5091	29
Unitor-SVRegressor_run1	.6353	.5744	.3521	.3285	.4941	37
Unitor-SVRegressor_run2	.6511	.5610	.3580	.3096	.4902	42
Unitor-SVRegressor_run3	.6027	.5489	.3269	.3192	.4716	52
UPC-AE	.6092	.5679	-.1268	.2090	.4037	65
UPC-AED	.4136	.4770	-.0852	.1662	.3050	83
UPC-AED_T	.5119	.6386	-.0464	.1235	.3671	72

Table 2: Results on the CORE task. The first rows on the left correspond to the baseline and to two publicly available systems, see text for details. Note: † signals team involving one of the organizers, ‡ for systems submitting past the 120 hour window.

system runs. For the TYPED task, 6 teams participated, submitting 14 system runs.[6]

Some submissions had minor issues: one team had a confidence score of 0 for all items (we replaced them by 100), and another team had a few Not-a-Number scores for the SMT dataset, which we replaced by 5. One team submitted the results past the 120 hours. This team, and the teams that included one of the organizers, are explicitly marked. We want to stress that in these teams the organizers did not allow the developers of the system to access any data or information which was not available for the rest of participants. After the submission deadline expired, the organizers published the gold standard in the task website, in order to ensure a transparent evaluation process.

[6]Due to lack of space we can't detail the full names of authors and institutions that participated.The interested reader can use the name of the runs in Tables 2 and 3 to find the relevant paper in these proceedings.

4.4 CORE Task Results

Table 2 shows the results of the CORE task, with runs listed in alphabetical order. The correlation in

Team and run	General	Author	People_involved	Time	Location	Event	Subject	Description	Mean	#
baseline	.6691	.4278	.4460	.5002	.4835	.3062	.5015	.5810	.4894	8
BUAP-RUN1	.6798	.6166	.0670	.2761	.0163	.1612	.5167	.5283	.3577	14
BUAP-RUN2	.6745	.6093	.1285	.3721	.0163	.1660	.5094	.5546	.3788	13
BUAP-RUN3	.6992	.6345	.1055	.1461	.0000	-.0668	.3729	.5120	.3004	15
BUT-1	.3686	.7468	.3920	.5725	.3604	.2906	.2270	.5882	.4433	9
ECNUCS-Run1	.6040	.7362	.3663	.4685	.3844	.4057	.5229	.6027	.5113	5
ECNUCS-Run2	.6064	.5684	.3663	.4685	.3844	.4057	.5563	.6027	.4948	7
PolyUCOMP-RUN1	.4888	.6940	.3223	.3820	.3621	.1625	.3962	.4816	.4112	12
PolyUCOMP-RUN2	.4893	.6940	.3253	.3777	.3628	.1968	.3962	.4816	.4155	11
PolyUCOMP-RUN3	.4915	.6940	.3254	.3737	.3667	.2207	.3962	.4816	.4187	10
UBC_UOS-RUN1†	.7256	.4568	.4467	.5762	.4858	.3090	.5015	.5810	.5103	6
UBC_UOS-RUN2†	.7457	.6618	.6518	.7466	.7244	.6533	.7404	.7751	.7124	4
UBC_UOS-RUN3†	.7461	.6656	.6544	.7411	.7257	.6545	.7417	.7763	.7132	3
Unitor-SVRegressor_lin	.7564	.8076	.6758	.7090	.7351	.6623	.7520	.7745	.7341	2
Unitor-SVRegressor_rbf	**.7981**	**.8158**	**.6922**	**.7471**	**.7723**	**.6835**	**.7875**	**.7996**	**.7620**	1

Table 3: Results on TYPED task. The first row corresponds to the baseline. Note: † signals team involving one of the organizers.

each dataset is given, followed by the mean correlation (the official measure), and the rank of the run. The baseline ranks 73. The highest correlations are for OnWN (84%, by deft) and HDL (78%, by UMBC), followed by FNWN (58%, by UMBC) and SMT (40%, by NTNU). This fits nicely with the inter-tagger correlations (respectively 87, 85, 70 and 65, cf. Section 3). It also shows that the systems get close to the human correlations in the OnWN and HDL dataset, with bigger differences for FNWN and SMT.

The result of the best run (by UMBC) is significantly different (p-value < 0.05) than all runs except the second best. The second best run is only significantly different to the runs ranking 7th and below, and the third best to the 14th run and below. The difference between consecutive runs was not significant. This indicates that many system runs performed very close to each other.

Only 13 runs included non-uniform confidence scores. In 10 cases the confidence value allowed to improve performance, sometimes as much as .11 absolute points. For instance, SXUCFN-run3 improves from .4773 to .5458. The most notable exception is MayoClinicNLP-r2CDT, which achieves a mean correlation of .5879 instead of .5572 if they provide uniform confidence values.

The Table also shows the results of TakeLab and DKPro. We train the DKPro and TakeLab-sts12 models on all the training and test STS 2012 data. We additionally train another variant system of TakeLab, TakeLab-best, where we use targeted training where the model yields the best performance for each test subset as follows: (1) HDL is trained on MSRpar 2012 data; (2) OnWN is trained on all 2012 data; (3) FnWN is trained on 2012 OnWN data; (4) SMT is trained on 2012 SMTeuroparl data. Note that Takelab-best is an upper bound, as the best combination is selected on the test dataset. TakeLab-sts12, TakeLab-best, DKPro rank as 58th, 27th and 6th in this year's system submissions, respectively. The different results yielded from TakeLab depending on the training data suggests that some STS systems are quite sensitive to the source of the sentence pairs, indicating that domain adaptation techniques could have a role in this task. On the other hand, DKPro performed extremely well when trained on all available training, with no special tweaking for each dataset.

4.5 TYPED Task Results

Table 3 shows the results of TYPED task. The columns show the correlation for each type of similarity, followed by the mean correlation (the official measure), and the rank of the run. The best system (from Unitor) is best in all types. The baseline ranked 8th, but the performance difference with the best system is quite significant. The best result is significantly different (p-value < 0.02) to all runs. The second and third best runs are only significantly different from the run ranking 5th and below. Note that in this dataset the correlations of the best system are higher than the inter-tagger correlations. This might indicate that the task has been solved, in the sense that the features used by the top systems are enough to characterize the problem and reach human performance, although the correlations of some

	Acronyms	Distributional memory	Distributional thesaurus	Monolingual corpora	Multilingual corpora	Opinion and Sentiment	Tables of paraphrases	Wikipedia	Wiktionary	Word embeddings	WordNet	Coreference	Dependency parse	Distributional similarity	KB Similarity	LDA	Lemmatizer	Lexical Substitution	Logical inference	Metaphor or Metonymy	Multiword recognition	Named Entity recognition	POS tagger	ROUGE package	Scoping	Search engine	Semantic Role Labeling	String similarity	Syntax	Textual entailment	Time and date resolution	Tree kernels	Word Sense Disambiguation
aolney-w3c3								x						x	x																		
BGU-1				x						x							x					x	x						x	x			
BGU-2				x						x							x					x	x						x	x			
BGU-3				x						x							x					x	x						x	x			
CFILT-APPROACH				x							x						x						x						x				
CLaC-Run1			x					x			x			x	x		x						x	x									
CLaC-Run2			x					x			x			x	x		x						x	x									
CLaC-Run3			x					x			x			x	x		x						x	x									
CNGL-LPSSVR				x										x			x						x						x				
CNGL-LPSSVRTL				x										x			x						x						x				
CNGL-LSSVR				x										x			x						x						x				
CPN-combined.RandSubSpace						x		x			x			x	x		x				x		x										
CPN-combined.SVM						x		x			x			x	x		x				x		x										
CPN-individual.RandSubSpace						x		x			x			x	x		x				x		x										
DeepPurple-length				x										x			x	x				x	x								x		
DeepPurple-linear				x										x			x	x				x	x								x		
DeepPurple-lineara				x										x			x	x				x	x								x		
deft-baseline				x					x		x			x																			
deft-baseline				x					x		x			x			x						x										
DLS@CU-charSemantic				x				x			x						x																
DLS@CU-charWordSemantic				x				x			x			x	x		x																
DLS@CU-charWordSemantic														x	x		x																
ECNUCS-Run1				x							x			x	x		x						x						x				
ECNUCS-Run2				x							x			x	x		x						x						x				
ECNUCS-Run3				x							x			x	x		x						x						x				
HENRY-run1	x			x		x	x	x			x				x		x	x															
HENRY-run2				x		x	x	x			x				x		x	x															
IBM_EG-run2				x	x		x							x				x				x											
IBM_EG-run5				x	x		x							x				x				x											
IBM_EG-run6				x	x		x							x				x															
ikernels-sys1				x				x			x		x	x	x		x					x	x						x			x	
ikernels-sys2				x				x			x		x	x	x		x					x	x						x			x	
ikernels-sys3				x				x			x		x	x	x		x					x	x						x			x	
INAOE-UPV-run1	x		x	x	x		x	x			x																						
INAOE-UPV-run2	x		x	x	x		x	x			x																						
INAOE-UPV-run3	x		x	x	x		x	x			x																						
KLUE-approach_1		x		x							x			x	x		x						x										
KLUE-approach_2		x		x							x				x		x						x										
KnCe2013-all								x	x		x						x				x	x	x						x				
KnCe2013-div								x	x		x						x				x	x	x						x				
KnCe2013-div								x	x		x						x				x	x	x						x				
LCL_Sapienza-ADW1											x						x						x										
LCL_Sapienza-ADW2											x						x						x										
LCL_Sapienza-ADW3											x						x						x										
LIPN-tAll				x				x			x			x	x		x					x	x			x			x				
LIPN-tSp				x				x			x			x	x		x					x	x			x			x				
MayoClinicNLP-r1wtCDT				x	x			x			x			x	x		x	x				x	x						x	x			
MayoClinicNLP-r2CDT				x	x			x			x			x	x		x	x				x	x						x	x			
MayoClinicNLP-r3wtCD				x	x			x			x			x	x		x	x				x	x						x	x			
NTNU-RUN1	x		x	x	x		x	x			x	x		x	x		x	x	x	x	x	x	x		x		x		x	x	x		x
NTNU-RUN2	x		x	x	x		x	x			x	x		x	x		x	x	x	x	x	x	x		x		x		x	x	x		x
NTNU-RUN3	x		x	x	x		x	x			x	x		x	x		x	x	x	x	x	x	x		x		x		x	x	x		x
PolyUCOMP-RUN1											x				x		x						x										
SOFTCARDINALITY-run1																	x																
SOFTCARDINALITY-run2				x										x			x																
SOFTCARDINALITY-run3				x										x			x																
SXUCFN-run1											x				x												x						
SXUCFN-run2											x				x												x						
SXUCFN-run3											x				x												x						
SXULLL-1											x				x																		
UCam-A								x						x			x												x				
UCam-B								x						x			x												x				
UCam-C								x						x			x												x				
UCSP-NC											x						x				x		x						x				
UMBC_EBIQUITY-galactus	x			x							x				x		x						x								x		
UMBC_EBIQUITY-ParingWords				x							x				x		x						x								x		
UMBC_EBIQUITY-saiyan	x			x							x				x		x						x								x		
UMCC_DLSI-1	x			x							x				x		x						x				x		x		x		x
UMCC_DLSI-2	x		x	x							x				x		x						x				x		x				x
UMCC_DLSI-3				x							x				x		x						x				x		x		x		x
UNIBA-2STEPSML			x	x				x			x			x	x		x					x	x						x		x		
UNIBA-DSM_PERM				x				x						x			x						x						x				
UNIBA STACKING			x	x				x			x			x	x		x					x	x						x		x		
Unimelb_NLP-bahar																	x											x					
Unimelb_NLP-concat				x				x	x		x			x		x	x						x			x		x					
Unimelb_NLP-stacking				x				x	x		x			x		x	x						x			x		x					
Unitor-SVRegressor_run1				x										x			x						x					x				x	
Unitor-SVRegressor_run2				x										x			x						x					x				x	
Unitor-SVRegressor_run3				x										x			x						x					x				x	
Total	11	2	12	54	12	5	11	36	7	3	54	3	3	48	40	2	67	14	3	3	10	24	55	3	3	4	9	6	34	9	13	6	6

Table 4: CORE task: Resources and tools used by the systems that submitted a description file. Leftmost columns correspond to the resources, and rightmost to tools, in alphabetic order.

types could be too low for practical use.

5 Tools and resources used

The organizers asked participants to submit a description file, making special emphasis on the tools and resources that were used. Tables 4 and 5 show schematically the tools and resources as reported by some of the participants for the CORE and TYPED tasks (respectively). In the last row, the totals show that WordNet and monolingual corpora were the most used resources for both tasks, followed by Wikipedia and the use of acronyms (for CORE and TYPED tasks respectively). Dictionaries, multilingual corpora, opinion and sentiment analysis, and lists and tables of paraphrases are also used.

For CORE, generic NLP tools such as lemmatization and PoS tagging are widely used, and to a lesser extent, distributional similarity, knowledge-based similarity, syntactic analysis, named entity recognition, lexical substitution and time and date resolution (in this order). Other popular tools are Semantic Role Labeling, Textual Entailment, String Similarity, Tree Kernels and Word Sense Disambiguation. Machine learning is widely used to combine and tune components (and so, it is not mentioned in the tables). Several less used tools are also listed but are used by three or less systems. The top scoring systems use most of the resources and tools listed (*UMBC_EBIQUITY-ParingWords*, *MayoClinicNLP-r3wtCD*). Other well ranked systems like *deft-baseline* are only based on distributional similarity. Although not mentioned in the descriptions files, some systems used the publicly available DKPro and Takelab systems.

For the TYPED task, the most used tools are lemmatizers, Named Entity Recognizers, and PoS taggers. Distributional and Knowledge-base similarity is also used, and at least four systems used syntactic analysis and time and date resolution.[7]

6 Conclusions and Future Work

We presented the 2013 *SEM shared task on Semantic Textual Similarity.[8] Two tasks were defined: a

	Acronyms	Monolingual corpora	Wikipedia	WordNet	Distributional similarity	KB Similarity	Lemmatizer	Multiword recognition	Named Entity recognition	POS tagger	Syntax	Time and date resolution	Tree kernels
BUT-1	x	x			x		x		x	x		x	
PolyUCOMP-RUN2				x			x		x	x			
ECNUCS-Run1							x		x	x			
ECNUCS-Run2		x		x	x	x	x		x	x			
PolyUCOMP-RUN1				x			x		x	x			
PolyUCOMP-RUN3				x			x		x	x			
UBC_UOS-RUN1	x	x	x	x	x	x	x	x	x	x		x	
UBC_UOS-RUN2	x	x	x	x	x	x	x	x	x	x	x	x	
UBC_UOS-RUN3	x	x	x	x	x	x	x	x	x	x	x	x	
Unitor-SVRegressor_lin		x			x		x		x	x	x		x
Unitor-SVRegressor_rbf		x			x		x		x	x	x		x
Total	4	7	3	7	7	4	11	3	11	11	4	4	2

Table 5: TYPED task: Resources and tools used by the systems that submitted a description file. Leftmost columns correspond to the resources, and rightmost to tools, in alphabetic order.

core task CORE similar to the STS 2012 task, and a new pilot on typed-similarity TYPED. We had 34 teams participate in both tasks submitting 89 system runs for CORE and 14 system runs for TYPED, in total amounting to a 103 system evaluations. CORE uses datasets which are related to but different from those used in 2012: news headlines, MT evaluation data, gloss pairs. The best systems attained correlations close to the human inter tagger correlations. The TYPED task characterizes, for the first time, the reasons why two items are deemed similar. The results on TYPED show that the training data provided allowed systems to yield high correlation scores, demonstrating the practical viability of this new task. In the future, we are planning on adding more nuanced evaluation data sets that include modality (belief, negation, permission, etc.) and sentiment. Also given the success rate of the TYPED task, however, the data in this pilot is relatively structured, hence in the future we are interested in investigating identifying reasons why two pairs of unstructured texts as those present in CORE are deemed similar.

Acknowledgements

We are grateful to the OntoNotes team for sharing OntoNotes to WordNet mappings (Hovy et al. 2006). We thank Language Weaver, INC, DARPA and LDC for providing the SMT data. This work is also partially funded by the Spanish Ministry of Education, Culture and Sport (grant FPU12/06243). This

[7]For a more detailed analysis, the reader is directed to the papers in this volume.

[8]All annotations, evaluation scripts and system outputs are available in the website for the task[9]. In addition, a collaboratively maintained site[10], open to the STS community, contains a comprehensive list of evaluation tasks, datasets, software and papers related to STS.

work was partially funded by the DARPA BOLT and DEFT programs.

We want to thank Nikolaos Aletras, German Rigau and Mark Stevenson for their help designing, annotating and collecting the typed-similarity data. The development of the typed-similarity dataset was supported by the PATHS project (http://paths-project.eu) funded by the European Community's Seventh Framework Program (FP7/2007-2013) under grant agreement no. 270082. The tasks were partially financed by the READERS project under the CHIST-ERA framework (FP7 ERA-Net). We thank Europeana and all contributors to Europeana for sharing their content through the API.

References

Eneko Agirre and Enrique Amigó. In prep. Exploring evaluation measures for semantic textual similarity. In *Unpublished manuscript*.

Eneko Agirre, Daniel Cer, Mona Diab, and Aitor Gonzalez-Agirre. 2012. Semeval-2012 task 6: A pilot on semantic textual similarity. In **SEM 2012: The First Joint Conference on Lexical and Computational Semantics – Volume 1: Proceedings of the main conference and the shared task, and Volume 2: Proceedings of the Sixth International Workshop on Semantic Evaluation (SemEval 2012)*, pages 385–393, Montréal, Canada, 7-8 June. Association for Computational Linguistics.

Collin F. Baker, Charles J. Fillmore, and John B. Lowe. 1998. The berkeley framenet project. In *COLING '98 Proceedings of the 17th international conference on Computational linguistics - Volume 1*.

Daniel Bar, Chris Biemann, Iryna Gurevych, and Torsten Zesch. 2012. Ukp: Computing semantic textual similarity by combining multiple content similarity measures. In *Proceedings of the 6th International Workshop on Semantic Evaluation, in conjunction with the 1st Joint Conference on Lexical and Computational Semantics*.

Clive Best, Erik van der Goot, Ken Blackler, Tefilo Garcia, and David Horby. 2005. Europe media monitor - system description. In *EUR Report 22173-En*, Ispra, Italy.

Markus Dreyer and Daniel Marcu. 2012. Hyter: Meaning-equivalent semantics for translation evaluation. In *Human Language Technologies: Conference of the North American Chapter of the Association of Computational Linguistics*.

Christiane Fellbaum. 1998. *WordNet: An Electronic Lexical Database*. MIT Press.

Eduard Hovy, Mitchell Marcus, Martha Palmer, Lance Ramshaw, and Ralph Weischedel. 2006. Ontonotes: The 90% solution. In *Proceedings of the Human Language Technology Conference of the North American Chapter of the ACL*.

W.H. Press, S.A. Teukolsky, W.T. Vetterling, and B.P. Flannery. 2002. *Numerical Recipes: The Art of Scientific Computing V 2.10 With Linux Or Single-Screen License*. Cambridge University Press.

Matthew Snover, Bonnie Dorr, Richard Schwartz, Linnea Micciulla, and John Makhoul. 2006. A study of translation edit rate with targeted human annotation. In *Proceedings of Association for Machine Translation in the Americas*.

Frane Šarić, Goran Glavaš, Mladen Karan, Jan Šnajder, and Bojana Dalbelo Bašić. 2012. Takelab: Systems for measuring semantic text similarity. In *Proceedings of the Sixth International Workshop on Semantic Evaluation (SemEval 2012)*, pages 441–448, Montréal, Canada, 7-8 June. Association for Computational Linguistics.

UMBC_EBIQUITY-CORE: Semantic Textual Similarity Systems

Lushan Han, Abhay Kashyap, Tim Finin
Computer Science and
Electrical Engineering
University of Maryland, Baltimore County
Baltimore MD 21250
{lushan1,abhay1,finin}@umbc.edu

James Mayfield and Jonathan Weese
Human Language Technology
Center of Excellence
Johns Hopkins University
Baltimore MD 21211
mayfield@jhu.edu, jonny@cs.jhu.edu

Abstract

We describe three semantic text similarity systems developed for the *SEM 2013 STS shared task and the results of the corresponding three runs. All of them shared a word similarity feature that combined LSA word similarity and WordNet knowledge. The first, which achieved the best mean score of the 89 submitted runs, used a simple term alignment algorithm augmented with penalty terms. The other two runs, ranked second and fourth, used support vector regression models to combine larger sets of features.

1 Introduction

Measuring semantic text similarity has been a research subject in natural language processing, information retrieval and artificial intelligence for many years. Previous efforts have focused on comparing two long texts (e.g., for document classification) or a short text with a long text (e.g., Web search), but there are a growing number of tasks requiring computing the semantic similarity between two sentences or other short text sequences. They include paraphrase recognition (Dolan et al., 2004), Twitter tweets search (Sriram et al., 2010), image retrieval by captions (Coelho et al., 2004), query reformulation (Metzler et al., 2007), automatic machine translation evaluation (Kauchak and Barzilay, 2006) and schema matching (Han et al., 2012).

There are three predominant approaches to computing short text similarity. The first uses information retrieval's vector space model (Meadow, 1992) in which each text is modeled as a "bag of words" and represented using a vector. The similarity between two texts is then computed as the cosine similarity of the vectors. A variation on this approach leverages web search results (e.g., snippets) to provide context for the short texts and enrich their vectors using the words in the snippets (Sahami and Heilman, 2006). The second approach is based on the assumption that if two sentences or other short text sequences are semantically equivalent, we should be able to align their words or expressions. The alignment quality can serve as a similarity measure. This technique typically pairs words from the two texts by maximizing the summation of the word similarity of the resulting pairs (Mihalcea et al., 2006). The third approach combines different measures and features using machine learning models. Lexical, semantic and syntactic features are computed for the texts using a variety of resources and supplied to a classifier, which then assigns weights to the features by fitting the model to training data (Saric et al., 2012).

For evaluating different approaches, the 2013 Semantic Textual Similarity (STS) task asked automatic systems to compute sentence similarity according to a scale definition ranging from 0 to 5, with 0 meaning unrelated and 5 semantically equivalent (Agirre et al., 2012; Agirre et al., 2013). The example sentence pair "The woman is playing the violin" and "The young lady enjoys listening to the guitar" is scored as only *1* and the pair "The bird is bathing in the sink" and "Birdie is washing itself in the water basin" is given a score of *5*.

The vector-space approach tends to be too shallow for the task, since solving it well requires discriminating word-level semantic differences and goes be-

*Second Joint Conference on Lexical and Computational Semantics (*SEM), Volume 1: Proceedings of the Main Conference and the Shared Task*, pages 44–52, Atlanta, Georgia, June 13-14, 2013.

yond simply comparing sentence topics or contexts. Our first run uses an *align-and-penalize* algorithm, which extends the second approach by giving penalties to the words that are poorly aligned. Our other two runs use a support vector regression model to combine a large number of general and domain specific features. An important and fundamental feature used by all three runs is a powerful semantic word similarity model based on a combination of Latent Semantic Analysis (LSA) (Deerwester et al., 1990; Landauer and Dumais, 1997) and knowledge from WordNet (Miller, 1995).

The remainder of the paper proceeds as follows. Section 2 presents the hybrid word similarity model. Section 3 describes the align-and-penalize approach used for the *PairingWords* run. In Section 4 we describe the SVM approach used for the *Galactus* and *Saiyan* runs. Section 5 discusses the results and is followed by a short conclusion.

2 Semantic Word Similarity Model

Our word similarity model was originally developed for the Graph of Relations project (UMBC, 2013a) which maps informal queries with English words and phrases for an RDF linked data collection into a SPARQL query. For this, we wanted a metric in which only the semantics of a word is considered and not its lexical category. For example, the verb "marry" should be semantically similar to the noun "wife". Another desiderata was that the metric should give highest scores and lowest scores in its range to similar and non-similar words, respectively. In this section, we describe how we constructed the model by combining LSA word similarity and WordNet knowledge.

2.1 LSA Word Similarity

LSA Word Similarity relies on the distributional hypothesis that words occurring in the same contexts tend to have similar meanings (Harris, 1968).

2.1.1 Corpus Selection and Processing

In order to produce a reliable word co-occurrence statistics, a very large and balanced text corpus is required. After experimenting with several corpus choices including Wikipedia, Project Gutenberg e-Books (Hart, 1997), ukWaC (Baroni et al., 2009), Reuters News stories (Rose et al., 2002) and LDC gigawords, we selected the Web corpus from the Stanford WebBase project (Stanford, 2001). We used the February 2007 crawl, which is one of the largest collections and contains 100 million web pages from more than 50,000 websites. The WebBase project did an excellent job in extracting textual content from HTML tags but still has abundant text duplications, truncated text, non-English text and strange characters. We processed the collection to remove undesired sections and produce high quality English paragraphs. We detected paragraphs using heuristic rules and only retrained those whose length was at least two hundred characters. We eliminated non-English text by checking the first twenty words of a paragraph to see if they were valid English words. We used the percentage of punctuation characters in a paragraph as a simple check for typical text. We removed duplicated paragraphs using a hash table. Finally, we obtained a three billion words corpus of good quality English, which is available at (Han and Finin, 2013).

2.1.2 Word Co-Occurrence Generation

We performed POS tagging and lemmatization on the WebBase corpus using the Stanford POS tagger (Toutanova et al., 2000). Word/term co-occurrences are counted in a moving window of a fixed size that scans the entire corpus[1]. We generated two co-occurrence models using window sizes ±1 and ±4 because we observed different natures of the models. ±1 window produces a context similar to the dependency context used in (Lin, 1998a). It provides a more precise context but only works for comparing words within the same POS. In contrast, a context window of ±4 words allows us to compute semantic similarity between words with different POS.

Our word co-occurrence models were based on a predefined vocabulary of more than 22,000 common English words and noun phrases. We also added to it more than 2,000 verb phrases extracted from WordNet. The final dimensions of our word co-occurrence matrices are $29{,}000 \times 29{,}000$ when words are POS tagged. Our vocabulary includes only open-class words (i.e. nouns, verbs, adjectives and adverbs). There are no proper nouns in the vocabulary with the only exception of country names.

[1]We used a stop-word list consisting of only the three articles "a", "an" and "the".

Word Pair	±4 model	±1 model
1. doctor_NN, physician_NN	0.775	0.726
2. car_NN, vehicle_NN	0.748	0.802
3. person_NN, car_NN	0.038	0.024
4. car_NN, country_NN	0.000	0.016
5. person_NN, country_NN	0.031	0.069
6. child_NN, marry_VB	0.098	0.000
7. wife_NN, marry_VB	0.548	0.274
8. author_NN, write_VB	0.364	0.128
9. doctor_NN, hospital_NN	0.473	0.347
10. car_NN, driver_NN	0.497	0.281

Table 1: Ten examples from the LSA similarity model

2.1.3 SVD Transformation

Singular Value Decomposition (SVD) has been found to be effective in improving word similarity measures (Landauer and Dumais, 1997). SVD is typically applied to a *word by document* matrix, yielding the familiar LSA technique. In our case we apply it to our *word by word* matrix. In literature, this variation of LSA is sometimes called HAL (Hyperspace Analog to Language) (Burgess et al., 1998).

Before performing SVD, we transform the raw word co-occurrence count f_{ij} to its log frequency $log(f_{ij}+1)$. We select the 300 largest singular values and reduce the 29K word vectors to 300 dimensions. The LSA similarity between two words is defined as the cosine similarity of their corresponding word vectors after the SVD transformation.

2.1.4 LSA Similarity Examples

Ten examples obtained using LSA similarity are given in Table 1. Examples 1 to 6 illustrate that the metric has a good property of differentiating similar words from non-similar words. Examples 7 and 8 show that the ± 4 model can detect semantically similar words even with different POS while the ± 1 model yields much worse performance. Example 9 and 10 show that highly related but not substitutable words can also have a strong similarity but the ± 1 model has a better performance in discriminating them. We call the ± 1 model and the ± 4 model as *concept similarity* and *relation similarity* respectively since the ± 1 model has a good performance on nouns and the ± 4 model is good at computing similarity between relations regardless of POS of words, such as "marry to" and "is the wife of".

2.2 Combining with WordNet Knowledge

Statistical word similarity measures have limitations. Related words can have similarity scores as high as what similar words get, as illustrated by "doctor" and "hospital" in Table 1. Word similarity is typically low for synonyms having many word senses since information about different senses are mashed together (Han et al., 2013). By using WordNet, we can reduce the above issues.

2.2.1 Boosting LSA similarity using WordNet

We increase the similarity between two words if any of the following relations hold.

- They are in the same WordNet synset.
- One word is the direct hypernym of the other.
- One word is the two-link indirect hypernym of the other.
- One adjective has a direct *similar to* relation with the other.
- One adjective has a two-link indirect *similar to* relation with the other.
- One word is a derivationally related form of the other.
- One word is the head of the gloss of the other or its direct hypernym or one of its direct hyponyms.
- One word appears frequently in the glosses of the other and its direct hypernym and its direct hyponyms.

We use the algorithm described in (Collins, 1999) to find a word gloss header. We require a minimum LSA similarity of 0.1 between the two words to filter out noisy data when extracting WordNet relations.

We define a word's "significant senses" to deal with the problem of WordNet trivial senses. The word "year", for example, has a sense "a body of students who graduate together" which makes it a synonym of the word "class". This causes problems because "year" and "class" are not similar, in general. A sense is significant, if any of the following conditions are met: (i) it is the first sense; (ii) its WordNet frequency count is not less than five; or (iii) its word form appears first in its synset's word form list and it has a WordNet sense number less than eight.

We assign path distance of zero to the category 1, path distance of one to the category 2, 4 and 6, and path distance of two to the other categories. The new similarity between word x and y by combining LSA similarity and WordNet relations is shown in the following equation

$$sim_{\oplus}(x, y) = sim_{LSA}(x, y) + 0.5e^{-\alpha D(x,y)} \quad (1)$$

where $D(x, y)$ is the minimal path distance between x and y. Using the $e^{-\alpha D(x,y)}$ to transform simple shortest path length has been demonstrated to be very effective according to (Li et al., 2003). The parameter α is set to be 0.25, following their experimental results. The ceiling of $sim_{\oplus}(x, y)$ remains 1.0 and we simply cut the excess.

2.2.2 Dealing with words of many senses

For a word w with many WordNet senses (currently ten or more), we use its synonyms with fewer senses (at most one third of that of w) as its substitutions in computing similarity with another word. Let S_x and S_y be the sets of all such substitutions of the words x and y respectively. The new similarity is obtained using Equation 2.

$$sim(x, y) = max\Big(\max_{s_x \in S_x \cup \{x\}} sim_{\oplus}(s_x, y), \max_{s_y \in S_y \cup \{y\}} sim_{\oplus}(x, s_y)\Big) \quad (2)$$

An online demonstration of a similar model developed for the GOR project is available (UMBC, 2013b), but it lacks some of this version's features.

3 Align-and-Penalize Approach

First we hypothesize that STS similarity between two sentences can be computed using

$$STS = T - P' - P'' \quad (3)$$

where T is the term alignments score, P' is the penalty for bad term alignments and P'' is the penalty for syntactic contradictions led by the alignments. However P'' had not been fully implemented and was not used in our STS submissions. We show it here just for completeness.

3.1 Aligning terms in two sentences

We start by applying the Stanford POS tagger to tag and lemmatize the input sentences. We use our predefined vocabulary, POS tagging data and simple regular expressions to recognize multi-word terms including noun and verb phrases, proper nouns, numbers and time. We ignore adverbs with frequency count larger than $500,000$ in our corpus and stop words with general meaning.

Equation 4 shows our aligning function g which finds the counterpart of term $t \in S$ in sentence S'.

$$g(t) = \underset{t' \in S'}{argmax}\ sim'(t, t') \quad (4)$$

$sim'(t, t')$ is a wrapper function over $sim(x, y)$ in Equation 2 that uses the *relation similarity* model. It compares numerical and time terms by their values. If they are equal, 1 is returned; otherwise 0. $sim'(t, t')$ provides limited comparison over pronouns. It returns 1 between subject pronouns *I*, *we*, *they*, *he*, *she* and their corresponding object pronouns. $sim'(t, t')$ also outputs 1 if one term is the acronym of the other term, or if one term is the head of the other term, or if two consecutive terms in a sentence match a single term in the other sentence (e.g. "long term" and "long-term"). $sim'(t, t')$ further adds support for matching words[2] not presented in our vocabulary using a simple string similarity algorithm. It computes character bigram sets for each of the two words without using padding characters. Dice coefficient is then applied to get the degree of overlap between the two sets. If it is larger than two thirds, $sim'(t, t')$ returns a score of 1; otherwise 0.

$g(t)$ is direction-dependent and does not achieve one-to-one mapping. This property is useful in measuring STS similarity because two sentences are often not exact paraphrases of one another. Moreover, it is often necessary to align multiple terms in one sentence to a single term in the other sentence, such as when dealing with repetitions and anaphora or, e.g., mapping "people writing books" to "writers".

Let S_1 and S_2 be the sets of terms in two input sentences. We define term alignments score T as the following equation shows.

$$\frac{\sum_{t \in S_1} sim'(t, g(t))}{2 \cdot |S_1|} + \frac{\sum_{t \in S_2} sim'(t, g(t))}{2 \cdot |S_2|} \quad (5)$$

[2] We use the regular expression "[A-Za-z][A-Za-z]*" to identify them.

3.2 Penalizing bad term alignments

We currently treat two kinds of alignments as "bad", as described in Equation 6. For the set B_i, we have an additional restriction that neither of the sentences has the form of a negation. In defining B_i, we used a collection of antonyms extracted from WordNet (Mohammad et al., 2008). Antonym pairs are a special case of disjoint sets. The terms "piano" and "violin" are also disjoint but they are not antonyms. In order to broaden the set B_i we will need to develop a model that can determine when two terms belong to disjoint sets.

$$\begin{aligned} A_i &= \{\langle t, g(t)\rangle \,|t \in S_i \wedge sim'(t, g(t)) < 0.05\} \\ B_i &= \{\langle t, g(t)\rangle \,|t \in S_i \wedge t \text{ is an antonym of } g(t)\} \\ & \qquad i \in \{1, 2\} \end{aligned} \tag{6}$$

We show how we compute P' in Equation 7.

$$\begin{aligned} P_i^A &= \frac{\sum_{\langle t,g(t)\rangle \in A_i} (sim'(t, g(t)) + w_f(t) \cdot w_p(t))}{2 \cdot |S_i|} \\ P_i^B &= \frac{\sum_{\langle t,g(t)\rangle \in B_i} (sim'(t, g(t)) + 0.5)}{2 \cdot |S_i|} \\ P' &= P_1^A + P_1^B + P_2^A + P_2^B \end{aligned} \tag{7}$$

The $w_f(t)$ and $w_p(t)$ terms are two weighting functions on the term t. $w_f(t)$ inversely weights the log frequency of term t and $w_p(t)$ weights t by its part of speech tag, assigning 1.0 to verbs, nouns, pronouns and numbers, and 0.5 to terms with other POS tags.

4 SVM approach

We used the scores from the align-and-penalize approach along with several other features to learn a support vector regression model. We started by applying the following preprocessing steps.

- The sentences were tokenized and POS-tagged using NLTK's (Bird, 2006) default Penn Treebank based tagger.
- Punctuation characters were removed from the tokens except for the decimal point in numbers.
- All numbers written as words were converted into numerals, e.g., "2.2 million" was replaced by "2200000" and "fifty six" by "56".
- All mentions of time were converted into military time, e.g., "5:40pm" was replaced by "1740" and "1h30am" by "0130".
- Abbreviations were expanded using a compiled list of commonly used abbreviations.
- About 80 stopwords were removed.

4.1 Ngram Matching

The sentence similarities are derived as a function of the similarity scores of their corresponding paired word ngrams. These features closely resemble the ones used in (Saric et al., 2012). For our system, we used unigrams, bigrams, trigrams and skip-bigrams, a special form of bigrams which allow for arbitrary distance between two tokens.

An ngram from the first sentence is exclusively paired with an ngram from the second which has the highest similarity score. Several similarity metrics are used to generate different features. For bigrams, trigrams and skip-bigrams, the similarity score for two ngrams is computed as the arithmetic mean of the similarity scores of the individual words they contain. For example, for the bigrams "he ate" and "she spoke", the similarity score is the average of the similarity scores between the words "he" and "she" and the words "ate" and "spoke".

The ngram overlap of two sentences is defined as "*the harmonic mean of the degree to which the second sentence covers the first and the degree to which the first sentence covers the second*" (Saric et al., 2012). Given sets S_1 and S_2 containing ngrams from sentences 1 and 2, and sets P_1 and P_2 containing their paired ngrams along with their similarity scores, the ngram overlap score for a given ngram type is computed using the following equation.

$$HM\left(\frac{\sum_{n\epsilon P_1} w(n).sim(n)}{\sum_{n\epsilon S_1} w(n)}, \frac{\sum_{n\epsilon P_2} w(n).sim(n)}{\sum_{n\epsilon S_2} w(n)}\right) \tag{8}$$

In this formula, HM is the harmonic mean, $w(n)$ is the weight assigned for the given ngram and $sim(n)$ is the similarity score of the paired word.

By default, all the ngrams are assigned a uniform weight of 1. But since different words carry different amount of information, e.g. "acclimatize" vs. "take", "cardiologist" vs. "person", we also use information content as weights. The information content of a word is as defined in (Saric et al., 2012).

$$ic(w) = ln\left(\frac{\sum_{w'\epsilon C} freq(w')}{freq(w)}\right) \tag{9}$$

Here C is the set of words in the corpus and $freq(w)$ is the frequency of a word in the corpus. The weight of an ngram is the sum of its constituent word weights. We use refined versions of Google ngram frequencies (Michel et al., 2011) from (Mem, 2008) and (Saric et al., 2012) to get the information content of the words. Words not in this list are assigned the average weight.

We used several word similarity metrics for ngram matching apart from the similarity metric described in section 2. Our baseline similarity metric was an exact string match which assigned a score of 1 if two tokens contained the same sequence of characters and 0 otherwise. We also used NLTK's library to compute WordNet based similarity measures such as Path Distance Similarity, Wu-Palmer Similarity (Wu and Palmer, 1994) and Lin Similarity (Lin, 1998b). For Lin Similarity, the Semcor corpus was used for the information content of words.

4.2 Contrast Scores

We computed contrast scores between two sentences using three different lists of antonym pairs (Mohammad et al., 2008). We used a large list containing 3.5 million antonym pairs, a list of about 22,000 antonym pairs from Wordnet and a list of 50,000 pairs of words with their degree of contrast. Contrast scores between two sentences were derived as a function of the number of antonym pairs between them similar to equation 8 but with negative values to indicate contrast scores.

4.3 Features

We constructed 52 features from different combinations of similarity metrics, their parameters, ngram types (unigram, bigram, trigram and skip-bigram) and ngram weights (equal weight vs. information content) for all sentence pairs in the training data.

- We used scores from the align-and-penalize approach directly as a feature.
- Using exact string match over different ngram types and ngram weights, we extracted eight features ($4 * 4$). We also developed four additional features ($2 * 2$) by includin stopwords in bigrams and trigrams, motivated by the nature of MSRvid dataset.
- We used the LSA boosted similarity metric in three modes: concept similarity, relation similarity and mixed mode, which used the concept model for nouns and relation model for verbs, adverbs and adjectives. A total of 24 features were extracted ($4 * 2 * 3$).
- For Wordnet-based similarity measures, we used uniform weights for Path and Wu-Palmer similarity and used the information content of words (derived from the Semcor corpus) for Lin similarity. Skip bigrams were ignored and a total of nine features were produced ($3 * 3$).
- Contrast scores used three different lists of antonym pairs. A total of six features were extracted using different weight values ($3 * 2$).

4.4 Support Vector Regression

The features described in 4.3 were used in different combinations to train several support vector regression (SVR) models. We used LIBSVM (Chang and Lin, 2011) to learn the SVR models and ran a grid search provided by (Saric et al., 2012) to find the optimal values for the parameters C, g and p. These models were then used to predict the scores for the test sets.

The *Galactus* system was trained on all of STS 2012 data and used the full set of 52 features. The FnWN dataset was handled slightly differently from the others. We observed that terms like "frame" and "entity" were used frequently in the five sample sentence pairs and treated them as stopwords. To accommodate the vast difference in sentence lengths, equation 8 was modified to compute the arithmetic mean instead of the harmonic mean.

The *Saiyan* system employed data-specific training and features. The training sets were subsets of the supplied STS 2012 dataset. More specifically, the model for headlines was trained on 3000 sentence pairs from MSRvid and MSRpar, SMT used 1500 sentence pairs from SMT europarl and SMT news, while OnWN used only the 750 OnWN sentence pairs from last year. The FnWN scores were directly used from the Align-and-Penalize approach. None of the models for *Saiyan* used contrast features and the model for SMT also ignored similarity scores from exact string match metric.

5 Results and discussion

Table 2 presents the official results of our three runs in the 2013 STS task. Each entry gives a run's Pearson correlation on a dataset as well as the rank of the run among all 89 runs submitted by the 35 teams. The last row shows the mean of the correlations and the overall ranks of our three runs.

We tested performance of the align-and-penalize approach on all of the 2012 STS datasets. It obtained correlation values of 0.819 on MSRvid, 0.669 on MSRpar, 0.553 on SMTeuroparl, 0.567 on SMTnews and 0.722 on OnWN for the test datasets, and correlation values of 0.814 on MSRvid, 0.707 on MSRpar and 0.646 on SMTeuroparl for the training datasets. The performance of the approach without using the antonym penalty is also tested, producing correlation scores of 0.795 on MSRvid, 0.667 on MSRpar, 0.554 on SMTeuroparl, 0.566 on SMTnew and 0.727 on OnWN, for the test datasets, and 0.794 on MSRvid, 0.707 on MSRpar and 0.651 on SMTeuroparl for the training datasets. The average of the correlation scores on all eight datasets with and without the antonym penalty is 0.6871 and 0.6826, respectively. Since the approach's performance was only slightly improved when the antonym penalty was used, we decided to not include this penalty in our *PairingWords* run in the hope that its simplicity would make it more robust.

During development, our SVM approach achieved correlations of 0.875 for MSRvid, 0.699 for MSRpar, 0.559 for SMTeuroparl, 0.625 for SMTnews and 0.729 for OnWN on the 2012 STS test data. Models were trained on their respective training sets while SMTnews used SMTeuroparl and OnWN used all the training sets. We experimented with different features and training data to study their influence on the performance of the models. We found that the unigram overlap feature, based on boosted LSA similarity and weighted by information content, could independently achieve very high correlations. Including more features improved the accuracy slightly and in some cases added noise. The difficulty in selecting data specific features and training for novel datasets is indicated by *Saiyan's* contrasting performance on headlines and OnWN datasets. The model used for Headlines was trained on data from seemingly different domains (MSRvid, MSRpar) while OnWN was trained only on OnWN from STS 2012. When the model for headlines dataset was used to predict the scores for OnWN, the correlation jumped from 0.55 to 0.71 indicating that the earlier model suffered from overfitting.

Dataset	Pairing	Galactus	Saiyan
Headlines (750 pairs)	0.7642 (3)	0.7428 (7)	**0.7838 (1)**
OnWN (561 pairs)	0.7529 (5)	0.7053 (12)	0.5593 (36)
FNWN (189 pairs)	**0.5818 (1)**	0.5444 (3)	0.5815 (2)
SMT (750 pairs)	0.3804 (8)	0.3705 (11)	0.3563 (16)
Weighted mean	**0.6181 (1)**	0.5927 (2)	0.5683 (4)

Table 2: Performance of our three systems on the four test sets.

Overfitting is not evident in the performance of *PairingWords* and *Galactus*, which have more consistent performance over all datasets. The relatively simple *PairingWords* system has two advantages: it is faster, since the current *Galactus* requires computing a large number of features; and its performance is more predictable, since training is not needed thus eliminating noise induced from diverse training sets.

6 Conclusion

We described three semantic text similarity systems developed for the *SEM 2013 STS shared task and the results of the corresponding three runs we submitted. All of the systems used a lexical similarity feature that combined POS tagging, LSA word similarity and WordNet knowledge.

The first run, which achieved the best mean score out of all 89 submissions, used a simple term alignment algorithm augmented with two penalty metrics. The other two runs, ranked second and fourth out of all submissions, used support vector regression models based on a set of more than 50 additional features. The runs differed in their feature sets, training data and procedures, and parameter settings.

Acknowledgments

This research was supported by AFOSR award FA9550-08-1-0265 and a gift from Microsoft.

References

[Agirre et al.2012] Eneko Agirre, Mona Diab, Daniel Cer, and Aitor Gonzalez-Agirre. 2012. Semeval-2012 task 6: a pilot on semantic textual similarity. In *Proceedings of the First Joint Conference on Lexical and Computational Semantics*, pages 385–393. Association for Computational Linguistics.

[Agirre et al.2013] Eneko Agirre, Daniel Cer, Mona Diab, Aitor Gonzalez-Agirre, and Weiwei Guo. 2013. *sem 2013 shared task: Semantic textual similarity, including a pilot on typed-similarity. In **SEM 2013: The Second Joint Conference on Lexical and Computational Semantics*. Association for Computational Linguistics.

[Baroni et al.2009] M. Baroni, S. Bernardini, A. Ferraresi, and E. Zanchetta. 2009. The wacky wide web: A collection of very large linguistically processed web-crawled corpora. *Language Resources and Evaluation*, 43(3):209–226.

[Bird2006] Steven Bird. 2006. Nltk: the natural language toolkit. In *Proceedings of the COLING/ACL on Interactive presentation sessions*, COLING-ACL '06, pages 69–72, Stroudsburg, PA, USA. Association for Computational Linguistics.

[Burgess et al.1998] C. Burgess, K. Livesay, and K. Lund. 1998. Explorations in context space: Words, sentences, discourse. *Discourse Processes*, 25:211–257.

[Chang and Lin2011] Chih-Chung Chang and Chih-Jen Lin. 2011. LIBSVM: A library for support vector machines. *ACM Transactions on Intelligent Systems and Technology*, 2:27:1–27:27.

[Coelho et al.2004] T.A.S. Coelho, Pável Pereira Calado, Lamarque Vieira Souza, Berthier Ribeiro-Neto, and Richard Muntz. 2004. Image retrieval using multiple evidence ranking. *IEEE Trans. on Knowl. and Data Eng.*, 16(4):408–417.

[Collins1999] Michael John Collins. 1999. *Head-driven statistical models for natural language parsing*. Ph.D. thesis, University of Pennsylvania.

[Deerwester et al.1990] Scott Deerwester, Susan T. Dumais, George W. Furnas, Thomas K. Landauer, and Richard Harshman. 1990. Indexing by latent semantic analysis. *Journal of the American Society for Information Science*, 41(6):391–407.

[Dolan et al.2004] Bill Dolan, Chris Quirk, and Chris Brockett. 2004. Unsupervised construction of large paraphrase corpora: exploiting massively parallel news sources. In *Proceedings of the 20th international conference on Computational Linguistics*, COLING '04. Association for Computational Linguistics.

[Ganitkevitch et al.2013] Juri Ganitkevitch, Benjamin Van Durme, and Chris Callison-Burch. 2013. PPDB: The paraphrase database. In *HLT-NAACL 2013*.

[Han and Finin2013] Lushan Han and Tim Finin. 2013. UMBC webbase corpus. http://ebiq.org/r/351.

[Han et al.2012] Lushan Han, Tim Finin, and Anupam Joshi. 2012. Schema-free structured querying of dbpedia data. In *Proceedings of the 21st ACM international conference on Information and knowledge management*, pages 2090–2093. ACM.

[Han et al.2013] Lushan Han, Tim Finin, Paul McNamee, Anupam Joshi, and Yelena Yesha. 2013. Improving Word Similarity by Augmenting PMI with Estimates of Word Polysemy. *IEEE Transactions on Knowledge and Data Engineering*, 25(6):1307–1322.

[Harris1968] Zellig Harris. 1968. *Mathematical Structures of Language*. Wiley, New York, USA.

[Hart1997] M. Hart. 1997. Project gutenberg electronic books. http://www.gutenberg.org/wiki/Main_Page.

[Kauchak and Barzilay2006] David Kauchak and Regina Barzilay. 2006. Paraphrasing for automatic evaluation. In *HLT-NAACL '06*, pages 455–462.

[Landauer and Dumais1997] T. Landauer and S. Dumais. 1997. A solution to plato's problem: The latent semantic analysis theory of the acquisition, induction, and representation of knowledge. In *Psychological Review, 104*, pages 211–240.

[Li et al.2003] Y. Li, Z.A. Bandar, and D. McLean. 2003. An approach for measuring semantic similarity between words using multiple information sources. *IEEE Transactions on Knowledge and Data Engineering*, 15(4):871–882.

[Lin1998a] Dekang Lin. 1998a. Automatic retrieval and clustering of similar words. In *Proc. 17th Int. Conf. on Computational Linguistics*, pages 768–774, Montreal, CN.

[Lin1998b] Dekang Lin. 1998b. An information-theoretic definition of similarity. In *Proceedings of the Fifteenth International Conference on Machine Learning*, ICML '98, pages 296–304, San Francisco, CA, USA. Morgan Kaufmann Publishers Inc.

[Meadow1992] Charles T. Meadow. 1992. *Text Information Retrieval Systems*. Academic Press, Inc.

[Mem2008] 2008. Google word frequency counts. http://bit.ly/10JdTRz.

[Metzler et al.2007] Donald Metzler, Susan Dumais, and Christopher Meek. 2007. Similarity measures for short segments of text. In *Proceedings of the 29th European conference on IR research*, pages 16–27. Springer-Verlag.

[Michel et al.2011] Jean-Baptiste Michel, Yuan K. Shen, Aviva P. Aiden, Adrian Veres, Matthew K. Gray, The Google Books Team, Joseph P. Pickett, Dale Hoiberg, Dan Clancy, Peter Norvig, Jon Orwant, Steven Pinker,

Martin A. Nowak, and Erez L. Aiden. 2011. Quantitative analysis of culture using millions of digitized books. *Science*, 331(6014):176–182, January 14.

[Mihalcea et al.2006] Rada Mihalcea, Courtney Corley, and Carlo Strapparava. 2006. Corpus-based and knowledge-based measures of text semantic similarity. In *Proceedings of the 21st national conference on Artificial intelligence*, pages 775–780. AAAI Press.

[Miller1995] G.A. Miller. 1995. WordNet: a lexical database for English. *Communications of the ACM*, 38(11):41.

[Mohammad et al.2008] Saif Mohammad, Bonnie Dorr, and Graeme Hirst. 2008. Computing word-pair antonymy. In *Proc. Conf. on Empirical Methods in Natural Language Processing and Computational Natural Language Learning (EMNLP-2008)*, October.

[Rose et al.2002] Tony Rose, Mark Stevenson, and Miles Whitehead. 2002. The reuters corpus volume 1 - from yesterdays news to tomorrows language resources. In *In Proceedings of the Third International Conference on Language Resources and Evaluation*, pages 29–31.

[Sahami and Heilman2006] Mehran Sahami and Timothy D. Heilman. 2006. A web-based kernel function for measuring the similarity of short text snippets. In *Proceedings of the 15th international conference on World Wide Web*, WWW '06, pages 377–386. ACM.

[Saric et al.2012] Frane Saric, Goran Glavas, Mladen Karan, Jan Snajder, and Bojana Dalbelo Basic. 2012. Takelab: systems for measuring semantic text similarity. In *Proceedings of the First Joint Conference on Lexical and Computational Semantics*, pages 441–448. Association for Computational Linguistics.

[Sriram et al.2010] Bharath Sriram, Dave Fuhry, Engin Demir, Hakan Ferhatosmanoglu, and Murat Demirbas. 2010. Short text classification in twitter to improve information filtering. In *Proceedings of the 33rd international ACM SIGIR conference on Research and development in information retrieval*, pages 841–842. ACM.

[Stanford2001] Stanford. 2001. Stanford WebBase project. http://bit.ly/WebBase.

[Toutanova et al.2000] Kristina Toutanova, Dan Klein, Christopher Manning, William Morgan, Anna Rafferty, and Michel Galley. 2000. Stanford log-linear part-of-speech tagger. http://nlp.stanford.edu/software/tagger.shtml.

[UMBC2013a] UMBC. 2013a. Graph of relations project. http://ebiq.org/j/95.

[UMBC2013b] UMBC. 2013b. Semantic similarity demonstration. http://swoogle.umbc.edu/SimService/.

[Wu and Palmer1994] Z. Wu and M. Palmer. 1994. Verb semantic and lexical selection. In *Proceedings of the 32nd Annual Meeting of the Association for Computational Linguistics (ACL-1994)*, pages 133–138, Las Cruces (Mexico).

iKernels-Core: Tree Kernel Learning for Textual Similarity

Aliaksei Severyn[1] and **Massimo Nicosia**[1] and **Alessandro Moschitti**[1,2]
[1]University of Trento, DISI, 38123 Povo (TN), Italy
{severyn,m.nicosia,moschitti}@disi.unitn.it
[2]Qatar Foundation, QCRI, Doha, Qatar
{amoschitti}@qf.org.qa

Abstract

This paper describes the participation of iKernels system in the Semantic Textual Similarity (STS) shared task at *SEM 2013. Different from the majority of approaches, where a large number of pairwise similarity features are used to learn a regression model, our model directly encodes the input texts into syntactic/semantic structures. Our systems rely on tree kernels to automatically extract a rich set of syntactic patterns to learn a similarity score correlated with human judgements. We experiment with different structural representations derived from constituency and dependency trees. While showing large improvements over the top results from the previous year task (STS-2012), our best system ranks 21st out of total 88 participated in the STS-2013 task. Nevertheless, a slight refinement to our model makes it rank 4th.

1 Introduction

Comparing textual data to establish the degree of semantic similarity is of key importance in many Natural Language Processing (NLP) tasks ranging from document categorization to textual entailment and summarization. The key aspect of having an accurate STS framework is the design of features that can adequately represent various aspects of the similarity between texts, e.g. using lexical, syntactic and semantic similarity metrics.

The majority of approaches to semantic textual similarity treat the input text pairs as feature vectors where each feature is a score corresponding to a certain type of similarity. This approach is conceptually easy to implement and STS-2012 (Agirre et al., 2012) has shown that the best systems were built following this idea, i.e. a number of features encoding similarity of an input text pair were combined in a single scoring model, such as Linear Regression or Support Vector Regression (SVR). One potential limitation of using only similarity features to represent a text pair is that of low representation power.

The novelty of our approach is that we encode the input text pairs directly into structural objects, e.g. trees, and rely on the power of kernel learning to extract relevant structures. This completely different from (Croce et al.,), where tree kernels where used to establish syntactic similarity and then plugged as similarity features. To link the documents in a pair we mark the nodes in the related structures with a special relational tag. In this way effective structural relational patterns are implicitly encoded in the trees and can be automatically learned by the kernel-based machine learning methods. We build our systems on top of the features used by two best systems from STS-2012 and combine them with the tree kernel models within the Support Vector Regression to derive a single scoring model. Since the test data used for evaluation in STS-2013 (Agirre et al., 2013) is different from the 2012 data provided for the system development, domain adaptation represents an additional challenge. To address this problem we augment our feature vector representation with features extracted from a text pair as a whole to capture individual properties of each dataset. Additionally, we experiment with a corpus type classifier and include its prediction score as additional features. Finally, we use stacking to combine several structural models into the feature vector representation.

*Second Joint Conference on Lexical and Computational Semantics (*SEM), Volume 1: Proceedings of the Main Conference and the Shared Task*, pages 53–58, Atlanta, Georgia, June 13-14, 2013.

In the following sections we describe our approach to combine structural representations with the pairwise similarity features in a single SVR learning framework. We then report results on both STS-2012 and 2013 tasks.

2 Structural Relational Similarity

In this section we first describe the kernel framework to combine structural and vector models, then we explain how to construct the tree models and briefly describe tree kernels we use to automatically extract the features.

2.1 Structural Kernel Learning

In supervised learning, given the labeled data $\{(\boldsymbol{x}_i, \boldsymbol{y}_i)\}_{i=1}^n$, the goal is to estimate a decision function $h(\boldsymbol{x}) = \boldsymbol{y}$ that maps input examples to the target variables. A conventional approach is to represent a pair of texts as a set of similarity features $\{f_i\}$, s.t. the predictions are computed as $h(\boldsymbol{x}) = \boldsymbol{w} \cdot \boldsymbol{x} = \sum_i w_i f_i$, where $\boldsymbol{w}$ is the model weight vector. Hence, the learning problem boils down to estimating the individual weight of each of the similarity feature f_i. One downside of such approach is that a great deal of similarity information carried by a given text pair is lost when modeled by single real-valued scores.

A more versatile approach in terms of the input representation relies on kernels. In a typical kernel machine, e.g. SVM, the prediction function for a test input $\boldsymbol{x}$ takes on the following form $h(\boldsymbol{x}) = \sum_i \alpha_i y_i K(\boldsymbol{x}, \boldsymbol{x}_i)$, where α_i are the model parameters estimated from the training data, y_i - target variables, $\boldsymbol{x}_i$ are support vectors, and $K(\cdot,\cdot)$ is a kernel function.

To encode both structural representation and similarity feature vectors of input text pairs $\boldsymbol{x}_i$ in a single model, we treat it as the following tuple: $\boldsymbol{x}_i = \langle \boldsymbol{x}_i^a, \boldsymbol{x}_i^b \rangle = \langle (\boldsymbol{t}_i^a, \boldsymbol{v}_i^a), (\boldsymbol{t}_i^b, \boldsymbol{v}_i^b) \rangle$, where $\boldsymbol{x}_i^a$ $\boldsymbol{x}_i^b$ are the first and the second document of $\boldsymbol{x}_i$, and $\boldsymbol{t}$ and $\boldsymbol{v}$ denote tree and vector representations respectively.

To compute a kernel between two text pairs $\boldsymbol{x}_i$ and $\boldsymbol{x}_j$ we define the following all-vs-all kernel, where all possible combinations of documents from each pair are considered: $K(\boldsymbol{x}_i, \boldsymbol{x}_j) = K(\boldsymbol{x}_i^a, \boldsymbol{x}_j^a) + K(\boldsymbol{x}_i^a, \boldsymbol{x}_j^b) + K(\boldsymbol{x}_i^b, \boldsymbol{x}_j^a) + K(\boldsymbol{x}_i^b, \boldsymbol{x}_j^b)$. Each of the kernel computations K between two documents $\boldsymbol{x}^a$ and $\boldsymbol{x}^b$ can be broken down into the following: $K(\boldsymbol{x}^a, \boldsymbol{x}^b) = K_{\text{TK}}(\boldsymbol{t}^a, \boldsymbol{t}^b) + K_{\text{fvec}}(\boldsymbol{v}^a, \boldsymbol{v}^b)$, where K_{TK} computes a tree kernel and K_{fvec} is a kernel over feature vectors, e.g. linear, polynomial or RBF, etc. Further in the text we refer to structural tree kernel models as `TK` and explicit feature vector representation as `fvec`.

Having defined a way to jointly model text pairs using structural `TK` representations along with the similarity features `fvec`, we next briefly review tree kernels and our relational structures derived from constituency and dependency trees.

2.2 Tree Kernels

We use tree structures as our base representation since they provide sufficient flexibility in representation and allow for easier feature extraction than, for example, graph structures. We use a Partial Tree Kernel (PTK) (Moschitti, 2006) to take care of automatic feature extraction and compute $K_{\text{TK}}(\cdot,\cdot)$.

PTK is a tree kernel function that can be effectively applied to both constituency and dependency parse trees. It generalizes a subset tree kernel (STK) (Collins and Duffy, 2002) that maps a tree into the space of all possible tree fragments constrained by the rule that the sibling nodes from their parents cannot be separated. Different from STK where the nodes in the generated tree fragments are constrained to include none or all of their direct children, PTK fragments can contain any subset of the features, i.e. PTK allows for breaking the production rules. Consequently, PTK generalizes STK generating an extremely rich feature space, which results in higher generalization ability.

2.3 Relational Structures

The idea of using relational structures to jointly model text pairs was previously proposed in (Severyn and Moschitti, 2012), where shallow syntactic structures derived from chunks and part-of-speech tags were used to represent question/answer pairs. In this paper, we define novel relational structures based on: (i) constituency and (ii) dependency trees.

Constituency tree. Each document in a given text pair is represented by its constituency parse tree. If a document contains multiple sentences they are merged in a single tree with a common root. To encode the structural relationships between docu-

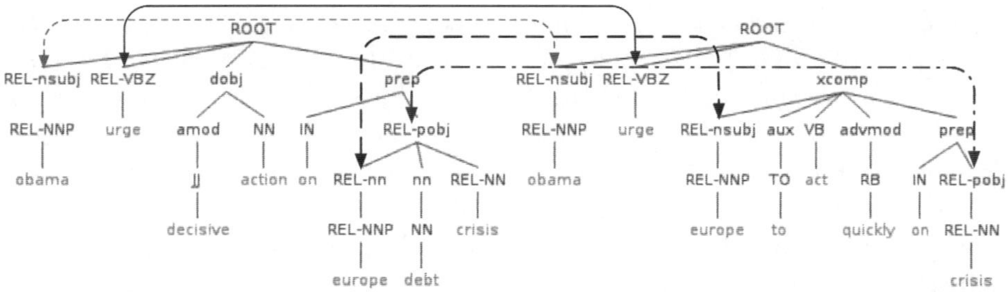

Figure 1: A dependency-based structural representation of a text pair. REL tag links related fragments.

ments in a pair a special REL tag is used to link the related structures. We adopt a simple strategy to establish such links: words from two documents that have a common lemma get their parents (POS tags) and grandparents, non-terminals, marked with a REL tag.

Dependency tree. We propose to use dependency relations between words to derive an alternative structural representation. In particular, dependency relations are used to link words in a way that words are always at the leaf level. This reordering of the nodes helps to avoid the situation where nodes with words tend to form long chains. This is essential for PTK to extract meaningful fragments. We also plug part-of-speech tags between the word nodes and nodes carrying their grammatical role. Again a special REL tag is used to establish relations between tree fragments. Fig. 1 gives an example of a dependency-based structure taken from STS-2013 *headlines* dataset.

3 Pairwise similarity features.

Along with the direct representation of input text pairs as structural objects our framework also encodes feature vectors (base), which we describe below.

3.1 Baseline features

We adopt similarity features from two best performing systems of STS-2012, which were publicly released: namely, the Takelab[1] system (Šarić et al., 2012) and the UKP Lab's system[2] (Bar et al., 2012). Both systems represent input texts with similarity features which combine multiple text similarity measures of varying complexity.

UKP provides metrics based on matching of character, word n-grams and common subsequences. It also includes features derived from Explicit Semantic Analysis vector comparisons and aggregation of word similarity based on lexical-semantic resources, e.g. WordNet. In total it provides 18 features.

Takelab includes n-gram matching of varying size, weighted word matching, length difference, WordNet similarity and vector space similarity where pairs of input sentences are mapped into Latent Semantic Analysis (LSA) space (Turney and Pantel, 2010). The features are computed over several sentence representations where stop words are removed and/or lemmas are used in place of raw tokens. The total number of Takelab's features is 21. Even though some of the UKP and Takelab features overlap we include all of them in a combined system with the total of 39 features.

3.2 iKernels features

Here we describe our additional features added to the fvec representation. First, we note that word frequencies used to compute weighted word matchings and the word-vector mappings to compute LSA similarities required by **Takelab** features are provided only for the vocabulary extracted from 2012 data. Hence, we use both STS-2012 and 2013 data to obtain the word counts and re-estimate LSA vector representations. For the former we extract unigram counts from Google Books Ngrams[3], while for the latter we use additional corpora as described below.

LSA similarity. To construct LSA word-vector mappings we use the following three sources: (i)

[1] http://takelab.fer.hr/sts/

[2] https://code.google.com/p/dkpro-similarity-asl/wiki/SemEval2013

[3] http://storage.googleapis.com/books/ngrams/books/datasetsv2.html

Aquaint[4], which consists of more than 1 million newswire documents, (ii) ukWaC (Baroni et al., 2009) - a 2 billion word corpus constructed from the Web, and (iii) and a collection of documents extracted from Wikipedia dump[5]. To extract LSA topics we use GenSim[6] software. We preprocess the data by lowercasing, removing stopwords and words with frequency lower than 5. Finally, we apply tf-idf weighting. For all representations we fix the number of dimensions to 250. For all corpora we use document-level representation, except for Wikipedia we also experimented with a sentence-level document representation, which typically provides a more restricted context for estimating word-document distributions.

Brown Clusters. In addition to vector representations derived from LSA, we extract word-vector mappings using Brown word clusters[7] (Turian et al., 2010), where words are organized into a hierarchy and each word is represented as a bit-string. We encode each word by a feature vector where each entry corresponds to a prefix extracted from its bit-string. We use prefix lengths in the following range: $k = \{4, 8, 12, 16, 20\}$. Finally, the document is represented as a feature vector composed by the individual word vectors.

Term-overlap features. In addition to the word overlap features computed by **UKP** and **Takelab** systems we also compute a cosine similarity over the following representations: (i) n-grams of part-of-speech tags (up to 4-grams), (ii) SuperSense tags (Ciaramita and Altun, 2006), (iii) named entities, and (iv) dependency triplets.

PTK similarity. We use PTK to provide a syntactic similarity score between documents in a pair: $\texttt{PTK}(a, b) = PTK(a, b)$, where as input representations we use *dependency* and *constituency* trees.

Explicit Semantic Analysis (ESA) similarity. ESA (Gabrilovich and Markovitch, 2007) represents input documents as vectors of Wikipedia concepts. To compute ESA features we use Lucene[8] to index documents extracted from a Wikipedia dump. Given a text pair we retrieve k top documents (i.e. Wikipedia concepts) and compute the metric by looking at the overlap of the concepts between the documents: $\texttt{esa}_k(a, b) = \frac{|W_a \bigcap W_b|}{k}$, where W_a is the set of concepts retrieved for document a. We compute `esa` features with $k \in \{10, 25, 50, 100\}$.

[4]http://www.ldc.upenn.edu/Catalog/docs/LDC2002T31/

[5]http://dumps.wikimedia.org/

[6]http://radimrehurek.com/gensim/

[7]http://metaoptimize.com/projects/wordreprs/

[8]http://lucene.apache.org/

3.3 Corpus type features

Here we describe two complementary approaches (`corpus`) in an attempt to alleviate the problem of domain adaptation, where the datasets used for training and testing are drawn from different sources.

Pair representation. We treat each pair of texts as a whole and extract the following sets of `corpus` features: plain bag-of-words, dependency triplets, production rules of the syntactic parse tree and a length feature, i.e. a log-normalized length of the combined text. Each feature set is normalized and added to the `fvec` model.

Corpus classifier. We use the above set of features to train a multi-class classifier to predict for each instance its most likely corpus type. Our categories correspond to five dataset types of STS-2012. Prediction scores for each of the dataset categories are then plugged as features into the final `fvec` representation. Our multi-class classifier is a one-vs-all binary SVM trained on the merged data from STS-2012. We apply 5-fold cross-validation scheme, s.t. for each of the held-out folds we obtain independent predictions. The accuracy (averaged over 5-folds) on the STS-2012 data is 92.0%.

3.4 Stacking

To integrate multiple TK models into a single model we apply a classifier stacking approach (Fast and Jensen, 2008). Each of the learned TK models is used to generate predictions which are then plugged as features into the final `fvec` representation, s.t. the final model uses only explicit feature vector representation. We apply a 5-fold cross-validation scheme to obtain prediction scores in the same manner as described above.

4 Experimental Evaluation

4.1 Experimental setup

To encode TK models along with the similarity feature vectors into a single regression scoring model,

	base			corpus			TK								
	U	T	I	B	O	M	C	D	ALL	Mean	MSRp	MSRv	SMTe	OnWN	SMTn
	•								0.7060	0.6087	0.6080	0.8390	0.2540	0.6820	0.4470
		•							0.7589	0.6863	0.6814	0.8637	0.4950	0.7091	0.5395
	•	•							0.8079	0.7161	0.7134	0.8837	0.5519	0.7343	0.5607
	•	•	•						0.8187	0.7137	0.7157	0.8833	0.5131	0.7355	0.5809
	•	•	•				•		0.8458	0.7047	0.6935	0.8953	0.5080	0.7101	0.5834
	•	•	•					•	0.8468	0.6954	0.6717	0.8902	0.4652	0.7089	0.6133
	•	•	•	•			•		0.8539	0.7132	0.6993	0.9005	0.4772	0.7189	0.6481
	•	•	•	•				•	0.8529	0.7249	0.7080	0.8984	0.5142	0.7263	0.6700
Sys$_1$	•	•	•	•			•	•	0.8546	0.7156	0.6989	0.8979	0.4884	0.7181	0.6609
Sys$_3$	•	•	•		•		•	•	0.8810	0.7416	0.7210	0.8971	0.5912	0.7328	0.6778
Sys$_2$	•	•	•			•	•	•	0.8705	0.7339	0.7039	0.9012	0.5629	0.7376	0.6656
	UKP$_{best}$								0.8239	0.6773	0.6830	0.8739	0.5280	0.6641	0.4937

Table 1: System configurations and results on STS-2012. Column set `base` lists 3 feature sets : UKP (U), Takelab (T) and iKernels (I); corpus type features (`corpus`) include plain features (B), corpus classifier (O), and manually encoded dataset category (M); `TK` contains constituency (C) and dependency-based (D) models. UKP$_{best}$ is the best system of STS-2012. First column shows configuration of our three system runs submitted to STS-2013.

we use an SVR framework implemented in SVM-Light-TK[9]. We use the following parameter settings `-t 5 -F 3 -W A -C +`, which specifies to use a combination of trees and feature vectors (`-C +`), PTK over trees (`-F 3`) computed in all-vs-all mode (`-W A`) and using polynomial kernel of degree 3 for the feature vector (active by default).

We report the following metrics employed in the final evaluation: *Pearson* correlation for individual test sets[10] and *Mean* – an average score weighted by the test set size.

4.2 STS-2012

For STS-2013 task the entire data from STS-2012 was provided for the system development. To compare with the best systems of the previous year we followed the same setup, where 3 datasets (*MSRp*, *MSRv* and *SMTe*) are used for training and 5 for testing (two "surprise" datasets were added: *OnWN* and *SMTn*). We use the entire training data to obtain a single model.

Table 1 summarizes the results using structural models (`TK`), pairwise similarity (`base`) and corpus type features (`corpus`). We first note, that combining all three features sets (`U`, `T` and `I`) provides a good match to the best system `UKP`$_{best}$. Next, adding TK models results in a large improvement beating the top results in STS-2012. Furthermore, using `corpus` features results in even greater improvement with the *Mean* $= 0.7416$ and Pearson *ALL* $= 0.8810$.

4.3 STS-2013

Below we specify the configuration for each of the submitted runs (also shown in Table 1) and report the results on the STS-2013 test sets: *headlines* (*head*), *OnWN*, *FNWN*, and *SMT*:

Sys$_1$: combines `base` features (`U`, `T` and `I`), TK models (`C` and `D`) and plain corpus type features (`B`). We use STS-2012 data to train a single model.

Sys$_2$: different from **Sys$_1$** where a single model trained on the entire data is used to make predictions, we adopt a different training/test setup to account for the different nature of the data used for training and testing. After performing manual analysis of the test data we came up with the following strategy to split the training data into two sets to learn two different models: *STMe* and *OnWN* (model$_1$) and *MSRp*, *SMTn* and *STMe* (model$_2$); model$_1$ is then used to get predictions for *OnWN*, *FNWN*, while model$_2$ is used for *SMT* and *headlines*.

Sys$_3$: same as **Sys$_1$** + a corpus type classifier `O` as described in Sec. 3.3.

Table 2 shows the resulting performance of our systems and the best UMBC system published in the final ranking. **Sys$_2$** appears the most accurate among our systems, which ranked 21st out of 88. Comparing to the best system across four datasets we observe that it performs reasonably well on the *headlines* dataset (it is 5th best), while completely fails on the *OnWN* and *FNWN* test sets. After performing

[9]http://disi.unitn.it/moschitti/Tree-Kernel.htm

[10]for STS-2012 we also report the results for a concatenation of all five test sets (`ALL`)

error analysis, we found that TK models underperform on *FNWN* and *OnWN* sets, which appear underrepresented in the training data from STS-2012. We build a new system ($\mathbf{Sys}_2^*$), which is based on $\mathbf{Sys}_2$, by making two adjustments in the setup: (i) we exclude *SMTe* from training to obtain predictions on *SMT* and *head* and (ii) we remove all TK features to train a model for *FNWN* and *OnWN*. This is motivated by the observation that text pairs from STS-2012 yield a paraphrase model, since the texts are syntactically very similar. Yet, two datasets from STS-2013 *FNWN*, and *OnWN* contain text pairs where documents exhibit completely different structures. This is misleading for our syntactic similarity model learned on the STS-2012.

System	head	OnWN	FNWN	SMT	Mean	Rank
UMBC	0.7642	0.7529	0.5818	0.3804	0.6181	1
$\mathbf{Sys}_2$	0.7465	0.5572	0.3875	0.3409	0.5339	21
$\mathbf{Sys}_1$	0.7352	0.5432	0.3842	0.3180	0.5188	28
$\mathbf{Sys}_3$	0.7395	0.4228	0.3596	0.3294	0.4919	40
$\mathbf{Sys}_2^*$	0.7538	0.6872	0.4478	0.3391	0.5732	4*

Table 2: Results on STS-2013.

5 Conclusions and Future Work

We have described our participation in STS-2013 task. Our approach treats text pairs as structural objects which provides much richer representation for the learning algorithm to extract useful patterns. We experiment with structures derived from constituency and dependency trees where related fragments are linked with a special tag. Such structures are then used to learn tree kernel models which can be efficiently combined with the a feature vector representation in a single scoring model. Our approach ranks 1st with a large margin w.r.t. to the best systems in STS-2012 task, while it is 21st according to the final rankings of STS-2013. Nevertheless, a small change in the system setup makes it rank 4th. Clearly, domain adaptation represents a big challenge in STS-2013 task. We plan to address this issue in our future work.

6 Acknowledgements

This research has been supported by the European Community's Seventh Framework Program (FP7/2007-2013) under the #288024 LiMoSINe project.

References

Eneko Agirre, Daniel Cer, Mona Diab, and Gonzalez-Agirre. 2012. Semeval-2012 task 6: A pilot on semantic textual similarity. In *First Joint Conference on Lexical and Computational Semantics (*SEM)*.

Eneko Agirre, Daniel Cer, Mona Diab, Aitor Gonzalez-Agirre, and Weiwei Guo. 2013. *sem 2013 shared task: Semantic textual similarity, including a pilot on typed-similarity. In **SEM 2013: The Second Joint Conference on Lexical and Computational Semantics*.

Daniel Bar, Chris Biemann, Iryna Gurevych, and Torsten Zesch. 2012. Ukp: Computing semantic textual similarity by combining multiple content similarity measures. In *Proceedings of the Sixth International Workshop on Semantic Evaluation (SemEval 2012)*.

Marco Baroni, Silvia Bernardini, Adriano Ferraresi, and Eros Zanchetta. 2009. The wacky wide web: a collection of very large linguistically processed web-crawled corpora. *Language Resources and Evaluation*, 43(3):209–226.

Massimiliano Ciaramita and Yasemin Altun. 2006. Broad-coverage sense disambiguation and information extraction with a supersense sequence tagger. In *EMNLP*.

Michael Collins and Nigel Duffy. 2002. New Ranking Algorithms for Parsing and Tagging: Kernels over Discrete Structures, and the Voted Perceptron. In *ACL*.

Danilo Croce, Paolo Annesi, Valerio Storch, and Roberto Basili. Unitor: Combining semantic text similarity functions through sv regression. In *SemEval 2012*.

Andrew S. Fast and David Jensen. 2008. Why stacked models perform effective collective classification. In *ICDM*.

Evgeniy Gabrilovich and Shaul Markovitch. 2007. Computing semantic relatedness using wikipedia-based explicit semantic analysis. In *IJCAI*.

A. Moschitti. 2006. Efficient convolution kernels for dependency and constituent syntactic trees. In *ECML*.

Aliaksei Severyn and Alessandro Moschitti. 2012. Structural relationships for large-scale learning of answer re-ranking. In *SIGIR*.

Joseph Turian, Lev Ratinov, and Yoshua Bengio. 2010. Word representations: a simple and general method for semi-supervised learning. In *ACL*.

Peter D. Turney and Patrick Pantel. 2010. From frequency to meaning: vector space models of semantics. *J. Artif. Int. Res.*, 37(1):141–188.

Frane Šarić, Goran Glavaš, Mladen Karan, Jan Šnajder, and Bojana Dalbelo Bašić. 2012. Takelab: Systems for measuring semantic text similarity. In *Proceedings of the Sixth International Workshop on Semantic Evaluation (SemEval 2012)*.

UNITOR-CORE_TYPED: Combining Text Similarity and Semantic Filters through SV Regression

Danilo Croce, Valerio Storch and Roberto Basili
Department of Enterprise Engineering
University of Roma, Tor Vergata
00133 Roma, Italy
{croce,storch,basili}@info.uniroma2.it

Abstract

This paper presents the UNITOR system that participated in the *SEM 2013 shared task on Semantic Textual Similarity (STS). The task is modeled as a Support Vector (SV) regression problem, where a similarity scoring function between text pairs is acquired from examples. The proposed approach has been implemented in a system that aims at providing high applicability and robustness, in order to reduce the risk of over-fitting over a specific datasets. Moreover, the approach does not require any manually coded resource (e.g. WordNet), but mainly exploits distributional analysis of unlabeled corpora. A good level of accuracy is achieved over the shared task: in the Typed STS task the proposed system ranks in 1st and 2nd position.

1 Introduction

Semantic Textual Similarity (STS) measures the degree of semantic equivalence between two phrases or texts. An effective method to compute similarity between sentences or semi-structured material has many applications in Natural Language Processing (Mihalcea et al., 2006) and related areas such as Information Retrieval, improving the effectiveness of semantic search engines (Sahami and Heilman, 2006), or databases, using text similarity in schema matching to solve semantic heterogeneity (Islam and Inkpen, 2008).

This paper describes the UNITOR system participating in both tasks of the *SEM 2013 shared task on Semantic Textual Similarity (STS), described in (Agirre et al., 2013):

- the **Core STS tasks**: given two sentences, s_1 and s_2, participants are asked to provide a score reflecting the corresponding text similarity. It is the same task proposed in (Agirre et al., 2012).
- the **Typed-similarity STS task**: given two semi-structured records t_1 and t_2, containing several typed fields with textual values, participants are asked to provide multiple similarity scores: the types of similarity to be studied include *location*, *author*, *people involved*, *time*, *events or actions*, *subject* and *description*.

In line with several participants of the STS 2012 challenge, such as (Banea et al., 2012; Croce et al., 2012a; Šarić et al., 2012), STS is here modeled as a Support Vector (SV) regression problem, where a SV regressor learns the similarity function over text pairs. The semantic relatedness between two sentences is first modeled in an unsupervised fashion by several similarity functions, each describing the analogy between the two texts according to a specific semantic perspective. We aim at capturing separately syntactic and lexical equivalences between sentences and exploiting either topical relatedness or paradigmatic similarity between individual words. Such information is then combined in a supervised schema through a scoring function $y = f(\vec{x})$ over individual measures from labeled data through SV regression: y is the gold similarity score (provided by human annotators), while $\vec{x}$ is the vector of the different individual scores, provided by the chosen similarity functions.

For the Typed STS task, given the specificity of the involved information and the heterogeneity of target scores, individual measures are not applied to entire texts. Specific phrases are filtered according to linguistic policies, e.g. words characterized by specific Part-of-Speech (POS), such as nouns and verbs, or Named Entity (NE) Category, i.e. men-

*Second Joint Conference on Lexical and Computational Semantics (*SEM), Volume 1: Proceedings of the Main Conference and the Shared Task*, pages 59–65, Atlanta, Georgia, June 13-14, 2013. ©2013 Association for Computational Linguistics

tions to specific name classes, such as of a PERSON, LOCATION or DATE. The former allows to focus the similarity functions over entities (nouns) or actions (verbs), while the latter allows to focus on some aspects connected with the targeted similarity functions, such as *person_involved*, *location* or *time*.

The proposed approach has been implemented in a system that aims at providing high applicability and robustness. This objective is pursued by adopting four similarity measures designed to avoid the risk of over-fitting over each specific dataset. Moreover, the approach does not require any manually coded resource (e.g. WordNet), but mainly exploits distributional analysis of unlabeled corpora. Despite of its simplicity, a good level of accuracy is achieved over the 2013 STS challenge: in the Typed STS task the proposed system ranks 1st and 2nd position (out of 18); in the Core STS task, it ranks around the 37th position (out of 90) and a simple refinement to our model makes it 19th.

In the rest of the paper, in Section 2, the employed similarity functions are described and the application of SV regression is presented. Finally, Section 3 discusses results on the *SEM 2013 shared task.

2 Similarity functions, regression and linguistic filtering

This section describes the approach behind the UNITOR system. The basic similarity functions and their combination via SV regressor are discussed in Section 2.1, while the linguistic filters are presented in Section 2.2.

2.1 STS functions

Each STS function depends on a variety of linguistic aspects in data, e.g. syntactic or lexical information. While their supervised combination can be derived through SV regression, different unsupervised estimators of STS exist.

Lexical Overlap. A basic similarity function is modeled as the *Lexical Overlap* (**LO**) between sentences. Given the sets W_a and W_b of words occurring in two generic texts t_a and t_b, LO is estimated as the *Jaccard Similarity* between the sets, i.e. LO=$\frac{|W_a \cap W_b|}{|W_a \cup W_b|}$. In order to reduce data sparseness, lemmatization is applied and each word is enriched with its POS to avoid the confusion between words from different grammatical classes.

Compositional Distributional Semantics. Other similarity functions are obtained by accounting for the syntactic composition of the lexical information involved in the sentences. Basic lexical information is obtained by a co-occurrence Word Space that is built according to (Sahlgren, 2006; Croce and Previtali, 2010). Every word appearing in a sentence is then projected in such space. A sentence can be thus represented neglecting its syntactic structure, by applying an *additive linear combination*, i.e. the so-called **SUM** operator. The similarity function between two sentences is then the cosine similarity between their corresponding vectors.

A second function is obtained by applying a *Distributional Compositional Semantics* operator, in line with the approaches introduced in (Mitchell and Lapata, 2010), and it is adopted to account for semantic composition. In particular, the approach described in (Croce et al., 2012c) has been applied. It is based on space projection operations over basic geometric lexical representations: syntactic bi-grams are projected in the so called *Support Subspace* (Annesi et al., 2012), aimed at emphasizing the semantic features shared by the compound words. The aim is to model semantics of syntactic bi-grams as projections in lexically-driven subspaces. In order to extend this approach to handle entire sentences, we need to convert them in syntactic representations compatible with the compositional operators proposed. A dependency grammar based formalism captures binary syntactic relations between the words, expressed as nodes in a dependency graph. Given a sentence, the parse structure is acquired and different triples (w_1, w_2, r) are generated, where w_1 is the relation governor, w_2 is the dependent and r is the grammatical type. In (Croce et al., 2012c) a simple approach is defined, and it is inspired by the notion of Soft Cardinality, (Jimenez et al., 2012). Given a triple set $T = \{t_1, \ldots, t_n\}$ extracted from a sentence S and a similarity $sim(t_i, t_j)$, the Soft Cardinality is estimated as $|S|'_{sim} \approx \sum_{t_i}^{|T|}(\sum_{t_j}^{|T|} sim(t_i, t_j)^p)^{-1}$, where parameter p controls the "softness" of the cardinality: with $p = 1$ element similarities are unchanged while higher value will tend to the Classical Cardinality measure. Notice that differently from the previous usage of the Soft Cardinality notion, we did not apply it to sets of individual words, but to the sets of dependencies (i.e. triples) derived from the two sentences. The sim function here can be thus replaced by any compositional operator among the ones discussed in (Annesi et al., 2012). Given two sentences, higher Soft Cardinality values mean that the elements in both sentences (i.e. triples) are different, while the lower values mean that common triples are identical or very similar, suggesting that sentences contain the same kind of information. Given the sets of triples A and B extracted from the two candidate sentences, our approach estimates a syntactically restricted soft cardinality operator, the *Syntactic Soft Cardinality* (**SSC**) as $SSC(A, B) = \frac{2|A \cap B|'}{|A|' + |B|'}$, as a "soft approximation" of Dice's coefficient calculated on both sets[1].

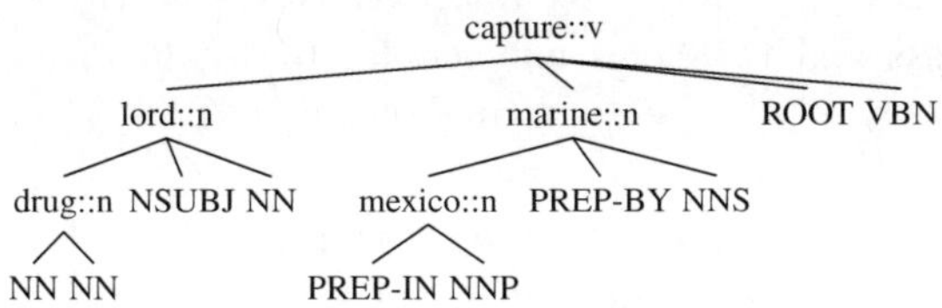

Figure 1: Lexical Centered Tree (LCT)

Convolution kernel-based similarity. The similarity function is here the *Smoothed Partial Tree Kernel* (**SPTK**) proposed in (Croce et al., 2011). SPTK is a generalized formulation of a Convolution Kernel function (Haussler, 1999), i.e. the Tree Kernel (TK), by extending the similarity between tree structures with a function of node similarity. The main characteristic of SPTK is its ability to measure the similarity between syntactic tree structures, which are partially similar and whose nodes can differ but are semantically related. One of the most important outcomes is that SPTK allows "embedding" external lexical information in the kernel function only through a similarity function among lexical nodes, namely words. Moreover, SPTK only requires this similarity to be a valid kernel itself. This means that such lexical information can be derived from lexical resources or it can be automatically acquired by a Word Space. The SPTK is applied to a specific tree representation that allowed to achieve state-of-the-art results on several complex semantic tasks, such as Question Classification (Croce et al., 2011) or Verb Classification (Croce et al., 2012b): each sentence is represented through the Lexical Centered Tree (LCT), as shown in Figure 1 for the sentence "*Drug lord captured by Marines in Mexico*". It is derived from the dependency parse tree: nodes reflect lexemes and edges encode their syntactic dependencies; then, we add to each lexical node two leftmost children, encoding the grammatical function and the POS-Tag respectively.

[1]Notice that, since the intersection $|A \cap B|'$ tends to be too strict, we approximate it from the union cardinality estimation $|A|' + |B|' - |A \cup B|'$.

Combining STSs with SV Regression The similarity functions described above provide scores capturing different linguistic aspects and an effective way to combine such information is made available by Support Vector (SV) regression, described in (Smola and Schölkopf, 2004). The idea is to learn a higher level model by weighting scores according to specific needs implicit in training data. Given similarity scores $\vec{x}_i$ for the i-th sentence pair, the regressor learns a function $y_i = f(\vec{x}_i)$, where y_i is the score provided by human annotators. Moreover, since the combination of kernel is still a kernel, we can apply polynomial and RBF kernels (Shawe-Taylor and Cristianini, 2004) to the regressor.

2.2 Semantic constraints for the Typed STS

Typed STS insists on records, i.e. sequence of typed textual fields, rather than on individual sentences. Our aim is to model the typed task with the same spirit as the core one, through a combination of different linguistic evidences, which are modeled through independent kernels. The overall similarity model described in 2.1 has been thus applied also to the typed task according to two main model changes:

- **Semantic Modeling**. Although SV regression is still applied to model one similarity type, each type depends on a subset of the multiple evidences originating from individual fields: one similarity type acts as a filter on the set of fields, on which kernels will be then applied.
- **Learning Constraints**. The selected *fields* provide different evidences to the regression steps. Correspondingly, each similarity type corresponds to specific kernels and features for its fields. These constraints are applied by selecting features and kernels for each field.

	dcTitle	dcSubject	dcDescription	dcCreator	dcDate	dcSource
author	-	-	PER	$*$	-	-
people_inv.	PER	PER	PER	-	-	-
time	DATE	DATE	DATE	-	$*$	-
location	LOC	LOC	LOC	-	-	-
event	$N, V, N \cup V$	$N, V, N \cup V$	$N, V, N \cup V$	-	-	-
subject	$N, V, J, N \cup J \cup V$	$N, V, J, N \cup J \cup V$	-	-	-	-
description	-	-	$N, V, J, N \cup J \cup V$	-	-	-
general	$+$	$+$	$+$	$*$	$*$	$*$

Table 1: Filtering Schema adopted for the Typed STS task.

Notice how some kernels loose significance in the typed STS task. Syntactic information is no useful so that no tree kernel and compositional kernel is applied here. Most of the fields are non-sentential[2]. Moreover, not all morpho-syntactic information are extracted as feature from some fields. Filters usually specify some syntactic categories or Named Entities (NEs): they are textual mentions to specific real-world categories, such as of PERSONS (PER), LOCATIONS (LOC) or DATES. They are detected in a field and made available as feature to the corresponding kernel: this introduces a bias on typed measures and emphasizes specific semantic aspects (e.g. places LOC or persons PER, in *location* or *author* measures, respectively). For example, in the sentence "*The chemist R.S. Hudson began manufacturing soap in the back of his small shop in West Bomich in 1837*", when POS tag filters are applied, only verbs (*V*), nouns (*N*) or adjectives (*J*) can be selected as features. This allows to focus on specific actions, e.g. the verb "*manufacture*", entities, e.g. nouns "*soap*" and "*shop*", or some properties, e.g. the adjective "*small*". When Named Entity categories are used, a mention to a person like "*R.S. Hudson*" or to a location, e.g. "*West Bomich*', or date, e.g. "*1837*", can be useful to model the the *person_involved*, the *location* or *time* similarity measures, respectively.

The Semantic Modeling and the Learning Constraints system adopted to model the Typed STS task are defined in Table 1. There rows are the different target similarities, while columns indicate document fields, such as `dcTitle`, `dcSubject`, `dcDescription`, `dcCreator`, `dcDate` and `dcSource`, as described in the *SEM 2013 shared task description. Each entry in the Table represents the feature set for that fields, i.e. POS tags (i.e. V, N, J) or Named Entity classes. The "$*$" symbol corresponds to all features, i.e. no restriction is applied to any POS tag or NE class. Finally, the *general* similarity function makes use of every NE class and POS tags adopted for that field in any measure, as expressed by the special notation $+$, i.e. "*all of the above features*".

Every feature set denoted in the Table 1 supports the application of a lexical kernel, such as the LO described in Section 2.1. When different POS tags are requested (such as N and V) multiple feature sets and kernels are made available. The "-" symbol means that the source field is fully neglected from the SV regression. As an example, the SV regressor for the *location* similarity has been acquired considering the fields `dcTitle`, `dcSubject`, `dcDescription`. Only features used for the kernel correspond to LOCATIONs (LOC). For each of the three feature, the LO and SUM similarity function has been applied, giving rise to an input 6-dimensional feature space for the regressor. Differently, in the *subject* similarity, nouns, adjectives and verbs are the only features adopted from the fields `dcSubject`, `dcTitle`, so that 8 feature sets are used to model these fields, giving rise to a 16-dimensional feature space.

3 Results and discussion

This section describes results obtained in the *SEM 2013 shared task. The experimental setup of different similarity functions is described in Section 3.1. Results obtained over the Core STS task and Typed STS task are described in Section 3.2 and 3.3.

[2]The `dcDescription` is also made of multiple sentences and it reduces the applicability of SPTK and SSC: parse trees have no clear alignment.

3.1 Experimental setup

In all experiments, sentences are processed with the Stanford CoreNLP[3] system, for Part-of-Speech tagging, lemmatization, named entity recognition[4] and dependency parsing.

In order to estimate the basic lexical similarity function employed in the SUM, SSC and SPTK operators, a co-occurrence Word Space is acquired through the distributional analysis of the UkWaC corpus (Baroni et al., 2009), a Web document collection made of about 2 billion tokens. The same setting of (Croce et al., 2012a) has been adopted for the space acquisition. The same setup described in (Croce et al., 2012c) is applied to estimate the SSC function. The similarity between pairs of syntactically restricted word compound is evaluated through a *Symmetric model*: it selects the best 200 dimensions of the space, selected by maximizing the component-wise product of each compound as in (Annesi et al., 2012), and combines the similarity scores measured in each couple subspace with the product function. The similarity score in each subspace is obtained by summing the cosine similarity of the corresponding projected words. The "soft cardinality" is estimated with the parameter $p = 2$.

The estimation of the semantically Smoothed Partial Tree Kernel (SPTK) is made available by an extended version of SVM-LightTK software[5] (Moschitti, 2006) implementing the smooth matching between tree nodes. Similarity between lexical nodes is estimated as the cosine similarity in the co-occurrence Word Space described above, as in (Croce et al., 2011). Finally, SVM-LightTK is employed for the SV regression learning to combine specific similarity functions.

3.2 Results over the Core STS

In the Core STS task, the resulting text similarity score is measured by the regressor: each sentence pair from all datasets is modeled according to a 13 dimensional feature space derived from the different functions introduced in Section 2.1, as follows.

The first 5 dimensions are derived by applying

	Run_1	Run_2	Run_3	Run_1^*
headlines	.635 (50)	**.651 (39)**	.603 (58)	.671 (30)
OnWN	**.574 (33)**	.561 (36)	.549 (40)	.637 (25)
FNWN	.352 (35)	**.358 (32)**	.327 (44)	.459 (7)
SMT	**.328 (39)**	.310 (49)	.319 (44)	.348 (21)
Mean	**.494 (37)**	.490 (42)	.472 (52)	.537 (19)

Table 2: Results over the Core STS task

the LO operator over lemmatized words in the noun, verb, adjective and adverb POS categories: 4 kernels look at individual categories, while a fifth kernel insists on the union of all POS. A second set of 5 dimensions is derived by the same application of the SUM operator to the same syntactic selection of features. The SPTK is then applied to estimate the similarity between the LCT structures derived from the dependency parse trees of sentences. Then, the SPTK is applied to derive an additional score without considering any specific similarity function between lexical nodes; in this setting, the SPTK can be considered as a traditional Partial Tree Kernel (Moschitti, 2006), in order to capture a more strict syntactical similarity between texts. The last score is generated by applying the SSC operator.

We participated in the *SEM challenge with three different runs. The main difference between each run is the dataset employed in the training phase and the employed kernel within the regressor. Without any specific information about the test datasets, a strategy to prevent the regressor to over-fit training material has been applied. We decided to use a training dataset that achieved the best results over datasets radically different from the training material in the STS challenge of Semeval 2012. In particular, for the FNWN and OnWN datasets, we arbitrarily selected the training material achieving best results over the 2012 surprise.OnWN; for the headlines and SMT datasets we maximized performance training over surprise.SMTnews. In $\mathbf{Run_1}$ the SVM regressor is trained using dataset combinations providing best results according to the above criteria: MSRpar, MSRvid, SMTeuroparl and surprise.OnWN are employed against FNWN and OnWN; MSRpar, SMTeuroparl and surprise.SMTnews are employed against headline and SMT. A linear kernel is applied when training the regressor. In $\mathbf{Run_2}$, differently from the previous one, the SVM regressor is

[3] http://nlp.stanford.edu/software/corenlp.shtml

[4] The TIME and DURATION classes are collapsed with DATE, while the PERSON and LOCATION classes are considered without any modification.

[5] http://disi.unitn.it/moschitti/Tree-Kernel.htm

	rank	general	author	people_inv.	time	location	event	subject	description	mean
Run_1	1	**.7981**	**.8158**	**.6922**	**.7471**	**.7723**	**.6835**	**.7875**	**.7996**	**.7620**
Run_2	2	.7564	.8076	.6758	.7090	.7351	.6623	.7520	.7745	.7341

Table 3: Results over the Typed STS task

trained using all examples from the training datasets. A linear kernel is applied when training the regressor. Finally, in $\mathbf{Run_3}$ the same training dataset selection schema of Run_1 is applied and a gaussian kernel is employed in the regressor.

Table 2 reports the general outcome for the UNITOR systems in term of Pearson Correlation. The best system, based on the linear kernel, ranks around the 35th position (out of 90 systems), that reflects the mean rank of all the systems in the ranking of the different datasets. The gaussian kernel, employed for the Run_3 does not provide any contribution, as it ranks 50th. We think that the main reason of these results is due to the intrinsic differences between training and testing datasets that have been heuristically coupled. This is first motivated by lower rank achieved by Run_2. Moreover, it is in line with the experimental findings of (Croce et al., 2012a), where a performance drop is shown when the regressor is trained over data that is not constrained over the corresponding source. In $\mathbf{Run_1^*}$ we thus optimized the system by manually selecting the training material that does provides best performance on the test dataset: MSRvid, SMTeuroparl and surprise.OnWN are employed against OnWN; surprise.OnWN against FNWN, SMTeuroparl against headlines; SMTeuroparl and surprise.SMTnews against SMT. A linear kernel within the regressor allow to reach the 19th position, even reducing the complexity of the representation to a five dimensional feature space: LO and SUM without any specific filter, SPTK, PTK and SSC.

3.3 Results over the Typed STS

SV regression has been also applied to the Typed STS task through seven type-specific regressors plus a *general* one. Each SV regressor insists on the LO and SUM kernel as applied to the features in Table 1. Notice that it was mainly due to the lack of rich syntactic structures in almost all fields.

As described in Section 2.2, a specific modeling strategy has been applied to derive the feature space of each target similarity. For example, the regressor associated with the *event* similarity score is fed with 18 scores. Each of the 3 fields, , i.e. `dcTitle`, `dcSubject` and `dcDescription`, provides the 2 kernels (LO and SUM) with 3 feature sets (i.e. N, V and $N \cup V$). In particular, the *general* similarity function considers all extracted features for each field, giving rise to a space of 51 dimensions. We participated in the task with two different runs, whose main difference is the adopted kernel within the SV regressor. In $\mathbf{Run_1}$, a *linear kernel* is used, while in $\mathbf{Run_2}$ a *RBF kernel* is applied.

Table 3 reports the general outcome for the UNITOR system. The adopted semantic modeling, as well as the selection of the proper information, e.g. the proper named entity, allows the system to rank in the 1st and 2nd positions (out of 18 systems). The proposed selection schema in Table 1 is very effective, as confirmed by the results for almost all typed similarity scores. Again, the RBF kernel does not improve result over the linear kernel. The impact of the proposed approach can be noticed for very specific scores, such as *time* and *location*, especially for text pairs where structured information is absent, such as in the `dcDate` field. Moreover, the regressor is not affected by the differences between training and test dataset as for the previous Core STS task. A deep result analysis showed that some similarity scores are not correctly estimated within pairs showing partial similarities. For example, the *events or actions* typed similarity is overestimated for the texts pairs "*The Octagon and Pavilions, Pavilion Garden, Buxton, c 1875*" and "*The Beatles, The Octagon, Pavillion Gardens, St John's Road, Buxton, 1963*" because they mention the same location (i.e. "*Pavillion Gardens*").

Acknowledgements This work has been partially supported by the Regione Lazio under the project PROGRESS-IT (FILAS-CR-2011-1089) and the Italian Ministry of Industry within the "Industria 2015" Framework, project DIVINO (MI01_00234).

References

Eneko Agirre, Daniel Cer, Mona Diab, and Aitor Gonzalez-Agirre. 2012. Semeval-2012 task 6: A pilot on semantic textual similarity. In **SEM 2012*, pages 385–393, Montréal, Canada, 7-8 June.

Eneko Agirre, Daniel Cer, Mona Diab, Aitor Gonzalez-Agirre, and Weiwei Guo. 2013. *sem 2013 shared task: Semantic textual similarity, including a pilot on typed-similarity. In **SEM 2013: The Second Joint Conference on Lexical and Computational Semantics*. Association for Computational Linguistics.

Paolo Annesi, Valerio Storch, and Roberto Basili. 2012. Space projections as distributional models for semantic composition. In *CICLing (1)*, Lecture Notes in Computer Science, pages 323–335. Springer.

Carmen Banea, Samer Hassan, Michael Mohler, and Rada Mihalcea. 2012. Unt: A supervised synergistic approach to semantic text similarity. In **SEM 2012*, pages 635–642, Montréal, Canada, 7-8 June. Association for Computational Linguistics.

Marco Baroni, Silvia Bernardini, Adriano Ferraresi, and Eros Zanchetta. 2009. The wacky wide web: a collection of very large linguistically processed web-crawled corpora. *Language Resources and Evaluation*, 43(3):209–226.

Danilo Croce and Daniele Previtali. 2010. Manifold learning for the semi-supervised induction of framenet predicates: An empirical investigation. In *Proceedings of the GEMS 2010 Workshop*, pages 7–16, Uppsala, Sweden.

Danilo Croce, Alessandro Moschitti, and Roberto Basili. 2011. Structured lexical similarity via convolution kernels on dependency trees. In *Proceedings of EMNLP*, Edinburgh, Scotland, UK.

Danilo Croce, Paolo Annesi, Valerio Storch, and Roberto Basili. 2012a. Unitor: Combining semantic text similarity functions through sv regression. In **SEM 2012*, pages 597–602, Montréal, Canada, 7-8 June.

Danilo Croce, Alessandro Moschitti, Roberto Basili, and Martha Palmer. 2012b. Verb classification using distributional similarity in syntactic and semantic structures. In *Proceedings of the 50th Annual Meeting of the Association for Computational Linguistics (Volume 1: Long Papers)*, pages 263–272, Jeju Island, Korea, July.

Danilo Croce, Valerio Storch, Paolo Annesi, and Roberto Basili. 2012c. Distributional compositional semantics and text similarity. *2012 IEEE Sixth International Conference on Semantic Computing*, 0:242–249.

David Haussler. 1999. Convolution kernels on discrete structures. Technical report, University of Santa Cruz.

Aminul Islam and Diana Inkpen. 2008. Semantic text similarity using corpus-based word similarity and string similarity. *ACM Trans. Knowl. Discov. Data*, 2:10:1–10:25, July.

Sergio Jimenez, Claudia Becerra, and Alexander Gelbukh. 2012. Soft cardinality: A parameterized similarity function for text comparison. In **SEM 2012*, pages 449–453, Montréal, Canada, 7-8 June. Association for Computational Linguistics.

Rada Mihalcea, Courtney Corley, and Carlo Strapparava. 2006. Corpus-based and knowledge-based measures of text semantic similarity. In *In AAAI06*.

Jeff Mitchell and Mirella Lapata. 2010. Composition in distributional models of semantics. *Cognitive Science*, 34(8):1388–1429.

Alessandro Moschitti. 2006. Efficient convolution kernels for dependency and constituent syntactic trees. In *ECML*, pages 318–329, Berlin, Germany, September. Machine Learning: ECML 2006, 17th European Conference on Machine Learning, Proceedings.

Mehran Sahami and Timothy D. Heilman. 2006. A web-based kernel function for measuring the similarity of short text snippets. In *Proceedings of the 15th international conference on World Wide Web*, WWW '06, pages 377–386, New York, NY, USA. ACM.

Magnus Sahlgren. 2006. *The Word-Space Model*. Ph.D. thesis, Stockholm University.

John Shawe-Taylor and Nello Cristianini. 2004. *Kernel Methods for Pattern Analysis*. Cambridge University Press, New York, NY, USA.

Alex J. Smola and Bernhard Schölkopf. 2004. A tutorial on support vector regression. *Statistics and Computing*, 14(3):199–222, August.

Frane Šarić, Goran Glavaš, Mladen Karan, Jan Šnajder, and Bojana Dalbelo Bašić. 2012. Takelab: Systems for measuring semantic text similarity. In **SEM 2012*, pages 441–448, Montréal, Canada, 7-8 June.

NTNU-CORE: Combining strong features for semantic similarity

Erwin Marsi, Hans Moen, Lars Bungum, Gleb Sizov, Björn Gambäck, André Lynum
Norwegian University of Science and Technology
Department of Computer and Information and Science
Sem Sælands vei 7-9
NO-7491 Trondheim, Norway
{emarsi,hansmoe,bungum,sizov,gamback,andrely}@idi.ntnu.no

Abstract

The paper outlines the work carried out at NTNU as part of the *SEM'13 shared task on Semantic Textual Similarity, using an approach which combines shallow textual, distributional and knowledge-based features by a support vector regression model. Feature sets include (1) aggregated similarity based on named entity recognition with WordNet and Levenshtein distance through the calculation of maximum weighted bipartite graphs; (2) higher order word co-occurrence similarity using a novel method called "Multi-sense Random Indexing"; (3) deeper semantic relations based on the RelEx semantic dependency relationship extraction system; (4) graph edit-distance on dependency trees; (5) reused features of the TakeLab and DKPro systems from the STS'12 shared task. The NTNU systems obtained 9th place overall (5th best team) and 1st place on the SMT data set.

1 Introduction

Intuitively, two texts are semantically similar if they roughly mean the same thing. The task of formally establishing semantic textual similarity clearly is more complex. For a start, it implies that we have a way to formally represent the intended meaning of all texts in all possible contexts, and furthermore a way to measure the degree of equivalence between two such representations. This goes far beyond the state-of-the-art for arbitrary sentence pairs, and several restrictions must be imposed. The Semantic Textual Similarity (STS) task (Agirre et al., 2012, 2013) limits the comparison to isolated sentences only (rather than complete texts), and defines similarity of a pair of sentences as the one assigned by human judges on a 0–5 scale (with 0 implying no relation and 5 complete semantic equivalence). It is unclear, however, to what extent two judges would agree on the level of similarity between sentences; Agirre et al. (2012) report figures on the agreement between the authors themselves of about 87–89%.

As in most language processing tasks, there are two overall ways to measure sentence similarity, either by data-driven (distributional) methods or by knowledge-driven methods; in the STS'12 task the two approaches were used nearly equally much. Distributional models normally measure similarity in terms of word or word co-occurrence statistics, or through concept relations extracted from a corpus. The basic strategy taken by NTNU in the STS'13 task was to use something of a "feature carpet bombing approach" in the way of first automatically extracting as many potentially useful features as possible, using both knowledge and data-driven methods, and then evaluating feature combinations on the data sets provided by the organisers of the shared task.

To this end, four different types of features were extracted. The first (Section 2) aggregates similarity based on named entity recognition with WordNet and Levenshtein distance by calculating maximum weighted bipartite graphs. The second set of features (Section 3) models higher order co-occurrence similarity relations using Random Indexing (Kanerva et al., 2000), both in the form of a (standard) sliding window approach and through a novel method called "Multi-sense Random Indexing" which aims to separate the representation of different senses of a term

*Second Joint Conference on Lexical and Computational Semantics (*SEM), Volume 1: Proceedings of the Main Conference and the Shared Task*, pages 66–73, Atlanta, Georgia, June 13-14, 2013.

from each other. The third feature set (Section 4) aims to capture deeper semantic relations using either the output of the RelEx semantic dependency relationship extraction system (Fundel et al., 2007) or an in-house graph edit-distance matching system. The final set (Section 5) is a straight-forward gathering of features from the systems that fared best in STS'12: TakeLab from University of Zagreb (Šarić et al., 2012) and DKPro from Darmstadt's Ubiquitous Knowledge Processing Lab (Bär et al., 2012).

As described in Section 6, Support Vector Regression (Vapnik et al., 1997) was used for solving the multi-dimensional regression problem of combining all the extracted feature values. Three different systems were created based on feature performance on the supplied development data. Section 7 discusses scores on the STS'12 and STS'13 test data.

2 Compositional Word Matching

Compositional word matching similarity is based on a one-to-one alignment of words from the two sentences. The alignment is obtained by maximal weighted bipartite matching using several word similarity measures. In addition, we utilise named entity recognition and matching tools. In general, the approach is similar to the one described by Karnick et al. (2012), with a different set of tools used. Our implementation relies on the ANNIE components in GATE (Cunningham et al., 2002) and will thus be referred to as `GateWordMatch`.

The processing pipeline for `GateWordMatch` is: (1) tokenization by ANNIE English Tokeniser, (2) part-of-speech tagging by ANNIE POS Tagger, (3) lemmatization by GATE Morphological Analyser, (4) stopword removal, (5) named entity recognition based on lists by ANNIE Gazetteer, (6) named entity recognition based on the JAPE grammar by the ANNIE NE Transducer, (7) matching of named entities by ANNIE Ortho Matcher, (8) computing WordNet and Levenstein similarity between words, (9) calculation of a maximum weighted bipartite graph matching based on similarities from 7 and 8.

Steps 1–4 are standard preprocessing routines. In step 5, named entities are recognised based on lists that contain locations, organisations, companies, newspapers, and person names, as well as date, time and currency units. In step 6, JAPE grammar rules are applied to recognise entities such as addresses, emails, dates, job titles, and person names based on basic syntactic and morphological features. Matching of named entities in step 7 is based on matching rules that check the type of named entity, and lists with aliases to identify entities as "US", "United State", and "USA" as the same entity.

In step 8, similarity is computed for each pair of words from the two sentences. Words that are matched as entities in step 7 get a similarity value of 1.0. For the rest of the entities and non-entity words we use *LCH* (Leacock and Chodorow, 1998) similarity, which is based on a shortest path between the corresponding senses in WordNet. Since word sense disambiguation is not used, we take the similarity between the nearest senses of two words. For cases when the WordNet-based similarity cannot be obtained, a similarity based on the Levenshtein distance (Levenshtein, 1966) is used instead. It is normalised by the length of the longest word in the pair. For the STS'13 test data set, named entity matching contributed to 4% of all matched word pairs; LCH similarity to 61%, and Levenshtein distance to 35%.

In step 9, maximum weighted bipartite matching is computed using the Hungarian Algorithm (Kuhn, 1955). Nodes in the bipartite graph represent words from the sentences, and edges have weights that correspond to similarities between tokens obtained in step 8. Weighted bipartite matching finds the one-to-one alignment that maximizes the sum of similarities between aligned tokens. Total similarity normalised by the number of words in both sentences is used as the final sentence similarity measure.

3 Distributional Similarity

Our distributional similarity features use Random Indexing (RI; Kanerva et al., 2000; Sahlgren, 2005), also employed in STS'12 by Tovar et al. (2012); Sokolov (2012); Semeraro et al. (2012). It is an efficient method for modelling higher order co-occurrence similarities among terms, comparable to Latent Semantic Analysis (LSA; Deerwester et al., 1990). It incrementally builds a term co-occurrence matrix of reduced dimensionality through the use of a sliding window and fixed size *index vectors* used for training *context vectors*, one per unique term.

A novel variant, which we have called "Multi-sense Random Indexing" (MSRI), inspired by Reisinger and Mooney (2010), attempts to capture one or more "*senses*" per unique term in an unsupervised manner, each sense represented as an individual vector in the model. The method is similar to classical sliding window RI, but each term can have multiple context vectors (referred to as "*sense vectors*" here) which are updated individually. When updating a term vector, instead of directly adding the index vectors of the neighbouring terms in the window to its context vector, the system first computes a separate *window vector* consisting of the sum of the index vectors. Then cosine similarity is calculated between the window vector and each of the term's sense vectors. Each similarity score is in turn compared to a set *similarity threshold*: if no score exceeds the threshold, the sentence vector is added as a new separate sense vector for the term; if exactly one score is above the threshold, the window vector is added to that sense vector; and if multiple scores are above the threshold, all the involved senses are merged into one sense vector, together with the window vector. This accomplishes an incremental clustering of senses in an unsupervised manner while retaining the efficiency of classical RI.

As data for training the models we used the CLEF 2004–2008 English corpus (approx. 130M words). Our implementation of RI and MSRI is based on JavaSDM (Hassel, 2004). For classical RI, we used stopword removal (using a customised versions of the English stoplist from the Lucene project), window size of 4+4, dimensionality set to 1800, 4 non-zeros, and unweighted index vector in the sliding window. For MSRI, we used a similarity threshold of 0.2, a vector dimensionality of 800, a non-zero count of 4, and window size of 5+5. The index vectors in the sliding window were shifted to create *direction vectors* (Sahlgren et al., 2008), and weighted by distance to the target term. Rare senses with a frequency below 10 were excluded. Other sliding-window schemes, including unweighted non-shifted vectors and *Random Permutation* (Sahlgren et al., 2008), were tested, but none outperformed the sliding-window schemes used.

Similarity between sentence pairs was calculated as the normalised maximal bipartite similarity between term pairs in each sentence, resulting in the following features: (1) `MSRI-Centroid`: each term is represented as the sum of its sense vectors; (2) `MSRI-MaxSense`: for each term pair, the sense-pair with max similarity is used; (3) `MSRI-Context`: for each term, its neighbouring terms within a window of 2+2 is used as context for picking a single, max similar, sense from the target term to be used as its representation; (4) `MSRI-HASenses`: similarity between two terms is computed by applying the Hungarian Algorithm to all their possible sense pair mappings; (5) `RI-Avg`: classical RI, each term is represented as a single context vector; (6) `RI-Hungarian`: similarity between two sentences is calculated using the Hungarian Algorithm. Alternatively, sentence level similarity was computed as the cosine similarity between sentence vectors composed of their terms' vectors. The corresponding features are (1) `RI-SentVectors-Norm`: sentence vectors are created by summing their constituent terms (i.e., context vectors), which have first been normalized; (2) `RI-SentVectors-TFIDF`: same as before, but TF*IDF weights are added.

4 Deeper Semantic Relations

Two deep strategies were employed to accompany the shallow-processed feature sets. Two existing systems were used to provide the basis for these features, namely the RelEx system (Fundel et al., 2007) from the OpenCog initiative (Hart and Goertzel, 2008), and an in-house graph-edit distance system developed for plagiarism detection (Røkenes, 2013).

RelEx outputs syntactic trees, dependency graphs, and *semantic frames* as this one for the sentence "*Indian air force to buy 126 Rafale fighter jets*":

```
Commerce_buy:Goods(buy,jet)
Entity:Entity(jet,jet)
Entity:Name(jet,Rafale)
Entity:Name(jet,fighter)
Possibilities:Event(hyp,buy)
Request:Addressee(air,you)
Request:Message(air,air)
Transitive_action:Beneficiary(buy,jet)
```

Three features were extracted from this: first, if there was an exact match of the frame found in s_1 with s_2; second, if there was a partial match until the first argument (`Commerce_buy:Goods(buy)`; and third if there was a match of the frame category

(`Commerce_buy:Goods`).

In STS'12, Singh et al. (2012) matched Universal Networking Language (UNL) graphs against each other by counting matches of relations and universal words, while Bhagwani et al. (2012) calculated WordNet-based word-level similarities and created a weighted bipartite graph (see Section 2). The method employed here instead looked at the graph edit distance between dependency graphs obtained with the Maltparser dependency parser (Nivre et al., 2006). Edit distance is the defined as the minimum of the sum of the costs of the edit operations (insertion, deletion and substitution of nodes) required to transform one graph into the other. It is approximated with a fast but suboptimal algorithm based on bipartite graph matching through the Hungarian algorithm (Riesen and Bunke, 2009).

5 Reused Features

The TakeLab '*simple*' system (Šarić et al., 2012) obtained 3rd place in overall Pearson correlation and 1st for normalized Pearson in STS'12. The source code[1] was used to generate all its features, that is, *n-gram overlap*, *WordNet-augmented word overlap*, *vector space sentence similarity*, *normalized difference*, *shallow NE similarity*, *numbers overlap*, and *stock index* features.[2] This required the full LSA vector space models, which were kindly provided by the TakeLab team. The word counts required for computing Information Content were obtained from Google Books Ngrams.[3]

The DKPro system (Bär et al., 2012) obtained first place in STS'12 with the second run. We used the source code[4] to generate features for the STS'12 and STS'13 data. Of the string-similarity features, we reused the *Longest Common Substring*, *Longest Common Subsequence* (with and without normalization), and *Greedy String Tiling* measures. From the character/word n-grams features, we used *Character n-grams* ($n = 2, 3, 4$), *Word n-grams by Containment w/o Stopwords* ($n = 1, 2$), *Word n-grams by Jaccard* ($n = 1, 3, 4$), and *Word n-grams by Jaccard w/o Stopwords* ($n = 2, 4$). Semantic similarity measures include *WordNet Similarity* based on the Resnik measure (two variants) and *Explicit Semantic Similarity* based on WordNet, Wikipedia or Wiktionary. This means that we reused all features from DKPro run 1 except for *Distributional Thesaurus*.

6 Systems

Our systems follow previous submissions to the STS task (e.g., Šarić et al., 2012; Banea et al., 2012) in that feature values are extracted for each sentence pair and combined with a gold standard score in order to train a Support Vector Regressor on the resulting regression task. A postprocessing step guarantees that all scores are in the $[0, 5]$ range and equal 5 if the two sentences are identical. SVR has been shown to be a powerful technique for predictive data analysis when the primary goal is to approximate a *function*, since the learning algorithm is applicable to continuous classes. Hence support vector *regression* differs from support vector machine *classification* where the goal rather is to take a *binary* decision. The key idea in SVR is to use a cost function for building the model which tries to ignore noise in training data (i.e., data which is too close to the prediction), so that the produced model in essence only depends on a more robust subset of the extracted features.

Three systems were created using the supplied annotated data based on Microsoft Research Paraphrase and Video description corpora (MSRpar and MSvid), statistical machine translation system output (SMTeuroparl and SMTnews), and sense mappings between OntoNotes and WordNet (OnWN). The first system (NTNU1) includes all TakeLab and DKPro features plus the `GateWordMatch` feature with the SVR in its default setting.[5] The training material consisted of all annotated data available, except for the SMT test set, where it was limited to SMTeuroparl and SMTnews. The NTNU2 system is similar to NTNU1, except that the training material for OnWN and FNWN excluded MSRvid and that the SVR parameter C was set to 200. NTNU3 is similar to NTNU1 except that *all* features available are included.

[1] `http://takelab.fer.hr/sts/`

[2] We did not use content n-gram overlap or skip n-grams.

[3] `http://storage.googleapis.com/books/ngrams/books/datasetsv2.html`, version 20120701, with 468,491,999,592 words

[4] `http://code.google.com/p/dkpro-similarity-asl/`

[5] RBF kernel, $\epsilon = 0.1$, $C = \#samples$, $\gamma = \frac{1}{\#features}$

Data	NTNU1	NTNU2	NTNU3
MSRpar	0.7262	0.7507	0.7221
MSRvid	0.8660	0.8882	0.8662
SMTeuroparl	0.5843	0.3386	0.5503
SMTnews	0.5840	0.5592	0.5306
OnWN	0.7503	0.6365	0.7200
mean	0.7022	0.6346	0.6779

Table 1: Correlation score on 2012 test data

Data	NTNU1		NTNU2		NTNU3	
	r	n	r	n	r	n
Head	0.7279	11	0.5909	59	0.7274	12
OnWN	0.5952	31	0.1634	86	0.5882	32
FNWN	0.3215	45	0.3650	27	0.3115	49
SMT	0.4015	2	0.3786	9	**0.4035**	**1**
mean	0.5519	9	0.3946	68	0.5498	12

Table 2: Correlation score and rank on 2013 test data

7 Results

System performance is evaluated using the Pearson product-moment correlation coefficient (r) between the system scores and the human scores. Results on the 2012 test data (i.e., 2013 development data) are listed in Table 1. This basically shows that except for the `GateWordMatch`, adding our other features tends to give slightly lower scores (cf. NTNU1 vs NTNU3). In addition, the table illustrates that optimizing the SVR according to cross-validated grid search on 2012 training data (here $C = 200$), rarely pays off when testing on unseen data (cf. NTNU1 vs NTNU2).

Table 2 shows the official results on the test data. These are generally in agreement with the scores on the development data, although substantially lower. Our systems did particularly well on SMT, holding first and second position, reasonably good on headlines, but not so well on the ontology alignment data, resulting in overall 9th (NTNU1) and 12th (NTNU3) system positions (5th best team). Table 3 lists the correlation score and rank of the ten best individual features per STS'13 test data set, and those among the top-20 overall, resulting from linear regression on a single feature. Features in boldface are genuinely new (i.e., described in Sections 2–4).

Overall the character n-gram features are the most informative, particularly for HeadLine and SMT. The reason may be that these not only capture word overlap (Ahn, 2011), but also inflectional forms and spelling variants.

The (weighted) distributional similarity features based on NYT are important for HeadLine and SMT, which obviously contain sentence pairs from the news genre, whereas the Wikipedia based feature is more important for OnWN and FNWN. WordNet-based measures are highly relevant too, with variants relying on path length outperforming those based on Resnik similarity, except for SMT.

As is to be expected, basic word and lemma unigram overlap prove to be informative, with overall unweighted variants resulting in higher correlation. Somewhat surprisingly, higher order n-gram overlaps ($n > 1$) seem to be less relevant. Longest common subsequence and substring appear to work particularly well for OnWN and FNWN, respectively.

`GateWordMatch` is highly relevant too, in agreement with earlier results on the development data. Although treated as a single feature, it is actually a combination of similarity features where an appropriate feature is selected for each word pair. This "vertical" way of combining features can potentially provide a more fine-grained feature selection, resulting in less noise. Indeed, if two words are matching as named entities or as close synonyms, less precise types of features such as character-based and data-driven similarity should not dominate the overall similarity score.

It is interesting to find that MSRI outperforms both classical RI and ESA (Gabrilovich and Markovitch, 2007) on this task. Still, the more advanced features, such as `MSRI-Context`, gave inferior results compared to `MSRI-Centroid`. This suggests that more research on MSRI is needed to understand how both training and retrieval can be optimised. Also, LSA-based features (see `tl.weight-dist-sim-wiki`) achieve better results than both MSRI, RI and ESA. Then again, larger corpora were used for training the LSA models. RI has been shown to be comparable to LSA (Karlgren and Sahlgren, 2001), and since a relatively small corpus was used for training the RI/MSRI models, there are reasons to believe that better scores can be achieved by both RI- and MSRI-based features by using more training data.

Features	HeadLine *r*	HeadLine n	OnWN *r*	OnWN n	FNWN *r*	FNWN n	SMT *r*	SMT n	Mean *r*	Mean n
CharacterNGramMeasure-3	0.72	2	0.39	2	0.44	3	**0.70**	**1**	**0.56**	**1**
CharacterNGramMeasure-4	0.69	3	0.38	5	0.45	2	0.67	6	0.55	2
CharacterNGramMeasure-2	**0.73**	**1**	0.37	9	0.34	10	0.69	2	0.53	3
tl.weight-dist-sim-wiki	0.58	14	0.39	3	**0.45**	**1**	0.67	5	0.52	4
tl.wn-sim-lem	0.69	4	**0.40**	**1**	0.41	5	0.59	10	0.52	5
GateWordMatch	0.67	8	0.37	11	0.34	11	0.60	9	0.50	6
tl.dist-sim-nyt	0.69	5	0.34	28	0.26	23	0.65	8	0.49	7
tl.n-gram-match-lem-1	0.68	6	0.36	16	0.37	8	0.51	14	0.48	8
tl.weight-dist-sim-nyt	0.57	17	0.37	14	0.29	18	0.66	7	0.47	9
tl.n-gram-match-lc-1	0.68	7	0.37	10	0.32	13	0.50	17	0.47	10
MCS06-Resnik-WordNet	0.49	26	0.36	22	0.28	19	0.68	3	0.45	11
TWSI-Resnik-WordNet	0.49	27	0.36	23	0.28	20	0.68	4	0.45	12
tl.weight-word-match-lem	0.56	18	0.37	16	0.37	7	0.50	16	0.45	13
MSRI-Centroid	0.60	13	0.36	17	0.37	9	0.45	19	0.45	14
tl.weight-word-match-olc	0.56	19	0.38	8	0.32	12	0.51	15	0.44	15
MSRI-MaxSense	0.58	15	0.36	15	0.31	14	0.45	20	0.42	16
GreedyStringTiling-3	0.67	9	0.38	6	0.31	15	0.34	29	0.43	17
ESA-Wikipedia	0.50	25	0.30	38	0.32	14	0.54	12	0.42	18
WordNGramJaccard-1	0.64	10	0.37	12	0.25	25	0.33	30	0.40	19
WordNGramContainment-1-stopword	0.64	25	0.38	7	0.25	24	0.32	31	0.40	20
RI-Hungarian	0.58	16	0.33	31	0.10	34	0.42	22	0.36	24
RI-AvgTermTerm	0.56	20	0.33	32	0.11	33	0.37	28	0.34	25
LongestCommonSubstring	0.40	29	0.30	39	0.42	4	0.37	27	0.37	26
ESA-WordNet	0.11	43	0.30	40	0.41	6	0.49	18	0.33	29
LongestCommonSubsequenceNorm	0.53	21	0.39	4	0.19	27	0.18	37	0.32	30
MultisenseRI-ContextTermTerm	0.39	31	0.33	33	0.28	21	0.15	38	0.29	33
MultisenseRI-HASensesTermTerm	0.39	32	0.33	34	0.28	22	0.15	39	0.29	34
RI-SentVectors-Norm	0.34	35	0.35	26	-0.01	51	0.24	35	0.23	39
RelationSimilarity	0.31	39	0.35	27	0.24	26	0.02	41	0.23	40
RI-SentVectors-TFIDF	0.27	40	0.15	50	0.08	40	0.23	36	0.18	41
GraphEditDistance	0.33	38	0.25	46	0.13	31	-0.11	49	0.15	42

Table 3: Correlation score and rank of the best features

8 Conclusion and Future Work

The NTNU system can be regarded as continuation of the most successful systems from the STS'12 shared task, combining shallow textual, distributional and knowledge-based features into a support vector regression model. It reuses features from the TakeLab and DKPro systems, resulting in a very strong baseline.

Adding new features to further improve performance turned out to be hard: only GateWordMatch yielded improved performance. Similarity features based on both classical and innovative variants of Random Indexing were shown to correlate with semantic textual similarity, but did not complement the existing distributional features. Likewise, features designed to reveal deeper syntactic (graph edit distance) and semantic relations (RelEx) did not add to the score.

As future work, we would aim to explore a vertical feature composition approach similar to GateWordMatch and contrast it with the "flat" composition currently used in our systems.

Acknowledgements

Thanks to TakeLab for source code of their '*simple*' system and the full-scale LSA models. Thanks to the team from Ubiquitous Knowledge Processing Lab for source code of their DKPro Similarity system.

References

Agirre, E., Cer, D., Diab, M., and Gonzalez-Agirre, A. (2012). SemEval-2012 Task 6: A pilot on semantic textual similarity. In *SEM (2012), pages 385–393.

Agirre, E., Cer, D., Diab, M., Gonzalez-Agirre, A., and Guo, W. (2013). *SEM 2013 Shared Task: Semantic textual similarity, including a pilot on typed-similarity. In **SEM 2013: The Second Joint Conference on Lexical and Computational Semantics*. Association for Computational Linguistics.

Ahn, C. S. (2011). *Automatically detecting authors' native language*. PhD thesis, Monterey, California. Naval Postgraduate School.

Banea, C., Hassan, S., Mohler, M., and Mihalcea, R. (2012). UNT: a supervised synergistic approach to semantic text similarity. In *SEM (2012), pages 635–642.

Bär, D., Biemann, C., Gurevych, I., and Zesch, T. (2012). UKP: Computing semantic textual similarity by combining multiple content similarity measures. In *SEM (2012), pages 435–440.

Bhagwani, S., Satapathy, S., and Karnick, H. (2012). sranjans : Semantic textual similarity using maximal weighted bipartite graph matching. In **SEM 2012: The First Joint Conference on Lexical and Computational Semantics – Volume 1: Proceedings of the main conference and the shared task, and Volume 2: Proceedings of the Sixth International Workshop on Semantic Evaluation (SemEval 2012)*, pages 579–585, Montréal, Canada. Association for Computational Linguistics.

Cunningham, H., Maynard, D., Bontcheva, K., and Tablan, V. (2002). GATE: A framework and graphical development environment for robust NLP tools and applications. In *Proceedings of the 40th Annual Meeting of the Association for Computational Linguistics*, pages 168–175, Philadelphia, Pennsylvania. ACL.

Deerwester, S., Dumais, S., Furnas, G., Landauer, T., and Harshman, R. (1990). Indexing by latent semantic analysis. *Journal of the American Society for Information Science*, 41(6):391–407.

Fundel, K., Küffner, R., and Zimmer, R. (2007). RelEx - Relation extraction using dependency parse trees. *Bioinformatics*, 23(3):365–371.

Gabrilovich, E. and Markovitch, S. (2007). Computing semantic relatedness using wikipedia-based explicit semantic analysis. In *Proceedings of The Twentieth International Joint Conference for Artificial Intelligence.*, pages 1606–1611.

Hart, D. and Goertzel, B. (2008). Opencog: A software framework for integrative artificial general intelligence. In *Proceedings of the 2008 conference on Artificial General Intelligence 2008: Proceedings of the First AGI Conference*, pages 468–472, Amsterdam, The Netherlands, The Netherlands. IOS Press.

Hassel, M. (2004). JavaSDM package.

Kanerva, P., Kristoferson, J., and Holst, A. (2000). Random indexing of text samples for latent semantic analysis. In Gleitman, L. and Josh, A., editors, *Proceedings of the 22nd Annual Conference of the Cognitive Science Society*, page 1036. Erlbaum.

Karlgren, J. and Sahlgren, M. (2001). From Words to Understanding. In Uesaka, Y., Kanerva, P., and Asoh, H., editors, *Foundations of real-world intelligence*, chapter 26, pages 294–311. Stanford: CSLI Publications.

Karnick, H., Satapathy, S., and Bhagwani, S. (2012). sranjans: Semantic textual similarity using maximal bipartite graph matching. In *SEM (2012), pages 579–585.

Kuhn, H. (1955). The Hungarian method for the assignment problem. *Naval research logistics quarterly*, 2:83–97.

Leacock, C. and Chodorow, M. (1998). Combining local context and WordNet similarity for word sense identification. *WordNet: An electronic lexical ....*

Levenshtein, V. I. (1966). Binary codes capable of correcting deletions, insertions and reversals. *Soviet Physics Doklady*, 10(8):707–710.

Nivre, J., Hall, J., and Nilsson, J. (2006). Maltparser: A data-driven parser-generator for dependency parsing. In *In Proc. of LREC-2006*, pages 2216–2219.

Reisinger, J. and Mooney, R. (2010). Multi-prototype vector-space models of word meaning. In *Human Language Technologies: The 2010 Annual Conference of the North American Chapter of the Association for Computational Linguistics*, number June, pages 109–117.

Riesen, K. and Bunke, H. (2009). Approximate graph edit distance computation by means of bipartite graph matching. *Image and Vision Computing*, 27(7):950–959.

Røkenes, H. (2013). Graph-Edit Distance Applied to the Task of Detecting Plagiarism. Master's thesis, Norwegian University of Science and Technology.

Sahlgren, M. (2005). An introduction to random indexing. In *Methods and Applications of Semantic Indexing Workshop at the 7th International Conference on Terminology and Knowledge Engineering, TKE*, volume 5.

Sahlgren, M., Holst, A., and Kanerva, P. (2008). Permutations as a Means to Encode Order in Word Space. *Proceedings of the 30th Conference of the Cognitive Science Society.*

Šarić, F., Glavaš, G., Karan, M., Šnajder, J., and Bašić, B. D. (2012). TakeLab: systems for measuring semantic text similarity. In *SEM (2012), pages 441–448.

*SEM (2012). *Proceedings of the First Joint Conference on Lexical and Computational Semantics (*SEM)*, volume 2: Proceedings of the Sixth International Workshop on Semantic Evaluation, Montreal, Canada. Association for Computational Linguistics.

Semeraro, G., Aldo, B., and Orabona, V. E. (2012). UNIBA: Distributional semantics for textual similarity. In *SEM (2012), pages 591–596.

Singh, J., Bhattacharya, A., and Bhattacharyya, P. (2012). janardhan: Semantic textual similarity using universal networking language graph matching. In **SEM 2012: The First Joint Conference on Lexical and Computational Semantics – Volume 1: Proceedings of the main conference and the shared task, and Volume 2: Proceedings of the Sixth International Workshop on Semantic Evaluation (SemEval 2012)*, pages 662–666, Montréal, Canada. Association for Computational Linguistics.

Sokolov, A. (2012). LIMSI: learning semantic similarity by selecting random word subsets. In *SEM (2012), pages 543–546.

Tovar, M., Reyes, J., and Montes, A. (2012). BUAP: a first approximation to relational similarity measuring. In *SEM (2012), pages 502–505.

Vapnik, V., Golowich, S. E., and Smola, A. (1997). Support vector method for function approximation, regression estimation, and signal processing. In Mozer, M. C., Jordan, M. I., and Petsche, T., editors, *Advances in Neural Information Processing Systems*, volume 9, pages 281–287. MIT Press, Cambridge, Massachusetts.

SXUCFN-Core: STS Models Integrating FrameNet Parsing Information

Sai Wang, Ru Li, RuiboWang, ZhiqiangWang, Xia Zhang
Shanxi University, Taiyuan, China
enrique.s.wang@gmail.com
{liru, wangruibo}@sxu.edu.cn
{zhiq.wang, caesarzhangx}@163.com

Abstract

This paper describes our system submitted to *SEM 2013 Semantic Textual Similarity (STS) core task which aims to measure semantic similarity of two given text snippets. In this shared task, we propose an interpolation STS model named Model_LIM integrating FrameNet parsing information, which has a good performance with low time complexity compared with former submissions.

1 Introduction

The goal of Semantic Textual Similarity (STS) is to measure semantic similarity of two given text snippets. STS has been recently proposed by Agirre et al. (2012) as a pilot task, which has close relationship with both tasks of Textual Entailment and Paraphrase, but not equivalent with them and it is more directly applicable to a number of NLP tasks such as Question Answering (Lin and Pantel, 2001), Text Summarization (Hatzivassiloglou et al., 1999), etc. And yet, the acquiring of sentence similarity has been the most important and basic task in STS. Therefore, the STS core task of *SEM 2013 conference, is formally defined as the degree of semantic equivalence between two sentences as follows:

- **5: completely equivalent,** as they *mean the same thing.*
- **4: mostly equivalent,** but some *unimportant details differ.*
- **3: roughly equivalent,** but some *important information differs/missing.*
- **2: not equivalent,** but share some *details.*
- **1: not equivalent,** but are *on the same topic.*
- **0: on different topics.**

In this paper, we attempt to integrate semantic information into STS task besides the lower-level word and syntactic information. Evaluation results show that our STS model could benefit from semantic parsing information of two text snippets. The rest of the paper is organized as follows: Section 2 reviews prior researches on STS. Section 3 illustrates three models measuring text similarity. Section 4 describes the linear interpolation model in detail. Section 5 provides the experimental results on the development set as well as the official results on all published datasets. Finally, Section 6 summarizes our paper with direction for future works.

2 Related Work

Several techniques have been developed for STS. The typical approach to finding the similarity between two text segments is to use simple word matching method. In order to improve this simple method, Mihalcea et al. (2006) combine two corpus-based and six knowledge-based measures of word similarity, but the cost of their algorithm is expensive. In contrast, our method treats words and texts in essentially the same way.

In 2012 STS task, 35 teams participate and submit 88 runs. The two top scoring systems are UKP

*Second Joint Conference on Lexical and Computational Semantics (*SEM), Volume 1: Proceedings of the Main Conference and the Shared Task*, pages 74–79, Atlanta, Georgia, June 13-14, 2013. ©2013 Association for Computational Linguistics

and Takelab. The former system (Bär et al., 2012) uses a simple log-linear regression model to combine multiple text similarity measures (related to content, structure and style) of varying complexity. While the latter system Takelab (Šarić et al., 2012) uses a support vector regression model with multiple features measuring word-overlap similarity and syntax similarity.

The results of them score over 80%, far exceeding that of a simple lexical baseline. But both share one characteristic: they integrate lexical and syntax information without semantic information, especially FrameNet parsing information. In addition, the complexity of these algorithms is very high. Therefore, we propose a different and simple model integrating FrameNet parsing information in this paper.

3 Linear Interpolation Model

In this paper, we propose a combination interpolation model which is constructed by the results of three similarity models based on words, WordNet, FrameNet , which are called $sim_{WD}(\cdot)$, $sim_{WN}(\cdot)$ and $sim_{FN}(\cdot)$ respectively. The overall similarity $sim_{LIM}(S_1, S_2)$ between a pair of texts S_1, S_2 is computed in the following equation:

$$sim_{LIM}(S_1, S_2) = \omega_1 \cdot sim_{WD}(S_1, S_2) + \omega_2 \cdot sim_{WN}(S_1, S_2) + \omega_3 \cdot sim_{FN}(S_1, S_2) \quad (1)$$

In which, ω_1, ω_2 and ω_3 are respectively the weights of the similarity models, i.e., $\omega_1 + \omega_2 + \omega_3 = 1$; and they are all positive hyperparameters. Now, we describe the three models used in this equation.

3.1 Similarity Based on Words

This model is motivated by Vector Space Model (Salton et al., 1975). We present each sentence as a vector in the multidimensional token space. Let S_c denote the set of all words in the c-th text snippets $(c = 1, 2)$; the words of bag is $W = S_1 \cup S_2$. Hence, the similarity of a pair of sentences, formally expressed as:

$$sim_{WD}(S_1, S_2) = \frac{\sum_{i=1}^{|W|} w_{1,i} \cdot w_{2,i}}{\sqrt{\sum_{i=1}^{|W|} w_{1,i}^2} \cdot \sqrt{\sum_{i=1}^{|W|} w_{2,i}^2}} \quad (2)$$

In which, we can find $w_{c,k} \in W(\ k = 1,2, \ldots, |W|;\ c = 1,2)$ by solving:

$$w_{c,k} = \begin{cases} 1, & if\ w_{c,k} \in S_c \\ 0, & otherwise \end{cases} \quad (3)$$

From these two equations above, we can see the more identical words in a text pair, the more similar the two snippets are. Whereas, by intuition, many high-frequency functional words would not be helpful to the estimation of the similarity given in Eq.(2). Therefore, in the preprocessing stage, we compute the word frequencies per dataset, and then remove the high frequency words (top 1% in frequency list) in each segment.

3.2 Similarity Based on WordNet

This model measures semantic similarity with the help of such resources that specifically encode relations between words or concepts like WordNet (Fellbaum, 1998). We use the algorithms by Lin (1998) on WordNet to compute the similarity between two words a and b, which we call $sim_{Lin}(a, b)$. Let S_1, S_2 be the two word sets of two given text snippets, we use the method below:

$$sim_{WN}(S_1, S_2) = \frac{\sum_{i=1}^{\min(|S_1|,|S_2|)} \max\left(sim_{Lin}(w_{1,i} \cdot w_{2,i})\right)}{\min(|S_1|,|S_2|)} \quad (4)$$

In which, $w_{c,i} \in S_c (c = 1,2)$. In the numerator of Eq.(4),we try to $max(\cdot)$, $avg(\cdot)$ and $mid(\cdot)$ respectively, then we find the $max(\cdot)$ is the best.

3.3 Similarity Based on FrameNet

FrameNet lexicon (Fillmore et al., 2003) is a rich linguistic resource containing expert knowledge about lexical and predicate-argument semantics in English. In a sentence, word or phrase tokens that evoke a frame are known as **targets**. Each frame definition also includes a set of **frame elements**, or **roles**, corresponding to different aspects of the concept represented by the frame, such as participants, props, and attributes. We use the term **argument** to refer to a sequence of word tokens annotated as filling a frame role.

All the data are automatically parsed by SEMFOR[1] (Das and Smith, 2012; Das and Smith,

[1] See http://www.ark.cs.cmu.edu/SEMAFOR/.

2011). Figure 1 shows the parser output of a sentence pair given in Microsoft Research Video Description Corpus with annotated targets, frames and role argument pairs. It can be noticed that FrameNet parsing information could give some clues of the similarity of two given snippets and we think that integrating this information could improve the accuracy of STS task. For example, the sentences in the Figure 1 both illustrate "somebody is moving". However, our model depends on the precision of that parser. If it would be improved, the results in STS task would be better.

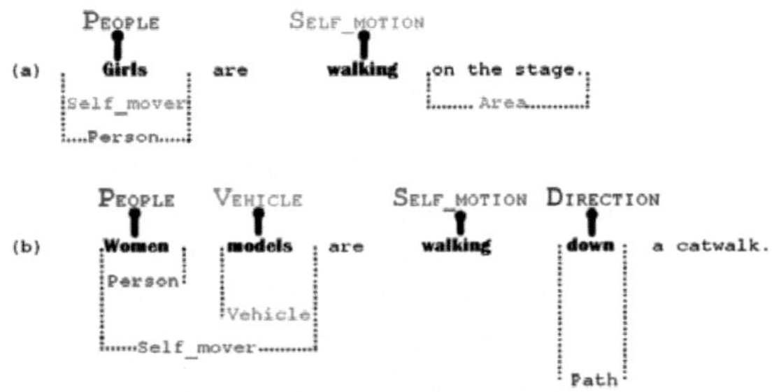

Figure 1: This is a pair of sentences in 2013 STS training data: *(a) Girls are walking on the stage; (b) Women models are walking down a catwalk.* The words in bold correspond to targets, which evoke semantic frames that are denoted in capital letters. Every frame is shown in a distinct color; the arguments of each frame are annotated with the same color, and marked below the sentence, at different levels; the spans marked in the block of dotted liens fulfill a specific role.

For a given sentence S_c $(c = 1,2)$ with a set of evoked frame $F_c = < f_1, f_2, ..., f_n >$ *(n is the number of evoked frames),* a set of target word with each frame $T_c = < t_1, t_2, ..., t_n >$ and the set of roles (namely, frame elements) $\mathfrak{R}_c = \{R_{c,1}, R_{c,2}, ..., R_{c,n}\}$, each frame contains one or more arguments $R_{c,i} = \{r_j\}$ *(i = 1, 2, ..., n; j is an integer that is greater or equal to zero).* Take Figure 1 as an example,

T_1 = <grils, walking>,
F_1 = <PEOPLE, SELF_MOTION>,
$\mathfrak{R}_1 = \{R_{1,1}, R_{1,2}\}$,
$R_{1,1}$ = {girls},
$R_{1,2}$ = {girls, on the stage};

T_2 = <women, models, walking, down>,
F_2 = <PEOPLE, VEHICLE, SELF_MOTION, DIRECTION>,
$\mathfrak{R}_2 = \{R_{2,1}, R_{2,2}, R_{2,3}, R_{2,4}\}$,
$R_{2,1}$ = {women}, $R_{2,2}$ = {models},
$R_{2,3}$ = {women models}, $R_{2,4}$ = {down}.

In order to compute $sim_{Fr}(\cdot)$ simply, we also use a interpolation model to combine the similarities based on target words $sim_{Tg}(\cdot)$, frames $sim_{Fr}(\cdot)$ and frame relations $sim_{Re}(\cdot)$. They are estimated as the following:

When computing the similarity on target word level $sim_{Tg}(S_1, S_2)$, we also consider each sentence as a vector of target words as is seen in Eq.(5).

$$T = T_1 \cup T_2;$$
$$sim_{Tg}(S_1, S_2) = \frac{\sum_{i=1}^{|T|} t_{1,i} \cdot t_{2,i}}{\sqrt{\sum_{i=1}^{|T|} t_{1,i}^2} \cdot \sqrt{\sum_{i=1}^{|T|} t_{2,i}^2}} \quad (5)$$

In which, we can find $t_{c,k} \in T(k = 1,2, ..., |T|; c = 1,2)$ by solving:

$$t_{c,k} = \begin{cases} 1, & if\ f_{c,j} \in F_c\ \mathbf{and}\ t_{c,k} \in T_c \\ & (j = 1,2, ..., |F|) \\ 0, & otherwise \end{cases} \quad (6)$$

Let $sim_{Fr}(S_1, S_2)$ be the similarity on frame level as shown in Eq.(7), with each sentence as a vector of frames. We define $f_{1,i}$, $f_{2,i}$ like $w_{c,k}$ in Eq.(3).

$$F = F_1 \cup F_2;$$
$$sim_{Fr}(S_1, S_2) = \frac{\sum_{i=1}^{|F|} f_{1,i} \cdot f_{2,i}}{\sqrt{\sum_{i=1}^{|F|} f_{1,i}^2} \cdot \sqrt{\sum_{i=1}^{|F|} f_{2,i}^2}} \quad (7)$$

Before computing the role relationship between the pair of sentences, we should find the **containment relationship** of each pair of frames in one sentence. We use a rule to define the containment relationship:

Given two frames $f_{c,i}$, $f_{c,j}$ in a sentence S_c, if $t_{c,j} \in R_{c,j}$ $(i \neq j)$, then $f_{c,j}$ contains $f_{c,i}$ - and that is $f_{c,i}$ is a child of $f_{c,j}$. After that we add them into the ***set of frame relationship*** $Rlt_c = \langle < f_{c,i}^k, f_{c,j}^k > \rangle_{k=0}^N = \langle rel_{c,k} \rangle_{k=0}^N, (k \geq 0)$.

We consider the relationship between two frames in a sentence as a 2-tuple, and again use Figure 1 as an example,

Rlt_1 = ⟨<PEOPLE, SELF_MOTION>⟩;
Rlt_2 = ⟨<PEOPLE, SELF_MOTION>, <VEHICLE, SELF_MOTION >⟩.

Besides, we do exactly the same with both frames, namely $rel_{c,i} \in Rlt_c$ (c = 1,2) the value of $rel_{c,i}$ is 1. The similarity on frame relationship level $sim_{Re}(S_1, S_2)$ presents each sentence as a vector of roles as shown in Eq.(8).

$$Rlt = Rlt_1 \cup Rlt_2; \tag{8}$$

$$sim_{Re}(S_1, S_2) = \frac{\sum_{i=1}^{|Rlt|} rel_{1,i} \cdot rel_{2,i}}{\sqrt{\sum_{i=1}^{|Rlt|} rel_{1,i}^2} \cdot \sqrt{\sum_{i=1}^{|Rlt|} rel_{2,i}^2}}$$

Lastly, the shallow semantic similarity between two given sentences is computed as:

$$Sim_{FN}(S_1, S_2) = \alpha \cdot sim_{Tg}(S_1, S_2) + \beta \cdot sim_{Fr}(S_1, S_2) + \gamma \cdot sim_{Re}(S_1, S_2) \tag{9}$$

In which, $\alpha + \beta + \gamma = 1$, and they are all positive hyperparameters. As shown in Figure 2, we plot the Pearson correlation (vertical axis) against the combination of parameters (horizontal axis) in all 2013 STS train data (2012 STS data). We notice that generally the Pearson correlation is fluctuates, and the correlation peak is found at 32, which in Table 1 is $\alpha=0.6, \beta=0.3, \gamma=0.1$.

ID	α	β	γ	ID	α	β	γ	ID	α	β	γ
1	1	0	0	23	0.7	0.2	0.1	45	0	0.4	0.6
2	0.9	0	0.1	24	0.6	0.2	0.2	46	0.5	0.5	0
3	0.8	0	0.2	25	0.5	0.2	0.3	47	0.4	0.5	0.1
4	0.7	0	0.3	26	0.4	0.2	0.4	48	0.3	0.5	0.2
5	0.6	0	0.4	27	0.3	0.2	0.5	49	0.2	0.5	0.3
6	0.5	0	0.5	28	0.2	0.2	0.6	50	0.1	0.5	0.4
7	0.4	0	0.6	29	0.1	0.2	0.7	51	0	0.5	0.5
8	0.3	0	0.7	30	0	0.2	0.8	52	0.4	0.6	0
9	0.2	0	0.8	31	0.7	0.3	0	53	0.3	0.6	0.1
10	0.1	0	0.9	32	0.6	0.3	0.1	54	0.2	0.6	0.2
11	0	0	1	33	0.5	0.3	0.2	55	0.1	0.6	0.3
12	0.9	0.1	0	34	0.4	0.3	0.3	56	0	0.6	0.4
13	0.8	0.1	0.1	35	0.3	0.3	0.4	57	0.3	0.7	0
14	0.7	0.1	0.2	36	0.2	0.3	0.5	58	0.2	0.7	0.1
15	0.6	0.1	0.3	37	0.1	0.3	0.6	59	0.1	0.7	0.2
16	0.5	0.1	0.4	38	0	0.3	0.7	60	0	0.7	0.3
17	0.4	0.1	0.5	39	0.6	0.4	0	61	0.2	0.8	0
18	0.3	0.1	0.6	40	0.5	0.4	0.1	62	0.1	0.8	0.1
19	0.2	0.1	0.7	41	0.4	0.4	0.2	63	0	0.8	0.2
20	0.1	0.1	0.8	42	0.3	0.4	0.3	64	0.1	0.9	0
21	0	0.1	0.9	43	0.2	0.4	0.4	65	0	0.9	0.1
22	0.8	0.2	0	44	0.1	0.4	0.5	66	0	1	0

Table 1: Different combinations of α, β, γ ($\alpha + \beta + \gamma = 1$) with ID that is horizontal axis in Figure 2. This table also apples to different combinations of $\omega_1, \omega_2, \omega_3$ ($\omega_1 + \omega_2 + \omega_3 = 1$) with ID that is horizontal axis in Figure 3.

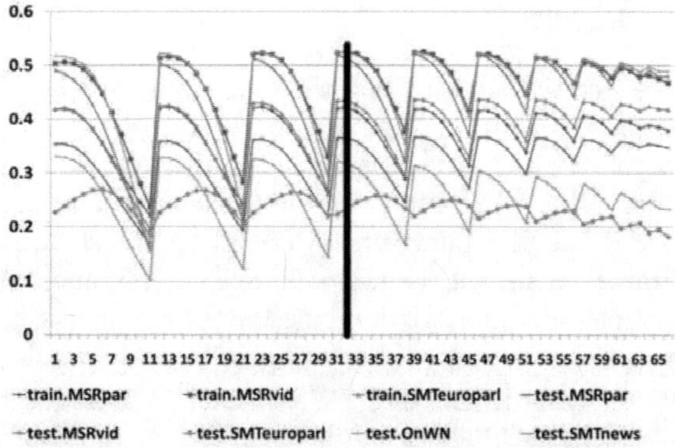

Figure 2: This graph shows the variation of Pearson correlation (vertical axis) in all 2013 STS train data (2012 STS data), with numbers (horizontal axis) indicating different combinations α, β, γ in Table 1 and when the value of result confidence is 100. The effect values are represented by a vertical line (i.e. ID = 32).

4 Tuning Hyperparameters

Eq.(1) is a very simple linear interpolation model, and we tune the hyperparameters on the whole 2012 STS data.

As shown in Figure 3,we plot the Pearson correlation (vertical axis) for the different combination of parameters ω_1, ω_2 and ω_3 (horizontal axis). We notice that generally the Pearson correlation fluctuates with a dropping tendency in most cases, and the correlation peak presents at 13, which in Table 1 is $\omega_1=0.8, \omega_2=0.1, \omega_3=0.1$.

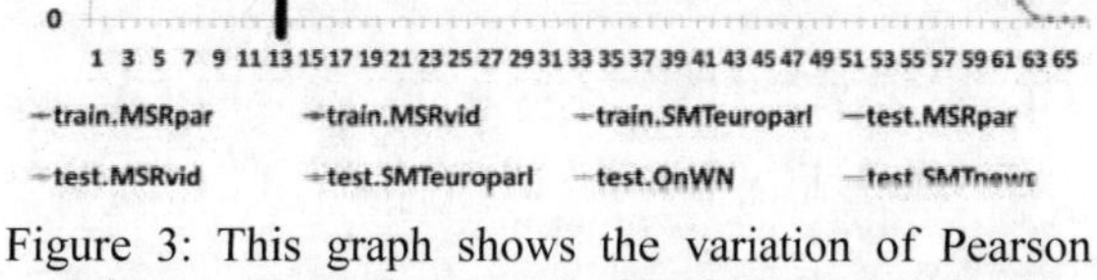

Figure 3: This graph shows the variation of Pearson correlation (vertical axis) in all 2013 STS train data (2012 STS data), with numbers (horizontal axis) indicating different combinations $\omega_1, \omega_2, \omega_3$ in Table 1 and when the value of result confidence is 100. The effect values are represented by a vertical line (i.e. ID = 13).

5 Results

We submit four runs: the first one (Model_WD) is based on word similarity; the second one (Model_WN) which is only using the similarity based on WordNet, is submitted with the team name of SXULLL; the third one (Model_FN) which uses FrameNet similarity defined in Section 3.3; and the last one in which we combine the three similarities described in Section 4 together with an interpolation model. In addition, we map our outputs multiply by five to the [0-5] range.

It is worth notice that in the first model, we lowercase all words and remove all numbers and punctuations. And in the third model, we extract all frame-semantic roles with SEMFOR.

In the experiment, we use eight datasets totally - namely MSRpar, MSRvid, SMTeuroparl, OnWN, SMTnews, headlines, FNWN and SMT - with their gold standard file to evaluate the performance of the submitted systems. Evaluation is carried out using the official scorer which computes Pearson correlation between the human rated similarity scores and the system's output. The final measure is the score that is weighted by the number of text pairs in each dataset ("Mean"). See Agirre et al. (2012) for a full description of the metrics.

5.1 Experiments on STS 2012 Data

There is no new train data in 2013, so we use 2012 data as train data. From Table 2, 3 we can see that the Model_LIM has better performance than the other three models.

	MSRpar	MSRvid	SMTeuroparl	Mean
Model_WD	0.4532	0.4487	0.6467	0.5153
Model_WN	0.2718	0.5410	0.6225	0.4774
Model_FN	0.4437	0.5530	0.5178	0.5048
Model_LIM	**0.4896**	**0.5533**	**0.6681**	**0.5696**

Table 2: Performances of the four models on 2012 train data. The highest correlation in each column is given in bold.

From Table 2, we notice that all the models except Model_FN, are apt to handle the SMTeuroparl that involves long sentences. For Model_FN, it performs well in computing on short and similarly structured texts such as MSRvid (This will be confirmed in test data later). Although WordNet and FrameNet model has a mere weight of 20% in Model_LIM (i.e. $\omega_1 + \omega_2 = 0.2$), the run which integrate more semantic information displays a consistent performance across the three train sets (especially in SMTeuroparl, the Pearson correlation rises from 0.5178 to 0.66808), when compared to the other three.

	MSRpar	MSRvid	SMTeuroparl	OnWN	SMTnews	Mean
Baseline	0.4334	0.2996	0.4542	0.5864	0.3908	0.4356
Model_WD	0.4404	0.5464	0.5059	0.6751	0.4583	0.5346
Model_WN	0.1247	0.6608	0.0637	0.4089	0.3436	0.3417
Model_FN	0.3830	0.6082	0.3537	0.6091	0.4061	0.4905
Model_LIM	0.4489	0.6301	0.5086	**0.6841**	0.4872	0.5631
UKP_run2	**0.6830**	**0.8739**	**0.5280**	0.6641	**0.4937**	**0.6773**

Table 3: Performances of our three models as well as the baseline and UKP_run2 (that is ranked 1 in last STS task) results on 2012 test data. The highest correlation in each column is given in bold.

The 2012 STS test results obtained by first ranking UKP_run2 and baseline system are shown in Table 3, it is interesting to notice that performance of Model_WD is similar with Model_LIM except on MSRvid, the text segments in which there are fewer identical words because of the semantic equivalence. For Model_FN, we can see it performs well on short and similarly structured texts (MSRvid and OnWN) as mentioned before. This is because the precision of FrameNet parser took effect on the FrameNet-based models performance. Compared to UKP_run2, the performance of Model_LIM is obviously better on OnWN set, while on SMTeuroparl and SMTnews this model scores slightly lower than UKP_run2. Finally, Model_LIM did not perform best on MSRpar and MSRvid compared with UKP_run2, but it has low time complexity and integrates semantic information.

5.2 Official Results on STS 2013 Test Data

Table 4 provides the official results of our submitted systems, along with the rank on each dataset. Generally, all results outperform the baseline, based on simple word overlap. However, the performance of Model_LIM is not always the best in the three runs for each dataset. From the table we can note that a particular model always performs well on the dataset including the lexicon on which the model is based on e.g. Model_WN in OnWN, Model_FN in FNWN. Besides, Model_WD and Model_LIM almost have same scores except in OnWN set, because in Model_LIM is included with WordNet resource.

	headlines	OnWN	FNWN	SMT	Mean
Baseline	0.5399 (66)	0.2828 (80)	0.2146 (66)	0.2861 (65)	0.3639 (73)
Model_WD	**0.6806 (24)**	0.5355 (44)	0.3181 (48)	0.3980 (4)	0.5198 (27)
Model_WN	0.4840 (78)	**0.7146 (12)**	0.0415 (83)	0.1543 (86)	0.3944 (69)
Model_FN	0.4881 (76)	0.6146 (27)	**0.4237 (9)**	0.3844 (6)	0.4797 (46)
Model_LIM	0.6761 (29)	0.6481 (23)	0.3025 (51)	**0.4003 (3)**	**0.5458 (14)**

Table 4: Performances of our systems as well as baseline on STS 2013 individual test data, accompanied by their rank (out of 90) shown in brackets. Scores in bold denote significant improvements over the baseline.

As seen from the system rank in table, the optimal runs in the three submitted system remain with Model_LIM. Not only Model_LIM performs best on two occasions, but also Model_FN ranks top ten twice, in FNWN and SMT respectively, we owe this result to the contribution of FrameNet parsing information.

6 Conclusion

We have tested all the models on published STS datasets. Compared with the official results, Model_LIM system is apt to handle the SMT that involves long sentences. Moreover, this system just integrates words, WordNet and FrameNet semantic information, thus it has low time complexity. There is still much room for improvement in our work. For example, we will attempt to use multivariate regression software to tuning the hyperparameters.

Acknowledgments

This work is supported by the National Nature Science Foundation of China (No.60970053), by the National High-tech Research and Development Projects (863) grant No.2006AA01Z142, by the State Language Commission of China No.YB125-19 as well as by the International Cooperation of Shanxi Province, Contracts 2010081044. And we would like to thank the organizer for the tremendous effort they put into formulating this challenging work.

References

Eneko Agirre, Daniel Cer, Mona Diab, and Aitor Gonzalez-Agirre. 2012. SemEval-2012 Task 6: A Pilot on Semantic Textual Similarity. In *Proceedings of the 6th International Workshop on Semantic Evaluation, in conjunction with the 1st Joint Conference on Lexical and Computational Semantics,* 385–393.

Dekang Lin, Patrick Pantel. 2001. Discovery of Inference Rules for Question Answering. *Natural Language Engineering,* 7(4):343-360.

Vasileios Hatzivassiloglou, Judith L. Klavans, and Eleazar Eskin. 1999. Detecting Text Similarity over Short Passages: Exploring Linguistic Feature Combinations via Machine Learning. In *proceedings of the Joint SIGDAT Conference on Empirical Methods in Natural Language Processing and Very Large Corpora,* 224-231.

Rada Mihalcea, Courtney Corley, and Carlo Strapparava. 2006. Corpus-based and Knowledge-based Measures of Text Semantic Similarity. In *Proceedings of the National Conference on Artificial Intelligence,* 21(1): 775-780.

Daniel Bär, Chris Biemann, Iryna Gurevych, and Torsten Zesch. 2012. UKP: Computing Semantic Textual Similarity by Combining Multiple Content Similarity Measures. In *Proceedings of the 6th International Workshop on Semantic Evaluation, in conjunction with the 1st Joint Conference on Lexical and Computational Semantics,* 435-440.

Frane Šarić, Goran Glavaš, Mladen Karan, Jan Šnajder, and Bojana Dalbelo Bašić. 2012. TakeLab: Systems for Measuring Semantic Text Similarity. In *Proceedings of the 6th International Workshop on Semantic Evaluation, in conjunction with the 1st Joint Conference on Lexical and Computational Semantics,* 441-448.

G. Salton, A. Wong, C.S. Yang. 1975. A Vector Space Model for Automatic Indexing. *Communications of the ACM,* 18(11):613-620.

C. J. Fillmore, C. R. Johnson and M. R.L. Petruck. 2003. Background to FrameNet. *International Journal of Lexicography,* 16: 235-250.

Dipanjan Das and Noah A. Smith. 2012. Graph-Based Lexicon Expansion with Sparsity-Inducing Penalties. In *Proceedings of the Conference of the North American Chapter of the Association for Computational Linguistics,* 677-687.

Dipanjan Das and Noah A. Smith. 2011. Semi-Supervised Frame-Semantic Parsing for Unknown Predicates. In *Proceedings of Annual Meeting of the Association for Computational Linguistics,* 1435-1444.

Christiane Fellbaum. 1998. *WordNet: An Electronic Lexical Database.* MIT Press.

Dekang Lin. 1998. An information-theoretic definition of similarity. In *Proceedings of International Conference on Machine Learning,* 296-340.

Distinguishing Common and Proper Nouns

Judita Preiss and **Mark Stevenson**
{j.preiss, r.m.stevenson}@sheffield.ac.uk
Department of Computer Science,
University of Sheffield
211 Portobello, Sheffield S1 4DP
United Kingdom

Abstract

We describe a number of techniques for automatically deriving lists of common and proper nouns, and show that the distinction between the two can be made automatically using a vector space model learning algorithm. We present a direct evaluation on the British National Corpus, and application based evaluations on Twitter messages and on automatic speech recognition (where the system could be employed to restore case).

1 Introduction

Some nouns are homographs (they have the same written form, but different meaning) which can be used to denote either a common or proper noun, for example the word *apple* in the following examples: (1) **Apple** designs and creates iPod (2) The **Apple** II series is a set of 8-bit home computers (3) The **apple** is the pomaceous fruit of the apple tree (4) For **apple** enthusiasts – tasting notes and apple identification.

The common and proper uses are not always as clearly distinct as in this example; for example, a specific instance of a common noun, e.g., *District Court* turns *court* into a proper noun.

While heuristically, proper nouns often start with a capital letter in English, capitalization can be inconsistent, incorrect or omitted, and the presence or absence of an article cannot be relied on.

The problem of distinguishing between common and proper usages of nouns has not received much attention within language processing, despite being an important component for many tasks including machine translation (Lopez, 2008; Hermjakob et al., 2008), sentiment analysis (Pang and Lee, 2008; Wilson et al., 2009) and topic tracking (Petrović et al., 2010). Approaches to the problem also have applications to tasks such as web search (Chen et al., 1998; Baeza-Yates and Ribeiro-Neto, 2011), and case restoration (e.g., in automatic speech recognition output) (Baldwin et al., 2009), but frequently involve the manual creation of a gazeteer (a list of proper nouns), which suffer not only from omissions but also often do not allow the listed words to assume their common role in text.

This paper presents methods for generating lists of nouns that have both common and proper usages (Section 2) and methods for identifying the type of usage (Section 3) which are evaluated using data derived automatically from the BNC (Section 4) and on two applications (Section 5). It shows that it is difficult to automatically construct lists of ambiguous nouns but also that they can be distinguished effectively using standard features from Word Sense Disambiguation.

2 Generating Lists of Nouns

To our knowledge, no comprehensive list of common nouns with proper noun usage is available. We develop a number of heuristics to generate such lists automatically.

Part of speech tags A number of part of speech (PoS) taggers assign different tags to common and proper nouns. Ambiguous nouns are identified by tagging a corpus and extracting those that have had both tags assigned, together with the frequency of occurrence of the common/proper usage. The CLAWS (Garside, 1987) and the RASP taggers

*Second Joint Conference on Lexical and Computational Semantics (*SEM), Volume 1: Proceedings of the Main Conference and the Shared Task*, pages 80–84, Atlanta, Georgia, June 13-14, 2013.

(Briscoe et al., 2006) were applied to the British National Corpus (BNC) (Leech, 1992) to generate the lists *BNCclaws* and *BNCrasp* respectively. In addition the RASP tagger was also run over the 1.75 billion word Gigaword corpus (Graff, 2003) to extract the list *Gigaword*.

Capitalization Nouns appearing intra-sententially with both lower and upper case first letters are assumed to be ambiguous. This technique is applied to the 5-grams from the Google corpus (Brants and Franz, 2006) and the BNC (creating the lists *5-grams* and *BNCcaps*).

Wikipedia includes disambiguation pages for ambiguous words which provide information about their potential usage. Wikipedia pages for nouns with senses (according to the disambiguation page) in a set of predefined categories were identified to form the list *Wikipedia*.

Named entity recognition The Stanford Named Entity Recogniser (Finkel et al., 2005) was run over the BNC and any nouns that occur in the corpus with both named entity and non-named entity tags are extracted to form the list *Stanford*.

WordNet The final heuristic makes use of WordNet (Fellbaum, 1998) which lists nouns that are often used as proper nouns with capitalisation. Nouns which appeared in both a capitalized and lowercased form were extracted to create the list *WordNet*.

Table 1 shows the number of nouns identified by each technique in the column labeled *words* which demonstrates that the number of nouns identified varies significantly depending upon which heuristic is used. A pairwise score is also shown to indicate the consistency between each list and two example lists, *BNCclaws* and *Gigaword*. It can be seen that the level of overlap is quite low and the various heuristics generate quite different lists of nouns. In particular the recall is low, in almost all cases less than a third of nouns in one list appear in the other.

One possible reason for the low overlap between the noun lists is mistakes by the heuristics used to extract them. For example, if a PoS tagger mistakenly tags just one instance of a common noun as proper then that noun will be added to the list extracted by the part of speech heuristic. Two filtering schemes were applied to improve the accuracy of the lists: (1) minimum frequency of occurrence, the noun must appear more than a set number of times in the corpus and (2) bias, the least common type of noun usage (i.e., common or proper) must account for more than a set percentage of all usages.

	words	BNCclaws		Gigaword	
		P	R	P	R
BNCclaws	41,110	100	100	31	2
BNCrasp	20,901	52	27	45	17
BNCcaps	18,524	56	26	66	21
5-grams	27,170	45	29	59	28
Gigaword	57,196	22	31	100	100
Wikipedia	7,351	49	9	59	8
WordNet	798	75	1	68	1
Stanford	64,875	43	67	26	29

Table 1: Pairwise comparison of lists. The nouns in each list are compared against the *BNCclaws* and *Gigaword* lists. Results are computed for P(recision) and R(ecall).

We experimented with various values for these filters and a selection of results is shown in Table 2, where *freq* is the minimum frequency of occurrence filter and *bias* indicates the percentage of the less frequent noun type.

	bias	freq	words	BNCclaws		Gigaword	
				P	R	P	R
BNCclaws	40	100	274	100	1	53	1
BNCrasp	30	100	253	94	1	85	0
5-grams	40	150	305	80	1	67	0
Stanford	40	200	260	87	1	47	0

Table 2: Pairwise comparison of lists with filtering

Precision (against *BNCclaws*) increased as the filters become more aggressive. However comparison with *Gigaword* does not show such high precision and recall is extremely low in all cases.

These experiments demonstrate that it is difficult to automatically generate a list of nouns that exhibit both common and proper usages. Manual analysis of the lists generated suggest that the heuristics can identify ambiguous nouns but intersecting the lists results in the loss of some obviously ambiguous nouns (however, their union introduces a large amount of noise). We select nouns from the lists created by these heuristics (such that the distribution of either the common or proper noun sense in the data was not less than 45%) for experiments in the following sections.[1]

[1]The 100 words selected for our evaluation are available at http://pastehtml.com/view/cjsbs4xvl.txt

3 Identifying Noun Types

We cast the problem of distinguishing between common and proper usages of nouns as a classification task and develop the following approaches.

3.1 Most frequent usage

A naive baseline is supplied by assigning each word its most frequent usage form (common or proper noun). The most frequent usage is derived from the training portion of labeled data.

3.2 n-gram system

A system based on n-grams was implemented using NLTK (Bird et al., 2009). Five-grams, four-grams, trigrams and bigrams from the training corpus are matched against a test corpus sentence, and results of each match are summed to yield a preferred use in the given context with a higher weight (experimentally determined) being assigned to longer n-grams. The system backs off to the most frequent usage (as derived from the training data).

3.3 Vector Space Model (VSM)

Distinguishing between common and proper nouns can be viewed as a classification problem. Treating the problem in this manner is reminiscent of techniques commonly employed in Word Sense Disambiguation (WSD). Our supervised approach is based on an existing WSD system (Agirre and Martinez, 2004) that uses a wide range of features:

- Word form, lemma or PoS bigrams and trigrams containing the target word.
- Preceding or following lemma (or word form) content word appearing in the same sentence as the target word.
- High-likelihood, salient, bigrams.
- Lemmas of all content words in the same sentence as the target word.
- Lemmas of all content words within a ± 4 word window of the target word.
- Non stopword lemmas which appear more than twice throughout the corpus.

Each occurrence of a common / proper noun is represented as a binary vector in which each position indicates the presence or absence of a feature. A centroid vector is created during the training phase for the common noun and the proper noun instances of a word. During the test phase, the centroids are compared to the vector of each test instance using the cosine metric, and the word is assigned the type of the closest centroid.

4 Evaluation

The approaches described in the previous section are evaluated on two data sets extracted automatically from the BNC. The **BNC-PoS** data set is created using the output from the CLAWS tagger. Nouns assigned the tag NP0 are treated as proper nouns and those assigned any other nominal tag as common nouns. (According to the BNC manual the NP0 tag has a precision 83.99% and recall 97.76%.[2]) This data set consists of all sentences in the BNC in which the target word appears. The second data set, **BNC-Capital**, is created using capitalisation information and consists of instances of the target noun that do not appear sentence-initially. Any instances that are capitalised are treated as proper nouns and those which are non-capitalised as common nouns.

Experiments were carried out using capitalised and decapitalized versions of the two test corpora. The decapitalised versions by lowercasing each corpus and using it for training and testing. Results are presented in Table 3. Ten fold cross validation is used for all experiments: i.e. 9/10th of the corpus were used to acquire the training data centroids and 1/10th was used for evaluation. The average performance over the 10 experiments is reported.

The vector space model (VSM) outperforms other approaches on both corpora. Performance is particularly high when capitalisation is included (*VSM w caps*). However, this approach still outperforms the baseline without case information (*VSM w/o caps*), demonstrating that using this simple approach is less effective than making use of local context.

[2]No manual annotation of common and proper nouns in this corpus exists and thus an exact accuracy figure for this corpus cannot be obtained.

	Gold standard	
	BNC-PoS	BNC-Capital
Most frequent	79%	67%
n-gram w caps	80%	77%
n-gram w/o caps	68%	56%
VSM w caps	90%	100%
VSM w/o caps	86%	80%

Table 3: BNC evaluation results

5 Applications

We also carried out experiments on two types of text in which capitalization information may not be available: social media and ASR output.

5.1 Twitter

As demonstrated in the BNC based evaluations, the system can be applied to text which does not contain capitalization information to identify proper nouns (and, as a side effect, enable the correction of capitalization). An example of such a dataset are the (up to) 140 character messages posted on Twitter.

There are some interesting observations to be made on messages downloaded from Twitter. Although some users choose to always tweet in lower case, the overall distribution of capitalization in tweets is high for the 100 words selected in Section 2 and only 3.7% of the downloaded tweets are entirely lower case. It also appeared that users who capitalize, do so fairly consistently.

This allows the creation of a dataset based on downloaded Twitter data[3]:

1. Identify purely lower case tweets containing the target word. These will form the test data (and are manually assigned usage).
2. Any non-sentence initial occurrences of the target word are used as training instances: lower case indicating a common instance, upper case indicating a proper instance.

14 words[4] were randomly selected from the list used in Section 4 and their lowercase tweet instances were manually annotated by a single annotator. The average proportion of proper nouns in the test data was 59%.

[3] `http://search.twitter.com/api`

[4] abbot, bull, cathedral, dawn, herald, justice, knight, lily, lodge, manor, park, president, raven and windows

Training corpus	MF	n-grams	VSM
Twitter	59%	40%	60%
BNCclaw decap	59%	44%	79%

Table 4: Results on the Twitter data

The results for the three systems are presented in Table 4. As the length of the average sentence in the Twitter data is only 15 words (compared to 27 words in the BNCclaws data for the same target words), the Twitter data is likely to be suffering sparseness issues. This hypothesis is partly supported by the increase in performance when the BNCclaws decapitalized data is added to the training data, however, the performance of the n-gram system remains below the most frequent use. On closer examination, this is likely due to the skew in the data – there are many more examples for the common use of each noun, and thus each context is much more likely to have been seen in this setting.

5.2 Automatic speech recognition

Most automatic speech recognition (ASR) systems do not provide capitalization. However, our system does not rely on capitalization information, and therefore can identify proper / common nouns even if capitalization is absent. Also, once proper nouns are identified, the system can be used to restore case – a feature which allows an evaluation to take place on this dataset. We use the TDT2 Test and Speech corpus (Cieri et al., 1999), which contains ASR and a manually transcribed version of news texts from six different sources, to demonstrate the usefulness of this system for this task.

The ASR corpus is restricted to those segments which contain an equal number of target word occurrences in the ASR text and the manually transcribed version, and all such segments are extracted. The gold standard, and the most frequent usage, are drawn from the manually transcribed data.

Again, results are based on an average performance obtained using a ten fold cross validation. Three versions of training data are used: the 9/10 of ASR data (with labels provided by the manual transcription), the equivalent 9/10 of lowercased manu-

Training corpus	MF	n-grams	VSM
Manual	66%	42%	73%
ASR	63%	41%	79%

Table 5: Results on the ASR data

ally transcribed data, and a combination of the two. The results can be seen in Table 5. The performance rise obtained with the VSM model when the ASR data is used is likely due to the repeated errors within this, which will not be appearing in the manually transcribed texts. The n-gram performance is greatly affected by the low volume of training data available, and again, a large skew within this.

6 Conclusion

We automatically generate lists of common and proper nouns using a number of different techniques. A vector space model technique for distinguishing common and proper nouns is found to achieve high performance when evaluated on the BNC. This greatly outperforms a simple n-gram based system, due to its better adaptability to sparse training data. Two application based evaluations also demonstrate the system's performance and as a side effect the system could serve as a technique for automatic case restoration.

Acknowledgments

The authors are grateful to the funding for this research received from Google (Google Research Award) and the UK Engineering and Physical Sciences Research Council (EP/J008427/1).

References

Agirre, E. and Martinez, D. (2004). The Basque Country University system: English and Basque tasks. In *Senseval-3: Third International Workshop on the Evaluation of Systems for the Semantic Analysis of Text*, pages 44–48.

Baeza-Yates, R. and Ribeiro-Neto, B. (2011). *Modern Information Retrieval: The Concepts and Technology Behind Search.* Addison Wesley Longman Limited, Essex.

Baldwin, T., Paul, M., and Joseph, A. (2009). Restoring punctuation and casing in English text. In *Proceedings of the 22nd Australian Joint Conference on Artificial Intelligence (AI09)*, pages 547–556.

Bird, S., Klein, E., and Loper, E. (2009). *Natural Language Processing with Python – Analyzing Text with the Natural Language Toolkit.* O'Reilly.

Brants, T. and Franz, A. (2006). Web 1T 5-gram v1.

Briscoe, T., Carroll, J., and Watson, R. (2006). The second release of the RASP system. In *Proceedings of the COLING/ACL 2006 Interactive Presentation Sessions.*

Chen, H., Huang, S., Ding, Y., and Tsai, S. (1998). Proper name translation in cross-language information retrieval. In *Proceedings of the 36th Annual Meeting of the Association for Computational Linguistics and 17th International Conference on Computational Linguistics, Volume 1*, pages 232–236, Montreal, Canada.

Cieri, C., Graff, D., Liberman, M., Martey, N., and Strassel, S. (1999). The TDT-2 text and speech corpus. In *Proceedings of DARPA Broadcast News Workshop*, pages 57–60.

Fellbaum, C., editor (1998). *WordNet: An Electronic Lexical Database and some of its Applications.* MIT Press, Cambridge, MA.

Finkel, J. R., Grenager, T., and Manning, C. (2005). Incorporating non-local information into information extraction systems by Gibbs sampling. In *Proceedings of the 43nd Annual Meeting of the Association for Computational Linguistics*, pages 363–370.

Garside, R. (1987). The CLAWS word-tagging system. In Garside, R., Leech, G., and Sampson, G., editors, *The Computational Analysis of English: A Corpus-based Approach.* London: Longman.

Graff, D. (2003). English Gigaword. Technical report, Linguistic Data Consortium.

Hermjakob, U., Knight, K., and Daumé III, H. (2008). Name translation in statistical machine translation - learning when to transliterate. In *Proceedings of ACL-08: HLT*, pages 389–397, Columbus, Ohio.

Leech, G. (1992). 100 million words of English: the British National Corpus. *Language Research*, 28(1):1–13.

Lopez, A. (2008). Statistical machine translation. *ACM Computing Surveys*, 40(3):1–49.

Pang, B. and Lee, L. (2008). Opinion mining and sentiment analysis. *Foundations and Trends in Information Retrieval*, Vol. 2(1-2):pp. 1–135.

Petrović, S., Osborne, M., and Lavrenko, V. (2010). Streaming first story detection with application to twitter. In *Human Language Technologies: The 2010 Annual Conference of the North American Chapter of the Association for Computational Linguistics*, pages 181–189, Los Angeles, California.

Wilson, T., Wiebe, J., and Hoffman, P. (2009). Recognizing contextual polarity: an exploration of features for phrase-level sentiment analysis. *Computational Linguistics*, 35(5).

UCAM-CORE: Incorporating structured distributional similarity into STS

Tamara Polajnar Laura Rimell Douwe Kiela
Computer Laboratory
University of Cambridge
Cambridge CB3 0FD, UK
{tamara.polajnar,laura.rimell,douwe.kiela}@cl.cam.ac.uk

Abstract

This paper describes methods that were submitted as part of the *SEM shared task on Semantic Textual Similarity. Multiple kernels provide different views of syntactic structure, from both tree and dependency parses. The kernels are then combined with simple lexical features using Gaussian process regression, which is trained on different subsets of training data for each run. We found that the simplest combination has the highest consistency across the different data sets, while introduction of more training data and models requires training and test data with matching qualities.

1 Introduction

The Semantic Textual Similarity (STS) shared task consists of several data sets of paired passages of text. The aim is to predict the similarity that human annotators have assigned to these aligned pairs. Text length and grammatical quality vary between the data sets, so our submissions to the task aimed to investigate whether models that incorporate syntactic structure in similarity calculation can be consistently applied to diverse and noisy data.

We model the problem as a combination of kernels (Shawe-Taylor and Cristianini, 2004), each of which calculates similarity based on a different view of the text. State-of-the-art results on text classification have been achieved with kernel-based classification algorithms, such as the support vector machine (SVM) (Joachims, 1998), and the methods here can be adapted for use in multiple kernel classification, as in Polajnar et al. (2011). The kernels are combined using Gaussian process regression (GPR) (Rasmussen and Williams, 2006). It is important to note that the combination strategy described here is only a different way of viewing the regression-combined mixture of similarity measures approach that is already popular in STS systems, including several that participated in previous SemEval tasks (Croce et al., 2012; Bär et al., 2012). Likewise, others, such as Croce et al. (2012), have used tree and dependency parse information as part of their systems; however, we use a tree kernel approach based on a novel encoding method introduced by Zanzotto et al. (2011) and from there derive two dependency-based methods.

In the rest of this paper we will describe our system, which consists of distributional similarity (Section 2.1), several kernel measures (Section 2.2), and a combination method (Section 2.3). This will be followed by the description of our three submissions (Section 3), and a discussion of the results (Section 4).

2 Methods

At the core of all the kernel methods is either surface, distributional, or syntactic similarity between sentence constituents. The methods themselves encode sentences into vectors or sets of vectors, while the similarity between any two vectors is calculated using cosine.

2.1 Distributional Similarity

Target words are the non-stopwords that occur within our training and test data. The two distributional methods we use here both represent target

*Second Joint Conference on Lexical and Computational Semantics (*SEM), Volume 1: Proceedings of the Main Conference and the Shared Task*, pages 85–89, Atlanta, Georgia, June 13-14, 2013.

words as vectors that encode word occurrence within a set of contexts. The first method is a variation on BEAGLE (Jones and Mewhort, 2007), which considers contexts to be words that surround targets. The second method is based on ESA (Gabrilovich and Markovitch, 2007), which considers contexts to be Wikipedia documents that contain target words.

To gather the distributional data with both of these approaches we used 316,305 documents from the September 2012 snapshot of Wikipedia. The training corpus for BEAGLE is generated by pooling the top 20 documents retrieved by querying the Wikipedia snapshot index for each target word in the training and test data sets.

2.1.1 BEAGLE

Random indexing (Kaski, 1998) is a technique for dimensionality reduction where pseudo-orthogonal bases are generated by randomly sampling a distribution. BEAGLE is a model where random indexing is used to represent word co-occurrence vectors in a distributional model.

Each context word is represented as a D-dimensional vector of normally distributed random values drawn from the Gaussian distribution

$$\mathcal{N}(0, \sigma^2), \text{ where } \sigma = \frac{1}{\sqrt{D}} \text{ and } D = 4096 \quad (1)$$

A target word is represented as the sum of the vectors of all the context words that occur within a certain context window around the target word. In BEAGLE this window is considered to be the sentence in which the target word occurs; however, to avoid segmenting the entire corpus, we assume the window to include 5 words to either side of the target. This method has the advantage of keeping the dimensionality of the context space constant even if more context words are added, but we limit the context words to the top 10,000 most frequent non-stopwords in the corpus.

2.1.2 ESA

ESA represents a target word as a weighted ranked list of the top N documents that contain the word, retrieved from a high quality collection. We used the BM25F (Robertson et al., 2004) weighting function and the top $N = 700$ documents. These parameters were chosen by testing on the WordSim353 dataset.[1] The list of retrieved documents can be represented as a very sparse vector whose dimensions match the number of documents in the collection, or in a more computationally efficient manner as a hash map linking document identifiers to the retrieval weights. Similarity between lists was calculated using the cosine measure augmented to work on the hash map data type.

2.2 Kernel Measures

In our experiments we use six basic kernel types, which are described below. Effectively we have eight kernels, because we also use the tree and dependency kernels with and without distributional information. Each kernel is a function which is passed a pair of short texts, which it then encodes into a specific format and compares using a defined similarity function. LK uses the regular cosine similarity function, but LEK, TK, DK, MDK, DGK use the following cosine similarity redefined for sets of vectors. If the texts are represented as sets of vectors X and Y, the set similarity kernel function is:

$$\kappa_{set}(X, Y) = \sum_i \sum_j \cos(\vec{x}_i, \vec{y}_j) \quad (2)$$

and normalisation is accomplished in the standard way for kernels by:

$$\kappa_{set-n}(X, Y) = \frac{\kappa_{set}(X, Y)}{\sqrt{(\kappa_{set}(X, X)\kappa_{set}(Y, Y))}} \quad (3)$$

LK - The **lexical kernel** calculates the overlap between the tokens that occur in each of the paired texts, where the tokens consist of Porter stemmed (Porter, 1980) non-stopwords. Each text is represented as a frequency vector of tokens that occur within it and the similarity between the pair is calculated using cosine.

LEK - The **lexical ESA kernel** represents each example in the pair as the set of words that do not occur in the intersection of the two texts. The similarity is calculated as in Equation (3) with X and Y being the ESA vectors of each word from the first and second text representations, respectively.

TK - The **tree kernel** representation is based on the definition by Zanzotto et al. (2011). Briefly,

[1] http://www.cs.technion.ac.il/~gabr/resources/data/wordsim353/

each piece of text is parsed[2]; the non-terminal nodes of the parse tree, stopwords, and out-of-dictionary terms are all assigned a new random vector (Equation 1); while the leaves that occurred in the BEAGLE training corpus are assigned their learned distributional vectors (Section 2.1.1).

Each subtree of a tree is encoded recursively as a vector, where the distributional vectors representing each node are combined using the circular convolution operator (Plate, 1994; Jones and Mewhort, 2007). The whole tree is represented as a set of vectors, one for each subtree.

DK - The **dependency kernel** representation encodes each dependency pair as a separate vector, discounting the labels. The non-stopword terminals are represented as their distributional vectors, while the stopwords and out-of-dictionary terms are given a unique random vector. The vector for the dependency pair is obtained via a circular convolution of the individual word vectors.

MDK - The **multiple dependency kernel** is constructed like the dependency kernel, but similarity is calculated separately between all the the pairs that share the same dependency label. The combined similarity for all dependency labels in the parse is then calculated using least squares linear regression. While at the later stage we use GPR to combine all of the different kernels, for MDK we found that linear regression provided better performance.

DGK - The **depgram kernel** represents each dependency pair as an ESA vector obtained by searching the ESA collection for the two words in the dependency pair joined by the *AND* operator. The DGK representation only contains the dependencies that occur in one similarity text or the other, but not in both.

2.3 Regression

Each of the kernel measures above is used to calculate a similarity score between a pair of texts. The different similarity scores are then combined using Gaussian process regression (GPR) (Rasmussen and Williams, 2006). GPR is a probabilistic regression method where the weights are modelled as Gaussian random variables. GPR is defined by a covariance function, which is akin to the kernel function in the support vector machine. We used the squared exponential isotropic covariance function (also known as the radial basis function):

$$cov(x_i, x_j) = p_1^2 e^{\frac{(x_i - x_j)^T \cdot (p_2 * I)^{-1} \cdot (x_i - x_j)}{2}} + p_3^2 \delta_{ij}$$

with parameters $p_1 = 1, p_2 = 1$, and $p_3 = 0.01$. We found that training for parameters increased overfitting and produced worse results in validation experiments.

3 Submitted Runs

We submitted three runs. This is not sufficient for a full evaluation of the new methods we proposed here, but it gives us an inkling of general trends. To choose the composition of the submissions, we used STS 2012 training data for training, and STS 2012 test data for validation (Agirre et al., 2012). The final submitted runs also used some of the STS 2012 test data for training.

Basic - With this run we were examining if a simple introduction of syntactic structure can improve over the baseline performance. We trained a GPR combination of the linear and tree kernels (LK-TK) on the MSRpar training data. In validation experiments we found that this data set in general gave the most consistent performance for regression training.

Custom - Here we tried to approximate the best training setup for each type of data. We only had training data for OnWN and for this dataset we were able to improve over the LK-TK setup; however, the settings for the rest of the data sets were guesses based on observations from the validation experiments and overall performed poorly. OnWN was trained on MSRpar train with LK and DK. The headlines model was trained on MSRpar train and Europarl test, with LK-LEK-TK-DK-TKND-DKND-MDK (trained on Europarl).[3] FNWN was trained on MSRpar train and OnWN test with LK-LEK-DGK-TK-DK-TKND-DKND. Finally, the SMT model

[2]Because many of the datasets contained incomplete or ungrammatical sentences, we had to approximate some parses. The parsing was done using the Stanford parser (Klein and Manning, 2003), which failed on some overly long sentences, which we therefore segmented at conjunctions or commas. Since our methods only compared subtrees of parses, we simply took the union of all the partial parses for a given sentence.

[3]TKND and DKND are the versions of the tree and dependency kernels where no distributional vectors were used.

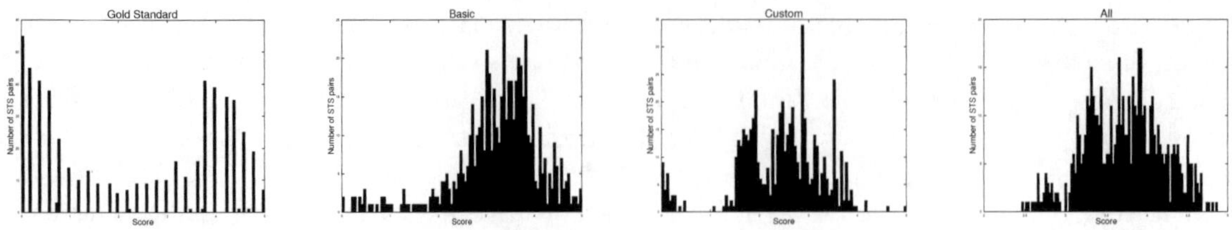

Figure 1: Score distributions of different runs on the OnWN dataset

was trained on MSRpar train and Europarl test with LK-LEK-TK-DK-TKND-DKND-MDK (trained on MSRpar).

All - As in the LK-TK experiment, we used the same model on all of the data sets. It was trained on all of the training data except MSRvid, using all eight kernel types defined above. In summary we used the LK-LEK-TK-TKND-DK-DKND-MDK-DGK kernel combination. MDK was trained on the 2012 training portion of MSRpar.

4 Discussion

From the shared task results in Table 1, we can see that Basic is our highest ranked run. It has also achieved the best performance on all data sets. The LK on its own improves slightly on the task baseline by removing stop words and using stemming, while the introduction of TK contributes syntactic and distributional information. With the Custom run, we were trying to manually estimate which training data would best reflect properties of particular test data, and to customise the kernel combination through validation experiments. The only data set for which this led to an improvement is OnWN, indicating that customised settings can be beneficial, but that a more scientific method for matching of training and test data properties is required. In the All run, we were examining the effects that maximising the amount of training data and the number of kernel measures has on the output predictions. The results show that swamping the regression with models and training data leads to overly normalised output and a decrease in performance.

	hdlns	OnWN	FNWN	SMT	mean	rank
BL	0.5399	0.2828	0.2146	0.2861	0.3639	71
Basic	0.6399	0.4440	0.3995	0.3400	0.4709	51
Cstm	0.4962	0.5639	0.1724	0.3006	0.4207	60
All	0.5510	0.3099	0.2385	0.1171	0.3200	78

Table 1: Shared task results: Pearson correlation with the gold standard

While the evaluation measure, Pearson correlation, does not take into account the shape of the output distribution, Figure 1 shows that this information may be a useful indicator of model quality and behaviour. In particular, the role of the regression component in our approach is to learn a transformation from the output distributions of the models to the distribution of the training data gold standard. This makes it sensitive to the choice of training data, which ideally would have similar characteristics to the individual kernels, as well as a similar gold standard distribution to the test data. We can see in Figure 1 that the training data and choice of kernels influence the output distribution.

Analysis of the minimum, first quartile, median, third quartile, and maximum statistics of the distributions in Figure 1 demonstrates that, while it is difficult to visually evaluate the similarities of the different distributions, the smallest squared error is between the gold standard and the Custom run. This suggests that properties other than the rank order may also be good indicators in training and testing of STS methods.

Acknowledgments

Tamara Polajnar is supported by the ERC Starting Grant, DisCoTex, awarded to Stephen Clark, and Laura Rimell and Douwe Kiela by EPSRC grant EP/I037512/1: A Unified Model of Compositional and Distributional Semantics: Theory and Applications.

References

Eneko Agirre, Daniel Cer, Mona Diab, and Aitor Gonzalez-Agirre. 2012. Semeval-2012 task 6: A pilot on semantic textual similarity. In **SEM 2012: The First Joint Conference on Lexical and Computational Semantics – Volume 1: Proceedings of the main conference and the shared task, and Volume 2: Proceedings of the Sixth International Workshop on Semantic Evaluation (SemEval 2012)*, pages 385–393, Montréal, Canada, 7-8 June. Association for Computational Linguistics.

Daniel Bär, Chris Biemann, Iryna Gurevych, and Torsten Zesch. 2012. UKP: Computing semantic textual similarity by combining multiple content similarity measures. In *Proceedings of the 6th International Workshop on Semantic Evaluation, held in conjunction with the 1st Joint Conference on Lexical and Computational Semantics*, pages 435–440, Montréal, Canada, June. Association for Computational Linguistics.

Danilo Croce, Paolo Annesi, Valerio Storch, and Roberto Basili. 2012. UNITOR: Combining semantic text similarity functions through sv regression. In *Proceedings of the 6th International Workshop on Semantic Evaluation, held in conjunction with the 1st Joint Conference on Lexical and Computational Semantics*, pages 597–602, Montréal, Canada, 7-8 June. Association for Computational Linguistics.

Evgeniy Gabrilovich and Shaul Markovitch. 2007. Computing semantic relatedness using wikipedia-based explicit semantic analysis. In *Proceedings of the 20th international joint conference on Artifical intelligence*, IJCAI'07, pages 1606–1611, San Francisco, CA, USA. Morgan Kaufmann Publishers Inc.

Thorsten Joachims. 1998. Text categorization with suport vector machines: Learning with many relevant features. In *Proceedings of the 10th European Conference on Machine Learning*, ECML '98, pages 137–142, London, UK, UK. Springer-Verlag.

Michael N. Jones and Douglas J. K. Mewhort. 2007. Representing word meaning and order information in a composite holographic lexicon. *Psychological Review*, 114:1–37.

S. Kaski. 1998. Dimensionality reduction by random mapping: fast similarity computation for clustering. In *Proceedings of the 1998 IEEE International Joint Conference on Neural Networks*, volume 1, pages 413–418 vol.1, May.

Dan Klein and Christopher D. Manning. 2003. Accurate unlexicalized parsing. In *Proceedings of the 41st Annual Meeting on Association for Computational Linguistics - Volume 1*, ACL '03, pages 423–430, Stroudsburg, PA, USA. Association for Computational Linguistics.

T. A. Plate. 1994. *Distributed Representations and Nested Compositional Structure*. Ph.D. thesis, University of Toronto.

T Polajnar, T Damoulas, and M Girolami. 2011. Protein interaction sentence detection using multiple semantic kernels. *J Biomed Semantics*, 2(1):1–1.

M. F. Porter. 1980. An algorithm for suffix stripping. *Program*, 14(3):130–137, July.

C. E. Rasmussen and C. K. I. Williams. 2006. *Gaussian Processes for Machine Learning*. MIT Press.

Stephen Robertson, Hugo Zaragoza, and Michael Taylor. 2004. Simple BM25 extension to multiple weighted fields. In *Proceedings of the thirteenth ACM international conference on Information and knowledge management*, CIKM '04, pages 42–49, New York, NY, USA. ACM.

John Shawe-Taylor and Nello Cristianini. 2004. *Kernel Methods for Pattern Analysis*. Cambridge University Press, New York, NY, USA.

Fabio Massimo Zanzotto and Lorenzo Dell'Arciprete. 2011. Distributed structures and distributional meaning. In *Proceedings of the Workshop on Distributional Semantics and Compositionality*, DiSCo '11, pages 10–15, Stroudsburg, PA, USA. Association for Computational Linguistics.

PolyUCOMP-CORE_TYPED: Computing Semantic Textual Similarity using Overlapped Senses

Jian Xu **Qin Lu**
The Hong Kong Polytechnic University
Department of Computing
Hung Hom, Kowloon, Hong Kong
{csjxu, csluqin}@comp.polyu.edu.hk

Abstract

The Semantic Textual Similarity (STS) task aims to exam the degree of semantic equivalence between sentences (Agirre et al., 2012). This paper presents the work of the Hong Kong Polytechnic University (PolyUCOMP) team which has participated in the STS core and typed tasks of SemEval-2013. For the STS core task, the PolyUCOMP system disambiguates words senses using contexts and then determine sentence similarity by counting the number of senses they shared. For the STS typed task, the string kernel (Lodhi et al., 2002) is used to compute similarity between two entities to avoid string variations in entities.

1 Introduction

Sentence similarity computation plays an important role in text summarization and social network applications (Erkan et al., 2004; Jin et al., 2011). The SemEval 2012 competition initiated a task targeted at Semantic Textual Similarity (STS) between sentence pairs (Agirre et al., 2012). Given a set of sentence pairs, participants are required to assign to each sentence pair a similarity score.

Because a sentence has only a limited amount of content words, it is difficult to determine sentence similarities. To solve this problem, Hatzivassiloglou et al. (1999) proposed to use linguistic features as indicators of text similarity to address the problem of sparse representation of sentences. Mihalcea et al. (2006) measured sentence similarity using component words in sentences. Li et al. (2006) proposed to incorporate the semantic vector and word order to calculate sentence similarity. Biemann et al. (2012) applied the log-linear regression model by combining the simple string based measures, for example, word ngrams and semantic similarity measures, for example, textual entailment. Similarly, Saric et al. (2012) used a support vector regression model which incorporates features computed from sentence pairs. The features are knowledge- and corpus-based word similarity, ngram overlaps, WordNet augmented word overlap, syntactic features and so on. Xu et al. (2012) combined semantic vectors with skip bigrams to determine sentence similarity, whereas the skip bigrams take into the sequential order between words.

In our approach to the STS task, words in sentences are assigned with appropriate senses using their contexts. Sentence similarity is computed by calculating the number of shared senses in both sentences since it is reasonable to assume that similar sentences should have more overlapping senses. For the STS-TYPED task, variations might occur in author names, people involved, time expression and location. Thus, string kernel is applied to compute similarity between entities because it can capture variations between entities. Moreover, for the event similarity in STS-TYPED task, semantic relatedness between verbs is derived the WordNet.

The rest of this paper is structured as follows. Section 2 describes sentence similarity using sense overlapping and string kernel. Section 3 gives the performance evaluation. Section 4 is the conclusion.

*Second Joint Conference on Lexical and Computational Semantics (*SEM), Volume 1: Proceedings of the Main Conference and the Shared Task*, pages 90–95, Atlanta, Georgia, June 13-14, 2013. ©2013 Association for Computational Linguistics

2 Similarity between Sentences

Words are used to convey meaning in a sentence. They are tagged with appropriate senses initially and then sentence similarity is calculated based on the number of shared senses.

2.1 Sense Overlapping

When comparing word features, we did not compare their surface equality, but we first conceptualize these words and then calculate their similarities based on the hierarchial structure in WordNet. For a word in a sentence, it will be assigned a WordNet sense. In this paper, we focus on the Word Sense Disambiguation (WSD) algorithm taken by Banerjee and Pederson (2003). They measured the semantic relatedness between concepts by counting the shared words in their WordNet glosses.

In WordNet, a word sense is represented by a synset which has a gloss that defines the concept that it represents. For example, the words *walking, afoot, ambulate* constitute a single synset which has gloss representations as follows,

walking: *the act of traveling by foot*
afoot: *traveling by foot*
ambulate: *walk about*

To lift the limitations of dictionary glosses which are fairly short with insufficient vocabulary, we utilize the glosses of related senses since we assume that words co-occur in one sentence share related senses and the more glosses two senses share, the more similar they are. Therefore, we extract not only glosses of target synset, but also the glosses of the hypernym, hyponym, meronym, holonym and troponym synsets of the target synset to form a synset context. Finally, we compare the sentence contexts with different synset contexts to determine which sense should be assigned to the words.

To disambiguate word senses, a window of contexts surrounding the the target word is specified and a set of candidate word senses are extracted for the content word (noun, verb, adjective) within that window. Let the current target word index $i = 0$ that is, w_0, the window size be $2n+1$ and $-n \leq i \leq +n$. Let $|w_i|$ be the number of senses for word w_i and the jth sense of w_i is $s_{i,j}$, where $1 \leq j \leq |w_i|$. Next is to assign an appropriate sense k to the target word. We achieve this by adding together the relatedness scores calculated by comparing the senses of the target word and senses of every non-target word within the window of context. The sense score for the current target word w_0 is defined as,

$$Sense_k = \sum_{i=-n}^{n} \sum_{j=1}^{|w_i|} relatedness(s_{0,k}, s_{i,j}) \tag{1}$$

The kth sense which has the biggest sense score will be chosen as the right sense for the target word w_0. Now remains the question of how to define the relatedness between two synsets. It is defined as,

$$\begin{aligned} relatedness(s_{0,k}, s_{i,j}) = \\ & score(gloss(s_{0,k}), gloss(s_{i,j})) \\ & +score(hype(s_{0,k}), hype(s_{i,j})) \\ & +score(hypo(s_{0,k}), hypo(s_{i,j})) \\ & +score(hype(s_{0,k}), gloss(s_{i,j})) \\ & +score(gloss(s_{0,k}), hype(s_{i,j})) \end{aligned} \tag{2}$$

In Equation 2, the score function counts the number of overlapping words between two glosses. However, if there is a phrasal n-word overlap, then a score of n^2 will be assigned, thus encouraging the longer n-word overlap. Let **V** denote the set of n-word overlaps shared between two glosses, the score is defined as,

$$score = \sum_{w \in \mathbf{V}} \|w\|^2 \tag{3}$$

where $\|w\|$ refers to the number of words in w. In so doing, we can have corresponding senses for the sentence *Castro celebrates 86th birthday Monday* as follows,

castro/10886929-n celebrate/02490877-v birthday/15250178-n monday/15163979-n

To find the n-word overlap, we found that contiguous words in two glosses lie in the diagonal of a matrix, take the senses *walk* and *afoot* for example, their glosses are,

walking: *the act of traveling by foot*
afoot: *traveling by foot*

Place the *walking* glosses in rows and *afoot* glosses in columns, we get the matrix representation in Figure 1,

		walk					
		the	act	of	traveling	by	foot
afoot	traveling				1		
	by					1	
	foot						1

Figure 1: n-word overlap representation

Figure 1 shows that *travel by foot* is a continuous sequence of words shared by two glosses. Steps to find n-word overlapping are:

(1) Construct a matrix for two sentences;

(2) Get continuous n-word overlapping, n is greater than 1;

(3) Set the cell values to 0 if they are contained in continuous n-word.

(4) Get the words (unigrams) which are shared by two sentences.

Take *a b c d* and *b c a d* for example, we will have the matrix as follows,

	b	c	a	d
a	0	0	1	0
b	**1**	0	0	0
c	0	**1**	0	0
d	0	0	0	1

Table 1: Matrix representation for two sentences

By the step 2, we will get the *b c* and its corresponding cells *cell(1,0)* and *cell(2,1)*. We then set the two cells to zero, and obtain an updated matrix as follows,

	b	c	a	d
a	0	0	1	0
b	**0**	0	0	0
c	0	**0**	0	0
d	0	0	0	1

Table 2: Updated matrix representation for two sentences

In Table 2, we found that *cell(0,2)* and *cell(3,3)* have values greater than zero. Therefore, a and b will be extracted the common terms.

This approach can also be applied to find common n-word overlaps between sentences, for example,

s_1: *Olli Heinonen, the Head of the International Atomic Energy Agency delegation to Iran, declared yesterday that the agency has reached an agreement with Tehran on the method of conducting the negotiations pertaining to its nuclear program.*

s_2: *leader of international atomic energy agency delegation to iran , olli heinonen said yesterday , that the agency concluded a mutual understanding with tehran on the way to manage talks depending upon its atomic program .*

We will have ngrams with n ranging from 1 to 7, such as,

unigram: *of, to, its, program, yesterday*

bigram: *olli heinonen*

trigram: *that the agency*

four-gram: *with tehran on the*

seven-gram: *international atomic energy agency delegation to iran*

Similarity between two sentences is calculated by counting the number of overlapped n-words. The similarity for s_1 and s_2 is, $(1+1+1+1+1)+(2)^2+(3)^2+(4)^2+(7)^2 = 83$.

2.2 String kernel

For the STS-TYPED task, when comparing whether people or authors are similar or not, we found that some entity mentions may have tiny variations, for example,

E Vincent Harris and *E.Vincent Harris*

The difference between the entities lies in fact that the second entity has one more dot. In this case, string kernel would be a good choice in verifying they are similar or not. If we consider n=2, we obtain 79-dimensional feature space where the two entities are mapped in Table 3.

In Table 3, λ is the decay factor, in the range of [0,1], that penalizes the longer distance of a subsequence. Formally, string kernel is defined as,

$$K_n(s,t) = \sum_{u \in \sum^n} \langle \phi_u(s) \cdot \phi_u(t) \rangle \qquad (4)$$

	ev	ei	en	$\cdots$	e.	$\cdots$	rs	is
$\phi(evincentharris)$	λ^2	$\lambda^3+\lambda^{13}$	$\lambda^2+\lambda^4+\lambda^7$	$\cdots$	0	$\cdots$	$\lambda^3+\lambda^4$	$\lambda^2+\lambda^{12}$
$\phi(e.vincentharris)$	λ^3	$\lambda^4+\lambda^{14}$	$\lambda^2+\lambda^5+\lambda^8$	$\cdots$	λ^2	$\cdots$	$\lambda^3+\lambda^4$	$\lambda^2+\lambda^{12}$

Table 3: Feature mapping for two entities

TEAM	headlines	OnWN	FNWN	SMT	mean	rank
RUN1	0.5176	0.1517	0.2496	0.2914	0.3284	77

Table 4: Experimental results for STS-CORE

where $\sum^n$ is the set of all possible subsequences of length n. u indicates an item in the set, for example, the subsequence ev in Table 3. $\phi_u(s)$ is the feature mapping of the subsequences in s. In so doing, we can have similarity between entities in Table 3 as follows:

$$K_n(s,t) = \lambda^2 \times \lambda^3 + (\lambda^3+\lambda^{13}) \times (\lambda^4+\lambda^{14}) + \cdots + (\lambda^3+\lambda^4) \times (\lambda^3+\lambda^4) + (\lambda^2+\lambda^{12}) \times (\lambda^2+\lambda^{12})$$

To avoid enumeration of all subsequences for similarity measurement, dynamic programming, similar to the method by Lodhi et al. (2002) is used here for similarity calculation.

3 Experiments

The STS-CORE task is to quantify how similar two sentences are. We simply use the sense overlapping approach to compute the similarity. Since this approach needs to find appropriate senses for each word based on its contexts. The number of contextual words is set to 5. Experiments are conducted on four datasets. They are: headlines mined from news sources by European Media, OnWN extracted from from WordNet and OntoNotes, FNWN from WordNet and FrameNet and SMT dataset from DARPA GALE HTER and HyTER. The results of our system (PolyUCOMP-RUN1) are given in Table 4 ,

Our system achieves rather lower performance in the OnWN and FNWN datasets. This is because it is difficult to use contextual terms to find the correct senses for words in sentences of these two datasets. Take the two sentences in OnWN dataset for example,

s_1: *the act of choosing among alternatives*

s_2: *the act of changing one thing for another thing.*

The valid concepts for the two sentences are:

c_1: *06532095-n 05790944-n*

c_2: *00030358-n 00126264-v 00002452-n 00002452-n*

c_1 and c_2 have no shared senses, resulting in a zero similarity between s_1 and s_2. However, s_1 and s_2 should have the same meaning. Moreover, in the FNWN dataset, the sentence lengths are unbalanced, for example,

s_1: *there exist a number of different possible events that may happen in the future. in most cases, there is an agent involved who has to consider which of the possible events will or should occur. a salient entity which is deeply involved in the event may also be mentioned.*

s_2: *doing as one pleases or chooses;*

s_1 has 48 tokens with punctuations being excluded and s_2 has only 6 tokens. This would affect our system performance as well.

For the STS-TYPED task, data set is taken from Europeana, which provides millions of books, paintings, films, museum objects and archival records that have been digitised throughout Europe. Each item has one line per type, where the type can be the title of a record, list of subject terms, textual description of the record, creator of the record and date of the record. Participating systems are supposed to compute similarities between semi-structured items. In this task, we take the strategies in Table 5,

$Jaccard$ denotes the Jaccard similarity measure. $Stringkernel + Jaccard$ means that two types are similar if they share many terms, for example,

TEAM	general	author	people	time	location	event	subject	description	mean	rank
RUN1	0.4888	0.6940	0.3223	0.3820	0.3621	0.1625	0.3962	0.4816	0.4112	12
RUN2	0.4893	0.6940	0.3253	0.3777	0.3628	0.1968	0.3962	0.4816	0.4155	11
RUN3	0.4915	0.6940	0.3254	0.3737	0.3667	0.2207	0.3962	0.4816	0.4187	10

Table 6: Experimental results for STS-TYPED

Type	Strategy
author	String kernel
people	String kernel + Jaccard
time	String kernel + Jaccard
location	String kernel + Jaccard
event	WordNet + Jaccard
subject	Sense overlapping
description	Sense overlapping

Table 5: Strategies for computing similarity

location; and string kernel is used to determine whether two locations are similar or not. For the type of event, we extract verbs from records and count the number of shared verbs between two records. The verb similarity is obtained through WordNet. The general similarity is equal to the average of the 7 scores. Also, Stanford CoreNLP tool[1] is used to extract author, date, time, location and handle part-of-speech tagging.

In this STS-TYPED task, we use string kernel and WordNet to determine whether two terms are similar and increase the number of counts if their similarity exceeds a certain threshold. Therefore, we have chosen 0.4, 0.5 and 0.6 in a heuristic manner and obtained three different runs. Experimental results are given in Table 6.

Since the types of $author$, $subject$ and $description$ are not related to either string kernel or WordNet, their performances remain unchanged during three runs.

4 Conclusions and Future Work

In the Semantic Textual Similarity task of SemEval-2013, to capture the meaning between sentences, we proposed to disambiguate word senses using contexts and then determine sentence similarity by counting the senses they shared. First, word senses are disambiguated by means of the contextual words. When determining similarity between two senses (synsets), n-word overlapping approach is used for counting the number of shared words in two glosses. Besides, string kernel is used to capture similarity between entities to avoid variations between entities. Our approach is simple and we will apply regression models to determine sentence similarity on the basis of these features in future work.

[1] http://nlp.stanford.edu/software/corenlp.shtml

References

Daniel B., Chris Biemann, Iryna Gurevych and Torsten Zesch. 2012. UKP: Computing Semantic Textual Similarity by Combining Multiple Content Similarity Measures. *Proceedings of the 6th International Workshop on Semantic Evaluation (SemEval 2012), in conjunction with the First Joint Conference on Lexical and Computational Semantics (*SEM 2012).*

Eneko Agirre, Daniel Cer, Mona Diab, and Aitor Gonzalez-Agirre. 2012. SemEval-2012 Task 6: A Pilot on Semantic Textual Similarity. *Proceedings of the 6th International Workshop on Semantic Evaluation (SemEval 2012), in conjunction with the First Joint Conference on Lexical and Computational Semantics (*SEM 2012).*

Frane Saric, Goran Glavas, Mladen Karan, Jan Snajder and Bojana Dalbelo Basia. 2012. TakeLab: Systems for Measuring Semantic Text Similarity. *Proceedings of the 6th International Workshop on Semantic Evaluation (SemEval 2012), in conjunction with the First Joint Conference on Lexical and Computational Semantics (*SEM 2012).*

Gunes Erkan and Dragomir R. Radev. 2004. Lexrank: Graph-based Lexical Centrality as Salience in Text Summarization. *Journal of Artificial Intelligence Research*, 22(2004):457–479.

Huma Lodhi, Craig Saunders, John Shawe-Taylor, Nello Cristianini, and Chris Watkins. 2002. Text Classification using String Kernels. *The Journal of Machine Learning Research*, 2(2002):419–444.

Jian Xu, Qin Lu and Zhengzhong Liu. 2012. PolyUCOMP: Combining Semantic Vectors with Skip-bigrams for Semantic Textual Similarity.

*Proceedings of the 6th International Workshop on Semantic Evaluation (SemEval 2012), in conjunction with the First Joint Conference on Lexical and Computational Semantics (*SEM 2012).*

Ou Jin, Nathan Nan Liu, Yong Yu and Qiang Yang 2011. Transferring Topical Knowledge from Auxiliary Long Text for Short Text Understanding. *Proceedings of the 20th ACM Conference on Information and Knowledge Management (ACM CIKM 2011).*

Rada Mihalcea and Courtney Corley. 2006. Corpusbased and Knowledge-based Measures of Text Semantic Similarity. *Proceeding of the Twenty-First National Conference on Artificial Intelligence and the Eighteenth Innovative Applications of Artificial Intelligence Conference..*

Satanjeev Banerjee and Ted Pedersen. 2003. Extended Gloss Overlaps as a Measure of Semantic Relatedness. *Proceedings of the 18th International Joint Conference on Artificial Intelligence.*

Vasileios Hatzivassiloglou, Judith L. Klavans , Eleazar Eskin. 1999. Detecting Text Similarity over Short Passages: Exploring Linguistic Feature Combinations via Machine Learning. *Proceeding of Empirical Methods in natural language processing and Very Large Corpora.*

Yuhua Li, David Mclean, Zuhair B, James D. O'shea and Keeley Crockett. 2006. Sentence Similarity Based on Semantic Nets and Corpus Statistics. *IEEE Transactions on Knowledge and Data Engineering*, 18(8):1138–1149.

HENRY-CORE: Domain Adaptation and Stacking for Text Similarity*

Michael Heilman and **Nitin Madnani**
Educational Testing Service
660 Rosedale Road
Princeton, NJ 08541, USA
{mheilman,nmadnani}@ets.org

Abstract

This paper describes a system for automatically measuring the semantic similarity between two texts, which was the aim of the 2013 Semantic Textual Similarity (STS) task (Agirre et al., 2013). For the 2012 STS task, Heilman and Madnani (2012) submitted the PERP system, which performed competitively in relation to other submissions. However, approaches including word and n-gram features also performed well (Bär et al., 2012; Šarić et al., 2012), and the 2013 STS task focused more on predicting similarity for text pairs from new domains. Therefore, for the three variations of our system that we were allowed to submit, we used stacking (Wolpert, 1992) to combine PERP with word and n-gram features and applied the domain adaptation approach outlined by Daume III (2007) to facilitate generalization to new domains. Our submissions performed well at most subtasks, particularly at measuring the similarity of news headlines, where one of our submissions ranked 2nd among 89 from 34 teams, but there is still room for improvement.

1 Introduction

We aim to develop an automatic measure of the semantic similarity between two short texts (e.g., sentences). Such a measure could be useful for various applications, including automated short answer scoring (Leacock and Chodorow, 2003; Nielsen et al., 2008), question answering (Wang et al., 2007), and machine translation evaluation (Przybocki et al., 2009).

In this paper, we describe our submissions to the 2013 Semantic Textual Similarity (STS) task (Agirre et al., 2013), which evaluated implementations of text-to-text similarity measures. Submissions were evaluated according to Pearson correlations between gold standard similarity values acquired from human raters and machine-produced similarity values. Teams were allowed to submit up to three submissions. For each submission, correlations were calculated separately for four subtasks: measuring similarity between news headlines ("headlines"), between machine translation outputs and human reference translations ("SMT"), between word glosses from OntoNotes (Pradhan and Xue, 2009) and WordNet (Fellbaum, 1998) ("OnWN"), and between frame descriptions from FrameNet (Fillmore et al., 2003) and glosses from WordNet ("FNWN"). A weighted mean of the correlations was also computed as an overall evaluation metric (the OnWn and FNWN datasets were smaller than the headlines and SMT datasets).

The suggested training data for the 2013 STS task was the data from the 2012 STS task (Agirre et al., 2012), including both the training and test sets for that year. The 2012 task was similar except that the data were from a different set of subtasks: measuring similarity between sentences from the Microsoft Research Paraphrase corpus (Dolan et al., 2004) ("MSRpar"), between sentences from the Microsoft Research Video Description corpus (Chen and Dolan, 2011) ("MSRvid"), and between human and machine translations of parliamentary

* System description papers for this task were required to have a team ID and task ID (e.g., "HENRY-CORE") as a prefix.

*Second Joint Conference on Lexical and Computational Semantics (*SEM), Volume 1: Proceedings of the Main Conference and the Shared Task*, pages 96–102, Atlanta, Georgia, June 13-14, 2013. ©2013 Association for Computational Linguistics

proceedings ("SMTeuroparl"). The 2012 task provided training and test sets for those three subtasks and also included two additional tasks with just test sets: a similar OnWN task, and measuring similarity between human and machine translations of news broadcasts ("SMTnews").

Heilman and Madnani (2012) described the PERP system and submitted it to the 2012 STS task. PERP measures the similarity of a sentence pair by finding a sequence of edit operations (e.g., insertions, deletions, substitutions, and shifts) that converts one sentence to the other. It then uses various features of the edits, with weights learned from labeled sentence pairs, to assign a similarity score. PERP performed well, ranking 7th out of 88 submissions from 35 teams according to the weighted mean correlation. However, PERP lacked some of the useful word and n-gram overlap features included in some of the other top-performing submissions. In addition, domain adaptation seemed more relevant for the STS 2013 task since in-domain data was available only for one (OnWN) of the four subtasks.

Therefore, in this work, we combine the PERP system with various word and n-gram features. We also apply the domain adaptation technique of Daume III (2007) to support generalization beyond the domains in the training data.

2 System Details

In this section, we describe the system we developed, and the variations of it that comprise our submissions to the 2013 STS task.

Our system is a linear model estimated using ridge regression, as implemented in the scikit-learn toolkit (Pedregosa et al., 2011). The system uses a 5-fold cross-validation grid search to tune the α penalty for ridge regression (with $\alpha \in 2^{\{-5,-4,\ldots,4\}}$). During development, we evaluated its performance on the full STS 2012 data (training and test) using 10-fold cross-validation, with the 5-fold cross-validation being used to tune within each training partition.

2.1 Features

Our full system uses the following features computed from an input sentence pair (s_1, s_2).

The system standardizes feature values to zero mean and unit variance by subtracting the feature's mean and dividing by its standard deviation. The means and standard deviations are estimated from the training set, or from each training partition during cross-validation.

2.1.1 n-gram Overlap Features

The system computes Jaccard similarity (i.e., the ratio of the sizes of the set intersection to the set union) for the following overlap features:

- character n-gram overlap ($n = 1 \ldots 12$). Note that this is computed from the entire original texts for a pair, including punctuation, whitespace, etc.
- word n-gram overlap ($n = 2 \ldots 8$). We do not include $n = 1$ here because it would be identical to the $n = 1$ version for the unordered word n-gram feature described next.
- unordered word n-gram overlap features ($n = 1 \ldots 3$). By unordered, we mean combinations (in the mathematical sense of "combinations") of word tokens, regardless of order. Note that these features are similar to the word n-gram overlap features except that the words need not be contiguous to match. For example, the text "John saw Mary" would result in the following unordered word n-grams: {*john*}, {*mary*}, {*saw*}, {*john, saw*}, {*mary, saw*}, {*john, mary*}, and {*john, mary, saw*}.

For the word and unordered n-gram overlap features, we computed two variants: one based on all tokens and one based on just content words, which we define as words that are not punctuation and do not appear in the NLTK (Bird et al., 2009) English stopword list. We lowercase everything for the word overlap measures but not for character overlap.

2.1.2 Length Features

The system includes various length-related features, where $L_{max} = \max(\text{length}(s_1), \text{length}(s_2))$, $L_{min} = \min(\text{length}(s_1), \text{length}(s_2))$, and $\text{length}(x)$ denotes the number of tokens in x. log denotes the natural logarithm.

- $\log(\frac{L_{max}}{L_{min}})$
- $\frac{L_{max} - L_{min}}{L_{max}}$

- $\log(\mathrm{L}_{min})$
- $\log(\mathrm{L}_{max})$
- $\log(|\mathrm{L}_{max} - \mathrm{L}_{min}| + 1)$

2.1.3 Sentiment Features

The system includes various features based on the proprietary sentiment lexicon described by Beigman Klebanov et al. (2012). Each word in this lexicon is associated with a 3-tuple specifying a distribution over three classes: positive, negative, and neutral. These distributions were estimated via crowdsourcing. If a word is not in the lexicon, we assume its positivity and negativity are zero.

We define the set of sentiment words in a sentence s as $\sigma(s) = \{w : \text{positivity}(w) > 0.5 \vee \text{negativity}(w) > 0.5\}$. We also define the positivity, negativity, and neutrality of a sentence as the sum over the corresponding values of individual words w. For example, $\text{positivity}(s) = \sum_{w \in s} \text{positivity}(w)$.

The system includes the following features:

- $\frac{\sigma(s_1) \cap \sigma(s_2)}{\sigma(s_1) \cup \sigma(s_2)}$ (i.e., the Jaccard similarity of the sentiment words)
- The cosine distance between $(\text{positivity}(s_1), \text{negativity}(s_1))$ and $(\text{positivity}(s_2), \text{negativity}(s_2))$
- $|\text{positivity}(s_1) - \text{positivity}(s_2)|$
- $|\text{negativity}(s_1) - \text{negativity}(s_2)|$
- $|\text{neutrality}(s_1) - \text{neutrality}(s_2)|$

2.1.4 PERP with Stacking

The system also incorporates the PERP system (Heilman and Madnani, 2012) (as briefly described in §1) as a feature in its model by using 10-fold stacking (Wolpert, 1992). Stacking is a procedure similar to k-fold cross-validation that allows one to use the output of one model as the input to another model, without requiring multiple training sets. A PERP model is iteratively trained on nine folds and then the PERP feature is computed for the tenth, producing PERP features for the whole training set, which are then used in the final regression model.

We trained PERP in a general manner using data from all the STS 2012 subtasks rather than training subtask-specific models. PERP was trained for 100 iterations.

We refer readers to Heilman and Madnani (2012) for a full description of PERP. Next, we provide details about modifications made to PERP since STS 2012. Although these details are not necessary to understand how the system works in general, we include them here for completeness.

- We extended PERP to model abbreviations as zero cost edits, using a list of common abbreviations extracted from Wikipedia.[1]
- In a similar vein, we also extended PERP to model multiword sequences with differing punctuation (e.g., "Built-In Test" → "Built In Test") as zero cost edits.
- We changed the stemming and synonymy edits in the original PERP (Heilman and Madnani, 2012) to be substitution edits that activate additional stemming and synonymy indicator features.
- We added an incentive to TERp's (Snover et al., 2009) original inference algorithm to prefer matching words when searching for a good edit sequence. We added this to avoid rare cases where other edits would have a negative costs, and then the same word in a sentence pair would be, for example inserted and deleted rather than matched.
- We fixed a minor bug in the inference algorithm, which appeared to only affect results on the MSRvid subtask in the STS 2012 task.
- We tweaked the learning algorithm by increasing the learning rate and not performing weight averaging.

2.2 Domain Adaptation

The system also uses the domain adaptation technique described by Daume III (2007) to facilitate generalization to new domains. Instead of having a single weight for each of the features described above, the system maintains a generic and a subtask-specific copy. For example, the content bigram overlap feature had six copies: a generic copy and one for each of the five subtasks in the training data from

[1] `http://en.wikipedia.org/wiki/List_of_acronyms_and_initialisms`, downloaded April 27, 2012

STS 2012 (i.e., OnWN, MSRpar, MSRvid, SMTeuroparl, SMTnews). And then for an instance from MSRpar, only the generic and MSRpar-specific versions of the feature will be active. For an instance from a new subtask (e.g., a test set instance), only the generic feature will be active.

We also included a generic intercept feature and intercept features for each subtask (these always had a value of 1). These help the model capture, for example, whether high or low similarities are more frequent in general, without having to use the other feature weights to do so.

2.3 Submissions

We submitted three variations of the system.

- **Run 1**: This run used all the features described above. In addition, we mapped the test subtasks to the training subtasks as follows so that the specific features would be active for test data from previously unseen but related subtasks: headlines to MSRpar, SMT to SMTnews, and FNWN to OnWN.
- **Run 2**: As in Run 1, this run used all the features described above. However, we did not map the STS 2013 subtasks to STS 2012 subtasks. Thus, the specific copies of features were only active for OnWN test set examples.
- **Run 3**: This run used all the features except for the PERP and sentiment features. Like Run 2, this run did not map subtasks.

3 Results

This section presents results on the STS 2012 data (our development set) and results for our submissions to STS 2013.

3.1 STS 2012 (development set)

Although we used cross-validation on the entire STS 2012 dataset during preliminary experiments (§2), in this section, we train the system on the original STS 2012 training set and report performance on the original STS 2012 test set, in order to facilitate comparison to submissions to that task. It is important to note that our system's results here may be somewhat optimistic since we had access to the STS 2012 test data and were using it for development, whereas the participants in the 2012 task only had access to the training data.

Table 1 presents the results. We include the results for our three submissions, the results for the top-ranked submission according to the weighted mean ("UKP"), the results for the best submission from Heilman and Madnani (2012) ("PERPphrases"), and the mean across all submissions. Note that while we compare to the PERP submission from Heilman and Madnani (2012), the results are not directly comparable since the version of PERP is not the same and since PERP was trained differently.

For Run 1 on the STS 2012 data, we mapped OnWN to MSRpar, and SMTnews to SMTeuroparl, similar to Heilman and Madnani (2012).

3.2 STS 2013 (unseen test set)

Table 2 presents results for our submissions to the 2013 STS task. We include results for our three submissions, results for the top-ranked submission according to the weighted mean, results for the baseline provided by the task organizers, and the mean across all submissions and the baseline from the organizers.[2]

Note that while our Run 2 submission outperformed the top-ranked UMBC submission on the headlines subtask, as shown in 2, there was another UMBC submission that performed better than Run 2 for the headlines subtask.

4 Discussion

The weighted mean correlation across tasks for our submissions was relatively poor compared to the top-ranked systems for STS 2013: our Run 1, Run 2, and Run 3 submissions beat the baseline and ranked 41st, 26th, and 48th, respectively, out of 89 submissions.

The primary reason for this result is that performance of our submissions was poor for the OnWN subtask, where, e.g., our Run 2 submission's correlation was $r = .4631$, compared to $r = .8431$ for the top-ranked submission for that subtask ("deft-baseline"). Upon investigation, we found that OnWN training and test data were very different in terms of their score distributions. The mean gold

[2]The STS 2013 results are from http://ixa2.si.ehu.es/sts/.

Submission	MSRpar	MSRvid	SMTeuroparl	OnWN	SMTnews	W. Mean
Run 1	.6461	.8060	.5014	.7073	.4876	.6577
Run 2	.6461	.8060	.5014	.7274	.4744	.6609
Run 3	.6369	.7904	.5101	.7010	.4985	.6529
UKP (top-ranked)	.6830	.8739	.5280	.6641	.4937	.6773
PERPphrases	.6397	.7200	.4850	.7124	.5312	.6399
mean-2012	.4894	.7049	.3958	.5557	.3731	.5286

Table 1: Pearson correlations for STS 2012 data for each subtask and then the weighted mean across subtasks. "UKP" was submitted by Bär et al. (2012), "PERPphrases" was submitted by Heilman and Madnani (2012), and "mean-2012" is the mean of all submissions to STS 2012.

Submission	headlines	OnWN	FNWN	SMT	W. Mean
Run 1	.7601	.4631	.3516	.2801	.4917
Run 2	.7645	.4631	.3905	.3593	.5229
Run 3	.7103	.3934	.3364	.3308	.4734
UMBC (top-ranked)	.7642	.7529	.5818	.3804	.6181
baseline	.5399	.2828	.2146	.2861	.3639
mean-2013	.6022	.5042	.2887	.2989	.4503

Table 2: Pearson correlations for STS 2013 data for each subtask and then the weighted mean across subtasks. "UMBC" = "UMBC_EBIQUITY-ParingWords", and "mean-2013" is the mean of the submissions to STS 2013 and the baseline.

standard similarity value for the STS 2012 OnWN data was 3.87 (with a standard deviation of 1.02), while the mean for the 2013 OnWN data was 2.31 (with a standard deviation of 1.76). We speculate that our system performed relatively poorly because it was expecting the OnWN data to include many highly similar sentences (as in the 2012 data). We hypothesize that incorporating more detailed WordNet information (only the PERP feature used WordNet, and only in a limited fashion, to check synonymy) and task-specific features for comparing definitions might have helped performance for the OnWN subtask.

If we ignore the definition comparison subtasks, and consider performance on just the headlines and SMT subtasks, the system performed quite well. Our Run 2 submission had a mean correlation of $r = .5619$ for those two subtasks, which would rank 5th among all submissions.

We have not fully explored the effects on performance of the domain adaptation approach used in the system, but our approach of mapping tasks used for our Run 1 submission did not seem to help. It seems better to keep a general model, as in Runs 2 and 3.

Additionally, we observe that the performance of Run 3, which did not use the PERP and sentiment features, was relatively good compared to Runs 1 and 2, which used all the features. This indicates that if speed and implementation simplicity are important concerns for an application, it may suffice to use relatively simple overlap and length features to measure semantic similarity.

The contribution of domain adaptation is not clear. Mapping novel subtasks to tasks for which training data is available (§2.3), in combination with the domain adaptation technique we used, did not generally improve performance. However, we leave to future work a detailed analysis of whether the domain adaptation approach (without mapping) is better than simply training a separate system for each subtask and using out-of-domain data when in-domain data is unavailable.

5 Conclusion

In this paper, we described a system for predicting the semantic similarity of two short texts. The system uses stacking to combine a trained edit-based similarity model (Heilman and Madnani, 2012) with simple features such as word and n-gram overlap, and it uses the technique described by Daume III (2007) to support generalization to domains not represented in the training data. We also presented evaluation results, using data from the STS 2012 and STS 2013 shared tasks, that indicate that the system performs competitively relative to other approaches for many tasks. In particular, we observed very good performance on the news headline similarity and MT evaluation subtasks of the STS 2013 shared task.

Acknowledgments

We would like to thank the STS 2013 task organizers for facilitating this research and Dan Blanchard for helping with scikit-learn.

References

Eneko Agirre, Daniel Cer, Mona Diab, and Aitor Gonzalez-Agirre. 2012. Semeval-2012 task 6: A pilot on semantic textual similarity. In **SEM 2012: The First Joint Conference on Lexical and Computational Semantics – Volume 1: Proceedings of the main conference and the shared task, and Volume 2: Proceedings of the Sixth International Workshop on Semantic Evaluation (SemEval 2012)*, pages 385–393, Montréal, Canada, 7-8 June. Association for Computational Linguistics.

Eneko Agirre, Daniel Cer, Mona Diab, Aitor Gonzalez-Agirre, and Weiwei Guo. 2013. *sem 2013 shared task: Semantic textual similarity, including a pilot on typed-similarity. In **SEM 2013: The Second Joint Conference on Lexical and Computational Semantics*. Association for Computational Linguistics.

Daniel Bär, Chris Biemann, Iryna Gurevych, and Torsten Zesch. 2012. UKP: Computing semantic textual similarity by combining multiple content similarity measures. In **SEM 2012: The First Joint Conference on Lexical and Computational Semantics – Volume 1: Proceedings of the main conference and the shared task, and Volume 2: Proceedings of the Sixth International Workshop on Semantic Evaluation (SemEval 2012)*, pages 435–440, Montréal, Canada, 7-8 June. Association for Computational Linguistics.

Beata Beigman Klebanov, Jill Burstein, Nitin Madnani, Adam Faulkner, and Joel Tetreault. 2012. Building sentiment lexicon(s) from scratch for essay data. In *Proceedings of the 13th International Conference on Intelligent Text Processing and Computational Linguistics (CICLing)*, New Delhi, India, March.

S. Bird, E. Klein, and E. Loper. 2009. *Natural Language Processing with Python*. O'Reilly Media.

David Chen and William Dolan. 2011. Collecting highly parallel data for paraphrase evaluation. In *Proceedings of the 49th Annual Meeting of the Association for Computational Linguistics: Human Language Technologies*, pages 190–200, Portland, Oregon, USA, June. Association for Computational Linguistics.

Hal Daume III. 2007. Frustratingly easy domain adaptation. In *Proceedings of the 45th Annual Meeting of the Association of Computational Linguistics*, pages 256–263, Prague, Czech Republic, June. Association for Computational Linguistics.

Bill Dolan, Chris Quirk, and Chris Brockett. 2004. Unsupervised construction of large paraphrase corpora: Exploiting massively parallel news sources. In *Proceedings of Coling 2004*, pages 350–356, Geneva, Switzerland, Aug 23–Aug 27. COLING.

C. Fellbaum. 1998. *WordNet: An Electronic Lexical Database*. Bradford Books.

Charles J. Fillmore, Christopher R. Johnson, and Miriam R.L. Petruck. 2003. Background to Framenet. *International Journal of Lexicography*, 16(3):235–250.

Michael Heilman and Nitin Madnani. 2012. ETS: Discriminative edit models for paraphrase scoring. In **SEM 2012: The First Joint Conference on Lexical and Computational Semantics – Volume 1: Proceedings of the main conference and the shared task, and Volume 2: Proceedings of the Sixth International Workshop on Semantic Evaluation (SemEval 2012)*, pages 529–535, Montréal, Canada, 7-8 June. Association for Computational Linguistics.

C. Leacock and M. Chodorow. 2003. c-rater: Scoring of short-answer questions. *Computers and the Humanities*, 37.

Rodney D. Nielsen, Wayne Ward, and James H. Martin. 2008. Classification errors in a domain-independent assessment system. In *Proceedings of the Third Workshop on Innovative Use of NLP for Building Educational Applications*, pages 10–18, Columbus, Ohio, June. Association for Computational Linguistics.

F. Pedregosa, G. Varoquaux, A. Gramfort, V. Michel, B. Thirion, O. Grisel, M. Blondel, P. Prettenhofer, R. Weiss, V. Dubourg, J. Vanderplas, A. Passos, D. Cournapeau, M. Brucher, M. Perrot, and E. Duchesnay. 2011. Scikit-learn: Machine learning in Python. *Journal of Machine Learning Research*, 12:2825–2830.

S. S. Pradhan and N. Xue. 2009. OntoNotes: The 90% solution. In *Proceedings of Human Language Technologies: The 2009 Annual Conference of the North*

American Chapter of the Association for Computational Linguistics, Companion Volume: Tutorial Abstracts, pages 11–12.

M. A. Przybocki, K. Peterson, S. Bronsart, and G. A. Sanders. 2009. The NIST 2008 metrics for machine translation challenge - overview, methodology, metrics, and results. *Machine Translation*, 23(2-3):71–103.

Matthew G. Snover, Nitin Madnani, Bonnie Dorr, and Richard Schwartz. 2009. TER-Plus: Paraphrase, semantic, and alignment enhancements to translation edit rate. *Machine Translation*, 23(2-3):117–127, September.

Frane Šarić, Goran Glavaš, Mladen Karan, Jan Šnajder, and Bojana Dalbelo Bašić. 2012. TakeLab: Systems for measuring semantic text similarity. In **SEM 2012: The First Joint Conference on Lexical and Computational Semantics – Volume 1: Proceedings of the main conference and the shared task, and Volume 2: Proceedings of the Sixth International Workshop on Semantic Evaluation (SemEval 2012)*, pages 441–448, Montréal, Canada, 7-8 June. Association for Computational Linguistics.

Mengqiu Wang, Noah A. Smith, and Teruko Mitamura. 2007. What is the Jeopardy model? a quasi-synchronous grammar for QA. In *Proceedings of the 2007 Joint Conference on Empirical Methods in Natural Language Processing and Computational Natural Language Learning (EMNLP-CoNLL)*, pages 22–32, Prague, Czech Republic, June. Association for Computational Linguistics.

David H. Wolpert. 1992. Stacked generalization. *Neural Networks*, 5:241–259.

DeepPurple: Lexical, String and Affective Feature Fusion for Sentence-Level Semantic Similarity Estimation

Nikolaos Malandrakis[1], **Elias Iosif**[2], **Vassiliki Prokopi**[2], **Alexandros Potamianos**[2], **Shrikanth Narayanan**[1]

[1]Signal Analysis and Interpretation Laboratory (SAIL), USC, Los Angeles, CA 90089, USA
[2]Department of ECE, Technical University of Crete, 73100 Chania, Greece
malandra@usc.edu, iosife@telecom.tuc.gr, vprokopi@isc.tuc.gr, potam@telecom.tuc.gr, shri@sipi.usc.edu

Abstract

This paper describes our submission for the *SEM shared task of Semantic Textual Similarity. We estimate the semantic similarity between two sentences using regression models with features: 1) n-gram hit rates (lexical matches) between sentences, 2) lexical semantic similarity between non-matching words, 3) string similarity metrics, 4) affective content similarity and 5) sentence length. Domain adaptation is applied in the form of independent models and a model selection strategy achieving a mean correlation of 0.47.

1 Introduction

Text semantic similarity estimation has been an active research area, thanks to a variety of potential applications and the wide availability of data afforded by the world wide web. Semantic textual similarity (STS) estimates can be used for information extraction (Szpektor and Dagan, 2008), question answering (Harabagiu and Hickl, 2006) and machine translation (Mirkin et al., 2009). Term-level similarity has been successfully applied to problems like grammar induction (Meng and Siu, 2002) and affective text categorization (Malandrakis et al., 2011). In this work, we built on previous research and our submission to SemEval'2012 (Malandrakis et al., 2012) to create a sentence-level STS model for the shared task of *SEM 2013 (Agirre et al., 2013).

Semantic similarity between words has been well researched, with a variety of knowledge-based (Miller, 1990; Budanitsky and Hirst, 2006) and corpus-based (Baroni and Lenci, 2010; Iosif and Potamianos, 2010) metrics proposed. Moving to sentences increases the complexity exponentially and as a result has led to measurements of similarity at various levels: lexical (Malakasiotis and Androutsopoulos, 2007), syntactic (Malakasiotis, 2009; Zanzotto et al., 2009), and semantic (Rinaldi et al., 2003; Bos and Markert, 2005). Machine translation evaluation metrics can be used to estimate lexical level similarity (Finch et al., 2005; Perez and Alfonseca, 2005), including BLEU (Papineni et al., 2002), a metric using word n-gram hit rates. The pilot task of sentence STS in SemEval 2012 (Agirre et al., 2012) showed a similar trend towards multi-level similarity, with the top performing systems utilizing large amounts of partial similarity metrics and domain adaptation (the use of separate models for each input domain) (Bär et al., 2012; Šarić et al., 2012).

Our approach is originally motivated by BLEU and primarily utilizes "hard" and "soft" n-gram hit rates to estimate similarity. Compared to last year, we utilize different alignment strategies (to decide which n-grams should be compared with which). We also include string similarities (at the token and character level) and similarity of affective content, expressed through the difference in sentence arousal and valence ratings. Finally we added domain adaptation: the creation of separate models per domain and a strategy to select the most appropriate model.

2 Model

Our model is based upon that submitted for the same task in 2012 (Malandrakis et al., 2012). To estimate semantic similarity metrics we use a supervised model with features extracted using corpus-

*Second Joint Conference on Lexical and Computational Semantics (*SEM), Volume 1: Proceedings of the Main Conference and the Shared Task*, pages 103–108, Atlanta, Georgia, June 13-14, 2013.

based word-level similarity metrics. To combine these metrics into a sentence-level similarity score we use a modification of BLEU (Papineni et al., 2002) that utilizes word-level semantic similarities, string level comparisons and comparisons of affective content, detailed below.

2.1 Word level semantic similarity

Co-occurrence-based. The semantic similarity between two words, w_i and w_j, is estimated as their pointwise mutual information (Church and Hanks, 1990): $I(i,j) = \log \frac{\hat{p}(i,j)}{\hat{p}(i)\hat{p}(j)}$, where $\hat{p}(i)$ and $\hat{p}(j)$ are the occurrence probabilities of w_i and w_j, respectively, while the probability of their co-occurrence is denoted by $\hat{p}(i,j)$. In our previous participation in SemEval12-STS task (Malandrakis et al., 2012) we employed a modification of the pointwise mutual information based on the maximum sense similarity assumption (Resnik, 1995) and the minimization of the respective error in similarity estimation. In particular, exponential weights α were introduced in order to reduce the overestimation of denominator probabilities. The modified metric $I_a(i,j)$, is defined as:

$$I_a(i,j) = \frac{1}{2}\left[\log \frac{\hat{p}(i,j)}{\hat{p}^{\alpha}(i)\hat{p}(j)} + \log \frac{\hat{p}(i,j)}{\hat{p}(i)\hat{p}^{\alpha}(j)}\right]. \quad (1)$$

The weight α was estimated on the corpus of (Iosif and Potamianos, 2012) in order to maximize word sense coverage in the semantic neighborhood of each word. The $I_a(i,j)$ metric using the estimated value of $\alpha = 0.8$ was shown to significantly outperform $I(i,j)$ and to achieve state-of-the-art results on standard semantic similarity datasets (Rubenstein and Goodenough, 1965; Miller and Charles, 1998; Finkelstein et al., 2002).

Context-based: The fundamental assumption behind context-based metrics is that *similarity of context implies similarity of meaning* (Harris, 1954). A contextual window of size $2H+1$ words is centered on the word of interest w_i and lexical features are extracted. For every instance of w_i in the corpus the H words left and right of w_i formulate a feature vector v_i. For a given value of H the context-based semantic similarity between two words, w_i and w_j, is computed as the cosine of their feature vectors: $Q^H(i,j) = \frac{v_i.v_j}{||v_i||\,||v_j||}$. The elements of feature vectors can be weighted according various schemes [(Iosif and Potamianos, 2010)], while, here we use a binary scheme.

Network-based: The aforementioned similarity metrics were used for the definition of a semantic network (Iosif and Potamianos, 2013; Iosif et al., 2013). A number of similarity metrics were proposed under either the *attributional similarity* (Turney, 2006) or the *maximum sense similarity* (Resnik, 1995) assumptions of lexical semantics[1].

2.2 Sentence level similarities

To utilize word-level semantic similarities in the sentence-level task we use a modified version of BLEU (Papineni et al., 2002). The model works in two passes: the first pass identifies exact matches (similar to baseline BLEU), the second pass compares non-matched terms using semantic similarity. Non-matched terms from the hypothesis sentence are compared with all terms of the reference sentence (regardless of whether they were matched during the first pass). In the case of bigram and higher order terms, the process is applied recursively: the bigrams are decomposed into two words and the similarity between them is estimated by applying the same method to the words. All word similarity metrics used are peak-to-peak normalized in the [0,1] range, so they serve as a "degree-of-match". The semantic similarity scores from term pairs are summed (just like n-gram hits) to obtain a BLEU-like hit-rate. Alignment is performed via maximum similarity: we iterate on the hypothesis n-grams, left-to-right, and compare each with the *most similar* n-gram in the reference. The features produced by this process are "soft" hit-rates (for 1-, 2-, 3-, 4-grams)[2]. We also use the "hard" hit rates produced by baseline BLEU as features of the final model.

2.3 String similarities

We use the following string-based similarity features: 1) Longest Common Subsequence Similarity (LCSS) (Lin and Och, 2004) based on the Longest Common Subsequence (LCS) character-based dy-

[1]The network-based metrics were applied only during the training phase of the shared task, due to time limitations. They exhibited almost identical performance as the metric defined by (1), which was used in the test runs.

[2]Note that the features are computed twice on each sentence pair and then averaged.

namic programming algorithm. LCSS represents the length of the longest string (or strings) that is a substring (or are substrings) of two or more strings. 2) Skip bigram co-occurrence measures the overlap of skip-bigrams between two sentences or phrases. A skip-bigram is defined as any pair of words in the sentence order, allowing for arbitrary gaps between words (Lin and Och, 2004). 3) Containment is defined as the percentage of a sentence that is contained in another sentence. It is a number between 0 and 1, where 1 means the hypothesis sentence is fully contained in the reference sentence (Broder, 1997). We express containment as the amount of n-grams of a sentence contained in another. The containment metric is not symmetric and is calculated as: $c(X, Y) = |S(X) \cap S(Y)|/S(X)$, where $S(X)$ and $S(Y)$ are all the n-grams of sentences X and Y respectively.

2.4 Affective similarity

We used the method proposed in (Malandrakis et al., 2011) to estimate affective features. Continuous (valence and arousal) ratings in $[-1, 1]$ of any term are represented as a linear combination of a function of its semantic similarities to a set of seed words and the affective ratings of these words, as follows:

$$\hat{v}(w_j) = a_0 + \sum_{i=1}^{N} a_i \, v(w_i) \, d_{ij}, \qquad (2)$$

where w_j is the term we mean to characterize, $w_1 ... w_N$ are the seed words, $v(w_i)$ is the valence rating for seed word w_i, a_i is the weight corresponding to seed word w_i (that is estimated as described next), d_{ij} is a measure of semantic similarity between w_i and w_j (for the purposes of this work, cosine similarity between context vectors is used). The weights a_i are estimated over the Affective norms for English Words (ANEW) (Bradley and Lang, 1999) corpus.

Using this model we generate affective ratings for every content word (noun, verb, adjective or adverb) of every sentence. We assume that these can adequately describe the affective content of the sentences. To create an "affective similarity metric" we use the difference of means of the word affective ratings between two sentences.

$$\hat{d}_{\text{affect}} = 2 - |\mu(\hat{v}(s_1)) - \mu(\hat{v}(s_2))| \qquad (3)$$

where $\mu(\hat{v}(s_i))$ the mean of content word ratings included in sentence i.

2.5 Fusion

The aforementioned features are combined using one of two possible models. The first model is a Multiple Linear Regression (MLR) model

$$\hat{D}_L = a_0 + \sum_{n=1}^{k} a_n \, f_k, \qquad (4)$$

where $\hat{D}_L$ is the estimated similarity, f_k are the unsupervised semantic similarity metrics and a_n are the trainable parameters of the model.

The second model is motivated by an assumption of cognitive scaling of similarity scores: we expect that the perception of hit rates is non-linearly affected by the length of the sentences. We call this the hierarchical fusion scheme. It is a combination of (overlapping) MLR models, each matching a range of sentence lengths. The first model D_{L1} is trained with sentences with length up to l_1, i.e., $l \leq l_1$, the second model D_{L2} up to length l_2 etc. During testing, sentences with length $l \in [1, l_1]$ are decoded with D_{L1}, sentences with length $l \in (l_1, l_2]$ with model D_{L2} etc. Each of these partial models is a linear fusion model as shown in (4). In this work, we use four models with $l_1 = 10$, $l_2 = 20$, $l_3 = 30$, $l_4 = \infty$.

Domain adaptation is employed, by creating separate models per domain (training data source). Beyond that, we also create a unified model, trained on all data to be used as a fallback if an appropriate model can not be decided upon during evaluation.

3 Experimental Procedure and Results

Initially all sentences are pre-processed by the CoreNLP (Finkel et al., 2005; Toutanova et al., 2003) suite of tools, a process that includes named entity recognition, normalization, part of speech tagging, lemmatization and stemming. We evaluated multiple types of preprocessing per unsupervised metric and chose different ones depending on the metric. Word-level semantic similarities, used for soft comparisons and affective feature extraction, were computed over a corpus of 116 million web snippets collected by posing one query for every word in the Aspell spellchecker (asp,) vocabulary to the Yahoo! search engine. Word-level emotional ratings in continuous valence and arousal scales were produced by a model trained on the ANEW dataset and using contextual similarities. Finally, string similarities were calculated over the original unmodified sentences.

Next, results are reported in terms of correlation between the generated scores and the ground truth, for each corpus in the shared task, as well as their weighted mean. **Feature selection** is applied to the large candidate feature set using a wrapper-based backward selection approach on the training data.The final feature set contains 15 features: soft hit rates calculated over content word 1- to 4-grams (4 features), soft hit rates calculated over unigrams per part-of-speech, for adjectives, nouns, adverbs, verbs (4 features), BLEU unigram hit rates for all words and content words (2 features), skip and containment similarities, containment normalized by sum of sentence lengths or product of sentence lengths (3 features) and affective similarities for arousal and valence (2 features).

Domain adaptation methods are the only difference between the three submitted runs. For all three runs we train one linear model per training set and a fallback model. For the first run, dubbed linear, the fallback model is linear and model selection during evaluation is performed by file name, therefore results for the OnWN set are produced by a model trained with OnWN data, while the rest are produced by the fallback model. The second run, dubbed length, uses a hierarchical fallback model and model selection is performed by file name. The third run, dubbed adapt, uses the same models as the first run and each test set is assigned to a model (i.e., the fallback model is never used). The test set - model (training) mapping for this run is: OnWN → OnWN, headlines → SMTnews, SMT → Europarl and FNWN → OnWN.

Table 1: Correlation performance for the linear model using lexical (L), string (S) and affect (A) features

Feature	headl.	OnWN	FNWN	SMT	mean
L	0.68	0.51	0.23	0.25	0.46
L+S	0.69	0.49	0.23	0.26	0.46
L+S+A	0.69	0.51	0.27	0.28	0.47

Results are shown in Tables 1 and 2. Results for the linear run using subsets of the final feature set are shown in Table 1. Lexical features (hit rates) are obviously the most valuable features. String similarities provided us with an improvement in the training set which is not reflected in the test set. Affect proved valuable, particularly in the most difficult sets of FNWN and SMT.

Table 2: Correlation performance on the evaluation set.

Run	headl.	OnWN	FNWN	SMT	mean
linear	0.69	0.51	0.27	0.28	0.47
length	0.65	0.51	0.25	0.28	0.46
adapt	0.62	0.51	0.33	0.30	0.46

Results for the three submission runs are shown in Table 2. Our best run was the simplest one, using a purely linear model and effectively no adaptation. Adding a more aggressive adaptation strategy improved results in the FNWN and SMT sets, so there is definitely some potential, however the improvement observed is nowhere near that observed in the training data or the same task of SemEval 2012. We have to question whether this improvement is an artifact of the rating distributions of these two sets (SMT contains virtually only high ratings, FNWN contains virtually only low ratings): such wild mismatches in priors among training and test sets can be mitigated using more elaborate machine learning algorithms (rather than employing better semantic similarity features or algorithms). Overall the system performs well in the two sets containing large similarity rating ranges.

4 Conclusions

We have improved over our previous model of sentence semantic similarity. The inclusion of string-based similarities and more so of affective content measures proved significant, but domain adaptation provided mixed results. While expanding the model to include more layers of similarity estimates is clearly a step in the right direction, further work is required to include even more layers. Using syntactic information and more levels of abstraction (e.g. concepts) are obvious next steps.

5 Acknowledgements

The first four authors have been partially funded by the PortDial project (Language Resources for Portable Multilingual Spoken Dialog Systems) supported by the EU Seventh Framework Programme (FP7), grant number 296170.

References

E. Agirre, D. Cer, M. Diab, and A. Gonzalez-Agirre. 2012. Semeval-2012 task 6: A pilot on semantic textual similarity. In *Proc. SemEval*, pages 385–393.

Eneko Agirre, Daniel Cer, Mona Diab, Aitor Gonzalez-Agirre, and Weiwei Guo. 2013. *sem 2013 shared task: Semantic textual similarity, including a pilot on typed-similarity. In *Proc. *SEM.*

Gnu aspell. `http://www.aspell.net`.

D. Bär, C. Biemann, I. Gurevych, and T. Zesch. 2012. Ukp: Computing semantic textual similarity by combining multiple content similarity measures. In *Proc. SemEval*, pages 435–440.

M. Baroni and A. Lenci. 2010. Distributional memory: A general framework for corpus-based semantics. *Computational Linguistics*, 36(4):673–721.

J. Bos and K. Markert. 2005. Recognising textual entailment with logical inference. In *Proceedings of the Human Language Technology Conference and Conference on Empirical Methods in Natural Language Processing*, page 628635.

M. Bradley and P. Lang. 1999. Affective norms for English words (ANEW): Stimuli, instruction manual and affective ratings. Technical report C-1. The Center for Research in Psychophysiology, University of Florida.

Andrei Z. Broder. 1997. On the resemblance and containment of documents. In *In Compression and Complexity of Sequences (SEQUENCES97*, pages 21–29. IEEE Computer Society.

A. Budanitsky and G. Hirst. 2006. Evaluating WordNet-based measures of semantic distance. *Computational Linguistics*, 32:13–47.

K. W. Church and P. Hanks. 1990. Word association norms, mutual information, and lexicography. *Computational Linguistics*, 16(1):22–29.

A. Finch, S. Y. Hwang, and E. Sumita. 2005. Using machine translation evaluation techniques to determine sentence-level semantic equivalence. In *Proceedings of the 3rd International Workshop on Paraphrasing*, page 1724.

J. R. Finkel, T. Grenager, and C. D. Manning. 2005. Incorporating non-local information into information extraction systems by gibbs sampling. In *Proceedings of the 43rd Annual Meeting on Association for Computational Linguistics*, pages 363–370.

L. Finkelstein, E. Gabrilovich, Y. Matias, E. Rivlin, Z. Solan, G. Wolfman, and E. Ruppin. 2002. Placing search in context: The concept revisited. *ACM Transactions on Information Systems*, 20(1):116–131.

S. Harabagiu and A. Hickl. 2006. Methods for Using Textual Entailment in Open-Domain Question Answering. In *Proceedings of the 21st International Conference on Computational Linguistics and 44th Annual Meeting of the Association for Computational Linguistics*, pages 905–912.

Z. Harris. 1954. Distributional structure. *Word*, 10(23):146–162.

E. Iosif and A. Potamianos. 2010. Unsupervised semantic similarity computation between terms using web documents. *IEEE Transactions on Knowledge and Data Engineering*, 22(11):1637–1647.

E. Iosif and A. Potamianos. 2012. Semsim: Resources for normalized semantic similarity computation using lexical networks. In *Proc. Eighth International Conference on Language Resources and Evaluation*, pages 3499–3504.

Elias Iosif and Alexandros Potamianos. 2013. Similarity Computation Using Semantic Networks Created From Web-Harvested Data. *Natural Language Engineering*, (submitted).

E. Iosif, A. Potamianos, M. Giannoudaki, and K. Zervanou. 2013. Semantic similarity computation for abstract and concrete nouns using network-based distributional semantic models. In *10th International Conference on Computational Semantics (IWCS)*, pages 328–334.

Chin-Yew Lin and Franz Josef Och. 2004. Automatic evaluation of machine translation quality using longest common subsequence and skip-bigram statistics. In *Proceedings of the 42nd Annual Meeting on Association for Computational Linguistics*, ACL '04, Stroudsburg, PA, USA. Association for Computational Linguistics.

P. Malakasiotis and I. Androutsopoulos. 2007. Learning textual entailment using svms and string similarity measures. In *Proceedings of of the ACL-PASCAL Workshop on Textual Entailment and Paraphrasing*, pages 42–47.

P. Malakasiotis. 2009. Paraphrase recognition using machine learning to combine similarity measures. In *Proceedings of the 47th Annual Meeting of ACL and the 4th Int. Joint Conference on Natural Language Processing of AFNLP*, pages 42–47.

N. Malandrakis, A. Potamianos, E. Iosif, and S. Narayanan. 2011. Kernel models for affective lexicon creation. In *Proc. Interspeech*, pages 2977–2980.

N. Malandrakis, E. Iosif, and A. Potamianos. 2012. DeepPurple: Estimating sentence semantic similarity using n-gram regression models and web snippets. In *Proc. Sixth International Workshop on Semantic Evaluation (SemEval) – The First Joint Conference on Lexical and Computational Semantics (*SEM)*, pages 565–570.

H. Meng and K.-C. Siu. 2002. Semi-automatic acquisition of semantic structures for understanding domain-specific natural language queries. *IEEE Transactions on Knowledge and Data Engineering*, 14(1):172–181.

G. Miller and W. Charles. 1998. Contextual correlates of semantic similarity. *Language and Cognitive Processes*, 6(1):1–28.

G. Miller. 1990. Wordnet: An on-line lexical database. *International Journal of Lexicography*, 3(4):235–312.

S. Mirkin, L. Specia, N. Cancedda, I. Dagan, M. Dymetman, and S. Idan. 2009. Source-language entailment modeling for translating unknown terms. In *Proceedings of the 47th Annual Meeting of ACL and the 4th Int. Joint Conference on Natural Language Processing of AFNLP*, pages 791–799.

K. Papineni, S. Roukos, T. Ward, and W.-J. Zhu. 2002. Bleu: a method for automatic evaluation of machine translation. In *Proceedings of the 40th Annual Meeting on Association for Computational Linguistics*, pages 311–318.

D. Perez and E. Alfonseca. 2005. Application of the bleu algorithm for recognizing textual entailments. In *Proceedings of the PASCAL Challenges Worshop on Recognising Textual Entailment.*

P. Resnik. 1995. Using information content to evaluate semantic similarity in a taxanomy. In *Proc. of International Joint Conference for Artificial Intelligence*, pages 448–453.

F. Rinaldi, J. Dowdall, K. Kaljurand, M. Hess, and D. Molla. 2003. Exploiting paraphrases in a question answering system. In *Proceedings of the 2nd International Workshop on Paraphrasing*, pages 25–32.

H. Rubenstein and J. B. Goodenough. 1965. Contextual correlates of synonymy. *Communications of the ACM*, 8(10):627–633.

I. Szpektor and I. Dagan. 2008. Learning entailment rules for unary templates. In *Proceedings of the 22nd International Conference on Computational Linguistics*, pages 849–856.

K. Toutanova, D. Klein, C. D. Manning, and Y. Singer. 2003. Feature-rich part-of-speech tagging with a cyclic dependency network. In *Proceedings of Conference of the North American Chapter of the Association for Computational Linguistics on Human Language Technology*, pages 173–180.

P. Turney. 2006. Similarity of semantic relations. *Computational Linguistics*, 32(3):379–416.

F. Šarić, G. Glavaš, M. Karan, J. Šnajder, and B. Dalbelo Bašić. 2012. Takelab: Systems for measuring semantic text similarity. In *Proc. SemEval*, pages 441–448.

F. Zanzotto, M. Pennacchiotti, and A. Moschitti. 2009. A machine-learning approach to textual entailment recognition. *Natural Language Engineering*, 15(4):551582.

UMCC_DLSI: Textual Similarity based on Lexical-Semantic features

Alexander Chávez, Antonio Fernández Orquín, Héctor Dávila, Yoan Gutiérrez, Armando Collazo, José I. Abreu
DI, University of Matanzas
Autopista a Varadero km 3 ½
Matanzas, Cuba.
{alexander.chavez, tony, hector.davila, yoan.gutierrez, armando.collazo, jose.abreu}@umcc.cu

Andrés Montoyo, Rafael Muñoz
DLSI, University of Alicante Carretera de San Vicente S/N Alicante, Spain.
{montoyo,rafael}@dlsi.ua.es

Abstract

This paper describes the specifications and results of UMCC_DLSI system, which participated in the Semantic Textual Similarity task (STS) of SemEval-2013. Our supervised system uses different types of lexical and semantic features to train a Bagging classifier used to decide the correct option. Related to the different features we can highlight the resource ISR-WN used to extract semantic relations among words and the use of different algorithms to establish semantic and lexical similarities. In order to establish which features are the most appropriate to improve STS results we participated with three runs using different set of features. Our best run reached the position 44 in the official ranking, obtaining a general correlation coefficient of 0.61.

1 Introduction

SemEval-2013 (Agirre *et al.*, 2013) presents the task Semantic Textual Similarity (STS) again. In STS, the participating systems must examine the degree of semantic equivalence between two sentences. The goal of this task is to create a unified framework for the evaluation of semantic textual similarity modules and to characterize their impact on NLP applications.

STS is related to Textual Entailment (TE) and Paraphrase tasks. The main difference is that STS assumes bidirectional graded equivalence between the pair of textual snippets.

In case of TE, the equivalence is directional (e.g. a student is a person, but a person is not necessarily a student). In addition, STS differs from TE and Paraphrase in that, rather than being a binary yes/no decision, STS is a similarity-graded notion (e.g. a student is more similar to a person than a dog to a person).

This graded bidirectional is useful for NLP tasks such as Machine Translation (MT), Information Extraction (IE), Question Answering (QA), and Summarization. Several semantic tasks could be added as modules in the STS framework, "*such as Word Sense Disambiguation and Induction, Lexical Substitution, Semantic Role Labeling, Multiword Expression detection and handling, Anaphora and Co-reference resolution, Time and Date resolution and Named Entity, among others*"[1]

1.1 Description of 2013 pilot task

This edition of SemEval-2013 remain with the same classification approaches that in their first version in 2012. The output of different systems was compared to the reference scores provided by SemEval-2013 gold standard file, which range from five to zero according to the next criterions[2]: (5) "The two sentences are equivalent, as they mean the same thing". (4) "The two sentences are mostly equivalent, but some unimportant details differ". (3) "The two sentences are roughly equivalent, but some important information differs/missing". (2) "The two sentences are not equivalent, but share some details". (1) "The two sentences are not

[1] http://www.cs.york.ac.uk/semeval-2012/task6/
[2] http://www.cs.york.ac.uk/semeval-2012/task6/data/uploads/datasets/train-readme.txt

*Second Joint Conference on Lexical and Computational Semantics (*SEM), Volume 1: Proceedings of the Main Conference and the Shared Task*, pages 109–118, Atlanta, Georgia, June 13-14, 2013.

equivalent, but are on the same topic". (0) "The two sentences are on different topics".

After this introduction, the rest of the paper is organized as follows. Section 3 shows the Related Works. Section 4 presents our system architecture and description of the different runs. In section 4 we describe the different features used in our system. Results and a discussion are provided in Section 5 and finally we conclude in Section 6.

2 Related Works

There are more extensive literature on measuring the similarity between documents than to between sentences. Perhaps the most recently scenario is constituted by the competition of SemEval-2012 task 6: A Pilot on Semantic Textual Similarity (Aguirre and Cerd, 2012). In SemEval-2012, there were used different tools and resources like stop word list, multilingual corpora, dictionaries, acronyms, and tables of paraphrases, "*but WordNet was the most used resource, followed by monolingual corpora and Wikipedia*" (Aguirre and Cerd, 2012).

According to Aguirre, Generic NLP tools were widely used. Among those that stand out were tools for lemmatization and POS-tagging (Aguirre and Cerd, 2012). On a smaller scale word sense disambiguation, semantic role labeling and time and date resolution. In addition, Knowledge-based and distributional methods were highly used. Aguirre and Cerd remarked on (Aguirre and Cerd, 2012) that alignment and/or statistical machine translation software, lexical substitution, string similarity, textual entailment and machine translation evaluation software were used to a lesser extent. It can be noted that machine learning was widely used to combine and tune components.

Most of the knowledge-based methods "*obtain a measure of relatedness by utilizing lexical resources and ontologies such as WordNet* (Miller *et al.*, 1990b) *to measure definitional overlap, term distance within a graphical taxonomy, or term depth in the taxonomy as a measure of specificity*" (Banea *et al.*, 2012).

Some scholars as in (Corley and Mihalcea, June 2005) have argue "*the fact that a comprehensive metric of text semantic similarity should take into account the relations between words, as well as the role played by the various entities involved in the interactions described by each of the two sentences*". This idea is resumed in the Principle of Compositionality, this principle posits that the meaning of a complex expression is determined by the meanings of its constituent expressions and the rules used to combine them (Werning *et al.*, 2005). Corley and Mihalcea in this article combined metrics of word-to-word similarity, and language models into a formula and they pose that this is a potentially good indicator of the semantic similarity of the two input texts sentences. They modeled the semantic similarity of a sentence as a function of the semantic similarity of the component words (Corley and Mihalcea, June 2005).

One of the top scoring systems at SemEval-2012 (Šarić *et al.*, 2012) tended to use most of the aforementioned resources and tools. They predict the human ratings of sentence similarity using a support-vector regression model with multiple features measuring word-overlap similarity and syntax similarity. They also compute the similarity between sentences using the semantic alignment of lemmas. First, they compute the word similarity between all pairs of lemmas from first to second sentence, using either the knowledge-based or the corpus-based semantic similarity. They named this method Greedy Lemma Aligning Overlap.

Daniel Bär presented the UKP system, which performed best in the Semantic Textual Similarity (STS) task at SemEval-2012 in two out of three metrics. It uses a simple log-linear regression model, trained on the training data, to combine multiple text similarity measures of varying complexity.

3 System architecture and description of the runs

As we can see in Figure 1, our three runs begin with the pre-processing of SemEval-2013's training set. Every sentence pair is tokenized, lemmatized and POS-tagged using Freeling 2.2 tool (Atserias *et al.*, 2006). Afterwards, several methods and algorithms are applied in order to extract all features for our Machine Learning System (MLS). Each run uses a particular group of features.

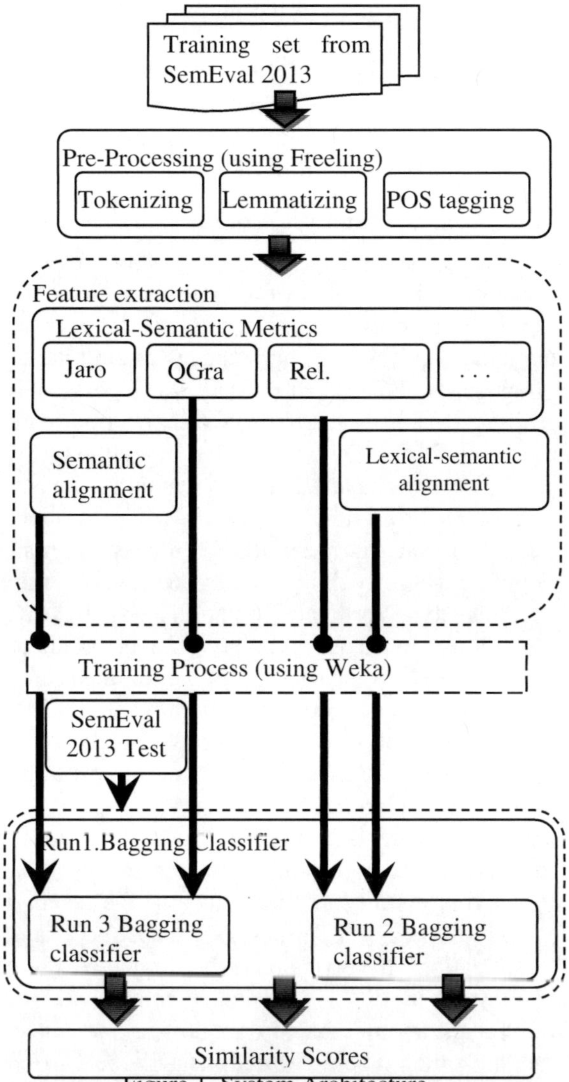

Figure 1. System Architecture.

The Run 1 (named **MultiSemLex**) is our main run. This takes into account all extracted features and trains a model with a Bagging classifier (Breiman, 1996) (using REPTree). The training corpus has been provided by SemEval-2013 competition, in concrete by the Semantic Textual Similarity task.

The Run 2 (named **MultiLex**) and Run 3 (named **MultiSem**) use the same classifier, but including different features. Run 2 uses (see Figure 1) features extracted from Lexical-Semantic Metrics (LS-M) described in section 4.1, and Lexical-Semantic Alignment (LS-A) described in section 4.2.

On the other hand, Run 3 uses features extracted only from Semantic Alignment (SA) described in section 4.3.

As a result, we obtain three trained models capable to estimate the similarity value between two phrases.

Finally, we test our system with the SemEval-2013 test set (see Table 14 with the results of our three runs). The following section describes the features extraction process.

4 Description of the features used in the Machine Learning System

Many times when two phrases are very similar, one sentence is in a high degree lexically overlapped by the other. Inspired in this fact we developed various algorithms, which measure the level of overlapping by computing a quantity of matching words in a pair of phrases. In our system, we used as features for a MLS lexical and semantic similarity measures. Other features were extracted from a lexical-semantic sentences alignment and a variant using only a semantic alignment.

4.1 Similarity measures

We have used well-known string based similarity measures like: Needleman-Wunch (sequence alignment), Smith-Waterman (sequence alignment), Smith-Waterman-Gotoh, Smith-Waterman-Gotoh-Windowed Affine, Jaro, Jaro-Winkler, Chapman-Length-Deviation, Chapman-Mean-Length, QGram-Distance, Block-Distance, Cosine Similarity, Dice Similarity, Euclidean Distance, Jaccard Similarity, Matching Coefficient, Monge-Elkan and Overlap-Coefficient. These algorithms have been obtained from an API (*Application Program Interface*) SimMetrics library v1.5 for .NET 2.0[3]. We obtained 17 features for our MLS from these similarity measures.

Using Levenshtein's edit distance (LED), we computed also two different algorithms in order to obtain the alignment of the phrases. In the first one, we considered a value of the alignment as the LED between two sentences. Contrary to (Tatu *et al.*, 2006), we do not remove the punctuation or stop words from the sentences,

[3] Copyright (c) 2006 by Chris Parkinson, available in http://sourceforge.net/projects/simmetrics/

neither consider different cost for transformation operation, and we used all the operations (deletion, insertion and substitution).

The second one is a variant that we named Double Levenshtein's Edit Distance (DLED) (see Table 9 for detail). For this algorithm, we used LED to measure the distance between the phrases, but in order to compare the words, we used LED again (Fernández *et al.*, 2012; Fernández Orquín *et al.*, 2009).

Another distance we used is an extension of LED named Extended Distance (in spanish distancia extendida (DEx)) (see (Fernández *et al.*, 2012; Fernández Orquín *et al.*, 2009) for details). This algorithm is an extension of the Levenshtein's algorithm, with which penalties are applied by considering what kind of transformation (insertion, deletion, substitution, or non-operation) and the position it was carried out, along with the character involved in the operation. In addition to the cost matrixes used by Levenshtein's algorithm, DEx also obtains the Longest Common Subsequence (LCS) (Hirschberg, 1977) and other helpful attributes for determining similarity between strings in a single iteration. It is worth noting that the inclusion of all these penalizations makes the DEx algorithm a good candidate for our approach.

In our previous work (Fernández Orquín *et al.*, 2009), DEx demonstrated excellent results when it was compared with other distances as (Levenshtein, 1965), (Neeedleman and Wunsch, 1970), (Winkler, 1999). We also used as a feature the Minimal Semantic Distances (Breadth First Search (BFS)) obtained between the most relevant concepts of both sentences. The relevant concepts pertain to semantic resources ISR-WN (Gutiérrez *et al.*, 2011; 2010a), as WordNet (Miller *et al.*, 1990a), WordNet Affect (Strapparava and Valitutti, 2004), SUMO (Niles and Pease, 2001) and Semantic Classes (Izquierdo *et al.*, 2007). Those concepts were obtained after having applied the Association Ratio (AR) measure between concepts and words over each sentence. (We refer reader to (Gutiérrez *et al.*, 2010b) for a further description).

Another attribute obtained by the system was a value corresponding with the sum of the smaller distances (using QGram-Distance) between the words or the lemmas of the phrase one with each words of the phrase two.

As part of the attributes extracted by the system, was also the value of the sum of the smaller distances (using Levenshtein) among stems, chunks and entities of both phrases.

4.2 Lexical-Semantic alignment

Another algorithm that we created is the Lexical-Semantic Alignment. In this algorithm, we tried to align the phrases by its lemmas. If the lemmas coincide we look for coincidences among parts-of-speech[4] (POS), and then the phrase is realigned using both. If the words do not share the same POS, they will not be aligned. To this point, we only have taken into account a lexical alignment. From now on, we are going to apply a semantic variant. After all the process, the non-aligned words will be analyzed taking into account its WordNet's relations (synonymy, hyponymy, hyperonymy, derivationally-related-form, similar-to, verbal group, entailment and cause-to relation); and a set of equivalences like abbreviations of months, countries, capitals, days and currency. In case of hyperonymy and hyponymy relation, words are going to be aligned if there is a word in the first sentence that is in the same relation (hyperonymy or hyponymy) with another one in the second sentence. For the relations "cause-to" and "implication" the words will be aligned if there is a word in the first sentence that causes or implicates another one in the second sentence. All the other types of relations will be carried out in bidirectional way, that is, there is an alignment if a word of the first sentence is a synonymous of another one belonging to the second one or vice versa.

Finally, we obtain a value we called alignment relation. This value is calculated as $FAV = NAW / NWSP$. Where FAV is the final alignment value, NAW is the number of aligned words, and $NWSP$ is the number of words of the shorter phrase. The FAV value is also another feature for our system. Other extracted attributes they are the quantity of aligned words and the quantity of not aligned words. The core of the alignment is carried out in different ways, which

[4] (noun, verb, adjective, adverbs, prepositions, conjunctions, pronouns, determinants, modifiers, etc.)

are obtained from several attributes. Each way can be compared by:

- the part-of-speech.
- the morphology and the part-of-speech.
- the lemma and the part-of-speech.
- the morphology, part-of-speech, and relationships of WordNet.
- the lemma, part-of-speech, and relationships of WordNet.

4.3 Semantic Alignment

This alignment method depends on calculating the semantic similarity between sentences based on an analysis of the relations, in ISR-WN, of the words that fix them.

First, the two sentences are pre-processed with Freeling and the words are classified according to their POS, creating different groups.

The distance between two words will be the distance, based on WordNet, of the most probable sense of each word in the pair, on the contrary of our previously system in SemEval 2012. In that version, we assumed the selected sense after apply a double Hungarian Algorithm (Kuhn, 1955), for more details please refer to (Fernández *et al.*, 2012). The distance is computed according to the equation (1):

$$d(x,y) = \sum_{i=0}^{i=m} w * r(L[i], L[i+1]); \quad (1)$$

Where L is the collection of synsets corresponding to the minimum path between nodes x and y, m is the length of L subtracting one, r is a function that search the relation connecting x and y nodes, w is a weight associated to the relation searched by r (see Table 1).

Relation	Weight
Hyponym, Hypernym	2
Member_Holonym, Member_Meronym, Cause, Entailment	5
Similar_To	10
Antonym	200
Other relation different to Synonymy	60

Table 1. Weights applied to WordNet relations.

Table 1 shows the weights associated to WordNet relations between two synsets.

Let us see the following example:

- We could take the pair 99 of corpus MSRvid (from training set of SemEval-2013) with a littler transformation in order to a better explanation of our method.

Original pair

A: A polar bear is running towards a group of walruses.

B: A polar bear is chasing a group of walruses.

Transformed pair:

A_1: A polar bear runs towards a group of cats.

B_1: A wale chases a group of dogs.

Later on, using equation (1), a matrix with the distances between all groups of both phrases is created (see Table 2).

GROUPS	polar	bear	runs	towards	group	cats
wale	Dist:=3	Dist:=2	Dist:=3	Dist:=5		Dist:=2
chases	Dist:=4	Dist:=3	Dist:=2	Dist:=4		Dist:=3
group					Dist:=0	
dogs	Dist:=3	Dist:=1	Dist:=4	Dist:=4		Dist:=1

Table 2. Distances between groups.

Using the Hungarian Algorithm (Kuhn, 1955) for Minimum Cost Assignment, each group of the first sentence is checked with each element of the second sentence, and the rest is marked as words that were not aligned.

In the previous example the words "toward" and "polar" are the words that were not aligned, so the number of non-aligned words is two. There is only one perfect match: "group-group" (match with cost=0). The length of the shortest sentence is four. The Table 3 shows the results of this analysis.

Number of exact coincidence	Total Distances of optimal Matching	Number of non-aligned Words
1	5	2

Table 3. Features from the analyzed sentences.

This process has to be repeated for nouns (see Table 4), verbs, adjective, adverbs, prepositions, conjunctions, pronouns, determinants, modifiers, digits and date times. On the contrary, the tables have to be created only with the similar groups of the sentences. Table 4 shows features extracted from the analysis of nouns.

GROUPS	bear	group	cats
wale	Dist := 2		Dist := 2
group		Dist := 0	
dogs	Dist := 1		Dist := 1

Table 4. Distances between groups of nouns.

Number of exact coincidence	Total Distances of optimal Matching	Number of non-aligned Words
1	3	0

Table 5. Feature extracted from analysis of nouns.

Several attributes are extracted from the pair of sentences (see Table 3 and Table 5). Three attributes considering only verbs, only nouns, only adjectives, only adverbs, only prepositions, only conjunctions, only pronouns, only determinants, only modifiers, only digits, and only date times. These attributes are:

- Number of exact coincidences
- Total distance of matching
- Number of words that do not match

Many groups have particular features according to their parts-of-speech. The group of the nouns has one more feature that indicates if the two phrases have the same number (plural or singular). For this feature, we take the average of the number of each noun in the phrase like a number of the phrase.

For the group of adjectives we added a feature indicating the distance between the nouns that modify it from the aligned adjectives, respectively.

For the verbs, we search the nouns that precede it, and the nouns that are next of the verb, and we define two groups. We calculated the distance to align each group with every pair of aligned verbs. The verbs have other feature that specifies if all verbs are in the same verbal time.

With the adverbs, we search the verb that is modified by it, and we calculate their distance from all alignment pairs.

With the determinants and the adverbs we detect if any of the alignment pairs are expressing negations (like don't, or do not) in both cases or not. Finally, we determine if the two phrases have the same principal action. For all this new features, we aid with Freeling tool.

As a result, we finally obtain 42 attributes from this alignment method. It is important to remark that this alignment process searches to solve, for each word from the rows (see Table 4) it has a respectively word from the columns.

4.4 Description of the alignment feature

From the alignment process, we extract different features that help us a better result of our MLS. Table 6 shows the group of features with lexical and semantic support, based on WordNet relation (named F1). Each of they were named with a prefix, a hyphen and a suffix. Table 7 describes the meaning of every prefix, and Table 8 shows the meaning of the suffixes.

Features
CPA_FCG, CPNA_FCG, SIM_FCG, CPA_LCG, CPNA_LCG, SIM_LCG, CPA_FCGR, CPNA_FCGR, SIM_FCGR, CPA_LCGR, CPNA_LCGR, SIM_LCGR

Table 6. F1. Semantic feature group.

Prefixes	Descriptions
CPA	Number of aligned words.
CPNA	Number of non-aligned words.
SIM	Similarity

Table 7. Meaning of each prefixes.

Prefixes	Compared words for...
FCG	Morphology and POS
LCG	Lemma and POS
FCGR	Morphology, POS and WordNet relation.
LCGR	Lemma, POS and WordNet relation.

Table 8. Suffixes for describe each type of alignment.

Features	Descriptions
LevForma	Levenshtein Distance between two phrases comparing words by morphology
LevLema	The same as above, but now comparing by lemma.
LevDoble	Idem, but comparing again by Levenshtein and accepting words match if the distance is ≤ 2.
DEx	Extended Distance
NormLevF, NormLevL	Normalized forms of LevForma and LevLema.

Table 9. F2. Lexical alignment measures.

Features
NWunch, SWaterman, SWGotoh, SWGAffine, Jaro, JaroW, CLDeviation, CMLength, QGramD, BlockD, CosineS, DiceS, EuclideanD, JaccardS, MaCoef, MongeElkan, OverlapCoef.

Table 10. Lexical Measure from SimMetrics library.

Features	Descriptions
AxAQGD_L	All against all applying QGramD and comparing by lemmas of the words.
AxAQGD_F	Same as above, but applying QGramD and comparing by morphology.
AxAQGD_LF	Idem, not only comparing by lemma but also by morphology.
AxALev_LF	All against all applying Levenhstein

	comparing by morphology and lemmas.
AxA_Stems	Idem, but applying Levenhstein comparing by the stems of the words.

Table 11. Aligning all against all.

Other features we extracted were obtained from the following similarity measures (named F2) (see Table 9 for detail).

We used another group named F3, with lexical measure extracted from SimMetric library (see Table 10 for detail).

Finally we used a group of five feature (named F4), extracted from all against all alignment (see Table 11 for detail).

4.5 Description of the training phase

For the training process, we used a supervised learning framework, including all the training set as a training corpus. Using ten-fold cross validation with the classifier mentioned in section 3 (experimentally selected).

As we can see in Table 12, the attributes corresponding with the Test 1 (only lexical attributes) obtain 0.7534 of correlation. On the other side, the attributes of the Test 2 (lexical features with semantic support) obtain 0.7549 of correlation, and all features obtain 0.7987. Being demonstrated the necessity to tackle the problem of the similarity from a multidimensional point of view (see Test 3 in the Table 12).

Features	Correlation on the training data of SemEval-2013		
	Test 1	Test 2	Test 3
F1		0.7549	0.7987
F2			
F3	0.7534		
F4			

Table 12. Features influence. Gray cells mean features are not taking into account.

5 Result and discussion

Semantic Textual Similarity task of SemEval-2013 offered two official measures to rank the systems[5]: Mean- the main evaluation value, Rank- gives the rank of the submission as ordered by the "mean" result.

[5]http://ixa2.si.ehu.es/sts/index.php?option=com_content&view=article&id=53&Itemid=61

Test data for the core test datasets, coming from the following:

Corpus	**Description**
Headlineas:	news headlines mined from several news sources by European Media Monitor using the RSS feed.
OnWN:	mapping of lexical resources OnWN. The sentences are sense definitions from WordNet and OntoNotes.
FNWN:	the sentences are sense definitions from WordNet and FrameNet.
SMT:	SMT dataset comes from DARPA GALE HTER and HyTER. One sentence is a MT output and the other is a reference translation where a reference is generated based on human post editing.

Table 13. Test Core Datasets.

Using these measures, our second run (Run 2) obtained the best results (see Table 14). As we can see in Table 14, our lexical run has obtained our best result, given at the same time worth result in our other runs. This demonstrates that tackling this problem with combining multiple lexical similarity measure produce better results in concordance to this specific test corpora.

To explain Table 14 we present following descriptions: caption in top row mean: 1- Headlines, 2- OnWN, 3- FNWN, 4- SMT and 5- mean.

Run	**1**	**R**	**2**	**R**	**3**	**R**	**4**	**R**	**5**	**R**
1	0.5841	60	0.4847	54	0.2917	52	0.2855	66	0.4352	58
2	0.6168	55	0.5557	39	0.3045	50	0.3407	28	0.4833	44
3	0.3846	85	0.1342	88	-0.0065	85	0.2736	72	0.2523	87

Table 14. Official SemEval-2013 results over test datasets. Ranking (R).

The Run 1 is our main run, which contains the junction of all attributes (lexical and semantic attributes). Table 14 shows the results of all the runs for a different corpus from test phase. As we can see, Run 1 did not obtain the best results among our runs.

Otherwise, Run 3 uses more semantic analysis than Run 2, from this; Run 3 should get better results than reached over the corpus of FNWN, because this corpus is extracted from FrameNet corpus (Baker *et al.*, 1998) (a semantic network). FNWN provides examples with high semantic content than lexical.

Run 3 obtained a correlation coefficient of 0.8137 for all training corpus of SemEval 2013, while Run 2 and Run 1 obtained 0.7976 and 0.8345 respectively with the same classifier (Bagging using REPTree, and cross validation with ten-folds). These results present a contradiction between test and train evaluation. We think it is consequence of some obstacles present in test corpora, for example:

In headlines corpus there are great quantity of entities, acronyms and gentilics that we not take into account in our system.

The corpus FNWN presents a non-balance according to the length of the phrases.

In OnWN -test corpus-, we believe that some evaluations are not adequate in correspondence with the training corpus. For example, in line 7 the goal proposed was 0.6, however both phrases are semantically similar. The phrases are:

- the act of lifting something
- the act of climbing something.

We think that 0.6 are not a correct evaluation for this example. Our system result, for this particular case, was 4.794 for Run 3, and 3.814 for Run 2, finally 3.695 for Run 1.

6 Conclusion and future works

This paper have introduced a new framework for recognizing Semantic Textual Similarity, which depends on the extraction of several features that can be inferred from a conventional interpretation of a text.

As mentioned in section 3 we have conducted three different runs, these runs only differ in the type of attributes used. We can see in Table 14 that all runs obtained encouraging results. Our best run was situated at 44th position of 90 runs of the ranking of SemEval-2013. Table 12 and Table 14 show the reached positions for the three different runs and the ranking according to the rest of the teams.

In our participation, we used a MLS that works with features extracted from five different strategies: String Based Similarity Measures, Semantic Similarity Measures, Lexical-Semantic Alignment and Semantic Alignment.

We have conducted the semantic features extraction in a multidimensional context using the resource ISR-WN, the one that allowed us to navigate across several semantic resources (WordNet, WordNet Domains, WordNet Affect, SUMO, SentiWordNet and Semantic Classes).

Finally, we can conclude that our system performs quite well. In our current work, we show that this approach can be used to correctly classify several examples from the STS task of SemEval-2013. Compared with the best run of the ranking (UMBC_EBIQUITY- ParingWords) (see Table 15) our main run has very close results in headlines (1), and SMT (4) core test datasets.

Run	1	2	3	4	5	6
(First)	0.7642	0.7529	0.5818	0.3804	0.6181	1
(Our) RUN 2	0.6168	0.5557	0.3045	0.3407	0.4833	44

Table 15. Comparison with best run (SemEval 2013).

As future work we are planning to enrich our semantic alignment method with Extended WordNet (Moldovan and Rus, 2001), we think that with this improvement we can increase the results obtained with texts like those in OnWN test set.

6.1 Team Collaboration

Is important to remark that our team has been working up in collaboration with INAOE (Instituto Nacional de Astrofísica, Óptica y Electrónica) and LIPN (Laboratoire d'Informatique de Paris-Nord), Université Paris 13 universities, in order to encourage the knowledge interchange and open shared technology. Supporting this collaboration, INAOE-UPV (Instituto Nacional de Astrofísica, Óptica y Electrónica and Universitat Politècnica de València) team, in concrete in INAOE-UPV-run 3 has used our semantic distances for nouns, adjectives, verbs and adverbs, as well as lexical attributes like LevDoble, NormLevF, NormLevL and Ext (see influence of these attributes in Table 12).

Acknowledgments

This research work has been partially funded by the Spanish Government through the project TEXT-MESS 2.0 (TIN2009-13391-C04), "Análisis de Tendencias Mediante Técnicas de Opinión Semántica" (TIN2012-38536-C03-03) and “Técnicas de Deconstrucción en la Tecnologías del Lenguaje Humano” (TIN2012-31224); and by the Valencian Government through the project PROMETEO (PROMETEO/2009/199).

Reference

Agirre, E.; D. Cer; M. Diab and W. Guo. *SEM 2013 Shared Task: Semantic Textual Similarity including a Pilot on Typed-Similarity. *SEM 2013: The Second Joint Conference on Lexical and Computational Semantics, Association for Computational Linguistics, 2013.

Aguirre, E. and D. Cerd. SemEval 2012 Task 6:A Pilot on Semantic Textual Similarity. First Join Conference on Lexical and Computational Semantic (*SEM), Montréal, Canada, Association for Computational Linguistics., 2012. 385-393 p.

Atserias, J.; B. Casas; E. Comelles; M. González; L. Padró and M. Padró. FreeLing 1.3: Syntactic and semantic services in an opensource NLP library. Proceedings of LREC'06, Genoa, Italy, 2006.

Baker, C. F.; C. J. Fillmore and J. B. Lowe. The berkeley framenet project. Proceedings of the 17th international conference on Computational linguistics-Volume 1, Association for Computational Linguistics, 1998. 86-90 p.

Banea, C.; S. Hassan; M. Mohler and R. Mihalcea. UNT:A Supervised Synergistic Approach to SemanticText Similarity. First Joint Conference on Lexical and Computational Semantics (*SEM), Montréal. Canada, Association for Computational Linguistics, 2012. 635–642 p.

Breiman, L. Bagging predictors Machine learning, 1996, 24(2): 123-140.

Corley, C. and R. Mihalcea. Measuring the Semantic Similarity of Texts, Association for Computational Linguistic. Proceedings of the ACL Work shop on Empirical Modeling of Semantic Equivalence and Entailment, pages 13–18, June 2005.

Fernández, A.; Y. Gutiérrez; H. Dávila; A. Chávez; A. González; R. Estrada; Y. Castañeda; S. Vázquez; A. Montoyo and R. Muñoz. UMCC_DLSI: Multidimensional Lexical-Semantic Textual Similarity. {*SEM 2012}: The First Joint Conference on Lexical and Computational Semantics -- Volume 1: Proceedings of the main conference and the shared task, and Volume 2: Proceedings of the Sixth International Workshop on Semantic Evaluation {(SemEval 2012)}, Montreal, Canada, Association for Computational Linguistics, 2012. 608--616 p.

Fernández Orquín, A. C.; J. Díaz Blanco; A. Fundora Rolo and R. Muñoz Guillena. Un algoritmo para la extracción de características lexicográficas en la comparación de palabras. IV Convención Científica Internacional CIUM, Matanzas, Cuba, 2009.

Gutiérrez, Y.; A. Fernández; A. Montoyo and S. Vázquez. Integration of semantic resources based on WordNet. XXVI Congreso de la Sociedad Española para el Procesamiento del Lenguaje Natural, Universidad Politécnica de Valencia, Valencia, SEPLN 2010, 2010a. 161-168 p. 1135-5948.

Gutiérrez, Y.; A. Fernández; A. Montoyo and S. Vázquez. UMCC-DLSI: Integrative resource for disambiguation task. Proceedings of the 5th International Workshop on Semantic Evaluation, Uppsala, Sweden, Association for Computational Linguistics, 2010b. 427-432 p.

Gutiérrez, Y.; A. Fernández; A. Montoyo and S. Vázquez Enriching the Integration of Semantic Resources based on WordNet Procesamiento del Lenguaje Natural, 2011, 47: 249-257.

Hirschberg, D. S. Algorithms for the longest common subsequence problem J. ACM, 1977, 24: 664–675.

Izquierdo, R.; A. Suárez and G. Rigau A Proposal of Automatic Selection of Coarse-grained Semantic Classes for WSD Procesamiento del Lenguaje Natural, 2007, 39: 189-196.

Kuhn, H. W. The Hungarian Method for the assignment problem Naval Research Logistics Quarterly, 1955, 2: 83–97.

Levenshtein, V. I. Binary codes capable of correcting spurious insertions and deletions of ones. Problems of information Transmission. 1965. pp. 8-17 p.

Miller, G. A.; R. Beckwith; C. Fellbaum; D. Gross and K. Miller. Five papers on WordNet. Princenton University, Cognositive Science Laboratory, 1990a.

Miller, G. A.; R. Beckwith; C. Fellbaum; D. Gross and K. Miller Introduction to WordNet: An On-line Lexical Database International Journal of Lexicography, 3(4):235-244., 1990b.

Moldovan, D. I. and V. Rus Explaining Answers with Extended WordNet ACL, 2001.

Neeedleman, S. and C. Wunsch A general method applicable to the search for similarities in the amino acid sequence of two proteins Mol. Biol, 1970, 48(443): 453.

Niles, I. and A. Pease. Origins of the IEEE Standard Upper Ontology. Working Notes of the IJCAI-2001 Workshop on the IEEE Standard Upper Ontology, Seattle, Washington, USA., 2001.

Šarić, F.; G. Glavaš; Mladenkaran; J. Šnajder and B. D. Basić. TakeLab: Systems for Measuring Semantic Text Similarity. Montréal, Canada, First Join Conference on Lexical and Computational Semantic (*SEM), pages 385-393. Association for Computational Linguistics., 2012.

Strapparava, C. and A. Valitutti. WordNet-Affect: an affective extension of WordNet. Proceedings of the 4th International Conference on Language Resources and Evaluation (LREC 2004), Lisbon, 2004. 1083-1086 p.

Tatu, M.; B. Iles; J. Slavick; N. Adrian and D. Moldovan. COGEX at the Second Recognizing Textual Entailment Challenge. Proceedings of the Second PASCAL Recognising Textual Entailment Challenge Workshop, Venice, Italy, 2006. 104-109 p.

Werning, M.; E. Machery and G. Schurz. The Compositionality of Meaning and Content, Volume 1: Foundational issues. ontos verlag [Distributed in] North and South America by Transaction Books, 2005. p. Linguistics & philosophy, Bd. 1. 3-937202-52-8.

Winkler, W. The state of record linkage and current research problems. Technical Report, Statistical Research Division, U.S, Census Bureau, 1999.

BUT-TYPED: Using domain knowledge for computing typed similarity

Lubomir Otrusina
Brno University of Technology
Faculty of Information Technology
IT4Innovations Centre of Excellence
Bozetechova 2, 612 66 Brno
Czech Republic
iotrusina@fit.vutbr.cz

Pavel Smrz
Brno University of Technology
Faculty of Information Technology
IT4Innovations Centre of Excellence
Bozetechova 2, 612 66 Brno
Czech Republic
smrz@fit.vutbr.cz

Abstract

This paper deals with knowledge-based text processing which aims at an intuitive notion of textual similarity. Entities and relations relevant for a particular domain are identified and disambiguated by means of semi-supervised machine learning techniques and resulting annotations are applied for computing typed-similarity of individual texts.

The work described in this paper particularly shows effects of the mentioned processes in the context of the *SEM 2013 pilot task on typed-similarity, a part of the Semantic Textual Similarity shared task. The goal is to evaluate the degree of semantic similarity between semi-structured records. As the evaluation dataset has been taken from Europeana – a collection of records on European cultural heritage objects – we focus on computing a semantic distance on field *author* which has the highest potential to benefit from the domain knowledge.

Specific features that are employed in our system BUT-TYPED are briefly introduced together with a discussion on their efficient acquisition. Support Vector Regression is then used to combine the features and to provide a final similarity score. The system ranked third on the attribute *author* among 15 submitted runs in the typed-similarity task.

1 Introduction

The goal of the pilot typed-similarity task lied in measuring a degree of semantic similarity between semi-structured records. The data came from the Europeana digital library[1] collecting millions of records on paintings, books, films, and other museum and archival objects that have been digitized throughout Europe. More than 2,000 cultural and scientific institutions across Europe have contributed to Europeana. There are many metadata fields attached to each item in the library, but only fields *title, subject, description, creator, date* and *source* were used in the task.

Having this collection, it is natural to expect that domain knowledge on relevant cultural heritage entities and their inter-relations will help to measure semantic closeness between particular items. When focusing on similarities in a particular field (a semantic type) that clearly covers a domain-specific aspect (such as field author/creator in our case), the significance of the domain knowledge should be the highest.

Intuitively, the semantic similarity among authors of two artworks corresponds to strengths of links that can be identified among the two (groups of) authors. As the gold standard for the task resulted from a Mechanical Turk experiment (Paolacci et al., 2010), it could be expected that close fields correspond to authors that are well known to represent the same style, worked in the same time or the same art branch (e. g., Gabriël Metsu and Johannes Vermeer), come from the same region (often guessed from the names), dealt with related topics (not necessarily in the artwork described by the record in question), etc. In addition to necessary evaluation of the intersection and the union of two author fields (leading naturally to the Jaccard similarity coeffi-

[1] http://www.europeana.eu/

*Second Joint Conference on Lexical and Computational Semantics (*SEM), Volume 1: Proceedings of the Main Conference and the Shared Task*, pages 119–123, Atlanta, Georgia, June 13-14, 2013.

cient on normalized name records – see below), it is therefore crucial to integrate means measuring the above-mentioned semantic links between identified authors.

Unfortunately, there is a lot of noise in the data used in the task. Since Europeana does not precisely define meaning and purpose of each particular field in the database, many mistakes come directly from the unmanaged importing process realized by participating institutions. Fields often mix content of various semantic nature and, occasionally, they are completely misinterpreted (e. g., field *creator* stands for the author, but, in many cases, it contains only the institution the data comes from). Moreover, the data in records is rather sparse – many fields are left empty even though the information to be filled in is included in original museum records (e. g., the author of an artwork is known but not entered).

The low quality of underlying data can be also responsible for results reported in related studies. For example, Aletras et al. (2012) evaluate semantic similarity between semi-structured items from Europeana. They use several measures including a simple normalized textual overlap, the extended Lesk measure, the cosine similarity, a Wikipedia-based model and the LDA (Latent Dirichlet Allocation). The study, restricted to fields *title, subject* and *description*, shows that the best score is obtained by the normalized overlap applied only to the title field. Any other combination of the fields decreased the performance. Similarly, sophisticated methods did not bring any improvement.

The particular gold standard (training/test data) used in the typed-similarity task is also problematic. For example, it provides estimates of location-based similarity even though it makes no sense for particular two records – no field mentions a location and it cannot be inferred from other parts). A throughout analysis of the task data showed that *creator* is the only field we could reasonably use in our experiments (although many issues discussed in previous paragraphs apply for the field as well). That is why we focus on similarities between author fields in this study.

While a plenty of measures for computing textual similarity have been proposed (Lin, 1998; Landauer et al., 1998; Sahlgren, 2005; Gabrilovich and Markovitch, 2007) and there is an active research in the fields of Textual Entailment (Negri et al., 2012), Paraphrase Identification (Lintean and Rus, 2010) and, recently, the Semantic Textual Similarity (Agirre et al., 2012), the semi-structured record similarity is a relatively new area of research. Even though we focus on a particular domain-specific field in this study, our work builds on previous results (Croce et al., 2012; Annesi et al., 2012) to pre-compute semantic closeness of authors based on available biographies and other related texts.

The rest of the paper is organized as follows: The next section introduces the key domain-knowledge processing step of our system which aims at recognizing and disambiguating entities relevant for the cultural heritage domain. The realized system and its results are described in Section 3. Finally, Section 4 briefly summarizes the achievements.

2 Entity Recognition and Disambiguation

A fundamental step in processing text in particular fields lies in identifying named entities relevant for similarity measuring. There is a need for a named entity recognition tool (NER) which identifies names and classifies referred entities into predefined categories. We take advantage of such a tool developed by our team within the DECIPHER project[2].

The DECIPHER NER is able to recognize artists relevant for the cultural heritage domain and, for most of them, to identify the branch of the arts they were primarily focused on (such as painter, sculptors, etc.). It also recognizes names of artworks, genres, art periods and movements and geographical features. In total, there are 1,880,985 recognizable entities from the art domain and more than 3,000,000 place names. Cultural-heritage entities come from various sources; the most productive ones are given in Table 1. The list of place names is populated from the Geo-Names database[3].

The tool takes lists of entities and constructs a finite state automaton to scan and annotate input texts. It is extremely fast (50,000 words per second) and has a relatively small memory footprint (less than 90 MB for all the data).

Additional information attached to entities is

[2]http://decipher-research.eu/

[3]http://www.geonames.org/

Source	# of entities
Freebase[4]	1,288,192
Getty ULAN[5]	528,921
VADS[6]	31,587
Arthermitage[7]	4,259
Artcyclopedia[8]	3,966

Table 1: Number of art-related entities from various sources

stored in the automaton too. A normalized form of a name and its semantic type is returned for each entity. Normalized forms enable identifying equivalent entities expressed differently in texts, e. g., Gabriël Metsu refers to the same person as Gabriel Metsu, US can stand for the United States (of America), etc. Type-specific information is also stored. It includes a detailed type (e. g., architect, sculptor, etc.), nationality, relevant periods or movements, and years of birth and death for authors. Types of geographical features (city, river), coordinates and the GeoNames database identifiers are stored for locations.

The tool is also able to disambiguate entities based on a textual context in which they appeared. Semantic types and simple rules preferring longer matches provide a primary means for this. For example, a text containing *Bobigny – Pablo Picasso*, refers probably to a station of the Paris Metro and does not necessarily deal with the famous Spanish artist. A higher level of disambiguation takes form of classification engines constructed for every ambiguous name from Wikipedia. A set of most specific terms characterizing each particular entity with a shared name is stored together with an entity identifier and used for disambiguation during the text processing phase. Disambiguation of geographical names is performed in a similar manner.

3 System Description and Results

To compute semantic similarity of two non-empty author fields, normalized textual content is compared by an exact match first. As there is no unified form defined for author names entered to the field, the next step applies the NER tool discussed in the previous section to the field text and tries to identify all mentioned entities. Table 2 shows examples of texts from author fields and their respective annotations (in the typewriter font).

Dates and places of birth and death as well as few specific keywords are put together and used in the following processing separately. To correctly annotate expressions that most probably refer to names of people not covered by the DECIPHER NER tool, we employ the Stanford NER[9] that is trained to identify names based on typical textual contexts.

The final similarity score for a pair of author fields is computed by means of the SVR combining specific features characterizing various aspects of the similarity. Simple Jaccard coefficient on recognized person names, normalized word overlap of the remaining text and its edit distance (to deal with typos) are used as basic features.

Places of births and deaths, author's nationality (e. g., Irish painter) and places of work (active in Spain and France) provide data to estimate location-based similarity of authors. Coordinates of each location are used to compute an average location for the author field. The distance between the average coordinates is then applied as a feature. Since types of locations (city, state, etc.) are also available, the number of unique location types for each item and the overlap between corresponding sets are also employed as features.

Explicitly mentioned dates as well as information provided by the DECIPHER NER are compared too. The time-similarity feature takes into account time overlap of the dates and time distance of an earlier and a later event.

Other features reflect an overlap between visual art branches represented by artists in question (Photographer, Architect, etc.), an overlap between their styles, genres and all other information available from external sources. We also employ a matrix of artistic influences that has been derived from a large collection of domain texts by means of relation extraction methods.

Finally, general relatedness of artists is precomputed from the above-mentioned collection by means of Random Indexing (RI), Explicit Semantic Analysis (ESA) and Latent Dirichlet Allocation (LDA) methods, stored in sparse matrices and entered as a final set of features to the SVR process.

The system is implemented in Python and takes

[9]http://nlp.stanford.edu/software/CRF-NER.shtml

Eginton, Francis; West, Benjamin <author name="Francis Eginton" url="http://www.freebase.com/m/0by1w5n"> Eginton, Francis</author>; <author name="Benjamin West" url="http://www.freebase.com/m/01z6r6">West, Benjamin</author>
Yossef Zaritsky Israeli, born Ukraine, 1891-1985 <author name="Joseph Zaritsky" url="http://www.freebase.com/m/0bh71xw" nationality="Israel" place_of_birth="Ukraine" date_of_birth="1891" date_of_death="1985">Yossef Zaritsky Israeli, born Ukraine, 1891-1985</author>
Man Ray (Emmanuel Radnitzky) 1890, Philadelphia – 1976, Paris <author name="Man Ray" alternate_name="Emmanuel Radnitzky" url="http://www.freebase.com/m/0gskj" date_of_birth="1890" place_of_birth="Philadelphia" date_of_death="1976" place_of_death="Paris"> Man Ray (Emmanuel Radnitzky) 1890, Philadelphia - 1976, Paris</author>

Table 2: Examples of texts in the author field and their annotations

advantage of several existing modules such as gensim[10] for RI, ESA and other text-representation methods, numpy[11] for Support Vector Regression (SVR) with RBF kernels, PyVowpal[12] for an efficient implementation of the LDA, and nltk[13] for general text pre-processing.

The resulting system was trained and tested on the data provided by the task organizers. The train and test sets consisted each of 750 pairs of cultural heritage records from Europeana along with the gold standard for the training set. The BUT-TYPED system reached score 0.7592 in the author field (cross-validated results, Pearson correlation) on the training set where 80 % were used for training whereas 20 % for testing. The score for the field on the testing set was 0.7468, while the baseline was 0.4278.

4 Conclusions

Despite issues related to the low quality of the gold standard data, the attention paid to the similarity computation on the chosen field showed to bear fruit. The realized system ranked third among 14 others in the criterion we focused on. Domain knowledge proved to significantly help in measuring semantic closeness between authors and the results correspond to an intuitive understanding of the similarity between artists.

[10]http://radimrehurek.com/gensim/

[11]http://www.numpy.org/

[12]https://github.com/shilad/PyVowpal

[13]http://nltk.org/

Acknowledgments

This work was partially supported by the EC's Seventh Framework Programme (FP7/2007-2013) under grant agreement No. 270001, and by the Centrum excellence IT4Innovations (ED1.1.00/02.0070).

References

Agirre, E., Diab, M., Cer, D., and Gonzalez-Agirre, A. (2012). Semeval-2012 task 6: A pilot on semantic textual similarity. In *Proceedings of the First Joint Conference on Lexical and Computational Semantics-Volume 1: Proceedings of the main conference and the shared task, and Volume 2: Proceedings of the Sixth International Workshop on Semantic Evaluation*, pages 385–393. Association for Computational Linguistics.

Aletras, N., Stevenson, M., and Clough, P. (2012). Computing similarity between items in a digital library of cultural heritage. *Journal on Computing and Cultural Heritage (JOCCH)*, 5(4):16.

Annesi, P., Storch, V., and Basili, R. (2012). Space projections as distributional models for semantic composition. In *Computational Linguistics and Intelligent Text Processing*, pages 323–335. Springer.

Croce, D., Annesi, P., Storch, V., and Basili, R. (2012). Unitor: combining semantic text similarity functions through sv regression. In *Proceedings of the First Joint Conference on Lexical and Computational Semantics-Volume 1: Proceedings of the main conference and the shared task, and Volume 2: Proceedings of the Sixth International Workshop on Semantic Evaluation*, pages 597–602. Association for Computational Linguistics.

Gabrilovich, E. and Markovitch, S. (2007). Computing semantic relatedness using wikipedia-based explicit semantic analysis. In *Proceedings of the 20th International Joint Conference on Artificial Intelligence*, pages 6–12.

Landauer, T., Foltz, P., and Laham, D. (1998). An introduction to latent semantic analysis. *Discourse processes*, 25(2):259–284.

Lin, D. (1998). An information-theoretic definition of similarity. In *Proceedings of the 15th International Conference on Machine Learning*, volume 1, pages 296–304. Citeseer.

Lintean, M. C. and Rus, V. (2010). Paraphrase identification using weighted dependencies and word semantics. *Informatica: An International Journal of Computing and Informatics*, 34(1):19–28.

Negri, M., Marchetti, A., Mehdad, Y., Bentivogli, L., and Giampiccolo, D. (2012). semeval-2012 task 8: Cross-lingual textual entailment for content synchronization. In *Proceedings of the First Joint Conference on Lexical and Computational Semantics-Volume 1: Proceedings of the main conference and the shared task, and Volume 2: Proceedings of the Sixth International Workshop on Semantic Evaluation*, pages 399–407. Association for Computational Linguistics.

Paolacci, G., Chandler, J., and Ipeirotis, P. (2010). Running experiments on amazon mechanical turk. *Judgment and Decision Making*, 5(5):411–419.

Sahlgren, M. (2005). An introduction to random indexing. In *Methods and Applications of Semantic Indexing Workshop at the 7th International Conference on Terminology and Knowledge Engineering, TKE 2005*. Citeseer.

ECNUCS: Measuring Short Text Semantic Equivalence Using Multiple Similarity Measurements

Tian Tian ZHU
Department of Computer Science and Technology
East China Normal University
51111201046@student.ecnu.edu.cn

Man LAN*
Department of Computer Science and Technology
East China Normal University
mlan@cs.ecnu.edu.cn

Abstract

This paper reports our submissions to the Semantic Textual Similarity (STS) task in *SEM Shared Task 2013. We submitted three Support Vector Regression (SVR) systems in core task, using 6 types of similarity measures, i.e., string similarity, number similarity, knowledge-based similarity, corpus-based similarity, syntactic dependency similarity and machine translation similarity. Our third system with different training data and different feature sets for each test data set performs the best and ranks 35 out of 90 runs. We also submitted two systems in typed task using string based measure and Named Entity based measure. Our best system ranks 5 out of 15 runs.

1 Introduction

The task of semantic textual similarity (STS) is to measure the degree of semantic equivalence between two sentences, which plays an increasingly important role in natural language processing (NLP) applications. For example, in text categorization (Yang and Wen, 2007), two documents which are more similar are more likely to be grouped in the same class. In information retrieval (Sahami and Heilman, 2006), text similarity improves the effectiveness of a semantic search engine by providing information which holds high similarity with the input query. In machine translation (Kauchak and Barzilay, 2006), sentence similarity can be applied for automatic evaluation of the output translation and the reference translations. In question answering (Mohler and Mihalcea, 2009), once the question and the candidate answers are treated as two texts, the answer text which has a higher relevance with the question text may have higher probability to be the right one.

The STS task in *SEM Shared Task 2013 consists of two subtasks, i.e., core task and typed task, and we participate in both of them. The core task aims to measure the semantic similarity of two sentences, resulting in a similarity score which ranges from 5 (semantic equivalence) to 0 (no relation). The typed task is a pilot task on typed-similarity between semi-structured records. The types of similarity to be measured include location, author, people involved, time, events or actions, subject and description as well as the general similarity of two texts (Agirre et al., 2013).

In this work we present a Support Vector Regression (SVR) system to measure sentence semantic similarity by integrating multiple measurements, i.e., string similarity, knowledge based similarity, corpus based similarity, number similarity and machine translation metrics. Most of these similarities are borrowed from previous work, e.g., (Bär et al., 2012), (Šaric et al., 2012) and (de Souza et al., 2012). We also propose a novel syntactic dependency similarity. Our best system ranks 35 out of 90 runs in core task and ranks 5 out of 15 runs in typed task.

The rest of this paper is organized as follows. Section 2 describes the similarity measurements used in this work in detail. Section 3 presents experiments and the results of two tasks. Conclusions and future work are given in Section 4.

*Second Joint Conference on Lexical and Computational Semantics (*SEM), Volume 1: Proceedings of the Main Conference and the Shared Task*, pages 124–131, Atlanta, Georgia, June 13-14, 2013. ©2013 Association for Computational Linguistics

2 Text Similarity Measurements

To compute semantic textual similarity, previous work has adopted multiple semantic similarity measurements. In this work, we adopt 6 types of measures, i.e., string similarity, number similarity, knowledge-based similarity, corpus-based similarity, syntactic dependency similarity and machine translation similarity. Most of them are borrowed from previous work due to their superior performance reported. Besides, we also propose two syntactic dependency similarity measures. Totally we get 33 similarity measures. Generally, these similarity measures are represented as numerical values and combined using regression model.

2.1 Preprocessing

Generally, we perform text preprocessing before we compute each text similarity measurement. Firstly, Stanford parser[1] is used for sentence tokenization and parsing. Specifically, the tokens *n't* and *'m* are replaced with *not* and *am*. Secondly, Stanford POS Tagger[2] is used for POS tagging. Thirdly, Natural Language Toolkit[3] is used for WordNet based Lemmatization, which lemmatizes the word to its nearest base form that appears in WordNet, for example, was is lemmatized as is, not *be*.

Given two short texts or sentences s_1 and s_2, we denote the word set of s_1 and s_2 as S_1 and S_2, the length (i.e., number of words) of s_1 and s_2 as $|S_1|$ and $|S_2|$.

2.2 String Similarity

Intuitively, if two sentences share more strings, they are considered to have higher semantic similarity. Therefore, we create 12 string based features in consideration of the common sequence shared by two texts.

Longest Common sequence (LCS). The widely used *LCS* is proposed by (Allison and Dix, 1986), which is to find the maximum length of a common subsequence of two strings and here the subsequence need to be contiguous. In consideration of the different length of two texts, we compute *LCS* similarity using Formula (1) as follows:

$$Sim_{LCS} = \frac{Length\_of\_LCS}{min(|S_1|, |S_2|)} \quad (1)$$

In order to eliminate the impacts of various forms of word, we also compute a *Lemma LCS* similarity score after sentences being lemmatized.

word n-grams. Following (Lyon et al., 2001), we calculate the *word n-grams* similarity using the Jaccard coefficient as shown in Formula (2), where p is the number of n-grams shared by s_1 and s_2, q and r are the number of n-grams not shared by s_1 and s_2, respectively.

$$Jacc = \frac{p}{p+q+r} \quad (2)$$

Since we focus on short texts, here only n=1,2,3,4 is used in this work. Similar with *LCS*, we also compute a *Lemma n-grams* similarity score.

Weighted Word Overlap (WWO). (Šaric et al., 2012) pointed out that when measuring sentence similarity, different words may convey different content information. Therefore, we consider to assign more importance to those words bearing more content information. To measure the importance of each word, we use Formula (3) to calculate the information content for each word w:

$$ic(w) = \ln \frac{\sum_{w' \in C} freq(w')}{freq(w)} \quad (3)$$

where C is the set of words in the corpus and $freq(w)$ is the frequency of the word w in the corpus. To compute $ic(w)$, we use the Web 1T 5-gram Corpus[4], which is generated from approximately one trillion word tokens of text from Web pages.

Obviously, the *WWO* scores between two sentences is non-symmetric. The *WWO* of s_2 by s_1 is given by Formula (4):

$$Sim_{wwo}(s_1, s_2) = \frac{\sum_{w \in S_1 \cap S_2} ic(w)}{\sum_{w' \in S_2} ic(w')} \quad (4)$$

Likewise, we can get $Sim_{wwo}(s_2, s_1)$ score. Then the final *WWO* score is the harmonic mean of $Sim_{wwo}(s_1, s_2)$ and $Sim_{wwo}(s_2, s_1)$. Similarly, we get a *Lemma WWO* score as well.

[1] http://nlp.stanford.edu/software/lex-parser.shtml
[2] http://nlp.stanford.edu/software/tagger.shtml
[3] http://nltk.org/
[4] http://www.ldc.upenn.edu/Catalog/docs/LDC2006T13

2.3 Knowledge Based Similarity

Knowledge based similarity approaches rely on a semantic network of words. In this work all knowledge-based word similarity measures are computed based on WordNet. For word similarity, we employ four WordNet-based similarity metrics: the ***Path*** similarity (Banea et al., 2012); the ***WUP*** similarity (Wu and Palmer, 1994); the ***LCH*** similarity (Leacock and Chodorow, 1998); the ***Lin*** similarity (Lin, 1998). We adopt the NLTK library (Bird, 2006) to compute all these word similarities.

In order to determine the similarity of sentences, we employ two strategies to convert the word similarity into sentence similarity, i.e., (1) the best alignment strategy (*align*) (Banea et al., 2012) and (2) the aggregation strategy (*agg*) (Mihalcea et al., 2006).

The best alignment strategy is computed as below:

$$Sim_{align}(s_1, s_2) = \frac{(\omega + \sum_{i=1}^{|\varphi|} \varphi_i) * (2|S_1||S_2|)}{|S_1| + |S_2|} \quad (5)$$

where ω is the number of shared terms between s_1 and s_2, list φ contains the similarities of non-shared words in shorter text, φ_i is the highest similarity score of the ith word among all words of the longer text. The aggregation strategy is calculated as below:

$$Sim_{agg}(s_1, s_2) = \frac{\sum_{w \in S_1}(maxSim(w, S_2) * ic(w))}{\sum_{w \in \{S_1\}} ic(w)} \quad (6)$$

where $maxSim(w, S_2)$ is the highest WordNet-based score between word w and all words of sentence S_2. To compute $ic(w)$, we use the same corpus as *WWO*, i.e., the Web 1T 5-gram Corpus. The final score of the aggregation strategy is the mean of $Sim_{agg}(s_1, s_2)$ and $Sim_{agg}(s_2, s_1)$. Finally we get 8 knowledge based features.

2.4 Corpus Based Similarity

Latent Semantic Analysis (LSA) (Landauer et al., 1997). In LSA, term-context associations are captured by means of a dimensionality reduction operation performing singular value decomposition (SVD) on the term-by-context matrix T, where T is induced from a large corpus. We use the TASA corpus[5] to obtain the matrix and compute the word similarity using *cosine* similarity of the two vectors of the words. After that we transform word similarity to sentence similarity based on Formula (5).

Co-occurrence Retrieval Model (CRM) (Weeds, 2003). *CRM* is based on a notion of substitutability. That is, the more appropriate it is to substitute word w_1 in place of word w_2 in a suitable natural language task, the more semantically similar they are. The degree of substitutability of w_2 with w_1 is dependent on the proportion of co-occurrences of w_1 that are also the co-occurrences of w_2, and the proportion of co-occurrences of w_2 that are also the co-occurrences of w_1. Following (Weeds, 2003), the *CRM* word similarity is computed using Formula (7):

$$Sim_{CRM}(w_1, w_2) = \frac{2 * |c(w_1) \cap c(w_2)|}{|c(w_1)| + |c(w_2)|} \quad (7)$$

where $c(w)$ is the set of words that co-occur with w. We use the 5-gram part of the Web 1T 5-gram Corpus to obtain $c(w)$. If two words appear in one 5-gram, we will treat one word as the co-occurring word of each other. To obtain $c(w)$, we propose two methods. In the first *CRM* similarity, we only consider the word w with $|c(w)| > 200$, and then take the top 200 co-occurring words ranked by the co-occurrence frequency as its $c(w)$. To relax restrictions, we also present an extended *CRM* (denoted by *ExCRM*), which extends the *CRM* list that all w with $|c(w)| > 50$ are taken into consideration, but the maximum of $|c(w)|$ is still set to 200. Finally, these two *CRM* word similarity measures are transformed to sentence similarity using Formula (5).

2.5 Syntactic Dependency Similarity

As (Šaric et al., 2012) pointed out that dependency relations of sentences often contain semantic information, in this work we propose two novel syntactic dependency similarity features to capture their possible semantic similarity.

Simple Dependency Overlap. First we measure the simple dependency overlap between two sentences based on matching dependency relations. Stanford Parser provides 53 dependency relations, for example:

$$nsubj(remain - 16, leader - 4)$$
$$dobj(return - 10, home - 11)$$

[5] http://lsa.colorado.edu/

where $nsubj$ (nominal subject) and $dobj$ (direct object) are two dependency types, $remain$ is the governing lemma and $leader$ is the dependent lemma. Two syntactic dependencies are considered equal when they have the same dependency type, governing lemma, and dependent lemma.

Let R_1 and R_2 be the set of all dependency relations in s_1 and s_2, we compute Simple Dependency Overlap using Formula (8):

$$Sim_{SimDep}(s_1, s_2) = \frac{2 * |R_1 \cap R_2| * |R_1||R_2|}{|R_1| + |R_2|} \quad (8)$$

Special Dependency Overlap. Several types of dependency relations are believed to contain the primary content of a sentence. So we extract three roles from those special dependency relations, i.e., *predicate*, *subject* and *object*. For example, from above dependency relation $dobj$, we can extract the object of the sentence, i.e., *home*. For each of these three roles, we get a similarity score. For example, to calculate $Sim_{predicate}$, we denote the sets of predicates of two sentences as S_{p1} and S_{p2}. We first use *LCH* to compute word similarity and then compute sentence similarity using Formula (5). Similarly, the Sim_{subj} and Sim_{obj} are obtained in the same way. In the end we average the similarity scores of the three roles as the final Special Dependency Overlap score.

2.6 Number Similarity

Numbers in the sentence occasionally carry similarity information. If two sentences contain different sets of numbers even though their sentence structure is quite similar, they may be given a low similarity score. Here we adopt two features following (Šaric et al., 2012), which are computed as follow:

$$\log(1 + |N_1| + |N_2|) \quad (9)$$

$$2 * |N_1 \cap N_2| / (|N_1| + |N_2|) \quad (10)$$

where N_1 and N_2 are the sets of all numbers in s_1 and s_2. We extract the number information from sentences by checking if the POS tag is *CD* (cardinal number).

2.7 Machine Translation Similarity

Machine translation (MT) evaluation metrics are designed to assess whether the output of a MT system is semantically equivalent to a set of reference translations. The two given sentences can be viewed as one input and one output of a MT system, then the MT measures can be used to measure their semantic similarity. We use the following 6 lexical level metrics (de Souza et al., 2012): *WER*, *TER*, *PER*, *NIST*, *ROUGE-L*, *GTM-1*. All these measures are obtained using the Asiya Open Toolkit for Automatic Machine Translation (Meta-) Evaluation[6].

3 Experiment and Results

3.1 Regression Model

We adopt LIBSVM[7] to build Support Vector Regression (SVR) model for regression. To obtain the optimal SVR parameters C, g, and p, we employ grid search with 10-fold cross validation on training data. Specifically, if the score returned by the regression model is bigger than 5 or less than 0, we normalize it as 5 or 0, respectively.

3.2 Core Task

The organizers provided four different test sets to evaluate the performance of the submitted systems. We have submitted three systems for core task, i.e., Run 1, Run 2 and Run 3. Run 1 is trained on all training data sets with all features except the number based features, because most of the test data do not contain number. Run 2 uses the same feature sets as Run 1 but different training data sets for different test data as listed in Table 1, where different training data sets are combined together as they have similar structures with the test data. Run 3 uses different feature sets as well as different training data sets for each test data. Table 2 shows the best feature sets used for each test data set, where "+" means the feature is selected and "-" means not selected. We did not use the whole feature set because in our preliminary experiments, some features performed not well on some training data sets, and they even reduced the performance of our system. To select features, we trained two SVR models for each feature, one with all features and another with all features except this feature. If the first model outperforms the second model, this feature is chosen.

Table 3 lists the performance of these three systems as well as the baseline and the best results on

[6]http://nlp.lsi.upc.edu/asiya/

[7]http://www.csie.ntu.edu.tw/ cjlin/libsvm/

Test	Training
Headline	MSRpar
OnWN+FNWN	MSRpar+OnWN
SMT	SMTnews+SMTeuroparl

Table 1: Different training data sets used for each test data set

type	Features	Headline	OnWN and FNWN	SMT
String Based	LCS	+	+	-
	Lemma LCS	+	+	-
	N-gram	+	1+2gram	1gram
	Lemma N-gram	+	1+2gram	1gram
	WWO	+	+	+
	Lemma WWO	+	+	+
Knowledge Based	Path,WUP,LCH,Lin +aligh	+	+	+
	Path,WUP,LCH,Lin +ic-weighted	+	+	+
Corpus Based	LSA	+	+	+
	CRM,ExCRM	+	+	+
Syntactic Dependency	Simple Dependency Overlap	+	+	+
	Special Dependency Overlap	+	-	+
Number	Number	+	-	-
MT	WER	-	+	+
	TER	-	+	+
	PER	+	+	+
	NIST	+	+	-
	ROUGE-L	+	+	+
	GTM-1	+	+	+

Table 2: Best feature combination for each data set

System	Mean	Headline	OnWN	FNWN	SMT
Best	0.6181	0.7642	0.7529	0.5818	0.3804
Baseline	0.3639	0.5399	0.2828	0.2146	0.2861
Run 1	0.3533	0.5656	0.2083	0.1725	0.2949
Run 2	0.4720	0.7120	0.5388	0.2013	0.2504
Run 3 (rank 35)	0.4967	0.6799	0.5284	0.2203	0.3595

Table 3: Final results on STS core task

STS core task in *SEM Shared Task 2013. For the three runs we submitted to the task organizers, Run 3 performs the best results and ranks 35 out of 90 runs. Run 2 performs much better than Run 1. It indicates that using different training data sets for different test sets indeed improves results. Run 3 outperforms Run 2 and Run 1. It shows that our feature selection process for each test data set does help improve the performance too. From this table, we find that different features perform different on different kinds of data sets and thus using proper feature subsets for each test data set would make improvement.

Besides, results on the four test data sets are quite different. *Headline* always gets the best result on each run and *OnWN* follows second. And results of *FNWN* and *SMT* are much lower than *Headline* and *OnWN*. One reason of the poor performance of *FNWN* may be the big length difference of sentence pairs. That is, sentence from WordNet is short while sentence from FrameNet is quite longer, and some samples even have more than one sentence (e.g. "*doing as one pleases or chooses*" VS "*there exist a number of different possible events that may happen in the future in most cases, there is an agent involved who has to consider which of the possible events will or should occur a salient entity which is deeply involved in the event may also be mentioned*"). As a result, even though the two sentences are similar in meaning, most of our measures would give low scores due to quite different sentence length.

In order to understand the contributions of each similarity measurement, we trained 6 SVR regression models based on 6 types on *MSRpar* data set. Table 4 presents the Pearson's correlation scores of the 6 types of measurements on *MSRpar*. We can see that the corpus-based measure achieves the best, then the knowledge-based measure and the MT measure follow. Number similarity performs surprisingly well, which benefits from the property of data set that *MSRpar* contains many numbers in sentences and the sentence similarity depends a lot on those numbers as well. The string similarity is not as good as the knowledge-based, the corpus-based and the MT similarity because of its disability of extracting semantic characteristics of sentence. Surprisingly, the Syntactic dependency similarity performs the worst. Since we only extract two features based on sentence dependency, they may not enough to capture the key semantic similarity information from the sentences.

3.3 Typed Task

For typed task, we also adopt a SVR model for each type. Since several previous similarity measures used for core task are not suitable for evaluation of the similarity of *people involved*, *time period*, *location* and *event or action involved*, we add two Named Entity Recognition (NER) based features. Firstly we use Stanford NER[8] to obtain person, location and date information from the whole text with NER tags of "PERSON", "LOCATION" and "DATE". Then for each list of entity, we get two feature values using the following two formulas:

Features	results
string	0.4757
knowledge-based	**0.5640**
corpus-based	**0.5842**
syntactic dependency	0.3528
number	**0.5278**
MT metrics	**0.5595**

Table 4: Pearson correlation of features of the six aspects on MSRpar

$$Sim_{NER\_Num}(L1_{NER}, L2_{NER}) = \frac{min(|L1_{NER}|, |L2_{NER}|)}{max(|L1_{NER}|, |L2_{NER}|)} \quad (11)$$

$$Sim_{NER}(L1_{NER}, L2_{NER}) = \frac{Num(equalpairs)}{|L1_{NER}| * |L2_{NER}|} \quad (12)$$

where L_{NER} is the list of one entity type from the text, and for two lists of NERs $L1_{NER}$ and $L2_{NER}$, there are $|L1_{NER}| * |L2_{NER}|$ NER pairs. $Num(equalpairs)$ is the number of equal pairs. Here we expand the condition of equivalence: two NERs are considered equal if one is part of another (e.g. "John Warson" VS "Warson"). Features and content we used for each similarity are presented in Table 5. For the three similarities: *people involved*, *time period*, *location*, we compute the two NER based features for each similarity with NER type of "PERSON", "LOCATION" and "DATE". And for *event or action involved*, we add the above 6 NER feature scores as its feature set. The NER based similarity used in *description* is the same as *event or action involved* but only based on "dcDescription" part of text. Besides, we add a length feature in *description*, which is the ratio of shorter length and longer length of descriptions.

[8]http://nlp.stanford.edu/software/CRF-NER.shtml

Type	Features	Content used
author	string based (+ knowledge based for Run2)	dcCreator
people involved	NER based	whole text
time period	NER based	whole text
location	NER based	whole text
event or action involved	NER based	whole text
subject	string based (+ knowledge based for Run2)	dcSubject
description	string based, NER based,length	dcDescription
General	the 7 similarities above	

Table 5: Feature sets and content used of 8 type similarities of Typed data

We have submitted two runs. Run 1 uses only string based and NER based features. Besides features used in Run 1, Run 2 also adds knowledge based features. Table 6 shows the performance of our two runs as well as the baseline and the best results on STS typed task in *SEM Shared Task 2013. Our Run 1 ranks 5 and Run 2 ranks 7 out of 15 runs. Run 2 performed worse than Run 1 and the possible reason may be the knowledge based method is not suitable for this kind of data. Furthermore, since we only use NER based features which involves three entities for these similarities, they are not enough to capture the relevant information for other types.

4 Conclusion

In this paper we described our submissions to the Semantic Textual Similarity Task in *SEM Shared Task 2013. For core task, we collect 6 types of similarity measures, i.e., string similarity, number similarity, knowledge-based similarity, corpus-based similarity, syntactic dependency similarity and machine translation similarity. And our Run 3 with different training data and different feature sets for each test data set ranks 35 out of 90 runs. For typed task, we adopt string based measure, NER based measure and knowledge based measure, our best system ranks 5 out of 15 runs. Clearly, these similarity measures are not quite enough. For the core task, in our future work we will consider the measures to evaluate the sentence difference as well. For the typed task, with the help of more advanced IE tools to extract more information regarding different types, we need to propose more methods to evaluate the similarity.

Acknowledgments

The authors would like to thank the organizers and reviewers for this interesting task and their helpful suggestions and comments, which improved the final version of this paper. This research is supported by grants from National Natural Science Foundation of China (No.60903093), Shanghai Pujiang Talent Program (No.09PJ1404500), Doctoral Fund of Ministry of Education of China (No.20090076120029) and Shanghai Knowledge Service Platform Project (No.ZF1213).

References

Eneko Agirre, Daniel Cer, Mona Diab, Aitor Gonzalez-Agirre, and Weiwei Guo. 2013. *sem 2013 shared task: Semantic textual similarity, including a pilot on typed-similarity. In **SEM 2013: The Second Joint Conference on Lexical and Computational Semantics*. Association for Computational Linguistics.

Lloyd Allison and Trevor I Dix. 1986. A bit-string longest-common-subsequence algorithm. *Information Processing Letters*, 23(5):305–310.

Carmen Banea, Samer Hassan, Michael Mohler, and Rada Mihalcea. 2012. Unt: A supervised synergistic approach to semantic text similarity. pages 635–642. First Joint Conference on Lexical and Computational Semantics (*SEM).

Daniel Bär, Chris Biemann, Iryna Gurevych, and Torsten Zesch. 2012. Ukp: Computing semantic textual similarity by combining multiple content similarity measures. pages 435–440. First Joint Conference on Lexical and Computational Semantics (*SEM).

Steven Bird. 2006. Nltk: the natural language toolkit. In *Proceedings of the COLING/ACL on Interactive presentation sessions*, pages 69–72. Association for Computational Linguistics.

System	general	author	people	time	location	event	subject	description	mean
Best	0.7981	0.8158	0.6922	0.7471	0.7723	0.6835	0.7875	0.7996	0.7620
Baseline	0.6691	0.4278	0.4460	0.5002	0.4835	0.3062	0.5015	0.5810	0.4894
Run 1	0.6040	0.7362	0.3663	0.4685	0.3844	0.4057	0.5229	0.6027	0.5113
Run 2	0.6064	0.5684	0.3663	0.4685	0.3844	0.4057	0.5563	0.6027	0.4948

Table 6: Final results on STS typed task

José Guilherme C de Souza, Matteo Negri, Trento Povo, and Yashar Mehdad. 2012. Fbk: Machine translation evaluation and word similarity metrics for semantic textual similarity. pages 624–630. First Joint Conference on Lexical and Computational Semantics (*SEM).

David Kauchak and Regina Barzilay. 2006. Paraphrasing for automatic evaluation. In *Proceedings of the main conference on Human Language Technology Conference of the North American Chapter of the Association of Computational Linguistics*, pages 455–462. Association for Computational Linguistics.

Thomas K Landauer, Darrell Laham, Bob Rehder, and Missy E Schreiner. 1997. How well can passage meaning be derived without using word order? a comparison of latent semantic analysis and humans. In *Proceedings of the 19th annual meeting of the Cognitive Science Society*, pages 412–417.

Claudia Leacock and Martin Chodorow. 1998. Combining local context and wordnet similarity for word sense identification. *WordNet: An electronic lexical database*, 49(2):265–283.

Dekang Lin. 1998. An information-theoretic definition of similarity. In *Proceedings of the 15th international conference on Machine Learning*, volume 1, pages 296–304. San Francisco.

Caroline Lyon, James Malcolm, and Bob Dickerson. 2001. Detecting short passages of similar text in large document collections. In *Proceedings of the 2001 Conference on Empirical Methods in Natural Language Processing*, pages 118–125.

Rada Mihalcea, Courtney Corley, and Carlo Strapparava. 2006. Corpus-based and knowledge-based measures of text semantic similarity. In *Proceedings of the national conference on artificial intelligence*, volume 21, page 775. Menlo Park, CA; Cambridge, MA; London; AAAI Press; MIT Press; 1999.

Michael Mohler and Rada Mihalcea. 2009. Text-to-text semantic similarity for automatic short answer grading. In *Proceedings of the 12th Conference of the European Chapter of the Association for Computational Linguistics*, pages 567–575. Association for Computational Linguistics.

Mehran Sahami and Timothy D Heilman. 2006. A web-based kernel function for measuring the similarity of short text snippets. In *Proceedings of the 15th international conference on World Wide Web*, pages 377–386. ACM.

Frane Šaric, Goran Glavaš, Mladen Karan, Jan Šnajder, and Bojana Dalbelo Bašic. 2012. Takelab: Systems for measuring semantic text similarity. pages 441–448. First Joint Conference on Lexical and Computational Semantics (*SEM).

Julie Elizabeth Weeds. 2003. *Measures and applications of lexical distributional similarity*. Ph.D. thesis, Citeseer.

Zhibiao Wu and Martha Palmer. 1994. Verbs semantics and lexical selection. In *Proceedings of the 32nd annual meeting on Association for Computational Linguistics*, pages 133–138. Association for Computational Linguistics.

Cha Yang and Jun Wen. 2007. Text categorization based on similarity approach. In *Proceedings of International Conference on Intelligence Systems and Knowledge Engineering (ISKE)*.

UBC_UOS-TYPED: Regression for Typed-similarity

Eneko Agirre
University of the Basque Country
Donostia, 20018, Basque Country
e.agirre@ehu.es

Nikolaos Aletras
University of Sheffield
Sheffield, S1 4DP, UK
n.aletras@dcs.shef.ac.uk

Aitor Gonzalez-Agirre
University of the Basque Country
Donostia, 20018, Basque Country
agonzalez278@ikasle.ehu.es

German Rigau
University of the Basque Country
Donostia, 20018, Basque Country
german.rigau@ehu.es

Mark Stevenson
University of Sheffield
Sheffield, S1 4DP, UK
m.stevenson@dcs.shef.ac.uk

Abstract

We approach the typed-similarity task using a range of heuristics that rely on information from the appropriate metadata fields for each type of similarity. In addition we train a linear regressor for each type of similarity. The results indicate that the linear regression is key for good performance. Our best system was ranked third in the task.

1 Introduction

The typed-similarity dataset comprises pairs of Cultural Heritage items from Europeana[1], a single access point to digitised versions of books, paintings, films, museum objects and archival records from institutions throughout Europe. Typically, the items comprise meta-data describing a cultural heritage item and, sometimes, a thumbnail of the item itself. Participating systems need to compute the similarity between items using the textual meta-data. In addition to general similarity, the dataset includes specific kinds of similarity, like similar author, similar time period, etc.

We approach the problem using a range of similarity techniques for each similarity types, these make use of information contained in the relevant meta-data fields.In addition, we train a linear regressor for each type of similarity, using the training data provided by the organisers with the previously defined similarity measures as features.

We begin by describing our basic system in Section 2, followed by the machine learning system in Section 3. The submissions are explained in Section 4. Section 5 presents our results. Finally, we draw our conclusions in Section 6.

2 Basic system

The items in this task are taken from Europeana. They cannot be redistributed, so we used the urls and scripts provided by the organizers to extract the corresponding metadata. We analysed the text in the metadata, performing lemmatization, PoS tagging, named entity recognition and classification (NERC) and date detection using Stanford CoreNLP (Finkel et al., 2005; Toutanova et al., 2003). A preliminary score for each similarity type was then calculated as follows:

- General: cosine similarity of **TF.IDF** vectors of tokens, taken from all fields.
- Author: cosine similarity of **TF.IDF** vectors of dc:Creator field.
- People involved, time period and location: cosine similarity of **TF.IDF** vectors of location/date/people entities recognized by NERC in all fields.
- Events: cosine similarity of **TF.IDF** vectors of event verbs and nouns. A list of verbs and nouns possibly denoting events was derived using the WordNet Morphosemantic Database[2].
- Subject and description: cosine similarity of **TF.IDF** vectors of respective fields.

IDF values were calculated using a subset of Europeana items (the Culture Grid collection), available internally. These preliminary scores were im-

[1] http://www.europeana.eu/

[2] urlhttp://wordnetcode.princeton.edu/standoff-files/morphosemantic-links.xls

*Second Joint Conference on Lexical and Computational Semantics (*SEM), Volume 1: Proceedings of the Main Conference and the Shared Task*, pages 132–137, Atlanta, Georgia, June 13-14, 2013.

proved using **TF.IDF** based on Wikipedia, UKB (Agirre and Soroa, 2009) and a more informed time similarity measure. We describe each of these processes in turn.

2.1 TF.IDF

A common approach to computing document similarity is to represent documents as Bag-Of-Words (BOW). Each BOW is a vector consisting of the words contained in the document, where each dimension corresponds to a word, and the weight is the frequency in the corresponding document. The similarity between two documents can be computed as the cosine of the angle between their vectors. This is the approached use above.

This approach can be improved giving more weight to words which occur in only a few documents, and less weight to words occurring in many documents (Baeza-Yates and Ribeiro-Neto, 1999). In our system, we count document frequencies of words using Wikipedia as a reference corpus since the training data consists of only 750 items associated with short textual information and might not be sufficient for reliable estimations. The **TF.IDF** similarity between items a and b is defined as:

$$sim_{\text{tf.idf}}(a,b) = \frac{\sum_{w\in a,b} \text{tf}_{w,a} \times \text{tf}_{w,b} \times \text{idf}_w^2}{\sqrt{\sum_{w\in a}(\text{tf}_{w,a} \times \text{idf}_w)^2} \times \sqrt{\sum_{w\in b}(\text{tf}_{w,b} \times \text{idf}_w)^2}}$$

where $\text{tf}_{w,x}$ is the frequency of the term w in $x \in \{a,b\}$ and idf_w is the inverted document frequency of the word w measured in Wikipedia. We substituted the preliminary general similarity score by the obtained using the **TF.IDF** presented in this section.

2.2 UKB

The semantic disambiguation UKB[3] algorithm (Agirre and Soroa, 2009) applies personalized PageRank on a graph generated from the English WordNet (Fellbaum, 1998), or alternatively, from Wikipedia. This algorithm has proven to be very competitive in word similarity tasks (Agirre et al., 2010).

To compute similarity using UKB we represent WordNet as a graph $G = (V, E)$ as follows: graph nodes represent WordNet concepts (synsets) and dictionary words; relations among synsets are represented by undirected edges; and dictionary words are linked to the synsets associated to them by directed edges.

Our method is provided with a pair of vectors of words and a graph-based representation of WordNet. We first compute the personalized PageRank over WordNet separately for each of the vector of words, producing a probability distribution over WordNet synsets. We then compute the similarity between these two probability distributions by encoding them as vectors and computing the cosine between the vectors. We present each step in turn.

Once personalized PageRank is computed, it returns a probability distribution over WordNet synsets. The similarity between two vectors of words can thus be implemented as the similarity between the probability distributions, as given by the cosine between the vectors.

We used random walks to compute improved similarity values for author, people involved, location and event similarity:

- Author: UKB over Wikipedia using person entities recognized by NERC in the dc:Creator field.
- People involved and location: UKB over Wikipedia using people/location entities recognized by NERC in all fields.
- Events: UKB over WordNet using event nouns and verbs recognized in all fields.

Results on the training data showed that performance using this approach was quite low (with the exception of events). This was caused by the large number of cases where the Stanford parser did not find entities which were in Wikipedia. With those cases on mind, we combined the scores returned by UKB with the similarity scores presented in Section 2 as follows: if UKB similarity returns a score, we multiply both, otherwise we return the square of the other similarity score. Using the multiplication of the two scores, the results on the training data improved.

2.3 Time similarity measure

In order to measure the time similarity between a pair of items, we need to recognize time expressions in both items. We assume that the year of

[3]http://ixa2.si.ehu.es/ukb/

creation or the year denoting when the event took place in an artefact are good indicators for time similarity. Therefore, information about years is extracted from each item using the following pattern: $[1|2][0-9]\{3\}$. Using this approach, each item is represented as a set of numbers denoting the years mentioned in the meta-data.

Time similarity between two items is computed based on the similarity between their associated years. Similarity between two years is defined as:

$$sim_{year}(y_1, y_2) = max\{0, 1 - |y1 - y2| * k\}$$

k is a parameter to weight the difference between two years, e.g. for $k = 0.1$ all items that have difference of 10 years or more assigned a score of 0. We obtained best results for $k = 0.1$.

Finally, time similarity between items a and b is computed as the maximum of the pairwise similarity between their associated years:

$$sim_{time}(a, b) = max_{\substack{\forall i \in a \\ \forall j \in b}}\{0, sim_{year}(a_i, b_j)\}$$

We substituted the preliminary time similarity score by the measure obtained using the method presented in this section.

3 Applying Machine Learning

The above heuristics can be good indicators for the respective kind of similarity, and can be thus applied directly to the task. In this section, we take those indicators as features, and use linear regression (as made available by Weka (Hall et al., 2009)) to learn models that fit the features to the training data.

We generated further similarity scores for general similarity, including Latent Dirichlet Allocation (LDA) (Blei et al., 2003), UKB and Wikipedia Link Vector Model (WLVM)(Milne, 2007) using information taken from all fields, as explained below.

3.1 LDA

LDA (Blei et al., 2003) is a statistical method that learns a set of latent variables called topics from a training corpus. Given a topic model, documents can be inferred as probability distributions over topics, θ. The distribution for a document i is denoted as θ_i. An LDA model is trained using the training set consisting of 100 topics using the *gensim* package[4]. The hyperparameters (α, β) were set to $\frac{1}{num\_of\_topics}$. Therefore, each item in the test set is represented as a topic distribution.

The similarity between a pair of items is estimated by comparing their topic distributions following the method proposed in Aletras et al. (2012; Aletras and Stevenson (2012). This is achieved by considering each distribution as a vector (consisting of the topics corresponding to an item and its probability) then computing the cosine of the angle between them, i.e.

$$sim_{LDA}(a, b) = \frac{\vec{\theta_a} \cdot \vec{\theta_b}}{|\vec{\theta_a}| \times |\vec{\theta_b}|}$$

where $\vec{\theta_a}$ is the vector created from the probability distribution generated by LDA for item a.

3.2 Pairwise UKB

We run UKB (Section 2.2) to generate a probability distribution over WordNet synsets for all of the words of all items. Similarity between two words is computed by creating vectors from these distributions and comparing them using the cosine of the angle between the two vectors. If a words does not appear in WordNet its similarity value to every other word is set to 0. We refer to that similarity metric as UKB here.

Similarity between two items is computed by performing pairwise comparison between their words, for each, selecting the highest similarity score:

$$sim(a, b) = \frac{1}{2}\left(\frac{\sum_{w_1 \in a} \arg\max_{w_2 \in b} UKB(w_1, w_2)}{|a|} + \frac{\sum_{w_2 \in b} \arg\max_{w_1 \in a} UKB(w_2, w_1)}{|b|}\right)$$

where a and b are two items, $|a|$ the number of tokens in a and $UKB(w_1, w_2)$ is the similarity between words w_1 and w_2.

3.3 WLVM

An algorithm described by Milne and Witten (2008) associates Wikipedia articles which are likely to be relevant to a given text snippet using machine learning techniques. We make use of that method to represent each item as a set of likely relevant Wikipedia

[4]http://pypi.python.org/pypi/gensim

articles. Then, similarity between Wikipedia articles is measured using the Wikipedia Link Vector Model (WLVM) (Milne, 2007). WLVM uses both the link structure and the article titles of Wikipedia to measure similarity between two Wikipedia articles. Each link is weighted by the probability of it occurring. Thus, the value of the weight w for a link $x \rightarrow y$ between articles x and y is:

$$w(x \rightarrow y) = |x \rightarrow y| \times \log \left(\sum_{z=1}^{t} \frac{t}{z \rightarrow y} \right)$$

where t is the total number of articles in Wikipedia. The similarity of articles is compared by forming vectors of the articles which are linked from them and computing the cosine of their angle. For example the vectors of two articles x and y are:

$$x = (w(x \rightarrow l_1), w(x \rightarrow l_2), ..., w(x \rightarrow l_n))$$
$$y = (w(y \rightarrow l_1), w(y \rightarrow l_2), ..., w(y \rightarrow l_n))$$

where x and y are two Wikipedia articles and $x \rightarrow l_i$ is a link from article x to article l_i.

Since the items have been mapped to Wikipedia articles, similarity between two items is computed by performing pairwise comparison between articles using WLVM, for each, selecting the highest similarity score:

$$sim(a,b) = \frac{1}{2}\left(\frac{\sum_{w_1 \in a} \arg\max_{w_2 \in b} WLVM(w_1, w_2)}{|a|} + \frac{\sum_{w_2 \in b} \arg\max_{w_1 \in a} WLVM(w_2, w_1)}{|b|} \right)$$

where a and b are two items, $|a|$ the number of Wikipedia articles in a and $WLVM(w_1, w_2)$ is the similarity between concepts w_1 and w_2.

4 Submissions

We selected three systems for submission. The first run uses the similarity scores of the basic system (Section 2) for each similarity types as follows:

- General: cosine similarity of **TF.IDF** vectors, IDF based on Wikipedia (as shown in Section 2.1).
- Author: product of the scores obtained obtained using **TF.IDF** vectors and UKB (as shown in Section 2.2) using only the data extracted from dc:Creator field.
- People involved and location: product of cosine similarity of **TF.IDF** vectors and UKB (as shown in Section 2.2) using the data extracted from all fields.
- Time period: time similarity measure (as shown in Section 2.3).
- Events: product of cosine similarity of **TF.IDF** vectors and UKB (as shown in Section 2.2) of event nouns and verbs recognized in all fields.
- Subject and description: cosine similarity of **TF.IDF** vectors of respective fields (as shown in Section 2).

For the second run we trained a ML model for each of the similarity types, using the following features:

- Cosine similarity of **TF.IDF** vectors as shown in Section 2 for the eight similarity types.
- Four new values for general similarity: **TF.IDF** (Section 2.1), LDA (Section 3.1), UKB and WLVM (Section 3.3).
- Time similarity as shown in Section 2.3.
- Events similarity computed using UKB initialized with the event nouns and verbs in all fields.

We decided not to use the product of **TF.IDF** and UKB presented in Section 2.2 in this system because our intention was to measure the power of the linear regression ML algorithm to learn on the given raw data.

The third run is similar, but includes all available features (21). In addition to the above, we included:

- Author, people involved and location similarity computed using UKB initialized with people/location recognized by NERC in dc:Creator field for author, and in all fields for people involved and location.
- Author, people involved, location and event similarity scores computed by the product of **TF.IDF** vectors and UKB values as shown in Section 2.2.

5 Results

Evaluation was carried out using the official scorer provided by the organizers, which computes the Pearson Correlation score for each of the eight similarity types plus an additional mean correlation.

Team and run	General	Author	People_involved	Time	Location	Event	Subject	Description	Mean
UBC_UOS-RUN1	0.7269	0.4474	0.4648	0.5884	0.4801	0.2522	0.4976	0.5389	0.5033
UBC_UOS-RUN2	0.7777	0.6680	0.6767	0.7609	0.7329	0.6412	0.7516	0.8024	0.7264
UBC_UOS-RUN3	**0.7866**	**0.6941**	**0.6965**	**0.7654**	**0.7492**	**0.6551**	**0.7586**	**0.8067**	**0.7390**

Table 1: Results of our systems on the training data, using cross-validation when necessary.

Team and run	General	Author	People_involved	Time	Location	Event	Subject	Description	Mean	Rank
UBC_UOS-RUN1	0.7256	0.4568	0.4467	0.5762	0.4858	0.3090	0.5015	0.5810	0.5103	6
UBC_UOS-RUN2	0.7457	0.6618	0.6518	**0.7466**	0.7244	0.6533	0.7404	0.7751	0.7124	4
UBC_UOS-RUN3	**0.7461**	**0.6656**	**0.6544**	0.7411	**0.7257**	**0.6545**	**0.7417**	**0.7763**	**0.7132**	**3**

Table 2: Results of our submitted systems.

5.1 Development

The three runs mentioned above were developed using the training data made available by the organizers. In order to avoid overfitting we did not change the default parameters of the linear regressor, and 10-fold cross-validation was used for evaluating the models on the training data. The results of our systems on the training data are shown on Table 1. The table shows that the heuristics (RUN1) obtain low results, and that linear regression improves results considerably in all types. Using the full set of features, RUN3 improves slightly over RUN2, but the improvement is consistent across all types.

5.2 Test

The test dataset was composed of 750 pairs of items. Table 2 illustrates the results of our systems in the test dataset. The results of the runs are very similar to those obtained on the training data, but the difference between RUN2 and RUN3 is even smaller. Our systems were ranked #3 (RUN 3), #4 (RUN 2) and #6 (RUN 1) among 14 systems submitted by 6 teams. Our systems achieved good correlation scores for almost all similarity types, with the exception of author similarity, which is the worst ranked in comparison with the rest of the systems.

6 Conclusions and Future Work

In this paper, we presented the systems submitted to the *SEM 2013 shared task on Semantic Textual Similarity. We combined some simple heuristics for each type of similarity, based on the appropriate metadata fields. The use of lineal regression improved the results considerably across all types. Our system fared well in the competition. We submitted three systems and the highest-ranked of these achieved the third best results overall.

Acknowledgements

This work is partially funded by the PATHS project (http://paths-project.eu) funded by the European Community's Seventh Framework Programme (FP7/2007-2013) under grant agreement no. 270082. Aitor Gonzalez-Agirre is supported by a PhD grant from the Spanish Ministry of Education, Culture and Sport (grant FPU12/06243).

References

Eneko Agirre and Aitor Soroa. 2009. Personalizing pagerank for word sense disambiguation. In *Proceedings of the 12th conference of the European chapter of the Association for Computational Linguistics (EACL-2009)*, Athens, Greece.

Eneko Agirre, Montse Cuadros, German Rigau, and Aitor Soroa. 2010. Exploring knowledge bases for similarity. In *Proceedings of the Seventh conference on International Language Resources and Evaluation (LREC10). European Language Resources Association (ELRA). ISBN: 2-9517408-6-7. Pages 373–377."*.

Nikolaos Aletras and Mark Stevenson. 2012. Computing similarity between cultural heritage items using multimodal features. In *Proceedings of the 6th Workshop on Language Technology for Cultural Heritage, Social Sciences, and Humanities*, pages 85–93, Avignon, France.

Nikolaos Aletras, Mark Stevenson, and Paul Clough. 2012. Computing similarity between items in a digital library of cultural heritage. *J. Comput. Cult. Herit.*, 5(4):16:1–16:19, December.

R. Baeza-Yates and B. Ribeiro-Neto. 1999. *Modern Information Retrieval*. Addison Wesley Longman Limited, Essex.

David M. Blei, Andrew Y. Ng, and Michael I. Jordan. 2003. Latent Dirichlet Allocation. *Journal of Machine Learning Research*, 3:993–1022, March.

Christiane Fellbaum. 1998. *WordNet: An Electronic Lexical Database*. MIT Press.

Jenny Rose Finkel, Trond Grenager, and Christopher Manning. 2005. Incorporating non-local information into information extraction systems by gibbs sampling. In *Proceedings of the 43rd Annual Meeting on Association for Computational Linguistics*, ACL '05, pages 363–370, Stroudsburg, PA, USA. Association for Computational Linguistics.

Mark Hall, Eibe Frank, Geoffrey Holmes, Bernhard Pfahringer, Peter Reutemann, and Ian H. Witten. 2009. The weka data mining software: an update. *SIGKDD Explor. Newsl.*, 11(1):10–18, November.

D. Milne and I. Witten. 2008. Learning to Link with Wikipedia. In *Proceedings of the ACM Conference on Information and Knowledge Management (CIKM'2008)*, Napa Valley, California.

D. Milne. 2007. Computing semantic relatedness using Wikipedia's link structure. In *Proceedings of the New Zealand Computer Science Research Student Conference*.

Kristina Toutanova, Dan Klein, Christopher D. Manning, and Yoram Singer. 2003. Feature-rich part-of-speech tagging with a cyclic dependency network. In *Proceedings of the 2003 Conference of the North American Chapter of the Association for Computational Linguistics on Human Language Technology - Volume 1*, NAACL '03, pages 173–180, Stroudsburg, PA, USA. Association for Computational Linguistics.

KnCe2013-CORE:Semantic Text Similarity by use of Knowledge Bases

Hermann Ziak
Know-Center GmbH
Graz University of Technology
Inffeldgasse 13/ 6. Stock
8010 Graz, Austria
hziak@know-center.at

Roman Kern
Know-Center GmbH
Graz University of Technology
Inffeldgasse 13/ 6. Stock
8010 Graz, Austria
rkern@know-center.at

Abstract

In this paper we describe KnCe2013-CORE, a system to compute the semantic similarity of two short text snippets. The system computes a number of features which are gathered from different knowledge bases, namely WordNet, Wikipedia and Wiktionary. The similarity scores derived from these features are then fed into several multilayer perceptron neuronal networks. Depending on the size of the text snippets different parameters for the neural networks are used. The final output of the neural networks is compared to human judged data. In the evaluation our system performed sufficiently well for text snippets of equal length, but the performance dropped considerably once the pairs of text snippets differ in size.

1 Introduction

The task of the semantic sentence similarity is to assign a score to a given pair of sentences. This score should reflect the degree by which the two sentences represent the same meaning. The semantic similarity of two sentences could then be used in a number of different application scenarios, for example it could help to improve the performance of information retrieval systems.

In the past, systems based on regression models in combination with well chosen features have demonstrated good performance on this topic[4] [6]. Therefore we took this approach as a starting point to develop our semantic similarity system; additionally, we integrated a number of existing knowledge bases into our system. With it, trained with the data discussed in the task specification of last year[1], we participated in the shared task of SEM 2013.

Additionally, to the similarity based on the features derived from the external knowledge bases, we employ a neural network to compute the final similarity score. The motivation to use a supervised machine learning algorithm has been the observation that the semantic similarity is heavily influenced by the context of the human evaluator. A financial expert for example would judge sentences with financial topics different to non financial experts, if occurring numbers differ from each other.

The remainder of the paper is organised as follows: In Section 2 we described our system, the main features and the neuronal network to combine different feature sets. In Section 3 the calculation method of our feature values is discribed. In Section 4 we report the results of our system based on our experiments and the submitted results of the test data. In Section 5 and 6 we discuss the results and the outcome of our work.

2 System Overview

2.1 Processing

Initially the system puts the sentence pairs of the whole training set through our annotation pipeline. After this process the sentence pairs are compared to each other by our different feature scoring algorithms. The result is a list of scores for each of these pairs where every score represents a feature or part of a feature. The processed sentences are now separated by their length and used to train the neuronal

*Second Joint Conference on Lexical and Computational Semantics (*SEM), Volume 1: Proceedings of the Main Conference and the Shared Task*, pages 138–142, Atlanta, Georgia, June 13-14, 2013.

network models for each length group. The testing data is also grouped based on the sentence length and the score for each pair is determined by a relevant model.

2.2 Token Features

The first set of features are simply the tokens from the two respective sentences. This feature set should perform well, if exactly the same words are used within the pair of sentences to be compared. But as soon as words are replaced by their synonyms or other semantically related words, this feature set will not be able to capture the true similarity. Used without other features it could even lead to false positive matches, for example given sentences with similar content but containing antonyms. The tokenizer used by our system was based on the OpenNLP maximum entropy tokenizer, which detects token boundaries based on probability model.

2.3 Wiktionary Features

While the collaboratively created encyclopedia Wikipedia receives a lot of attention from the general public, as well as the research community, the free dictionary Wiktionary[1] is far lesser known. The Wiktionary dictionary stores the information in a semi-structured way using Wikimedia syntax, where a single page represents a single word or phrase. Therefore we developed a parser to extract relevant information. In our case we were especially interested in semantically related terms, where the semantic relationship is:

Representations: Set of word forms for a specific term. These terms are expected to indicate the highest semantic similarity. This includes all flexions, for example the 's' suffix for plural forms.

Synonyms: List of synonyms for the term.

Hyponyms: List of more specific terms.

Hypernym: Terms which represent more general terms.

Antonym: List of terms, which represent an opposing sense.

Related Terms: Terms, with a semantic relationship, which does not fall in the aforementioned categories. For example related terms for 'bank' are 'bankrupt'. Related terms represent only a weak semantic similarity.

Derived Terms: Terms, with overlapping word forms, such as 'bank holiday', 'bankroll' and 'databank' for the term 'bank'. From all the semantic relationship types, derived terms are the weakest indicator for their similarities.

[1] http://en.wiktionary.org

2.4 WordNet Features

The WordNet[5][2] features were generated identically to the Wiktionary features. We used the WordNet off line database and the provided library to get a broader knowledge base. Therefore we extract the semantically related terms of each token and saved each class of relation. Where each dependency class produced an one value in the final feature score list of the sentence pairs.

2.5 Wikification Feature

We applied a Named Entity Recognition component, which has been trained using Wikipedia categories as input. Given a sentence it will annotate all found concepts that match a Wikipedia article, together with a confidence score. So for every found entry by the annotator there is a list of possible associated topics. The confidence score can then be used to score the topic information, in the final step the evaluation values where calculated as follows:

$$score_{wiki}(s_1, s_2) = \frac{|T_1 \cap T_2|}{norm(T_1, T_2)}$$

where T_1 and T_2 are the set of topics of the two sentences and $norm$ is the mean of the confidence scores of the topics.

2.6 Other Features

Although we mainly focused our approach on the three core features above, others seemed to be useful to improve the performance of the system of which some are described below.

Numbers and Financial Expression Feature: Some sentence pairs showed particular variations between the main features and their actual score. Many of these sentence pairs where quite similar in their semantic topic but contained financial expressions or numbers that differed. Therefore these expressions where extracted and compared against each other with a descending score.

NGrams Feature: The ngram overlapping feature is based on a noun-phrase detection which returns the noun-phrases in different ngrams. This noun-phrase detection is a pos tagger pattern which matches multiple nouns preceding adjectives and determiners. In both sentences the ngrams where extracted and compared to each other returning only the biggest overlapping. In the end, to produce the evaluation values, the word-count of the overlapping ngrams were taken.

3 Distance calculation

For the calculation of the distance of the different features we chose a slightly modified version of the Jacquard similarity coefficient.

$$Jsc(w, l) = \frac{w}{l}$$

Where in this case w stands for the intersection of the selected feature, and l for $\frac{l_a + l_b}{2}$ where l_a and l_b are the length of the sentences with or without stop-words depending on the selected feature. The assumption was that for some features the gap between sentences where one has many stop-words and sentences with none would have a crucial impact but for others it would be detrimental. In regard to this we used, depending on the feature, the words or words excluding stop-words.

3.1 Scoring

One of the main issues at the beginning of our research was how to signal the absence of features to the neuronal network. As our feature scores depend on the length of the sentence, the absence of a particular feature (e.g. financial values) and detected features without intersections (e.g. none of the found financial values in the sentences are intersecting) in the sentence pairs would lead to the same result.

Therefore we applied two different similarity scores based on the feature set. They differ in the result they give, if there is no overlap between the two feature sets.

For a simple term similarity we defined our similarity score as

$$score(w, s, l) = \begin{cases} -1 & : s = 0 \; or \; w = 0 \\ Jsc(w, l) & : w > 0 \end{cases}$$

where w stands for the intersections and S for the word-count of the sentences. The system returns the similarity of -1 for no overlap, which signals no similarity at all. For fully overlapping feature sets, the score is 1.

For other features, where we did not expect them to occur in every sentence, for example numbers or financial terms, the similarity score was defined as follows:

$$score(w, s, l) = \begin{cases} 1 & : s = 0 \; or \; w = 0 \\ Jsc(w, l) & : w > 0 \end{cases}$$

In this case the score would yield 1 decreasing for non overlapping feature sets and will drop to -1 the more features differentiated. This redefines the normal state as equivalent to a total similarity of all found features and only if features differ this value drops.

3.2 Sentence Length Grouping

From tests with the training data we found that our system performed very diversly with both long and short sentences although our features where normalized to the sentence length. To cover this problem we separated the whole collection of training data into different groups based on their length, each of the groups were later used to train their own model. Finally the testing data were also divided into this groups and were applied on the group model.

3.3 Neural Network

We applyied multilayer perceptron neuronal networks on the individual sentence length groups. So for each group of sentence length we computed separately the weights of the neural network. To model the neural networks we used the open-source library Neuroph.[2]. This network was defined with a 48-input layer, which represented the extracted feature scores, 4 hidden layers, and a 1-output layer which represents the similarity score of the sentences. For the runs referenced by table 1 and 2 we used 400000 iterations, which gave us the best results in our tests, with a maximum error of 0.001 and a learning rate of 0.001

[2] http://neuroph.sourceforge.net

4 Evaluation and Results

The following results of our system where produced by our test-run after the challenge deadline. For the first run we split each training set in halfe, self-evident without the use of the datasets published after the challenge, and used the other half to validate our system. See table 1 for result, which contain our system.

	MSRvid	MSRpar	SMTeuroparl
Grouping	0.69	0.55	0.50
Without Grouping	0.66	0.52	0.62

Table 1: Run with and without sentence length grouping on the training set

For the validation the whole 2013 test set was used as it wasnot used for training. In table 2 the results of our system on the test-set are listed. When using the sentence length grouping and without sentence length grouping just using a single neural network for all sentence similarities.

	FNWN	headlines	OnWN	SMT
Grouping	0.08	0.66	0.62	0.21
Without Grouping	0.38	0.62	0.39	0.25

Table 2: Results of our system with and without sentence length grouping on the test set

Finally, we report the results from the original evaluation of the STS-SharedTask in table 3.

	FNWN	headlines	OnWN	SMT
KnCe2013-all	0.11	0.35	0.35	0.16
KnCe2013-diff	0.13	0.40	0.35	0.18
KnCe2013-set	0.04	0.05	-0.15	-0.06

Table 3: The submission to the challenge

5 Discussion

Based on the results we can summarize that our submitted system, worked well for data with very short and simple sentences, such as the MSRvid; however for the longer the sentences the performance declined. The grouping based on the input length worked well for sentences of similar length when compared, as we used the average length of both sentences to group them, but it seamed to fail for sentences with very diverse lengths like in the FNWN data set as shown in table 2. Comparing the results of the official submission to the test runs of our system it underperformed in all datasets. We assume that the poor results in the submission run were caused by badly chosen training settings.

6 Conclusion

In our system for semantic sentence similarity we tried to integrate a number of external knowledge bases to improve its performance. (Viz. WordNet, Wikipedia, Wiktionary) Furthermore, we integrated a neural network component to replicate the similarity score assigned by human judges. We used different sets of neural networks, depending on the size of the sentences. In the evaluation we found that our system worked well for the most datasets. But as soon as the pairs of sentences differed too much in size, or the sentences were very long, the performance decreased. In future work we will consider to tackle this problem with partial matching[3] and to introduces features to extract core statements of short texts.

Acknowledgements

The Know-Center is funded within the Austrian COMET Program - Competence Centers for Excellent Technologies - under the auspices of the Austrian Federal Ministry of Transport, Innovation and Technology, the Austrian Federal Ministry of Economy, Family and Youth and by the State of Styria. COMET is managed by the Austrian Research Promotion Agency FFG.

References

[1] Eneko Agirre, Daniel Cer, Mona Diab, and Aitor González. Semeval-2012 task 6: A pilot on semantic textual similarity. In *SEM 2012: The First Joint Conference on Lexical and Computational Semantics (SemEval 2012)*, Montreal, Canada, 2012.

[2] Christiane Fellbaum, editor. *WordNet: An Electronic Lexical Database.* MIT Press, Cambridge, MA, 1998.

[3] Prodromos Malakasiotis and Ion Androutsopoulos. Learning textual entailment using svms and string similarity measures.

[4] Nikos Malandrakis, Elias Iosif, and Alexandros Potamianos. Deeppurple: estimating sentence semantic similarity using n-gram regression models and web snippets. In *Proceedings of the First Joint Conference on Lexical and Computational Semantics - Volume 1: Proceedings of the main conference and the shared task, and Volume 2: Proceedings of the Sixth International Workshop on Semantic Evaluation*, SemEval '12, pages 565–570, Stroudsburg, PA, USA, 2012. Association for Computational Linguistics.

[5] George A. Miller. Wordnet: a lexical database for english. *Commun. ACM*, 38(11):39–41, November 1995.

[6] Frane Šarić, Goran Glavaš, Mladen Karan, Jan Šnajder, and Bojana Dalbelo Bašić. Takelab: Systems for measuring semantic text similarity. In *Proceedings of the Sixth International Workshop on Semantic Evaluation (SemEval 2012)*, pages 441–448, Montréal, Canada, 7-8 June 2012. Association for Computational Linguistics.

UPC-CORE: What Can Machine Translation Evaluation Metrics and Wikipedia Do for Estimating Semantic Textual Similarity?

Alberto Barrón-Cedeño[1,2] **Lluís Màrquez**[1] **Maria Fuentes**[1] **Horacio Rodríguez**[1] **Jordi Turmo**[1]
[1] TALP Research Center, Universitat Politècnica de Catalunya
Jordi Girona Salgado 1–3, 08034, Barcelona, Spain
[2] Facultad de Informática, Universidad Politécnica de Madrid
Boadilla del Monte, 28660 Madrid, Spain
albarron, lluism, mfuentes, horacio, turmo @lsi.upc.edu

Abstract

In this paper we discuss our participation to the 2013 Semeval Semantic Textual Similarity task. Our core features include (*i*) a set of metrics borrowed from automatic machine translation, originally intended to evaluate automatic against reference translations and (*ii*) an instance of explicit semantic analysis, built upon opening paragraphs of Wikipedia 2010 articles. Our similarity estimator relies on a support vector regressor with RBF kernel. Our best approach required 13 machine translation metrics + explicit semantic analysis and ranked 65 in the competition. Our post-competition analysis shows that the features have a good expression level, but overfitting and —mainly— normalization issues caused our correlation values to decrease.

1 Introduction

Our participation to the 2013 Semantic Textual Similarity task (STS) (Agirre et al., 2013)[1] was focused on the CORE problem: GIVEN TWO SENTENCES, s_1 AND s_2, QUANTIFIABLY INFORM ON HOW SIMILAR s_1 AND s_2 ARE. We considered real-valued features from four different sources: (*i*) a set of linguistic measures computed with the Asiya Toolkit for Automatic MT Evaluation (Giménez and Màrquez, 2010b), (*ii*) an instance of explicit semantic analysis (Gabrilovich and Markovitch, 2007), built on top of Wikipedia articles, (*iii*) a dataset predictor, and (*iv*) a subset of the features available in Takelab's Semantic Text Similarity system (Šarić et al., 2012).

Our approaches obtained an overall modest result compared to other participants (best position: 65 out of 89). Nevertheless, our post-competition analysis shows that the low correlation was caused mainly by a deficient data normalization strategy.

The paper distribution is as follows. Section 2 offers a brief overview of the task. Section 3 describes our approach. Section 4 discuss our experiments and obtained results. Section 5 provides conclusions.

2 Task Overview

Detecting two similar text fragments is a difficult task in cases where the similarity occurs at semantic level, independently of the implied lexicon (e.g in cases of dense paraphrasing). As a result, similarity estimation models must involve features other than surface aspects. The STS task is proposed as a challenge focused in short English texts of different nature: from automatic machine translation alternatives to human descriptions of short videos. The test partition also included texts extracted from news headlines and FrameNet–Wordnet pairs.

The range of similarity was defined between 0 (no relation) up to 5 (semantic equivalence). The gold standard values were averaged from different human-made annotations. The expected system's output was composed of a real similarity value, together with an optional confidence level (our confidence level was set constant).

Table 1 gives an overview of the development (2012 training and test) and test datasets. Note that both collections extracted from SMT data are highly biased towards the maximum similarity values (more than 75% of the instances have a similar-

[1] `http://ixa2.si.ehu.es/sts/`

*Second Joint Conference on Lexical and Computational Semantics (*SEM), Volume 1: Proceedings of the Main Conference and the Shared Task*, pages 143–147, Atlanta, Georgia, June 13-14, 2013.

Table 1: Overview of sub-collections in the development and test datasets, including number of instances and distribution of similarity values (in percentage) as well as mean, minimum, and maximum lengths.

		similarity distribution					length		
dataset	instances	[0,1)	[1,2)	[2,3)	[3,4)	[4,5]	mean	min	max
dev-[train + test]									
MSRpar	1,500	1.20	8.13	17.13	**48.73**	24.80	17.84	**5**	30
MSRvid	1,500	31.00	14.13	15.47	20.87	18.53	6.66	2	24
SMTEuroparl	1,193	0.67	0.42	1.17	12.32	**85.4**	21.13	1	72
OnWN	750	2.13	2.67	10.40	25.47	59.33	7.57	1	34
SMTnews	399	1.00	0.75	5.51	13.03	79.70	11.72	2	28
test									
headlines	750	15.47	22.00	16.27	24.67	21.60	7.21	3	22
OnWN	561	**36.54**	9.80	7.49	17.11	29.05	7.17	**5**	22
FNWN	189	34.39	**29.63**	**28.57**	6.88	0.53	19.90	3	71
SMT	750	0.00	0.27	3.47	20.40	75.87	**26.40**	1	**96**

ity higher than 4) and include the longest instances. On the other hand, the FNWN instances are shifted towards low similarity levels (more than 60% have a similarity lower than 2).

3 Approach

Our similarity assessment model relies upon SVM^{light}'s support vector regressor, with RBF kernel (Joachims, 1999).[2] Our model estimation procedure consisted of two steps: parameter definition and backward elimination-based feature selection. The considered features belong to four families, briefly described in the following subsections.

3.1 Machine Translation Evaluation Metrics

We consider a set of linguistic measures originally intended to evaluate the quality of automatic translation systems. These measures compute the quality of a translation by comparing it against one or several reference translations, considered as gold standard. A straightforward application of these measures to the problem at hand is to consider s_1 as the reference and s_2 as the automatic translation, or vice versa. Some of the metrics are not symmetric so we compute similarity between s_1 and s_2 in both directions and average the resulting scores.

The measures are computed with the Asiya Toolkit for Automatic MT Evaluation (Giménez and Màrquez, 2010b). The only pre-processing carried out was tokenization (Asiya performs additional inbox pre-processing operations, though). We considered a sample from three similarity families, which was proposed in (Giménez and Màrquez, 2010a) as a varied and robust metric set, showing good correlation with human assessments.[3]

Lexical Similarity Two metrics of Translation Error Rate (Snover et al., 2006) (i.e. the estimated human effort to convert s_1 into s_2): -TER and -TER$_{pA}$. Two measures of lexical precision: BLEU (Papineni et al., 2002) and NIST (Doddington, 2002). One measure of lexical recall: ROUGE$_W$ (Lin and Och, 2004). Finally, four variants of METEOR (Banerjee and Lavie, 2005) (*exact, stemming, synonyms,* and *paraphrasing*), a lexical metric accounting for F-Measure.

Syntactic Similarity Three metrics that estimate the similarity of the sentences over dependency parse trees (Liu and Gildea, 2005): DP-HWCMi$_c$-4 for grammatical categories chains, DP-HWCMi$_r$-4 over grammatical relations, and DP-O$_r(\star)$ over words ruled by non-terminal nodes. Also, one measure that estimates the similarity over constituent parse trees: CP-STM$_4$ (Liu and Gildea, 2005).

Semantic Similarity Three measures that estimate the similarities over semantic roles (i.e. arguments and adjuncts): SR-O$_r$, SR-M$_r(\star)$, and SR-O$_r(\star)$. Additionally, two metrics that estimate similarities over discourse representations: DR-O$_r(\star)$ and DR-O$_{rp}(\star)$.

[2]We also tried with linear kernels, but RBF always obtained better results.

[3]Asiya is available at http://asiya.lsi.upc.edu. Full descriptions of the metrics are available in the Asiya Technical Manual v2.0, pp. 15–21.

3.2 Explicit Semantic Analysis

We built an instance of Explicit Semantic Analysis (ESA) (Gabrilovich and Markovitch, 2007) with the first paragraph of $100k$ Wikipedia articles (dump from 2010).Pre-processing consisted of tokenization and lemmatization.

3.3 Dataset Prediction

Given the similarity shifts in the different datasets (cf. Table 1), we tried to predict what dataset an instance belonged to on the basis of its vocabulary. We built binary maxent classifiers for each dataset in the development set, resulting in five dataset likelihood features: dMSRpar, dSMTeuroparl, dMSRvid, dOnWN, and dSMTnews.[4] Pre-processing consisted of tokenization and lemmatization.

3.4 Baseline

We considered the features included in the Takelab Semantic Text Similarity system (Šarić et al., 2012), one of the top-systems in last year competition. This system is used as a black box. The resulting features are named tklab_n, where $n = [1, 21]$.

Our runs departed from three increasing subsets of features: **AE** machine translation evaluation metrics and explicit semantic analysis, **AED** the previous set plus dataset prediction, and **AED_T** the previous set plus Takelab's baseline features (cf. Table 3). We performed a feature normalization, which relied on the different feature's distribution over the entire dataset. Firstly, features were bounded in the range $\mu \pm 3 * \sigma^2$ in order to reduce the potentially negative impact of outliers. Secondly, we normalized according to the z-score (Nardo et al., 2008, pp. 28, 84); i.e. $x = (x - \mu)/\sigma$. As a result, each real-valued feature distribution in the dataset has $\mu = 0$ and $\sigma = 1$. During the model tuning stage we tried with other numerous normalization options: normalizing each dataset independently, together with the training set, and without normalization at all. Normalizing according to the entire dev-test dataset led to the best results

[4] We used the Stanford classifier; http://nlp.stanford.edu/software/classifier.shtml

Table 2: Tuning process: parameter definition and feature selection. Number of features at the **b**eginning and **e**nd of the feature selection step included.

run	parameter def.				feature sel.		
	c	γ	ϵ	corr	b	e	corr
AE	3.7	0.06	0.3	0.8257	19	14	0.8299
AED	3.8	0.03	0.2	0.8413	24	19	0.8425
AED_T	2.9	0.02	0.3	0.8761	45	33	0.8803

4 Experiments and Results

Section 4.1 describes our model tuning strategy. Sections 4.2 and 4.3 discuss the official and post-competition results.

4.1 Model Tuning

We used only the dev-train partition (2012 training) for tuning. By means of a 10-fold cross validation process, we defined the trade-off (c), gamma (γ), and tube width (ϵ) parameters for the regressor and performed a backward-elimination feature selection process (Witten and Frank, 2005, p. 294), independently for the three experiments.

The results for the cross-validation process are summarized in Table 2. The three runs allow for correlations higher than 0.8. On the one hand, the best regressor parameters obtain better results as more features are considered, still with very small differences. On the other hand, the low correlation increase after the feature selection step shows that a few features are indeed irrelevant.

A summary of the features considered in each experiment (also after feature selection) is displayed in Table 3. The correlation obtained over the dev-test partition are $corr_{AE} = 0.7269$, $corr_{AED} = 0.7638$, and $corr_{AED_T} = 0.8044$ —it would have appeared in the top-10 ranking of the 2012 competition.

4.2 Official Results

We trained three new regressors with the features considered relevant by the tuning process, but using the entire development dataset. The test 2013 partition was normalized again by means of z-score, considering the means and standard deviations of the entire test dataset. Table 4 displays the official results. Our best approach —**AE**—, was positioned in rank 65. The worst results of run **AED** can be explained by the difference in the nature of the test respect to

Table 3: Features considered at the beginning of each run, represented as empty squares (□). Filled squares (■) represent features considered relevant after feature selection.

Feature	AE	AED	AED_T	Feature	AE	AED	AED_T	Feature	AED_T
DP-HWCM_c-4	■	■	■	METEOR-pa	■	■	■	tklab_7	■
DP-HWCM_r-4	■	■	■	METEOR-st	□	■	□	tklab_8	■
DP-Or(⋆)	■	■	■	METEOR-sy	■	■	□	tklab_9	■
CP-STM-4	□	□	■	ESA	■	■	■	tklab_10	□
SR-Or(⋆)	□	□	■	dMSRpar		■	□	tklab_11	■
SR-Mr(⋆)	■	■	■	dSMTeuroparl		■	■	tklab_12	■
SR-Or	■	■	■	dMSRvid		■	□	tklab_13	■
DR-Or(⋆)	□	■	■	dOnWN		□	□	tklab_14	■
DR-Orp(⋆)	■	■	■	dSMTnews		□	□	tklab_15	■
BLEU	■	■	□	tklab_1			□	tklab_16	■
NIST	■	■	■	tklab_2			■	tklab_17	■
-TER	■	■	■	tklab_3			■	tklab_18	■
-TERp-A	■	■	■	tklab_4			■	tklab_19	■
ROUGE-W	■	■	□	tklab_5			■	tklab_20	□
METEOR-ex	□	□	■	tklab_6			□	tklab_21	■

Table 4: Official results for the three runs (rank included).

run	headlines	OnWN	FNWN	SMT	mean
AE (65)	0.6092	0.5679	-0.1268	0.2090	0.4037
AED (83)	0.4136	0.4770	-0.0852	0.1662	0.3050
AED_T (72)	0.5119	0.6386	-0.0464	0.1235	0.3671

Table 5: Post-competition experiments results

run	headlines	OnWN	FNWN	SMT	mean
AE (*a*)	0.6210	0.5905	-0.0987	0.2990	0.4456
AE (*b*)	0.6072	0.4767	-0.0113	0.3236	0.4282
AE (*c*)	0.6590	0.6973	0.1547	0.3429	0.5208

the development dataset. **AED_T** obtains worst results than **AE** on the *headlines* and *SMT* datasets. The reason behind this behavior can be in the difference of vocabularies respect to that stored in the Takelab system (it includes only the vocabulary of the development partition). This could be the same reason behind the drop in performance with respect to the results previously obtained on the dev-test partition (cf. Section 4.1).

4.3 Post-Competition Results

Our analysis of the official results showed the main issue was normalization. Thus, we performed a manifold of new experiments, using the same configuration as in run **AE**, but applying other normalization strategies: (*a*) z-score normalization, but ignoring the FNWN dataset (given its shift through low values); (*b*) z-score normalization, but considering independent means and standard deviations for each test dataset; and (*c*) without normalizing any of dataset (including the regressor one).

Table 5 includes the results. (*a*) makes evident that the instances in FNWN represent "anomalies" that harm the normalized values of the rest of subsets. Run (*b*) shows that normalizing the test sets independently is not a good option, as the regressor is trained considering overall normalizations, which explains the correlation decrease. Run (*c*) is completely different: not normalizing any dataset — both in development and test— reduces the influence of the datasets to each other and allows for the best results. Indeed, this configuration would have advanced practically forty positions at competition time, locating us in rank 27.

Estimating the adequate similarities over *FNWN* seems particularly difficult for our systems. We observe two main factors. (*i*) *FNWN* presents an important similarity shift respect to the other datasets: nearly 90% of the instances similarity is lower than 2.5 and (*ii*) the average lengths of s_1 and s_2 are very different: 30 vs 9 words. These characteristics made it difficult for our MT evaluation metrics to estimate proper similarity values (be normalized or not).

We performed two more experiments over FNWN: training regressors with ESA as the only feature, before and after normalization. The correlation was 0.16017 and 0.3113, respectively. That is, the normalization mainly affects the MT features.

5 Conclusions

In this paper we discussed on our participation to the 2013 Semeval Semantic Textual Similarity task. Our approach relied mainly upon a combination of automatic machine translation evaluation metrics and explicit semantic analysis. Building an RBF support vector regressor with these features allowed us for a modest result in the competition (our best run was ranked 65 out of 89).

Acknowledgments

We would like to thank the organizers of this challenging task for their efforts.

This research work was partially carried out during the tenure of an ERCIM "Alain Bensoussan" Fellowship. The research leading to these results received funding from the EU FP7 Programme 2007-2013 (grants 246016 and 247762). Our research work is partially supported by the Spanish research projects OpenMT-2 and SKATER (TIN2009-14675-C03, TIN2012-38584-C06-01).

References

Eneko Agirre, Daniel Cer, Mona Diab, Aitor Gonzalez Agirre, and Weiwei Guo. 2013. *SEM 2013 Shared Task: Semantic Textual Similarity, including a Pilot on Typed-Similarity. In **SEM 2013: The Second Joint Conference on Lexical and Computational Semantics*. Association for Computational Linguistics.

Satanjeev Banerjee and Alon Lavie. 2005. METEOR: An Automatic Metric for MT Evaluation with Improved Correlation with Human Judgments. In Goldstein et al. (Goldstein et al., 2005), pages 65–72.

George Doddington. 2002. Automatic Evaluation of Machine Translation Quality Using N-Gram Co-occurrence Statistics. In *Proceedings of the Second International Conference on Human Language Technology Research*, pages 138–145, San Francisco, CA. Morgan Kaufmann Publishers Inc.

Evgeniy Gabrilovich and Shaul Markovitch. 2007. Computing Semantic Relatedness Using Wikipedia-based Explicit Semantic Analysis. In *Proceedings of the 20th International Joint Conference on Artificial Intelligence*, pages 1606–1611, San Francisco, CA, USA. Morgan Kaufmann Publishers Inc.

Jesús Giménez and Lluís Màrquez. 2010a. Asiya: An Open Toolkit for Automatic Machine Translation (Meta-)Evaluation. *The Prague Bulletin of Mathematical Linguistics*, (94).

Jesús Giménez and Lluís Màrquez. 2010b. Linguistic Measures for Automatic Machine Translation Evaluation. *Machine Translation*, 24(3–4):209–240.

Jade Goldstein, Alon Lavie, Chin-Yew Lin, and Clare Voss, editors. 2005. *Proceedings of the ACL Workshop on Intrinsic and Extrinsic Evaluation Measures for Machine Translation and/or Summarization*. Association for Computational Linguistics.

Thorsten Joachims, 1999. *Advances in Kernel Methods – Support Vector Learning*, chapter Making large-Scale SVM Learning Practical. MIT Press.

Chin-Yew Lin and Franz Josef Och. 2004. Automatic Evaluation of Machine Translation Quality Using Longest Common Subsequence and Skip-Bigram Statistics. In *Proceedings of the 42nd Annual Meeting of the Association for Computational Linguistics (ACL 2002)*, Stroudsburg, PA. Association for Computational Linguistics.

Ding Liu and Daniel Gildea. 2005. Syntactic Features for Evaluation of Machine Translation. In Goldstein et al. (Goldstein et al., 2005), pages 25–32.

Michela Nardo, Michaela Saisana, Andrea Saltelli, Stefano Tarantola, Anders Hoffmann, and Enrico Giovannini. 2008. *Handbook on Constructing Composite Indicators: Methodology and User Guide*. OECD Publishing.

Kishore Papineni, Salim Roukos, Todd Ward, and Wei-Jing Zhu. 2002. BLEU: A Method for Automatic Evaluation of Machine Translation. In *Proceedings of the 40th Annual Meeting of the Association for Computational Linguistics (ACL 2002)*, pages 311–318, Philadelphia, PA. Association for Computational Linguistics.

Matthew Snover, Bonnie Dorr, Richard Schwartz, Linnea Micciulla, and John Makhoul. 2006. A Study of Translation Edit Rate with Targeted Human Annotation. In *Proceedings of Association for Machine Translation in the Americas*, pages 223–231.

Frane Šarić, Goran Glavaš, Mladen Karan, Jan Šnajder, and Bojana Dalbelo Bašić. 2012. TakeLab: Systems for Measuring Semantic Text. In *First Joint Conference on Lexical and Computational Semantics (*SEM)*, pages 441–448, Montréal, Canada. Association for Computational Linguistics.

Ian H. Witten and Eibe Frank. 2005. *Data Mining: Practical Machine Learning Tools and Techniques*. Morgan Kaufmann, San Francisco, CA, 2 edition.

MayoClinicNLP–CORE: Semantic representations for textual similarity

Stephen Wu
Mayo Clinic
Rochester, MN 55905
wu.stephen@mayo.edu

Dongqing Zhu & Ben Carterette
University of Delaware
Newark, DE 19716
{zhu,carteret}@cis.udel.edu

Hongfang Liu
Mayo Clinic
Rochester, MN 55905
liu.hongfang@mayo.edu

Abstract

The Semantic Textual Similarity (STS) task examines semantic similarity at a sentence-level. We explored three representations of semantics (implicit or explicit): named entities, semantic vectors, and structured vectorial semantics. From a DKPro baseline, we also performed feature selection and used source-specific linear regression models to combine our features. Our systems placed 5th, 6th, and 8th among 90 submitted systems.

1 Introduction

The Semantic Textual Similarity (STS) task (Agirre et al., 2012; Agirre et al., 2013) examines semantic similarity at a sentence-level. While much work has compared the semantics of terms, concepts, or documents, this space has been relatively unexplored. The 2013 STS task provided sentence pairs and a 0–5 human rating of their similarity, with training data from 5 sources and test data from 4 sources.

We sought to explore and evaluate the usefulness of several semantic representations that have had recent significance in research or practice. First, information extraction (IE) methods often implicitly consider named entities as ad hoc semantic representations, for example, in the clinical domain. Therefore, we sought to evaluate similarity based on named entity-based features. Second, in many applications, an effective means of incorporating distributional semantics is Random Indexing (RI). Thus we consider three different representations possible within Random Indexing (Kanerva et al., 2000; Sahlgren, 2005). Finally, because compositional distributional semantics is an important research topic (Mitchell and Lapata, 2008; Erk and Padó, 2008), we sought to evaluate a principled composition strategy: structured vectorial semantics (Wu and Schuler, 2011).

The remainder of this paper proceeds as follows. Section 2 overviews our similarity metrics, and Section 3 overviews the systems that were defined on these metrics. Competition results and additional analyses are in Section 4. We end with discussion on the results in Section 5.

2 Similarity measures

Because we expect semantic similarity to be multi-layered, we expect that we will need many similarity measures to approximate human similarity judgments. Rather than reinvent the wheel, we have chosen to introduce features that complement existing successful feature sets. We utilized 17 features from DKPro Similarity and 21 features from TakeLab, i.e., the two top-performing systems in the 2012 STS task, as a solid baseline.

These are summarized in Table 1. We introduce 3 categories of new similarity metrics, 9 metrics in all.

2.1 Named entity measures

Named entity recognition provides a common approximation of semantic content for the information extraction perspective. We define three simple similarity metrics based on named entities. First, we computed the *named entity overlap* (exact string matches) between the two sentences, where NE_k was the set of named entities found in sentence S_k. This is the harmonic mean of how closely $S1$

*Second Joint Conference on Lexical and Computational Semantics (*SEM), Volume 1: Proceedings of the Main Conference and the Shared Task*, pages 148–154, Atlanta, Georgia, June 13-14, 2013.

Table 1: Full feature pool in MayoClinicNLP systems. The proposed MayoClinicNLP metrics are meant to complement DKPro (Bär et al., 2012) and TakeLab (Šarić et al., 2012) metrics.

DKPro metrics (17)	TakeLab metrics (21)	Custom MayoClinicNLP metrics (9)
n-grams/WordNGramContainmentMeasure_1_stopword-filtered	t_ngram/UnigramOverlap	
n-grams/WordNGramContainmentMeasure_2_stopword-filtered	t_ngram/BigramOverlap	
n-grams/WordNGramJaccardMeasure_1	t_ngram/TrigramOverlap	
n-grams/WordNGramJaccardMeasure_2_stopword-filtered	t_ngram/ContentUnigramOverlap	
n-grams/WordNGramJaccardMeasure_3	t_ngram/ContentBigramOverlap	
n-grams/WordNGramJaccardMeasure_4	t_ngram/ContentTrigramOverlap	
n-grams/WordNGramJaccardMeasure_4_stopword-filtered		
	t_words/WeightedWordOverlap	custom/StanfordNerMeasure_overlap.txt
	t_words/GreedyLemmaAligningOverlap	custom/StanfordNerMeasure_aligngst.txt
	t_words/WordNetAugmentedWordOverlap	custom/StanfordNerMeasure_alignlcs.txt
esa/ESA_Wiktionary	t_vec/LSAWordSimilarity_NYT	custom/SVSePhrSimilarityMeasure.txt
esa/ESA_WordNet	t_vec/LSAWordSimilarity_weighted_NYT	custom/SVSeTopSimilarityMeasure.txt
	t_vec/LSAWordSimilarity_weighted_Wiki	custom/SemanticVectorsSimilarityMeasure_d200_wr0.txt
		custom/SemanticVectorsSimilarityMeasure_d200_wr6b.txt
		custom/SemanticVectorsSimilarityMeasure_d200_wr6d.txt
		custom/SemanticVectorsSimilarityMeasure_d200_wr6p.txt
n-grams/CharacterNGramMeasure_2	t_other/RelativeLengthDifference	
n-grams/CharacterNGramMeasure_3	t_other/RelativeInfoContentDifference	
n-grams/CharacterNGramMeasure_4	t_other/NumbersSize	
string/GreedyStringTiling_3	t_other/NumbersOverlap	
string/LongestCommonSubsequenceComparator	t_other/NumbersSubset	
string/LongestCommonSubsequenceNormComparator	t_other/SentenceSize	
string/LongestCommonSubstringComparator	t_other/CaseMatches	
	t_other/StocksSize	
	t_other/StocksOverlap	

matches $S2$, and how closely $S2$ matches $S1$:

$$\text{sim}_{neo}(S1, S2) = 2 \cdot \frac{|NE_1 \cap NE_2|}{|NE_1| + |NE_2|} \quad (1)$$

Additionally, we relax the constraint of requiring exact string matches between the two sentences by using the longest common subsequence (Allison and Dix, 1986) and greedy string tiling (Wise, 1996) algorithms. These metrics give similarities between two strings, rather than two sets of strings as we have with NE_1 and NE_2. Thus, we follow previous work in greedily aligning these named entities (Lavie and Denkowski, 2009; Šarić et al., 2012) into pairs. Namely, we compare each pair $(ne_{i,1}, ne_{j,2})$ of named entity strings in NE_1 and NE_2. The highest-scoring pair is entered into a set of pairs, P. Then, the next highest pair is added to P if neither named entity is already in P, and discarded otherwise; this continues until there are no more named entities in either NE_1 or NE_2.

We then define two named entity aligning measures that use the longest common subsequence (LCS) and greedy string tiling (GST) fuzzy string matching algorithms:

$$\text{sim}_{nea}(S1, S2) = \frac{\sum_{(ne_1, ne_2) \in P} f(ne_1, ne_2)}{\max\left(|NE_1|, |NE_2|\right)} \quad (2)$$

where $f(\cdot)$ is either the LCS or GST algorithm.

In our experiments, we performed named entity recognition with the Stanford NER tool using the standard English model (Finkel et al., 2005). Also, we used UKP's existing implementation of LCS and GST (Šarić et al., 2012) for the latter two measures.

2.2 Random indexing measures

Random indexing (Kanerva et al., 2000; Sahlgren, 2005) is another distributional semantics framework for representing terms as vectors. Similar to LSA (Deerwester et al., 1990), an index is created that represents each term as a semantic vector. But in random indexing, each term is represented by an elemental vector $\mathbf{e}_t$ with a small number of randomly-generated non-zero components. The intuition for this means of dimensionality reduction is that these randomly-generated elemental vectors are like quasi-orthogonal bases in a traditional geometric semantic space, rather than, e.g., 300 fully orthogonal dimensions from singular value decomposition (Landauer and Dumais, 1997). For a *standard model* with random indexing, a contextual term vector $\mathbf{c}_{t,\text{std}}$ is the the sum of the elemental vectors corresponding to tokens in the document. All contexts for a particular term are summed and normalized to produce a final term vector $\mathbf{v}_{t,\text{std}}$.

Other notions of context can be incorporated into

this model. Local co-occurrence context can be accounted for in a *basic sliding-window model* by considering words within some window radius r (instead of a whole document). Each instance of the term t will have a contextual vector $\mathbf{c}_{t,\text{win}} = \mathbf{e}_{t-r} + \cdots + \mathbf{e}_{t-1} + \mathbf{e}_{t+1} + \cdots + \mathbf{e}_{t+r}$; context vectors for each instance (in a large corpus) would again be added and normalized to create the overall vector $\mathbf{v}_{t,\text{win}}$.

A *directional model* doubles the dimensionality of the vector and considers left- and right-context separately (half the indices for left-context, half for right-context), using a permutation to achieve one of the two contexts. A *permutated positional model* uses a position-specific permutation function to encode the relative word positions (rather than just left- or right-context) separately. Again, $\mathbf{v}_t$ would be summed and normalized over all instances of $\mathbf{c}_t$.

Sentence vectors from any of these 4 Random Indexing-based models (standard, windowed, directional, positional) are just the sum of the vectors for each term $\mathbf{v}_S = \sum_{t \in S} \mathbf{v}_t$. We define 4 separate similarity metrics for STS as:

$$\text{sim}_{RI}(S1, S2) = \cos(\mathbf{v}_{S1}, \mathbf{v}_{S2}) \qquad (3)$$

We used the semantic vectors package (Widdows and Ferraro, 2008; Widdows and Cohen, 2010) in the default configuration for the standard model. For the windowed, directional, and positional models, we used a 6-word window radius with 200 dimensions and a seed length of 5. All models were trained on the raw text of the Penn Treebank Wall Street Journal corpus and a 100,075-article subset of Wikipedia.

2.3 Semantic vectorial semantics measures

Structured vectorial semantics (SVS) composes distributional semantic representations in syntactic context (Wu and Schuler, 2011). Similarity metrics defined with SVS inherently explore the qualities of a fully interactive syntax–semantics interface. While previous work evaluated the syntactic contributions of this model, the STS task allows us to evaluate the phrase-level semantic validity of the model. We summarize SVS here as bottom-up vector composition and parsing, then continue on to define the associated similarity metrics.

Each token in a sentence is modeled generatively as a vector $\mathbf{e}_\gamma$ of latent referents i_γ in syntactic context c_γ; each element in the vector is defined as:

$$\mathbf{e}_\gamma[i_\gamma] = \mathsf{P}(x_\gamma \,|\, lci_\gamma), \quad \text{for preterm } \gamma \qquad (4)$$

where l_γ is a constant for preterminals.

We write SVS vector composition between two word (or phrase) vectors in linear algebra form,[1] assuming that we are composing the semantics of two children $\mathbf{e}_\alpha$ and $\mathbf{e}_\beta$ in a binary syntactic tree into their parent $\mathbf{e}_\gamma$:

$$\mathbf{e}_\gamma = \mathbf{M} \odot (\mathbf{L}_{\gamma\times\alpha} \cdot \mathbf{e}_\alpha) \odot (\mathbf{L}_{\gamma\times\beta} \cdot \mathbf{e}_\beta) \cdot \mathbf{1} \qquad (5)$$

$\mathbf{M}$ is a diagonal matrix that encapsulates probabilistic syntactic information; the $\mathbf{L}$ matrices are linear transformations that capture how semantically relevant child vectors are to the resulting vector (e.g., $\mathbf{L}_{\gamma\times\alpha}$ defines the the relevance of $\mathbf{e}_\alpha$ to $\mathbf{e}_\gamma$). These matrices are defined such that the resulting $\mathbf{e}_\gamma$ is a semantic vector of consistent $\mathsf{P}(x_\gamma \,|\, lci_\gamma)$ probabilities. Further detail is in our previous work (Wu, 2010; Wu and Schuler, 2011).

Similarity metrics can be defined in the SVS space by comparing the distributions of the composed $\mathbf{e}_\gamma$ vectors — i.e., our similarity metric is a comparison of the vector semantics at different phrasal nodes. We define two measures, one corresponding to the top node $c_\triangle$ (e.g., with a syntactic constituent $c_\triangle$ = 'S'), and one corresponding to the left and right largest child nodes (e.g.,, $c_\angle$ = 'NP' and $c_\measuredangle$ = 'VP' for a canonical subject–verb–object sentence in English).

$$\begin{aligned}
&\text{sim}_{\textit{svs-top}}(S1, S2) = \cos(\mathbf{e}_{\triangle(S1)}, \mathbf{e}_{\triangle(S2)}) && (6)\\
&\text{sim}_{\textit{svs-phr}}(S1, S2) = \max(\\
&\quad \text{avgsim}(\mathbf{e}_{\angle(S1)}, \mathbf{e}_{\angle(S2)}; \mathbf{e}_{\measuredangle(S1)}, \mathbf{e}_{\measuredangle(S2)}), \\
&\quad \text{avgsim}(\mathbf{e}_{\angle(S1)}, \mathbf{e}_{\measuredangle(S2)}; \mathbf{e}_{\measuredangle(S1)}, \mathbf{e}_{\angle(S2)})) && (7)
\end{aligned}$$

where avgsim() is the harmonic mean of the cosine similarities between the two pairs of arguments. Top-level similarity comparisons in (6) amounts to comparing the semantics of a whole sentence. The phrasal similarity function $\text{sim}_{\textit{svs-phr}}(S1, S2)$ in (7) thus seeks to semantically align the two largest subtrees, and weight them. Compared to $\text{sim}_{\textit{svs-top}}$,

[1] We define the operator $\odot$ as point-by-point multiplication of two diagonal matrices and $\mathbf{1}$ as a column vector of ones, collapsing a diagonal matrix onto a column vector.

the phrasal similarity function $\text{sim}_{svs\text{-}phr}(S1, S2)$ assumes there might be some information captured in the child nodes that could be lost in the final composition to the top node.

In our experiments, we used the parser described in Wu and Schuler (2011) with 1,000 headwords and 10 relational clusters, trained on the Wall Street Journal treebank.

3 Feature combination framework

The similarity metrics of Section 2 were calculated for each of the sentence pairs in the training set, and later the test set. In combining these metrics, we extended a DKPro Similarity baseline (3.1) with feature selection (3.2) and source-specific models and classification (3.3).

3.1 Linear regression via DKPro Similarity

For our baseline (MayoClinicNLPr1wtCDT), we used the UIMA-based DKPro Similarity system from STS 2012 (Bär et al., 2012). Aside from the large number of sound similarity measures, this provided linear regression through the WEKA package (Hall et al., 2009) to combine all of the disparate similarity metrics into a single one, and some preprocessing. Regression weights were determined on the whole training set for each source.

3.2 Feature selection

Not every feature was included in the final linear regression models. To determine the best of the 47 (DKPro–17, TakeLab–21, MayoClinicNLP–9) features, we performed a full forward-search on the space of similarity measures. In forward-search, we perform 10-fold cross-validation on the training set for each measure, and pick the best one; in the next round, that best metric is retained, and the remaining metrics are considered for addition. Rounds continue until all the features are exhausted, though a stopping-point is noted when performance no longer increases.

3.3 Subdomain source models and classification

There were 5 sources of data in the training set: paraphrase sentence pairs (MSRpar), sentence pairs from video descriptions (MSRvid), MT evaluation sentence pairs (MTnews and MTeuroparl) and gloss pairs (OnWN). In our submitted runs, we trained a separate, feature-selected model based on cross-validation for each of these data sources. In training data on cross-validation tests, training domain-specific models outperformed training a single conglomerate model.

In the test data, there were 4 sources, with 2 appearing in training data (OnWN, SMT) and 2 that were novel (FrameNet/Wordnet sense definitions (FNWN), European news headlines (headlines)). We examined two different strategies for applying the 5-source trained models on these 4 test sets. Both of these strategies rely on a multiclass random forest *classifier*, which we trained on the 47 similarity metrics.

First, for each sentence pair, we considered the final similarity score to be a weighted combination of the similarity score from each of the 5 source-specific similarity models. The combination weights were determined by utilizing the classifier's confidence scores. Second, the final similarity was chosen as the single source-specific similarity score corresponding to the classifier's output class.

4 Evaluation

The MayoClinicNLP team submitted three systems to the STS-Core task. We also include here a post-hoc run that was considered as a possible submission.

r1wtCDT This run used the 47 metrics from DKPro, TakeLab, and MayoClinicNLP as a feature pool for feature selection. Source-specific similarity metrics were combined with classifier-confidence-score weights.

r2CDT Same feature pool as run 1. Best-match (as determined by classifier) source-specific similarity metric was used rather than a weighted combination.

r3wtCD TakeLab features were removed from the feature pool (before feature selection). Same source combination as run 1.

r4ALL Post-hoc run using all 47 metrics, but training a single linear regression model rather than source-specific models.

Table 2: Performance comparison.

TEAM NAME	headlines	rank	OnWN	rank	FNWN	rank	SMT	rank	mean	rank
UMBC_EBIQUITY-ParingWords	0.7642		0.7529		0.5818		0.3804		0.6181	1
UMBC_EBIQUITY-galactus	0.7428		0.7053		0.5444		0.3705		0.5927	2
deft-baseline	0.6532		0.8431		0.5083		0.3265		0.5795	3
MayoClinicNLP-r4ALL	0.7275		0.7618		0.4359		0.3048		0.5707	
UMBC_EBIQUITY-saiyan	0.7838		0.5593		0.5815		0.3563		0.5683	4
MayoClinicNLP-r3wtCD	0.6440	43	0.8295	2	0.3202	47	0.3561	17	0.5671	5
MayoClinicNLP-r1wtCDT	0.6584	33	0.7775	4	0.3735	26	0.3605	13	0.5649	6
CLaC-RUN2	0.6921		0.7366		0.3793		0.3375		0.5587	7
MayoClinicNLP-r2CDT	0.6827	23	0.6612	20	0.396	17	0.3946	5	0.5572	8
NTNU-RUN1	0.7279		0.5952		0.3215		0.4015		0.5519	9
CLaC-RUN1	0.6774		0.7667		0.3793		0.3068		0.5511	10

4.1 Competition performance

Table 2 shows the top 10 runs of 90 submitted in the STS-Core task are shown, with our three systems placing 5th, 6th, and 8th. Additionally, we can see that run 4 would have placed 4th. Notice that there are significant source-specific differences between the runs. For example, while run 4 is better overall, runs 1–3 outperform it on all but the headlines and FNWN datasets, i.e., the test datasets that were not present in the training data. Thus, it is clear that the source-specific models are beneficial when the training data is in-domain, but a combined model is more beneficial when no such training data is available.

4.2 Feature selection analysis

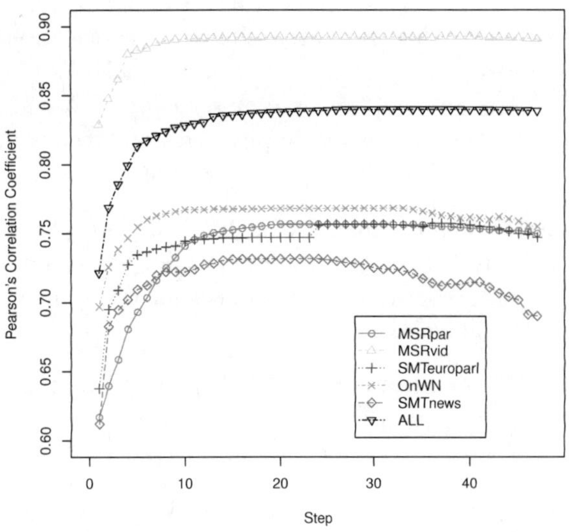

Figure 1: Performance curve of feature selection for **r1wtCDT**, **r2CDT**, and **r4ALL**

Due to the source-specific variability among the runs, it is important to know whether the forward-search feature selection performed as expected. For source specific models (runs 1 and 3) and a combined model (run 4), Figure 1 shows the 10-fold cross-validation scores on the training set as the next feature is added to the model. As we would expect, there is an initial growth region where the first features truly complement one another and improve performance significantly. A plateau is reached for each of the models, and some (e.g., SMTnews) even decay if too many noisy features are added.

The feature selection curves are as expected. Because the plateau regions are large, feature selection could be cut off at about 10 features, with gains in efficiency and perhaps little effect on accuracy.

The resulting selected features for some of the trained models are shown in Table 3.

4.3 Contribution of MayoClinicNLP metrics

We determined whether including MayoClinicNLP features was any benefit over a feature-selected DKPro baseline. Table 4 analyzes this question by adding each of our measures in turn to a baseline feature-selected DKPro (dkselected). Note that this baseline was extremely effective; it would have ranked 4th in the STS competition, outperforming our run 4. Thus, metrics that improve this baseline must truly be complementary metrics. Here, we see that only the phrasal SVS measure is able to improve performance overall, largely by its contributions to the most difficult categories, FNWN and SMT. In fact, that system (dkselected + SVSePhrSimilarityMeasure) represents the best-performing run of any that was produced in our framework.

Table 3: Top retained features for several linear regression models.

OnWN - r1wtCDT and r2CDT (15 shown/19 selected)	SMTnews - r1wtCDT and r2CDT (15 shown/17 selected)	All - r4ALL (29 shown/29 selected)
t_ngram/ContentUnigramOverlap	t_other/RelativeInfoContentDifference	t_vec/LSAWordSimilarity_weighted_NYT
t_other/RelativeInfoContentDifference	n-grams/CharacterNGramMeasure_2	n-grams/CharacterNGramMeasure_2
t_vec/LSAWordSimilarity_weighted_NYT	t_other/CaseMatches	string/LongestCommonSubstringComparator
esa/ESA_Wiktionary	string/GreedyStringTiling_3	t_other/NumbersOverlap
t_ngram/ContentBigramOverlap	**custom/RandomIndexingMeasure_d200_wr6p**	t_words/WordNetAugmentedWordOverlap
n-grams/CharacterNGramMeasure_2	**custom/StanfordNerMeasure_overlap**	n-grams/WordNGramJaccardMeasure_1
t_words/WordNetAugmentedWordOverlap	t_vec/LSAWordSimilarity_weighted_NYT	n-grams/CharacterNGramMeasure_3
t_ngram/BigramOverlap	t_other/SentenceSize	t_other/SentenceSize
string/GreedyStringTiling_3	**custom/RandomIndexingMeasure_d200_wr0**	t_other/RelativeInfoContentDifference
string/LongestCommonSubsequenceNormComparator	**custom/SVSePhrSimilarityMeasure**	t_ngram/ContentBigramOverlap
custom/RandomIndexingMeasure_d200_wr0	esa/ESA_Wiktionary	n-grams/WordNGramJaccardMeasure_4
custom/StanfordNerMeasure_aligngst	string/LongestCommonSubstringComparator	t_other/NumbersSize
custom/StanfordNerMeasure_alignlcs	t_other/NumbersSize	t_other/NumbersSubset
custom/StanfordNerMeasure_overlap	n-grams/WordNGramContainmentMeasure_2_stopword-filtered	**custom/SVSePhrSimilarityMeasure**
custom/SVSePhrSimilarityMeasure	**custom/SVSeTopSimilarityMeasure**	**custom/SemanticVectorsSimilarityMeasure_d200_wr6p**
		esa/ESA_WordNet
OnWN - r3wtCD (7 shown/7 selected)	SMTnews - r3wtCD (15 shown/23 selected)	esa/ESA_Wiktionary
esa/ESA_Wiktionary	string/GreedyStringTiling_3	string/LongestCommonSubsequenceComparator
string/LongestCommonSubsequenceComparator	**custom/StanfordNerMeasure_overlap**	string/LongestCommonSubsequenceNormComparator
string/GreedyStringTiling_3	n-grams/CharacterNGramMeasure_2	n-grams/WordNGramContainmentMeasure_1_stopword-filtered
string/LongestCommonSubsequenceNormComparator	**custom/RandomIndexingMeasure_d200_wr6p**	word-sim/MCS06_Resnik_WordNet
string/LongestCommonSubstringComparator	n-grams/CharacterNGramMeasure_3	t_ngram/ContentUnigramOverlap
word-sim/MCS06_Resnik_WordNet	string/LongestCommonSubsequenceComparator	n-grams/WordNGramContainmentMeasure_2_stopword-filtered
n-grams/WordNGramContainmentMeasure_2_stopword-filtered	**custom/StanfordNerMeasure_aligngst**	n-grams/WordNGramJaccardMeasure_2_stopword-filtered
	custom/SVSePhrSimilarityMeasure	t_ngram/UnigramOverlap
	esa/ESA_Wiktionary	t_ngram/BigramOverlap
	esa/ESA_WordNet	t_other/StocksSize
	n-grams/WordNGramContainmentMeasure_2_stopword-filtered	t_words/GreedyLemmaAligningOverlap
	n-grams/WordNGramJaccardMeasure_1	t_other/StocksOverlap
	string/LongestCommonSubstringComparator	
	custom/RandomIndexingMeasure_d200_wr6d	
	custom/RandomIndexingMeasure_d200_wr0	

Table 4: Adding customized features one at a time into optimized DKPro feature set. Models are trained across all sources.

	headlines	OnWN	FNWN	SMT	mean
dkselected	0.70331	0.79752	0.38358	0.31744	0.571319
dkselected + SVSePhrSimilarityMeasure	0.70178	0.79644	**0.38685**	**0.32332**	**0.572774**
dkselected + RandomIndexingMeasure_d200_wr0	0.70054	0.79752	**0.38432**	0.31615	0.570028
dkselected + SVSeTopSimilarityMeasure	0.69873	0.79522	**0.38815**	0.31723	0.569533
dkselected + RandomIndexingMeasure_d200_wr6d	0.69944	**0.79836**	**0.38416**	0.31397	0.569131
dkselected + RandomIndexingMeasure_d200_wr6b	0.69992	**0.79788**	**0.38435**	0.31328	0.568957
dkselected + RandomIndexingMeasure_d200_wr6p	0.69878	**0.79848**	0.37876	0.31436	0.568617
dkselected + StanfordNerMeasure_aligngst	0.69446	0.79502	**0.38703**	0.31497	0.567212
dkselected + StanfordNerMeasure_overlap	0.69468	0.79509	**0.38703**	0.31466	0.567200
dkselected + StanfordNerMeasure_alignlcs	0.69451	0.79486	**0.38657**	0.31394	0.566807
(dk + all custom) selected	0.70311	0.79887	0.37477	0.31665	0.570586

Also, we see some source-specific behavior. None of our introduced measures are able to improve the headlines similarities. However, random indexing improves OnWN scores, several strategies improve the FNWN metric, and $\text{sim}_{svs\text{-}phr}$ is the only viable performance improvement on the SMT corpus.

5 Discussion

Mayo Clinic's submissions to Semantic Textual Similarity 2013 performed well, placing 5th, 6th, and 8th among 90 submitted systems. We introduced similarity metrics that used different means to do compositional distributional semantics along with some named entity-based measures, finding some improvement especially for phrasal similarity from structured vectorial semantics. Throughout, we utilized forward-search feature selection, which enhanced the performance of the models. We also used source-based linear regression models and considered unseen sources as mixtures of existing sources; we found that in-domain data is necessary for smaller, source-based models to outperform larger, conglomerate models.

Acknowledgments

Thanks to the developers of the UKP DKPro system and the TakeLab system for making their code available. Also, thanks to James Masanz for initial implementations of some similarity measures.

References

Eneko Agirre, Mona Diab, Daniel Cer, and Aitor Gonzalez-Agirre. 2012. Semeval-2012 task 6: A pilot on semantic textual similarity. In *Proceedings of the First Joint Conference on Lexical and Computational Semantics-Volume 1: Proceedings of the main conference and the shared task, and Volume 2: Proceedings of the Sixth International Workshop on Semantic Evaluation*, pages 385–393. Association for Computational Linguistics.

Eneko Agirre, Daniel Cer, Mona Diab, Aitor Gonzalez-Agirre, and Weiwei Guo. 2013. *sem 2013 shared task: Semantic textual similarity, including a pilot on typed-similarity. In **SEM 2013: The Second Joint Conference on Lexical and Computational Semantics*. Association for Computational Linguistics.

Lloyd Allison and Trevor I Dix. 1986. A bit-string longest-common-subsequence algorithm. *Information Processing Letters*, 23(5):305–310.

Daniel Bär, Chris Biemann, Iryna Gurevych, and Torsten Zesch. 2012. Ukp: Computing semantic textual similarity by combining multiple content similarity measures. In *Proceedings of the First Joint Conference on Lexical and Computational Semantics-Volume 1: Proceedings of the main conference and the shared task, and Volume 2: Proceedings of the Sixth International Workshop on Semantic Evaluation*, pages 435–440. Association for Computational Linguistics.

Scott Deerwester, Susan Dumais, George W. Furnas, Thomas K. Landauer, and Richard Harshman. 1990. Indexing by latent semantic analysis. *Journal of the American Society for Information Science*, 41(6):391–407.

Katrin Erk and Sebastian Padó. 2008. A structured vector space model for word meaning in context. In *Proceedings of EMNLP 2008*.

Jenny Rose Finkel, Trond Grenager, and Christopher Manning. 2005. Incorporating non-local information into information extraction systems by gibbs sampling. In *Proceedings of the 43rd Annual Meeting on Association for Computational Linguistics*, pages 363–370. Association for Computational Linguistics.

Mark Hall, Eibe Frank, Geoffrey Holmes, Bernhard Pfahringer, Peter Reutemann, and Ian H. Witten. 2009. The weka data mining software: an update. *SIGKDD Explor. Newsl.*, 11(1):10–18, November.

Pentti Kanerva, Jan Kristofersson, and Anders Holst. 2000. Random indexing of text samples for latent semantic analysis. In *Proceedings of the 22nd annual conference of the cognitive science society*, volume 1036. Citeseer.

T.K. Landauer and S.T. Dumais. 1997. A Solution to Plato's Problem: The Latent Semantic Analysis Theory of Acquisition, Induction, and Representation of Knowledge. *Psychological Review*, 104:211–240.

Alon Lavie and Michael J Denkowski. 2009. The meteor metric for automatic evaluation of machine translation. *Machine translation*, 23(2-3):105–115.

Jeff Mitchell and Mirella Lapata. 2008. Vector-based models of semantic composition. In *Proceedings of ACL-08: HLT*, pages 236–244, Columbus, OH.

M. Sahlgren. 2005. An introduction to random indexing. In *Methods and Applications of Semantic Indexing Workshop at the 7th International Conference on Terminology and Knowledge Engineering, TKE*, volume 5.

Frane Šarić, Goran Glavaš, Mladen Karan, Jan Šnajder, and Bojana Dalbelo Bašić. 2012. Takelab: Systems for measuring semantic text similarity. In *Proceedings of the Sixth International Workshop on Semantic Evaluation (SemEval 2012)*, pages 441–448, Montréal, Canada, 7-8 June. Association for Computational Linguistics.

Dominic Widdows and Trevor Cohen. 2010. The semantic vectors package: New algorithms and public tools for distributional semantics. In *Semantic Computing (ICSC), 2010 IEEE Fourth International Conference on*, pages 9–15. IEEE.

D. Widdows and K. Ferraro. 2008. Semantic vectors: a scalable open source package and online technology management application. *Proceedings of the Sixth International Language Resources and Evaluation (LREC'08)*, pages 1183–1190.

Michael J Wise. 1996. Yap3: Improved detection of similarities in computer program and other texts. In *ACM SIGCSE Bulletin*, volume 28, pages 130–134. ACM.

Stephen Wu and William Schuler. 2011. Structured composition of semantic vectors. In *Proceedings of the International Conference on Computational Semantics*.

Stephen Tze-Inn Wu. 2010. *Vectorial Representations of Meaning for a Computational Model of Language Comprehension*. Ph.D. thesis, Department of Computer Science and Engineering, University of Minnesota.

SRIUBC-Core: Multiword Soft Similarity Models for Textual Similarity

Eric Yeh
SRI International
Menlo Park, CA USA
yeh@ai.sri.com

Eneko Agirre
University of Basque Country
Donostia, Basque Country
e.agirre@ehu.es

Abstract

In this year's Semantic Textual Similarity evaluation, we explore the contribution of models that provide soft similarity scores across spans of multiple words, over the previous year's system. To this end, we explored the use of neural probabilistic language models and a TF-IDF weighted variant of Explicit Semantic Analysis. The neural language model systems used vector representations of individual words, where these vectors were derived by training them against the context of words encountered, and thus reflect the distributional characteristics of their usage. To generate a similarity score between spans, we experimented with using tiled vectors and Restricted Boltzmann Machines to identify similar encodings. We find that these soft similarity methods generally outperformed our previous year's systems, albeit they did not perform as well in the overall rankings. A simple analysis of the soft similarity resources over two word phrases is provided, and future areas of improvement are described.

1 Introduction

For this year's Semantic Textual Similarity (STS) evaluation, we built upon the best performing system we deployed last year with several methods for exploring the soft similarity between windows of words, instead of relying just on single token-to-token similarities. From the previous year's evaluation, we were impressed by the performance of features derived from bigrams and skip bigrams. Bigrams capture the relationship between two concurrent words, while skip bigrams can capture longer distance relationships. We found that characterizing the overlap in skip bigrams between the sentences in a STS problem pair proved to be a major contributor to last year's system's performance.

Skip bigrams were matched on two criteria, lexical matches, and via part of speech (POS). Lexical matching is brittle, and even if the match were made on lemmas, we lose the ability to match against synonyms. We could rely on the token-to-token similarity methods to account for these non-lexical similarities, but these do not account for sequence nor dependencies in the sentencees. Using POS based matching allows for a level of generalization, but at a much broader level. What we would like to have is a model that can capture these long distance relationships at a level that is less broad than POS matching, but allows for a soft similarity scoring between words. In addition, the ability to encompass a larger window without having to manually insert skips would be desirable as well.

To this end we decided to explore the use of neural probabilistic language models (NLPM) for capturing this kind of behavior (Bengio et al., 2003). NLPMs represent individual words as real valued vectors, often at a much lower dimensionality than the original vocabulary. By training these representations to maximize a criterion such as log-likelihood of target word given the other words in its neighborhood, the word vectors themselves can capture commonalities between words that have been used in similar contexts. In previous studies, these vectors themselves can capture distributionally derived similarities, by directly comparing the word vectors themselves using simple measures such as

*Second Joint Conference on Lexical and Computational Semantics (*SEM), Volume 1: Proceedings of the Main Conference and the Shared Task*, pages 155–161, Atlanta, Georgia, June 13-14, 2013. ©2013 Association for Computational Linguistics

Euclidean distance (Collobert and Weston, 2008).

In addition, we fielded a variant of Explicit Semantic Analysis (Gabrilovich and Markovitch, 2009) that used TF-IDF weightings, instead of using the raw concept vectors themselves. From previous experiments, we found that using TF-IDF weightings on the words in a pair gave a boost in performance over sentence length comparisons and above, so this simple modification was incorporated into our system.

In order to identify the contribution of these soft similarity methods against last year's system, we fielded three systems:

1. **System 1**, the system from the previous year, incorporating semantic similarity resources, precision focused and Bilingual Evaluation Understudy (BLEU) overlaps (Papineni et al., 2002), and several types of skip-bigrams.

2. **System 2**, features just the new NLPM scores and TFIDF-ESA.

3. **System 3**, combines System 1 and System 2.

For the rest of this system description, we briefly describe the previous year's system (System 1), the TFIDF weighted Explicit Semantic Analysis, and the NLPM systems. We then describe the experiment setup, and follow up with results and analysis.

2 System 1

The system we used in SemEval 2012 consisted of the following components:

1. Resource based word-to-word similarities, combined using a Semantic Matrix (Fernando and Stevenson, 2008).

2. Cosine-based lexical overlap measure.

3. Bilingual Evaluation Understudy (BLEU) (Papineni et al., 2002) lexical overlap.

4. Precision focused part-of-speech (POS) features.

5. Lexical match skip-bigram overlap.

6. Precision focused skip-bigram POS features.

The Semantic Matrix assesses similarity between a pair s_1 and s_2 by summing over all of the word to word similarities between the pair, subject to normalization, as given by Formula 1.

$$\mathrm{sim}(s_1, s_2) = \frac{\mathbf{v}_1^T \mathbf{W} \mathbf{v}_2}{\|\mathbf{v_1}\| \, \|\mathbf{v_2}\|} \quad (1)$$

The matrix $\mathbf{W}$ is a symmetric matrix that encodes the word to word similarities, derived from the underlying resources this is drawn from. From the previous year's assessment, we used similarities derived from Personalized PageRank (Agirre et al., 2010) over WordNet (Fellbaum, 1998), the Explicit Semantic Analysis (Gabrilovich and Markovitch, 2009) concept vector signatures for each lemma, and the Dekang Lin Proximity-based Thesaurus [1].

The cosine-based lexical overlap measure simply measures the cosine similarity, using strict lexical overlap, between the sentence pairs. The BLEU, precision focused POS, and skip-bigrams are directional measures, which measure how well a target sentence matches a source sentence. To score pair of sentences, we simply averaged the score where one sentence is the source, the other the target, and then vice versa. These directional measures were originally used as a precision focused means to assess the quality of machine translations output against reference translations. Following (Finch et al., 2005), these measures have also been shown to be good for assessing semantic similarity between pairs of sentences.

For BLEU, we measured how well ngrams of order one through four were matched by the target sentence, matching solely on lexical matches, or POS matches. Skip bigrams performed similarly, except the bigrams were not contiguous. The precision focused POS features assess how well each POS tag found in the source sentence has been matched in the target sentence, where the matches are first done via a lemma match.

To combine the scores from these features, we used the LIBSVM Support Vector Regression (SVR) package (Chang and Lin, 2011), trained on the training pair gold scores. Per the previous year, we used a radial basis kernel with a degree of three.

[1] http://webdocs.cs.ualberta.ca/ lindek/downloads.htm

For a more in-depth description of System 1, please refer to (Yeh and Agirre, 2012).

3 TFIDF-ESA

This year instead of using Explicit Semantic Analysis (ESA) to populate a word-by-word similarity matrix, we used ESA to derive a similarity score between the sentences in a STS pair. For a given sentence, we basically treated it as an IR query against the ESA concept-base: we tokenized the words, extracted the ESA concept vectors, and performed a TFIDF weighted average to arrive at the sentence vector. A cutoff of the top 1000 scoring concepts was further applied, per previous experience, to improve performance. The similarity score for two sentence vectors was computed using cosine similarity.

4 Neural Probabilistic Language Models

Neural probabilistic language models represent words as real valued vectors, where these vectors are trained to jointly capture the distributional statistics of their context words and the positions these words occur at. These representations are usually at a much lower dimensionality than that of the original vocabulary, forcing some form of compression to occur in the vocabulary. The intent is to train a model that can account for words that have not been observed in a given context before, but that word vector has enough similarity to another word that has been encountered in that context before.

Earlier models simply learnt how to model the next word in a sequence, where each word in the vocabulary is initially represented by a randomly initialized vector. For each instance, a larger vector is assembled from the concatenation of the vectors of the words observed, and act as inputs into a model. This model itself is optimized to maximize the likelihood of the next word in the observed sequence, with the errors backpropagated through the vectors, with the parameters for the vectors being tied (Bengio et al., 2003).

In later studies, these representations are the product of training a neural network to maximize the margin between the scores it assigns to observed "correct" examples, which should have higher scores, and "corrupted examples," where the token of interest is swapped out to produce an incorrect example and preferably a lower score. As shown in (Collobert and Weston, 2008) and then (Huang et al., 2012), simple distance measures using the representations derived from this process are both useful for assessing word similarity and relatedness. For this study, we used the contextually trained language vectors provided by (Huang et al., 2012), which were trained to maximize the margin between training pairs and to account for document context as well. The dimensionality of these vectors was 50.

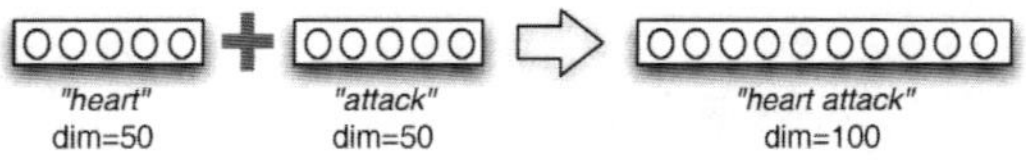

Figure 1: Vector Window encoding for the phrase *"heart attack."*

As we are interested in capturing information at a level greater than individual words, we used two methods to combine these NLPM word vectors to represent an order n ngram: a **Vector Window** where we simply concatenated the word vectors, and one that relied on encodings learnt by **Restricted Boltzmann Machines**.

For this work, we experimented with generating encodings for ngrams sized 2,3,5,10, and 21. The smaller sizes correspond to commonly those commonly used to match ngrams, while the larger ones were used to take advantage of the reduced sparsity. Similarities between a pair of ngram encodings is given similarity of their vector encodings.

4.1 Vector Window

The most direct way to encode an order n ngram as a vector is to concatenate the n NLPM word vectors together, in order. For example, to encode *"heart attack"*, the vectors for *"heart"* and *"attack"*, both with dimensionality 50, are linked together to form a larger vector with dimensionality 100 (Figure 1).

For size n vector windows where the total number of tokens is less than n, we pad the left and right sides of the window with a "negative" token, which was selected to be a vector that, on the average, is anticorrelated with all the vectors in the vocabulary.

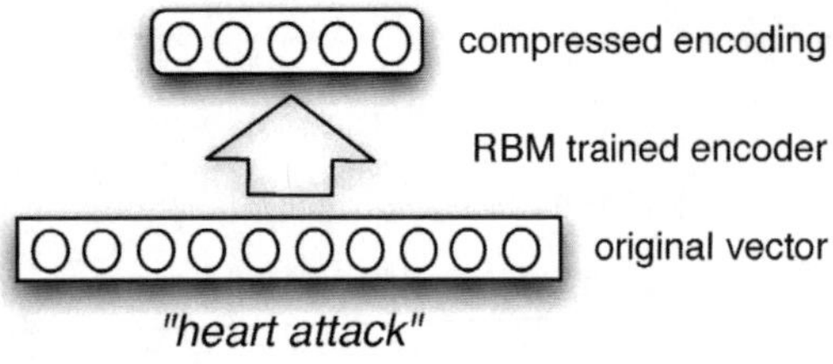

Figure 2: Using a RBM trained compressor to generate a compressed encoding of *"heart attack."*

4.2 Restricted Boltzmann Machines

Although the word vectors we used were trained against a ten word context, the vector windows may not be able to describe similarities at multiword level, as the method is still performing comparisons at a word-to-word level. For example the vector window score for the related phrases *heart attack* and *cardiac arrest* is 0.35. In order to account for similarities at a multiword level, we trained Restricted Boltzmann Machines (RBM) to further encode these vector windows (Hinton, 2002). A RBM is a bipartite undirected graphical model, where the only edges are between a layer of input variables and a layer of latent variables. The latent layer consists of sigmoid units, allowing for non-linear combinations of the inputs. The training objective is to learn a set of weights that maximize the likelihood of training observations, and given the independences inherent, in the model it can be trained quickly and effectively via Contrastive Divergence. The end effect is the system attempts to force the latent layer to learn an encoding of the input variables, usually at a lower dimensionality. In our case, by compressing their distributional representations we hope to amplify significant similarities between multiword expressions, albeit for those of the same size.

To derive a RBM based encoding, we first generate a vector window for the ngram, and then used the trained RBM to arrive at the compressed vector (Figure 2). As before, we derive a similarity score between two RBM based encodings by comparing their cosine distance.

Following the above example, the vectors from an RBM trained system for *heart attack* and *cardiac arrest* score the pair at a higher similarity, 0.54. For phrases that are unrelated, comparing *door key* with *cardiac arrest* gives a score of -0.14 with the vector window, and RBM this is -0.17.

To train a RBM encoder for order n ngrams, we generated n sized vector windows over ngrams drawn from the English language articles in Wikipedia. The language dump was filtered to larger sized articles, in order to avoid pages likely to be content-free, such as redirects. The training set size consisted of 35,581,434 words, which was split apart into 1,519,256 sentences using the OpenNLP sentence splitter tool [2]. The dimensionality of the encoding layer was set to 50 for window sizes 2,3,5, and 200 for the larger windows.

4.3 Combining word and ngram similarity scores

In order to produce an overall similarity score, we used a variant of the weighted variant of the similarity combination method given in (Mihalcea et al., 2006). Here, we generated a directional similarity score from a source to target by the following,

$$\text{sim}(S,T) = \frac{\sum_{s \in S} maxSim(s,T)}{|S|} \tag{2}$$

where $maxSim(s,T)$ represents the maximum similarity between the token s and the set of tokens in the target sentence, T. In the case of ngrams with order 2 or greater, we treat each ngram as a token for the combination.

$$\text{avgsim}(T_1,T_2) = \frac{1}{2}\left(\text{sim}(T_1,T_2) + \text{sim}(T_2,T_1)\right) \tag{3}$$

Unlike the original method, we treated each term equally, in order to account for ngrams with order 2 and above. We also did not filter based off of the part of speech, relying on the scores themselves to help perform the filtering.

In addition to the given word window sizes, we also directly assess the word-to-word similarity scores by comparing the word vectors directly, using a window size of one.

5 Evaluation Setup

System 2, the TFIDF-ESA score for a pair is a feature. For each of the given ngram sizes, we treated

[2] http://opennlp.apache.org/

Training (2012)	Test (2013)
Surprise1 (ONWN)	FNWN
MSRPar	Headlines
Surprise1 (ONWN)	ONWN
Surprise2 (SMT)	SMT

Table 1: Train (2012) and Test (2013) sets used to train the regressors.

the ngram similarity scores from the Vector Window and RBM methods as individual features. System 3 combines the features from System 2 with those from System 1. For Systems 2 and 3, the SVR setup used by System 1 was used to develop scorers. As no training immediate training sets were provided for the evaluation sets, we used the train and test partitions given in Table 1, training on both the 2012 train and test data, where gold scores were available.

6 Results and Discussion

The results of our three runs are given in the top half of Table 2. To get a better sense of the contribution of the new components, we also ran the NLPM vector window and RBM window models and TFIDF-ESA components individually against the test sets. The NLPM system was trained using the same SVR setup as the main experiment.

In order to provide a lexical match comparison for the NLPM system, we experimented with a ngram matching system, where ngrams of size 1,2,3,5,10, and 21 were used to generate similarity scores via the same combination method as the NLPM models. Here, hard matching was performed, where matching ngrams were given a score of 1, else 0. Again, we used the main experiment SVR setup to combine the scores from the various ngram sizes.

We found that overall the previous year's system did not perform adequately on the evaluation datasets, short of the *headlines* dataset. Oddly enough, TFIDF-ESA by itself would have arrived at a good correlation with *OnWN*: one possible explanation for this would be the fact that TFIDF-ESA by itself is essentially an order-free "bag of words" model that assesses soft token to token similarity. As the other systems incorporate either some notion of sequence and/or require strict lexical matching, it is possible that characterization does not help with the *OnWN* sense definitions.

Combining the new features with the previous year's system gave poorer performance; a preliminary assessment over the training sets showed some degree of overfitting, likely due to high correlation between the NLPM features and last year's directional measures.

When using the same combination method, ngram matching via lexical content over ngrams gave poorer results than those from NLPM models, as given in Table 2. This would also argue for identifying better combination methods than the averaged maximum similarity method used here.

What is interesting to note is that the NLPM and TFIDF-ESA systems do not rely on any part of speech information, nor hand-crafted semantic similarity resources. Instead, these methods are derived from large scale corpora, and generally outperformed the previous year's system which relied on that extra information.

To get a better understanding of the NLPM and TFIDF-ESA models, we compared how the components would score the similarity between pairs of two word phrases, given in Table 3. At least over this small sampling we genearted, we found that in general the RBM method tended to have a much wider range of scores than the Vector Window, although both methods were very correlated. Both systems had very low correlation with TFIDF-ESA.

7 Future Work

One area of improvement would be to develop a better method for combining the various ngram similarity scores provided by the NLPMs. When using lexical matching of ngrams, we found that the combination method used here proved inferior to the directional measures from the previous year's systems. This would argue for a better way to use the NLPMs. As training STS pairs are available with gold scores, this would argue for some form of supervised training. For training similarities between multiword expressions, proxy measures for similarity, such as the Normalized Google Distance (Cilibrasi and Vitányi, 2004), may be feasible.

Another avenue would be to allow the NLPM methods to encode arbitrary sized text spans, as the current restriction on spans being the same size is

System	headlines	OnWN	FNWN	SMT	mean	rank
SRIUBC-system1 (Baseline)	0.6083	0.2915	0.2790	0.3065	0.4011	66
SRIUBC-system2 (NLPM, TFIDF-ESA)	0.6359	0.3664	0.2713	0.3476	0.4420	57
SRIUBC-system3 (Combined)	0.5443	0.2843	0.2705	0.3275	0.3842	70
NLPM	0.5791	0.3157	0.3211	0.2698	0.3714	
TFIDF-ESA	0.5739	0.7222	0.1781	0.2980	0.4431	
Lex-only	0.5455	0.3237	0.2095	0.3146	0.3483	

Table 2: Pearson correlation of systems against the test datasets (top). The test set performance for the new Neural Probabilistic Language Model (NLPM) and TFIDF-ESA components are given, along with a lexical-only variant for comparison (bottom).

String 1	String 2	Vec. Window	RBM Window	TFIDF-ESA
heart attack	cardiac arrest	0.354	0.544	0.182
door key	cardiac arrest	-0.14	-0.177	0
baby food	cat food	0.762	0.907	0.079
dog food	cat food	0.886	0.914	0.158
rotten food	baby food	0.482	0.473	0.071
frozen solid	thawed out	0.046	-0.331	0.102
severely burnt	frozen stiff	-0.023	-0.155	0
uphill slog	raced downhill	0.03	-0.322	0.043
small cat	large dog	0.817	0.905	0.007
ran along	sprinted by	0.31	0.238	0.004
ran quickly	jogged rapidly	0.349	0.327	0.001
deathly ill	very sick	0.002	0.177	0.004
ran to	raced to	0.815	0.829	0.013
free drinks	drinks free	0.001	0.042	1
door key	combination lock	0.098	0.093	0.104
frog blast	vent core	0.003	0.268	0.004

Table 3: Cosine similarity of two input strings, as given by the vectors generated from the Vector Window size 2, RBM Window size 2, and TFIDF-ESA.

unrealistic. One possibility is to use recurrent neural network techniques to generate this type of encoding.

Finally, the size of the Wikipedia dump used to train the Restricted Boltzmann Machines could be at issue, as 35 million words could be considered small compared to the full range of expressions we would wish to capture, especially for the larger window spans. A larger training corpus may be needed to fully see the benefit from RBMs.

Acknowledgments

Supported by the Artificial Intelligence Center at SRI International. The views and conclusions contained herein are those of the authors and should not be interpreted as necessarily representing the official policies or endorsements, either expressed or implied, of the Artificial Intelligence Center, or SRI International.

References

Eneko Agirre, Montse Cuadros, German Rigau, and Aitor Soroa. 2010. Exploring knowledge bases for similarity. In *Proceedings of the International Conference on Language Resources and Evaluation 2010.*

Yoshua Bengio, Réjean Ducharme, Pascal Vincent, and Christian Janvin. 2003. A neural probabilistic language model. *Journal of Machine Learning Research*, 3:1137–1155.

Chih-Chung Chang and Chih-Jen Lin. 2011. LIBSVM: A library for support vector machines. *ACM Transac-*

tions on Intelligent Systems and Technology, 2:27:1–27:27.

Rudi Cilibrasi and Paul M. B. Vitányi. 2004. The google similarity distance. *CoRR*, abs/cs/0412098.

R. Collobert and J. Weston. 2008. A unified architecture for natural language processing: Deep neural networks with multitask learning. In *International Conference on Machine Learning, ICML*.

Christine Fellbaum. 1998. *WordNet - An Electronic Lexical Database*. MIT Press.

Samuel Fernando and Mark Stevenson. 2008. A semantic similarity approach to paraphrase detection. In *Computational Linguistics UK (CLUK 2008) 11th Annual Research Colloqium*.

Andrew Finch, Young-Sook Hwang, and Eiichio Sumita. 2005. Using machine translation evaluation techniques to determine sentence-level semantic equivalence. In *Proceedings of the Third International Workshop on Paraphrasing (IWP 2005)*, pages 17–24, Jeju Island, South Korea.

Evgeniy Gabrilovich and Shaul Markovitch. 2009. Wikipedia-based semantic interpretation. *Journal of Artificial Intelligence Research*, 34:443–498.

Geoffrey E. Hinton. 2002. Training products of experts by minimizing contrastive divergence. *Neural Computation*, 14(8):1771–1800.

Eric H. Huang, Richard Socher, Christopher D. Manning, and Andrew Y. Ng. 2012. Improving Word Representations via Global Context and Multiple Word Prototypes. In *Annual Meeting of the Association for Computational Linguistics (ACL)*.

Rada Mihalcea, Courtney Corley, and Carlo Strapparava. 2006. Corpus-based and knowledge-based measures of text semantic similarity. In *Proceedings of the American Association for Artificial Intelligence (AAAI 2006)*, Boston, Massachusetts, July.

Kishore Papineni, Salim Roukos, Todd Ward, and Wei-Jing Zhu. 2002. Bleu: a method for automatic evaluation of machine translation. In *Proceedings of the 40th Annual Meeting on Association for Computational Linguistics*, ACL '02, pages 311–318, Stroudsburg, PA, USA. Association for Computational Linguistics.

Eric Yeh and Eneko Agirre. 2012. Sri and ubc: Simple similarity features for semantic textual similarity. In *Proceedings of SemEval 2012*.

LIPN-CORE: Semantic Text Similarity using n-grams, WordNet, Syntactic Analysis, ESA and Information Retrieval based Features

Davide Buscaldi, Joseph Le Roux,
Jorge J. García Flores
Laboratoire d'Informatique de Paris Nord,
CNRS, (UMR 7030)
Université Paris 13, Sorbonne Paris Cité,
F-93430, Villetaneuse, France
{buscaldi, joseph.le-roux, jgflores}
@lipn.univ-paris13.fr

Adrian Popescu
CEA, LIST,
Vision & Content
Engineering Laboratory
F-91190 Gif-sur-Yvette, France
adrian.popescu@cea.fr

Abstract

This paper describes the system used by the LIPN team in the Semantic Textual Similarity task at *SEM 2013. It uses a support vector regression model, combining different text similarity measures that constitute the features. These measures include simple distances like Levenshtein edit distance, cosine, Named Entities overlap and more complex distances like Explicit Semantic Analysis, WordNet-based similarity, IR-based similarity, and a similarity measure based on syntactic dependencies.

1 Introduction

The Semantic Textual Similarity task (STS) at *SEM 2013 requires systems to grade the degree of similarity between pairs of sentences. It is closely related to other well known tasks in NLP such as textual entailment, question answering or paraphrase detection. However, as noticed in (Bär et al., 2012), the major difference is that STS systems must give a *graded*, as opposed to binary, answer.

One of the most successful systems in *SEM 2012 STS, (Bär et al., 2012), managed to grade pairs of sentences accurately by combining focused measures, either simple ones based on surface features (*ie* n-grams), more elaborate ones based on lexical semantics, or measures requiring external corpora such as Explicit Semantic Analysis, into a robust measure by using a log-linear regression model.

The LIPN-CORE system is built upon this idea of combining simple measures with a regression model to obtain a robust and accurate measure of textual similarity, using the individual measures as features for the global system. These measures include simple distances like Levenshtein edit distance, cosine, Named Entities overlap and more complex distances like Explicit Semantic Analysis, WordNet-based similarity, IR-based similarity, and a similarity measure based on syntactic dependencies.

The paper is organized as follows. Measures are presented in Section 2. Then the regression model, based on Support Vector Machines, is described in Section 3. Finally we discuss the results of the system in Section 4.

2 Text Similarity Measures

2.1 WordNet-based Conceptual Similarity (Proxigenea)

First of all, sentences p and q are analysed in order to extract all the included WordNet synsets. For each WordNet synset, we keep noun synsets and put into the set of synsets associated to the sentence, C_p and C_q, respectively. If the synsets are in one of the other POS categories (verb, adjective, adverb) we look for their derivationally related forms in order to find a related noun synset: if there is one, we put this synsets in C_p (or C_q). For instance, the word "playing" can be associated in WordNet to synset `(v)play#2`, which has two derivationally related forms corresponding to synsets `(n)play#5` and `(n)play#6`: these are the synsets that are added to the synset set of the sentence. No disambiguation process is carried out, so we take all possible meanings into account.

Given C_p and C_q as the sets of concepts contained in sentences p and q, respectively, with $|C_p| \geq |C_q|$,

*Second Joint Conference on Lexical and Computational Semantics (*SEM), Volume 1: Proceedings of the Main Conference and the Shared Task*, pages 162–168, Atlanta, Georgia, June 13-14, 2013. ©2013 Association for Computational Linguistics

the conceptual similarity between p and q is calculated as:

$$ss(p,q) = \frac{\sum_{c_1 \in C_p} \max_{c_2 \in C_q} s(c_1, c_2)}{|C_p|} \quad (1)$$

where $s(c_1, c_2)$ is a conceptual similarity measure. Concept similarity can be calculated by different ways. For the participation in the 2013 Semantic Textual Similarity task, we used a variation of the Wu-Palmer formula (Wu and Palmer, 1994) named "ProxiGenea" (from the french Proximité Généalogique, genealogical proximity), introduced by (Dudognon et al., 2010), which is inspired by the analogy between a family tree and the concept hierarchy in WordNet. Among the different formulations proposed by (Dudognon et al., 2010), we chose the ProxiGenea3 variant, already used in the STS 2012 task by the IRIT team (Buscaldi et al., 2012). The ProxiGenea3 measure is defined as:

$$s(c_1, c_2) = \frac{1}{1 + d(c_1) + d(c_2) - 2 \cdot d(c_0)} \quad (2)$$

where c_0 is the most specific concept that is present both in the synset path of c_1 and c_2 (that is, the Least Common Subsumer or LCS). The function returning the depth of a concept is noted with d.

2.2 IC-based Similarity

This measure has been proposed by (Mihalcea et al., 2006) as a corpus-based measure which uses Resnik's Information Content (IC) and the Jiang-Conrath (Jiang and Conrath, 1997) similarity metric:

$$s_{jc}(c_1, c_2) = \frac{1}{IC(c_1) + IC(c_2) - 2 \cdot IC(c_0)} \quad (3)$$

where IC is the information content introduced by (Resnik, 1995) as $IC(c) = -\log P(c)$.

The similarity between two text segments T_1 and T_2 is therefore determined as:

$$sim(T_1, T_2) = \frac{1}{2}\left(\frac{\sum_{w \in \{T_1\}} \max_{w_2 \in \{T_2\}} ws(w, w_2) * idf(w)}{\sum_{w \in \{T_1\}} idf(w)} + \frac{\sum_{w \in \{T_2\}} \max_{w_1 \in \{T_1\}} ws(w, w_1) * idf(w)}{\sum_{w \in \{T_2\}} idf(w)}\right) \quad (4)$$

where $idf(w)$ is calculated as the inverse document frequency of word w, taking into account Google Web 1T (Brants and Franz, 2006) frequency counts. The semantic similarity between words is calculated as:

$$ws(w_i, w_j) = \max_{c_i \in W_i, c_j in W_j} s_{jc}(c_i, c_j). \quad (5)$$

where W_i and W_j are the sets containing all synsets in WordNet corresponding to word w_i and w_j, respectively. The IC values used are those calculated by Ted Pedersen (Pedersen et al., 2004) on the British National Corpus[1].

2.3 Syntactic Dependencies

We also wanted for our systems to take syntactic similarity into account. As our measures are lexically grounded, we chose to use dependencies rather than constituents. Previous experiments showed that converting constituents to dependencies still achieved best results on out-of-domain texts (Le Roux et al., 2012), so we decided to use a 2-step architecture to obtain syntactic dependencies. First we parsed pairs of sentences with the LORG parser[2]. Second we converted the resulting parse trees to Stanford dependencies[3].

Given the sets of parsed dependencies D_p and D_q, for sentence p and q, a dependency $d \in D_x$ is a triple (l, h, t) where l is the dependency label (for instance, *dobj* or *prep*), h the governor and t the dependant. We define the following similarity measure between two syntactic dependencies $d_1 = (l_1, h_1, t_1)$ and $d_2 = (l_2, h_2, t_2)$:

$$dsim(d_1, d_2) = Lev(l_1, l_2) * \frac{idf_h * s_{WN}(h_1, h_2) + idf_t * s_{WN}(t_1, t_2)}{2} \quad (6)$$

where $idf_h = \max(idf(h_1), idf(h_2))$ and $idf_t = \max(idf(t_1), idf(t_2))$ are the inverse document frequencies calculated on Google Web 1T for the governors and the dependants (we retain the maximum for each pair), and s_{WN} is calculated using formula 2, with two differences:

- if the two words to be compared are antonyms, then the returned score is 0;

[1] http://www.d.umn.edu/~tpederse/similarity.html

[2] https://github.com/CNGLdlab/LORG-Release

[3] We used the default built-in converter provided with the Stanford Parser (2012-11-12 revision).

- if one of the words to be compared is not in WordNet, their similarity is calculated using the Levenshtein distance.

The similarity score between p and q, is then calculated as:

$$s_{SD}(p,q) = \max\left(\frac{\sum_{d_i \in D_p} \max_{d_j in D_q} dsim(d_i,d_j)}{|D_p|}, \frac{\sum_{d_i \in D_q} \max_{d_j in D_p} dsim(d_i,d_j)}{|D_q|}\right) \quad (7)$$

2.4 Information Retrieval-based Similarity

Let us consider two texts p and q, an Information Retrieval (IR) system S and a document collection D indexed by S. This measure is based on the assumption that p and q are similar if the documents retrieved by S for the two texts, used as input queries, are ranked similarly.

Let be $L_p = \{d_{p1}, \ldots, d_{pK}\}$ and $L_q = \{d_{q1}, \ldots, d_{qK}\}$, $d_{x_i} \in D$ the sets of the top K documents retrieved by S for texts p and q, respectively. Let us define $s_p(d)$ and $s_q(d)$ the scores assigned by S to a document d for the query p and q, respectively. Then, the similarity score is calculated as:

$$sim_{IR}(p,q) = 1 - \frac{\sum_{d \in L_p \cap L_q} \frac{\sqrt{(s_p(d) - s_q(d))^2}}{\max(s_p(d), s_q(d))}}{|L_p \cap L_q|} \quad (8)$$

if $|L_p \cap L_q| \neq \emptyset$, 0 otherwise.

For the participation in this task we indexed a collection composed by the AQUAINT-2[4] and the English NTCIR-8[5] document collections, using the Lucene[6] 4.2 search engine with BM25 similarity. The K value was empirically set to 20 after some tests on the STS 2012 data.

2.5 ESA

Explicit Semantic Analysis (Gabrilovich and Markovitch, 2007) represents meaning as a weighted vector of Wikipedia concepts. Weights are supposed to quantify the strength of the relation between a word and each Wikipedia concept using the *tf-idf* measure. A text is then represented as a high-dimensional real valued vector space spanning all along the Wikipedia database. For this particular task we adapt the *research-esa* implementation (Sorg and Cimiano, 2008)[7] to our own home-made weighted vectors corresponding to a Wikipedia snapshot of February 4th, 2013.

2.6 N-gram based Similarity

This feature is based on the Clustered Keywords Positional Distance (CKPD) model proposed in (Buscaldi et al., 2009) for the passage retrieval task.

The similarity between a text fragment p and another text fragment q is calculated as:

$$sim_{ngrams}(p,q) = \frac{\sum_{\forall x \in Q} h(x,P) \frac{1}{d(x, x_{max})}}{\sum_{i=1}^{n} w_i} \quad (9)$$

Where P is the set of n-grams with the highest weight in p, where all terms are also contained in q; Q is the set of all the possible n-grams in q and n is the total number of terms in the longest passage. The weights for each term and each n-gram are calculated as:

- w_i calculates the weight of the term t_I as:

$$w_i = 1 - \frac{log(n_i)}{1 + log(N)} \quad (10)$$

Where n_i is the frequency of term t_i in the Google Web 1T collection, and N is the frequency of the most frequent term in the Google Web 1T collection.

- the function $h(x,P)$ measures the weight of each n-gram and is defined as:

$$h(x, P_j) = \begin{cases} \sum_{k=1}^{j} w_k & \text{if } x \in P_j \\ 0 & \text{otherwise} \end{cases} \quad (11)$$

[4] http://www.nist.gov/tac/data/data_desc.html#AQUAINT-2

[5] http://metadata.berkeley.edu/NTCIR-GeoTime/ntcir-8-databases.php

[6] http://lucene.apache.org/core

[7] http://code.google.com/p/research-esa/

Where w_k is the weight of the *k-th* term (see Equation 10) and *j* is the number of terms that compose the n-gram x;

- $\frac{1}{d(x,x_{max})}$ is a distance factor which reduces the weight of the *n*-grams that are far from the heaviest *n*-gram. The function $d(x, x_{max})$ determines numerically the value of the separation according to the number of words between a *n*-gram and the heaviest one:

$$d(x, x_{max}) = 1 + k \cdot ln(1 + L) \quad (12)$$

where *k* is a factor that determines the importance of the distance in the similarity calculation and *L* is the number of words between a *n*-gram and the heaviest one (see Equation 11). In our experiments, k was set to 0.1, the default value in the original model.

2.7 Other measures

In addition to the above text similarity measures, we used also the following common measures:

2.7.1 Cosine

Given $\mathbf{p} = (w_{p_1}, \ldots, w_{p_n})$ and $\mathbf{q} = (w_{q_1}, \ldots, w_{q_n})$ the vectors of $tf.idf$ weights associated to sentences p and q, the cosine distance is calculated as:

$$sim_{cos}(\mathbf{p}, \mathbf{q}) = \frac{\sum_{i=1}^{n} w_{p_i} \times w_{q_i}}{\sqrt{\sum_{i=1}^{n} {w_{p_i}}^2} \times \sqrt{\sum_{i=1}^{n} {w_{q_i}}^2}} \quad (13)$$

The idf value was calculated on Google Web 1T.

2.7.2 Edit Distance

This similarity measure is calculated using the Levenshtein distance as:

$$sim_{ED}(p, q) = 1 - \frac{Lev(p, q)}{\max(|p|, |q|)} \quad (14)$$

where $Lev(p, q)$ is the Levenshtein distance between the two sentences, taking into account the characters.

2.7.3 Named Entity Overlap

We used the Stanford Named Entity Recognizer by (Finkel et al., 2005), with the 7 class model trained for MUC: Time, Location, Organization, Person, Money, Percent, Date. Then we calculated a per-class overlap measure (in this way, "France" as an Organization does not match "France" as a Location):

$$O_{NER}(p, q) = \frac{2 * |N_p \cap N_q|}{|N_p| + |N_q|} \quad (15)$$

where N_p and N_q are the sets of NEs found, respectively, in sentences p and q.

3 Integration of Similarity Measures

The integration has been carried out using the ν-Support Vector Regression model (ν-SVR) (Schölkopf et al., 1999) implementation provided by LIBSVM (Chang and Lin, 2011), with a radial basis function kernel with the standard parameters ($\nu = 0.5$).

4 Results

In order to evaluate the impact of the different features, we carried out an ablation test, removing one feature at a time and training a new model with the reduced set of features. In Table 2 we show the results of the ablation test for each subset of the *SEM 2013 test set; in Table 1 we show the same test on the whole test set. Note: the results have been calculated as the Pearson correlation test on the whole test set and not as an average of the correlation scores calculated over the composing test sets.

Feature Removed	Pearson	Loss
None	0.597	0
N-grams	0.596	0.10%
WordNet	0.563	3.39%
SyntDeps	0.602	−0.43%
Edit	0.584	1.31%
Cosine	0.596	0.10%
NE Overlap	0.603	0.53%
IC-based	0.598	−0.10%
IR-Similarity	0.510	**8.78%**
ESA	0.601	−0.38%

Table 1: Ablation test for the different features on the whole 2013 test set.

	FNWN		Headlines		OnWN		SMT	
Feature	**Pearson**	**Loss**	**Pearson**	**Loss**	**Pearson**	**Loss**	**Pearson**	**Loss**
None	0.404	0	0.706	0	0.694	0	0.301	0
N-grams	0.379	2.49%	0.705	0.12%	0.698	−0.44%	0.289	1.16%
WordNet	0.376	**2.80%**	0.695	1.09%	0.682	1.17%	0.278	2.28%
SyntDeps	0.403	0.08%	0.699	0.70%	0.679	1.49%	0.284	1.62%
Edit	0.402	0.19%	0.689	1.70%	0.667	2.72%	0.286	1.50%
Cosine	0.393	1.03%	0.683	2.38%	0.676	1.80%	0.303	−0.24%
NE Overlap	0.410	−0.61%	0.700	0.67%	0.680	1.37%	0.285	1.58%
IC-based	0.391	1.26%	0.699	0.75%	0.669	2.50%	0.283	1.76%
IR-Similarity	0.426	−2.21%	0.633	**7.33%**	0.589	**10.46%**	0.249	**5.19%**
ESA	0.391	1.22%	0.691	1.57%	0.702	−0.81%	0.275	2.54%

Table 2: Ablation test for the different features on the different parts of the 2013 test set.

	FNWN	Headlines	OnWN	SMT	ALL
N-grams	0.285	0.532	0.459	0.280	0.336
WordNet	0.395	**0.606**	0.552	0.282	0.477
SyntDeps	0.233	0.409	0.345	0.323	0.295
Edit	0.220	0.536	0.089	**0.355**	0.230
Cosine	0.306	0.573	0.541	0.244	0.382
NE Overlap	0.000	0.216	0.000	0.013	0.020
IC-based	**0.413**	0.540	**0.642**	0.285	0.421
IR-based	0.067	0.598	0.628	0.241	**0.541**
ESA	0.328	0.546	0.322	0.289	0.390

Table 3: Pearson correlation calculated on individual features.

The ablation test show that the IR-based feature showed up to be the most effective one, especially for the headlines subset (as expected), and, quite surprisingly, on the OnWN data. In Table 3 we show the correlation between each feature and the result (feature values normalised between 0 and 5): from this table we can also observe that, on average, IR-based similarity was better able to capture the semantic similarity between texts. The only exception was the FNWN test set: the IR-based similarity returned a 0 score 178 times out of 189 (94.1%), indicating that the indexed corpus did not fit the content of the FNWN sentences. This result shows also the limits of the IR-based similarity score which needs a large corpus to achieve enough coverage.

4.1 Shared submission with INAOE-UPV

One of the files submitted by INAOE-UPV, `INAOE-UPV-run3` has been produced using seven features produced by different teams: INAOE, LIPN and UMCC-DLSI. We contributed to this joint submission with the IR-based, WordNet and cosine features.

5 Conclusions and Further Work

In this paper we introduced the LIPN-CORE system, which combines semantic, syntactic an lexical measures of text similarity in a linear regression model. Our system was among the best 15 runs for the STS task. According to the ablation test, the best performing feature was the IR-based one, where a sentence is considered as a query and its meaning represented as a set of documents indexed by an IR system. The second and third best-performing measures were WordNet similarity and Levenshtein's edit distance. On the other hand, worst performing similarity measures were Named Entity Overlap, Syntactic Dependencies and ESA. However, a correlation analysis calculated on the features taken one-by-one shows that the contribution of a feature on the overall regression result does not correspond to the actual capability of the measure to represent the semantic similarity between the two texts. These results raise the methodological question of how to combine semantic, syntactic and lexical similarity measures in order to estimate the impact of the different strategies used on each dataset.

Further work will include richer similarity measures, like quasi-synchronous grammars (Smith and Eisner, 2006) and random walks (Ramage et al., 2009). Quasi-synchronous grammars have been used successfully for paraphrase detection (Das and Smith, 2009), as they provide a fine-grained modeling of the alignment of syntactic structures, in a very flexible way, enabling partial alignments and the inclusion of external features, like Wordnet lexical relations for example. Random walks have been used effectively for paraphrase recognition and as a feature for recognizing textual entailment. Finally, we will continue analyzing the question of how to combine a wide variety of similarity measures in such a way that they tackle the semantic variations of each dataset.

Acknowledgments

We would like to thank the Quaero project and the LabEx EFL[8] for their support to this work.

References

[Bär et al.2012] Daniel Bär, Chris Biemann, Iryna Gurevych, and Torsten Zesch. 2012. Ukp: Computing semantic textual similarity by combining multiple content similarity measures. In *Proceedings of the 6th International Workshop on Semantic Evaluation, held in conjunction with the 1st Joint Conference on Lexical and Computational Semantics*, pages 435–440, Montreal, Canada, June.

[Brants and Franz2006] Thorsten Brants and Alex Franz. 2006. Web 1t 5-gram corpus version 1.1.

[Buscaldi et al.2009] Davide Buscaldi, Paolo Rosso, José Manuel Gómez, and Emilio Sanchis. 2009. Answering questions with an n-gram based passage retrieval engine. *Journal of Intelligent Information Systems (JIIS)*, 34(2):113–134.

[Buscaldi et al.2012] Davide Buscaldi, Ronan Tournier, Nathalie Aussenac-Gilles, and Josiane Mothe. 2012. Irit: Textual similarity combining conceptual similarity with an n-gram comparison method. In *Proceedings of the 6th International Workshop on Semantic Evaluation (SemEval 2012)*, Montreal, Quebec, Canada.

[Chang and Lin2011] Chih-Chung Chang and Chih-Jen Lin. 2011. LIBSVM: A library for support vector machines. *ACM Transactions on Intelligent Systems and Technology*, 2:27:1–27:27. Software available at `http://www.csie.ntu.edu.tw/~cjlin/libsvm`.

[Das and Smith2009] Dipanjan Das and Noah A. Smith. 2009. Paraphrase identification as probabilistic quasi-synchronous recognition. In *Proc. of ACL-IJCNLP*.

[Dudognon et al.2010] Damien Dudognon, Gilles Hubert, and Bachelin Jhonn Victorino Ralalason. 2010. Proxigénéa : Une mesure de similarité conceptuelle. In *Proceedings of the Colloque Veille Stratégique Scientifique et Technologique (VSST 2010)*.

[Finkel et al.2005] Jenny Rose Finkel, Trond Grenager, and Christopher Manning. 2005. Incorporating non-local information into information extraction systems by gibbs sampling. In *Proceedings of the 43rd Annual Meeting on Association for Computational Linguistics*, ACL '05, pages 363–370, Stroudsburg, PA, USA. Association for Computational Linguistics.

[Gabrilovich and Markovitch2007] Evgeniy Gabrilovich and Shaul Markovitch. 2007. Computing semantic relatedness using wikipedia-based explicit semantic analysis. In *Proceedings of the 20th international joint conference on Artifical intelligence*, IJCAI'07, pages 1606–1611, San Francisco, CA, USA. Morgan Kaufmann Publishers Inc.

[Jiang and Conrath1997] J.J. Jiang and D.W. Conrath. 1997. Semantic similarity based on corpus statistics and lexical taxonomy. In *Proc. of the Int'l. Conf. on Research in Computational Linguistics*, pages 19–33.

[Le Roux et al.2012] Joseph Le Roux, Jennifer Foster, Joachim Wagner, Rasul Samad Zadeh Kaljahi, and Anton Bryl. 2012. DCU-Paris13 Systems for the SANCL 2012 Shared Task. In *The NAACL 2012 First Workshop on Syntactic Analysis of Non-Canonical Language (SANCL)*, pages 1–4, Montréal, Canada, June.

[Mihalcea et al.2006] Rada Mihalcea, Courtney Corley, and Carlo Strapparava. 2006. Corpus-based and knowledge-based measures of text semantic similarity. In *Proceedings of the 21st national conference on Artificial intelligence - Volume 1*, AAAI'06, pages 775–780. AAAI Press.

[Pedersen et al.2004] Ted Pedersen, Siddharth Patwardhan, and Jason Michelizzi. 2004. Wordnet::similarity: measuring the relatedness of concepts. In *Demonstration Papers at HLT-NAACL 2004*, HLT-NAACL–

[8] `http://www.labex-efl.org`

Demonstrations '04, pages 38–41, Stroudsburg, PA, USA. Association for Computational Linguistics.

[Ramage et al.2009] Daniel Ramage, Anna N. Rafferty, and Christopher D. Manning. 2009. Random walks for text semantic similarity. In *Proceedings of the 2009 Workshop on Graph-based Methods for Natural Language Processing*, pages 23–31. The Association for Computer Linguistics.

[Resnik1995] Philip Resnik. 1995. Using information content to evaluate semantic similarity in a taxonomy. In *Proceedings of the 14th international joint conference on Artificial intelligence - Volume 1*, IJCAI'95, pages 448–453, San Francisco, CA, USA. Morgan Kaufmann Publishers Inc.

[Schölkopf et al.1999] Bernhard Schölkopf, Peter Bartlett, Alex Smola, and Robert Williamson. 1999. Shrinking the tube: a new support vector regression algorithm. In *Proceedings of the 1998 conference on Advances in neural information processing systems II*, pages 330–336, Cambridge, MA, USA. MIT Press.

[Smith and Eisner2006] David A. Smith and Jason Eisner. 2006. Quasi-synchronous grammars: Alignment by soft projection of syntactic dependencies. In *Proceedings of the HLT-NAACL Workshop on Statistical Machine Translation*, pages 23–30, New York, June.

[Sorg and Cimiano2008] Philipp Sorg and Philipp Cimiano. 2008. Cross-lingual Information Retrieval with Explicit Semantic Analysis. In *Working Notes for the CLEF 2008 Workshop*.

[Wu and Palmer1994] Zhibiao Wu and Martha Palmer. 1994. Verbs semantics and lexical selection. In *Proceedings of the 32nd annual meeting on Association for Computational Linguistics*, ACL '94, pages 133–138, Stroudsburg, PA, USA. Association for Computational Linguistics.

UNIBA-CORE: Combining Strategies for Semantic Textual Similarity

Annalina Caputo **Pierpaolo Basile** **Giovanni Semeraro**
Department of Computer Science
University of Bari Aldo Moro
Via E. Orabona, 4 - 70125 Bari, Italy
{annalina.caputo, pierpaolo.basile, giovanni.semeraro}@uniba.it

Abstract

This paper describes the UNIBA participation in the Semantic Textual Similarity (STS) core task 2013. We exploited three different systems for computing the similarity between two texts. A system is used as baseline, which represents the best model emerged from our previous participation in STS 2012. Such system is based on a distributional model of semantics capable of taking into account also syntactic structures that glue words together. In addition, we investigated the use of two different learning strategies exploiting both syntactic and semantic features. The former uses ensemble learning in order to combine the best machine learning techniques trained on 2012 training and test sets. The latter tries to overcome the limit of working with different datasets with varying characteristics by selecting only the more suitable dataset for the training purpose.

1 Introduction

Semantic Textual Similarity is the task of computing the similarity between any two given texts. The task, in its core formulation, aims at capturing the different kinds of similarity that emerge from texts. Machine translation, paraphrasing, synonym substitution or text entailment are some fruitful methods exploited for this purpose. These techniques, along with other methods for estimating the text similarity, were successfully employed via machine learning approaches during the 2012 task.

However, the STS 2013 core task (Agirre et al., 2013) differs from the 2012 formulation in that it provides a test set which is similar to the training, but not drawn from the same set of data. Hence, in order to generalize the machine learning models trained on a group of datasets, we investigate the use of combination strategies. The objective of combination strategies, known under the name of *ensemble learning*, is that of reducing the bias-variance decomposition through reducing the variance error. Hence, this class of methods should be more robust with respect to previously unseen data. Among the several ensemble learning alternatives, we exploit the *stacked generalization* (STACKING) algorithm (Wolpert, 1992). Moreover, we investigate the use of a two-steps learning algorithm (2STEPSML). In this method the learning algorithm is trained using only the dataset most similar to the instance to be predicted. The first step aims at predicting the dataset more similar to the given pair of texts. Then the second step makes use of the previously trained algorithm to predict the similarity value. The baseline for the evaluation is represented by our best system (DSM_PERM) resulting from our participation in the 2012 task. After introducing the general models behind our systems in Section 2, Section 3 describes the evaluation setting of our systems along with the experimental results. Then, some conclusions and remarks close the paper.

2 General Models

2.1 Dependency Encoding via Vector Permutations

Distributional models are effective methods for representing word paradigmatic relations in a simple

*Second Joint Conference on Lexical and Computational Semantics (*SEM), Volume 1: Proceedings of the Main Conference and the Shared Task*, pages 169–175, Atlanta, Georgia, June 13-14, 2013.

way through vector spaces (Mitchell and Lapata, 2008). These spaces are built taking into account the word context, hence the resulting vector representation is such that the distance between vectors reflects their similarity. Although several definitions of context are possible (e.g. a sliding window of text, the word order or syntactic dependencies), in their plain definition these kinds of models account for just one type of context at a time. To overcome this limitation, we exploit a method to encode more definitions of context in the same vector exploiting the vector permutations (Caputo et al., 2012). This technique, which is based on Random Indexing as a means for computing the distributional model, is based on the idea that when the components of a highly sparse vector are shuffled, the resulting vector is nearly orthogonal to the original one. Hence, vector permutation represents a way for generating new random vectors in a predetermined manner. Different word contexts can be encoded using different types of permutations. In our distributional model system (DSM_PERM), we encode the syntactic dependencies between words rather than the mere co-occurrence information. In this way, word-vector components bear the information about both co-occurring and syntactically related words. In this distributional space, a text can be easily represented as the superposition of its words. Then, the vector representation of a text is given by adding the vector representation of its words, and the similarity between texts come through the cosine of the angle between their vector representations.

2.2 Stacking

Stacking algorithms (Wolpert, 1992) are a way of combining different types of learning algorithms reducing the variance of the system. In this model, the meta-learner tries to predict the real value of an instance combining the outputs of other machine learning methods.

Figure 1 shows how the learning process takes place. The level-0 represents the ensemble of different models to be trained on the same dataset. The level-0 outputs build up the level-1 dataset: an instance at this level is represented by the numeric values predicted by each level-0 model along with the gold standard value. Then, the objective of the level-1 learning model is to learn how to combine the level-0 outputs in order to provide the best prediction.

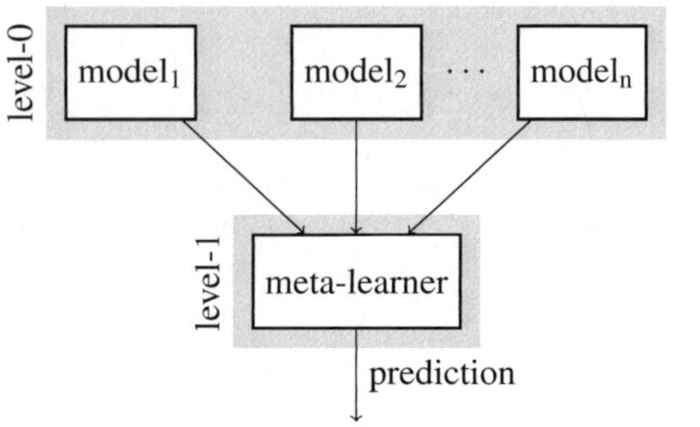

Figure 1: Stacking algorithm

2.3 Two steps learning algorithm

Given an ensemble of datasets with different characteristics, this method is based on the idea that when instances come from a specific dataset, the learning algorithm trained on that dataset outperforms the same algorithm trained on the whole ensemble.

Hence, the two steps algorithm tries to overcome the problem of dealing with different datasets having different characteristics through a classification model.

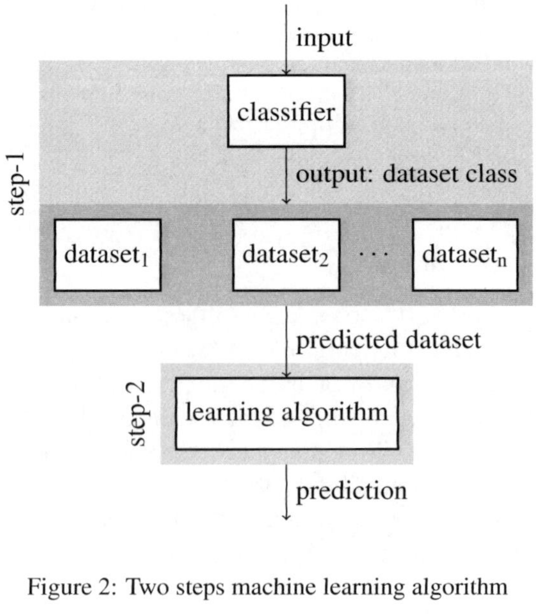

Figure 2: Two steps machine learning algorithm

In the first step (Figure 2), a different class is assigned to each dataset. The classifier is trained on a set of instances whose classes correspond to the dataset numbers. Then, given a new instance the output of this step will be the dataset to be used for training the learning algorithm in the step 2. In the second step, the learning algorithm is trained on the dataset choose in the first step. The output of this step is the predicted similarity between the two texts. Through these steps, it is possible to select the dataset with the characteristics more similar to a given instance, and exploit just this set of data for learning the algorithm.

2.4 Features

Both STACKING and 2STEPSML systems rely on several kinds of features, which vary from lexical to semantic ones. Features are grouped in seven main classes, as follows:

1. **Character/string/annotation**-based features: the length of the longest common contiguous substring between the texts; the Jaccard index of both tokens and lemmas; the Levenshtein distance between texts; the normalized number of common 2-grams, 3-grams and 4-grams; the total number of tokens and characters; the difference in tokens and characters between texts; the normalized difference with respect to the max text length in tokens and characters between texts. Exploiting other linguistic annotations extracted by Stanford CoreNLP[1], we compute the Jaccard index between PoS-tags and named entities. Using WordNet we extract the Jaccard index between the first sense and its super-sense tag.

2. **Textual Similarity**-based features: a set of features based on the textual similarity proposed by Mihalcea (Mihalcea et al., 2006). Given two texts T_1 and T_2 the similarity is computed as follows:

$$sim(T_1, T_2) = \frac{1}{2}\left(\frac{\sum_{w \in T_1} maxSim(w, T_2)}{\sum_{w \in T_1} idf(w)} + \frac{\sum_{w \in T_2} maxSim(w, T_1)}{\sum_{w \in T_2} idf(w)}\right) \quad (1)$$

We adopt several similarity measures using semantic distributional models (see Section 2.5), the Resnik's knowledge-based approach (Resnik, 1995) and the point-wise mutual information as suggested by Turney (Turney, 2001) computed on British National Corpus[2]. For all the features, the *idf* is computed relying on UKWaC corpus[3] (Baroni et al., 2009).

3. **Head similarity**-based features: this measure takes into account the maximum similarity between the roots of each text. The roots are extracted using the dependency parser provided by Stanford CoreNLP. The similarity is computed according to the distributional semantic models proposed in Section 2.5.

4. **ESA similarity**: computes the similarity between texts using the Explicit Semantic Analysis (ESA) approach (Gabrilovich and Markovitch, 2007). For each text we extract the ESA vector built using the English Wikipedia, and then we compute the similarity as the cosine similarity between the two ESA vectors.

5. **Paraphrasing** features: this is a very simple measure which counts the number of possible paraphrasings belonging to the two texts. Given two texts T_1 and T_2, for each token in T_1 a list of paraphrasings is extracted using a dictionary[4]. If T_2 contains one of the paraphrasing in the list, the score is incremented by one. The final score is divided by the number of tokens in T_1. The same score is computed taking into account T_2. Finally, the two score are added and divided by 2.

6. **Greedy Lemma Aligning Overlap** features: this measure computes the similarity between texts using the semantic alignment of lemmas as proposed by Šarić et al. (2012). In order to compute the similarity between lemmas, we exploit the distributional semantic models described in Section 2.5.

[1] Available at: http://nlp.stanford.edu/software/corenlp.shtml

[2] Available at: http://www.natcorp.ox.ac.uk/

[3] Available at: http://wacky.sslmit.unibo.it/

[4] English Thesaurus for StarDict available at https://aur.archlinux.org/packages/stardict-thesaurus-ee/

7. **Compositional** features: we build several similarity features using the distributional semantic models described in Section 2.5 and a compositional operator based on sum. This approach is thoroughly explained in Section 2.6

2.5 Distributional semantic models

In several features proposed in our approaches, the similarity between words is computed using Distributional Semantic Models. These models represent word meanings through contexts: the different meanings of a word can be accounted for by looking at the different contexts wherein the word occurs. This insight can beautifully be expressed by the geometrical representation of words as vectors in a *semantic space*. Each term is represented as a vector whose components are contexts surrounding the term. In this way, the meaning of a term across a corpus is thoroughly conveyed by the contexts it appears in, where a context may typically be the set of co-occurring words in a document, in a sentence or in a window of surrounding terms.

In particular, we take into account two main classes of models: Simple Distributional Spaces and Structured Semantic Spaces. The former considers as context the co-occurring words, the latter takes into account both co-occurrence and syntactic dependency between words.

Simple Distributional Spaces rely on Latent Semantic Analysis (LSA) and Random Indexing (RI) in order to reduce the dimension of the co-occurrences matrix. Moreover, we use an approach which applies LSA to the matrix produced by RI.

Structured Semantic Spaces are based on two techniques to encode syntactic information into the vector space. The first approach uses the vector permutation of random vector in RI to encode the syntactic role (head or dependent) of a word. The second method is based on Holographic Reduced Representation, in particular using convolution between vectors, to encode syntactic information.

Adopting distributional semantic models, each word can be represented as a vector in a geometric space. The similarity between two words can be easily computed taking into account the cosine similarity between word vectors.

All models are described in Basile et al. (2012).

2.6 Compositional features

In Distributional Semantic Models, given the vector representations of two words, it is always possible to compute their similarity as the cosine of the angle between them.

However, texts are composed by several terms, so in order to compute the similarity between them we need a method to compose words occurring in these texts. It is possible to combine words through the vector addition (+). This operator is similar to the superposition defined in connectionist systems (Smolensky, 1990), and corresponds to the point-wise sum of components:

$$\mathbf{p} = \mathbf{u} + \mathbf{v} \tag{2}$$

where $p_i = u_i + v_i$

The addition is a commutative operator, which means that it does not take into account any order or underlying structures existing between words. In this first study, we do not exploit more complex methods to combine word vectors. We plan to investigate them in future work.

Given a text p, we denote with $\mathbf{p}$ its vector representation obtained applying addition operator (+) to the vector representation of terms it is composed of. Furthermore, it is possible to compute the similarity between two texts exploiting the cosine similarity between vectors.

Formally, if $a = a_1, a_2...a_n$ and $b = b_1, b_2...b_m$ are two texts, we build two vectors $\mathbf{a}$ and $\mathbf{b}$ which represent respectively the two texts in a semantic space. Vector representations for the two texts are built applying the addition operator to the vector representation of words belonging to them:

$$\begin{aligned} \mathbf{a} &= a_1 + a_2 + \ldots + a_n \\ \mathbf{b} &= b_1 + b_2 \ldots + b_m \end{aligned} \tag{3}$$

The similarity between $\mathbf{a}$ and $\mathbf{b}$ is computed as the cosine similarity between them.

3 Experimental evaluation

SemEval-2013 STS is the second attempt to provide a "*unified framework for the evaluation of modular semantic textual similarity and to characterize their impact on NLP applications*". The task consists in computing the similarity between pair of texts, returning a similarity score. The test set is composed by data coming from the following datasets: news headlines (headlines); mapping of lexical resources from Ontonotes to Wordnet (OnWN) and from FrameNet to WordNet (FNWN); and evaluation of machine translation (SMT).

The training data for STS-2013 is made up by training and testing data from the previous edition of STS-2012 task. During the 2012 edition, STS provided participants with three training data: MSR-Paraphrase, MSR-Video, STMeuropar; and five testing data: MSR-Paraphrase, MSR-Video, STMeuropar, SMTnews and OnWN. It is important to note that part of 2012 test sets were made up from the same sources of the training sets. On the other hand, STS-2013 training and testing are very different, making the prediction task a bit harder.

Humans rated each pair of texts with values from 0 to 5. The evaluation is performed by comparing the humans scores against system performance through Pearson's correlation with the gold standard for the four datasets.

3.1 System setup

For the evaluation, we built the distributional spaces using the WaCkypedia_EN corpus[5]. WaCkypedia_EN is based on a 2009 dump of the English Wikipedia (about 800 million tokens) and includes information about: part-of-speech, lemma and a full dependency parsing performed by MaltParser (Nivre et al., 2007). The structured spaces described in Subsections 2.1 and 2.5 are built exploiting information about term windows and dependency parsing supplied by WaCkypedia. The total number of dependencies amounts to about 200 million.

The RI system is implemented in Java and relies on some portions of code publicly available in the Semantic Vectors package (Widdows and Ferraro, 2008), while for LSA we exploited the publicly available C library SVDLIBC[6].

We restricted the vocabulary to the 50,000 most frequent terms, with stop words removal and forcing the system to include terms which occur in the dataset.

Semantic space building involves some parameters. In particular, each semantic space needs to set up the dimension k of the space. All spaces use a dimension of 500 (resulting in a 50,000$\times$500 matrix). The number of non-zero elements in the random vector is set to 10. When we apply LSA to the output space generated by the Random Indexing we hold all the 500 dimensions, since during the tuning we observed a drop in performance when a lower dimension was set. The co-occurrence distance w between terms was set up to 4.

In order to compute the similarity between the vector representations of text using UNIBA-DSM_PERM, we used the cosine similarity, and then we multiplied by 5 the obtained value.

The two supervised methods, UNIBA-2STEPML and UNIBA-STACKING, are developed in Java using Weka[7] to implement the learning algorithms. Regarding the stacking approach (UNIBA-STACKING) we used for the level-0 the following models: Gaussian Process with polynomial kernel, Gaussian Process with RBF kernel, Linear Regression, Support Vector regression with polynomial kernel, and decision tree. The level-1 model uses a Gaussian Process with RBF kernel. In the first step of UNIBA-2STEPML we adopt Support Vector Machine, while in the second one we use Support Vector Machine for regression. In both steps, the RBF-Kernel is used. Features are normalized removing non alphanumerics characters. In all the learning algorithms, we use the default parameters set by Weka. As future work, we plan to perform a tuning step in order to set the best parameters.

The choice of the learning algorithms for both UNIBA-STACKING and UNIBA-2STEPSML systems was performed after a tuning phase where only the STS-2012 training datasets were exploited. Table 1 reports the values obtained by our three systems on the STS-2012 test sets. After the tuning, we came up with the learning algorithms to employ in the level-0 and level-1 of UNIBA-STACKING and in step-1 and step-2 of UNIBA-2STEPSML. Then, the training of both UNIBA-STACKING and UNIBA-2STEPSML was performed on all STS-2012 datasets (training and test data).

[5]http://wacky.sslmit.unibo.it/doku.php?id=corpora

[6]http://tedlab.mit.edu/ dr/SVDLIBC/

	MSRpar	MSRvid	SMTeuroparl	OnWN	SMTnews	mean
UNIBA-2STEPSML	.6056	.8573	.6233	.5079	.4533	.7016
UNIBA-DSM_PERM	.4349	.7592	.5324	.6593	.4559	.6172
UNIBA-STACKING	.6473	.8727	.5344	.6646	.4604	.7714

Table 1: STS-2012 test results of Pearson's correlation.

	headlines	OnWN	FNWN	SMT	mean	rank
UNIBA- 2STEPSML	.4255	.4801	.1832	.2710	.3673	71
UNIBA- DSM_PERM	.6319	4910	.2717	.3155	.4610	54
UNIBA- STACKING	.6275	.4658	.2111	.2588	.4293	61

Table 2: Evaluation results of Pearson's correlation for individual datasets.

3.2 Evaluation results

Evaluation results on the STS-2013 data are reported in Table 2. Among the three systems, UNIBA-DSM_PERM obtained the best performances on both individual datasets and in the overall evaluation metric (mean), which computes the Pearson's correlation considering all datasets combined in a single one. The best system ranked 54 over a total of 90 submissions, while UNIBA-STACKING and UNIBA-2STEPSML ranked 61 and 71 respectively. These results are at odds with those reported in Table 1. During the test on 2012 dataset, UNIBA-STACKING gave the best result, followed by UNIBA-2STEPSML, while UNIBA-DSM_PERM gave the worst performance. The UNIBA-STACKING system corroborated our hypothesis giving also the best results on those datasets not exploited during the training phase of the system (OnWN, SMTnews). Conversely, UNIBA-2STEPSML reported a different trend showing its weakness with respect to a high variance in the data, and performing worse than UNIBA-DSM_PERM on the OnWN and SMTnews datasets.

However, the evaluation results have refuted our hypothesis, even with the use of the stacking system. The independence from a training set makes the UNIBA-DSM_PERM system more robust than other supervised algorithms, even though it is not able to give always the best performance on individual datasets, as highlighted by results in Table 1.

[7]http://www.cs.waikato.ac.nz/ml/weka/

4 Conclusions

This paper reports on UNIBA participation in Semantic Textual Similarity 2013 core task. In this task edition, we exploited both distributional models and machine learning techniques to build three systems. A distributional model, which takes into account the syntactic structure that relates words in a corpus, has been used as baseline. Moreover, we investigate the use of two machine learning techniques as a means to make our systems more independent from the training data. However, the evaluation results have highlighted the higher robustness of the distributional model with respect to these systems.

Acknowledgments

This work fulfils the research objectives of the PON 02_00563_3470993 project "VINCENTE - A Virtual collective INtelligenCe ENvironment to develop sustainable Technology Entrepreneurship ecosystems" funded by the Italian Ministry of University and Research (MIUR).

References

Eneko Agirre, Daniel Cer, Mona Diab, Aitor Gonzalez-Agirre, and Weiwei Guo. 2013. *sem 2013 shared task: Semantic textual similarity, including a pilot on typed-similarity. In **SEM 2013: The Second Joint Conference on Lexical and Computational Semantics*. Association for Computational Linguistics.

Marco Baroni, Silvia Bernardini, Adriano Ferraresi, and Eros Zanchetta. 2009. The WaCky Wide Web: a collection of very large linguistically processed web-crawled corpora. *Language Resources and Evaluation*, 43(3):209–226.

Pierpaolo Basile, Annalina Caputo, and Giovanni Semeraro. 2012. A study on compositional semantics of words in distributional spaces. In *Sixth IEEE International Conference on Semantic Computing, ICSC 2012, Palermo, Italy, September 19-21, 2012*, pages 154–161. IEEE Computer Society.

Annalina Caputo, Pierpaolo Basile, and Giovanni Semeraro. 2012. Uniba: Distributional semantics for textual similarity. In **SEM 2012: The First Joint Conference on Lexical and Computational Semantics – Volume 1: Proceedings of the main conference and the shared task, and Volume 2: Proceedings of the Sixth International Workshop on Semantic Evaluation (SemEval 2012)*, pages 591–596, Montréal, Canada, 7-8 June. Association for Computational Linguistics.

Evgeniy Gabrilovich and Shaul Markovitch. 2007. Computing semantic relatedness using Wikipedia-based explicit semantic analysis. In *Proceedings of the 20th international joint conference on artificial intelligence*, volume 6, page 12.

Rada Mihalcea, Courtney Corley, and Carlo Strapparava. 2006. Corpus-based and knowledge-based measures of text semantic similarity. In *Proceedings of the national conference on artificial intelligence*, volume 21, pages 775–780. Menlo Park, CA; Cambridge, MA; London; AAAI Press; MIT Press.

Jeff Mitchell and Mirella Lapata. 2008. Vector-based models of semantic composition. In Kathleen McKeown, Johanna D. Moore, Simone Teufel, James Allan, and Sadaoki Furui, editors, *ACL 2008, Proceedings of the 46th Annual Meeting of the Association for Computational Linguistics, June 15-20, 2008, Columbus, Ohio, USA*, pages 236–244. The Association for Computer Linguistics.

Joakim Nivre, Johan Hall, Jens Nilsson, Atanas Chanev, Gülsen Eryigit, Sandra Kübler, Svetoslav Marinov, and Erwin Marsi. 2007. Maltparser: A language-independent system for data-driven dependency parsing. *Natural Language Engineering*, 13(2):95–135.

Philip Resnik. 1995. Using information content to evaluate semantic similarity. In *Proceedings of the 14th International Joint Conference on Artificial Intelligence*, pages 448–453.

Paul Smolensky. 1990. Tensor product variable binding and the representation of symbolic structures in connectionist systems. *Artificial Intelligence*, 46(1-2):159–216, November.

Peter Turney. 2001. Mining the web for synonyms: PMI-IR versus LSA on TOEFL. In *Proceedings of the Twelfth European Conference on Machine Learning (ECML-2001)*, pages 491–502.

Frane Šarić, Goran Glavaš, Mladen Karan, Jan Šnajder, and Bojana Dalbelo Bašić. 2012. Takelab: Systems for measuring semantic text similarity. In **SEM 2012: The First Joint Conference on Lexical and Computational Semantics – Volume 1: Proceedings of the main conference and the shared task, and Volume 2: Proceedings of the Sixth International Workshop on Semantic Evaluation (SemEval 2012)*, pages 441–448, Montréal, Canada, 7-8 June. Association for Computational Linguistics.

Dominic Widdows and Kathleen Ferraro. 2008. Semantic Vectors: A Scalable Open Source Package and Online Technology Management Application. In Nicoletta Calzolari, Khalid Choukri, Bente Maegaard, Joseph Mariani, Jan Odjik, Stelios Piperidis, and Daniel Tapias, editors, *Proceedings of the 6th International Conference on Language Resources and Evaluation (LREC2008)*, pages 1183–1190, Marrakech, Morocco. European Language Resources Association (ELRA).

David H. Wolpert. 1992. Stacked generalization. *Neural networks*, 5(2):241–259, February.

DLS@CU-CORE: A Simple Machine Learning Model of Semantic Textual Similarity

Md. Arafat Sultan, Steven Bethard, Tamara Sumner
Institute of Cognitive Science and Department of Computer Science
University of Colorado, Boulder, CO 80309
{arafat.sultan, steven.bethard, sumner}@colorado.edu

Abstract

We present a system submitted in the Semantic Textual Similarity (STS) task at the Second Joint Conference on Lexical and Computational Semantics (*SEM 2013). Given two short text fragments, the goal of the system is to determine their semantic similarity. Our system makes use of three different measures of text similarity: word n-gram overlap, character n-gram overlap and semantic overlap. Using these measures as features, it trains a support vector regression model on SemEval STS 2012 data. This model is then applied on the STS 2013 data to compute textual similarities. Two different selections of training data result in very different performance levels: while a correlation of 0.4135 with gold standards was observed in the official evaluation (ranked 63rd among all systems) for one selection, the other resulted in a correlation of 0.5352 (that would rank 21st).

1 Introduction

Automatically identifying the semantic similarity between two short text fragments (e.g. sentences) is an important research problem having many important applications in natural language processing, information retrieval, and digital education. Examples include automatic text summarization, question answering, essay grading, among others.

However, despite having important applications, semantic similarity identification at the level of short text fragments is a relatively recent area of investigation. The problem was formally brought to attention and the first solutions were proposed in 2006 with the works reported in (Mihalcea et al., 2006) and (Li et al., 2006). Work prior to these focused primarily on large documents (or individual words) (Mihalcea et al., 2006). But the sentence-level granularity of the problem is characterized by factors like high specificity and low topicality of the expressed information, and potentially small lexical overlap even between very similar texts, asking for an approach different from those that were designed for larger texts.

Since its inception, the problem has seen a large number of solutions in a relatively small amount of time. The central idea behind most solutions is the identification and alignment of semantically similar or related words across the two sentences, and the aggregation of these similarities to generate an overall similarity score (Mihalcea et al., 2006; Islam and Inkpen, 2008; Šarić et al., 2012).

The Semantic Textual Similarity task (STS) organized as part of the Semantic Evaluation Exercises (see (Agirre et al., 2012) for a description of STS 2012) provides a common platform for evaluation of such systems via comparison with human-annotated similarity scores over a large dataset.

In this paper, we present a system which was submitted in STS 2013. Our system is based on very simple measures of lexical and character-level overlap, semantic overlap between the two sentences based on word relatedness measures, and surface features like the sentences' lengths. These measures are used as features for a support vector regression model that we train with annotated data from SemEval STS 2012. Finally, the trained model is applied on the STS 2013 test pairs.

Our approach is inspired by the success of similar systems in STS 2012: systems that combine multiple measures of similarity using a machine learning model to generate an overall score (Bär et al., 2012; Šarić et al., 2012). We wanted to investigate how a minimal system of this kind, making use of very few external resources, performs on a large dataset. Our experiments reveal that the performance of such a system depends highly on the training data. While training on one dataset yielded a best

*Second Joint Conference on Lexical and Computational Semantics (*SEM), Volume 1: Proceedings of the Main Conference and the Shared Task*, pages 176–180, Atlanta, Georgia, June 13-14, 2013.

correlation (among our three runs, described later in this document) of only 0.4135 with the gold scores, training on another dataset showed a considerably higher correlation of 0.5352.

2 Computation of Text Similarity: System Overview

In this section, we present a high-level description of our system. More details on extraction of some of the measures of similarity are provided in Section 3.

Given two input sentences S_1 and S_2, our algorithm can be described as follows:

1. Compute semantic overlap (8 features):
    a. Lemmatize S_1 and S_2 using a memory-based lemmatizer[1] and remove all stop words.
    b. Compute the degree to which the concepts in S_1 are covered by semantically similar concepts in S_2 and vice versa (see Section 3 for details). The result of this step is two different 'degree of containment' values (S_1 in S_2 and vice versa).
    c. Compute the minimum, maximum, arithmetic mean and harmonic mean of the two values to use as features in the machine learning model.
    d. Repeat steps 1a through 1c for a weighted version of semantic overlap where each word in the first sentence is assigned a weight which is proportional to its specificity in a selected corpus (see Section 3).
2. Compute word n-gram overlap (16 features):
    a. Extract n-grams (for $n = 1, 2, 3, 4$) of all words in S_1 and S_2 for four different setups characterized by the four different value combinations of the two following variables: lemmatization (*on* and *off*), stopWordsRemoved (*on* and *off*).
    b. Compute the four measures (min, max, arithmetic and harmonic mean) for each value of n.
3. Compute character n-gram overlap (16 features):
    a. Repeat all steps in 2 above for character n-grams ($n = 2, 3, 4, 5$).
4. Compute sentence length features (2 features):
    a. Compute the lengths of S_1 and S_2; and the minimum and maximum of the two values.
    b. Include the ratio of the maximum to the minimum and the difference between the maximum and minimum in the feature set.
5. Train a support vector regression model on the features extracted in steps 1 through 4 above using data from SemEval 2012 STS (see Section 4 for specifics on the dataset). We used the LibSVM implementation of SVR in WEKA.
6. Apply the model on STS 2013 test data.

3 Semantic Overlap Measures

In this section, we describe the computation of the two sets of semantic overlap measures mentioned in step 1 of the algorithm in Section 2.

We compute semantic overlap between two sentences by first computing the semantic relatedness among their constituent words. Automatically computing the semantic relatedness between words is a well-studied problem and many solutions to the problem have been proposed. We compute word relatedness in two forms: semantic relatedness and string similarity. For semantic relatedness, we utilize two web services. The first one concerns a resource named ConceptNet (Liu and Singh, 2004), which holds a large amount of common sense knowledge concerning relationships between real-world entities. It provides a web service[2] that generates word relatedness scores based on these relationships. We will use the term $CNrel(w_1, w_2)$ to denote the relatedness of the two words w_1 and w_2 as generated by ConceptNet.

We also used the web service[3] provided by another resource named Wikipedia Miner (Milne and Witten, 2013). While ConceptNet successfully captures common sense knowledge about words and concepts, Wikipedia Miner specializes in identifying relationships between scientific concepts powered by Wikipedia's vast repository of scientific information (for example, *Einstein* and relativity). We will use the term $WMrel(w_1, w_2)$ to denote the relatedness of the two words w_1 and w_2 as generated by Wikipedia Miner. Using two systems enabled us

[1] http://www.clips.ua.ac.be/pages/MBSP#lemmatizer
[2] http://conceptnet5.media.mit.edu/data/5.1/assoc/c/en/cat? filter=/c/en/dog&limit=1
[3] http://wikipedia-miner.cms.waikato.ac.nz/services/compare? term1=cat&term2=dog

to increase the coverage of our word similarity computation algorithm.

Each of these web services return a score in the range [0, 1] where 0 represents no relatedness and 1 represents complete similarity. A manual inspection of both services indicates that in almost all cases where the services' word similarity scores deviate from what would be the human-perceived similarity, they generate lower scores (i.e. lower than the human-perceived score). This is why we take the maximum of the two services' similarity scores for any given word pair as their semantic relatedness:

$$semRel(w_1, w_2) = \max\{CNrel(w_1, w_2), WMrel(w_1, w_2)\}$$

We also compute the string similarity between the two words by taking a weighted combination of the normalized lengths of their longest common substring, subsequence and prefix (normalization is done for each of the three by dividing its length with the length of the smaller word). We will refer to the string similarity between words w_1 and w_2 as $stringSim(w_1, w_2)$. This idea is taken from (Islam and Inkpen, 2008); the rationale is to be able to find the similarity between (1) words that have the same lemma but the lemmatizer failed to lemmatize at least one of the two surface forms successfully, and (2) words at least one of which has been misspelled. We take the maximum of the string similarity and the semantic relatedness between two words as the final measure of their similarity:

$$sim(w_1, w_2) = \max\{semRel(w_1, w_2), stringSim(w_1, w_2)\}$$

At the sentence level, our first set of semantic overlap measures (step 1b) is an unweighted measure that treats all content words equally. More specifically, after the preprocessing in step 1a of the algorithm, we compute the degree of semantic coverage of concepts expressed by individual content words in S_1 by S_2 using the following equation:

$$cov_{uw}(S_1, S_2) = \frac{\sum_{s \in S_1} \left[\max_{t \in S_2}\{sim(s,t)\}\right]}{|S_1|}$$

where $sim(s, t)$ is the similarity between the two lemmas s and t.

We also compute a weighted version of semantic coverage (step 1d in the algorithm) by incorporating the specificity of each word (measured by its *information content*) as shown in the equation below:

$$cov_w(S_1, S_2) = \frac{\sum_{s \in S_1} \left[\max_{t \in S_2}\{ic(s).sim(s,t)\}\right]}{|S_1|}$$

where $ic(w)$ stands for the information content of the word w. Less common words (across a selected corpus) have high information content:

$$ic(w) = \ln \frac{\sum_{w' \in C} f(w')}{f(w)}$$

where C is the set of all words in the chosen corpus and $f(w)$ is the frequency of the word w in the corpus. We have used the Google Unigram Corpus[4] to assign the required frequencies to these words.

4 Evaluation

The STS 2013 test data consists of four datasets: two datasets consisting of gloss pairs (*OnWN*: 561 pairs and *FNWN*: 189 pairs), a dataset of machine translation evaluation pairs (*SMT*: 750 pairs) and a dataset consisting of news headlines (*headlines*: 750 pairs). For each dataset, the output of a system is evaluated via comparison with human-annotated similarity scores and measured using the Pearson Correlation Coefficient. Then a weighted sum of the correlations for all datasets are taken to be the final score, where each dataset's weight is the proportion of sentence pairs in that dataset.

We computed the similarity scores using three different feature sets (for our three runs) for the support vector regression model:

1. All features mentioned in Section 2. This set of features were used in our run 1.
2. All features except word n-gram overlap (experiments on STS 2012 test data revealed that using word n-grams actually lowers the performance of our model, hence this decision). These are the features that were used in our run 2.
3. Only character n-gram and length features (just to test the performance of the model without

[4] http://googleresearch.blogspot.com/2006/08/all-our-n-gram-are-belong-to-you.html

any semantic features). Our run 3 was based on these features.

We trained the support vector regression model on two different training datasets, both drawn from STS 2012 data:

1. In the first setup, we chose the training datasets from STS 2012 that we considered the most similar to the test dataset. The only exception was the *FNWN* dataset, for which we selected the all the datasets from 2012 because no single dataset from STS 2012 seemed to have similarity with this dataset. For the *OnWN* test dataset, we selected the *OnWN* dataset from STS 2012. For both *headlines* and *SMT*, we selected *SMT-news* and *SMTeuroparl* from STS 2012. The rationale behind this selection was to train the machine learning model on a distribution similar to the test data.
2. In the second setup, we aggregated all datasets (train and test) from STS 2012 and used this combined dataset to train the three models that were later applied on each STS 2013 test data. Here the rationale is to train on as much data as possible.

Table 1 shows the results for the first setup. This is the performance of the set of scores which we actually submitted in STS 2013. The first four columns show the correlations of our system with the gold standard for all runs. The rightmost column shows the overall weighted correlations. As we can see, run 1 with all the features demonstrated the best performance among the three runs. There was a considerable drop in performance in run 3 which did not utilize any semantic similarity measure.

Table 1. Results for manually selected training data

Run	headlines	OnWN	FNWN	SMT	Total
1	.4921	.3769	.4647	.3492	.4135
2	.4669	.4165	.3859	.3411	.4056
3	.3867	.2386	.3726	.3337	.3309

As evident from the table, evaluation results did not indicate a particularly promising system. Our best system ranked 63rd among the 90 systems evaluated in STS 2013. We further investigated to find out the reason: is the set of our features insufficient to capture text semantic similarity, or were the training data inappropriate for their corresponding test data? This is why we experimented with the second setup discussed above. Following are the results:

Table 2. Results for combined training data

Run	headlines	OnWN	FNWN	SMT	Total
1	.6854	.5981	.4647	.3518	.5339
2	.7141	.5953	.3859	.349	.5352
3	.6998	.4826	.3726	.3365	.4971

As we can see in Table 2, the correlations for all feature sets improved by more than 10% for each run. In this case, the best system with correlation 0.5352 would rank 21st among all systems in STS 2013. These results indicate that the primary reason behind the system's previous bad performance (Table 1) was the selection of an inappropriate dataset. Although it was not clear in the beginning which of the two options would be the better, this second experiment reveals that selecting the largest possible dataset to train is the better choice for this dataset.

5 Conclusions

In this paper, we have shown how simple measures of text similarity using minimal external resources can be used in a machine learning setup to compute semantic similarity between short text fragments. One important finding is that more training data, even when drawn from annotations on different sources of text and thus potentially having different feature value distributions, improve the accuracy of the model in the task. Possible future expansion includes use of more robust concept alignment strategies using semantic role labeling, inclusion of structural similarities of the sentences (e.g. word order, syntax) in the feature set, incorporating word sense disambiguation and more robust strategies of concept weighting into the process, among others.

References

Eneko Agirre, Daniel Cer, Mona Diab, and Aitor Gonzalez-Agirre. 2012. SemEval-2012 Task 6: a pilot on semantic textual similarity. In *Proceedings of the First Joint Conference on Lexical and Computational Semantics*. ACL, Stroudsburg, PA, USA, 385-393.

Daniel Bär, Chris Biemann, Iryna Gurevych, and Torsten Zesch. 2012. UKP: computing semantic textual similarity by combining multiple content similarity measures. In *Proceedings of the First Joint Conference on Lexical and Computational Semantics*. ACL, Stroudsburg, PA, USA, 435-440.

Aminul Islam and Diana Inkpen. 2008. Semantic text similarity using corpus-based word similarity and string similarity. *ACM Trans. Knowl. Discov. Data* 2, 2, Article 10 (July 2008), 25 pages.

Yuhua Li, David Mclean, Zuhair A. Bandar, James D. O'Shea, and Keeley Crockett. 2006. Sentence similarity based on semantic nets and corpus statistics. *IEEE Transactions on Knowledge and Data Engineering*, vol.18, no.8, 1138-1150.

Hugo Liu and Push Singh. 2004. ConceptNet — a practical commonsense reasoning tool-kit. *BT Technology Journal* 22, 4 (October 2004), 211-226.

Rada Mihalcea, Courtney Corley, and Carlo Strapparava. 2006. Corpus-based and knowledge-based measures of text semantic similarity. In *Proceedings of the 21st national conference on Artificial intelligence - Volume 1* (AAAI'06), Anthony Cohn (Ed.), Vol. 1. AAAI Press 775-780.

David Milne and Ian H. Witten. 2013. An open-source toolkit for mining Wikipedia. *Artif. Intell.* 194 (January 2013), 222-239.

Frane Šarić, Goran Glavaš, Mladen Karan, Jan Šnajder, and Bojana Dalbelo Bašić.Šarić. 2012. TakeLab: systems for measuring semantic text similarity. In *Proceedings of the First Joint Conference on Lexical and Computational Semantics*. ACL, Stroudsburg, PA, USA, 441-448.

KLUE-CORE: A regression model of semantic textual similarity

Paul Greiner and **Thomas Proisl** and **Stefan Evert** and **Besim Kabashi**
Friedrich-Alexander-Universität Erlangen-Nürnberg
Department Germanistik und Komparatistik
Professur für Korpuslinguistik
Bismarckstr. 6
91054 Erlangen, Germany
{paul.greiner,thomas.proisl,stefan.evert,besim.kabashi}@fau.de

Abstract

This paper describes our system entered for the *SEM 2013 shared task on Semantic Textual Similarity (STS). We focus on the core task of predicting the semantic textual similarity of sentence pairs.

The current system utilizes machine learning techniques trained on semantic similarity ratings from the *SEM 2012 shared task; it achieved rank 20 out of 90 submissions from 35 different teams. Given the simple nature of our approach, which uses only WordNet and unannotated corpus data as external resources, we consider this a remarkably good result, making the system an interesting tool for a wide range of practical applications.

1 Introduction

The *SEM 2013 shared task on Semantic Textual Similarity (Agirre et al., 2013) required participants to implement a software system that is able to predict the semantic textual similarity (STS) of sentence pairs. Being able to reliably measure semantic similarity can be beneficial for many applications, e.g. in the domains of MT evaluation, information extraction, question answering, and summarization.

For the shared task, STS was measured on a scale ranging from 0 (indicating no similarity at all) to 5 (semantic equivalence). The system predictions were evaluated against manually annotated data.

2 Description of our approach

Our system KLUE-CORE uses two approaches to estimate STS between pairs of sentences: a distributional bag-of-words model inspired by Schütze (1998), and a simple alignment model that links each word in one sentence to the semantically most similar word in the other sentence. For the alignment model, word similarities were obtained from WordNet (using a range of state-of-the-art path-based similarity measures) and from two distributional semantic models (DSM).

All similarity scores obtained in this way were passed to a ridge regression learner in order to obtain a final STS score. The predictions for new sentence pairs were then transformed to the range $[0, 5]$, as required by the task definition.

2.1 The training data

We trained our system on manually annotated sentence pairs from the STS task at SemEval 2012 (Agirre et al., 2012). Pooling the STS 2012 training and test data, we obtained 5 data sets from different domains, comprising a total of 5 343 sentence pairs annotated with a semantic similarity score in the range $[0, 5]$. The data sets are paraphrase sentence pairs (MSRpar), sentence pairs from video descriptions (MSRvid), MT evaluation sentence pairs (MTnews and MTeuroparl), and glosses from two different lexical semantic resources (OnWN).

All sentence pairs were pre-processed with TreeTagger (Schmid, 1995)[1] for part-of-speech annotation and lemmatization.

[1] http://www.ims.uni-stuttgart.de/forschung/ressourcen/werkzeuge/treetagger.html

*Second Joint Conference on Lexical and Computational Semantics (*SEM), Volume 1: Proceedings of the Main Conference and the Shared Task*, pages 181–186, Atlanta, Georgia, June 13-14, 2013. ©2013 Association for Computational Linguistics

2.2 Similarity on word level

Our alignment model (Sec. 2.3.1) is based on similarity scores for pairs of words. We obtained a total of 11 different word similarity measures from WordNet (Miller et al., 1990) and in a completely unsupervised manner from distributional semantic models.

2.2.1 WordNet

We computed three state-of-the-art WordNet similarity measures, namely path similarity, Wu-Palmer similarity and Leacock-Chodorow similarity (Budanitsky and Hirst, 2006). As usual, for each pair of words the synsets with the highest similarity score were selected. For all three measures, we made use of the implementations provided as part of the Natural Language ToolKit for Python (Bird et al., 2009).

2.2.2 Distributional semantics

Word similarity scores were also obtained from two DSM: Distributional Memory (Baroni and Lenci, 2010) and a model compiled from a version of the English Wikipedia.[2] For Distributional Memory, we chose the collapsed $W \times W$ matricization, resulting in a $30\,686 \times 30\,686$ matrix that was further reduced to 300 latent dimensions using randomized SVD (Halko et al., 2009). For the Wikipedia DSM, we used a L2/R2 context window and mid-frequency feature terms, resulting in a $77\,598 \times 30\,484$ matrix. Co-occurrence frequency counts were weighted using sparse log-likelihood association scores with a square root transformation, and reduced to 300 latent dimensions with randomized SVD. In both cases, target terms are POS-disambiguated lemmas of content words, and the angle between vectors was used as a distance measure (equivalent to cosine similarity).

For each DSM, we computed the following semantic distances: (i) *angle*: the angle between the two word vectors; (ii) *fwdrank*: the (logarithm of the) forward neighbour rank, i.e. which rank the second word occupies among the nearest neighbours of the first word; (iii) *bwdrank*: the (logarithm of the) backward neighbour rank, i.e. which rank the first word occupies among the nearest neighbours of the second word; (iv) *rank*: the (logarithm of the) arithmetic mean of forward and backward neighbour rank; (v) *lowrank*: the (logarithm of the) harmonic mean of forward and backward neighbour rank.

A composite *similarity* score in the range $[0, 1]$ was obtained by linear regression on all five distance measures, using the WordSim-353 noun similarity ratings (Finkelstein et al., 2002) for parameter estimation. This score is referred to as *similarity* below. Manual inspection showed that word pairs with *similarity* < 0.7 were completely unrelated in many cases, so we also included a "strict" version of *similarity* with all lower scores set to 0. We further included *rank* and *angle*, which were linearly transformed to similarity values in the range $[0, 1]$.

2.3 Similarity on sentence level

Similarity scores for sentence pairs were obtained in two different ways: with a simple alignment model based on the word similarity scores from Sec. 2.2 (described in Sec. 2.3.1) and with a distributional bag-of-words model (described in Sec. 2.3.2).

2.3.1 Similarity by word alignment

The sentence pairs were preprocessed in the following way: input words were transformed to lowercase; common stopwords were eliminated; and duplicate words within each sentence were deleted. For the word similarity scores from Sec. 2.2.2, POS-disambiguated lemmas according to the TreeTagger annotation were used.

Every word of the first sentence in a given pair was then compared with every word of the second sentence, resulting in a matrix of similarity scores for each of the word similarity measures described in Sec. 2.2. Since we were not interested in an asymmetric notion of similarity, matrices were set up so that the shorter sentence in a pair always corresponds to the rows of the matrix, transposing the similarity matrix if necessary. From each matrix, two similarity scores for the sentence pair were computed: the arithmetic mean of the row maxima (marked as *short* in Tab. 4), and the artihmetic mean of the column maxima (marked as *long* in Tab. 4).

This approach corresponds to a simple word alignment model where each word in the shorter sentence is aligned to the semantically most similar word in the longer sentence (*short*), and vice versa (*long*). Note that multiple source words may be aligned to the same target word, and target words can remain

[2] For this purpose, we used the pre-processed and linguistically annotated Wackypedia corpus available from `http://wacky.sslmit.unibo.it/`.

unaligned without penalty. Semantic similarities are then averaged across all alignment pairs.

In total, we obtained 22 sentence similarity scores from this approach.

2.3.2 Distributional similarity

We computed distributional similarity between the sentences in each pair directly using bag-of-words centroid vectors as suggested by Schütze (1998), based on the two word-level DSM introduced in Sec. 2.2.2.

For each sentence pair and DSM, we computed (i) the angle between the centroid vectors of the two sentences and (ii) a z-score relative to all other sentences in the same data set of the training or test collection. Both values are measures of semantic distance, but are automatically transformed into similarity measures by the regression learner (Sec. 2.4).

For the z-scores, we computed the semantic distance (i.e. angle) between the first sentence of a given pair and the second sentences of *all* word pairs in the same data set. The resulting list of angles was standardized to z-scores, and the z-score corresponding to the second sentence from the given pair was used as a measure of forward similarity between the first and second sentence. In the same way, a backward z-score between the second and first sentence was determined. We used the average of the forward and backward z-score as our second STS measure.

The z-transformation was motivated by our observation that there are substantial differences between the individual data sets in the STS 2012 training and test data. For some data sets (MSRpar and MSRvid), sentences are often almost identical and even a single-word difference can result in low similarity ratings; for other data sets (e.g. OnWN), similarity ratings seem to be based on the general state of affairs described by the two sentences rather than their particular wording of propositional content. By using other sentences in the same data set as a frame of reference, corpus-based similarity scores can roughly be calibrated to the respective notion of STS.

In total, we obtained 4 sentence (dis)similarity scores from this approach. Because of technical issues, only the z-score measures were used in the submitted system. The experiments in Sec. 3 also focus on these z-scores.

2.4 The regression model

The 24 individual similarity scores described in Sec. 2.3.1 and 2.3.2 were combined into a single STS prediction by supervised regression.

We conducted experiments with various machine learning algorithms implemented in the Python library scikit-learn (Pedregosa et al., 2011). In particular, we tested linear regression, regularized linear regression (ridge regression), Bayesian ridge regression, support vector regression and regression trees. Our final system submitted to the shared task uses ridge regression, a shrinkage method applied to linear regression that uses a least-squares regularization on the regression coefficients (Hastie et al., 2001, 59). Intuitively speaking, the regularization term discourages large value of the regression coefficients, which makes the learning technique less prone to overfitting quirks of the training data, especially with large numbers of features.

We tried to optimise our results by training the individual regressors for each test data set on appropriate portions of the training data. For our task submission, we used the following training data based on educated guesses inspired by the very small amount of development data provied: for the headlines test set we trained on both glosses and statistical MT data, for the OnWN and FNWN test sets we trained on glosses only (OnWN), and for the SMT test set we trained on statistical MT data only (MTnews and MTeuroparl). We decided to omit the Microsoft Research Paraphrase Corpus (MSRpar and MSRvid) because we felt that the types of sentence pairs in this corpus were too different from the development data.

For our submission, we used all 24 features described in Sec. 2.3 as input for the ridge regression algorithm. Out of 90 submissions by 35 teams, our system ranked on place 20.[3]

3 Experiments

In this section, we describe some post-hoc experiments on the STS 2013 test data, which we performed in order to find out whether we made good decisions regarding the machine learning method, training data,

[3]This paper describes the run listed as KLUE-approach_2 in the official results. The run KLUE-approach_1 was produced by the same system without the bag-of-words features (Sec. 2.3.2); it was only submitted as a safety backup.

similarity features, and other parameters. Results of our submitted system are typeset in italics, the best results in each column are typeset in bold font.

3.1 Machine learning algorithms

Tab. 1 gives an overview of the performance of various machine learning algorithms. All regressors were trained on the same combinations of data sets (see Sec. 2.4 above) using all available features, and evaluated on the STS 2013 test data. Overall, our choice of ridge regression is justified. Especially for the OnWN test set, however, support vector regression is considerably better (it would have achieved rank 11 instead of 17 on this test set). If we had happened to use the best learning algorithm for each test set, we would have achieved a mean score of 0.54768 (putting our submission at rank 14 instead of 20).

3.2 Regularization strength

We also experimented with different regularization strengths, as determined by the parameter α of the ridge regression algorithm (see Tab. 2). Changing α from its default value $\alpha = 1$ does not seem to have a large impact on the performance of the regressor. Setting $\alpha = 2$ for all test sets would have minimally improved the mean score (rank 19 instead of 20). Even choosing the optimal α for each test set would only have resulted in a slightly improved mean score of 0.53811 (also putting our submission at rank 19).

3.3 Composition of training data

As described above, we suspected that using different combinations of the training data for different test sets might lead to better results. The overview in Tab. 3 confirms our expectations. We did, however, fail to correctly guess the optimal combinations for each test set. We would have obtained the best results by training on glosses (OnWN) for the headlines test set (rank 35 instead of 40 in this category), by training on MSR data (MSRpar and MSRvid) for the OnWN (rank 11 instead of 17) and FNWN test sets (rank 9 instead of 10), and by combining glosses and machine translation data (OnWN, MTnews MTeuroparl) for the SMT test set (rank 30 instead of 33). Had we found the optimal training data for each test set, our system would have achieved a mean score of 0.55021 (rank 11 instead of 20).

3.4 Features

For our submission, we used all the features described in Sec. 2. Tab. 4 shows what results each group of features would have achieved by itself (all runs use ridge regression, default $\alpha = 1$ and the same combinations of training data as in our submission).

In Tab. 4, the line labelled *wp500* shows the results obtained using only word-alignment similarity scores (Sec. 2.3.1) based on the Wikipedia DSM (Sec. 2.2.2) as features. The following two lines give separate results for the alignments from shorter to longer sentence, i.e. row maxima (*wp500-short*) and from longer to shorter sentence, i.e. column maxima (*wp500-long*), respectively. Below are corresponding results for word alignments based on Distributional Memory (*dm*, *dm-short*, *dm-long*) and WordNet similarity as described in Sec. 2.2.1 (*WN*, *WN-short*, *WN-long*). The line labelled *bow* represents the two z-score similarities obtained from distributional bag-of-words models (Sec. 2.3.2); *bow-wp500* (Wikipedia DSM) and *bow-dm* (Distributional Memory) each correspond to a single distributional feature.

Combining all the available features indeed results in the highest mean score. However, for OnWN and SMT a subset of the features would have led to better results. Using only the bag-of-words scores would have improved the results for the OnWN test set by a considerable margin (rank 8 instead of 17), using only the alignment scores based on WordNet would have improved the results for the SMT test set (rank 17 instead of 33). If we had used the optimal subset of features for each test set, the mean score would have increased to 0.55556 (rank 9 instead of 20).

4 Conclusion

Our experiments show that it is essential for high-quality semantic textual similarity to adapt a corpus-based system carefully to each particular data set (choice of training data, feature engineering, tuning of machine learning algorithm). Many of our educated guesses for parameter settings turned out to be fairly close to the optimal values, though there would have been some room for improvement.

Overall, our simple approach, which makes very limited use of external resources, performs quite well – achieving rank 20 out of 90 submissions – and will be a useful tool for many real-world applications.

	headlines	OnWN	FNWN	SMT	mean
Ridge Regression	*0.65102*	*0.68693*	*0.41887*	***0.33599***	***0.53546***
Linear Regression	**0.65184**	0.68118	0.39707	0.32756	0.52966
Bayesian Ridge	0.65164	0.68962	**0.42344**	0.33003	0.53474
SVM SVR	0.52208	**0.73330**	0.40479	0.30810	0.49357
Decision Tree	0.29320	0.50633	0.05022	0.17072	0.28510

Table 1: Evaluation results for different machine learning algorithms

α	headlines	OnWN	FNWN	SMT	mean
1	*0.65102*	*0.68693*	*0.41887*	*0.33599*	*0.53546*
0.01	0.65184	0.68129	0.39773	0.32773	0.52980
0.1	**0.65186**	0.68224	0.40246	0.32900	0.53087
0.5	0.65161	0.68492	0.41346	0.33311	0.53374
0.9	0.65114	0.68660	0.41816	0.33560	0.53523
2	0.64941	0.68917	**0.42290**	**0.33830**	**0.53659**
5	0.64394	**0.69197**	0.42265	0.33669	0.53491

Table 2: Evaluation results for different regularization strengths of the ridge regression learner

	headlines	OnWN	FNWN	SMT	mean
def	**0.65440**	*0.68693*	*0.41887*	0.32694	0.53357
smt	0.65322	0.62643	0.24895	*0.33599*	0.50684
def+smt	*0.65102*	0.59665	0.24953	**0.33867**	0.49962
msr	0.63633	**0.73396**	**0.43073**	0.33168	**0.54185**
def+smt+msr	0.65008	0.65093	0.39636	0.28645	0.50777
$approach_2$	*0.65102*	*0.68693*	*0.41887*	*0.33599*	*0.53546*

Table 3: Evaluation results for different training sets ("$approach_2$" refers to our shared task submission, cf. Sec. 2.4)

	headlines	OnWN	FNWN	SMT	mean
wp500	0.57099	0.59199	0.31740	0.31320	0.46899
wp500-long	0.57837	0.59012	0.30909	0.30075	0.46614
wp500-short	0.58271	0.58845	0.34205	0.29474	0.46794
dm	0.42129	0.55945	0.21139	0.27426	0.38910
dm-long	0.40709	0.56511	0.28993	0.23826	0.38037
dm-short	0.44780	0.53555	0.28709	0.24484	0.38853
WN	0.63654	0.65149	0.41025	**0.35624**	0.52783
WN-long	0.62749	0.63828	0.39684	0.33399	0.51297
WN-short	0.64986	0.66175	0.41441	0.33350	0.52759
bow	0.52384	**0.74046**	0.31917	0.24611	0.46808
bow-wp500	0.52726	0.73624	0.32797	0.24460	0.46841
bow-dm	0.21908	0.66873	0.17096	0.20176	0.32138
all	***0.65102***	*0.68693*	***0.41887***	*0.33599*	***0.53546***

Table 4: Evaluation results for different sets of similarity scores as features (cf. Sec. 3.4)

References

Eneko Agirre, Daniel Cer, Mona Diab, Aitor Gonzalez-Agirre, and Weiwei Guo. 2012. Semeval-2012 task 6: A pilot on semantic textual similarity. In *First Joint Conference on Lexical and Computational Semantics*, pages 385–393. Association for Computational Linguistics.

Eneko Agirre, Daniel Cer, Mona Diab, Aitor Gonzalez-Agirre, and Weiwei Guo. 2013. *sem 2013 shared task: Semantic textual similarity, including a pilot on typed-similarity. In **SEM 2013: The Second Joint Conference on Lexical and Computational Semantics*. Association for Computational Linguistics.

Marco Baroni and Alessandro Lenci. 2010. Distributional Memory: A general framework for corpus-based semantics. *Computational Linguistics*, 36(4):673–712.

Steven Bird, Ewan Klein, and Edward Loper. 2009. *Natural Language Processing with Python*. O'Reilly Media, Sebastopol, CA. Online version available at `http://www.nltk.org/book`.

Alexander Budanitsky and Graeme Hirst. 2006. Evaluating WordNet-based measures of lexical semantic relatedness. *Computational Linguistics*, 32(1):13–47.

Lev Finkelstein, Evgeniy Gabrilovich, Yossi Matias, Ehud Rivlin, Zach Solan, Gadi Wolfman, and Eytan Ruppin. 2002. Placing search in context: The concept revisited. *ACM Transactions on Information Systems*, 20(1):116–131.

N. Halko, P. G. Martinsson, and J. A. Tropp. 2009. Finding structure with randomness: Stochastic algorithms for constructing approximate matrix decompositions. Technical Report 2009-05, ACM, California Institute of Technology, September.

Trevor Hastie, Robert Tibshirani, and Jerome Friedman. 2001. *The Elements of Statistical Learning. Data Mining, Inference, and Prediction*. Springer, New York, NY.

George A. Miller, Richard Beckwith, Christiane Fellbaum, Derek Gross, and Katherine J. Miller. 1990. Introduction to WordNet: An on-line lexical database. *International Journal of Lexicography*, 3(4):235–244.

F. Pedregosa, G. Varoquaux, A. Gramfort, V. Michel, B. Thirion, O. Grisel, M. Blondel, P. Prettenhofer, R. Weiss, V. Dubourg, J. Vanderplas, A. Passos, D. Cournapeau, M. Brucher, M. Perrot, and E. Duchesnay. 2011. Scikit-learn: Machine learning in Python. *Journal of Machine Learning Research*, 12:2825–2830.

Helmut Schmid. 1995. Improvements in part-of-speech tagging with an application to German. In *Proceedings of the EACL SIGDAT-Workshop*, pages 47–50, Dublin.

Hinrich Schütze. 1998. Automatic word sense discrimination. *Computational Linguistics*, 24(1):97–123.

IBM_EG-CORE: Comparing multiple Lexical and NE matching features in measuring Semantic Textual similarity

Sara Noeman
IBM Cairo Technology and Development Center
Giza, Egypt
P.O. Box 166 Al-Ahram
noemans@eg.ibm.com

Abstract

We present in this paper the systems we participated with in the Semantic Textual Similarity task at SEM 2013. The Semantic Textual Similarity Core task (STS) computes the degree of semantic equivalence between two sentences where the participant systems will be compared to the manual scores, which range from 5 (semantic equivalence) to 0 (no relation). We combined multiple text similarity measures of varying complexity. The experiments illustrate the different effect of four feature types including direct lexical matching, idf-weighted lexical matching, modified BLEU N-gram matching and named entities matching. Our team submitted three runs during the task evaluation period and they ranked number 11, 15 and 19 among the 90 participating systems according to the official Mean Pearson correlation metric for the task. We also report an unofficial run with mean Pearson correlation of 0.59221 on STS2013 test dataset, ranking as the 3rd best system among the 90 participating systems.

1 Introduction

The Semantic Textual Similarity (STS) task at SEM 2013 is to measure the degree of semantic equivalence between pairs of sentences as a graded notion of similarity. Text Similarity is very important to many Natural Language Processing applications, like extractive summarization (Salton et al., 1997), methods for automatic evaluation of machine translation (Papineni et al., 2002), as well as text summarization (Lin and Hovy, 2003). In Text Coherence Detection (Lapata and Barzilay, 2005), sentences are linked together by similar or related words. For Word Sense Disambiguation, researchers (Banerjee and Pedersen, 2003; Guo and Diab, 2012a) introduced a sense similarity measure using the sentence similarity of the sense definitions. In this paper we illustrate the different effect of four feature types including direct lexical matching, idf-weighted lexical matching, modified BLEU N-gram matching and named entities matching. The rest of this paper will proceed as follows, Section 2 describes the four text similarity features used. Section 3 illustrates the system description, data resources as well as Feature combination. Experiments and Results are illustrated in section 4. then we report our conclusion and future work.

2 Text Similarity Features

Our system measures the semantic textual similarity between two sentences through a number of matching features which should cover four main dimensions: i) Lexical Matching ii) IDF-weighted Lexical Matching iii) Contextual sequence Matching (Modified BLEU Score), and iv) Named Entities Matching.

First we introduce the alignment technique used. For a sentence pair {s1, s2} matching is done in each direction separately to detect the sub-sentence of s1 matched to s2 and then detect the sub-sentence of s2 matched to s1. For each word *wi* in s1 we search for its match *wj* in s2 according to matching features.

S1: w0 w1 w2 w3 w4 …... wi …... wn
S2: w0 w1 w2 w3 w4 ....wj .... wm

*Second Joint Conference on Lexical and Computational Semantics (*SEM), Volume 1: Proceedings of the Main Conference and the Shared Task*, pages 187–193, Atlanta, Georgia, June 13-14, 2013.

2.1 Lexical Matching:

In this feature we handle the two sentences as bags of words to be matched using three types of matching, given that all stop words are cleaned out before matching:

I) Exact word matching.

II) Stemmed word matching: I used Porter Stemming algorithm (M.F. Porter, 1980) in matching, where it is a process for removing the commoner morphological and inflectional endings from words in English. Stemming will render inflections like "requires, required, requirements, ..." to "requir" so they can be easily matched

III) Synonyms matching: we used a corpus based dictionary of 58,921 entries and their equivalent synonyms. The next section describes how we automatically generated this language resource.

2.2 IDF-weighted Lexical Matching

We used the three matching criteria used in *Lexical Matching* after weighting them with Inverse-Document-Frequency. we applied the aggregation strategy by Mihalcea et al. (2006): The sum of the idf-weighted similarity scores of each word with the best-matching counterpart in the other text is computed in both directions. For a sentence pair s1, s2, if s1 consists of m words $\{w_0, w_1, \ldots, w_{(m-1)}\}$ and s2 consists of n words $\{w_0, w_1, \ldots, w_{(n-1)}\}$,after cleaning stop words from both, and the matched words are "@Matched_word_List" of "k" words, then

$$Similarity(S1, S2) = \frac{\sum_{w \in MatchS1S2} idf(w)}{\sum_{w \in S1} idf(w)};$$

$$Similarity(S2, S1) = \frac{\sum_{w \in MatchS1S2} idf(w)}{\sum_{w \in S2} idf(w)};$$

2.3 Contextual Sequence Matching (Modified BLEU score)

We used a modified version of Bleu score to measure n-gram sequences matching, where for sentence pair s1, s2 we align the matched words between them (through exact, stem, synonyms match respectively). Bleu score as presented by (K. Papineni et al., 2002) is an automated method for evaluating Machine Translation. It compares *n*-grams of the candidate translation with the *n*-grams of the reference human translation and counts the number of matches. These matches are position independent, where candidate translations with unmatched length to reference translations are penalized with *Sentence brevity penalty*.

This helps in measuring n-gram similarity in sentences structure. We define "matched sequence" of a sentence S1 as the sequence of words {wi, wi+1, wi+2, ….. wj}, where wi, and wj are the first and last words in sentence S1 that are matched with words in S2.

For example in sentence pair S1, S2:

S1: Today's great Pax Europa and today's pan-European prosperity depend on this.

S2: Large Pax Europa of today, just like current prosperity paneuropéenne, depends on it.

After stemming:

S1: todai's great pax europa and todai's pan-european prosper depend on thi.

S2: larg pax europa of todai, just like current prosper paneuropéenn, depend on it.

"Matched sequence of S1":

[**todai** 's great **pax europa** todai 's pan - european **prosper depend**]

"Matched sequence of S2":

[**pax europa todai** just like current **prosper** paneuropéenn **depend**]

We measure the Bleu score such that:

Bleu{S1, S2} = &BLEU(S1_stemmed,"*Matched sequence of S2*");

Bleu{S2, S1} = &BLEU(S2_stemmed,"*Matched sequence of S1*");

The objective of trimming the excess words outside the "Matched Sequence" range, before matching is to make use of the *Sentence brevity penalty* in case sentence pair S1, S2 may be not similar but having matched lengths.

2.4 Named Entities Matching

Named entities carry an important portion of sentence semantics. For example:
Sentence1: In **Nigeria** , **Chevron** has been accused by the **All - Ijaw** indigenous **people** of **instigating violence** against them and actually paying **Nigerian soldiers** to shoot **protesters** at the **Warri naval base** .
Sentence2: In **Nigeria** , the whole ijaw indigenous showed **Chevron** to encourage the **violence** against them and of up to pay **Nigerian soldiers** to shoot the **demonstrators** at the **naval base** from **Warri** .
The underlined words are Named entities of different types "COUNTRY, ORG, PEOPLE, LOC, EVENT_VIOLENCE" which capture the most important information in each sentence. Thus named entities matching is a measure of semantic matching between the sentence pair.

3 System Description

3.1 Data Resources and Processing

All data is tokenized, stemmed, and stop words are cleaned.

Corpus based resources:

i. **Inverse Document Frequency (IDF) language resource:** The document frequency ***df(t)*** of a term ***t*** is defined as the number of documents in a large collection of documents that contain a term ***"t"***. Terms that are likely to appear in most of the corpus documents reflect less importance than words that appear in specific documents only. That's why the **Inverse Document Frequency** is used as a measure of term importance in information retrieval and text mining tasks. We used the LDC English Gigaword Fifth Edition (LDC2011T07) to generate our idf dictionary. LDC Gigaword contains a huge collection of newswire from (afp, apw, cna, ltw, nyt, wpb, and xin). The generated idf resource contains 5,043,905 unique lower cased entries, and then we generated a stemmed version of the idf dictionary contains 4,677,125 entries. The equation below represents the idf of term t where N is the total number of documents in the corpus.

$$idf_t = \log \frac{N}{df_t}$$

ii. **English Synonyms Dictionary:** Using the Phrase table of an Arabic-to-English Direct Translation Model, we generated English-to-English phrase table using the double-link of English-to-Arabic and Arabic-to-English phrase translation probabilities over all pivot Arabic phrases. Then English-to-English translation probabilities are normalized over all generated English synonyms. **(**Chris Callison-Burch et al, 2006**)** used a similar technique to generate paraphrases to improve their SMT system**.** Figure (1) shows the steps:

```
For each English Phrase "e1"
{
  @ar_phrases = list of Arabic Phrases aligned to "e"
  in the phrase table;
  For each a (@ar_phrases)
   {
      @en_phrases = list of English phrases aligned
      to "a" in the phrase table;

       For each e2 (@en_phrases)
       {
          $Prob(e2\e1) = Prob(a\e1)*Prob(e2\a);
       }
   }
}
```

Figure(1) English phrase-to-phrase synonyms generation from E2A phrase table.

In our system we used the phrase table of the Direct Translation Model 2 (DTM2) (Ittycheriah and Roukos, 2007) SMT system, where each sentence pair in the training corpus was word-aligned, e.g. using a MaxEnt aligner (Ittycheriah and Roukos, 2005) or an HMM aligner (Ge, 2004). then Block Extraction step is done. The generated phrase table contains candidate phrase to phrase translation pairs with source-to-target and target-to source translation probabilities. However the open source Moses SMT system (Koehn et al., 2007) can be used in the same way to generate a synonyms dictionary from phrase table.

By applying the steps in figure (1):
a) English phrase-to-phrase synonyms table (or English-to-English phrase table), by applying the steps in a generic way.
b) English word-to-word synonyms table, by limiting the generation over English single word phrases.
For example, to get all possible synonyms of the English word "bike", we used all the Arabic phrases that are aligned to "bike" in the phrase table {دراجة, الدراجات , البسكليت, البسكلات},
P: 1905645 14 0.0142582 0.170507 | دراجة | bike |
P: 1910841 25 0.0262152 0.221198 | الدراجات | bike |
P: 2127826 4 0.0818182 0.0414747 | البسكليت | bike |
P: 2396796 2 0.375 0.0138249 | البسكلات | bike |
then we get all the English words in the phrase table aligned to these Arabic translations {دراجة, الدراجات , البسكليت, البسكلات }
This results in an English word-to-word synonyms list for the word "bike" like this:

bike:
motorcycle 0.365253185010659
bicycle 0.198195663512781
cycling 0.143290354808692
motorcycles 0.0871686646772204
bicycles 0.0480779974950311
cyclists 0.0317670845504069
motorcyclists 0.0304152910853553
cyclist 0.0278451740161998
riding 0.0215366691148431
motorbikes 0.0148697281155676

Dictionary based resources:

- **WordNet (Miller, 1995):** is a large lexical database of English. Nouns, verbs, adjectives and adverbs are grouped into sets of cognitive synonyms (synsets), each expressing a distinct concept. Synsets are interlinked by means of conceptual-semantic and lexical relations. WordNet groups words together based on their meanings and interlinks not just word forms—strings of letters—but specific senses of words. As a result, words that are found in close proximity to one another in the network are semantically disambiguated. Second, WordNet labels the semantic relations among words. Using WordNet, we can measure the semantic similarity or relatedness between a pair of concepts (or word senses), and by extension, between a pair of sentences. We use the similarity measure described in (Wu and Palmer, 1994) which finds the path length to the root node from the least common subsumer (LCS) of the two word senses which is the most specific word sense they share as an ancestor.

3.2 Feature Combination

The feature combination step uses the pre-computed similarity scores. Each of the text similarity features can be given a weight that sets its importance. Mathematically, the text similarity score between two sentences can be formulated using a cost function weighting the similarity features as follows: N.B.: The similarity score according to the features above is considered as a directional score.

Similarity(s1, s2) = [w1*Lexical_Score(s1, s2) +
w2*IDF_Lexical_Score(s1, s2) +
w3*Modified_BLEU(s1, s2) +
w4*NE_Score(s1, s2)] / (w1+w2+w3+w4)
Similarity(s2, s1) = [w1*Lexical_Score(s2, s1) +
w2*IDF_Lexical_Score(s2, s1) +
w3*Modified_BLEU(s2, s1) +
w4*NE_Score(s2, s1)] / (w1+w2+w3+w4)
Overall_Score = 5/2*[Similarity(s1, s2)+Similarity(s2, s1)]

where w1, w2, w3, w4 are the weights assigned to the similarity features (lexical, idf-weighted, modified_BLEU, and NE_Match features respectively). The similarity score will be normalized over (w1+w2+w3+w4).
In our experiments, the weights are tuned manually without applying machine learning techniques. We used both *SEM 2012 training and testing data sets for tuning these weights to get the best feature weighting combination to get highest Pearson Correlation score.

4 Experiments and Results

Submitted Runs
Our experiments showed that some features are more dominant in affecting the similarity scoring than others. We performed a separate experiment for each of the four feature types to illustrate their effect on textual semantic similarity measurement

using direct lexical matching, stemming matching, synonyms matching, as well as (stem+synonyms) matching. Table (1) reports the mean Pearson correlation results of these experiments on STS2012-test dataset

	Direct	Stem only	Synonyms only	Synonyms + Stem
NE	0.303	0.297	0.306	0.304
BLEU	0.439	0.446	0.469	0.453
Lexical	0.59	0.622	0.611	0.624
IDF	0.488	0.632	0.504	**0.634**

Table (1) reports the mean Pearson score for NE, BLEU, Lexical, and idf-weighted matching features respectively on STS2012-test dataset.

The submitted runs IBM_EG-run2, IBM_EG-run5, IBM_EG-run6 are the three runs with feature weighting and experiment set up that performed best on STS 2012 training and testing data sets.

Run 2: In this run the word matching was done on exact, and synonyms match only. Stemmed word matching was not introduced in this experiment. we tried the following weighting between similarity feature scores, where we decreased the weight of BLEU scoring feature to 0.5, and increased the idf_Lexical match weight of 3.5. this is because our initial tuning experiments showed that increasing the idf lexical weight compared to BLEU weight gives improved results. The NE matching feature weight was as follows:

NE_weight = 1.5* percent of NE word to sentence word count
= 1.5* (NE_words_count/Sentence_word_count)

Run 5: In this experiment we introduced Porter stemming word matching, as well as stemmed synonyms matching (after generating a stemmed version of the synonyms dictionary). BLEU score feature was removed from this experiment, while keeping the idf-weight= 3, lexical-weight = 1, and NE-matching feature weight = 1.

Run 6: For this run we kept only IDF-weighted lexical matching feature which proved to be the dominant feature in the previous runs, in addition to Porter stemming word matching, and stemmed synonyms matching.

Data: the training data of STS 2013 Core task consist of the STS 2012 train and test data. This data covers 5 datasets: paraphrase sentence pairs (MSRpar), sentence pairs from video descriptions (MSRvid), MT evaluation sentence pairs (SMTnews and SMTeuroparl) and gloss pairs (OnWN).

Results on Training Data

System outputs will be evaluated according to the official scorer which computes weighted Mean Pearson Correlation across the evaluation datasets, where the weight depends on the number of pairs in each dataset.

Table (2), reports the results achieved on each of the STS 2012 training dataset. While table (3), reports the results achieved on STS 2012 test dataset.

	IBM_run2	IBM_run5	IBM_run6
Mean	0.59802	0.64170	**0.68395**
MSRpar	0.61607	**0.63870**	0.62629
MSRvid	0.70356	0.80879	**0.83722**
SMTeuroparl	0.47173	0.47403	**0.58627**

Table (2) Results on STS 2012 training datasets.

	IBM_run2	IBM_run5	IBM_run6
Mean	0.59408	0.62614	**0.63365**
MSRpar	0.56059	0.59108	**0.61306**
MSRvid	0.73189	0.79960	**0.87154**
SMTeuroparl	0.51480	**0.50563**	0.41298
OnWN	0.62927	0.65760	**0.67136**
SMTnews	0.42305	**0.44551**	0.40819

Table (3) Results on STS 2012 test datasets.

Results on Test Data:

The best configuration of our system was **IBM_EG-run6** which was ranked #11 for the evaluation metric Mean (r = 0.5502) when submitted during the task evaluation period . **Run6** as illustrated before was planned to measure idf-weighted lexical matching feature only, over Porter stemmed, and stemmed synonyms words. **However** when revising this experiment set up during preparing the paper, after the evaluation period, we found that the English-to-English synonyms table was not correctly loaded during matching, thus skipping synonyms matching feature from this run. So the official result **IBM_EG-run6** reports only idf-weighted matching over Porter stemmed bag of words. By fixing this and replicating the experiment **IBM_EG-run6-UnOfficial** as planned to be, the mean Pearson correlation jumps 4 points (**r = 0.59221**) which ranks this system as the 3rd system among 90 submitted systems very slightly below the 2nd system (only 0.0006 difference on the mean correlation metric). In table (4), we report the official results achieved on STS 2013 test data. While table (5), reports the unofficial results achieved after activating the synonyms matching feature in **IBM_EG-run6 (unofficial)** and comparing this run to the best two reported systems.

	IBM_EG-run2	**IBM_EG-run5**	**IBM_EG-run6**
headlines	0.7217	0.7410	**0.7447**
OnWN	0.6110	0.5987	**0.6257**
FNWN	0.3364	0.4133	**0.4381**
SMT	**0.3460**	0.3426	0.3275
Mean	0.5365	0.5452	**0.5502**
Rank	**#19**	**#15**	**#11**

Table (4) Official Results on STS 2013 test datasets.

	UMBC_EBIQUITY-ParingWords	UMBC_EBIQUITY-galactus	**IBM_EG-run6 (UnOfficial)**
headlines	0.7642	0.7428	**0.77241**
OnWN	0.7529	0.7053	**0.70103**
FNWN	0.5818	0.5444	**0.44356**
SMT	0.3804	0.3705	**0.36807**
Mean	0.6181	0.5927	**0.59221**
Rank	#1	#2	#3

Table (5) UnOfficial Result after activating the synonyms matching feature in **IBM_EG-run6** compared to the best two performing systems in the evaluation.

Results of un-official run:

One unofficial run was performed after the evaluation submission deadline due to the tight schedule of the evaluation. This experiment introduces the effect of WordNet Wu and Palmer similarity measure on the configuration of Run5 (Porter stemming word matching, with synonyms matching, zero weight for BLEU score feature, while keeping the idf-weight= 3, lexical-weight = 1, and NE-matching feature weight = 1)

Table (6) reports the unofficial result achieved on STS 2013 test data, compared to the Official run **IBM_Eg-run5**.

	Unofficial-Run	**IBM_EG-run5**
Mean	0.52682	**0.5452**
headlines	0.70018	**0.7410**
OnWN	0.60371	0.5987
FNWN	0.35691	**0.4133**
SMT	0.33875	**0.3426**

Table (6) Un-Official Result on STS 2013 test datasets.

From the results in Table (6) it is clear that Corpus based synonyms matching outperforms dictionary-based WordNet matching over SEM2013 testset.

5 Conclusion

We proposed an unsupervised approach for measuring semantic textual similarity based on Lexical matching features (with porter stemming matching and synonyms matching), idf-Lexical matching features, Ngram Frquency (Modified BLEU) matching feature, as well as Named Entities matching feature combined together with a weighted cost function. Our experiments proved that idf-weighted Lexical matching in addition to porter stemming and synonyms-matching features perform best on most released evaluation datasets. Our best system officially ranked number 11 among 90 participating system reporting a Pearson Mean correlation score of 0.5502. However our best experimental set up "idf-weighted Lexical matching in addition to porter stemming and synonyms-matching" reported in an unofficial run a mean correlation score of **0.59221** which ranks the system as number 3 among the 90 participating systems. In our future work we intend to try some machine learning algorithms (like AdaBoost for example) for weighting our similarity matching feature scores. Also we plan to extend the usage of synonyms matching from the word level to the n-gram phrase matching level, by modifying the BLEU Score N-gram matching function to handle synonym phrases matching.

Acknowledgments

We would like to thank the reviewers for their constructive criticism and helpful comments.

References

Alfred. V. Aho and Jeffrey D. Ullman. 1972. *The Theory of Parsing, Translation and Compiling*, volume 1. Prentice-Hall, Englewood Cliffs, NJ.

American Psychological Association. 1983. *Publications Manual.* American Psychological Association, Washington, DC.

Association for Computing Machinery. 1983. *Computing Reviews*, 24(11):503-512.

Ashok K. Chandra, Dexter C. Kozen, and Larry J.Stockmeyer. 1981. Alternation. *Journal of the Association for Computing Machinery*, 28(1):114-133.

C. Y. Lin and E. H. Hovy. 2003. *Automatic evaluation of summaries using n-gram co-occurrence statistics.* In Proceedings of Human Language Technology Conference (HLT-NAACL 2003), Edmonton, Canada, May.

Chris Callison-Burch, Philipp Koehn, and Miles Osborne. 2006. *Improved statistical machine translation using paraphrases.* In Proceedings of HLT-NAACL.

Dan Gusfield. 1997. *Algorithms on Strings, Trees and Sequences*. Cambridge University Press, Cambridge, UK.

G. Salton and C. Buckley. 1997. *Term weighting approaches in automatic text retrieval.* In Readings in Information Retrieval. Morgan Kaufmann Publishers, San Francisco, CA.

Ittycheriah, A. and Roukos, S. (2007). *Direct translation model 2.* In Human Language Technologies 2007: The Conference of the North American Chapter of the Association for Computational Linguistics; Proceedings of the Main Conference, pp.57–64, Rochester, NY.

K. Papineni, S. Roukos, T. Ward, and W. Zhu. 2002. *Bleu: a method for automatic evaluation of machine translation.* In Proceedings of the 40th Annual Meeting of the Association for Computational Linguistics, Cambridge, UK.

M. Lapata and R. Barzilay. 2005. *Automatic evaluation of text coherence: Models and representations.* In Proceedings of the 19th International Joint Conference on Artificial Intelligence, Edinburgh.

P. Koehn, F.J. Och, and D. Marcu. 2003. *Statistical Phrase-Based Translation.* Proc. Of the Human Language Technology Conference, HLTNAACL' 2003, May.

Philipp Koehn, Hieu Hoang, Alexandra Birch, Chris Callison-Burch, Marcello Federico, Nicola Bertoldi, Brooke Cowan, Wade Shen, Christine Moran, Richard Zens, Chris Dyer, Ondˇrej Bojar, Alexandra Constantin, and Evan Herbst. 2007. *Moses: Open Source Toolkit for Statistical Machine Translation.* In Proceedings of the ACL 2007 Demo and Poster Sessions, pages 177–180.

R. Mihalcea , C. Corley, and C. Strapparava 2006. *Corpus-based and knowledge-based measures of text semantic similarity.* In Proceedings of the American Association for Artificial Intelligence. (Boston, MA).

Satanjeev Banerjee and Ted Pedersen. 2003. *Extended gloss overlaps as a measure of semantic relatedness.* In Proceedings of the 18th International Joint Conference on Artificial Intelligence, pages 805–810.

Ted Pedersen, Siddharth Patwardhan, and Jason Michelizzi, 2004, *WordNet::Similarity - Measuring the Relatedness of Concepts*. Proceedings of Fifth Annual Meeting of the North American Chapter of the Association for Computational Linguistics (NAACL-2004).

Wu, Z., and Palmer, M. 1994. *Verb semantics and lexical selection.* In 32nd Annual Meeting of the Association for Computational Linguistics, 133–138.

Weiwei Guo and Mona Diab. 2012a. *Learning the latent semantics of a concept from its definition.* In Proceedings of the 50th Annual Meeting of the Association for Computational Linguistics.

SOFTCARDINALITY-CORE: Improving Text Overlap with Distributional Measures for Semantic Textual Similarity

Sergio Jimenez, Claudia Becerra
Universidad Nacional de Colombia
Ciudad Universitaria,
edificio 453, oficina 114
Bogotá, Colombia
sgjimenezv@unal.edu.co
cjbecerrac@unal.edu.co

Alexander Gelbukh
CIC-IPN
Av. Juan Dios Bátiz, esq. Av. Mendizábal,
Col. Nueva Industrial Vallejo,
CP 07738, DF, México
www.gelbukh.com

Abstract

Soft cardinality has been shown to be a very strong text-overlapping baseline for the task of measuring semantic textual similarity (STS), obtaining 3rd place in SemEval-2012. At *SEM-2013 shared task, beside the plain text-overlapping approach, we tested within soft cardinality two distributional word-similarity functions derived from the ukWack corpus. Unfortunately, we combined these measures with other features using regression, obtaining positions 18th, 22nd and 23rd among the 90 participants systems in the official ranking. Already after the release of the gold standard annotations of the test data, we observed that using only the similarity measures without combining them with other features would have obtained positions 6th, 7th and 8th; moreover, an arithmetic average of these similarity measures would have been 4th(*mean*=0.5747). This paper describes both the 3 systems as they were submitted and the similarity measures that would obtained those better results.

1 Introduction

The task of textual semantic similarity (STS) consists in providing a similarity function on pairs of texts that correlates with human judgments. Such a function has many practical applications in NLP tasks (e.g. summarization, question answering, textual entailment, paraphrasing, machine translation evaluation, among others), which makes this task particularly important. Numerous efforts have been devoted to this task (Lee et al., 2005; Mihalcea et al., 2006) and major evaluation campaigns have been held at SemEval-2012 (Agirre et al., 2012) and in *SEM-2013 (Agirre et al., 2013).

The experimental setup of STS in 2012 consisted of three data sets, roughly divided in 50% for training and for testing, which contained text pairs manually annotated as a gold standard. Furthermore, two data sets were provided for surprise testing. The measure of performance was the average of the correlations per data set weighted by the number of pairs in each data set (*mean*). The best performing systems were UKP (Bär et al., 2012) *mean*=0.6773, TakeLab (Šaric et al., 2012) *mean*=0.6753 and soft cardinality (Jimenez et al., 2012) *mean*=0.6708. UKP and TakeLab systems used a large number of resources (see (Agirre et al., 2012)) such as dictionaries, a distributional thesaurus, monolingual corpora, Wikipedia, WordNet, distributional similarity measures, KB similarity, POS tagger, machine learning and others. Unlike those systems, the soft cardinality approach used mainly text overlapping and conventional text preprocessing such as removing of stop words, stemming and *idf* term weighting. This shows that the additional gain in performance from using external resources is small and that the soft cardinality approach is a very challenging baseline for the STS task. Soft cardinality has been previously shown (Jimenez and Gelbukh, 2012) to be also a good baseline for other applications such as information retrieval, entity matching, paraphrase detection and recognizing textual entailment.

Soft cardinality approach to constructing similarity functions (Jimenez et al., 2010) consists in using any cardinality-based resemblance coefficient (such as Jaccard or Dice) but substituting the classical set

*Second Joint Conference on Lexical and Computational Semantics (*SEM), Volume 1: Proceedings of the Main Conference and the Shared Task*, pages 194–201, Atlanta, Georgia, June 13-14, 2013.

cardinality with a softened counting function called soft cardinality. For example, the soft cardinality of a set containing three very similar elements is close to (though larger than) 1, while for three very different elements it is close to (though less than) 3. To use the soft cardinality with texts, they are represented as sets of words, and a word-similarity function is used for the soft counting of the words. For the sake of completeness, we give a brief overview of the soft-cardinality method in Section 3.

The resemblance coefficient used in our participation is a modified version of Tversky's ratio model (Tversky, 1977). Apart from the two parameters of this coefficient, a new parameter was included and functions *max* and *min* were used to make it symmetrical. The rationale for this new coefficient is given in Section 2.

Three word similarity features used in our systems are described in Section 4. The one is a measure of character q-gram overlapping, which reuses the coefficient proposed in Section 2; this measure is described in subsection 4.1. The other two ones are distributional measures obtained from the ukWack corpus (Baroni et al., 2009), which is a collection of web-crawled documents containing about 1.9 billion words in English. The second measure is, again, a reuse of the coefficient specified in Section 2, but using instead sets of occurrences (and co-occurrences) of words in sentences in the ukWack corpus; this measure is described in subsection 4.2. Finally, the third one, which is a normalized version of pointwise mutual information (PMI), is described in subsection 4.3.

The parameters of the three text-similarity functions derived from the combination of the proposed coefficient of resemblance (Section 2), the soft cardinality (Section 3) and the three word-similarity measures (Section 4) were adjusted to maximize the correlation with the 2012 STS gold standard data. At this point, these soft-cardinality similarity functions can provide predictions for the test data. However, we decided to test the approach of learning a resemblance function from the training data instead of using a preset resemblance coefficient. Basically, most resemblance coefficients are ternary functions $F(x, y, z)$ where $x = |A|$, $y = |B|$ and $z = |A \cap B|$: e.g. Dice coefficient is $F(x, y, z) = {}^{2z}/_{x+y}$ and Jaccard is $F(x, y, z) = {}^{z}/_{x+y-z}$. Thus, this function can be learned using a regression model, providing cardinalities *x*, *y* and *z* as features and the gold standard value as the target function. The results obtained for the text-similarity functions and the regression approach are presented in Section 7.

Unfortunately, when using a regressor trained with 2012 STS data and tested with 2013 surprise data we observed that the results worsened rather than improved. A short explanation of this is overfitting. A more detailed discussion of this, together with an assessment of the performance gain obtained by the use of distributional measures is provided in Section 8.

Finally, in Section 9 the conclusions of our participation in this evaluation campaign are presented.

2 Symmetrical Tversky's Ratio Model

In the field of mathematical psychology Tversky proposed the ratio model (TRM) (Tversky, 1977) motivated by the imbalance that humans have on the selection of the referent to compare things. This model is a parameterized resemblance coefficient to compare two sets A and B given by the following expression:

$$\mathbf{trm}(A, B) = \frac{|A \cap B|}{\alpha|A \setminus B| + \beta|B \setminus A| + |A \cap B|},$$

Having $\alpha, \beta \geq 0$. The numerator represents the commonality between A and B, and the denominator represents the referent for comparison. Parameters α and β represent the preference in the selection of A or B as referent. Tversky associated the set cardinality, to the stimuli of the objects being compared. Let us consider a Tversky's example of the 70s: A is North Corea, B is red China and stimuli is the prominence of the country. When subjects assessed the similarity between A and B, they tended to select the country with less prominence as referent. Tversky observed that α was larger than β when subjects compared countries, symbols, texts and sounds. Our motivation is to use this model by adjusting the parameters α and β for better modeling human similarity judgments for short texts.

However, this is not a symmetric model and the parameters α and β, have the dual interpretation of modeling the asymmetry in the referent selection, while controlling the balance between $|A \cap B|$ and

$|A - B| + |B - A|$ as well. The following reformulation, called symmetric TRM (**strm**), is intended to address these issues:

$$\mathbf{strm}(A, B) = \frac{c}{\beta\left(\alpha a + (1-\alpha)\, b\right) + c}, \quad (1)$$

$a = \min(|A - B|, |B - A|)$, $b = \max(|A - B|, |B - A|)$ and $c = |A \cap B| + bias$. In $\mathbf{strm}$, α models only the balance between the differences in the cardinalities of A and B, and β models the balance between $|A \cap B|$ and $|A - B| + |B - A|$. Furthermore, the use of functions min and max makes the measure to be symmetric. Although the motivation for the $bias$ parameter is empirical, we believe that this reduces the effect of the common features that are frequent and therefore less informative, e.g. stop words. Note that for $\alpha = 0.5$,$\beta = 1$ and $bias = 0$, $\mathbf{strm}$ is equivalent to Dice's coefficient. Similarity, for $\alpha = 0.5$,$\beta = 2$ and $bias = 0$, $\mathbf{strm}$ is equivalent to the Jaccard's coefficient.

3 Soft Cardinality

The cardinality of a set is its number of elements. By definition, the sets do not allow repeated elements, so if a collection of elements contains repetitions its cardinality is the number of different elements. The classical set cardinality does not take into account similar elements, i.e. only the identical elements in a collection counted once. The soft cardinality (Jimenez et al., 2010) considers not only identical elements but also similar using an auxiliary similarity function **sim**, which compares pairs of elements. This cardinality can be calculated for a collection of elements A with the following expression:

$$|A|' = \sum_{i=1}^{n} w_i \left(\sum_{j=1}^{n} \mathbf{sim}(a_i, a_j)^p \right)^{-1} \quad (2)$$

$A = \{a_1, a_2, \ldots, a_n\}$; $w_i \geq 0$; $p \geq 0$; $1 > \mathbf{sim}(x, y) \geq 0$, $x \neq y$; and $\mathbf{sim}(x, x) = 1$. The parameter p controls the degree of "softness" of the cardinality. This formulation has the property of reproducing classical cardinality when p is large and/or when **sim** is a rigid function that returns 1 only for identical elements and 0 otherwise. The coefficients w_i are the weights associated with each element. In text applications elements a_i are words and weights w_i represent the importance or informative character of each word (e.g. *idf* weights). The apostrophe is used to differentiate soft cardinality from the classic set cardinality.

4 Word Similarity

Analogous to the STS, the word similarity is the task of measuring the relationship of a couple of words in a way correlated with human judgments. Since when Rubenstein and Goodenough (1965) provided the first data set, this task has been addressed primarily through semantic networks (Resnik, 1999; Pedersen et al., 2004) and distributional measures (Agirre et al., 2009). However, other simpler approaches such as edit-distance (Levenshtein, 1966) and stemming (Porter, 1980) can also be used. For instance, the former identifies the similarity between "song" and "sing", and later that between "sing" and "singing". This section presents three approaches for word similarity that can be plugged into the soft cardinality expression in eq. 2.

4.1 *Q*-grams similarity

Q-grams are the collection of consecutive-overlapped sub-strings of length q obtained from the character string in a word. For instance, the 2-grams (bi-grams) and 3-grams (trigrams) representation of the word "sing" are {'#s', 'si', 'in', 'ng', 'g#'} and {'#si', 'sin', 'ing', 'ng#'} respectively. The character '#' is a padding character that distinguishes q-grams at the beginning and ending of a word. If the number of characters in a word is greater or equal than q its representation in q-grams is the word itself (e.g. the 6-grams in "sing" are {'sing'}). Moreover, the 1-grams (unigrams) and 0-grams representations of "sing" are {'s', 'i', 'n', 'g'} and {'sing'}. A word can also be represented by combining multiple representations of q-grams. For instance, the combined representation of "sing" using 0-grams, unigrams, and bi-grams is {'sing', 's', 'i', 'n', 'g', '#s', 'si', 'in', 'ng', 'g#'}, denoted by [0:2]-grams. In practice a range $[q_1 : q_2]$ of q-grams can be used having $0 \leq q_1 < q_2$.

The proposed word-similarity function (named $\mathbf{qgrams}$) first represents a pair of words using $[q_1 : q_2]$-grams and then compares them reusing the $\mathbf{strm}$ coefficient (eq.1). The parameters of the

qgrams function are q_1, q_2, α_{qgrams}, β_{qgrams}, and $bias_{qgrams}$. These parameters are sub-scripted to distinguish them from their counterparts at the text-similarity functions.

4.2 Context-Set Distributional Similarity

The hypothesis of this measure is that the co-occurrence of two words in a sentence is a hint of the possible relationship between them. Let us define $\mathrm{sf}(t)$ as the sentence frequency of a word *t* in a corpus. The sentence frequency is equivalent to the well known document frequency but uses sentences instead of documents. Similarly $\mathrm{sf}(t_A \wedge t_B)$ is the number of sentences where words t_A and t_B co-occur. The idea is to compute a similarity function between t_A and t_B representing them as A and B, which are sets of the sentences where t_A and t_B occur. Similarly, $A \cap B$ is the set of sentences where both words co-occur. The required cardinalities can be obtained from the sentence frequencies by: $|A| = \mathrm{sf}(t_A)$; $|B| = \mathrm{sf}(t_B)$ and $|A \cap B| = \mathrm{sf}(t_A \wedge t_B)$. These cardinalities are combined reusing again the **strm** coefficient (eq. 1) to obtain a word-similarity function. The parameters of this function, which we refer to it as **csds**, are α_{csds}, β_{csds} and $bias_{csds}$.

4.3 Normalized Point-wise Mutual Information

The pointwise mutual information (PMI) is a measure of relationship between two random variables. PMI is calculated by the following expression:

$$\mathbf{pmi}(t_A, t_B) = \log_2\left(\frac{P(t_A \wedge t_B)}{P(t_A) \cdot P(t_B)}\right)$$

PMI has been used to measure the relatedness of pairs of words using the number of the hits returned by a search engine (Turney, 2001; Bollegala et al., 2007). However, PMI cannot be used directly as **sim** function in eq.2. The alternative is to normalize it dividing it by $\log_2(P(t_A \wedge t_B))$ obtaining a value in the $[1, -1]$ interval. This measure returns 1 for complete co-occurrence, 0 for independence and -1 for "never" co-occurring. Given that the results in the interval (0,-1] are not relevant, the final normalized-trimmed expression is:

$$\mathbf{npmi}(t_A, t_B) = \max\left[\frac{\mathbf{pmi}(t_A, t_B)}{\log_2(P(t_A \wedge t_B))}, 0\right] \quad (3)$$

The probabilities required by PMI can be obtained by MLE using sentence frequencies in a large corpus: $P(t_A) \approx \frac{\mathrm{sf}(t_A)}{S}$, $P(t_B) \approx \frac{\mathrm{sf}(t_B)}{S}$,and $P(t_A \wedge t_B) \approx \frac{\mathrm{sf}(t_A \wedge t_B)}{S}$. Where S is the total number of sentences in the corpus.

5 Text-similarity Functions

The "building blocks" proposed in sections 2, 3 and 4, are assembled to build three text-similarity functions, namely $\mathbf{STS_{qgrams}}$, $\mathbf{STS_{csds}}$ and $\mathbf{STS_{npmi}}$. The first component is the **strm** resemblance coefficient (eq. 1), which takes as arguments a pair of texts represented as bags of words with importance weights associated with each word. In the following subsection 5.1 a detailed description of the procedure for obtaining such weighted bag-of-words is provided.

The **strm** coefficient is enhanced by replacing the classical cardinality by the soft cardinality, which exploits two resources: importance weights associated with each word (weights w_i) and pairwise comparisons among words (**sim**). Unlike $\mathbf{STS_{qgrams}}$ measure, $\mathbf{STS_{csds}}$ and $\mathbf{STS_{npmi}}$ measures require statistics from a large corpus. A brief description of the used corpus and the method for obtaining such statistics is described in subsection 5.2. Finally, the three proposed text-similarity functions contain free parameters that need to be adjusted. The method used to get those parameters is described in subsection 5.3.

5.1 Preprocessing and Term Weighting

All training and test texts were preprocessed with the following sequence of actions: *i*) text strings were tokenized, *ii*) uppercase characters are converted into lower-cased equivalents, *iii*) stop-words were removed, *iv*) punctuation marks were removed, and *v*) words were stemmed using Porter's algorithm (1980). Then each stemmed word was weighted with *idf* (Jones, 2004) calculated using the entire collection of texts.

5.2 Sentence Frequencies from Corpus

The sentence frequencies $\mathrm{sf}(t)$ and $\mathrm{sf}(t_A \wedge t_B)$ required by **csds** and **npmi** word-similarity functions were obtained from the ukWack corpus (Baroni et al., 2009). This corpus has roughly 1.9 billion words, 87.8 millions of sentences and 2.7 millions of documents. The corpus was iterated sentence by sentence with the same preprocessing that was described in the previous section, looking for all occurrences of words and word pairs from the full training and test texts. The target words were stored in a trie, making the entire corpus iteration took about 90 minutes in a laptop with 4GB and a 1.3Ghz processor.

5.3 Parameter optimization

The three proposed text-similarity functions have several parameters: p exponent in the soft cardinality; α, β, and $bias$ in $\mathbf{strm}$ coefficient; their sub-scripted versions in $\mathbf{qgrams}$ and $\mathbf{csds}$ word-similarity functions; and finally $q_1$and q_2 for $\mathbf{qgrams}$ function. Parameter sets for each of the three text-similarity functions were optimized using the full STS-SemEval-2012 data. The function to maximize was the correlation between similarity scores against the gold standard in the training data. The set of parameters for each similarity function were optimized using a greedy hill-climbing approach by using steps of 0.01 for all parameters except q_1 and q_2 that used 1 as step. The initial values were $p = 1$, $\alpha = 0.5$, $\beta = 1$, $bias = 0$, $q_1 = 2$ and $q_2 = 3$. All parameters were optimized until improvement in the function to maximize was below 0.0001. The obtained values are :

$\mathbf{STS_{qgrams}}$ $p = 1.32$,$\alpha = 0.52$, $\beta = 0.64$, $bias = -0.45$, $q_1 = 0$, $q_2 = 2$, $\alpha_{qgrams} = 0.95$, $\beta_{qgrams} = 1.44$, $bias_{qgrams} = -0.44$.

$\mathbf{STS_{csds}}$ $p = 0.5$, $\alpha = 0.63$, $\beta = 0.69$, $bias = -2.05$, $\alpha_{csds} = 1.34$, $\beta_{csds} = 2.57$, $bias_{csds} = -1.22$.

$\mathbf{STS_{npmi}}$ $p = 6.17$,$\alpha = 0.83$, $\beta = 0.64$, $bias = -2.11$.

6 Regression for STS

The use of regression is motivated by the following experiment. First, a synthetic data set with 1,000 instances was generated with the following three features: $|A| = RandomBetween(1, 100)$, $|B| = RandomBetween(1, 100)$ and $|A \cap B| = RandomBetween(0, min[|A|, |B|])$. Secondly, a linear regressor was trained using the Dice's coefficient (i.e. $2|A \cap B|/|A| + |B|$) as target function. The Pearson correlation obtained using 4-fold cross-validation as method of evaluation was $r = 0.93$. Besides, a Reduced Error Pruning (REP) tree (Witten and Frank, 2005) boosted with 30 iterations of Bagging (Breiman, 1996) was used instead of the linear regressor obtaining $r = 0.99$. We concluded that a particular resemblance coefficient can be accurately approximated using a nonlinear regression algorithm and training data.

#1	$\mathbf{STS_{sim}}$	#11	$\|A \cap B\|'/\|A\|'$
#2	$\|A\|'$	#12	$\|A \cap B\|'/\|B\|'$
#3	$\|B\|'$	#13	$\|A\|' \cdot \|B\|'$
#4	$\|A \cap B\|'$	#14	$\|A \cap B\|'/\|A \cup B\|'$
#5	$\|A \cup B\|'$	#15	$2 \cdot \|A \cap B\|'/\|A\|'+\|B\|'$
#6	$\|A \setminus B\|'$	#16	$\|A \cap B\|/\mathrm{min}[\|A\|, \|B\|]$
#7	$\|B \setminus A\|'$	#17	$\|A \cap B\|'/\mathrm{max}[\|A\|', \|B\|']$
#8	$\|A \cup B - A \cap B\|'$	#18	$\|A \cap B\|'/\sqrt{\|A\|' \cdot \|B\|'}$
#9	$\|A - B\|'/\|A\|'$	#19	$\frac{\|A \cap B\|'+\|A\|'+\|B\|'}{2 \cdot \|A\|' \cdot \|B\|'}$
#10	$\|B - A\|'/\|B\|'$	#20	gold standard

Table 1: Feature set for regression

This approach can be used for replacing the **strm** coefficient by a similarity function learned from STS training data. The three features used in the previous experiment were extended to a total of 19 (see table 1) plus the gold standard as target. The feature #1 is the score of the corresponding text-similarity function described in the previous section. Three sets of features were constructed, each with 19 features using the soft cardinality in combination with the word-similarity functions $\mathbf{qgrams}$, $\mathbf{csds}$ and $\mathbf{npmi}$. Let us name these feature sets as *fs:qgrams*, *fs:csds* and *fs:npmi*. The submission labeled *run1* was obtained using the feature set *fs:qgrams* (19 features). The submission labeled *run2* was obtained using the aggregation of *fs:qgrams* and *fs:csds* ($19 \times 2 = 38$ features). Finally, *run3* was the aggregation of *fs:grams*, *fs:csds* and *fs:npmi* ($19 \times 3 = 57$ features).

7 Results in *SEM 2013 Shared Task

In this section three groups of systems are described by using the functions and models proposed in the previous sections. The first group (and simplest)

Data set	$\mathbf{STS_{qgrams}}$	$\mathbf{STS_{csds}}$	$\mathbf{STS_{npmi}}$	*average*
headlines	**0.7625**	0.7243	0.7379	0.7562
OnWN	0.7022	0.7050	0.6832	**0.7063**
FNWM	0.2704	0.3713	**0.4215**	0.3940
SMT	0.3151	0.3325	**0.3408**	0.3402
mean	0.5570	0.5592	0.5653	**0.5747**
rank	8	7	6	**4**

Table 2: Unofficial results using text-similarity functions

Data set	*run1*	*run2*	*run3*
headlines	0.7591	0.7632	**0.7640**
OnWN	0.7159	0.7239	**0.7485**
FNWM	0.2806	**0.3679**	0.3487
SMT	0.2820	0.2786	**0.2952**
mean	0.5491	0.5586	**0.5690**
rank	14	8	**4**

Table 3: Unofficial results using linear regression

of systems consist in using the scores of the three text-similarity functions $\mathbf{STS_{qgrams}}$, $\mathbf{STS_{csds}}$ and $\mathbf{STS_{npmi}}$. Table 2 shows the unofficial results of these three systems. The bottom row shows the positions that these systems would have obtained if they had been submitted to the *SEM shared task 2013. The last column shows the results of a system that combines the scores of three measures on a single score calculating the arithmetic mean. This is the best performing system obtained with the methods described in this paper.

Tables 3 and 4 show unofficial and official results of the method described in section 6 using linear regression and Bagging (30 iterations)+REP tree respectively. These results were obtained using WEKA (Hall et al., 2009).

8 Discussion

Contrary to the observation we made in training data, the methods that used regression to predict the gold standard performed poorly compared with the text similarity functions proposed in Section 5. That is, the results in Table 2 overcome those in Tables 3 and 4. Also in training data, Bagging+REP tree surpassed linear regression, but, as can be seen in tables 3 and 4 the opposite happened in test data. This is a clear symptom of overfitting. However, the *OnWN*

Data set	*run1*	*run2*	*run3*
headlines	0.6410	**0.6713**	0.6603
OnWN	0.7360	**0.7412**	0.7401
FNWM	0.3442	**0.3838**	0.3347
SMT	**0.3035**	0.2981	0.2900
mean	0.5273	**0.5402**	0.5294
rank	23	**18**	22

Table 4: Official results of the submitted runs to STS *SEM 2013 shared task using Bagging + REP tree for regression

data set was an exception, which obtained the best results using linear regression. *OnWN* was the only one among the 2013 data sets that was not a surprise data set. Probably the 5.97% relative improvement obtained in *run3* by the linear regression versus the best result in Table 2 may be justified owing to some patterns discovered by the linear regressor in the OnWN'2012 training data which are projected on the OnWN'2013 test data.

It is worth noting that in all three sets of results, the lowest *mean* was consistently obtained by the text-overlapping methods, namely $\mathbf{STS_{qgrams}}$ and *run1*. The relative improvement in *mean* due to the use of distributional measures against the text-overlapping methods was 3.18%, 3.62% and 2.45% in each set of results (see Tables 2, 3 and 4). In *FNWM* data set, the biggest improvements achieved 55.88%, 31.11% and 11.50% respectively in the three groups of results, followed by *SMT* data set. Both in *FNWN* data set as in *SMT*, the texts are systematically longer than those found in *OnWN* and *headlines*. This result suggests that the improvement due to distributional measures is more significant in longer texts than in the shorter ones.

Lastly, it is also important to notice that the $\mathbf{STS_{qgrams}}$ text-similarity function obtained $mean = 0.5570$, which proved again to be a very strong text-overlapping baseline for the STS task.

9 Conclusions

We participated in the CORE-STS shared task in *SEM 2013 with satisfactory results obtaining positions 18th, 22nd, and 23rd in the official ranking. Our systems were based on a new parameterized resemblance coefficient derived from the Tversky's ratio model in combination with the soft cardinality. The three proposed text-similarity functions used q-grams overlapping and distributional measures obtained from the ukWack corpus. These text-similarity functions would have been attained positions 6th, 7th and 8th in the official ranking, besides a simple average of them would have reached the 4thplace. Another important conclusion was that the plain text-overlapping method was consistently improved by the incremental use of the proposed distributional measures. This result was most noticeable in long texts.

In conclusion, the proposed text-similarity functions proved to be competitive despite their simplicity and the few resources used.

Acknowledgments

This research was funded in part by the Systems and Industrial Engineering Department, the Office of Student Welfare of the National University of Colombia, Bogotá, and through a grant from the Colombian Department for Science, Technology and Innovation, Colciencias, proj. 1101-521-28465 with funding from "El Patrimonio Autónomo Fondo Nacional de Financiamiento para la Ciencia, la Tecnología y la Innovación, Francisco José de Caldas." The Section 2 was proposed during the first author's internship at Microsoft Research in 2012. The third author recognizes the support from Mexican Government (SNI, COFAA-IPN, SIP 20131702, CONACYT 50206-H) and CONACYT–DST India (proj. 122030 "Answer Validation through Textual Entailment"). Entailment").

References

Eneko Agirre, Enrique Alfonseca, Keith Hall, Jana Kravalova, Marius Pasca, and Aitor Soroa. 2009. A study on similarity and relatedness using distributional and WordNet-based approaches. In *Proceedings of Human Language Technologies: The 2009 Annual Conference of the North American Chapter of the Association for Computational Linguistics*, NAACL '09, pages 19–27, Stroudsburg, PA, USA. Association for Computational Linguistics.

Eneko Agirre, Daniel Cer, Mona Diab, and Gonzalez-Agirre Aitor. 2012. SemEval-2012 task 6: A pilot on semantic textual similarity. In *Proceedings of the 6th International Workshop on Semantic Evaluation (SemEval@*SEM 2012)*, Montreal,Canada. Association for Computational Linguistics.

Eneko Agirre, Daniel Cer, Mona Diab, Aitor Gonzalez-Agirre, and Weiwei Guo. 2013. *SEM 2013 shared task: Semantic textual similarity, including a pilot on typed-similarity. Atlanta, Georgia, USA. Association for Computational Linguistics.

Daniel Bär, Chris Biemann, Iryna Gurevych, and Torsten Zesch. 2012. UKP: computing semantic textual similarity by combining multiple content similarity measures. In *Proceedings of the 6th International Workshop on Semantic Evaluation (SemEval *SEM 2012)*, Montreal, Canada. Association for Computational Linguistics.

Marco Baroni, Silvia Bernardini, Adriano Ferraresi, and Eros Zanchetta. 2009. The WaCky wide web: a collection of very large linguistically processed web-crawled corpora. *Language resources and evaluation*, 43(3):209–226.

Danushka Bollegala, Yutaka Matsuto, and Mitsuru Ishizuka. 2007. Measuring semantic similarity between words using web search engines. In *Proceedings of the 16th international conference on World Wide Web*, WWW '07, pages 757–766, New York, NY, USA. ACM.

Leo Breiman. 1996. Bagging predictors. *Machine Learning*, 24(2):123–140.

Mark Hall, Frank Eibe, Geoffrey Holmes, and Bernhard Pfahringer. 2009. The WEKA data mining software: An update. *SIGKDD Explorations*, 11(1):10–18.

Sergio Jimenez and Alexander Gelbukh. 2012. Baselines for natural language processing tasks. *Appl. Comput. Math.*, 11(2):180–199.

Sergio Jimenez, Fabio Gonzalez, and Alexander Gelbukh. 2010. Text comparison using soft cardinality. In Edgar Chavez and Stefano Lonardi, editors, *String Processing and Information Retrieval*, volume 6393 of *LNCS*, pages 297–302. Springer, Berlin, Heidelberg.

Sergio Jimenez, Claudia Becerra, and Alexander Gelbukh. 2012. Soft cardinality: A parameterized similarity function for text comparison. In *Proceedings of the 6th International Workshop on Semantic Evaluation (SemEval *SEM 2012)*, Montreal, Canada.

Karen Spärck Jones. 2004. A statistical interpretation of term specificity and its application in retrieval. *Journal of Documentation*, 60(5):493–502, October.

Michael D Lee, B.M. Pincombe, and Matthew Welsh. 2005. An empirical evaluation of models of text document similarity. *IN COGSCI2005*, pages 1254–1259.

Vladimir I. Levenshtein. 1966. Binary codes capable of correcting deletions, insertions, and reversals. *Soviet Physics Doklady*, 10(8):707–710.

Rada Mihalcea, Courtney Corley, and Carlo Strapparava. 2006. Corpus-based and knowledge-based measures of text semantic similarity. In *In AAAI'06*, pages 775–780.

Ted Pedersen, Siddharth Patwardhan, and Jason Michelizzi. 2004. WordNet::Similarity: measuring the relatedness of concepts. In *Proceedings HLT-NAACL–Demonstration Papers*, Stroudsburg, PA, USA. Association for Computational Linguistics.

Martin Porter. 1980. An algorithm for suffix stripping. *Program*, 3(14):130–137, October.

Phillip Resnik. 1999. Semantic similarity in a taxonomy: An information-based measure and its application to problems of ambiguity in natural language. *Journal of Artificial Intelligence Research*, 11:95–130.

Herbert Rubenstein and John B. Goodenough. 1965. Contextual correlates of synonymy. *Commun. ACM*, 8(10):627–633, October.

Frane Šaric, Goran Glavaš, Mladen Karan, Jan Šnajder, and Bojana Dalbelo Bašic. 2012. TakeLab: systems for measuring semantic text similarity. In *Proceedings of the 6th International Workshop on Semantic Evaluation (SemEval *SEM 2012)*, Montreal, Canada. Association for Computational Linguistics.

Peter D. Turney. 2001. Mining the web for synonyms: PMI-IR versus LSA on TOEFL. In Luc De Raedt and Peter Flach, editors, *Machine Learning: ECML 2001*, number 2167 in Lecture Notes in Computer Science, pages 491–502. Springer Berlin Heidelberg, January.

Amos Tversky. 1977. Features of similarity. *Psychological Review*, 84(4):327–352, July.

I.H. Witten and E. Frank. 2005. *Data Mining: Practical Machine Learning Tools and Techniques*. Morgan Kaufmann Publishers Inc., San Francisto, CA, 2nd edition.

CLaC-CORE: Exhaustive Feature Combination for Measuring Textual Similarity

Ehsan Shareghi
CLaC Laboratory
Concordia University
Montreal, QC H3G 1M8, CANADA
eh_share@cse.concordia.ca

Sabine Bergler
CLaC Laboratory
Concordia University
Montreal, QC H3G 1M8, CANADA
bergler@cse.concordia.ca

Abstract

CLaC-CORE, an exhaustive feature combination system ranked 4th among 34 teams in the Semantic Textual Similarity shared task STS 2013. Using a core set of 11 lexical features of the most basic kind, it uses a support vector regressor which uses a combination of these lexical features to train a model for predicting similarity between sentences in a two phase method, which in turn uses all combinations of the features in the feature space and trains separate models based on each combination. Then it creates a meta-feature space and trains a final model based on that. This two step process improves the results achieved by single-layer standard learning methodology over the same simple features. We analyze the correlation of feature combinations with the data sets over which they are effective.

1 Introduction

The Semantic Textual Similarity (STS) shared task aims to find a unified way of measuring similarity between sentences. In fact, sentence similarity is a core element of tasks trying to establish how two pieces of text are related, such as Textual Entailment (RTE) (Dagan et al., 2006), and Paraphrase Recognition (Dolan et al., 2004). The STS shared task was introduced for SemEval-2012 and was selected as its first shared task. Similar in spirit, STS differs from the well-known RTE shared tasks in two important points: it defines a graded similarity scale to measure similarity of two texts, instead of RTE's binary yes/no decision and the similarity relation is considered to be symmetrical, whereas the entailment relation of RTE is inherently unidirectional.

The leading systems in the 2012 competition used a variety of very simple lexical features. Each system combines a different set of related features. CLaC Labs investigated the different combination possibilities of these simple lexical features and measured their performance on the different data sets. Originally conceived to explore the space of all possible feature combinations for 'feature combination selection', a two-step method emerged that deliberately compiles and trains all feature combinations exhaustively and then trains an SVM regressor using all combination models as its input features. It turns out that this technique is not nearly as prohibitive as imagined and achieves statistically significant improvements over the alternative of feature selection or of using any one single combination individually.

We propose the method as a viable approach when the characteristics of the data are not well understood and no satisfactory training set is available.

2 Related Work

Recently, systems started to approach measuring similarity by combining different resources and methods. For example, the STS-2012 shared task's leading UKP (Bär et al., 2012) system uses n-grams, string similarity, WordNet, and ESA, and a regressor. In addition, they use MOSES, a statistical machine translation system (Koehn et al., 2007), to translate each English sentence into Dutch, German, and Spanish and back into English in an effort to increase their training set of similar text pairs.

*Second Joint Conference on Lexical and Computational Semantics (*SEM), Volume 1: Proceedings of the Main Conference and the Shared Task*, pages 202–206, Atlanta, Georgia, June 13-14, 2013.

TakeLab (Šaric et al., 2012), in place two of the 2012 STS shared task, uses n-gram models, two WordNet-based measures, LSA, and dependencies to align subject-verb-object predicate structures. Including named-entities and number matching in the feature space improved performance of their support vector regressor.

(Shareghi and Bergler, 2013) illustrates two experiments with STS-2012 training and test sets using the basic core features of these systems, outperforming the STS-2012 task's highest ranking systems. The STS-2013 submission CLaC-CORE uses the same two-step approach.

3 CLaC Methodology

Preprocessing consists of tokenizing, lemmatizing, sentence splitting, and part of speech (POS) tagging. We extract two main categories of lexical features: explicit and implicit.

3.1 Explicit Lexical Features

Sentence similarity at the explicit level is based solely on the input text and measures the similarity between two sentences either by using an n-gram model (*ROUGE-1, ROUGE-2, ROUGE-SU4*) or by reverting to string similarity (longest common subsequence, *jaro, ROUGE-W*):

Longest Common Subsequence (Allison and Trevor, 1986) compare the length of the longest sequence of characters, not necessarily consecutive ones, in order to detect similarities

Jaro (Jaro, 1989) identifies spelling variation between two inputs based on the occurrence of common characters between two text segments at a certain distance

ROUGE-W (Lin et al., 2004a), a weighted version of *longest common subsequence*, takes into account the number of the consecutive characters in each match, giving higher score for those matches that have larger number of consecutive characters in common. This metric was developed to measure the similarity between machine generated text summaries and a manually generated gold standard

ROUGE-1 unigrams (Lin et al., 2004a)

ROUGE-2 bigrams (Lin et al., 2004a)

ROUGE-SU4 4-Skip bigrams (including Unigrams) (Lin et al., 2004a)

3.2 Implicit Lexical Features

Sentence similarity at the implicit level uses external resources to make up for the lexical gaps that go otherwise undetected at the explicit level. The synonymy of *bag* and *suitcase* is an example of an implicit similarity. This type of implicit similarity can be detected using knowledge sources such as WordNet or Roget's Thesaurus based on the WordNet::Similarity package (Pedersen et al., 2004) and combination techniques (Mihalcea et al., 2006). For the more semantically challenging non-ontologigal relations, for example *sanction* and *Iran*, which lexica do not provide, co-occurrence-based measures like ESA are more robust. We use:

Lin (Lin, 1998) uses the Brown Corpus of American English to calculate information content of two concepts' least common subsumer. Then he scales it using the sum of the information content of the compared concepts

Jiang-Conrath (Jiang and Conrath, 1997) uses the conditional probability of encountering a concept given an instance of its parent to calculate the information content. Then they define the distance between two concepts to be the sum of the difference between the information content of each of the two given concepts and their least common subsumer

Roget's Thesaurus is another lexical resource and is based on well-crafted concept classification and was created by professional lexicographers. It has a nine-level ontology and doesn't have one of the major drawbacks of WordNet, which is lack of links between part of speeches. According to the schema proposed by (Jarmasz and Szpakowicz, 2003) the distance of two terms decreases within the interval of [0,16], as the the common head that subsumes them moves from top to the bottom and becomes more specific. The electronic version of Roget's Thesaurus which was developed by (Jarmasz and Szpakowicz, 2003) was used for extracting this score

Explicit Semantic Analyzer (Gabrilovich and Markovitch, 2007) In order to have broader coverage on word types not represented in lexical resources, specifically for named entities, we add explicit semantic analyzer (ESA) generated features to our feature space

3.3 CLaC-CORE

CLaC-CORE first generates all combinations of the 11 basic features (*jaro, Lemma, lcsq, ROUGE-W, ROUGE-1, ROUGE-2, ROUGE-SU4, roget, lin, jcn, esa*), that is $2^{11} - 1 = 2047$ non-empty combinations. The *Two Phase Model Training* step trains a separate Support Vector Regressor (SVR) for each combination creating 2047 *Phase One Models*. These $2^N - 1$ predicted scores per text data item form a new feature vector called *Phase Two Features*, which feed into a SVR to train our *Phase Two Model*.

On a standard 2 core computer with $\leq$100 GB of RAM using multi-threading (thread pool of size 200, a training process per thread) it took roughly 15 hours to train the 2047 Phase One Models on 5342 text pairs and another 17 hours to build the Phase Two Feature Space for the training data. Building the Phase Two Feature Space for the test sets took roughly 7.5 hours for 2250 test pairs.

For the current submissions we combine all training sets into one single training set used in all of our submissions for the STS 2013 task.

4 Analysis of Results

Our three submission for STS-2013 compare a baseline of *Standard Learning* (RUN-1)with two versions of our *Two Phase Learning* (RUN-2, RUN-3). For the *Standard Learning* baseline, one regressor was trained on the training set on all 11 *Basic Features* and tested on the test sets. For the remaining runs the *Two Phase Learning* method was used. All our submissions use the same 11 *Basic Features*. *RUN-2* is our main contribution. *RUN-3* is identical to *RUN-2* except for reducing the number of support vectors and allowing larger training errors in an effort to assess the potential for speedup. This was done by decreasing the value of γ (in the *RBF* kernel) from 0.01 to 0.0001, and decreasing the value of C (error weight) from 1 to 0.01. These parameters resulted in a smoother and simpler decision surface but negatively affected the performance for *RUN-3* as shown in Table 1.

The STS shared task-2013 used the Pearson Correlation Coefficient as the evaluation metric. The results of our experiments are presented in Table 1. The results indicate that the proposed method, *RUN-2*, was successful in improving the results achieved by our baseline *RUN-1* ever so slightly (the confidence invervals at 5% differ to .016 at the upper end) and far exceeds the reduced computation version of *RUN-3*.

	rank	headlines	OnWN	FNWN	SMT
RUN-1	10	0.6774	0.7667	0.3793	0.3068
RUN-2	7	0.6921	0.7367	0.3793	0.3375
RUN-3	46	0.5276	0.6495	0.4158	0.3082
STS-bl	73	0.5399	0.2828	0.2146	0.2861

Table 1: CLaC-CORE runs and STS baseline performance

4.1 Successful Feature Combinations

Having trained separate models based on each subset of features we can use the predicted scores generated by each of these models to calculate their correlations to assess which of the feature combinations were more effective in making predictions and how this most successful combination varies bewteen the different datasets.

	best	**worst**
headlines	[ROUGE-1 ROUGE-SU4 esa lem]	[jcn lem lcsq]
	0.7329	0.3375
OnWN	[ROUGE-1 ROUGE-SU4 esa lin jcn roget lem lcsq ROUGE-W]	[jaro]
	0.7768	0.1425
FNWN	[roget ROUGE-1 ROUGE-SU4]	[ROUGE-2 lem lcsq]
	0.4464	-0.0386
SMT	[lin jcn roget ROUGE-1]	[esa lcsq]
	0.3648	0.2305

Table 2: Best and worst feature combination performance on test set

Table 2 lists the best and worst feature combinations on each test set. *ROUGE-1* (denoted by RO-1), unigram overlap, is part of all four best performing subsets. The features *ROUGE-SU4* and *Roget's* appear in three of the best four feature combinations, making Roget's the best performing lexicon-based feature outperforming WordNet features on this task. *esa*, *lin*, *jcn* are part of two of the best subsets, where *lin* and *jcn* occur together both times, suggesting synergy. Looking at the worst performing feature combinations is also instructive and suggests that *lcsq* was not an effective feature (despite being at the heart of the more successful *ROUGE-W* measure).

We also analyze performance of individual features over different datasets. Table 3 lists all the features and, instead of looking at only the best combination, takes the top three best combinations for each test and compares how many times each feature has occurred in the resulting 12 combinations (first column). Three clear classes of effectiveness emerge, high (10-7), medium (6-4), and low (3-0). Next, we observe that the test sets differ in the average length of the data: *headlines* and *OnWN* glosses are very short, in contrast to the other two. Table 3 shows in fact contrastive feature behavior for these two categories (denoted by short and long). The last column reports the number of time a feature has occurred in the best combinations (out of 4). Again, *ROUGE-1*, *ROUGE-SU4*, and *roget* prove effective across different test sets. *esa* and *lem* seem most reliable when we deal with short text fragments, while *roget* and *ROUGE-SU4* are most valuable on longer texts. The individual most valuable features overall are *ROUGE-1*, *ROUGE-SU4*, and *roget*.

Features	total (/12)	short (/6)	long (/6)	best (/4)
esa	6	6	0	2
lin	6	3	3	2
jcn	4	1	3	2
roget	9	3	6	3
lem	6	6	0	2
jaro	0	0	0	0
lcsq	3	3	0	1
ROUGE-W	7	4	3	1
ROUGE-1	10	6	4	4
ROUGE-2	3	1	2	0
ROUGE-SU4	10	5	5	3

Table 3: Feature contribution to the three best results over four datasets

5 Conclusion

CLaC-CORE investigated the performance possibilities of different feature combinations for 11 basic lexical features that are frequently used in semantic distance measures. By exhaustively training all combinations in a two-phase regressor, we were able to establish a few interesting observations.

First, our own baseline of simply training a SVM regressor on all 11 basic features achieves rank 10 and outperforms the baseline used for the shared task. It should probably become the new standard baseline.

Second, our two-phase exhaustive model, while resource intensive, is not at all prohibitive. If the knowledge to pick appropriate features is not available and if not enough training data exists to perform feature selection, the exhaustive method can produce results that outperform our baseline and one that is competitive in the current field (rank 7 of 88 submissions). But more importantly, this method allows us to forensically analyze feature combination behavior contrastively. We were able to establish that unigrams and 4-skip bigrams are most versatile, but surprisingly that Roget's Thesaurus outperforms the two leading WordNet-based distance measures. In addition, *ROUGE-W*, a weighted longest common subsequence algorithm that to our knowledge has not previously been used for similarity measurements shows to be a fairly reliable measure for all data sets, in contrast to longest common subsequence, which is among the lowest performers.

We feel that the insight we gained well justified the expense of our approach.

Acknowledgments

We are grateful to Michelle Khalife and Jona Schuman for their comments and feedback on this work. This work was financially supported by the Natural Sciences and Engineering Research Council of Canada (NSERC).

References

Adam Kilgarriff, Pavel Rychly, Pavel Smrz, and David Tugwell. 2004. ITRI-04-08 The Sketch Engine. *Information Technology*.

Alex J. Smola and Bernhard Schölkopf. 2004. A Tutorial on Support Vector Regression. *Statistics and Computing*, 14(3).

Alexander Budanitsky and Graeme Hirst. 2006. Evaluating WordNet-based Measures of Lexical Semantic Relatedness. *Computational Linguistics*, 32(1).

Chin-Yew Lin. 2004a. ROUGE: A Package for Automatic Evaluation of Summaries. In *Text Summarization Branches Out: Proceedings of the ACL-04 Workshop*.

Chin-Yew Lin and Franz Josef Och. 2004b. Automatic Evaluation of Machine Translation Quality Using Longest Common Subsequence and Skip-Bigram Statistics. In *Proceedings of the 42nd Annual Meeting on Association for Computational Linguistics*. Association for Computational Linguistics.

Christiane Fellbaum 2010. WordNet. *Theory and Applications of Ontology: Computer Applications*. Springer.

Daniel Bär, Chris Biemann, Iryna Gurevych, and Torsten Zesch. 2012. UKP: Computing Semantic Textual Similarity by Combining Multiple Content Similarity Measures. In *Proceedings of the 6th International Workshop on Semantic Evaluation (SemEval 2012), in conjunction with the First Joint Conference on Lexical and Computational Semantics*.

Dekang Lin. 1998. An Information-Theoretic Definition of Similarity. In *Proceedings of the 15th International Conference on Machine Learning*, volume 1.

Ehsan Shareghi, Sabine Bergler. 2013. Feature Combination for Sentence Similarity. To appear in *Proceedings of the 26st Conference of the Canadian Society for Computational Studies of Intelligence (Canadian AI'13). Advances in Artificial Intelligence*, Regina, SK, Canada. Springer-Verlag Berlin Heidelberg.

Eneko Agirre, Daniel Cer, Mona Diab, and Aitor Gonzalez-Agirre. 2012. Semeval-2012 Task 6: A Pilot on Semantic Textual Similarity. In *Proceedings of the 6th International Workshop on Semantic Evaluation (SemEval 2012), in conjunction with the First Joint Conference on Lexical and Computational Semantics*.

Evgeniy Gabrilovich and Shaul Markovitch. 2007. Computing Semantic Relatedness Using Wikipedia-based Explicit Semantic Analysis. In *Proceedings of the 20th International Joint Conference on Artificial Intelligence*.

Frane Šaric, Goran Glavaš, Mladen Karan, Jan Šnajder, and Bojana Dalbelo Bašic. 2012. TakeLab: Systems for Measuring Semantic Text Similarity. In *Proceedings of the 6th International Workshop on Semantic Evaluation (SemEval 2012), in conjunction with the First Joint Conference on Lexical and Computational Semantics*.

Ido Dagan, Oren Glickman, and Bernardo Magnini. 2006. The Pascal Recognising Textual Entailment Challenge. *Machine Learning Challenges. Evaluating Predictive Uncertainty, Visual Object Classification, and Recognising Tectual Entailment*.

Jay J. Jiang and David W. Conrath. 1997. Semantic Similarity Based on Corpus Statistics and Lexical Taxonomy. *Proceedings of the 10th International Conference on Research on Computational Linguistics*.

Lloyd Allison and Trevor I. Dix. 1986. A Bit-String Longest-Common-Subsequence Algorithm. *Information Processing Letters*, 23(5).

Mario Jarmasz and Stan Szpakowicz. 2003. Rogets Thesaurus and Semantic Similarity. In *Proceedings of the Conference on Recent Advances in Natural Language Processing*.

Mark Hall, Eibe Frank, Geoffrey Holmes, Bernhard Pfahringer, Peter Reutemann, and Ian H. Witten. 2009. The WEKA Data Mining Software: an Update. *ACM SIGKDD Explorations Newsletter*, 11(1).

Matthew A. Jaro. 1989. Advances in Record-Linkage Methodology as Applied to Matching the 1985 Census of Tampa, Florida. *Journal of the American Statistical Association*.

Philip Koehn, Hieu Hoang, Alexandra Birch, Chris Callison-Burch, Marcelo Federico, Nicola Bertoldi, Brooke Cowan, Wade Shen, Christine Moran, Richard Zens, Chris Dyer, Ondřej Bojar. 2007. Moses: Open Source Toolkit for Statistical Machine Translation. In *Proceedings of the 45th Annual Meeting of the ACL on Interactive Poster and Demonstration Sessions*. Association for Computational Linguistics.

Rada Mihalcea, Courtney Corley, and Carlo Strapparava. 2006. Corpus-based and Knowledge-based Measures of Text Semantic Similarity. In *Proceedings of the National Conference on Artificial Intelligence*.

Ted Pedersen, Siddharth Patwardhan and Jason Michelizzi. 2004. WordNet:: Similarity: Measuring the Relatedness of Concepts. In *Demonstration Papers at North American Chapter of the Association for Computational Linguistics: Human Language Technologies*. Association for Computational Linguistics.

William B. Dolan, Chris Quirk, and Chris Brockett. 2004. Unsupervised Construction of Large Paraphrase Corpora: Exploiting Massively Parallel News Sources. In *Proceedings of the 20th International Conference on Computational Linguistics*. Association for Computational Linguistics.

UniMelb_NLP-CORE: Integrating predictions from multiple domains and feature sets for estimating semantic textual similarity

Spandana Gella,[♣] **Bahar Salehi,**[♠♣] **Marco Lui,**[♠♣]
Karl Grieser,[♣] **Paul Cook,**[♣] and **Timothy Baldwin,**[♠♣]
♠ NICTA Victoria Research Laboratory
♣ Department of Computing and Information Systems, The University of Melbourne
sgella@student.unimelb.edu.au, bsalehi@student.unimelb.edu.au
mhlui@unimelb.edu.au, kgrieser@student.unimelb.edu.au
paulcook@unimelb.edu.au, tb@ldwin.net

Abstract

In this paper we present our systems for calculating the degree of semantic similarity between two texts that we submitted to the Semantic Textual Similarity task at SemEval-2013. Our systems predict similarity using a regression over features based on the following sources of information: string similarity, topic distributions of the texts based on latent Dirichlet allocation, and similarity between the documents returned by an information retrieval engine when the target texts are used as queries. We also explore methods for integrating predictions using different training datasets and feature sets. Our best system was ranked 17th out of 89 participating systems. In our post-task analysis, we identify simple changes to our system that further improve our results.

1 Introduction

Semantic Textual Similarity (STS) measures the degree of semantic similarity or equivalence between a pair of short texts. STS is related to many natural language processing applications such as text summarisation (Aliguliyev, 2009), machine translation, word sense disambiguation, and question answering (De Boni and Manandhar, 2003; Jeon et al., 2005).

Two short texts are considered similar if they both convey similar messages. Often it is the case that similar texts will have a high degree of lexical overlap, although this isn't always so. For example, *SC dismissed government's review plea in Vodafone tax case* and *SC dismisses govt's review petition on Vodafone tax verdict* are semantically similar. These texts have matches in terms of exact words (*SC*, *Vodafone*, *tax*), morphologically-related words (*dismissed* and *dismisses*), and abbreviations (*government's* and *govt's*). However, the usages (senses) of *plea* and *petition*, and *case* and *verdict* are also similar.

One straightforward way of estimating semantic similarity of two texts is by using approaches based on the similarity of the surface forms of the words they contain. However, such methods are not capable of capturing similarity or relatedness at the lexical level, and moreover, they do not exploit the context in which individual words are used in a target text. Nevertheless, a variety of knowledge sources — including part-of-speech, collocations, syntax, and domain — can be used to identify the usage or sense of words in context (McRoy, 1992; Agirre and Martinez, 2001; Agirre and Stevenson, 2006) to address these issues.

Despite their limitations, string similarity measures have been widely used in previous semantic similarity tasks (Agirre et al., 2012; Islam and Inkpen, 2008). Latent variable models have also been used to estimate the semantic similarity between words, word usages, and texts (Steyvers and Griffiths, 2007; Lui et al., 2012; Guo and Diab, 2012; Dinu and Lapata, 2010).

In this paper, we consider three different ways of measuring semantic similarity based on word and word usage similarity:

1. **String-based similarity** to measure surface-level lexical similarity, taking into account morphology and abbreviations (e.g., *dismisses* and *dismissed*, and *government's* and *govt's*);

*Second Joint Conference on Lexical and Computational Semantics (*SEM), Volume 1: Proceedings of the Main Conference and the Shared Task*, pages 207–215, Atlanta, Georgia, June 13-14, 2013.

2. **Latent variable models** of similarity to capture words that have different surface forms, but that have similar meanings or that can be used in similar contexts (e.g., *petition* and *plea*, *verdict* and *case*); and

3. **Topical/domain similarity** of the texts with respect to the similarity of documents in an external corpus (based on information-retrieval methods) that are relevant to the target texts.

We develop features based on all three of these knowledge sources to capture semantic similarity from a variety of perspectives. We build a regression model, trained on STS training data which has semantic similarity scores for pairs of texts, to learn weights for the features and rate the similarity of test instances. Our approach to the task is to explore the utility of novel features or features that have not performed well in previous research, rather than combine these features with the myriad of features that have been proposed by others for the task.

2 Text Similarity Measures

In this section we describe the various features used in our system.

2.1 String Similarity Measures (SS)

Our first set of features contains various string similarity measures (SS), which compare the target texts in terms of the words they contain and the order of the words (Islam and Inkpen, 2008). In the SemEval 2012 STS task (Agirre et al., 2012) such features were used by several participants (Biggins et al., 2012; Bär et al., 2012; Heilman and Madnani, 2012), including the first-ranked team (Bär et al., 2012) who considered string similarity measures alongside a wide range of other features.

For our string similarity features, the texts were lemmatized using the implementation of Lancaster Stemming in NLTK 2.0 (Bird, 2006), and all punctuation was removed. Limited stopword removal was carried out by eliminating the words *a*, *and*, and *the*. The output of each string similarity measure is normalized to the range of $[0, 1]$, where 0 indicates that the texts are completely different, while 1 means they are identical. The normalization method for each feature is described in Salehi and Cook (to appear), wherein the authors applied string similarity measures successfully to the task of predicting the compositionality of multiword expressions.

Identical Unigrams (IU): This feature measures the number of words shared between the two texts, irrespective of word order.

Longest Common Substring (LCS): This measures the longest sequence of words shared between the two texts. For example, the longest common substring between the following sentences is bolded:

> A woman and man **are dancing in the** rain.
> A couple **are dancing in the** street.

Levenshtein (LEV1): Levenshtein distance (also known as edit distance) calculates the number of basic word-level edit operations (insertion, deletion and substitution) to transform one text into the other:

Levenshtein with substitution penalty (LEV2): This feature is a variant of LEV1 in which substitution is considered as two edit operations: an insertion and a deletion (Baldwin, 2009).

Smith Waterman (SW): This method is designed to locally align two sequences of amino acids (Smith and Waterman, 1981). The algorithm looks for the longest similar regions by maximizing the number of matches and minimizing the number of insertion/deletion/substitution operations necessary to align the two sequences. In other words, it finds the longest common sequence while tolerating a small number of differences. We call this sequence, the "aligned sequence". It has length equal to or greater than the longest common sequence.

Not Aligned Words (NAW): As mentioned above, SW looks for similar regions in the given texts. Our last string similarity feature shows the number of identical words not aligned by the SW algorithm. We used this feature to examine how similar the unaligned words are.

These six features (IU, LCS, LEV1, LEV2, SW, and NAW) form our string similarity (SS) features. LEV2, SW, and NAW have not been previously considered for STS.

2.2 Topic Modelling Similarity Measures (TM)

The topic modelling features (TM) are based on Latent Dirichlet Allocation (LDA), a generative probabilistic model in which each document is modeled as a distribution over a finite set of topics, and each topic is represented as a distribution over words (Blei et al., 2003). We build a topic model on a background corpus, and then for each target text we create a topic vector based on the topic allocations of its content words, based on the method developed by Lui et al. (2012) for predicting word usage similarity.

The choice of the number of topics, T, can have a big impact on the performance of this method. Choosing a small T might give overly-broad topics, while a large T might lead to uninterpretable topics (Steyvers and Griffiths, 2007). Moreover smaller numbers of topics have been shown to perform poorly on both sentence similarity (Guo and Diab, 2012) and word usage similarity tasks (Lui et al., 2012). We therefore build topic models for 33 values of T in the range $2, 3, 5, 8, 10, 50, 80, 100, 150, 200, ...1350$.

The background corpus used for generating the topic models is similar to the COL-WTMF system (Guo and Diab, 2012) from the STS-2012 task, which outperformed LDA. In particular, we use sense definitions from WordNet, Wiktionary and all sentences from the Brown corpus. Similarity between two texts is measured on the basis of the similarity between their topic distributions. We consider three vector-based similarity measures here: Cosine similarity, Jensen-Shannon divergence and KL divergence. Thus for each target text pair we extract 99 features corresponding to the 3 similarity measures for each of the 33 T settings. These features are used as the TM feature set in the systems described below.

2.3 IR Similarity Measures (IR)

The information retrieval–based features (IR) were based on a dump of English Wikipedia from November 2009. The entire dump was stripped of markup and tokenised using the OpenNLP tokeniser. The tokenised documents were then parsed into TREC format, with each article forming an individual document. These documents were indexed using the Indri IR engine[1] with stopword removal. Each of the two target texts was issued as a full text query (without any phrases) to Indri, and the first 1000 documents for each text were returned, based on Okapi term weighting (Robertson and Walker, 1994). These resultant document lists were then converted into features using a number of set- and rank-based measures: Dice's coefficient, Jaccard index, average overlap, and rank-biased overlap (the latter two are described in Webber et al. (2010)). The first two are based on simple set overlap and ignore the ranks; average overlap takes into account the rank, but equally weights high- and low-ranking documents; and rank-biased overlap weights higher-ranked items higher.

In addition to comparisons of the document rankings for a given target text pair, we also considered a method that compared the top-ranking documents themselves. To compare two texts, we obtain the top-100 documents using each text as a query as above. We then calculate the similarity between these two sets of resultant documents using the χ^2-based corpus similarity measure of Kilgarriff (2001). In this method the χ^2 statistic is calculated for the 500 most frequent words in the union of the two sets of documents (corpora), and is interpreted as the similarity between the sets of documents.

These 5 IR features (4 rank-based, and 1 document-based) are novel in the context of STS, and are used in the compound systems described below.

3 Compound systems

3.1 Ridge regression

Each of our features represents a (potentially noisy) measurement of the semantic textual similarity between two texts. However, the scale of our features varies, e.g., $[0, 1]$ for the string similarity features vs. unbounded for KL divergence (one of the topic modelling features). To learn the mapping between these features and the graded $[0, 5]$ scale of the shared task, we made use of a statistical technique known as *ridge regression*, as implemented in `scikit-learn`.[2] Ridge regression is a form of linear regression where the loss function is the ordi-

[1] http://www.lemurproject.org/indri/

[2] http://scikit-learn.org

nary least squares, but with an additional L2 regularization term. In our empirical evaluation, we found that ridge regression outperformed linear regression on our feature set. For brevity, we only present results from ridge regression.

3.2 Domain Adaptation

Domain adaptation (Daumé and Marcu, 2006) is the general term applied to techniques for using labelled data from a related distribution to label data from a target distribution. For the 2013 Shared Task, no training data was provided for the target datasets, making domain adaptation an important consideration. In this work, we assume that each dataset represents a different domain, and on this basis develop approaches that are sensitive to inter-domain differences.

We tested two simple approaches to including domain information in our trained model. The first approach, which we will refer to as *flagging*, simply involves appending a boolean vector to each training instance to indicate which training dataset it came from. The vector has length D, equal to the number of training datasets (3 for this task, because we train on the STS 2012 training data). All the values of the vector are 0, except for a single 1 according to the dataset that the training instance is drawn from. For test data, the entire vector consists of 0s.

The second approach we considered is based on metalearning, and we will refer to it as *domain stacking*. In domain stacking, we train a regressor for each domain (the level 0 regressors (Wolpert, 1992)). Each of these regressors is then applied to a test instance to produce a predicted value (the level 0 prediction). These predictions are then combined using a second regressor (the level 1 regressor), to produce a final prediction for each instance (the level 1 prediction). This approach is closely related to *feature stacking* (Lui, 2012) and *stacked generalization* (Wolpert, 1992). A general principle of metalearning is to combine multiple weaker ("less accurate") predictors — termed level 0 predictors — to produce a stronger ("more accurate") predictor — the level 1 predictor. In stacked generalization, the level 0 predictors are different learning algorithms. In feature stacking, they are the same algorithm trained on different subsets of features, in this work corresponding to different methods for estimating STS (Section 2). In domain stacking, the level 0 predictions are obtained from subsets of the training data, where each subset corresponds to all the instances from a single dataset (e.g. MSRpar or SMTeuroparl). In terms of subsampling the training data, this technique is related to *bagging* (Breiman, 1996). However, rather than generating new training sets by uniform sampling across the whole pool of training data, we treat each domain in the training dataset as a unique sample. Finally, we also experiment with *feature-domain stacking*, in which the level 0 predictions are obtained from the cross product of subsets of the training data (as per domain stacking) and subsets of the feature set (as per feature stacking). We report results for all 3 variants in Section 5.

This framework of feature-domain stacking can be applied with any regression or classification algorithm (indeed, the level 0 and level 1 predictors could be trained using different algorithms). In this work, all our regressors are trained using ridge regression (Section 3.1).

4 Submitted Runs

In this section we describe the three official runs we submitted to the shared task.

4.1 Run1 — Bahar

For this run we used just the SS feature set, augmented with flagging for domain adaptation. Ridge regression was used to train a regressor across the three training datasets (MSRvid, MSRpar, SMTeuroparl). Each instance was then labelled using the output of the regressor, and the output range was linearly re-scaled to $[0, 5]$ as it occasionally produced values outside of this range. Although this approach approximates STS using only lexical textual similarity, it was our best-performing system on the training data (Table 1). Furthermore the SS features are appealing because of their simplicity and because they do not make use of any external resources.

4.2 Run2 — Concat

In this run, we concatenated the feature vectors from all three of our feature sets (SS, TM and IR), and again trained a regressor on the union of the MSRvid, MSRpar and SMTeuroparl training datasets. As in Run1, the output of the regression

FSet	FL	FS	DS	MSRpar	MSRvid	SMTeuroparl	Ave
SS				0.522	0.537	0.526	0.528
(*) SS	✓			**0.552**	0.533	**0.562**	**0.549**
TM				0.270	0.479	0.425	0.391
TM	✓			0.250	0.580	0.427	0.419
IR				0.264	**0.759**	0.407	0.477
IR	✓			0.291	0.754	0.400	0.482
(+) ALL				0.401	0.543	0.513	0.485
ALL	✓			0.377	0.595	0.516	0.496
ALL		✓		0.385	0.587	0.520	0.497
ALL			✓	0.452	0.637	0.472	0.521
ALL	✓	✓		0.429	0.619	0.526	0.524
ALL		✓	✓	0.429	0.627	0.526	0.527
(−) ALL	✓	✓	✓	0.441	0.645	0.527	0.538

Table 1: Pearson's ρ for each feature set (FSet), as well as combinations of feature sets and adaptation strategies, on each **training** dataset, and the micro-average over all training datasets. (*), (+), and (−) denote Run1, Run2, and Run3, respectively, our submissions to the shared task; FL=Flagging, FS=Feature stacking, DS=Domain stacking.

FSet	FL	FS	DS	OnWN	FNWN	Headlines	SMT	Ave
SS				0.340	0.366	0.688	0.325	0.453
(*) SS	✓			0.349	**0.381**	0.711	0.350	0.473
TM				0.648	0.358	0.516	0.209	0.433
TM	✓			0.701	0.368	0.614	0.287	0.506
IR				0.561	-0.006	0.610	0.228	0.419
IR	✓			0.596	0.002	0.621	0.256	0.441
(+) ALL				0.679	0.337	0.709	0.323	0.542
ALL	✓			**0.704**	0.365	0.718	0.344	**0.560**
ALL		✓		0.673	0.298	0.714	0.324	0.539
ALL			✓	0.618	0.264	0.717	**0.357**	0.534
ALL	✓	✓		0.658	0.309	**0.721**	0.330	0.540
ALL		✓	✓	0.557	0.142	0.694	0.280	0.475
(−) ALL	✓	✓	✓	0.614	0.186	0.706	0314	0.509

Table 2: Pearson's ρ for each feature set (FSet), as well as combinations of feature sets and adaptation strategies, on each **test** dataset, and the micro-average over all test datasets. (*), (+), and (−) denote Run1, Run2, and Run3, respectively, our submissions to the shared task; FL=Flagging, FS=Feature stacking, DS=Domain stacking.

was also linearly re-scaled to the $[0, 5]$ range. Unlike the previous run, the flagging approach to domain adaptation was not used. This approach reflects a simple application of machine learning to integrating data from multiple feature sets and training datasets, and provides a useful point of comparison against more sophisticated approaches (i.e., Run3).

4.3 Run3 — Stacking

In this run, we focused on an alternative method to integrating information from multiple feature sets and training datasets, namely feature-domain stacking, as discussed in Section 3.2. In this approach, we train nine regressors using ridge regression on each combination of the three training datasets and three feature sets. Thus, the level 1 representation for each instance is a vector of nine predictions. For the training data, when computing the level 1 features for the same training dataset from which a given instance is drawn, 10-fold cross-validation is used. Ridge regression is again used to combine the level 1 representations and produce the final prediction for each instance. In addition to this, we also simultaneously apply the flagging approach to domain adaptation. This approach incorporates all of our domain adaptation efforts, and in initial experiments on the training data (Table 1) it was our second-best system.

5 Results

For the STS 2013 task, the organisers advised participants to make use of the STS 2012 data; we took this to mean only the *training* data. In our post-task analysis, we realised that the entire 2012 dataset, including the testing data, could be used. All our official runs were trained only on the training data for the 2012 task (made up of MSRpar, MSRvid and SMTeuroparl). We first discuss preliminary findings training and testing on the (STS 2012) training data, and then present results for the (2013) test data. Post-submission, we re-trained our systems including the 2012 test data.

5.1 Experiments on Training Data

We evaluated our models based on a leave-one-out cross-validation across the 3 training datasets. Thus, for each of the training datasets, we trained a separate model using features from the other two. We considered approaches based on each individual feature set, with and without flagging. We further considered combinations of feature sets using feature concatenation, as well as feature and domain stacking, again with and without flagging.[3] Results are

[3] We did not consider domain stacking with flagging.

FSet	FL	FS	DS	OnWN (δ)	FNWN (δ)	Headlines (δ)	SMT (δ)	Ave (δ)
SS				0.3566 (+.0157)	0.3741 (+.0071)	0.6994 (+.0111)	0.3386 (+.0131)	0.4663 (+.0133)
(*) SS	✓			0.3532 (+.0042)	0.3809 (−.0004)	0.7122 (+.0003)	0.3417 (−.0090)	0.4714 (−.0016)
TM				0.6748 (+.0265)	0.3939 (+.0349)	0.5930 (+.0770)	0.2563 (+.0472)	0.4844 (+.0514)
TM	✓			0.6269 (−.0743)	0.3519 (−.0162)	0.5999 (−.0142)	0.2653 (−.0223)	0.4743 (−.0317)
IR				0.6632 (+.1015)	0.1026 (+.1093)	0.6383 (−.0281)	0.2987 (+.0701)	0.4863 (+.0673)
IR	✓			0.6720 (+.0755)	0.0861 (+.0841)	0.6316 (+.0097)	0.2811 (+.0244)	0.4790 (+.0680)
(+) ALL				**0.6976** (+.0006)	0.4350 (+.0976)	0.7071 (−.0014)	0.3329 (+.0099)	0.5571 (+.0151)
ALL	✓			0.6667 (−.0373)	0.4138 (+.0490)	0.7210 (+.0029)	0.3335 (−.0105)	0.5524 (−.0076)
ALL		✓		0.6889 (+.0149)	0.4620 (+.1636)	0.7309 (+.0167)	0.3538 (+.0295)	**0.5721** (+.0331)
ALL			✓	0.6765 (−.0185)	**0.4675** (+.1578)	**0.7337** (+.0126)	0.3552 (+.0252)	0.5709 (+.0369)
ALL	✓	✓		0.6369 (+.0208)	0.3615 (+.0970)	0.7233 (+.0060)	**0.3736** (+.0157)	0.5554 (+.0154)
ALL		✓	✓	0.6736 (+**.1165**)	0.4250 (+**.2821**)	0.7237 (+**0.0297**)	0.3404 (+**0.0603**)	0.5583(+**.0833**)
(−) ALL	✓	✓	✓	0.6772 (+.0632)	0.3992 (+.2127)	0.7315 (+.0251)	0.3300 (+0.0186)	0.5572 (+.0482)

Table 3: Pearson's ρ for each feature set (FSet), as well as combinations of feature sets and adaptation strategies, on each **test** dataset, and the micro-average over all test datasets, using features from all 2012 data (test + train). (*), (+), and (−) denote Run1, Run2, and Run3, respectively, our submissions to the shared task; FL=Flagging, FS=Feature stacking, DS=Domain stacking. δ denotes the difference in system performance after adding the additional training data.

reported in Table 1.

The best results on the training data were achieved using only our SS feature set with flagging (Run1), with an average Pearson's ρ of 0.549. This feature set also gave the best performance on MSRpar and SMTeuroparl, although the IR feature set was substantially better on MSRvid. On the training datasets, our approaches that combine feature sets did not give an improvement over the best individual feature set on any dataset, or overall.

5.2 Test Set Results

STS 2013 included four different test sets. Table 2 presents the Pearson's ρ for the same methods as Section 5.1 — including our submitted runs — on the test data. Run1 drops in performance on the test set as compared to the training set, where the other two runs are more consistent, suggesting that lexical similarity does not generalise well cross-domain. Table 4 shows that all of our systems performed above the baseline on each dataset, except Run3 on FNWN. Table 4 also shows that Run2 consistently performed well on all the datasets when compared to the median of all the systems submitted to the task (Agirre et al., to appear).

Run2, which was based on the concatenation of all the feature sets, performed well compared to the stacking-based approaches on the test set, whereas the stacking approaches all outperformed Run2 on the training datasets. This is likely due to the SS features being more effective for STS prediction in the training datasets as compared to the test datasets. Based on the training datasets, the stacking approaches placed greater weight on the predictions from the SS feature set. This hypothesis is supported by the result on Headlines, where the SS feature set does relatively well, and thus the stacking approaches tend to outperform the simple concatenation-based method. Finally, an extension of Run2 with flagging (not submitted to the shared task) was the best of our methods on the test data.

5.3 Error Analysis

To better understand the behaviour of our systems, we examined test instances and made the following observations. Systems based entirely on the TM features and domain adaptation consistently performed well on sentence pairs for which all of our other systems performed poorly. One example is the following OnWN pair, which corresponds to definitions of *newspaper*: *an enterprise or company that publishes newsprint* and *a business firm that publishes newspapers*. Because these texts do not share many common words, the SS features cannot capture their semantic similarity.

Stacking based approaches performed well on text pairs which are complex to comprehend, e.g., *Two German tourists, two pilots killed in Kenya air crash* and *Senator Reid involved in Las Vegas car crash*, where the individual methods tend to score lower

System	Headlines	OnWN	FNWN	SMT	Ave
(+) Run1	.711 (15)	.349 (71)	.381 (23)	.351 (18)	.473 (49)
(+) Run2	.709 (17)	.679 (18)	.337 (33)	.323 (43)	.542 (17)
(+) Run3	.706 (18)	.614 (28)	.187 (71)	.314 (47)	.509 (29)
Best	.718 (14)	.704 (15)	.365 (28)	.344 (24)	.560 (7)
(∗) Run1	.712 (14)	.353 (70)	.381 (23)	.341 (25)	.471 (54)
(∗) Run2	.707 (18)	.697 (14)	.435 (9)	.332 (35)	.557 (9)
(∗) Run3	.731 (11)	.677 (19)	.399 (17)	.330 (38)	.557 (8)
(∗) Best	.730 (11)	.688 (17)	.462 (7)	.353 (18)	.572 (4)
Baseline	.540 (67)	.283 (81)	.215 (67)	.286 (65)	.364 (73)
Median	.640 (45)	.528 (45)	.327 (45)	.318 (45)	.480 (45)
Best-Score	.783 (1)	.843 (1)	.581 (1)	.403 (1)	.618 (1)

Table 4: Pearson's ρ (and projected ranking) of runs. The upper 4 runs are trained only on STS 2012 training data. (+) denotes runs that were submitted for evaluation. (∗) denotes systems trained on STS 2012 training and test data. For comparison, we include "Best", the highest-scoring parametrization of our system from our post-task analysis (Table 3). We also include the organiser's baseline, as well as the median and best systems for each dataset across all competitors.

than the human rating, but stacking was able to predict a higher score (presumably based on the fact that no method predicted the text pair to be strongly *dis*similar; rather, all methods predicted there to be somewhat low similarity).

In some cases, the texts are on a similar topic, but semantically different, e.g., *Nigeria mourns over 193 people killed in plane crash* and *Nigeria opens probe into deadly air crash.* In such cases, systems based on SS features and stacking perform well. Systems based on TM and IR features, on the other hand, tend to predict overly-high scores because the texts relate to similar topics and tend to have similar relevant documents in an external corpus.

5.4 Results with the Full Training dataset

We re-trained all the above systems by extending the training data to include the 2012 test data. Scores on the 2013 test datasets and the change in Pearson's ρ after adding the extra training data (denoted δ) are presented in Table 3.

In general, the addition of the 2012 test data to the training dataset improves the performance of the system, though this is often not the case for the flagging approach to domain adaptation, which in some instances drops in performance after adding the additional training data. The biggest improvements were seen for feature-domain stacking, particularly on FNWN. This suggests that feature-domain stacking is more sensitive to the similarity between training data and test data than flagging, but also that it is better able to cope with variety in training domains than flagging. Given that the pool of annotated data for the STS task continues to increase, feature-domain stacking is a promising approach to exploiting the differences between domains to improve overall STS performance.

To facilitate comparison with the published results for the 2013 STS task, we present a condensed summary of our results in Table 4, which shows the absolute score as well as the projected ranking of each of our systems. It also includes the median and baseline results for comparison.

6 Conclusions and Future Work

In this paper we described our approach to the STS SemEval-2013 shared task. While we did not achieve high scores relative to the other submitted systems on any of the datasets or overall, we have identified some novel feature sets which we show to have utility for the STS task. We have also compared our proposed method's performance with a larger training dataset. In future work, we intend to consider alternative ways for combining features learned from different domains and training datasets. Given the strong performance of our string similarity features on particular datasets, we also intend to consider combining string and distributional similarity to capture elements of the texts that are not currently captured by our string similarity features.

Acknowledgments

This work was supported by the European Erasmus Mundus Masters Program in Language and Communication Technologies from the European Commission.

NICTA is funded by the Australian government as represented by Department of Broadband, Communication and Digital Economy, and the Australian Research Council through the ICT Centre of Excellence program.

References

Eneko Agirre and David Martinez. 2001. Knowledge sources for word sense disambiguation. In *Text, Speech and Dialogue*, pages 1–10. Springer.

Eneko Agirre and Mark Stevenson. 2006. Knowledge sources for wsd. In Eneko Agirre and Philip Edmonds, editors, *Word Sense Disambiguation*, volume 33 of *Text, Speech and Language Technology*, pages 217–251. Springer Netherlands.

Eneko Agirre, Daniel Cer, Mona Diab, and Aitor Gonzalez-Agirre. 2012. Semeval-2012 task 6: A pilot on semantic textual similarity. In **SEM 2012: The First Joint Conference on Lexical and Computational Semantics – Volume 1: Proceedings of the main conference and the shared task, and Volume 2: Proceedings of the Sixth International Workshop on Semantic Evaluation (SemEval 2012)*, pages 385–393, Montréal, Canada, 7-8 June. Association for Computational Linguistics.

Eneko Agirre, Daniel Cer, Mona Diab, Aitor Gonzalez-Agirre, and Weiwei Guo. to appear. *sem 2013 shared task: Semantic textual similarity, including a pilot on typed-similarity. In **SEM 2013: The Second Joint Conference on Lexical and Computational Semantics*, Atlana, USA. Association for Computational Linguistics.

Ramiz M Aliguliyev. 2009. A new sentence similarity measure and sentence based extractive technique for automatic text summarization. *Expert Systems with Applications*, 36(4):7764–7772.

Timothy Baldwin. 2009. The hare and the tortoise: Speed and reliability in translation retrieval. *Machine Translation*, 23(4):195–240.

Daniel Bär, Chris Biemann, Iryna Gurevych, and Torsten Zesch. 2012. Ukp: Computing semantic textual similarity by combining multiple content similarity measures. In **SEM 2012: The First Joint Conference on Lexical and Computational Semantics – Volume 1: Proceedings of the main conference and the shared task, and Volume 2: Proceedings of the Sixth International Workshop on Semantic Evaluation (SemEval 2012)*, pages 435–440, Montréal, Canada, 7-8 June. Association for Computational Linguistics.

Sam Biggins, Shaabi Mohammed, Sam Oakley, Luke Stringer, Mark Stevenson, and Judita Preiss. 2012. University_of_sheffield: Two approaches to semantic text similarity. In **SEM 2012: The First Joint Conference on Lexical and Computational Semantics – Volume 1: Proceedings of the main conference and the shared task, and Volume 2: Proceedings of the Sixth International Workshop on Semantic Evaluation (SemEval 2012)*, pages 655–661, Montréal, Canada, 7-8 June. Association for Computational Linguistics.

Steven Bird. 2006. NLTK: The Natural Language Toolkit. In *Proceedings of the COLING/ACL 2006 Interactive Presentation Sessions*, pages 69–72, Sydney, Australia, July. Association for Computational Linguistics.

David M. Blei, Andrew Y. Ng, and Michael I. Jordan. 2003. Latent Dirichlet allocation. *Journal of Machine Learning Research*, 3:993–1022.

Leo Breiman. 1996. Bagging predictors. *Machine learning*, 24(2):123–140.

Hal Daumé, III and Daniel Marcu. 2006. Domain adaptation for statistical classifiers. *Journal of Artificial Intelligence Research*, 26(1):101–126, May.

Marco De Boni and Suresh Manandhar. 2003. The use of sentence similarity as a semantic relevance metric for question answering. In *Proceedings of the AAAI Symposium on New Directions in Question Answering*, Stanford, USA.

Georgiana Dinu and Mirella Lapata. 2010. Measuring distributional similarity in context. In *Proceedings of the 2010 Conference on Empirical Methods in Natural Language Processing*, pages 1162–1172, Cambridge, MA, October. Association for Computational Linguistics.

Weiwei Guo and Mona Diab. 2012. Weiwei: A simple unsupervised latent semantics based approach for sentence similarity. In **SEM 2012: The First Joint Conference on Lexical and Computational Semantics – Volume 1: Proceedings of the main conference and the shared task, and Volume 2: Proceedings of the Sixth International Workshop on Semantic Evaluation (SemEval 2012)*, pages 586–590, Montréal, Canada, 7-8 June. Association for Computational Linguistics.

Michael Heilman and Nitin Madnani. 2012. Ets: Discriminative edit models for paraphrase scoring. In **SEM 2012: The First Joint Conference on Lexical and Computational Semantics – Volume 1: Proceedings of the main conference and the shared task, and Volume 2: Proceedings of the Sixth International Workshop on Semantic Evaluation (SemEval 2012)*, pages 529–535, Montréal, Canada, 7-8 June. Association for Computational Linguistics.

Aminul Islam and Diana Inkpen. 2008. Semantic text similarity using corpus-based word similarity and string similarity. *ACM Transactions on Knowledge Discovery from Data (TKDD)*, 2(2):10.

Jiwoon Jeon, W. Bruce Croft, and Joon Ho Lee. 2005. Finding similar questions in large question and answer archives. In *Proceedings of the 14th ACM international conference on Information and knowledge management*, CIKM '05, pages 84–90, New York, NY, USA. ACM.

Adam Kilgarriff. 2001. Comparing corpora. *International Journal of Corpus Linguistics*, 6(1):97–133.

Marco Lui, Timothy Baldwin, and Diana McCarthy. 2012. Unsupervised estimation of word usage similarity. In *Proceedings of the Australasian Language Technology Association Workshop 2012*, pages 33–41, Dunedin, New Zealand, December.

Marco Lui. 2012. Feature stacking for sentence classification in evidence-based medicine. In *Proceedings of the Australasian Language Technology Association Workshop 2012*, pages 134–138, Dunedin, New Zealand, December.

Susan W McRoy. 1992. Using multiple knowledge sources for word sense discrimination. *Computational Linguistics*, 18(1):1–30.

Stephen E Robertson and Steve Walker. 1994. Some simple effective approximations to the 2-poisson model for probabilistic weighted retrieval. In *Proceedings of the 17th annual international ACM SIGIR conference on Research and development in information retrieval*, SIGIR '94, pages 232–241, Dublin, Ireland.

Bahar Salehi and Paul Cook. to appear. Predicting the compositionality of multiword expressions using translations in multiple languages. In **SEM 2013: The Second Joint Conference on Lexical and Computational Semantics*, Atlana, USA. Association for Computational Linguistics.

TF Smith and MS Waterman. 1981. Identification of common molecular subsequences. *Molecular Biology*, 147:195–197.

Mark Steyvers and Tom Griffiths. 2007. Probabilistic topic models. *Handbook of latent semantic analysis*, 427(7):424–440.

William Webber, Alistair Moffat, and Justin Zobel. 2010. A similarity measure for indefinite rankings. *ACM Transactions on Information Systems (TOIS)*, 28(4):20.

David H. Wolpert. 1992. Stacked generalization. *Neural Networks*, 5:241–259.

CFILT-CORE: Semantic Textual Similarity using Universal Networking Language

Avishek Dan
IIT Bombay
Mumbai, India
avishekdan@cse.iitb.ac.in

Pushpak Bhattacharyya
IIT Bombay
Mumbai, India
pb@cse.iitb.ac.in

Abstract

This paper describes the system that was submitted in the *SEM 2013 Semantic Textual Similarity shared task. The task aims to find the similarity score between a pair of sentences. We describe a Universal Networking Language (UNL) based semantic extraction system for measuring the semantic similarity. Our approach combines syntactic and word level similarity measures along with the UNL based semantic similarity measures for finding similarity scores between sentences.

1 Introduction

Semantic Textual Similarity is the task of finding the degree of semantic equivalence between a pair of sentences. The core Semantic Textual Similarity shared task of *SEM 2013 (Agirre et al., 2013) is to generate a score in the range 0-5 for a pair of sentences depending on their semantic similarity. Textual similarity finds applications in information retrieval and it is closely related to textual entailment. Universal Networking Language (UNL) (Uchida, 1996) is an ideal mechanism for semantics representation. Our system first converts the sentences into a UNL graph representation and then matches the graphs to generate the semantic relatedness score. Even though the goal is to judge sentences based on their semantic relatedness, our system incorporates some lexical and syntactic similarity measures to make the system robust in the face of data sparsity.

Section 2 give a brief introduction to UNL. Section 3 decribes the English Enconverter developed by us. Section 4 discusses the various similarity measures used for the task. Section 5 mentions the corpus used for training and testing. Section 6 describes the method used to train the system and Section 7 presents the results obtained on the task datasets.

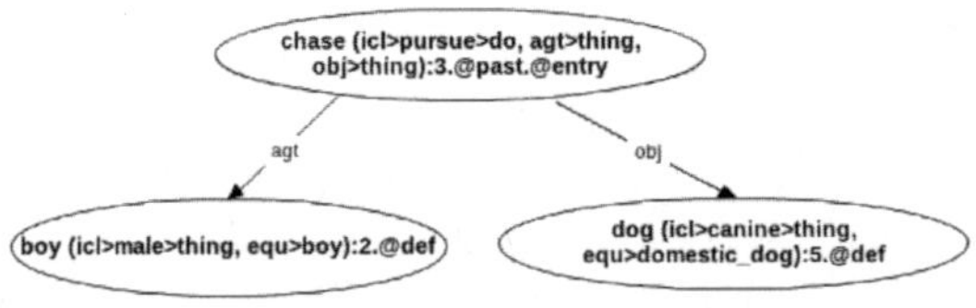

Figure 1: UNL Graph for *'The boy chased the dog'*

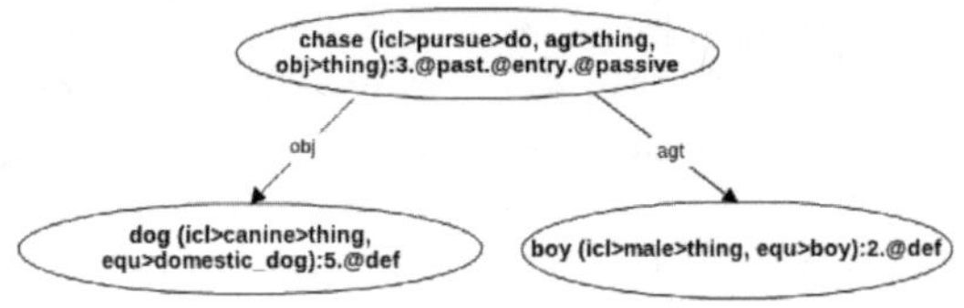

Figure 2: UNL Graph for *'The dog was chased by the boy'*

2 Universal Networking Language

Universal Networking Language (UNL) is an interlingua that represents a sentence in a language independent, unambiguous form. The three main building blocks of UNL are relations, universal words and attributes. UNL representations have a graphical structure with concepts being represented as nodes (universal words) and interactions between concepts being represented by edges (relations) between the nodes. Figure 1 shows the UNL graph correspond-

*Second Joint Conference on Lexical and Computational Semantics (*SEM), Volume 1: Proceedings of the Main Conference and the Shared Task*, pages 216–220, Atlanta, Georgia, June 13-14, 2013.

ing to the sentence *'The boy chased the dog.'* The conversion from a source language to UNL is called enconversion. The reverse process of generating a natural language sentence from UNL is called deconversion. The enconversion process is markedly more difficult than the deconversion process due to the inherent ambiguity and idiosyncracy of natural language.

UNL representation captures the semantics independent of the structure of the language. Figures 1 and 2 show the UNL representation of two structurally different sentences which convey the same meaning. The UNL graph structure remains the same with an additional attribute on the main verb of figure 2 indicating the voice of the sentence.

2.1 Universal Words

Universal words (UWs) are language independent concepts that are linked to various language resources. The UWs used by us are linked to the Princeton WordNet and various other language WordNet synsets. UWs consist of a head word which is the word in its lemma form. For example, in figure 2 the word *chased* is shown in its lemma form as *chased.* The head word is followed by a constraint list which is used to disambiguate it. For example, *chase* icl (includes) *pursue* indicates that chase as a type of pursuing is indicated here. Complex concepts are represented by hypernodes, which are UNL graphs themselves.

2.2 Relations

Relations are two place functions that imdicate the relationship between UWs. Some of the commonly used relations are agent (agt), object (obj), instrument (ins), place (plc). For example, in figure 1 the relation *agt* between *boy* and *chase* indicates that the boy is the doer of the action.

2.3 Attribute

Attributes are one place functions that convey various morphological and pragmatic information. For example, in figure 1 the attribute *past* indicates that the verb is in the past tense.

3 UNL Generation

The conversion from English to UNL involves augmenting the sentence with various factors such as POS tags, NER tags and dependency parse tree relations and paths. The suitable UW generation is achieved through a word sense disambiguation (WSD) system trained on a tourism corpus. The WSD system maps the words to Wordnet 2.1 synset ids. The attribute and relation generation is achieved through a combination of rule-base and classifiers trained on a small corpus. We use a nearest neighbor classifier trained on the EOLSS corpus for generating relations. The attributes are generated by conditional random fields trained on the IGLU corpus. The attribute generation is a word level phenomena, hence attributes for complex UWs cannot be generated by the classifiers. The steps are described in detail.

3.1 Parts of Speech Tagging

The Stanford POS tagger using the WSJ corpus trained PCFG model is used to tag the sentences. Penn Treebank style tags are generated.

3.2 Word Sense Disambiguation

A Supervised Word Sense Disambiguation (WSD) tool trained in Tourism domain is used. The WSD system takes a sequence of tagged words and provides the WordNet synset ids of all nouns, verbs, adjectives and adverbs in the sequence. The accuracy of the system is depends on the length of the input sentence.

3.3 Named Entity Recognition

Stanford Named Entity Recognizer is used to tag the words in the sentence. The tags may be PERSON, LOCATION or ORGANIZATION.

3.4 Parsing and Clause Marking

Stanford Parser is used to parse the sentences. Rules based on the constituency parse are used to identify the clause boundaries. The dependency parse is used for clause type detection. It is also used in the later stages of UNL generation.

The clauses are converted into separate simple sentences for further processing. Independent clauses can be trivially separated since they have complete sentential structure of their own. Dependent clauses are converted into complete sentences using rules based on the type of clause. For example, for the sentence, *That he is a good sprinter, is known to all*, containing a nominal clause, the simple sentences obtained are *he is a good sprinter* and *it is known to all.* Here the dependent clause is replaced by the anaphora *it* to generate the sentence corresponding to the main clause.

3.5 UW Generation

WordNet synset ids obtained from the WSD system and the parts of speech tags are used to generate the UWs. The head word is the English sentence in its lemma form. The constraint list is generated from the WordNet depending on the POS tag.

3.6 Relation Generation

Relations are generated by a combination of rule base and corpus based techniques. Rules are written using parts of speech tags, named entity tags and parse dependency relations. The corpus based techniques are used when insufficient rules exist for relation generation. We use a corpus of about 28000 sentences consisting of UNL graphs for WordNet glosses obtained from the UNDL foundation. This technique tries to find similar examples from the corpus and assigns the observed relation label to the new part of the sentence.

3.7 Attribute Generation

Attributes are a combination of morphological features and pragmatic information. Attribute generation can be considered to be a sequence labeling task on the words. A conditional random field trained on the corpus described in section 5.1 is used for attribute generation.

4 Similarity Measures

We broadly define three categories of similarity measures based on our classification of perception of similarity.

4.1 Word based Similarity Measure

Word based similarity measures consider the sentences as sets-of-words. These measures are motivated by our view that sentences having a lot of common words will appear quite similar to a human user. The sentences are tokenized using Stanford Parser. The Jaccard coefficient (Agirre and Ghosh and Mooney, 2000) compares the similarity or diversity of two sets. It is the ratio of size of intersection to the size of union of two sets. We define a new measure based on the Jaccard similarity coefficient that captures the relatedness between words. The tokens in the set are augmented with related words from Princeton WordNet. (Pedersen and Patwardhan and Michelizzi, 2004) As a preprocessing step, all the tokens are stemmed using WordNet Stemmer. For each possible sense of each stem, its synonyms, antonyms, hypernyms and holonyms are added to the set as applicable. For example, hypernyms are added only when the token appears as a noun or verb in the WordNet. The scoring function used is defined as

$$ExtJSim(S1, S2) = \frac{|ExtS1 \cap ExtS2|}{|S1 \cup S2|}$$

The following example illustrates the intuition behind this similarity measure.

- I am cooking chicken in the house.
- I am grilling chicken in the kitchen.

The measure generates a similarity score of 1 since grilling is a kind of cooking (hypernymy) and kitchen is a part of house (holonymy).

4.2 Syntactic Similarity Measures

Structural similarity as an indicator of textual similarity is captured by the syntactic similarity measures. Parses are obtained for the pair of English sentences using Stanford Parser. The parser is run on the English PCFG model. The dependency graphs of the two sentences are matched to generate the similarity score. A dependency graph consists of a number of dependency relations of the form *dep(word1, word2)* where dep is the type of relation and word1 and word2 are the words between which the relation holds. A complete match of a dependency relation contributes 1 to the score whereas a match of only the words in the relation contributes 0.75 to the score.

$$SynSim(S1, S2) = \frac{|S1 \cap S2|}{|S1 \cup S2|} + 0.75 * \frac{\sum_{a \in S1, b \in S2} [[a.w1 = b.w1 \& a.w2 = b.w2]]}{|S1 \cup S2|}$$

Here S1 and S2 represent the set of dependency relations.

An extended syntactic similarity measure in which exact word matchings are replaced by a match within a set formed by extending the word with related words as described in 4.1 is also used.

4.3 Semantic Similarity Measure

Semantic similarity measures try to capture the similarity in the meaning of the sentences. The UNL graphs generated for the two sentences are compared using the formula given below. In addition, synonymy is no more used for enriching the word bank since UWs by design are mapped to synsets, hence all synonyms are equivalent in a UNL graph.

$$SemSim(S1, S2) = \frac{|S1 \cap S2|}{|S1 \cup S2|} + \sum_{a \in S1, b \in S2} (0.75* \frac{[[a.w1 = b.w1 \& a.w2 = b.w2]]}{|S1 \cup S2|} + 0.75* \frac{[[a.r = b.r \& a.Ew1 = b.Ew1 \& a.Ew2 = b.Ew2]]}{|S1 \cup S2|} + 0.6 * \frac{[[a.Ew1 = b.Ew1 \& a.Ew2 = b.Ew2]]}{|S1 \cup S2|})$$

5 Corpus

The system is trained on the Semantic Textual Similarity 2012 task data. The training dataset consists of 750 pairs from the MSR-Paraphrase corpus, 750 sentences from the MSR-Video corpus and 734 pairs from the SMTeuroparl corpus.

The test set contains headlines mined from several news sources mined by European Media Monitor, sense definitions from WordNet and OntoNotes, sense definitions from WordNet and FrameNet, sentences from DARPA GALE HTER and HyTER, where one sentence is a MT output and the other is a reference translation.

Each corpus contains pairs of sentences with an associated score from 0 to 5. The scores are given based on whether the sentences are on different topics (0), on the same topic but have different content (1), not equivalent but sharing some details (2), roughly equivalent with some inportant information missing or differing (3), mostly important while differing in some unimportant details (4) or completely equivalent (5).

Table 1: Results

Corpus	CFILT	Best Results
Headlines	0.5336	0.7642
OnWN	0.2381	0.7529
FNWN	0.2261	0.5818
SMT	0.2906	0.3804
Mean	0.3531	0.6181

6 Training

The several scores are combined by training a Linear Regression model. We use the inbuilt libaries of Weka to learn the weights. To compute the probability of a test sentence pair, the following formula is used.

$$score(S1, S2) = c + \sum_{i=1}^{5} \lambda_i score_i(S1, S2)$$

7 Results

The test dataset contained many very long sentences which could not be parsed by the Stanford parser used by the UNL system. In addition, the performance of the WSD system led to numerous false negatives. Hence erroneous output were produced in these cases. In these cases, the word based similarity measures somewhat stabilized the scores. Table 1 summarizes the results.

The UNL system is not robust enough to handle large sentences with long distance relationships which leads to poor performance on the OnWN and FNWN datasets.

8 Conclusion and Future Work

The approach discussed in the paper shows promise for the small sentences. The ongoing development of UNL is expected to improve the accuracy of the system. Tuning the scoring parameters on a development set instead of arbitrary values may improve results. A log-linear model instead of the linear combination of scores may capture the relationships between the scores in a better way.

References

Eneko Agirre and Daniel Cer and Mona Diab and Aitor Gonzalez-Agirre and Weiwei Guo. *SEM 2013

Shared Task: Semantic Textual Similarity, including a Pilot on Typed-Similarity. *SEM 2013: The Second Joint Conference on Lexical and Computational Semantics. Association for Computational Linguistics.

Hiroshi Uchida. UNL: Universal Networking LanguageAn Electronic Language for Communication, Understanding, and Collaboration. 1996. UNU/IAS/UNL Center, Tokyo.

Alexander Strehl and Joydeep Ghosh and Raymond Mooney Impact of similarity measures on web-page clustering. 2000. Workshop on Artificial Intelligence for Web Search (AAAI 2000).

Ted Pedersen and Siddharth Patwardhan and Jason Michelizzi WordNet:: Similarity: measuring the relatedness of concepts. 2004. Demonstration Papers at HLT-NAACL 2004. Association for Computational Linguistics.

CPN-CORE: A Text Semantic Similarity System Infused with Opinion Knowledge

Carmen Banea[♭*], **Yoonjung Choi**[‡], **Lingjia Deng**[‡], **Samer Hassan**[§], **Michael Mohler**[◇]
Bishan Yang[√], **Claire Cardie**[√], **Rada Mihalcea**[♭†], **Janyce Wiebe**[‡]

[♭]University of North Texas
Denton, TX

[‡]University of Pittsburgh
Pittsburgh, PA

[§]Google Inc.
Mountain View, CA

[◇]Language Computer Corp.
Richardson, TX

[√]Cornell University
Ithaca, NY

Abstract

This article provides a detailed overview of the CPN text-to-text similarity system that we participated with in the Semantic Textual Similarity task evaluations hosted at *SEM 2013. In addition to more traditional components, such as knowledge-based and corpus-based metrics leveraged in a machine learning framework, we also use opinion analysis features to achieve a stronger semantic representation of textual units. While the evaluation datasets are not designed to test the similarity of opinions, as a component of textual similarity, nonetheless, our system variations ranked number 38, 39 and 45 among the 88 participating systems.

1 Introduction

Measures of text similarity have been used for a long time in applications in natural language processing and related areas. One of the earliest applications of text similarity is perhaps the vector-space model used in information retrieval, where the document most relevant to an input query is determined by ranking documents in a collection in reversed order of their angular distance with the given query (Salton and Lesk, 1971). Text similarity has also been used for relevance feedback and text classification (Rocchio, 1971), word sense disambiguation (Lesk, 1986; Schutze, 1998), and extractive summarization (Salton et al., 1997), in the automatic evaluation of machine translation (Papineni et al., 2002), text summarization (Lin and Hovy, 2003), text coherence (Lapata and Barzilay, 2005) and in plagiarism detection (Nawab et al., 2011).

Earlier work on this task has primarily focused on simple lexical matching methods, which produce a similarity score based on the number of lexical units that occur in both input segments. Improvements to this simple method have considered stemming, stopword removal, part-of-speech tagging, longest subsequence matching, as well as various weighting and normalization factors (Salton and Buckley, 1997). While successful to a certain degree, these lexical similarity methods cannot always identify the *semantic* similarity of texts. For instance, there is an obvious similarity between the text segments "she owns a dog" and "she has an animal," yet these methods will mostly fail to identify it.

More recently, researchers have started to consider the possibility of combining the large number of word-to-word semantic similarity measures (e.g., (Jiang and Conrath, 1997; Leacock and Chodorow, 1998; Lin, 1998; Resnik, 1995)) within a semantic similarity method that works for entire texts. The methods proposed to date in this direction mainly consist of either bipartite-graph matching strategies that aggregate word-to-word similarity into a text similarity score (Mihalcea et al., 2006; Islam and Inkpen, 2009; Hassan and Mihalcea, 2011; Mohler et al., 2011), or data-driven methods that perform component-wise additions of semantic vector representations as obtained with corpus measures such as latent semantic analysis (Landauer et al., 1997), explicit semantic analysis (Gabrilovich and Markovitch, 2007), or salient semantic analysis

* carmen.banea@gmail.com
† rada@cs.unt.edu

*Second Joint Conference on Lexical and Computational Semantics (*SEM), Volume 1: Proceedings of the Main Conference and the Shared Task*, pages 221–228, Atlanta, Georgia, June 13-14, 2013. ©2013 Association for Computational Linguistics

(Hassan and Mihalcea, 2011).

In this paper, we describe the system variations with which we participated in the *SEM 2013 task on semantic textual similarity (Agirre et al., 2013). The system builds upon our earlier work on corpus-based and knowledge-based methods of text semantic similarity (Mihalcea et al., 2006; Hassan and Mihalcea, 2011; Mohler et al., 2011; Banea et al., 2012), while also incorporating opinion aware features. Our observation is that text is not only similar on a semantic level, but also with respect to opinions. Let us consider the following text segments: "she owns a dog" and "I believe she owns a dog." The question then becomes how similar these text fragments truly are. Current systems will consider the two sentences semantically equivalent, yet to a human, they are not. A belief is not equivalent to a fact (and for the case in point, the person may very well have a cat or some other pet), and this should consequently lower the relatedness score. For this reason, we advocate that STS systems should also consider the opinions expressed and their equivalence. While the *SEM STS task is not formulated to evaluate this type of similarity, we complement more traditional corpus and knowledge-based methods with opinion aware features, and use them in a meta-learning framework in an arguably first attempt at incorporating this type of information to infer text-to-text similarity.

2 Related Work

Over the past years, the research community has focused on computing semantic relatedness using methods that are either knowledge-based or corpus-based. Knowledge-based methods derive a measure of relatedness by utilizing lexical resources and ontologies such as WordNet (Miller, 1995) to measure definitional overlap, term distance within a graphical taxonomy, or term depth in the taxonomy as a measure of specificity. We explore several of these measures in depth in Section 3.3.1. On the other side, corpus-based measures such as Latent Semantic Analysis (LSA) (Landauer et al., 1997), Explicit Semantic Analysis (ESA) (Gabrilovich and Markovitch, 2007), Salient Semantic Analysis (SSA) (Hassan and Mihalcea, 2011), Pointwise Mutual Information (PMI) (Church and Hanks, 1990), PMI-IR (Turney, 2001), Second Order PMI (Islam and Inkpen, 2006), Hyperspace Analogues to Language (Burgess et al., 1998) and distributional similarity (Lin, 1998) employ probabilistic approaches to decode the semantics of words. They consist of unsupervised methods that utilize the contextual information and patterns observed in raw text to build semantic profiles of words. Unlike knowledge-based methods, which suffer from limited coverage, corpus-based measures are able to induce a similarity between any given two words, as long as they appear in the very large corpus used as training.

3 Semantic Textual Similarity System

3.1 Task Setup

The STS task consists of labeling one sentence pair at a time, based on the semantic similarity existent between its two component sentences. Human assigned similarity scores range from 0 (no relation) to 5 (semantivally equivalent). The *SEM 2013 STS task did not provide additional labeled data to the training and testing sets released as part of the STS task hosted at SEMEVAL 2012 (Agirre et al., 2012); our system variations were trained on SEMEVAL 2012 data.

The test sets (Agirre et al., 2013) consist of text pairs extracted from headlines (*headlines*, 750 pairs), sense definitions from WordNet and OntoNotes (*OnWN*, 561 pairs), sense definitions from WordNet and FrameNet (*FNWN*, 189 pairs), and data used in the evaluation of machine translation systems (*SMT*, 750 pairs).

3.2 Resources

Various subparts of our framework use several resources that are described in more detail below.

Wikipedia[1] is the most comprehensive encyclopedia to date, and it is an open collaborative effort hosted on-line. Its basic entry is an *article* which in addition to describing an entity or an event also contains hyperlinks to other pages within or outside of Wikipedia. This structure (articles and hyperlinks) is directly exploited by semantic similarity methods such as ESA (Gabrilovich and Markovitch, 2007), or SSA (Hassan and Mihalcea, 2011)[2].

[1] `www.wikipedia.org`

[2] In the experiments reported in this paper, all the corpus-based methods are trained on the English Wikipedia download from October 2008.

WordNet (Miller, 1995) is a manually crafted lexical resource that maintains semantic relationships such as synonymy, antonymy, hypernymy, etc., between basic units of meaning, or *synsets*. These relationships are employed by various knowledge-based methods to derive semantic similarity.

The MPQA corpus (Wiebe and Riloff, 2005) is a newswire data set that was manually annotated at the expression level for opinion-related content. Some of the features derived by our opinion extraction models were based on training on this corpus.

3.3 Features

Our system variations derive the similarity score of a given sentence-pair by integrating information from knowledge, corpus, and opinion-based sources[3].

3.3.1 Knowledge-Based Features

Following prior work from our group (Mihalcea et al., 2006; Mohler and Mihalcea, 2009), we employ several WordNet-based similarity metrics for the task of sentence-level similarity. Briefly, for each open-class word in one of the input texts, we compute the maximum semantic similarity[4] that can be obtained by pairing it with any open-class word in the other input text. All the word-to-word similarity scores obtained in this way are summed and normalized to the length of the two input texts. We provide below a short description for each of the similarity metrics employed by this system.

The **shortest path** ($Path$) similarity is equal to:

$$Sim_{path} = \frac{1}{length} \quad (1)$$

where $length$ is the length of the shortest path between two concepts using node-counting.

The **Leacock & Chodorow** (Leacock and Chodorow, 1998) (LCH) metric is equal to:

$$Sim_{lch} = -\log \frac{length}{2 * D} \quad (2)$$

where $length$ is the length of the shortest path between two concepts using node-counting, and D is the maximum depth of the taxonomy.

The **Lesk** ($Lesk$) similarity of two concepts is defined as a function of the overlap between the corresponding definitions, as provided by a dictionary. It is based on an algorithm proposed by Lesk (1986) as a solution for word sense disambiguation.

The **Wu & Palmer** (Wu and Palmer, 1994) (WUP) similarity metric measures the depth of two given concepts in the WordNet taxonomy, and the depth of the least common subsumer (LCS), and combines these figures into a similarity score:

$$Sim_{wup} = \frac{2 * depth(LCS)}{depth(concept_1) + depth(concept_2)} \quad (3)$$

The measure introduced by **Resnik** (Resnik, 1995) (RES) returns the information content (IC) of the LCS of two concepts:

$$Sim_{res} = IC(LCS) \quad (4)$$

where IC is defined as:

$$IC(c) = -\log P(c) \quad (5)$$

and $P(c)$ is the probability of encountering an instance of concept c in a large corpus.

The measure introduced by **Lin** (Lin, 1998) (Lin) builds on Resnik's measure of similarity, and adds a normalization factor consisting of the information content of the two input concepts:

$$Sim_{lin} = \frac{2 * IC(LCS)}{IC(concept_1) + IC(concept_2)} \quad (6)$$

We also consider the **Jiang & Conrath** (Jiang and Conrath, 1997) (JCN) measure of similarity:

$$Sim_{jnc} = \frac{1}{IC(concept_1) + IC(concept_2) - 2 * IC(LCS)} \quad (7)$$

3.3.2 Corpus Based Features

While most of the corpus-based methods induce semantic profiles in a word-space, where the semantic profile of a word is expressed in terms of its co-occurrence with other words, LSA, ESA and SSA rely on a concept-space representation, thus expressing a word's semantic profile in terms of the implicit (LSA), explicit (ESA), or salient (SSA) concepts. This departure from the sparse word-space to a denser, richer, and unambiguous concept space resolves one of the fundamental problems in semantic relatedness, namely the vocabulary mismatch.

Latent Semantic Analysis (LSA) (Landauer et al., 1997). In LSA, term-context associations are captured by means of a dimensionality reduction operated by a singular value decomposition (SVD)

[3]The abbreviation in italics accompanying each method allows for cross-referencing with the results listed in Table 2.

[4]We use the WordNet::Similarity package (Pedersen et al., 2004).

on the term-by-context matrix $\mathbf{T}$, where the matrix is induced from a large corpus. This reduction entails the abstraction of meaning by collapsing similar contexts and discounting noisy and irrelevant ones, hence transforming the real world term-context space into a word-latent-concept space which achieves a much deeper and concrete semantic representation of words[5].

Random Projection (RP) (Dasgupta, 1999). In RP, a high dimensional space is projected onto a lower dimensional one, using a randomly generated matrix. (Bingham and Mannila, 2001) show that unlike LSA or principal component analysis (PCA), RP is computationally efficient for large corpora, while also retaining accurate vector similarity and yielding comparable results.

Explicit Semantic Analysis (ESA) (Gabrilovich and Markovitch, 2007). ESA uses encyclopedic knowledge in an information retrieval framework to generate a semantic interpretation of words. It relies on the distribution of words inside Wikipedia articles, thus building a semantic representation for a given word using a word-document association.

Salient Semantic Analysis (SSA) (Hassan and Mihalcea, 2011). SSA incorporates a similar semantic abstraction as ESA, yet it uses salient concepts gathered from encyclopedic knowledge, where a "concept" represents an unambiguous expression which affords an encyclopedic definition. Saliency in this case is determined based on the word being hyperlinked in context, implying that it is highly relevant to the given text.

In order to determine the similarity of two text fragments, we employ two variations: the typical cosine similarity (cos) and a best alignment strategy ($align$), which we explain in more detail in the paragraph below. Both variations were paired with the ESA, and SSA systems resulting in four similarity scores that were used as features by our meta-system, namely ESA_{cos}, ESA_{align}, SSA_{cos}, and SSA_{align}; in addition, we also used BOW_{cos}, LSA_{cos}, and RP_{cos}.

Best Alignment Strategy ($align$). Let T_a and T_b be two text fragments of size a and b respectively. After removing all stopwords, we first determine the number of shared terms (ω) between T_a and T_b. Second, we calculate the semantic relatedness of all possible pairings between non-shared terms in T_a and T_b. We further filter these possible combinations by creating a list φ which holds the strongest semantic pairings between the fragments' terms, such that each term can only belong to one and only one pair.

$$Sim(T_a, T_b) = \frac{(\omega + \sum_{i=1}^{|\varphi|} \varphi_i) \times (2ab)}{a+b} \quad (8)$$

where φ_i is the similarity score for the ith pairing.

3.3.3 Opinion Aware Features

We design opinion-aware features to capture sentence similarity on the subjectivity level based on the output of three subjectivity analysis systems. Intuitively, two sentences are similar in terms of subjectivity if there exists similar opinion expressions which also share similar opinion holders.

OpinionFinder (Wilson et al., 2005) is a publicly available opinion extraction model that annotates the subjectivity of new text based on the presence (or absence) of words or phrases in a large lexicon. The system consists of a two step process, by feeding the sentences identified as subjective or objective by a rule-based high-precision classifier to a high-recall classifier that iteratively learns from the remaining corpus. For each sentence in a STS pair, the two classifiers provide two predictions; a subjectivity similarity score (*SUBJSL*) is computed as follows. If both sentences are classified as subjective or objective, the score is 1; if one is subjective and the other one is objective, the score is -1; otherwise it is 0. We also make use of the output of the subjective expression identifier in OpinionFinder. We first record how many expressions the two sentences have: feature *NUMEX1* and *NUMEX2*. Then we compare how many tokens these expressions share and we normalize by the total number of expressions (feature *EXPR*).

We compute the difference between the probabilities of the two sentences being subjective (*SUBJDIFF*), by employing a logistic regression classifier using LIBLINEAR (Fan et al., 2008) trained on the MPQA corpus. The smaller the difference, the more similar the sentences are in terms of subjectivity.

We also employ features produced by the opinion-extraction model of Yang and Cardie (Yang and Cardie, 2012), which is better suited to process ex-

[5] We use the LSA implementation available at `code.google.com/p/semanticvectors/`.

pressions of arbitrary length. Specifically, for each sentence, we extract subjective expressions and generate the following features. *SUBJCNT* is a binary feature which is equal to 1 if both sentences contain a subjective expression. *DSEALGN* marks the number of shared words between subjective expressions in two sentences, while *DSESIM* represents their similarity beyond the word level. We represent the subjective expressions in each sentence as a feature vector, containing unigrams extracted from the expressions, their part-of-speech, their WordNet hypernyms and their subjectivity label[6], and compute the cosine similarity between the feature vectors. The holder of the opinion expressions is extracted with the aid of a dependency parser[7]. In most cases, the opinion holder and the opinion expression are related by the dependency relation *subj*. This relation is used to expand the verb dependents in the opinion expression and identify the opinion holder or *AGENT*.

3.4 Meta-learning

Each metric described above provides one individual score for every sentence-pair in both the training and test set. These scores then serve as input to a meta-learner, which adjusts their importance, and thus their bearing on the overall similarity score predicted by the system. We experimented with regression and decision tree based algorithms by performing 10-fold cross validation on the 2012 training data; these types of learners are particularly well suited to maintain the ordinality of the semantic similarity scores (i.e. a score of 4.5 is closer to either 4 or 5, implying that the two sentences are mostly or fully equivalent, while also being far further away from 0, implying no semantic relatedness between the two sentences). We obtained consistent results when using support vector regression with polynomial kernel (Drucker et al., 1997; Smola and Schoelkopf, 1998) (SVR) and random subspace meta-classification with tree learners (Ho, 1998) ($RandSubspace$)[8].

We submitted three system variations based on the training corpus (*first word* in the system name) or the learning methodology (*second word*) used: $comb.RandSubspace$, $comb.SVR$ and $indv.RandSubspace$. For $comb$, training was performed on the merged version of the entire 2012 SEMEVAL dataset. For $indv$, predictions for $OnWN$ and SMT test data were based on training on matching $OnWN$ and SMT[9] data from 2012, predictions for the other test sets were computed using the combined version ($comb$).

System	FNWN	headlines	OnWN	SMT	Mean
comb.RandSubSpace	0.331	**0.677**	0.514	0.337	**0.494**
comb.SVR	**0.362**	0.669	0.510	**0.341**	**0.494**
indv.RandSubspace	0.331	**0.677**	**0.548**	0.277	0.483
baseline-tokencos	0.215	0.540	0.283	0.286	0.364

Table 1: Evaluation results (Agirre et al., 2013).

4 Results and Discussion

Table 2 lists the correlations obtained between the scores assigned by each one of the features we used and the scores assigned by the human judges. It is interesting to note that overall, corpus-based measures are stronger performers compared to knowledge-based measures. The top contenders in the former group are ESA_{align}, SSA_{align}, LSA_{cos}, and RP_{cos}, indicating that these methods are able to leverage a significant amount of semantic information from text. While LSA_{cos} achieves high correlations on many of the datasets, replacing the singular value decomposition operation by random projection to a lower-dimension space (RP) achieves competitive results while also being computationally efficient. This observation is in line with prior literature (Bingham and Mannila, 2001). Among the knowledge-based methods, JCN and $Path$ achieve high performance on more than five of the datasets. In some cases, particularly on the 2013 test data, the shortest path method ($Path$) peforms better or on par with the performance attained by other knowledge-based measures, despite its computational simplicity. While opinion-based measures do not exhibit the same high correlation, we should remember that none of the datasets displays consistent opinion content, nor were they annotated with this aspect in mind, in order for this information to be properly leveraged and evaluated.

[6]Label is based on the OpinionFinder subjectivity lexicon (Wiebe et al., 2005).

[7]nlp.stanford.edu/software/

[8]Included with the Weka framework (Hall et al., 2009); we used the default values for both algorithms.

[9]The SMT training set is a combination of $SMTeuroparl$ (in this paper abbreviated as $SMTep$) and $SMTnews$ data.

	Train 2012			Test 2012					Test 2013			
Feature	SMTep	MSRpar	MSRvid	SMTep	MSRpar	MSRvid	OnWN	SMTnews	FNWN	headlines	OnWN	SMT
Knowledge-based measures												
JCN	**0.51**	**0.49**	**0.63**	0.48	0.48	0.64	0.62	0.28	0.38	**0.72**	0.71	**0.34**
LCH	0.45	0.48	0.49	0.47	**0.49**	0.54	0.54	0.3	0.39	0.69	0.69	0.32
$Lesk$	0.5	0.48	0.59	**0.5**	0.47	0.63	**0.64**	**0.4**	0.4	0.71	0.7	0.33
Lin	0.48	**0.49**	0.54	0.48	0.48	0.56	0.57	0.27	0.28	0.65	0.66	0.3
$Path$	0.5	**0.49**	0.62	0.48	**0.49**	**0.65**	0.62	0.35	**0.43**	**0.72**	**0.73**	**0.34**
RES	0.48	0.47	0.55	0.49	0.47	0.6	0.62	0.33	0.28	0.64	0.7	0.31
WUP	0.42	0.46	0.38	0.44	0.48	0.42	0.48	0.26	0.19	0.55	0.6	0.25
Corpus-based measures												
BOW_cos	0.51	0.47	0.69	0.32	0.44	0.71	0.66	0.37	0.34	0.68	0.52	0.32
ESA_cos	0.53	0.34	0.71	0.44	0.3	0.77	0.63	0.44	0.34	0.55	0.35	0.27
ESA_align	0.55	**0.56**	0.75	**0.49**	**0.52**	0.78	0.69	0.38	**0.46**	**0.71**	0.47	**0.34**
SSA_cos	0.4	0.34	0.63	0.4	0.22	0.71	0.6	0.42	0.35	0.48	0.47	0.26
SSA_align	0.54	**0.56**	0.74	**0.49**	0.51	0.77	0.68	0.38	0.44	0.69	0.46	**0.34**
LSA_cos	**0.65**	0.48	0.76	0.36	0.45	**0.79**	0.67	**0.45**	0.25	0.63	**0.61**	0.32
RP_cos	0.6	0.49	**0.78**	0.46	0.43	**0.79**	**0.7**	**0.45**	0.38	0.68	0.57	**0.34**
Opinion-aware measures												
$AGENT$	0.16	0.15	0.05	0.11	0.12	0.03	n/a	-0.01	n/a	**0.08**	-0.04	0.11
$DSEALGN$	**0.18**	0.2	**0.11**	0.05	0.11	**0.11**	0.07	0.06	-0.1	**0.08**	0.13	0.1
$DSESIM$	0.12	0.15	0.05	0.1	0.08	0.07	0.04	**0.08**	0.05	**0.08**	0.04	0.08
$EXPR$	0.17	0.19	0.06	0.18	**0.18**	0.02	0.07	0	0.13	**0.08**	**0.18**	**0.17**
$NUMEX1$	0.12	**0.22**	-0.03	0.07	0.16	-0.05	-0.01	-0.01	-0.01	-0.03	0.08	0.1
$NUMEX2$	-0.25	0.19	0.01	0.06	0.14	-0.03	0.01	0.06	0.09	-0.05	0.03	0.11
$SUBJCNT$	0.14	0.19	0.01	0.09	0.07	0.03	0.02	**0.08**	0.05	0.05	0.05	0.09
$SUBJDIFF$	-0.07	-0.07	-0.17	-0.27	-0.13	-0.22	-0.17	-0.12	-0.04	-0.12	-0.2	-0.12
$SUBJSL$	0.15	-0.11	0.07	**0.23**	0.01	0.07	**0.11**	-0.08	**0.15**	0.07	-0.03	0

Table 2: Correlation of individual features for the training and test sets with the gold standard.

Nonetheless, we notice several promising features, such as $DSEALIGN$ and $EXPR$. Lower correlations seem to be associated with shorter spans of text, since when averaging all opinion-based correlations per dataset, $MSRvid$ (x2), $OnWN$ (x2), and $headlines$ display the lowest average correlation, ranging from 0 to 0.03. This matches the expectation that opinionated content can be easier identified in longer contexts, as additional subjective elements amount to a stronger prediction. The other seven datasets consist of longer spans of text; they display an average opinion-based correlation between 0.07 and 0.12, with the exception of $FNWN$ and $SMTnews$ at 0.04 and 0.01, respectively.

Our systems performed well, ranking 38, 39 and 45 among the 88 competing systems in *SEM 2013 (see Table 1), with the best being *comb.SVR* and *comb.RandSubspace*, both with a mean correlation of 0.494. We noticed from our participation in SEMEVAL 2012 (Banea et al., 2012), that training and testing on the same type of data achieves the best results; this receives further support when considering the performance of the *indv.RandSubspace* variation on the OnWN data[10], which exhibits a 0.034 correlation increase over our next best system (*comb.RandSubspace*). While we do surpass the bag-of-words cosine baseline (*baseline-tokencos*) computed by the task organizers by a 0.13 difference in correlation, we fall short by 0.124 from the performance of the best system in the STS task.

5 Conclusions

To participate in the STS *SEM 2013 task, we constructed a meta-learner framework that combines traditional knowledge and corpus-based methods, while also introducing novel opinion analysis based metrics. While the *SEM data is not particularly suited for evaluating the performance of opinion features, this is nonetheless a first step toward conducting text similarity research while also considering the subjective dimension of text. Our system variations ranked 38, 39 and 45 among the 88 participating systems.

Acknowledgments

This material is based in part upon work supported by the National Science Foundation CAREER award #0747340 and IIS awards #1018613,

[10]The SMT test data is not part of the same corpus as either $SMTep$ or $SMTnews$.

#0208798 and #0916046. This work was supported in part by DARPA-BAA-12-47 DEFT grant #12475008. Any opinions, findings, and conclusions or recommendations expressed in this material are those of the authors and do not necessarily reflect the views of the National Science Foundation or the Defense Advanced Research Projects Agency.

References

E. Agirre, D. Cer, M. Diab, and A. Gonzalez. 2012. Semeval-2012 task 6: A pilot on semantic textual similarity. In *Proceedings of the 6th International Workshop on Semantic Evaluation (SemEval 2012), in conjunction with the First Joint Conference on Lexical and Computational Semantics (*SEM 2012)*.

E. Agirre, D. Cer, M. Diab, A. Gonzalez-Agirre, and W. Guo. 2013. *SEM 2013 Shared Task: Semantic Textual Similarity, including a Pilot on Typed-Similarity. In *Proceedings of the Second Joint Conference on Lexical and Computational Semantics (*SEM 2013)*, Atlanta, GA, USA.

C. Banea, S. Hassan, M. Mohler, and R. Mihalcea. 2012. UNT: A supervised synergistic approach to semantic text similarity. In *Proceedings of the First Joint Conference on Lexical and Computational Semantics (*SEM 2012)*, pages 635–642, Montreal, Canada.

E. Bingham and H. Mannila. 2001. Random projection in dimensionality reduction: applications to image and text data. In *Proceedings of the seventh ACM SIGKDD international conference on Knowledge discovery and data mining (KDD 2001)*, pages 245–250, San Francisco, CA, USA.

C. Burgess, K. Livesay, and K. Lund. 1998. Explorations in context space: words, sentences, discourse. *Discourse Processes*, 25(2):211–257.

K. Church and P. Hanks. 1990. Word association norms, mutual information, and lexicography. *Computational Linguistics*, 16(1):22–29.

S. Dasgupta. 1999. Learning mixtures of Gaussians. In *40th Annual Symposium on Foundations of Computer Science (FOCS 1999)*, pages 634–644, New York, NY, USA.

H. Drucker, C. J. Burges, L. Kaufman, A. Smola, and Vladimir Vapnik. 1997. Support vector regression machines. *Advances in Neural Information Processing Systems*, 9:155–161.

R. Fan, K. Chang, C. Hsieh, X. Wang, and C. Lin. 2008. Liblinear: A library for large linear classification. *The Journal of Machine Learning Research*, 9:1871–1874.

E. Gabrilovich and S. Markovitch. 2007. Computing semantic relatedness using Wikipedia-based explicit semantic analysis. In *Proceedings of the 20th AAAI International Conference on Artificial Intelligence (AAAI'07)*, pages 1606–1611, Hyderabad, India.

M. Hall, E. Frank, G. Holmes, B. Pfahringer, P. Reutemann, and Ian H. Witten. 2009. The WEKA data mining software: An update. *SIGKDD Explorations*, 11(1).

S. Hassan and R. Mihalcea. 2011. Measuring semantic relatedness using salient encyclopedic concepts. *Artificial Intelligence, Special Issue*.

T. K. Ho. 1998. The Random Subspace Method for Constructing Decision Forests. *IEEE Transactions on Pattern Analysis and Machine Intelligence*, 20(8):832–844.

A. Islam and D. Inkpen. 2006. Second order co-occurrence PMI for determining the semantic similarity of words. In *Proceedings of the 5th Conference on Language Resources and Evaluation (LREC 06)*, volume 2, pages 1033–1038, Genoa, Italy, July.

A. Islam and D. Inkpen. 2009. Semantic Similarity of Short Texts. In Nicolas Nicolov, Galia Angelova, and Ruslan Mitkov, editors, *Recent Advances in Natural Language Processing V*, volume 309 of *Current Issues in Linguistic Theory*, pages 227–236. John Benjamins, Amsterdam & Philadelphia.

J. J. Jiang and D. W. Conrath. 1997. Semantic similarity based on corpus statistics and lexical taxonomy. In *International Conference Research on Computational Linguistics (ROCLING X)*, pages 9008+, September.

T. K. Landauer, T. K. L, D. Laham, B. Rehder, and M. E. Schreiner. 1997. How well can passage meaning be derived without using word order? a comparison of latent semantic analysis and humans.

M. Lapata and R. Barzilay. 2005. Automatic evaluation of text coherence: Models and representations. In *Proceedings of the 19th International Joint Conference on Artificial Intelligence*, Edinburgh.

C. Leacock and M. Chodorow. 1998. Combining local context and WordNet similarity for word sense identification. In *WordNet: An Electronic Lexical Database*, pages 305–332.

M. Lesk. 1986. Automatic sense disambiguation using machine readable dictionaries: how to tell a pine cone from an ice cream cone. In *SIGDOC '86: Proceedings of the 5th annual international conference on Systems documentation*, pages 24–26, New York, NY, USA. ACM.

C. Lin and E. Hovy. 2003. Automatic evaluation of summaries using n-gram co-occurrence statistics. In *Proceedings of Human Language Technology Conference (HLT-NAACL 2003)*, Edmonton, Canada, May.

D. Lin. 1998. An information-theoretic definition of similarity. In *Proceedings of the Fifteenth Interna-*

tional Conference on Machine Learning, pages 296–304, Madison, Wisconsin.

R. Mihalcea, C. Corley, and C. Strapparava. 2006. Corpus-based and knowledge-based measures of text semantic similarity. In *Proceedings of the American Association for Artificial Intelligence (AAAI 2006)*, pages 775–780, Boston, MA, US.

G. A. Miller. 1995. WordNet: a Lexical database for English. *Communications of the Association for Computing Machinery*, 38(11):39–41.

M. Mohler and R. Mihalcea. 2009. Text-to-text semantic similarity for automatic short answer grading. In *Proceedings of the European Association for Computational Linguistics (EACL 2009)*, Athens, Greece.

M. Mohler, R. Bunescu, and R. Mihalcea. 2011. Learning to grade short answer questions using semantic similarity measures and dependency graph alignments. In *Proceedings of the Association for Computational Linguistics – Human Language Technologies (ACL-HLT 2011)*, Portland, Oregon, USA.

R. M. A. Nawab, M. Stevenson, and P. Clough. 2011. External plagiarism detection using information retrieval and sequence alignment: Notebook for PAN at CLEF 2011. In *Proceedings of the 5th International Workshop on Uncovering Plagiarism, Authorship, and Social Software Misuse (PAN 2011)*.

K. Papineni, S. Roukos, T. Ward, and W. Zhu. 2002. Bleu: a method for automatic evaluation of machine translation. In *Proceedings of the 40th Annual Meeting of the Association for Computational Linguistics*, pages 311–318, Philadelphia, PA.

T. Pedersen, S. Patwardhan, and J. Michelizzi. 2004. WordNet:: Similarity-Measuring the Relatedness of Concepts. *Proceedings of the National Conference on Artificial Intelligence*, pages 1024–1025.

P. Resnik. 1995. Using information content to evaluate semantic similarity in a taxonomy. In *In Proceedings of the 14th International Joint Conference on Artificial Intelligence*, pages 448–453.

J. Rocchio, 1971. *Relevance feedback in information retrieval.* Prentice Hall, Ing. Englewood Cliffs, New Jersey.

G. Salton and C. Buckley. 1997. Term weighting approaches in automatic text retrieval. In *Readings in Information Retrieval*. Morgan Kaufmann Publishers, San Francisco, CA.

G. Salton and M. Lesk, 1971. *The SMART Retrieval System: Experiments in Automatic Document Processing*, chapter Computer evaluation of indexing and text processing. Prentice Hall, Ing. Englewood Cliffs, New Jersey.

G. Salton, A. Singhal, M. Mitra, and C. Buckley. 1997. Automatic text structuring and summarization. *Information Processing and Management*, 2(32).

H. Schutze. 1998. Automatic word sense discrimination. *Computational Linguistics*, 24(1):97–124.

A. Smola and B. Schoelkopf. 1998. A tutorial on support vector regression. NeuroCOLT2 Technical Report NC2-TR-1998-030.

P. D. Turney. 2001. Mining the Web for Synonyms: PMI-IR versus LSA on TOEFL. In *Proceedings of the 12th European Conference on Machine Learning (ECML'01)*, pages 491–502, Freiburg, Germany.

J. Wiebe and E. Riloff. 2005. Creating subjective and objective sentence classifiers from unannotated texts. In *Proceedings of the 6th international conference on Computational Linguistics and Intelligent Text Processing (CICLing 2005)*, pages 486–497, Mexico City, Mexico.

J. Wiebe, T. Wilson, and C. Cardie. 2005. Annotating expressions of opinions and emotions in language. *Language Resources and Evaluation*, 39(2-3):165–210.

T. Wilson, P. Hoffmann, S. Somasundaran, J. Kessler, Janyce Wiebe, Yejin Choi, Claire Cardie, Ellen Riloff, and Siddharth Patwardhan. 2005. OpinionFinder: A system for subjectivity analysis. In *Proceedings of HLT/EMNLP on Interactive Demonstrations*, pages 34–35, Vancouver, BC, Canada.

Z. Wu and M. Palmer. 1994. Verbs semantics and lexical selection. In *Proceedings of the 32nd annual meeting on Association for Computational Linguistics*, pages 133—-138, Las Cruces, New Mexico.

B. Yang and C. Cardie. 2012. Extracting opinion expressions with semi-markov conditional random fields. In *Proceedings of the conference on Empirical Methods in Natural Language Processing*. Association for Computational Linguistics.

INAOE_UPV-CORE: Extracting Word Associations from Document Corpora to estimate Semantic Textual Similarity

Fernando Sánchez-Vega
Manuel Montes-y-Gómez
Luis Villaseñor-Pineda
Laboratorio de Tecnologías del Lenguaje,
Instituto Nacional de Astrofísica, Óptica y
Electrónica (INAOE), Mexico.
{fer.callotl,mmontesg,villasen}
@inaoep.mx

Paolo Rosso
Natural Language Engineering Lab., ELiRF,
Universitat Politècnica de València, Spain
prosso@dsic.upv.es

Abstract

This paper presents three methods to evaluate the Semantic Textual Similarity (STS). The first two methods do not require labeled training data; instead, they automatically extract semantic knowledge in the form of word associations from a given reference corpus. Two kinds of word associations are considered: co-occurrence statistics and the similarity of word contexts. The third method was done in collaboration with groups from the Universities of Paris 13, Matanzas and Alicante. It uses several word similarity measures as features in order to construct an accurate prediction model for the STS.

1 Introduction

Even with the current progress of the natural language processing, evaluating the semantic text similarity is an extremely challenging task. Due to the existence of multiple semantic relations among words, the measuring of text similarity is a multi-factorial and highly complex task (Turney, 2006).

Despite the difficulty of this task, it remains as one of the most attractive research topics for the NLP community. This is because the evaluation of text similarity is commonly used as an internal module in many different tasks, such as, information retrieval, question answering, document summarization, etc. (Resnik, 1999). Moreover, most of these tasks require determining the "semantic" similarity of texts showing stylistic differences or using polysemicwords (Hliaoutakis et al., 2006).

The most popular approach to evaluate the semantic similarity of words and texts consists in using the semantic knowledge expressed in ontologies (Resnik, 1999); commonly, WorldNet is used for this purpose (Fellbaum, 2005). Unfortunately, despite the great effort that has been the creation of WordNet, it is still far to cover all existing words and senses (Curran, 2003).Therefore, the semantic similarity methods that use this resource tend to reduce their applicability to a restricted domain and to a specific language.

We recognize the necessity of having and using manually-constructed semantic-knowledge sources in order to get precise assessments of the semantic similarity of texts, but, in turn, we also consider that it is possible to obtain good estimations of these similarities using less-expensive, and perhaps broader, information sources. In particular our proposal is to automatically extract the semantic knowledge from large amounts of raw data samples i.e. document corpora without labels.

In this paper we describe two different strategies to compute the semantic similarity of words from a reference corpus. The first strategy uses word co-occurrence statistics. It determines that two words are associated (in meaning) if they tend to be used together, in the same documents or contexts. The second strategy measures the similarity of words by taking into consideration second order word co-occurrences. It defines two words as associated if they are used in similar contexts (i.e., if they co-occur with similar words). The following section describes the implementation of these two strategies for our participation at the STS-SEM 2013 task, as well as their combination with the measures designed by the groups from the Universities of Matanzas, Alicante and Paris 13.

*Second Joint Conference on Lexical and Computational Semantics (*SEM), Volume 1: Proceedings of the Main Conference and the Shared Task*, pages 229–233, Atlanta, Georgia, June 13-14, 2013. ©2013 Association for Computational Linguistics

2 Participation in STS-SEM2013

The Semantic Textual Similarity (STS) task consists of estimated the value of semantic similarity between two texts,D_1 and D_2 for now on.

As we mentioned previously, our participation in the STS task of SEM 2013 considered two different approaches that aimed to take advantage of the language knowledge latent in a given reference corpus. By applying simple statistics we obtained a semantic similarity measure between words, and then we used this semantic word similarity (SWS) to get a sentence level similarity estimation. We explored two alternatives for measuring the semantic similarity of words, the first one, called SWS_{ocurr}, uses the co-occurrence of words in a limited context[1],and the second, $SWS_{context}$, compares the contexts of the words using the vector model and cosine similarity to achieve this comparison. It is important to point out that using the vector space model directly, without any spatial transformation as those used by other approaches[2], we could get greater control in the selection of the features used for the extraction of knowledge from the corpus. It is also worth mentioning that we applied a stemming procedure to the sentences to be compared as well as to all documents from the reference corpus. We represented the texts D_1 and D_2 by bags of tokens, which means that our approaches did not take into account the word order.

Following we present our baseline method, then, we introduce the two proposed methods as well as a method done in collaboration with other groups. The idea of this shared-method is to enhance the estimation of the semantic textual similarity by combining different and diverse strategies for computing word similarities.

2.1 STS-baseline method

Given textsD_1 and D_2, their textual similarity is given by:

$$STS - Baseline = MIN(SIM(D_1, D_2), SIM(D_2, D_1))$$

where

$$SIM(D_i, D_j) = \frac{1}{|D_i|} \sum_{t_k \in D_i} 1(t_k \in D_j)$$

This measure is based on a direct matching of tokens. It simply counts the number of tokens from one text D_i that also exist in the other text D_j. Because STS is a symmetrical attribute, unlike Textual Entailment (Agirre et al., 2012), we designed it as a symmetric measure. We assumed that the relationship between both texts is at least equal to their smaller asymmetric similarity.

2.2 The proposed STS methods

These methods incorporate semantic knowledge extracted from a reference corpus. They aim to take advantage of the latent semantic knowledge from a large document collection. Because the extracted knowledge from the reference corpus is at word level, these methods for STS use the same basic –word matching– strategy for comparing the sentences like the baseline method. Nevertheless, they allow a soft matching between words by incorporating information about their semantic similarity.

The following formula shows the proposed modification to the *SIM* function in order to incorporate information of the semantic word similarity (SWS). This modification allowed us not only to match words with exactly the same stem but also to link different but semantically related words.

$$SIM(D_i, D_j) = \sum_{t_m \in D_i} MAX\left(\bigcup_{t_n \in D_j} SWS(t_m, t_n) \right)$$

We propose two different strategies to compute the semantic word similarity (SWS), STS_{Occur} and STS_{Contex}. The following subsections describe in detail these two strategies.

2.2.1 STS based on word co-occurrence

SWS_{Occur} uses a reference corpus to get a numerical approximation of the semantic similarity between two terms $t_i$and t_j (when these terms have not the same stem). As shown in the following formula, SWS_{occur} takes values between 0 and 1; 0 indicates that it does not exist any text sample in the corpus that contains both terms, whereas, 1 indicates that they always occur together.

[1] In the experiments we considered a window (context) formed of 15 surrounding words.

[2] Such as Latent Semantic Analysis (LSA) (Turney, 2005).

$$SWS_{occur}\left(t_i, t_j\right) = \begin{cases} t_i = t_j & 1 \\ other & \dfrac{\#(t_i, t_j)}{MIN(\#(t_i), \#(t_j))} \end{cases}$$

where $\#\left(t_i, t_j\right)$ is the number of times that t_i and t_j co-occur and $\#(t_i)$ and $\#\left(t_j\right)$ are the number of times that terms t_i and t_j occur in the reference corpus respectively.

2.2.2 STS based on context similarity

$SWS_{context}$ is based on the idea that two terms are semantically closer if they tend to be used in similar contexts. This measure uses the well-known vector space model and cosine similarity to compare the terms' contexts. In a first step, we created a context vector for each term, which captures all the terms that appear around it in the whole reference corpus. Then, we computed the semantic similarity of two terms by the following formula.

$$SWS_{context}\left(t_i, t_j\right) = \begin{cases} t_i = t_j & 1 \\ other & SIMCOS(\vec{T_i}, \vec{T_j}) \end{cases}$$

where the cosine similarity, *SIMCOS*, is calculated on the vectors $\vec{T_i}$ and $\vec{T_j}$ corresponding to the vector space model representation of terms t_i and t_j, as indicated in the following equation:

$$SIMCOS(\vec{T_i}, \vec{T_j}) = \frac{\sum_{k \in |V|} t_{ik} \cdot t_{jk}}{|\vec{T_i}| \cdot |\vec{T_j}|}$$

It is important to point out that *SIMCOS* is calculated on a "predefined" vocabulary of interest; the appropriate selection of this vocabulary helps to get a better representation of terms, and, consequently, a more accurate estimation of their semantic similarities.

2.3 STS based on a combination of measures

In addition to our main methods we also developed a method that combines our SWS measures with measures proposed by other two research groups, namely:

- LIPN (Laboratoire d'Informatique de Paris-Nord, Université Paris 13, France).
- UMCC_DLSI (Universidad de Matanzas Camilo Cienfuegos, Cuba, in conjuction with the Departamento de Lenguajes y Sistemas Informáticos, Universidad de Alicante, Spain).

The main motivation for this collaboration was to investigate the relevance of using diverse strategies for computing word similarities and the effectiveness of their combination for estimating the semantic similarity of texts.

The proposed method used a set of measures provided by each one of the groups. These measures were employed as features to obtained a prediction model for the STS. Table 1 summarizes the used measures. For the generation and fitting of the model we used three approaches: linear regression, a Gaussian process and a multilayer neural network.

Description	Team	#	Mean Rank	Best Rank
Based on IR measures	LIPN	2	2.0	1
Based on distance on WordNet	LIPN	2	8.5	2
STS-Context	INAOE-UPV	1	4.0	4
Complexity of the sentences	INAOE-UPV	34	27.8	5
STS-Occur	INAOE UPV	1	7.0	7
Based on the alignment of particulars POS.	UMCC_DLSI	12	40.9	18
n-gram overlap	LIPN	1	20.0	20
Based on Edit distance	UMCC_DLSI	4	42.6	27
Syntactic dependencies overlap	LIPN	1	29.0	29
Levenshtein's distance	LIPN	1	42.0	42
Named entity overlap	LIPN	1	57.0	57

Table 1. General description of the features used by the shared method. The second column indicates the source team for each group of features; the third column indicates the number of used features from each group; the last two columns show the information gain rank of each group of features over the training set.

3 Implementation considerations

The extraction of knowledge for the computation of the *SWS* was performed over the Reuters-21578 collection. This collection was selected because it is a well-known corpus and also because it includes documents covering a wide range of topics.

Due to time and space restrictions we could not consider all the vocabulary from the reference corpus; the vocabulary selection was conducted by taking the best 20,000 words according to the transition point method (Pinto et al., 2006). This method selects the terms associated to the main topics of the corpus, which presumably contain more information for estimating the semantic similarity of words. We also preserved the vocabulary from the evaluation samples, provided they also occur in the reference corpus. The size of the vocabulary used in the experiments and the size of the corpus and test set vocabularies are shown in Table 2.

Experiment's Vocabulary	Selected Vocabulary	Ref. Corpus Vocabulary	Evaluation Vocabulary
26724	20000	31213	11491

Table 2. Number of different stems from each of the considered vocabularies

4 Evaluation and Results

The methods proposed by our group do not require to be trained, i.e., they do not require tagged data, only a reference corpus, therefore, it was possible to evaluate them on the whole training set available this year. Table 3 shows their results on this set.

Method	Correlation
STS-Baseline	0.455
STS-Occur	0.500
STS-Contex	0.511

Table 3. Correlation values of the proposed methods and our baseline method with human judgments.

Results in Table 3 show that the use of the co-occurrence information improves the correlation with human judgments. It also shows that the use of context information further improves the results. One surprising finding was the competitive performance of our baseline method; it is considerably better than the previous year's baseline result (0.31).

In order to evaluate the method done in collaboration with LIPN and UMCC_DLSI, we carried out several experiments using the features provided by each group independently and in conjunction with the others. The experiments were performed over the whole training set by means of two-fold cross-validation. The individual and global results are shown in Table 4.

As shown in Table 4, the result corresponding to the combination of all features clearly outperformed the results obtained by using each team´s features independently. Moreover, the best combination of features, containing selected features from the three teams, obtained a correlation value very close to last year's winner result.

Featured by Group	Perdition Model	Correlation
LIPN	Gaussian Process	0.587
LIPN	Lineal Regression	0.701
LIPN	Multilayer-NN	0.756
UMCC_DLSI	Gaussian Process	0.388
UMCC_DLSI	Lineal Regression	0.388
UMCC_DLSI	Multilayer-NN	0.382
INAOE-UPV	Gaussian Process	0.670
INAOE-UPV	Lineal Regression	0.674
INAOE-UPV	Multilayer-NN	0.550
ALL	Gaussian Process	0.770
ALL	Lineal Regression	0.777
ALL	Multilayer-NN	0.633
SELECTED-SET	Multilayer-NN	0.808
LAST YEAR´S WINNER	Simple log-linear regression	0.823

Table 4. Results obtained by the different subsets of features, from the different participating groups.

4.1 Officials Runs

For the official runs (refer to Table 5) we submitted the results corresponding to the STS_{Occur} and $STS_{Context}$ methods. We also submitted a result from the method done in collaboration with LIPN and UMCC_DLSI. Due to time restrictions we were not able to submit the results from our best configuration; we submitted the results for the linear regression model using all the features (second best result from Table 4).Table 5 shows the results in the four evaluation sub-collections; Headlines comes from news headlines, OnWN and FNWN contain pair senses definitions from WordNet and other resources, finally, SMT are translations from automatic machine translations and from the reference human translations.

As shown in Table 5, the performances of the two proposed methods by our group were very close. We hypothesize that this result could be caused by the use of a larger vocabulary for the computation of co-occurrence statistics than for the calculation of the context similarities. We had to use a smaller vocabulary for the later because its higher computational cost.

Finally, Table 5 also shows that the method done in collaboration with the other groups obtained our best results, confirming that using more information about the semantic similarity of words allows improving the estimation of the semantic similarity of texts. The advantage of this approach over the two proposed methods was especially clear on the OnWN and FNWN datasets, which were created upon WordNet information. Somehow this result was predictable since several measures from this "share-method" use WordNet information to compute the semantic similarity of words. However, this pattern was not the same for the other two (WordNet unrelated) datasets. In these other two collections, the average performance of our two proposed methods, without using any expensive and manually constructed resource, improved by 4% the results from the share-method.

Method	Headlines	OnWN	FNWN	SMT	MEAN
STS-Occur	0.639	0.324	0.271	0.349	0.433
STS-Contex	0.639	0.326	0.266	0.345	0.431
Collaboration	0.646	0.629	0.409	0.304	0.508

Table 4. Correlation values from our official runs over the four sub-datasets.

5 Conclusions

The main conclusion of this experiment is that it is possible to extract useful knowledge from raw corpora for evaluating the semantic similarity of texts. Other important conclusion is that the combination of methods (or word semantic similarity measures) helps improving the accuracy of STS. As future work we plan to carry out a detailed analysis of the used measures, with the aim of determining their complementariness and a better way for combining them. We also plan to evaluate the impact of the size and vocabulary richness of the reference corpus on the accuracy of the proposed STS methods.

Acknowledgments

This work was done under partial support of CONACyT project Grants: 134186, and Scholarship 224483. This work is the result of the collaboration in the framework of the WIQEI IRSES project (Grant No. 269180) within the FP 7 Marie Curie. The work of the last author was in the framework the DIANA-APPLICATIONS-Finding Hidden Knowledge in Texts: Applications (TIN2012-38603-C02-01) project, and the VLC/CAMPUS Microcluster on Multimodal Interaction in Intelligent Systems. We also thank the teams from the Universities of Paris 13, Matanzas and Alicante for their willingness to collaborate with us in this evalaution exercise.

References

AngelosHliaoutakis, GiannisVarelas, EpimeneidisVoutsakis, Euripides G. M. Petrakis, EvangelosMilios, 2006, *Information Retrieval by Semantic Similarity*, Intern. Journal on Semantic Web and Information Systems: Special Issue of Multimedia Semantics (IJSWIS), 3(3): 55–73.

Carmen Banea, Samer Hassan, Michael Mohler and RadaMihalcea, 2012, *UNT: A Supervised Synergistic Approach to Semantic Text Similarity*, SEM 2012: The First Joint Conference on Lexical and Computational Semantics, Proceedings of the Sixth International Workshop on Semantic Evaluation (SemEval 2012), Montreal, Vol. 2: 635-642.

Christiane Fellbaum,2005, *WordNet and wordnets*, Encyclopedia of Language and Linguistics, Second Ed., Oxford, Elsevier: 665-670.

David Pinto, Hector Jiménez H. and Paolo Rosso. *Clustering abstracts of scientific texts using the Transition Point technique*, Proc. 7th Int. Conf. on Comput. Linguistics and Intelligent Text Processing, CICLing-2006, Springer-Verlag, LNCS(3878): 536-546.

EnekoAgirre, Daniel Cer, Mona Diab and Aitor Gonzalez-Agirre, *SemEval-2012 Task 6: A Pilot on Semantic Textual Similarity*. SEM 2012: The First Joint Conference on Lexical and Computational Semantics, Proceedings of the Sixth International Workshop on Semantic Evaluation (SemEval2012), Montreal, Vol. 2: 386-393.

James Richard Curran, 2003, *Doctoral Thesis: From Distributional to Semantic Similarity*, Institute for Communicating and Collaborative Systems, School of Informatics, University of Edinburgh.

Peter D. Turney, 2005, Measuring semantic similarity by latent relational analysis, IJCAI'05 Proceedings of the 19th international joint conference on Artificial intelligence, Edinburgh, Scotland: 1136-1141

Peter D. Turney, 2006, *Similarity of Semantic Relations*, Computational Linguistics, Vol. 32, No. 3: 379-416.

Philip Resnik, 1999, *Semantic Similarity in a Taxonomy: An Information-Based Measure and its Application to Problems of Ambiguity in Natural Language*, Journal of Artificial Intelligence Research, Vol. 11: 95-130.

CNGL-CORE: Referential Translation Machines for Measuring Semantic Similarity

Ergun Biçici
Centre for Next Generation Localisation,
Dublin City University, Dublin, Ireland.
ebicici@computing.dcu.ie

Josef van Genabith
Centre for Next Generation Localisation,
Dublin City University, Dublin, Ireland.
josef@computing.dcu.ie

Abstract

We invent referential translation machines (RTMs), a computational model for identifying the translation acts between any two data sets with respect to a reference corpus selected in the same domain, which can be used for judging the semantic similarity between text. RTMs make quality and semantic similarity judgments possible by using retrieved relevant training data as interpretants for reaching shared semantics. An MTPP (machine translation performance predictor) model derives features measuring the closeness of the test sentences to the training data, the difficulty of translating them, and the presence of acts of translation involved. We view semantic similarity as paraphrasing between any two given texts. Each view is modeled by an RTM model, giving us a new perspective on the binary relationship between the two. Our prediction model is the 15th on some tasks and 30th overall out of 89 submissions in total according to the official results of the Semantic Textual Similarity (STS 2013) challenge.

1 Semantic Textual Similarity Judgments

We introduce a fully automated judge for semantic similarity that performs well in the semantic textual similarity (STS) task (Agirre et al., 2013). STS is a degree of semantic equivalence between two texts based on the observations that "vehicle" and "car" are more similar than "wave" and "car". Accurate prediction of STS has a wide application area including: identifying whether two tweets are talking about the same thing, whether an answer is correct by comparing it with a reference answer, and whether a given shorter text is a valid summary of another text.

The translation quality estimation task (Callison-Burch et al., 2012) aims to develop quality indicators for translations at the sentence-level and predictors without access to a reference translation. Bicici et al. (2013) develop a top performing machine translation performance predictor (MTPP), which uses machine learning models over features measuring how well the test set matches the training set relying on extrinsic and language independent features.

The semantic textual similarity (STS) task (Agirre et al., 2013) addresses the following problem. Given two sentences S_1 and S_2 in the same language, quantify the degree of similarity with a similarity score, which is a number in the range $[0, 5]$. The *semantic textual similarity prediction problem* involves finding a function f approximating the semantic textual similarity score given two sentences, S_1 and S_2:

$$f(S_1, S_2) \approx q(S_1, S_2). \quad (1)$$

We approach f as a supervised learning problem with (S_1, S_2, $q(S_1, S_2)$) tuples being the training data and $q(S_1, S_2)$ being the target similarity score.

We model the problem as a translation task where one possible interpretation is obtained by translating S_1 (the source to translate, S) to S_2 (the target translation, T). Since linguistic processing can reveal deeper similarity relationships, we also look at the translation task at different granularities of information: plain text (R for regular) , after lemmatization (L), after part-of-speech (POS) tagging (P), and after removing 128 English stop-words (S) [1]. Thus,

[1] http://anoncvs.postgresql.org/cvsweb.cgi/pgsql/

*Second Joint Conference on Lexical and Computational Semantics (*SEM), Volume 1: Proceedings of the Main Conference and the Shared Task*, pages 234–240, Atlanta, Georgia, June 13-14, 2013.

we obtain 4 different perspectives on the binary relationship between S_1 and S_2.

2 Referential Translation Machine (RTM)

Referential translation machines (RTMs) we develop provide a computational model for quality and semantic similarity judgments using retrieval of relevant training data (Biçici and Yuret, 2011a; Biçici, 2011) as interpretants for reaching shared semantics (Biçici, 2008). We show that RTM achieves very good performance in judging the semantic similarity of sentences and we can also use RTM to automatically assess the correctness of student answers to obtain better results (Biçici and van Genabith, 2013) than the state-of-the-art (Dzikovska et al., 2012).

RTM is a computational model for identifying the acts of translation for translating between any given two data sets with respect to a reference corpus selected in the same domain. RTM can be used for automatically judging the semantic similarity between texts. An RTM model is based on the selection of common training data relevant and close to both the training set and the test set where the selected relevant set of instances are called the interpretants. Interpretants allow shared semantics to be possible by behaving as a reference point for similarity judgments and providing the context. In semiotics, an interpretant I interprets the signs used to refer to the real objects (Biçici, 2008). RTMs provide a model for computational semantics using interpretants as a reference according to which semantic judgments with translation acts are made. Each RTM model is a data translation model between the instances in the training set and the test set. We use the FDA (Feature Decay Algorithms) instance selection model for selecting the interpretants (Biçici and Yuret, 2011a) from a given corpus, which can be monolingual when modeling paraphrasing acts, in which case the MTPP model (Section 2.1) is built using the interpretants themselves as both the source and the target side of the parallel corpus. RTMs map the training and test data to a space where translation acts can be identified. We view that acts of translation are ubiquitously used during communication:

Every act of communication is an act of translation (Bliss, 2012).

src/backend/snowball/stopwords/

Translation need not be between different languages and paraphrasing or communication also contain acts of translation. When creating sentences, we use our background knowledge and translate information content according to the current context.

Given a training set `train`, a test set `test`, and some monolingual corpus $\mathcal{C}$, preferably in the same domain as the training and test sets, the RTM steps are:

1. $T = \texttt{train} \cup \texttt{test}$.
2. select$(T, \mathcal{C}) \rightarrow \mathcal{I}$
3. MTPP$(\mathcal{I}, \texttt{train}) \rightarrow \mathcal{F}_{\texttt{train}}$
4. MTPP$(\mathcal{I}, \texttt{test}) \rightarrow \mathcal{F}_{\texttt{test}}$
5. learn$(M, \mathcal{F}_{\texttt{train}}) \rightarrow \mathcal{M}$
6. predict$(\mathcal{M}, \mathcal{F}_{\texttt{test}}) \rightarrow \hat{q}$

Step 2 selects the interpretants, $\mathcal{I}$, relevant to the instances in the combined training and test data. Steps 3, 4 use $\mathcal{I}$ to map `train` and `test` to a new space where similarities between translation acts can be derived more easily. Step 5 trains a learning model M over the training features, $\mathcal{F}_{\texttt{train}}$, and Step 6 obtains the predictions. RTM relies on the representativeness of $\mathcal{I}$ as a medium for building translation models for translating between `train` and `test`.

Our encouraging results in the STS task provides a greater understanding of the acts of translation we ubiquitously use when communicating and how they can be used to predict the performance of translation, judging the semantic similarity between text, and evaluating the quality of student answers. RTM and MTPP models are not data or language specific and their modeling power and good performance are applicable across different domains and tasks. RTM expands the applicability of MTPP by making it feasible when making monolingual quality and similarity judgments and it enhances the computational scalability by building models over smaller but more relevant training data as interpretants.

2.1 The Machine Translation Performance Predictor (MTPP)

In machine translation (MT), pairs of source and target sentences are used for training statistical MT (SMT) models. SMT system performance is affected by the amount of training data used as well as the *closeness* of the test set to the training set. MTPP (Biçici et al., 2013) is a top performing machine translation performance predictor, which uses machine learning models over features measuring how well the test set matches the training set to predict the quality of a translation without using a reference translation. MTPP measures the coverage of individual test sentence features and syntactic structures found in the training set and derives feature functions measuring the closeness of test sentences to the available training data, the difficulty of translating the sentence, and the presence of acts of translation for data transformation.

2.2 MTPP Features for Translation Acts

MTPP uses n-gram features defined over text or common cover link (CCL) (Seginer, 2007) structures as the basic units of information over which similarity calculations are made. Unsupervised parsing with CCL extracts links from base words to head words, which allow us to obtain structures representing the grammatical information instantiated in the training and test data. Feature functions use statistics involving the training set and the test sentences to determine their closeness. Since they are language independent, MTPP allows quality estimation to be performed extrinsically. Categories for the 289 features used are listed below and their detailed descriptions are presented in (Biçici et al., 2013) where the number of features are given in $\{\#\}$.

- *Coverage* $\{110\}$: Measures the degree to which the test features are found in the training set for both S ($\{56\}$) and T ($\{54\}$).
- *Synthetic Translation Performance* $\{6\}$: Calculates translation scores achievable according to the n-gram coverage.
- *Length* $\{4\}$: Calculates the number of words and characters for S and T and their ratios.
- *Feature Vector Similarity* $\{16\}$: Calculates the similarities between vector representations.
- *Perplexity* $\{90\}$: Measures the fluency of the sentences according to language models (LM). We use both forward ($\{30\}$) and backward ($\{15\}$) LM based features for S and T.
- *Entropy* $\{4\}$: Calculates the distributional similarity of test sentences to the training set.
- *Retrieval Closeness* $\{24\}$: Measures the degree to which sentences close to the test set are found in the training set.
- *Diversity* $\{6\}$: Measures the diversity of co-occurring features in the training set.
- *IBM1 Translation Probability* $\{16\}$: Calculates the translation probability of test sentences using the training set (Brown et al., 1993).
- *Minimum Bayes Retrieval Risk* $\{4\}$: Calculates the translation probability for the translation having the minimum Bayes risk among the retrieved training instances.
- *Sentence Translation Performance* $\{3\}$: Calculates translation scores obtained according to $q(T, R)$ using BLEU (Papineni et al., 2002), NIST (Doddington, 2002), or F_1 (Biçici and Yuret, 2011b) for q.
- *Character n-grams* $\{4\}$: Calculates the cosine between the character n-grams (for n=2,3,4,5) obtained for S and T (Bär et al., 2012).
- *LIX* $\{2\}$: Calculates the LIX readability score (Wikipedia, 2013; Björnsson, 1968) for S and T. [2]

3 Experiments

STS contains sentence pairs from news headlines (headlines), sense definitions from semantic lexical resources (OnWN is from OntoNotes (Pradhan et al., 2007) and WordNet (Miller, 1995) and FNWN is from FrameNet (Baker et al., 1998) and WordNet), and statistical machine translation (SMT) (Agirre et al., 2013). STS challenge results are evaluated with the Pearson's correlation score (r).

The test set contains 2250 (S_1, S_2) sentence pairs with 750, 561, 189, and 750 sentences from each type respectively. The training set contains 5342 sentence pairs with 1500 each from MSRpar and MSRvid (Microsoft Research paraphrase and video description corpus (Agirre et al., 2012)), 1592 from SMT, and 750 from OnWN.

3.1 RTM Models

We obtain CNGL results for the STS task as follows. For each perspective described in Section 1, we build an RTM model. Each RTM model views the STS task from a different perspective using the 289 features extracted dependent on the interpretants using MTPP. We extract the features both on

[2] LIX=$\frac{A}{B} + C\frac{100}{A}$, where A is the number of words, C is words longer than 6 characters, B is words that start or end with any of ".", ":", "!", "?" similar to (Hagström, 2012).

	r	R	P	L	S	R+P	R+L	R+S	L+P	<u>L+S</u>	L+S TL	R+P+L	R+P+S	<u>L+P+S</u>	<u>L+P+S TL</u>	R+P+L+S	R+P+L+S TL
$S_1 \rightarrow S_2$	RR	.7904	.7502	.8200	.7788	.8074	.8232	.8101	.8247	.8218	.8509	.8266	.8172	.8304	.8530	.8323	.8499
	SVR	.8311	.8060	.8443	.8330	.8404	.8517	.8498	.8501	<u>.8593</u>	.8556	.8496	.8422	<u>.8586</u>	<u>.8579</u>	.8527	.8564
$S_2 \rightarrow S_1$	RR	.7922	.7651	.8169	.7891	.8064	.8196	.8136	.8219	.8257	.8257	.8226	.8164	.8284	.8284	.8313	.8324
	SVR	.8308	.8165	.8407	.8302	.8361	.8506	.8467	.8510	.8567	.8567	.8525	.8460	.8588	.8588	.8575	.8574
$S_1 \rightleftarrows S_2$	RR	.8079	.787	.8279	.8101	.8216	.8333	.8275	.8346	.8375	.8409	.8361	.8312	.8412	.8434	.8432	.844
	SVR	.8397	.8237	.8554	.841	.8432	.857	.851	.8557	.8605	.8626	.8505	.8505	.8591	.8622	.8602	.8588

Table 1: CV performance on the training set with tuning. <u>Underlined</u> are the settings we use in our submissions. RTM models in directions $S_1 \rightarrow S_2$, $S_2 \rightarrow S_1$, and the bi-directional models $S_1 \rightleftarrows S_2$ are displayed.

the training set and the test set. The training corpus used is the English side of an out-of-domain corpus on European parliamentary discussions, Europarl (Callison-Burch et al., 2012) [3]. In-domain corpora are likely to improve the performance. We use the Stanford POS tagger (Toutanova et al., 2003) to obtain the perspectives P and L. We use the training corpus to build a 5-gram target LM.

We use ridge regression (RR) and support vector regression (SVR) with RBF kernel (Smola and Schölkopf, 2004). Both of these models learn a regression function using the features to estimate a numerical target value. The parameters that govern the behavior of RR and SVR are the regularization λ for RR and the C, ϵ, and γ parameters for SVR. At testing time, the predictions are bounded to obtain scores in the range $[0, 5]$. We perform tuning on a subset of the training set separately for each RTM model and optimize against the performance evaluated with R^2, the coefficient of determination.

We do not build a separate model for different types of sentences and instead use all of the training set for building a large prediction model. We also use transductive learning since using only the relevant training data for training can improve the performance (Biçici, 2011). Transductive learning is performed at the sentence level where for each test instance, we select 1250 relevant training instances using the cosine similarity metric over the feature vectors and build an individual model for the test instance and predict the similarity score.

[3] We use WMT'13 corpora from www.statmt.org/wmt13/.

3.2 Training Results

Table 1 lists the 10-fold cross-validation (CV) results on the training set for RR and SVR for different RTM systems using optimized parameters. As we combine different perspectives, the performance improves and we use the L+S with SVR for run 1 (LSSVR), L+P+S with SVR for run 2 (LPSSVR), and L+P+S with SVR using transductive learning for run 3 (LPSSVRTL) all in the translation direction $S_1 \rightarrow S_2$. Lemmatized RTM, L, performs the best among the individual perspectives. We also build RTM models in the direction $S_2 \rightarrow S_1$, which gives similar results. The last main row combines them to obtain the bi-directional results, $S_1 \rightleftarrows S_2$, which improves the performance. Each additional perspective adds another 289 features to the representation and the bi-directional results double the number of features. Thus, $S_1 \rightleftarrows S_2$ L+P+S is using 1734 features.

3.3 STS Challenge Results

Table 2 presents the STS challenge r and ranking results containing our CNGL submissions, the best system result, and the mean results over all submissions. There were 89 submissions from 35 competing systems (Agirre et al., 2013). The results are ranked according to the mean r obtained. We also include the mean result over all of the submissions and its corresponding rank.

According to the official results, CNGL-LSSVR is the 30th system from the top based on the mean r obtained and CNGL-LPSSVR is 15th according to the results on OnWN out of 89 submissions in total.

System	head	OnWN	FNWN	SMT	mean	rank
CNGL-LSSVR	.6552	.6943	.2016	.3005	.5086	30
CNGL-LPSSVRTL	.6385	.6756	.1823	.3098	.4998	33
CNGL-LPSSVR	.6510	.6971	.1180	.2861	.4961	36
UMBC-EB.-PW	.7642	.7529	.5818	.3804	.6181	1
mean	.6071	.5089	.2906	.3004	.4538	57

Table 2: STS challenge r and ranking results ranked according to the mean r obtained. head is headlines and mean is the mean of all submissions.

CNGL submissions perform unexpectedly low in the FNWN task and only slightly better than the average in the SMT task. The lower performance is likely to be due to using an out-of-domain corpus for building the RTM models and it may also be due to using and optimizing a single model for all types of tasks.

3.4 Bi-directional RTM Models

The STS task similarity score is directional invariant: $q(S_1, S_2) = q(S_2, S_1)$. We develop RTM models in the reverse direction and obtain bi-directional RTM models by combining both. Table 3 lists the bi-directional results on the STS challenge test set after tuning, which shows that slight improvement in the scores are possible when compared with Table 2. Transductive learning improves the performance in general. We also compare with the performance obtained when combining uni-directional models with mean, min, or max functions. Taking the minimum performs better than other combination approaches and can achieve $r = 0.5129$ with TL. One can also take the individual confidence scores obtained for each score when combining scores.

4 Conclusion

Referential translation machines provide a clean and intuitive computational model for automatically measuring semantic similarity by measuring the acts of translation involved and achieve to be the 15th on some tasks and 30th overall in the STS challenge out of 89 submissions in total. RTMs make quality and semantic similarity judgments possible based on the retrieval of relevant training data as interpretants for reaching shared semantics.

	System	head	OnWN	FNWN	SMT	mean
LS	mean	.6552	.6943	.2016	.3005	.5086
	mean TL	.6397	.6808	.1776	.3147	.5028
	min	.6512	.6947	.2003	.2984	.5066
	min TL	.6416	.6853	.1903	.3143	.5055
	max	.6669	.6680	.1867	.2737	.4958
	max TL	.6493	.6805	.1846	.3127	.5059
	$S_1 \rightleftarrows S_2$	.6388	.6695	.1667	.2999	.4938
	$S_1 \rightleftarrows S_2$ TL	.6285	.6686	.0918	.2931	.4816
LPS	mean	.6510	.6971	.1179	.2861	.4961
	mean TL	.6524	.6918	.1940	.3176	.5121
	min	.6608	.6953	.1704	.2922	.5053
	min TL	.6509	.6864	.1792	.3156	.5084
	max	.6588	.6800	.1355	.2868	.4961
	max TL	.6493	.6805	.1846	.3127	.5059
	$S_1 \rightleftarrows S_2$	.6251	.6843	.0677	.2994	.4845
	$S_1 \rightleftarrows S_2$ TL	.6370	.6978	.0951	.2980	.4936
RLPS	mean	.6517	.7136	.1002	.2880	.4996
	mean TL	.6383	.6841	.2434	.3063	.5059
	min	.6615	.7099	.1644	.2877	.5072
	min TL	.6606	.6987	.1972	.3059	.5129
	max	.6589	.7019	.0995	.2935	.5008
	max TL	.6362	.6896	.2044	.3153	.5063
	$S_1 \rightleftarrows S_2$	.6300	.7011	.0817	.2798	.4850
	$S_1 \rightleftarrows S_2$ TL	.6321	.6956	.1995	.3128	.5052

Table 3: Bi-directional STS challenge r and ranking results ranked according to the mean r obtained. We combine the two directions by taking the mean, min, or the max or use the bi-directional RTM model $S_1 \rightleftarrows S_2$.

Acknowledgments

This work is supported in part by SFI (07/CE/I1142) as part of the Centre for Next Generation Localisation (www.cngl.ie) at Dublin City University and in part by the European Commission through the QTLaunchPad FP7 project (No: 296347). We also thank the SFI/HEA Irish Centre for High-End Computing (ICHEC) for the provision of computational facilities and support.

References

Eneko Agirre, Daniel Cer, Mona Diab, and Aitor Gonzalez-Agirre. 2012. Semeval-2012 task 6: A pilot on semantic textual similarity. In **SEM 2012: The First Joint Conference on Lexical and Computational Semantics – Volume 1: Proceedings of the main conference and the shared task, and Volume 2: Proceedings of the Sixth International Workshop on Semantic Evaluation (SemEval 2012)*, pages 385–393, Montréal, Canada, 7-8 June. Association for Computational Linguistics.

Eneko Agirre, Daniel Cer, Mona Diab, Aitor Gonzalez-Agirre, and Weiwei Guo. 2013. *SEM 2013 shared task: Semantic textual similarity, including a pilot on typed-similarity. In **SEM 2013: The Second Joint Conference on Lexical and Computational Semantics*. Association for Computational Linguistics.

Collin F. Baker, Charles J. Fillmore, and John B. Lowe. 1998. The berkeley framenet project. In *Proceedings of the 36th Annual Meeting of the Association for Computational Linguistics and 17th International Conference on Computational Linguistics - Volume 1*, ACL '98, pages 86–90, Stroudsburg, PA, USA. Association for Computational Linguistics.

Daniel Bär, Chris Biemann, Iryna Gurevych, and Torsten Zesch. 2012. Ukp: Computing semantic textual similarity by combining multiple content similarity measures. In **SEM 2012: The First Joint Conference on Lexical and Computational Semantics – Volume 1: Proceedings of the main conference and the shared task, and Volume 2: Proceedings of the Sixth International Workshop on Semantic Evaluation (SemEval 2012)*, pages 435–440, Montréal, Canada, 7-8 June. Association for Computational Linguistics.

Ergun Biçici and Josef van Genabith. 2013. CNGL: Grading student answers by acts of translation. In **SEM 2013: The First Joint Conference on Lexical and Computational Semantics and Proceedings of the Seventh International Workshop on Semantic Evaluation (SemEval 2013)*, Atlanta, Georgia, USA, 14-15 June. Association for Computational Linguistics.

Ergun Biçici and Deniz Yuret. 2011a. Instance selection for machine translation using feature decay algorithms. In *Proceedings of the Sixth Workshop on Statistical Machine Translation*, pages 272–283, Edinburgh, Scotland, July. Association for Computational Linguistics.

Ergun Biçici and Deniz Yuret. 2011b. RegMT system for machine translation, system combination, and evaluation. In *Proceedings of the Sixth Workshop on Statistical Machine Translation*, pages 323–329, Edinburgh, Scotland, July. Association for Computational Linguistics.

Ergun Biçici, Declan Groves, and Josef van Genabith. 2013. Predicting sentence translation quality using extrinsic and language independent features. *Machine Translation*.

Ergun Biçici. 2011. *The Regression Model of Machine Translation*. Ph.D. thesis, Koç University. Supervisor: Deniz Yuret.

Ergun Biçici. 2008. Consensus ontologies in socially interacting multiagent systems. *Journal of Multiagent and Grid Systems*.

Carl Hugo Björnsson. 1968. *Läsbarhet*. Liber.

Chris Bliss. 2012. Comedy is translation, February. http://www.ted.com/talks/chris_bliss_comedy_is_translation.html.

Peter F. Brown, Stephen A. Della Pietra, Vincent J. Della Pietra, and Robert L. Mercer. 1993. The mathematics of statistical machine translation: Parameter estimation. *Computational Linguistics*, 19(2):263–311, June.

Chris Callison-Burch, Philipp Koehn, Christof Monz, Matt Post, Radu Soricut, and Lucia Specia. 2012. Findings of the 2012 workshop on statistical machine translation. In *Proceedings of the Seventh Workshop on Statistical Machine Translation*, pages 10–51, Montréal, Canada, June. Association for Computational Linguistics.

George Doddington. 2002. Automatic evaluation of machine translation quality using n-gram co-occurrence statistics. In *Proceedings of the second international conference on Human Language Technology Research*, pages 138–145, San Francisco, CA, USA. Morgan Kaufmann Publishers Inc.

Myroslava O. Dzikovska, Rodney D. Nielsen, and Chris Brew. 2012. Towards effective tutorial feedback for explanation questions: A dataset and baselines. In *Proceedings of the 2012 Conference of the North American Chapter of the Association for Computational Linguistics: Human Language Technologies*, pages 200–210, Montréal, Canada, June. Association for Computational Linguistics.

Kenth Hagström. 2012. Swedish readability calculator. https://github.com/keha76/Swedish-Readability-Calculator.

George A. Miller. 1995. Wordnet: a lexical database for english. *Communications of the ACM*, 38(11):39–41, November.

Kishore Papineni, Salim Roukos, Todd Ward, and Wei-Jing Zhu. 2002. BLEU: a method for automatic evaluation of machine translation. In *Proceedings of 40th Annual Meeting of the Association for Computational Linguistics*, pages 311–318, Philadelphia, Pennsylvania, USA, July. Association for Computational Linguistics.

Sameer S. Pradhan, Eduard H. Hovy, Mitchell P. Marcus, Martha Palmer, Lance A. Ramshaw, and Ralph M. Weischedel. 2007. Ontonotes: a unified relational semantic representation. *Int. J. Semantic Computing*, 1(4):405–419.

Yoav Seginer. 2007. *Learning Syntactic Structure*. Ph.D. thesis, Universiteit van Amsterdam.

Alex J. Smola and Bernhard Schölkopf. 2004. A tutorial on support vector regression. *Statistics and Computing*, 14(3):199–222, August.

Kristina Toutanova, Dan Klein, Christopher D. Manning, and Yoram Singer. 2003. Feature-rich part-of-speech tagging with a cyclic dependency network. In *Proceedings of the 2003 Conference of the North American Chapter of the Association for Computational Linguistics on Human Language Technology - Volume 1*, NAACL '03, pages 173–180, Stroudsburg, PA, USA. Association for Computational Linguistics.

Wikipedia. 2013. Lix. http://en.wikipedia.org/wiki/LIX.

A Dataset of Syntactic-Ngrams over Time from a Very Large Corpus of English Books

Yoav Goldberg
Bar Ilan University*
yoav.goldberg@gmail.com

Jon Orwant
Google Inc.
orwant@google.com

Abstract

We created a dataset of syntactic-ngrams (counted dependency-tree fragments) based on a corpus of 3.5 million English books. The dataset includes over 10 billion distinct items covering a wide range of syntactic configurations. It also includes temporal information, facilitating new kinds of research into lexical semantics over time. This paper describes the dataset, the syntactic representation, and the kinds of information provided.

1 Introduction

The distributional hypothesis of Harris (1954) states that properties of words can be captured based on their contexts. The consequences of this hypothesis have been leveraged to a great effect by the NLP community, resulting in algorithms for inferring syntactic as well as semantic properties of words (see e.g. (Turney and Pantel, 2010; Baroni and Lenci, 2010) and the references therein).

In this paper, we describe a very large dataset of *syntactic*-ngrams, that is, structures in which the contexts of words are based on their respective position in a syntactic parse tree, and not on their sequential order in the sentence: the different words in the ngram may be far apart from each other in the sentence, yet close to each other syntactically. See Figure 1 for an example of a syntactic-ngram.

The utility of syntactic contexts of words for constructing vector-space models of word meanings is well established (Lin, 1998; Lin and Pantel, 2001; Padó and Lapata, 2007; Baroni and Lenci, 2010). Syntactic relations are successfully used for modeling selectional preferences (Erk and Padó, 2008; Erk et al., 2010; Ritter et al., 2010; Séaghdha, 2010), and dependency paths are also used to infer binary relations between words (Lin and Pantel, 2001; Wu and Weld, 2010). The use of syntactic-ngrams holds promise also for improving the accuracy of core NLP tasks such as syntactic language-modeling (Shen et al., 2008) and syntactic-parsing (Chen et al., 2009; Sagae and Gordon, 2009; Cohen et al., 2012), though most successful attempts to improve syntactic parsing by using counts from large corpora are based on sequential rather than syntactic information (Koo et al., 2008; Bansal and Klein, 2011; Pitler, 2012), we believe this is because large-scale datasets of syntactic counts are not readily available. Unfortunately, most work utilizing counts from large textual corpora does not use a standardized corpora for constructing their models, making it very hard to reproduce results and challenging to compare results across different studies.

Our aim in this work is not to present new methods or results, but rather to provide a new kind of a large-scale (based on corpora about 100 times larger than previous efforts) high-quality and standard resource for researchers to build upon. Instead of focusing on a specific task, we aim to provide a flexible resource that could be adapted to many possible tasks.

Specifically, the contribution of this work is in creating a dataset of syntactic-ngrams which is:

- Derived from a very large (345 billion words) corpus spanning a long time period.
- Covers a wide range of syntactic phenomena and is adaptable to many use cases.
- Based on state-of-the-art syntactic processing in a modern syntactic representation.
- Broken down by year of occurrence, as well

*Work performed while at Google.

*Second Joint Conference on Lexical and Computational Semantics (*SEM), Volume 1: Proceedings of the Main Conference and the Shared Task*, pages 241–247, Atlanta, Georgia, June 13-14, 2013. ©2013 Association for Computational Linguistics

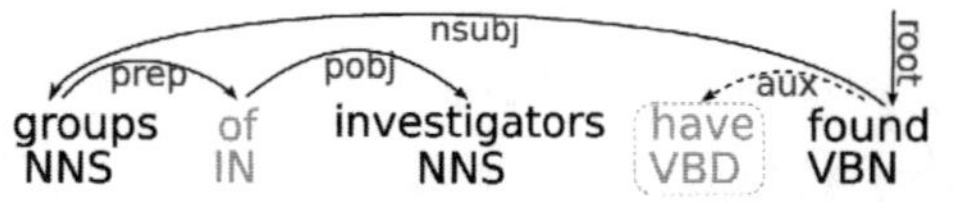

Figure 1: A syntactic ngram appearing 112 times in the *extended-biarcs* set, which include structures containing three content words (see Section 4). Grayed items are non-content words and are not included in the word count. The dashed auxiliary "have" is a functional marker (see Section 3), appearing only in the *extended-** sets.

- as some coarse-grained regional and genre distinctions (British, American, Fiction).
- Freely available for non-commercial use. [1]

After describing the underlying syntactic representation, we will present our definition of a syntactic-ngram, and detail the kinds of syntactic-ngrams we chose to include in the dataset. Then, we present details of the corpus and the syntactic processing we performed.

With respect to previous efforts, the dataset has the following distinguishing characteristics:

Temporal Dimension A unique aspect of our dataset is the temporal dimension, allowing inspection of how the contexts of different words vary over time. For example, one could examine how the meaning of a word evolves over time by looking at the contexts it appears in within different time periods. Figure 2 shows the cosine similarity between the word "rock" and the words "stone" and "jazz" from year 1930 to 2000, showing that rock acquired a new meaning around 1968.

Large syntactic contexts Previous efforts of providing syntactic counts from large scale corpora (Baroni and Lenci, 2010) focus on relations between two content words. Our dataset include structures covering much larger tree fragments, some of them including 5 or more content words. By including such structures we hope to encourage research exploring higher orders of interactions, for example modeling the relation between adjectives of two conjoined nouns, the interactions between subjects and objects of verbs, or fine-grained selectional preferences of verbs and nouns.

[1]The dataset is made publicly available under the Creative Commons Attribution-Non Commercial ShareAlike 3.0 Unported License: http://creativecommons.org/licenses/by-nc-sa/3.0/legalcode.

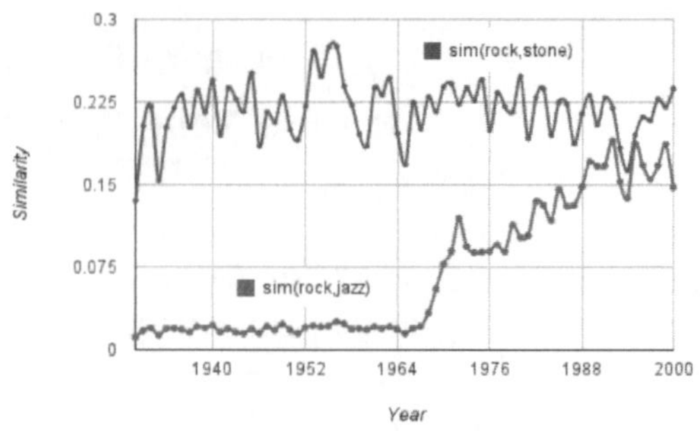

Figure 2: Word-similarity over time: The word "rock" starts to become similar to "jazz" around 1968. The plot shows the cosine similarity between the immediate syntactic contexts of of the word "rock" in each year, to the immediate syntactic contexts of the words "jazz" (in red) and "stone" (in blue) aggregated over all years.

A closely related effort to add syntactic annotation to the books corpus is described in Lin et al. (2012). That effort emphasize an interactive query interface covering several languages, in which the underlying syntactic representations are linear-ngrams enriched with universal part-of-speech tags, as well as first order unlabeled dependencies. In contrast, our emphasis is not on an easy-to-use query interface but instead a useful and flexible resource for computational-minded researchers. We focus on English and use finer-grained English-specific POS-tags. The syntactic analysis is done using a more accurate parser, and we provide counts over *labeled* tree fragments, covering a diverse set of tree-fragments many of which include more than two content words.

Counted Fragments instead of complete trees While some efforts provide complete parse trees from large corpora (Charniak, 2000; Baroni et al., 2009; Napoles et al., 2012), we instead provide counted tree fragments. We believe that our form of aggregate information is of more immediate use than the raw parse trees. While access to the parse trees may allow for somewhat greater flexibility in the kinds of questions one could ask, it also comes with a very hefty price tag in terms of the required computational resources: while counting seems trivial, it is, in fact, quite demanding computationally when done on such a scale, and requires a massive infrastructure. By lifting this burden of NLP researchers, we hope to free them to tackle interesting research questions.

2 Underlying Syntactic Representation

We assume the part-of-speech tagset of the Penn Treebank (Marcus et al., 1993). The syntactic representation we work with is based on dependency-grammar. Specifically, we use labeled dependency trees following the "basic" variant of the Stanford-dependencies scheme (de Marneffe and Manning, 2008b; de Marneffe and Manning, 2008a).

Dependency grammar is a natural choice, as it emphasizes individual words and explicitly models the connections between them. Stanford dependencies are appealing because they model relations between content words directly, without intervening functional markers (so in a construction such as "wanted to know" there is a direct relation `(wanted, know)` instead of two relation `(wanted, to)` and `(to, know)`. This facilitates focusing on meaning-bearing content words and including the maximal amount of information in an ngram.

3 Syntactic-ngrams

We define a syntactic-ngram to be a rooted connected dependency tree over k words, which is a subtree of a dependency tree over an entire sentence. For each of the k words in the ngram, we provide information about the word-form, its part-of-speech, and its dependency relation to its head. The ngram also indicates the relative ordering between the different words (the order of the words in the syntactic-ngram is the same as the order in which the words appear in the underlying sentence) but not the distance between them, nor an indication whether there is a missing material between the nodes. Examples of syntactic-ngrams are provided in Figures 1 and 3.

Content-words and Functional-markers We distinguish between *content-words* which are meaning bearing elements and *functional-markers*, which serve to add polarity, modality or definiteness information to the meaning bearing elements, but do not carry semantic meaning of their own, such as the auxiliary verb "have" in Figure 1. Specifically, we treat words with a dependency-label of `det, poss, neg, aux, auxpass, ps, mark, complm` and `prt` as functional-markers. With the exception of `poss`, these are all closed-class categories. All other words except for prepositions and conjunctions are treated as content-words. A syntactic-ngram of order n includes exactly n content words. It may optionally include all of the functional-markers that modify the content-words.

Conjunctions and Prepositions Conjunctions and Prepositions receive a special treatment. When a coordinating word ("and", "or", "but") appears as part of a conjunctive structure (e.g. "X, Y, and Z"), it is treated as a non-content word. Instead, it is always included in the syntactic-ngrams that include the conjunctive relation it is a part of, allowing to differentiate between the various kinds of conjunctions. An example is seen in Figure 3d, in which the relation `conj(efficient, effective)` is enriched with the coordinating word "or". When a coordinating word does not explicitly take part in a conjunction relation (e.g. "But, ...") it is treated as a content word.

When a preposition is part of a prepositional modification (i.e. in the middle of the pair `(prep, pcomp)` or `(prep, pobj)`), such as the word "of" in Figures 1 and 3h and the word "as" in Figure 3e, it is treated as a non-content word, and is always included in a syntactic-ngram whenever the words it connects are included. In cases of ellipsis or other cases where there is no overt pobj or pcomp ("he is hard to deal with") the preposition is treated as a content word.[2]

Multiword Expressions Some multiword expressions are recognized by the parser. Whenever a content word in an ngram has modifiers with the `mwe` relation, they are included in the ngram.

4 The Provided Ngram Types

We aimed to include a diverse set of relations, with maximal emphasis on relations between content-bearing words, while still retaining access to defi-

[2]This treatment of prepositions and conjunction is similar to the "collapsed" variant of Stanford Dependencies (de Marneffe and Manning, 2008a), in which preposition- and conjunction-words do not appear as nodes in the tree but are instead annotated on the dependency label between the content words they connect, e.g. `prep_with(saw, telescope)`. However, we chose to represent the preposition or conjunction as a node in the tree rather than moving it to the dependency label as it retains the information about the location of the function word with respect to the other words in the structure, is consistent with cases in which one of the content words is not present, and does not blow up the label-set size.

niteness, modality and polarity if they are desired. The dataset includes the following types of syntactic structures:

nodes (47M items) consist of a single content word, and capture the syntactic role of that word (as in Figure 3a). For example, we can learn that the pronoun "he" is predominantly used as a subject, and that "help" as a noun is over 4 times more likely to appear in object than in subject position.

arcs (919M items) consist of two content words, and capture direct dependency relations such as "subject of", "adverbial modifier of" and so on (see Figure 3c,3d for examples). These correspond to "dependency triplets" as used in Lin (1998) and most other work on syntax-based semantic similarity.

biarcs (1.78B items) consist of three content words (either a word and its two daughters, or a child-parent-grandparent chain) and capture relations such as "subject verb object", "a noun and two adjectivial modifiers", "verb, object and adjectivial modifier of the object" and many others.

triarcs (1.87B items) consist of four content words (example in Figure 3f). The locality of the dependency representation causes this set of three-arcs structures to be large, sparse and noisy – many of the relations may appear random because some arcs are in many cases almost independent given the others. However, some of the relations are known to be of interest, and we hope more of them will prove to be of interest in the future. Some of the interesting relations include:

- modifiers of the head noun of the subject or object in an SVO construction: ((small,boy), ate, cookies), (boy, ate, (tasty, cookies)), and with abstraction: adjectives that a boy likes to eat: (boy, ate, (tasty, *))
- arguments of an embeded verb (said, (boy, ate, cookie)), (said, ((small, boy), ate))
- modifiers of conjoined elements ((small, boy) (young, girl)) , ((small, *) (young, *))
- relative clause constructions (boy, (girl, with-cookies, saw))

quadarcs (187M items) consist of 5 content words (example in Figure 3h). In contrast to the previous datasets, this set includes only a subset of the possible relations involving 5 content words. We chose to focus on relations which are attested in the literature (Padó and Lapata 2007; Appendix A), namely structures consisting of two chains of length 2 with a single head, e.g. ((small, boy), ate, (tasty, cookie)).

extended-nodes, extended-arcs, extended-biarcs, extended-triarcs, extended-quadarcs (80M, 1.08B, 1.62B, 1.71B, and 180M items) Like the above, but the functional markers of each content words are included as well (see examples in Figures 3b, 3e, 3g). These structures retain information regarding aspects such as modality, polarity and definiteness, distinguishing, e.g. "his red car" from "her red car", "will go" from "should go" and "a best time" from "the best time".

verbargs (130M items) This set of ngrams consist of verbs with all their immediate arguments, and can be used to study interactions between modifiers of a verb, as well as subcategorization frames. These structures are also useful for syntactic language modeling, as all the daughters of a verb are guaranteed to be present.

nounargs (275M items) This set of ngrams consist of nouns with all their immediate arguments.

verbargs-unlex, nounargs-unlex (114M, 195M items) Like the above, but only the head word and the top-1000 occurring words in the English-1M subcorpus are lexicalized – other words are replaced with a `*W*` symbol. By abstracting away from non-frequent words, we include many of the larger syntactic configurations that will otherwise be pruned away by our frequency threshold. These could be useful for inspecting fine-grained syntactic subcategorization frames.

5 Corpora and Syntactic Processing

The dataset is based on the English Google Books corpus. This is the same corpus used to derive the Google Books Ngrams, and is described in detail in Michel et al. (2011). The corpus consists of the text of 3,473,595 English books which were published between 1520 and 2008, with the majority of the content published after 1800. We provide counts based on the entire corpus, as well as on several subsets of it:

English 1M Uniformly sampled 1 million books.
Fiction Works of Fiction.
American English Books published in the US.
British English Books published in Britain.

The sizes of the different corpora are detailed in Table 1.

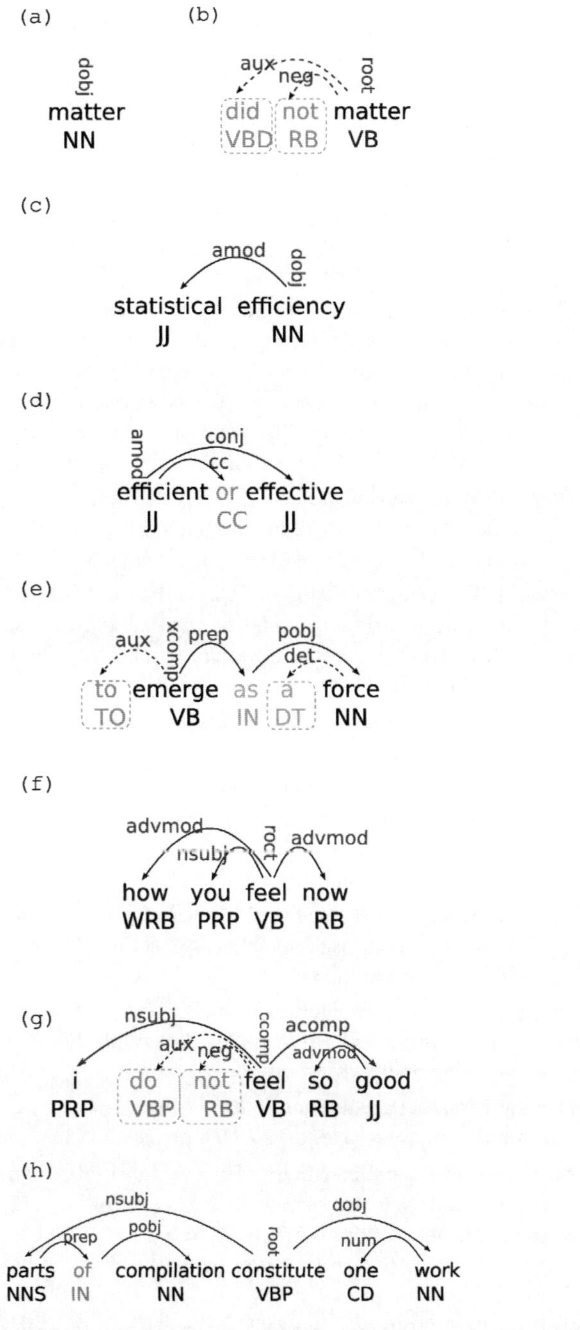

Figure 3: Syntactic-ngram examples. Non-content words are grayed, functional markers appearing only in the extended-* collections are dashed. (a) node (b) extended-node (c) arcs (d) arcs, including the coordinating word (e) extended-arcs, including a preposition (f) triarcs (g) extended-triarcs (h) quadarcs, including a preposition.

Counts Each syntactic ngram in each of the sub-corpora is coupled with a corpus-level count as well as counts from each individual year. To keep the data manageable, we employ a frequency threshold of 10 on the corpus-level count.

Corpus	# Books	# Pages	# Sentences	# Tokens
All	3.5M	925.7M	17.6B	345.1B
1M	1M	291.1M	5.1B	101.3B
Fiction	817K	231.3M	4.7B	86.1B
American	1.4M	387.6M	7.9B	146.2B
British	423K	124.9M	2.4B	46.1B

Table 1: Corpora sizes.

Data Processing We ignored pages with over 600 white-spaces (which are indicative of OCR errors or non-textual content), as well as sentences of over 60 tokens. Table 1 details the sizes of the various corpora.

After OCR, sentence splitting and tokenization, the corpus went through several stages of syntactic processing: part-of-speech tagging, syntactic parsing, and syntactic-ngrams extraction.

Part-of-speech tagging was performed using a first order CRF tagger, which was trained on a union of the Penn WSJ Corpus (Marcus et al., 1993), the Brown corpus (Kucera and Francis, 1967) and the Questions Treebank (Judge et al., 2006). In addition to the diverse training material, the tagger makes use of features based on word-clusters derived from tri-grams of the Books corpus. These cluster-features make the tagger more robust on the books domain. For further details regarding the tagger, see Lin et al. (2012).

Syntactic parsing was performed using a re-implementation of a beam-search shift-reduce dependency parser (Zhang and Clark, 2008) with a beam of size 8 and the feature-set described in Zhang and Nivre (2011). The parser was trained on the same training data as the tagger after 4-way jack-knifing so that the parser is trained on data with predicted part-of-speech tags. The parser provides state-of-the-art syntactic annotations for English.[3]

[3]Evaluating the quality of syntactic annotation on such a varied dataset is a challenging task on its own right – the underlying corpus includes many different genres spanning different time periods, as well as varying levels of digitization and OCR quality. It is extremely difficult to choose a representative sample to manually annotate and evaluate on, and we believe no single number will do justice to describing the annotation quality across the entire dataset. On top of that, we then aggregate fragments and filter based on counts, further changing the data distribution. We feel that it is better not to provide any numbers than to provide inaccurate, misleading or uninformative num-

6 Conclusion

We created a dataset of syntactic-ngrams based on a very large literary corpus. The dataset contains over 10 billion unique items covering a wide range of syntactic structures, and includes a temporal dimension.

The dataset is available for download at `http://storage.googleapis.com/books/syntactic-ngrams/index.html`

Acknowledgments

We would like to thank the members of Google's extended syntactic-parsing team (Ryan McDonald, Keith Hall, Slav Petrov, Dipanjan Das, Hao Zhang, Kuzman Ganchev, Terry Koo, Michael Ringgaard and, at the time, Joakim Nivre) for many discussions, support, and of course the creation and maintenance of an extremely robust parsing infrastructure. We further thank Fernando Pereira for supporting the project, and Andrea Held and Supreet Chinnan for their hard work in making this possible. Sebastian Padó, Marco Baroni, Alessandro Lenci, Jonathan Berant and Dan Klein provided valuable input that helped shape the final form of this resource.

References

Mohit Bansal and Dan Klein. 2011. Web-scale features for full-scale parsing. In *ACL*, pages 693–702.

Marco Baroni and Alessandro Lenci. 2010. Distributional memory: A general framework for corpus-based semantics. *Computational Linguistics*, 36(4):673–721.

Marco Baroni, Silvia Bernardini, Adriano Ferraresi, and Eros Zanchetta. 2009. The wacky wide web: a collection of very large linguistically processed web-crawled corpora. *Language Resources and Evaluation*, 43(3):209–226.

Eugene Charniak. 2000. Bllip 1987-89 wsj corpus release 1. In *Linguistic Data Consortium*, Philadelphia.

Wenliang Chen, Jun'ichi Kazama, Kiyotaka Uchimoto, and Kentaro Torisawa. 2009. Improving dependency parsing with subtrees from auto-parsed data. In *EMNLP*, pages 570–579.

bers. We therefore chose not to provide a numeric estimation of syntactic-annotation quality, but note that we used a state-of-the-art parser, and believe most of its output to be correct, although we do expect a fair share of annotation errors as well.

Raphael Cohen, Yoav Goldberg, and Michael Elhadad. 2012. Domain adaptation of a dependency parser with a class-class selectional preference model. In *Proceedings of ACL 2012 Student Research Workshop*, pages 43–48, Jeju Island, Korea, July. Association for Computational Linguistics.

Marie-Catherine de Marneffe and Christopher D. Manning. 2008a. Stanford dependencies manual. Technical report, Stanford University.

Marie-Catherine de Marneffe and Christopher D. Manning. 2008b. The stanford typed dependencies representation. In *Coling 2008: Proceedings of the workshop on Cross-Framework and Cross-Domain Parser Evaluation*, CrossParser '08, pages 1–8, Stroudsburg, PA, USA. Association for Computational Linguistics.

Katrin Erk and Sebastian Padó. 2008. A structured vector space model for word meaning in context. In *Proceedings of EMNLP*, Honolulu, HI. To appear.

Katrin Erk, Sebastian Padó, and Ulrike Padó. 2010. A flexible, corpus-driven model of regular and inverse selectional preferences. *Computational Linguistics*, 36(4):723–763.

Zellig Harris. 1954. Distributional structure. *Word*, 10(23):146–162.

John Judge, Aoife Cahill, and Josef van Genabith. 2006. Questionbank: Creating a corpus of parse-annotated questions. In *Proc. of ACL*, pages 497–504. Association for Computational Linguistics.

Terry Koo, Xavier Carreras, and Michael Collins. 2008. Simple semi-supervised dependency parsing. In *Proc. of ACL*, pages 595–603.

Henry Kucera and W. Nelson Francis. 1967. *Computational Analysis of Present-Day American English*. Brown University Press.

Dekang Lin and Patrick Pantel. 2001. Dirt: discovery of inference rules from text. In *KDD*, pages 323–328.

Yuri Lin, Jean-Baptiste Michel, Erez Aiden Lieberman, Jon Orwant, Will Brockman, and Slav Petrov. 2012. Syntactic annotations for the google books ngram corpus. In *ACL (System Demonstrations)*, pages 169–174.

Dekang Lin. 1998. Automatic retrieval and clustering of similar words. In *Proceedings of the 36th Annual Meeting of the Association for Computational Linguistics and 17th International Conference on Computational Linguistics - Volume 2*, ACL '98, pages 768–774, Stroudsburg, PA, USA. Association for Computational Linguistics.

Mitchell P. Marcus, Beatrice Santorini, and Mary Ann Marcinkiewicz. 1993. Building a large annotated corpus of English: The Penn Treebank. *Computational Linguistics*, 19:313–330.

Jean-Baptiste Michel, Yuan Kui Shen, Aviva Presser Aiden, Adrian Veres, Matthew K. Gray, The Google Books Team, Joseph P. Pickett, Dale Hoiberg, Dan Clancy, Peter Norvig, Jon Orwant, Steven Pinker, Martin A. Nowak, and Erez Lieberman Aiden. 2011. Quantitative analysis of culture using millions of digitized books. *Science*, 331(6014):176–182.

Courtney Napoles, Matthew Gormley, and Benjamin Van Durme. 2012. Annotated gigaword. In *AKBC-WEKEX Workshop at NAACL 2012*, June.

Sebastian Padó and Mirella Lapata. 2007. Dependency-based construction of semantic space models. *Computational Linguistics*, 33(2):161–199.

Emily Pitler. 2012. Attacking parsing bottlenecks with unlabeled data and relevant factorizations. In *ACL*, pages 768–776.

Alan Ritter, Mausam, and Oren Etzioni. 2010. A latent dirichlet allocation method for selectional preferences. In *ACL*, pages 424–434.

Kenji Sagae and Andrew S. Gordon. 2009. Clustering words by syntactic similarity improves dependency parsing of predicate-argument structures. In *IWPT*, pages 192–201.

Diarmuid Ó Séaghdha. 2010. Latent variable models of selectional preference. In *ACL*, pages 435–444.

Libin Shen, Jinxi Xu, and Ralph M. Weischedel. 2008. A new string-to-dependency machine translation algorithm with a target dependency language model. In *ACL*, pages 577–585.

P.D. Turney and P. Pantel. 2010. From frequency to meaning: Vector space models of semantics. *Journal of Artificial Intelligence Research*, 37(1):141–188.

Fei Wu and Daniel S. Weld. 2010. Open information extraction using wikipedia. In *ACL*, pages 118–127.

Yue Zhang and Stephen Clark. 2008. A tale of two parsers: Investigating and combining graph-based and transition-based dependency parsing. In *Proc. of EMNLP*, pages 562–571.

Yue Zhang and Joakim Nivre. 2011. Transition-based dependency parsing with rich non-local features. In *Proceedings of the 49th Annual Meeting of the Association for Computational Linguistics: Human Language Technologies*, pages 188–193.

Unsupervised Word Usage Similarity in Social Media Texts

Spandana Gella,[♣] **Paul Cook,**[♣] and **Bo Han**[♠♣]
[♠] NICTA Victoria Research Laboratory
[♣] Department of Computing and Information Systems, The University of Melbourne
sgella@student.unimelb.edu.au, paulcook@unimelb.edu.au,
hanb@student.unimelb.edu.au

Abstract

We propose an unsupervised method for automatically calculating word usage similarity in social media data based on topic modelling, which we contrast with a baseline distributional method and Weighted Textual Matrix Factorization. We evaluate these methods against a novel dataset made up of human ratings over 550 Twitter message pairs annotated for usage similarity for a set of 10 nouns. The results show that our topic modelling approach outperforms the other two methods.

1 Introduction

In recent years, with the growing popularity of social media applications, there has been a steep rise in the amount of "post"-based user-generated text (including microblog posts, status updates and comments) (Bennett, 2012). This data has been identified as having potential for applications ranging from trend analysis (Lau et al., 2012a) and event detection (Osborne et al., 2012) to election outcome prediction (O'Connor et al., 2010). However, given that posts are generally very short, noisy and lacking in context, traditional NLP approaches tend to perform poorly over social media data (Hong and Davison, 2010; Ritter et al., 2011; Han et al., 2012).

This is the first paper to address the task of lexical semantic interpretation in microblog data based on word usage similarity. Word usage similarity (USIM: Erk et al. (2009)) is a relatively new paradigm for capturing similarity in the usages of a given word independently of any lexicon or sense inventory. The task is to rate on an ordinal scale the similarity in usage between two different usages of the same word. In doing so, it avoids common issues in conventional word sense disambiguation, relating to sense underspecification, the appropriateness of a static sense inventory to a given domain, and the inability to capture similarities/overlaps between word senses. As an example of USIM, consider the following pairing of Twitter posts containing the target word *paper*:

1. Deportation of Afghan Asylum Seekers from Australia : This **paper** aims to critically evaluate a newly signed agree.

2. @USER has his number on a piece of **paper** and I walkd off!

The task is to predict a real-valued number in the range $[1, 5]$ for the similarity in the respective usages of *paper*, where 1 indicates the usages are completely different and 5 indicates they are identical.

In this paper we develop a new USIM dataset based on Twitter data. In experiments on this dataset we demonstrate that an LDA-based topic modelling approach outperforms a baseline distributional semantic approach and Weighted Textual Matrix Factorization (WTMF: Guo and Diab (2012a)). We further show that context expansion using a novel hashtag-based strategy improves both the LDA-based method and WTMF.

2 Related Work

Word sense disambiguation (WSD) is the task of determining the particular sense of a word from a given set of pre-defined senses (Navigli, 2009). It

*Second Joint Conference on Lexical and Computational Semantics (*SEM), Volume 1: Proceedings of the Main Conference and the Shared Task*, pages 248–253, Atlanta, Georgia, June 13-14, 2013.

contrasts with word sense induction (WSI), where the senses of a given target word are induced from an unannotated corpus of usages, and the induced senses are then used to disambiguate each token usage of the word (Manandhar et al., 2010; Lau et al., 2012b). WSD and WSI have been the predominant paradigms for capturing and evaluating lexical semantics, and both assume that each usage corresponds to exactly one of a set of discrete senses of the target word, and that any prediction other than the "correct" sense is equally wrong.

Erk et al. (2009) showed that, given a sense inventory, there is a high likelihood of multiple senses being compatible with a given usage, and proposed USIM as a means of capturing the similarity in usage between a pairing of usages of a given word. As part of their work, they released a dataset, which Lui et al. (2012) recently developed a topic modelling approach over. Based on extensive experimentation, they demonstrated the best results with a single topic model for all target words based on full document context. Our topic modelling-based approach to USIM builds off the approach of Lui et al. (2012). Guo and Diab (2012a) observed that, when applied to short texts, the effectiveness of latent semantic approaches can be boosted by expanding the text to include "missing" words. Based on this, they proposed Weighted Textual Matrix Factorization (WTMF), based on weighted matrix factorization (Srebro and Jaakkola, 2003). Here we experiment with both LDA based topic modeling and WTMF to estimate word similarities in twitter data. LDA based topic modeling has been earlier studied on Twitter data for tweet classification (Ramage et al., 2010) and tweet clustering (Jin et al., 2011).

3 Data Preparation

This section describes the construction of the USIM-tweet dataset based on microblog posts ("tweets") from Twitter. We describe the pre-processing steps taken to sample the tweets in our datasets, outline the annotation process, and then describe the background corpora used in our experiments.

3.1 Data preprocessing

Around half of Twitter is non-English (Hong et al., 2011), so our first step was to automatically identify English tweets using `langid.py` (Lui and Baldwin, 2012). We next performed lexical normalization using the dictionary of Han et al. (2012) to convert lexical variants (e.g., *tmrw*) to their standard forms (e.g., *tomorrow*) and reduce data sparseness. As our target words, we chose the 10 nouns from the original USIM dataset of Erk et al. (2009) (*bar*, *charge*, *execution*, *field*, *figure*, *function*, *investigator*, *match*, *paper*, *post*), and identified tweets containing the target words as nouns using the CMU Twitter POS tagger (Owoputi et al., 2012).

3.2 Annotation Settings and Data

To collect word usage similarity scores for Twitter message pairs, we used a setup similar to that of Erk et al. (2009) using Amazon Mechanical Turk: we asked the annotators to rate each sentence pair with an integer score in the range $[1, 5]$ using similar annotation guidelines to Erk et al. We randomly sampled twitter messages from the TREC 2011 microblog dataset,[1] and for each of our 10 nouns, we collected 55 pairs of messages satisfying the preprocessing described in Section 3.1. These 55 pairs are chosen such that each tweet has at least 4 content words (nouns, verbs, adjectives and adverbs) and at least 70+% of its post-normalized tokens in the Aspell dictionary (v6.06)[2]; these restrictions were included in an effort to ensure the tweets would contain sufficient linguistic content to be interpretable.[3] We created 110 Mechanical Turk jobs (referred to as HITs), with each HIT containing 5 randomly-selected message pairs. For this annotation the tweets were presented in their original form, i.e., without lexical normalisation applied. Each HIT was completed by 10 "turkers", resulting in a total of 5500 annotations. The annotation was restricted to turkers based in the United States having had at least 95% of their previous HITs accepted. In total, the annotation was carried out by 68 turkers, each completing between 1 and 100 HITs.

To detect outlier annotators, we calculated the average Spearman correlation score (ρ) of every annotator by correlating their annotation values with every other annotator and taking the average. We

[1] `http://trec.nist.gov/data/tweets/`

[2] `http://aspell.net/`

[3] In future analyses we intend to explore the potential impact of these restrictions on the resulting dataset.

Word	Orig	Exp	Word	Orig	Exp
bar	180k	186k	function	26k	27k
charge	41k	43k	investigator	17k	19k
execution	28k	30k	field	72k	75k
figure	28k	29k	match	126k	133k
paper	210k	218k	post	299k	310k

Table 1: The number of tweets for each word in each background corpus ("Orig" = ORIGINAL; "Exp" = EXPANDED; RANDEXPANDED, not shown, contains the same number of tweets as EXPANDED).

accepted all the annotations of annotators whose average ρ is greater than 0.6; this corresponded to 95% of the annotators. Two annotators had a negative average ρ and their annotations (only 4 HITs total) were discarded. For the other annotators (i.e., $0 \leq \rho \leq 0.6$), we accepted each of their HITs on a case by case basis; a HIT was accepted only if at least 2 out of 5 of the annotations for that HIT were within ± 2.0 of the mean for that annotation based on the judgments of the other turkers. (21 HITS were discarded using this heuristic.) We further eliminated 7 HITS which have incomplete judgments. In total only 32 HITs (of the 1100 HITs completed) were discarded through these heuristics. The weighted average Spearman correlation over all annotators after this filtering is 0.681, which is somewhat higher than the inter-annotator agreement of 0.548 reported by Erk et al. (2009). This dataset is available for download.

3.3 Background Corpus

We created three background corpora based on data from the Twitter Streaming API in February 2012 (only tweets satisfying the preprocessing steps in Section 3.1 were chosen).

ORIGINAL: 1 million tweets which contain at least one of the 10 target nouns;

EXPANDED: ORIGINAL plus an additional 40k tweets containing at least 1 hashtag attested in ORIGINAL with an average frequency of use of 10–35 times/hour (medium frequency);

RANDEXPANDED: ORIGINAL plus 40k randomly sampled tweets containing the same target nouns.

We select medium-frequency hashtags because low-frequency hashtags tend to be ad hoc and non-thematic in nature, while high-frequency hashtags are potentially too general to capture *usage* similarity. Statistics for ORIGINAL and EXPANDED/RANDEXPANDED are shown in Table 1. RANDEXPANDED is sampled such that it has the same number of tweets as EXPANDED.

4 Methodology

We propose an LDA topic modelling-based approach to the USIM task, which we contrast with a baseline distributional model and WTMF. In all these methods, the similarity between two word usages is measured using cosine similarity between the vector representation of each word usage.

4.1 Baseline

We represent each target word usage in a tweet as a second-order co-occurrence vector (Schütze, 1998). A second-order co-occurrence vector is built from the centroid (summation) of all the first-order co-occurrence vectors of the context words in the same tweet as the target word.

The first-order co-occurrence vector for a given target word represents the frequency with which that word co-occurs in a tweet with other context words. Each first-order vector is built from all tweets which contain a context word and the target word categorized as noun in the background corpus, thus sensitizing the first-order vector to the target word. We use the most frequent 10000 words (excluding stopwords) in the background corpus as our first-order vector dimensions/context words. Context words (dimensions) in the first-order vectors are weighted by mutual information.

Second-order co-occurrence is used as the context representation to reduce the effects of data sparseness in the tweets (which cannot be more than 140 codepoints in length).

4.2 Weighted Textual Matrix Factorization

WTMF (Guo and Diab, 2012b) addresses the data sparsity problem suffered by many latent variable

Model	ORIGINAL	EXPANDED	RANDEXPANDED
Baseline	0.09	0.08	0.09
WTMF	0.02	0.09	0.06
LDA	**0.20**	**0.29**	0.18

Table 2: Spearman rank correlation (ρ) for each method based on each background corpus. The best result for each corpus is shown in **bold**.

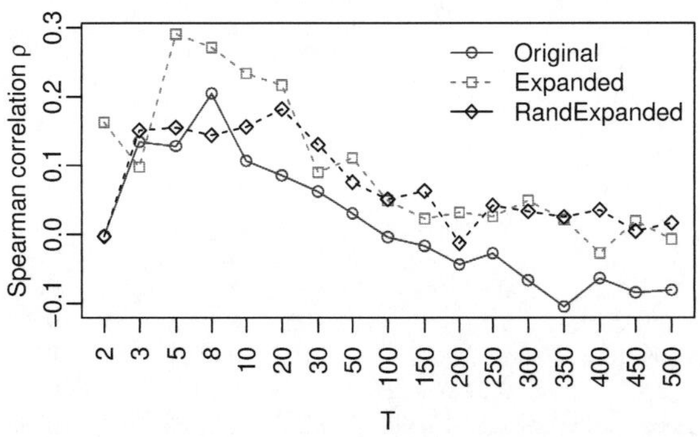

Figure 1: Spearman rank correlation (ρ) for LDA for varying numbers of topics (T) using different background corpora.

models by predicting "missing" words on the basis of the message content, and including them in the vector representation. Guo and Diab showed WTMF to outperform LDA on the SemEval-2012 semantic textual similarity task (STS) (Agirre et al., 2012). The semantic space required for this model as applied here is built from the background tweets corresponding to the target word. We experimented with the missing weight parameter w_m of WTMF in the range $[0.05, 0.01, 0.005, 0.0005]$ and with dimensions K=100 and report the best results ($w_m = 0.0005$).

4.3 Topic Modelling

Latent Dirichlet Allocation (LDA) (Blei et al., 2003) is a generative model in which a document is modeled as a finite mixture of topics, where each topic is represented as a multinomial distribution of words. We treat each tweet as a document. Topics sensitive to each target word are generated from its corresponding background tweets. We topic model each target word individually,[4] and create a topic vector for each word usage based on the topic allocations of the context words in that usage. We use Gibbs sampling in Mallet (McCallum, 2002) for training and inference of the LDA model. We experimented with the number of topics T for each target word ranging from 2 to 500. We optimized the hyper parameters by choosing those which best fit the data every 20 iterations over a total of 800 iterations, following 200 burn-in iterations.

[4]Unlike Lui et al. (2012) we found a single topic model for all target words to perform very poorly.

5 Results

We evaluate the above methods for word usage similarity on the dataset constructed in Section 3.2. We evaluate our models against the mean human ratings using Spearman's rank correlation. Table 2 presents results for each method using each background corpus. The results for LDA are for the optimal setting for T (8, 5, and 20 for ORIGINAL, EXPANDED, and RANDEXPANDED, respectively). LDA is superior to both the baseline and WTMF using each background corpus. The performance of LDA improves for EXPANDED but not RANDEXPANDED, over ORIGINAL, demonstrating the effectiveness of our hashtag based corpus expansion strategy.

In Figure 1 we plot the rank correlation of LDA across all words against the number of topics (T). As the number of topics increases beyond a certain number, the rank correlation decreases. LDA trained on EXPANDED consistently outperforms ORIGINAL and RANDEXPANDED for lower values of T (i.e., $T <= 20$).

In Table 3, we show results for LDA over each target word, for ORIGINAL and EXPANDED. (Results for RANDEXPANDED are not shown but are similar to ORIGINAL.) Results are shown for the optimal T for each lemma, and the optimal T over all lemmas. Optimizing T for each lemma gives an indication of the upperbound of the performance of LDA, and unsurprisingly gives better performance than us-

Lemma	ORIGINAL		EXPANDED	
	Per lemma	Global	Per lemma	Global
	ρ (T)	ρ (T=8)	ρ (T)	ρ (T=5)
bar	0.39 (10)	**0.28**	**0.35 (50)**	0.1
charge	**0.27 (30)**	0.04	**0.33 (20)**	−0.08
execution	**0.43 (8)**	**0.43**	**0.58 (5)**	**0.58**
field	**0.46 (5)**	**0.33**	**0.53 (10)**	0.32
figure	0.24 (150)	0.06	0.24 (250)	0.14
function	**0.44 (8)**	**0.44**	**0.40 (10)**	**0.27**
investigator	**0.3 (30)**	0.05	**0.50 (5)**	**0.50**
match	**0.28 (5)**	0.26	**0.45 (5)**	**0.45**
paper	**0.29 (30)**	0.20	0.32 (30)	0.22
post	0.1 (3)	−0.13	0.2 (30)	−0.01

Table 3: Spearman's ρ using LDA for the optimal T for each lemma (Per lemma) and the best T over all lemmas (Global) using ORIGINAL and EXPANDED. ρ values that are significant at the 0.05 level are shown in **bold**.

ing a fixed T for all lemmas. This suggests that approaches that learn an appropriate number of topics (e.g., HDP, (Teh et al., 2006)) could give further improvements; however, given the size of the dataset, the computational cost of HDP could be a limitation.

Contrasting our results with a fixed number of topics to those of Lui et al. (2012), our highest rank correlation of 0.29 ($T = 5$ using EXPANDED) is higher than the 0.11 they achieved over the original USIM dataset (where the documents offer an order of magnitude more context). The higher inter-annotator agreement for USIM-tweet compared to the original USIM dataset (Section 3.2), combined with this finding, demonstrates that USIM over microblog data is indeed a viable task.

Returning to the performance of LDA relative to WTMF in Table 2, the poor performance of WTMF is somewhat surprising here given WTMF's encouraging performance on the somewhat similar SemEval-2012 STS task. This difference is possibly due to the differences in the tasks: usage similarity measures the similarity of the usage of a target word while STS measures the similarity of two texts. Differences in domain — i.e., Twitter here and more standard text for STS — could also be a factor. WTMF attempts to alleviate the data sparsity problem by adding information from "missing" words in a text by assigning a small weight to these missing words. Because of the prevalence of lexical variation on Twitter, some missing words might be counted multiple times (e.g., *coool*, *kool*, and *kewl* all meaning roughly *cool*) thus indirectly assigning higher weights to the missing words leading to the lower performance of WTMF compared to LDA.

6 Summary

We have analysed word usage similarity in microblog data. We developed a new dataset (USIM-tweet) for usage similarity of nouns over Twitter. We applied a topic modelling approach to this task, and contrasted it with baseline and benchmark methods. Our results show that the LDA-based approach outperforms the other methods over microblog data. Moreover, our novel hashtag-based corpus expansion strategy substantially improves the results.

In future work, we plan to expand our annotated dataset, experiment with larger background corpora, and explore alternative corpus expansion strategies. We also intend to further analyse the difference in performance LDA and WTMF on similar data.

Acknowledgements

We are very grateful to Timothy Baldwin for his tremendous help with this work. We additionally thank Diana McCarthy for her insightful comments on this paper. We also acknowledge the European Erasmus Mundus Masters Program in Language and Communication Technologies from the European Commission.

NICTA is funded by the Australian government as represented by Department of Broadband, Communication and Digital Economy, and the Australian Research Council through the ICT Centre of Excellence programme.

References

Eneko Agirre, Daniel Cer, Mona Diab, and Aitor Gonzalez-Agirre. 2012. Semeval-2012 task 6: A pilot on semantic textual similarity. In *Proceedings of the Sixth International Workshop on Semantic Evaluation (SemEval 2012)*, pages 385–393, Montreal, Canada.

Shea Bennett. 2012. Twitter on track for 500 million total users by March, 250 million active users by end of 2012. `http://www.mediabistro.com/alltwitter/twitter-active-total-users_b17655.`

David M. Blei, Andrew Y. Ng, and Michael I. Jordan. 2003. Latent Dirichlet allocation. *Journal of Machine Learning Research*, 3:993–1022.

Katrin Erk, Diana McCarthy, and Nicholas Gaylord. 2009. Investigations on word senses and word usages. In *Proceedings of the Joint conference of the 47th Annual Meeting of the Association for Computational Linguistics and the 4th International Joint Conference on Natural Language Processing of the Asian Federation of Natural Language Processing (ACL-IJCNLP 2009)*, pages 10–18, Singapore.

Weiwei Guo and Mona Diab. 2012a. Modeling sentences in the latent space. In *Proc. of the 50th Annual Meeting of the Association for Computational Linguistics*, pages 864–872, Jeju, Republic of Korea.

Weiwei Guo and Mona Diab. 2012b. Weiwei: A simple unsupervised latent semantics based approach for sentence similarity. In *Proceedings of the First Joint Conference on Lexical and Computational Semantics (*SEM 2012)*, pages 586–590, Montreal, Canada.

Bo Han, Paul Cook, and Timothy Baldwin. 2012. Automatically constructing a normalisation dictionary for microblogs. In *Proceedings of the Joint Conference on Empirical Methods in Natural Language Processing and Computational Natural Language Learning 2012*, pages 421–432, Jeju, Republic of Korea.

Liangjie Hong and Brian D Davison. 2010. Empirical study of topic modeling in twitter. In *Proc. of the First Workshop on Social Media Analytics*, pages 80–88.

Lichan Hong, Gregoria Convertino, and Ed H. Chi. 2011. Language matters in Twitter: A large scale study. In *Proceedings of the 5th International Conference on Weblogs and Social Media (ICWSM 2011)*, pages 518–521, Barcelona, Spain.

Ou Jin, Nathan N Liu, Kai Zhao, Yong Yu, and Qiang Yang. 2011. Transferring topical knowledge from auxiliary long texts for short text clustering. In *Proc. of the 20th ACM International Conference on Information and Knowledge Management*, pages 775–784.

Jey Han Lau, Nigel Collier, and Timothy Baldwin. 2012a. On-line trend analysis with topic models: #twitter trends detection topic model online. In *Proceedings of the 24th International Conference on Computational Linguistics (COLING 2012)*, pages 1519–1534, Mumbai, India.

Jey Han Lau, Paul Cook, Diana McCarthy, David Newman, and Timothy Baldwin. 2012b. Word sense induction for novel sense detection. In *Proceedings of the 13th Conference of the European Chapter of the Association for Computational Linguistics (EACL 2012)*, pages 591–601, Avignon, France.

Marco Lui and Timothy Baldwin. 2012. langid.py: An off-the-shelf language identification tool. In *Proceedings of the 50th Annual Meeting of the Association for Computational Linguistics (ACL 2012) Demo Session*, pages 25–30, Jeju, Republic of Korea.

Marco Lui, Timothy Baldwin, and Diana McCarthy. 2012. Unsupervised estimation of word usage similarity. In *Proceedings of the Australasian Language Technology Workshop 2012 (ALTW 2012)*, pages 33–41, Dunedin, New Zealand.

Suresh Manandhar, Ioannis Klapaftis, Dmitriy Dligach, and Sameer Pradhan. 2010. SemEval-2010 Task 14: Word sense induction & disambiguation. In *Proceedings of the 5th International Workshop on Semantic Evaluation*, pages 63–68, Uppsala, Sweden.

Andrew Kachites McCallum. 2002. Mallet: A machine learning for language toolkit. `http://mallet.cs.umass.edu`.

Roberto Navigli. 2009. Word sense disambiguation: A survey. *ACM Computing Surveys*, 41(2).

Brendan O'Connor, Ramnath Balasubramanyan, Bryan R. Routledge, and Noah A. Smith. 2010. From tweets to polls: Linking text sentiment to public opinion time series. In *Proceedings of the 4th International Conference on Weblogs and Social Media*, pages 122–129, Washington, USA.

Miles Osborne, Sasa Petrović, Richard McCreadie, Craig Macdonald, and Iadh Ounis. 2012. Bieber no more: First story detection using Twitter and Wikipedia. In *Proceedings of the SIGIR 2012 Workshop on Time-aware Information Access*, Portland, USA.

Olutobi Owoputi, Brendan O'Connor, Chris Dyer, Kevin Gimpel, and Nathan Schneider. 2012. Part-of-speech tagging for Twitter: Word clusters and other advances. Technical Report CMU-ML-12-107, Carnegie Mellon University.

Daniel Ramage, Susan Dumais, and Dan Liebling. 2010. Characterizing microblogs with topic models. In *International AAAI Conference on Weblogs and Social Media*, volume 5, pages 130–137.

Alan Ritter, Sam Clark, Mausam, and Oren Etzioni. 2011. Named entity recognition in tweets: An experimental study. In *Proceedings of the 2011 Conference on Empirical Methods in Natural Language Processing*, pages 1524–1534, Edinburgh, UK.

Hinrich Schütze. 1998. Automatic word sense discrimination. *Computational Linguistics*, 24(1):97–123.

Nathan Srebro and Tommi Jaakkola. 2003. Weighted low-rank approximations. In *Proceedings of the 20th International Conference on Machine Learning*, Washington, USA.

Yee Whye Teh, Michael I. Jordan, Matthew J. Beal, and David M. Blei. 2006. Hierarchical Dirichlet processes. *Journal of the American Statistical Association*, 101:1566–1581.

Keynote Address:
More Words and Bigger Pictures

David Forsyth
University of Illinois
Urbana-Champaign
daf@illinois.edu

Abstract

Object recognition is a little like translation: a picture (text in a source language) goes in, and a description (text in a target language) comes out. I will use this analogy, which has proven fertile, to describe recent progress in object recognition.

We have very good methods to spot some objects in images, but extending these methods to produce descriptions of images remains very difficult. The description might come in the form of a set of words, indicating objects, and boxes or regions spanned by the object. This representation is difficult to work with, because some objects seem to be much more important than others, and because objects interact. An alternative is a sentence or a paragraph describing the picture, and recent work indicates how one might generate rich structures like this. Furthermore, recent work suggests that it is easier and more effective to generate descriptions of images in terms of chunks of meaning ("person on a horse") rather than just objects ("person"; "horse").

Finally, if the picture contains objects that are unfamiliar, then we need to generate useful descriptions that will make it possible to interact with them, even though we don't know what they are.

About the Speaker

David Forsyth is currently a full professor at U. Illinois at Urbana-Champaign, where he moved from U.C Berkeley, where he was also full professor. He has published over 130 papers on computer vision, computer graphics and machine learning. He has served as program chair and as general chair for various international conferences on computer vision. He received an IEEE technical achievement award for 2005 for his research and became an IEEE fellow in 2009. His textbook, "Computer Vision: A Modern Approach" (joint with J. Ponce and published by Prentice Hall) is widely adopted as a course text. A second edition appeared in 2011. He was named editor in chief of IEEE TPAMI for a term starting in Jan 2013.

*Second Joint Conference on Lexical and Computational Semantics (*SEM), Volume 1: Proceedings of the Main Conference and the Shared Task*, page 254, Atlanta, Georgia, June 13-14, 2013. ©2013 Association for Computational Linguistics

Exploring Vector Space Models to Predict the Compositionality of German Noun-Noun Compounds

Sabine Schulte im Walde and Stefan Müller and Stephen Roller
Institut für Maschinelle Sprachverarbeitung
Universität Stuttgart
Pfaffenwaldring 5b, 70569 Stuttgart, Germany
{schulte,muellesn,roller}@ims.uni-stuttgart.de

Abstract

This paper explores two hypotheses regarding vector space models that predict the compositionality of German noun-noun compounds: (1) Against our intuition, we demonstrate that window-based rather than syntax-based distributional features perform better predictions, and that not adjectives or verbs but nouns represent the most salient part-of-speech. Our overall best result is state-of-the-art, reaching Spearman's $\rho = 0.65$ with a word-space model of nominal features from a 20-word window of a 1.5 billion word web corpus. (2) While there are no significant differences in predicting compound–modifier vs. compound–head ratings on compositionality, we show that the modifier (rather than the head) properties predominantly influence the degree of compositionality of the compound.

1 Introduction

Vector space models and distributional information have been a steadily increasing, integral part of lexical semantic research over the past 20 years. On the one hand, *vector space models* (see Turney and Pantel (2010) and Erk (2012) for two recent surveys) have been exploited in psycholinguistic (Lund and Burgess, 1996) and computational linguistic research (Schütze, 1992) to explore the notion of "similarity" between a set of target objects within a geometric setting. On the other hand, the *distributional hypothesis* (Firth, 1957; Harris, 1968) has been exploited to determine co-occurrence features for vector space models that best describe the words, phrases, sentences, etc. of interest.

While the emergence of vector space models is increasingly pervasive within data-intensive lexical semantics, and even though useful features have been identified in general terms:[1] when it comes to a specific semantic phenomenon, we need to explore the relevant distributional features in order to investigate the respective phenomenon. Our research is interested in the meaning of German compounds. More specifically, we aim to predict the degrees of compositionality of German noun-noun compounds (e.g., *Feuerwerk* 'fire works') with regard to the meanings of their constituents (e.g., *Feuer* 'fire' and *Werk* 'opus'). This prediction uses vector space models, and our goal is to identify salient features that determine the degree of compositionality of the compounds by relying on the distributional similarities between the compounds and their constituents.

In this vein, we systematically explore window-based and syntax-based contextual clues. Since the targets in our vector space models are all nouns (i.e., the compound nouns, the modifier nouns, and the head nouns), our hypothesis is that ***adjectives and verbs are expected to provide salient distributional properties***, as adjective/verb meaning and noun meaning are in a strong interdependent relationship. Even more, we expect adjectives and verbs that are syntactically bound to the nouns under consideration (syntax-based, i.e., attributive adjectives and subcategorising verbs) to outperform those that "just" appear in the window contexts of the nouns (window-based). In order to investigate this first

[1] See Agirre et al. (2009) and Bullinaria and Levy (2007; 2012), among others, for systematic comparisons of co-occurrence features on various semantic relatedness tasks.

*Second Joint Conference on Lexical and Computational Semantics (*SEM), Volume 1: Proceedings of the Main Conference and the Shared Task*, pages 255–265, Atlanta, Georgia, June 13-14, 2013.

hypothesis, we compare window-based and syntax-based distributional features across parts-of-speech.

Concerning a more specific aspect of compound meaning, we are interested in the contributions of the *modifier* noun versus *head* noun properties with regard to the meaning of the noun-noun compounds. While there has been prior psycholinguistic research on the constituent contributions (e.g., Gagné and Spalding (2009; 2011)), computational linguistics has not yet paid much attention to this issue, as far as we know. Our hypothesis is that ***the distributional properties of the head constituents are more salient than the distributional properties of the modifier constituents in predicting the degree of compositionality of the compounds***. In order to assess this second hypothesis, we compare the vector space similarities between the *compounds and their modifier constituents* with those of the *compounds and their head constituents*, with regard to the overall most successful features.

The paper is organised as follows. Section 2 introduces the compound data that is relevant for this paper, i.e., the noun-noun compounds and the compositionality ratings. Section 3 performs and discusses the vector space experiments to explore our hypotheses, and Section 4 describes related work.

2 Data

2.1 German Noun-Noun Compounds

Compounds are combinations of two or more simplex words. Traditionally, a number of criteria (such as compounds being syntactically inseparable, and that compounds have a specific stress pattern) have been proposed, in order to establish a border between compounds and non-compounds. However, Lieber and Stekauer (2009a) demonstrated that none of these tests are universally reliable to distinguish compounds from other types of derived words.

Compounds have thus been a recurrent focus of attention within theoretical, cognitive, and in the last decade also within computational linguistics. Recent evidence of this strong interest are the Handbook of Compounding (Lieber and Stekauer, 2009b) on theoretical perspectives, and a series of workshops[2] and special journal issues with respect to multi-word expressions (including various types of compounds) and the computational perspective (Journal of Computer Speech and Language, 2005; Language Resources and Evaluation, 2010; ACM Transactions on Speech and Language Processing, to appear).

Our focus of interest is on German noun-noun compounds (see Fleischer and Barz (2012) for a detailed overview and Klos (2011) for a recent detailed exploration), such as *Ahornblatt* 'maple leaf', *Feuerwerk* 'fireworks', and *Obstkuchen* 'fruit cake' where both the grammatical head (in German, this is the rightmost constituent) and the modifier are nouns. More specifically, we are interested in the degrees of compositionality of German noun-noun compounds, i.e., the semantic relatedness between the meaning of a compound (e.g., *Feuerwerk*) and the meanings of its constituents (e.g., *Feuer* 'fire' and *Werk* 'opus').

Our work is based on a selection of noun compounds by von der Heide and Borgwaldt (2009), who created a set of 450 concrete, depictable German noun compounds according to four compositionality classes: compounds that are transparent with regard to both constituents (e.g., *Ahornblatt* 'maple leaf'); compounds that are opaque with regard to both constituents (e.g., *Löwenzahn* 'lion+tooth → dandelion'); compounds that are transparent with regard to the modifier but opaque with regard to the head (e.g., *Feuerzeug* 'fire+stuff → lighter'); and compounds that are opaque with regard to the modifier but transparent with regard to the head (e.g., *Fliegenpilz* 'fly+mushroom → toadstool').

From the compound set by von der Heide and Borgwaldt, we disregarded noun compounds with more than two constituents (in some cases, the modifier or the head was complex itself) as well as compounds where the modifiers were not nouns. Our final set comprises a subset of their compounds including 244 two-part noun-noun compounds.

2.2 Compositionality Ratings

von der Heide and Borgwaldt (2009) collected human ratings on compositionality for all their 450 compounds. The compounds were distributed over 5 lists, and 270 participants judged the degree of compositionality of the compounds with respect to their first as well as their second constituent, on

[2] www.multiword.sourceforge.net

Compounds			Mean Ratings and Standard Deviations			
whole	literal meanings of constituents		whole	modifier	head	mean range
Ahornblatt 'maple leaf'	maple	leaf	6.03 ± 1.49	**5.64** ± 1.63	**5.71** ± 1.70	(1) high/high
Postbote 'post man'	mail	messenger	6.33 ± 0.96	**5.87** ± 1.55	**5.10** ± 1.99	
Seezunge 'sole'	sea	tongue	1.85 ± 1.28	**3.57** ± 2.42	**3.27** ± 2.32	(2) mid/mid
Windlicht 'storm lamp'	wind	light	3.52 ± 2.08	**3.07** ± 2.12	**4.27** ± 2.36	
Löwenzahn 'dandelion'	lion	tooth	1.66 ± 1.54	**2.10** ± 1.84	**2.23** ± 1.92	(3) low/low
Maulwurf 'mole'	mouth	throw	1.58 ± 1.43	**2.21** ± 1.68	**2.76** ± 2.10	
Fliegenpilz 'toadstool'	fly/bow tie	mushroom	2.00 ± 1.20	**1.93** ± 1.28	**6.55** ± 0.63	(4) low/high
Flohmarkt 'flea market'	flea	market	2.31 ± 1.65	**1.50** ± 1.22	**6.03** ± 1.50	
Feuerzeug 'lighter'	fire	stuff	4.58 ± 1.75	**5.87** ± 1.01	**1.90** ± 1.03	(5) high/low
Fleischwolf 'meat chopper'	meat	wolf	1.70 ± 1.05	**6.00** ± 1.44	**1.90** ± 1.42	

Table 1: Examples of compound ratings.

a scale between 1 (definitely opaque) and 7 (definitely transparent). For each compound–constituent pair, they collected judgements from 30 participants, and calculated the rating mean and the standard deviation. We refer to this set as our ***compound–constituent ratings***.

A second experiment collected human ratings on compositionality for our subset of 244 noun-noun compounds. In this case, we asked the participants to provide a unique score for each compound as a whole, again on a scale between 1 and 7. The collection was performed via Amazon Mechanical Turk (AMT)[3]. We randomly distributed our subset of 244 compounds over 21 batches, with 12 compounds each, in random order. In order to control for spammers, we also included two German fake compound nouns into each of the batches, in random positions of the lists. If participants did not recognise the fake words, all of their ratings were rejected. We collected between 27 and 34 ratings per target compound. For each of the compounds we calculated the rating mean and the standard deviation. We refer to this second set as our ***compound whole ratings***.

Table 1 presents example mean ratings for the compound–constituent ratings as well as for the compound whole ratings, accompanied by the standard deviations. We selected two examples each for five categories of mean ratings: the compound–constituent ratings were (1) high or (2) mid or (3) low with regard to both constituents; the compound–constituent ratings were (4) low with regard to the modifier but high with regard to the head; (5) vice versa. Roller et al. (2013) performed a thorough analysis of the two sets of ratings, and assessed their reliability from several perspectives.

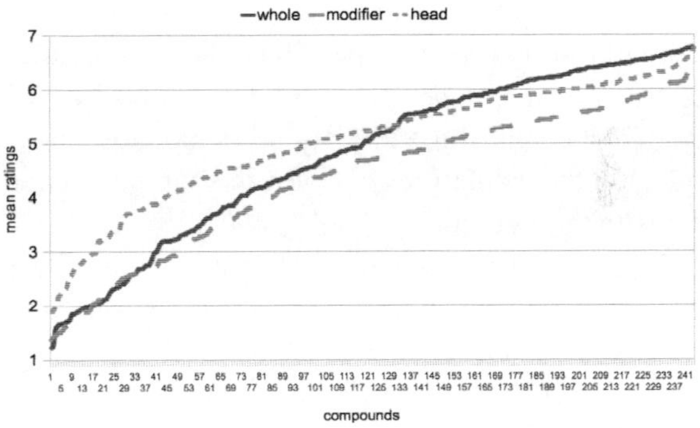

Figure 1: Distribution of compound ratings.

Figure 1 shows how the mean ratings for the compounds as a whole, for the compound–modifier pairs as well as for the compound–head pairs are distributed over the range $[1, 7]$: For each set, we independently sorted the 244 values and plotted them. The purpose of the figure is to illustrate that the ratings for our 244 noun-noun compounds are not particularly skewed to any area within the range.[4]

Figure 2 again shows the mean ratings for the compounds as a whole as well as for the compound–constituent pairs, but in this case only the compound whole ratings were sorted, and the compound–constituent ratings were plotted against the compound whole ratings. According to the plot, the compound–modifier ratings (red) seem to correlate better with the compound whole ratings than the compound–head ratings (yellow) do. This intuition will be confirmed in Section 3.1.

[3]www.mturk.com

[4]The illustration idea was taken from Reddy et al. (2011b).

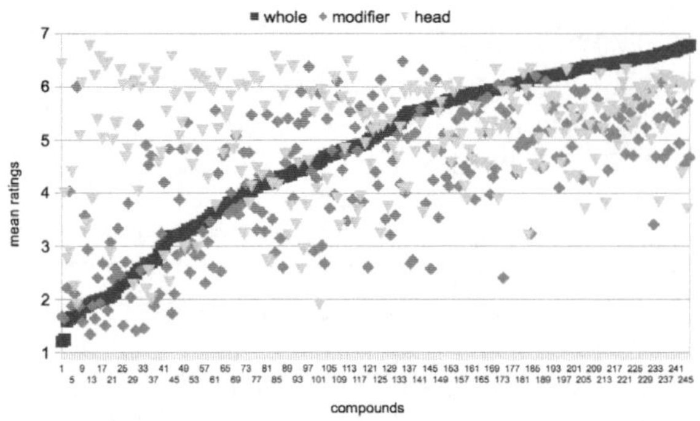

Figure 2: Compounds ratings sorted by *whole* ratings.

3 Vector Space Models (VSMs)

The goal of our vector space models is to identify distributional features that are salient to predict the degree of compositionality of the compounds, by relying on the similarities between the compound and constituent properties.

In all our vector space experiments, we used co-occurrence frequency counts as induced from German web corpora, and calculated *local mutual information (LMI)*[5] values (Evert, 2005), to instantiate the empirical properties of our target nouns with regard to the various corpus-based features. LMI is a measure from information theory that compares the observed frequencies O with expected frequencies E, taking marginal frequencies into account:

$$LMI = O \times log \frac{O}{E},$$

with E representing the product of the marginal frequencies over the sample size.[6] In comparison to (pointwise) mutual information (Church and Hanks, 1990), LMI improves the problem of propagating low-frequent events, by multiplying mutual information by the observed frequency.

Relying on the LMI vector space models, the *cosine* determined the distributional similarity between the compounds and their constituents, which was in turn used to predict the compositionality between the compound and the constituents, assuming that the stronger the distributional similarity (i.e., the *cosine* values), the larger the degree of compositionality.

[5]Alternatively, we also used the raw frequencies in all experiments below. The insights into the various features were identical to those based on LMI, but the predictions were worse.

[6]See `http://www.collocations.de/AM/` for a more detailed illustration of association measures (incl. LMI).

The vector space predictions were evaluated against the human ratings on the degree of compositionality, using the Spearman Rank-Order Correlation Coefficient ρ (Siegel and Castellan, 1988). The ρ correlation is a non-parametric statistical test that measures the association between two variables that are ranked in two ordered series. In Section 3.3 we will compare the overall effect of the various feature types and correlate all 488 compound–modifier and compound–head predictions against the ratings at the same time; in Section 3.4 we will compare the different effects of the features for compound–modifier pairs vs. compound–head pairs and thus correlate 244 predictions in both cases.

After introducing a baseline and an upper bound for our vector space experiments in Section 3.1 as well as our web corpora in Section 3.2, Section 3.3 presents window-based in comparison to syntax-based vector space models (distinguishing various part-of-speech features). In Section 3.4 we then focus on the contribution of modifiers vs. heads in the vector space models, with regard to the overall most successful features.

3.1 Baseline and Upper Bound

Table 2 presents the baseline and the upper bound values for the vector space experiments. The *baseline* in the first two lines follows a procedure performed by Reddy et al. (2011b), and relies on a *random assignment* of rating values $[1, 7]$ to the compound–modifier and the compound–head pairs. The 244 random values for the compound–constituent pairs were then each correlated against the compound whole ratings. The random compound–modifier ratings show a baseline correlation of $\rho = 0.0959$ with the compound whole ratings, and the random compound–head ratings show a baseline correlation of $\rho = 0.1019$ with the compound whole ratings.

The *upper bound* in the first two lines shows the correlations between the human ratings from the two experiments, i.e., between the 244 compound whole ratings and the respective compound–modifier and compound–head ratings. The compound–modifier ratings exhibit a strong correlation with the compound whole ratings ($\rho = 0.6002$), while the correlation between the compound–head ratings and the compound whole ratings is not even moderate

Function	ρ	
	Baseline	Upper Bound
modifier only	.0959	.6002
head only	.1019	.1385
addition	.1168	.7687
multiplication	.1079	.7829

Table 2: Baseline/Upper bound ρ correlations.

($\rho = 0.1385$). Obviously, the semantics of the modifiers had a much stronger impact on the semantic judgements of the compounds, thus confirming our intuition from Section 2.2.

The lower part of the table shows the respective baseline and upper bound values when the compound–modifier ratings and the compound–head ratings were combined by standard arithmetic operations, cf. Widdows (2008) and Mitchell and Lapata (2010), among others: the compound–modifier and compound–head ratings were treated as vectors, and the vector features (i.e., the compound–constituent ratings) were added/multiplied to predict the compound whole ratings. As in the related work, the arithmetic operations strengthen the predictions, and multiplication reached an upper bound of $\rho = 0.7829$, thus outperforming not only the head-only but also the modifier-only upper bound.

3.2 German Web Corpora

Most of our experiments rely on the *sdeWaC* corpus (Faaß et al., 2010), a cleaned version of the German web corpus *deWaC* created by the *WaCky* group (Baroni et al., 2009). The corpus cleaning had focused mainly on removing duplicates from the *deWaC*, and on disregarding sentences that were syntactically ill-formed (relying on a parsability index provided by a standard dependency parser (Schiehlen, 2003)). The sdeWaC contains approx. 880 million words and can be downloaded from `http://wacky.sslmit.unibo.it/`.

While the sdeWaC is an attractive corpus choice because it is a web corpus with a reasonable size, and yet has been cleaned and parsed (so that we can induce syntax-based distributional features), it has one serious drawback for a window-based approach (and, in general, for corpus work going beyond the sentence border): The sentences in the corpus have been sorted alphabetically, so going beyond the sentence border is likely to entering a sentence that did not originally precede or follow the sentence of interest. So window co-occurrence in the sdeWaC actually refers to x words to the left and right BUT within the same sentence. Thus, enlarging the window size does not effectively change the co-occurrence information any more at some point. For this reason, we additionally use *WebKo*, a predecessor version of the sdeWaC, which comprises more data (approx. 1.5 billion words in comparison to 880 million words) and is not alphabetically sorted, but is less clean and had not been parsed (because it was not clean enough).

3.3 Window-based vs. Syntax-based VSMs

Window-based Co-Occurrence When applying window-based co-occurrence features to our vector space models, we specified a corpus, a part-of-speech and a window size, and then determined the co-occurrence strengths of our compound nouns and their constituents with regard to the respective context words. For example, when restricting the part-of-speech to adjectives and the window size to 5, we counted how often our targets appeared with any adjectives in a window of five words to the left and to the right. We looked at lemmas, and deleted any kind of sentence punctuation. In general, we checked windows of sizes 1, 2, 5, 10, and 20. In one case we extended the window up to 100 words.

The window-based models compared the effect of varying the parts-of-speech of the co-occurring words, motivated by the hypothesis that adjectives and verbs were expected to provide salient distributional properties. So we checked which parts-of-speech provided specific insight into the distributional similarity between nominal compounds and nominal constituents: We used common nouns vs. adjectives vs. main verbs that co-occurred with the target nouns in the corpora. Figure 3 illustrates the behaviour of the Spearman Rank-Order Correlation Coefficient values ρ over the window sizes 1, 2, 5, 10, and 20 within sdeWaC (sentence-internal) and WebKo (beyond sentence borders), when restricting and combining the co-occurring parts-of-speech. It is clear from the figure that relying on nouns was the best choice, even better than combining nouns with adjectives and verbs. The differences for nouns vs. adjectives or verbs in the 20-word windows were

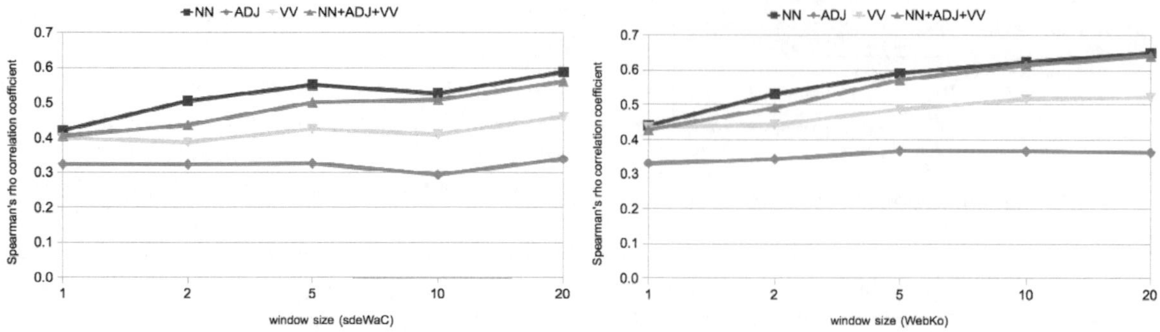

Figure 3: Window-based sdeWaC and WebKo ρ correlations across part-of-speech features.

significant.[7] Furthermore, the larger WebKo data outperformed the cleaned sdeWaC data, reaching an optimal prediction of $\rho = 0.6497$.[8] The corpus differences for NN and NN+ADJ+VV were significant.

As none of the window lines had reached an optimal correlation with a window size of 20 yet (i.e., the correlation values were still increasing), we enlarged the window size up to 100 words, in order to check on the most successful window size. We restricted the experiment to nominal features (with nouns representing the overall most successful features). The correlations did not increase with larger windows: the optimal prediction was still performed at a window size of 20.

Syntax-based Co-Occurrence When applying syntax-based co-occurrence features to our vector space models, we relied only on the sdeWaC corpus because WebKo was not parsed and thus did not provide syntactic information. We specified a syntax-based feature type and then determined the co-occurrence strengths of our compounds and constituents with regard to the respective context words.

In order to test our hypothesis that syntax-based information is more salient than window-based information to predict the compositionality of our compound nouns, we compared a number of potentially salient syntactic features for noun similarity: the syntactic functions of nouns in verb subcategorisation (intransitive and transitive subjects; direct and PP objects), and those categories that frequently modify nouns or are modified by nouns (adjectives and prepositions). With regard to subcategorisation functions, verbs subcategorising our target nouns represented the dimensions in the vector space models. For example, we used all verbs as vector dimensions that took our targets as direct objects, and vector values were based on these syntactic co-occurrences. For a noun like *Buch* 'book', the strongest verb dimensions were *lesen* 'read', *schreiben* 'write', and *kaufen* 'buy'. With regard to modification, we considered the adjectives and prepositions that modified our target nouns, as well as the prepositions that were modified by our target nouns. For the noun *Buch*, strong modifying adjective dimensions were *neu* 'new', *erschienen* 'published', and *heilig* 'holy'; strong modifying preposition dimensions were *in* 'in', *mit* 'with', and *zu* 'on'; and strong modified preposition dimensions were *von* 'by', *über* 'about', and *für* 'for'.

Figure 4 demonstrates that the potentially salient syntactic functions had different effects on predicting compositionality. The top part of the figure shows the modification-based correlations, the middle part shows the subcategorisation-based correlations, and at the bottom of the figure we repeat the ρ correlation values for window-based adjectives and verbs (within a window of 20 words) from the sdeWaC. The syntax-based predictions by modification and subcategorisation were all significantly worse than the predictions by the respective window-based parts-of-speech. Furthermore, the figure shows that there are strong differences with regard to the types of syntactic functions, when predicting compositionality: Relying on our target nouns as transitive subjects of verbs is al-

[7] All significance tests in this paper were performed by Fisher r-to-z transformation.

[8] For a fair corpus comparison, we repeated the experiments with WebKo on sentence-internal data. It still outperformed the sdeWaC corpus.

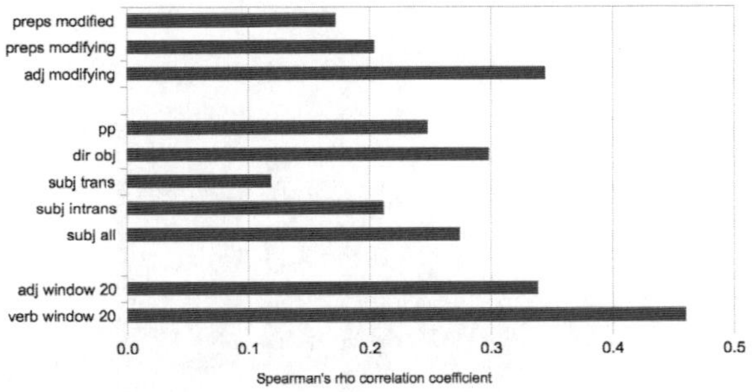

Figure 4: Syntax-based correlations.

most useless ($\rho = 0.1194$); using the intransitive subject function improves the prediction ($\rho = 0.2121$); interestingly, when abstracting over subject (in)transitivity, i.e., when we use all verbs as vector space features that appeared with our target nouns as subjects –independently whether this was an intransitive or a transitive subject– was again more successful ($\rho = 0.2749$). Relying on our noun targets as direct objects is again slightly better ($\rho = 0.2988$); as pp objects it is again slightly worse ($\rho = 0.2485$). None of these differences were significant, though.

Last but not least, we concatenated all syntax-based features to a large syntactic VSM (and we also considered variations of syntax-based feature set concatenations), but the results of any unified combinations were clearly below the best individual predictions. So the best syntax-based predictors were adjectives that modified our compound and constituent nouns, with $\rho = 0.3455$, which however just (non-significantly) outperformed the best adjective setting in our window-based vector space ($\rho = 0.3394$). Modification by prepositions did not provide salient distributional information, with $\rho = 0.2044/0.1725$ relying on modifying/modified prepositions.

In sum, attributive adjectives and verbs that subcategorised our target nouns as direct objects were the most salient syntax-based distributional features but nevertheless predicted worse than "just" window-based adjectives and verbs, respectively.

3.4 Role of Modifiers vs. Heads

This section tests our hypothesis that *the distributional properties of the head constituents are more salient than the distributional properties of the modifier constituents in predicting the degree of compositionality of the compounds*. Our rating data enables us to explore the modifier/head distinction with regard to two perspectives.

Perspective (i): Salient Features for Compound–Modifier vs. Compound–Head Pairs Instead of correlating all 488 compound–constituent predictions against the ratings, we distinguished between the 244 compound–modifier predictions and the 244 compound–head predictions. This perspective allowed us to distinguish between the salience of the various feature types with regard to the semantic relatedness between compound–modifier pairs vs. compound–head pairs.

Figure 5 presents the correlation values when predicting the degrees of compositionality of compound–modifier (***M***$_-$ in the left panel) vs. compound–head (***H***$_-$ in the right panel) pairs, as based on the window features and the various parts-of-speech. The prediction of the parts-of-speech is

NN $>$ NN+ADJ+VV $>$ VV $>$ ADJ

and –with few exceptions– the predictions are improving with increasing window sizes, as the overall predictions in the previous section did. But while in smaller window sizes the predictions of the compound–head ratings are better than those of the compound–modifier ratings, this difference vanishes with larger windows. With regard to a window size of 20 there is no significant difference between predicting the semantic relatedness between compound–modifier vs. compound–head pairs.

When using the syntactic features to predict the degrees of compositionality of compound–modifier vs. head–compound pairs, in all but one of the syntactic feature types the verb subcategorisation as well as the modification functions allowed a stronger prediction of compound–head ratings in comparison to compound–modifier ratings. The only syntactic feature that was significantly better to predict compound–modifier ratings was relying on transitive subjects. In sum, the predictions based on syntactic features in most but not all cases behaved in accordance with our hypothesis.

As in our original experiments in Section 3.3, the syntax-based features were significantly outperformed by the window-based features. The syntactic features reached an optimum of $\rho = 0.2224$ and $\rho = 0.3502$ for predicting modifier–compound

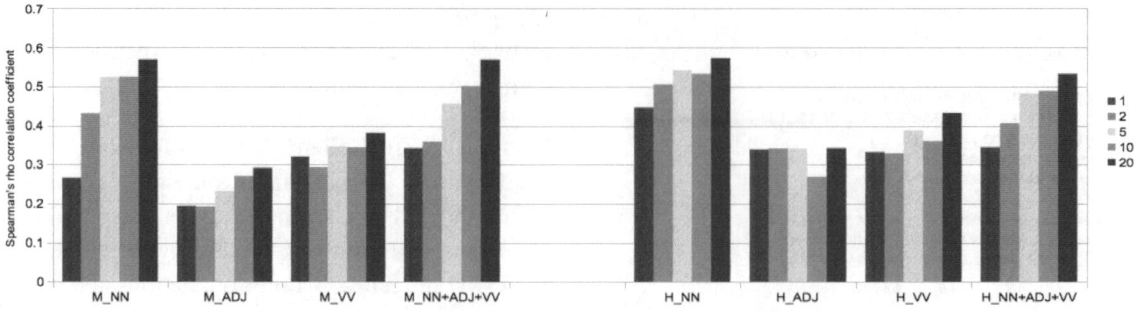

Figure 5: Window-based correlations (modifiers vs. heads).

vs. head–compound degrees of compositionality (in both cases relying on attributive adjectives), in comparison to $\rho = 0.5698$ and $\rho = 0.5745$ when relying on nouns in a window of 20 words.

Perspective (ii): Contribution of Modifiers/Heads to Compound Meaning This final analysis explores the contributions of the modifiers and of the heads with regard to the compound meaning, by correlating only one type of compound–constituent predictions with the compound whole ratings. I.e., we predicted the compositionality of the compound by the distributional similarity between the compound and only one of its constituents, checking if the meaning of the compound is determined more by the meaning of the modifier or the head. This analysis is in accordance with the upper bound in Section 3.1, where the compound–constituent ratings were correlated with the compound whole ratings.

Figure 6 presents the correlation values when determining the compound whole ratings by only compound–modifier predictions, or only compound–head predictions, or by adding or multiplying the modifier and head predictions. The underlying features rely on a 20-word window (adjectives, verbs, nouns, and across parts-of-speech). It is striking that in three out of four cases the predictions of the compound whole ratings were performed similarly well (i) by only the compound–modifier predictions, and (ii) by multiplying the compound–modifier and the compound–head predictions. So, as in the calculation of the upper bound, the distributional semantics of the modifiers had a much stronger impact on the semantics of the compound than the distributional semantics of the heads did.

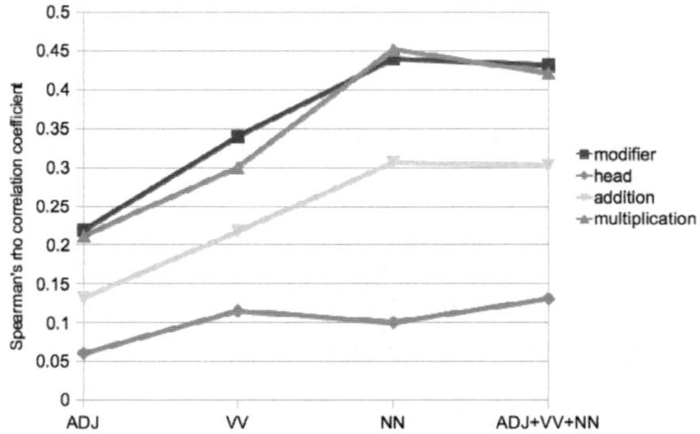

Figure 6: Predicting the compound whole ratings.

3.5 Discussion

The vector space models explored two hypotheses to predict the compositionality of German noun-noun compounds by distributional features. Regarding hypothesis 1, we demonstrated that –against our intuitions– not adjectives or verbs whose meanings are strongly interdependent with the meanings of nouns provided the most salient distributional information, but that relying on nouns was the best choice, in combination with a 20-word window, reaching state-of-the-art $\rho = 0.6497$. The larger but less clean web corpus *WebKo* outperformed the smaller but cleaner successor *sdeWaC*. Furthermore, the syntax-based predictions by adjective/preposition modification and by verb subcategorisation (as well as various concatenations of syntactic VSMs) were all worse than the predictions by the respective window-based parts-of-speech.

Regarding hypothesis 2, we distinguished the contributions of modifiers vs. heads to the compound meaning from two perspectives. (i) The predictions of the compound–modifier vs. compound–

head ratings did not differ significantly when using features from increasing window sizes, but with small window sizes the compound–head ratings were predicted better than the compound–modifier ratings. This insight fits well to the stronger impact of syntax-based features on compound–head in comparison to compound–modifier predictions because –even though German is a language with comparably free word order– we can expect many syntax-based features (especially attributive adjectives and prepositions) to appear in close vicinity to the nouns they depend on or subcategorise. We conclude that the features that are salient to predict similarities between the compound–modifier vs. the compound–head pairs are different, and that based on small windows the distributional similarity between compounds and heads is stronger than between compounds and modifiers, but based on larger contexts this difference vanishes. (ii) With regard to the overall meaning of the compound, the influence of the modifiers was not only much stronger in the human ratings (cf. Section 2) and in the upper bound (cf. Section 3.1), but also in the vector space models (cf. Figure 6). While this insight contradicts our second hypothesis (that the head properties are more salient than the modifier properties in predicting the compositionality of the compound), it fits into a larger picture that has primarily been discussed in psycholinguistic research on compound meaning, where various factors such as the semantic relation between the modifier and the head (Gagné and Spalding, 2009) and the modifier properties, inferential processing and world knowledge (Gagné and Spalding, 2011) were taken into account. However, also in psycholinguistic studies that explore the semantic role of modifiers and heads in noun compounds there is no agreement about which constituent properties are inherited by the compound.

4 Related Work

Most computational approaches to model the meaning or compositionality of compounds have been performed for English, including work on *particle verbs* (McCarthy et al., 2003; Bannard, 2005; Cook and Stevenson, 2006); *adjective-noun combinations* (Baroni and Zamparelli, 2010; Boleda et al., 2013); and *noun-noun compounds* (Reddy et al., 2011b; Reddy et al., 2011a). Most closely related to our work is Reddy et al. (2011b), who relied on window-based distributional models to predict the compositionality of English noun-noun compounds. Their gold standard also comprised compound–constituent ratings as well as compound whole ratings, but the resources had been cleaned more extensively, and they reached $\rho = 0.714$.

Concerning vector space explorations and semantic relatedness in more general terms, Bullinaria and Levy (2007; 2012) also systematically assessed a range of factors in VSMs (corpus type and size, window size, association measures, and corpus preprocessing, among others) against four semantic tasks, however not including compositionality ratings. Similarly, Agirre et al. (2009) compared and combined a WordNet-based and various distributional models to predict the pair similarity of the 65 Rubenstein and Goodenough word pairs and the 353 word pairs in WordSim353. They varied window sizes, dependency relations and raw words in the models. On WordSim353, they reached $\rho = 0.66$, which is slightly better than our best result, but at the same time the dataset is smaller.

Concerning computational models of German compounds, there is not much previous work. Our own work (Schulte im Walde, 2005; Kühner and Schulte im Walde, 2010) has addressed the degrees of compositionality of German particle verbs. Zinsmeister and Heid (2004) are most closely related to our current study. They suggested a distributional model to identify lexicalised German noun compounds by comparing the verbs that subcategorise the noun compound with those that subcategorise the head noun as direct objects.

5 Conclusion

This paper presented experiments to predict the compositionality of German noun-noun compounds. Our overall best result is state-of-the-art, reaching Spearman's $\rho = 0.65$ with a word-space model of nominal features from a 20-word window of a 1.5 billion word web corpus. Our experiments demonstrated that (1) window-based features outperformed syntax-based features, and nouns outperformed adjectives and verbs; (2) the modifier properties predominantly influenced the compositionality.

References

Eneko Agirre, Enrique Alfonseca, Keith Hall, Jana Kravalova, Marius Pasca, and Aitor Soroa. 2009. A Study on Similarity and Relatedness Using Distributional and WordNet-based Approaches. In *Proceedings of the North American Chapter of the Association for Computational Linguistics and Human Language Technologies Conference*, pages 19–27, Boulder, Colorado.

Collin Bannard. 2005. Learning about the Meaning of Verb–Particle Constructions from Corpora. *Computer Speech and Language*, 19:467–478.

Marco Baroni and Roberto Zamparelli. 2010. Nouns are Vectors, Adjectives are Matrices: Representing Adjective-Noun Constructions in Semantic Space. In *Proceedings of the 2010 Conference on Empirical Methods in Natural Language Processing*, pages 1183–1193, Cambridge, MA, October.

Marco Baroni, Silvia Bernardini, Adriano Ferraresi, and Eros Zanchetta. 2009. The WaCky Wide Web: A Collection of Very Large Linguistically Processed Web-Crawled Corpora. *Language Resources and Evaluation*, 43(3):209–226.

Gemma Boleda, Marco Baroni, Nghia The Pham, and Louise McNally. 2013. On Adjective-Noun Composition in Distributional Semantics. In *Proceedings of the 10th International Conference on Computational Semantics*, Potsdam, Germany.

John A. Bullinaria and Joseph P. Levy. 2007. Extracting Semantic Representations from Word Co-Occurrence Statistics: A Computational Study. *Behavior Research Methods*, 39(3):510–526.

John A. Bullinaria and Joseph P. Levy. 2012. Extracting Semantic Representations from Word Co-Occurrence Statistics: Stop-Lists, Stemming, and SVD. *Behavior Research Methods*, 44:890–907.

Kenneth W. Church and Patrick Hanks. 1990. Word Association Norms, Mutual Information, and Lexicography. *Computational Linguistics*, 16(1):22–29.

Paul Cook and Suzanne Stevenson. 2006. Classifying Particle Semantics in English Verb-Particle Constructions. In *Proceedings of the ACL/COLING Workshop on Multiword Expressions: Identifying and Exploiting Underlying Properties*, Sydney, Australia.

Katrin Erk. 2012. Vector Space Models of Word Meaning and Phrase Meaning: A Survey. *Language and Linguistics Compass*, 6(10):635–653.

Stefan Evert. 2005. *The Statistics of Word Co-Occurrences: Word Pairs and Collocations*. Ph.D. thesis, Institut für Maschinelle Sprachverarbeitung, Universität Stuttgart.

Gertrud Faaß Ulrich Heid, and Helmut Schmid. 2010. Design and Application of a Gold Standard for Morphological Analysis: SMOR in Validation. In *Proceedings of the 7th International Conference on Language Resources and Evaluation*, pages 803–810, Valletta, Malta.

John R. Firth. 1957. *Papers in Linguistics 1934-51*. Longmans, London, UK.

Wolfgang Fleischer and Irmhild Barz. 2012. *Wortbildung der deutschen Gegenwartssprache*. de Gruyter.

Christina L. Gagné and Thomas L. Spalding. 2009. Constituent Integration during the Processing of Compound Words: Does it involve the Use of Relational Structures? *Journal of Memory and Language*, 60:20–35.

Christina L. Gagné and Thomas L. Spalding. 2011. Inferential Processing and Meta-Knowledge as the Bases for Property Inclusion in Combined Concepts. *Journal of Memory and Language*, 65:176–192.

Zellig Harris. 1968. Distributional Structure. In Jerold J. Katz, editor, *The Philosophy of Linguistics*, Oxford Readings in Philosophy, pages 26–47. Oxford University Press.

Verena Klos. 2011. *Komposition und Kompositionalität*. Number 292 in Reihe Germanistische Linguistik. Walter de Gruyter, Berlin.

Natalie Kühner and Sabine Schulte im Walde. 2010. Determining the Degree of Compositionality of German Particle Verbs by Clustering Approaches. In *Proceedings of the 10th Conference on Natural Language Processing*, pages 47–56, Saarbrücken, Germany.

Rochelle Lieber and Pavol Stekauer. 2009a. Introduction: Status and Definition of Compounding. In *The Oxford Handbook on Compounding* (Lieber and Stekauer, 2009b), chapter 1, pages 3–18.

Rochelle Lieber and Pavol Stekauer, editors. 2009b. *The Oxford Handbook of Compounding*. Oxford University Press.

Kevin Lund and Curt Burgess. 1996. Producing High-Dimensional Semantic Spaces from Lexical Co-Occurrence. *Behavior Research Methods, Instruments, and Computers*, 28(2):203–208.

Diana McCarthy, Bill Keller, and John Carroll. 2003. Detecting a Continuum of Compositionality in Phrasal Verbs. In *Proceedings of the ACL-SIGLEX Workshop on Multiword Expressions: Analysis, Acquisition and Treatment*, Sapporo, Japan.

Jeff Mitchell and Mirella Lapata. 2010. Composition in Distributional Models of Semantics. *Cognitive Science*, 34:1388–1429.

Siva Reddy, Ioannis P. Klapaftis, Diana McCarthy, and Suresh Manandhar. 2011a. Dynamic and Static Prototype Vectors for Semantic Composition. In *Proceedings of the 5th International Joint Conference on*

Natural Language Processing, pages 705–713, Chiang Mai, Thailand.

Siva Reddy, Diana McCarthy, and Suresh Manandhar. 2011b. An Empirical Study on Compositionality in Compound Nouns. In *Proceedings of the 5th International Joint Conference on Natural Language Processing*, pages 210–218, Chiang Mai, Thailand.

Stephen Roller, Sabine Schulte im Walde, and Silke Scheible. 2013. The (Un)expected Effects of Applying Standard Cleansing Models to Human Ratings on Compositionality. In *Proceedings of the 9th Workshop on Multiword Expressions*, Atlanta, GA.

Michael Schiehlen. 2003. A Cascaded Finite-State Parser for German. In *Proceedings of the 10th Conference of the European Chapter of the Association for Computational Linguistics*, pages 163–166, Budapest, Hungary.

Sabine Schulte im Walde. 2005. Exploring Features to Identify Semantic Nearest Neighbours: A Case Study on German Particle Verbs. In *Proceedings of the International Conference on Recent Advances in Natural Language Processing*, pages 608–614, Borovets, Bulgaria.

Hinrich Schütze. 1992. Dimensions of Meaning. In *Proceedings of Supercomputing*, pages 787–796.

Sidney Siegel and N. John Castellan. 1988. *Nonparametric Statistics for the Behavioral Sciences*. McGraw-Hill, Boston, MA.

Peter D. Turney and Patrick Pantel. 2010. From Frequency to Meaning: Vector Space Models of Semantics. *Journal of Artificial Intelligence Research*, 37:141–188.

Claudia von der Heide and Susanne Borgwaldt. 2009. Assoziationen zu Unter-, Basis- und Oberbegriffen. Eine explorative Studie. In *Proceedings of the 9th Norddeutsches Linguistisches Kolloquium*, pages 51–74.

Dominic Widdows. 2008. Semantic Vector Products: Some Initial Investigations. In *Proceedings of the 2nd Conference on Quantum Interaction*, Oxford, UK.

Heike Zinsmeister and Ulrich Heid. 2004. Collocations of Complex Nouns: Evidence for Lexicalisation. In *Proceedings of Konvens*, Vienna, Austria.

Predicting the Compositionality of Multiword Expressions Using Translations in Multiple Languages

Bahar Salehi[♣♡] **and Paul Cook**[♡]
♣ NICTA Victoria Research Laboratory
♡ Department of Computing and Information Systems
The University of Melbourne
Victoria 3010, Australia
bsalehi@student.unimelb.edu.au, paulcook@unimelb.edu.au

Abstract

In this paper, we propose a simple, language-independent and highly effective method for predicting the degree of compositionality of multiword expressions (MWEs). We compare the translations of an MWE with the translations of its components, using a range of different languages and string similarity measures. We demonstrate the effectiveness of the method on two types of English MWEs: noun compounds and verb particle constructions. The results show that our approach is competitive with or superior to state-of-the-art methods over standard datasets.

1 Compositionality of MWEs

A multiword expression (MWE) is any combination of words with lexical, syntactic or semantic idiosyncrasy (Sag et al., 2002; Baldwin and Kim, 2009), in that the properties of the MWE are not predictable from the component words. For example, with *ad hoc*, the fact that neither *ad* nor *hoc* are standalone English words, makes *ad hoc* a lexically-idiosyncratic MWE; with *shoot the breeze*, on the other hand, we have semantic idiosyncrasy, as the meaning of "to chat" in usages such as *It was good to shoot the breeze with you*[1] cannot be predicted from the meanings of the component words *shoot* and *breeze*.

Semantic idiosyncrasy has been of particular interest to NLP researchers, with research on binary compositional/non-compositional MWE classification (Lin, 1999; Baldwin et al., 2003), or a three-way compositional/semi-compositional/non-compositional distinction (Fazly and Stevenson, 2007). There has also been research to suggest that MWEs span the entire continuum from full compositionality to full non-compositionality (McCarthy et al., 2003; Reddy et al., 2011).

Investigating the degree of MWE compositionality has been shown to have applications in information retrieval and machine translation (Acosta et al., 2011; Venkatapathy and Joshi, 2006). As an example of an information retrieval system, if we were looking for documents relating to *rat race* (meaning "an exhausting routine that leaves no time for relaxation"[2]), we would not be interested in documents on rodents. These results underline the need for methods for broad-coverage MWE compositionality prediction.

In this research, we investigate the possibility of using an MWE's translations in multiple languages to measure the degree of the MWE's compositionality, and investigate how literal the semantics of each component is within the MWE. We use Panlex to translate the MWE and its components, and compare the translations of the MWE with the translations of its components using string similarity measures. The greater the string similarity, the more compositional the MWE is.

Whereas past research on MWE compositionality has tended to be tailored to a specific MWE type (McCarthy et al., 2007; Kim and Baldwin, 2007; Fazly et al., 2009), our method is applicable to any MWE type in any language. Our experiments

[1]The example is taken from http://www.thefreedictionary.com

[2]This definition is from WordNet 3.1.

*Second Joint Conference on Lexical and Computational Semantics (*SEM), Volume 1: Proceedings of the Main Conference and the Shared Task*, pages 266–275, Atlanta, Georgia, June 13-14, 2013.

over two English MWE types demonstrate that our method is competitive with state-of-the-art methods over standard datasets.

2 Related Work

Most previous work on measuring MWE compositionality makes use of lexical, syntactic or semantic properties of the MWE. One early study on MWE compositionality was Lin (1999), who claimed that the distribution of non-compositional MWEs (e.g. *shoot the breeze*) differs significantly from the distribution of expressions formed by substituting one of the components with a semantically similar word (e.g. *shoot the wind*). Unfortunately, the method tends to fall down in cases of high statistical idiosyncrasy (or "institutionalization"): consider *frying pan* which is compositional but distributionally very different to phrases produced through word-substitution such as *sauteing pan* or *frying plate*.

Some research has investigated the syntactic properties of MWEs, to detect their compositionality (Fazly et al., 2009; McCarthy et al., 2007). The assumption behind these methods is that non-compositional MWEs are more syntactically fixed than compositional MWEs. For example, *make a decision* can be passivised, but *shoot the breeze* cannot. One serious problem with syntax-based methods is their lack of generalization: each type of MWE has its own characteristics, and these characteristics differ from one language to another. Moreover, some MWEs (such as noun compounds) are not flexible syntactically, no matter whether they are compositional or non-compositional (Reddy et al., 2011).

Much of the recent work on MWEs focuses on their semantic properties, measuring the semantic similarity between the MWE and its components using different resources, such as WordNet (Kim and Baldwin, 2007) or distributional similarity relative to a corpus (e.g. based on Latent Semantic Analysis: Schone and Jurafsky (2001), Bannard et al. (2003), Reddy et al. (2011)). The size of the corpus is important in methods based on distributional similarity. Unfortunately, however, large corpora are not available for all languages.

Reddy et al. (2011) hypothesize that the number of common co-occurrences between a given MWE and its component words indicates the degree of compositionality of that MWE. First, the co-occurrences of a given MWE/word are considered as the values of a vector. They then measure the Cosine similarity between the vectors of the MWE and its components. Bannard et al. (2003) presented four methods to measure the compositionality of English verb particle constructions. Their best result is based on the previously-discussed method of Lin (1999) for measuring compositionality, but uses a more-general distributional similarity model to identify synonyms.

Recently, a few studies have investigated using parallel corpora to detect the degree of compositionality (Melamed, 1997; Moirón and Tiedemann, 2006; de Caseli et al., 2010; Salehi et al., 2012). The general approach is to word-align the source and target language sentences and analyse alignment patterns for MWEs (e.g. if the MWE is always aligned as a single "phrase", then it is a strong indicator of non-compositionality). de Caseli et al. (2010) consider non-compositional MWEs to be those candidates that align to the same target language unit, without decomposition into word alignments. Melamed (1997) suggests using mutual information to investigate how well the translation model predicts the distribution of words in the target text given the distribution of words in the source text. Moirón and Tiedemann (2006) show that entropy is a good indicator of compositionality, because word alignment models are often confused by non-compositional MWEs. However, this assumption does not always hold, especially when dealing with high-frequency non-compositional MWEs. Salehi et al. (2012) tried to solve this problem with high frequency MWEs by using word alignment in both directions.[3] They computed backward and forward entropy to try to remedy the problem with especially high-frequency phrases. However, their assumptions were not easily generalisable across languages, e.g., they assume that the relative frequency of a specific type of MWE (light verb constructions) in Persian is much greater than in English.

Although methods using bilingual corpora are intuitively appealing, they have a number of drawbacks. The first and the most important problem

[3]The IBM models (Brown et al., 1993), e.g., are not bidirectional, which means that the alignments are affected by the alignment direction.

is data: they need large-scale parallel bilingual corpora, which are available for relatively few language pairs. Second, since they use statistical measures, they are not suitable for measuring the compositionality of MWEs with low frequency. And finally, most experiments have been carried out on English paired with other European languages, and it is not clear whether the results translate across to other language pairs.

3 Resources

In this research, we use the translations of MWEs and their components to estimate the relative degree of compositionality of a MWE. There are several resources available to translate words into various languages such as Babelnet (Navigli and Ponzetto, 2010),[4] Wiktionary,[5] Panlex (Baldwin et al., 2010) and Google Translate.[6] As we are ideally after broad coverage over multiple languages and MWEs/component words in a given language, we exclude Babelnet and Wiktionary from our current research. Babelnet covers only six languages at the time of writing this paper, and in Wiktionary, because it is constantly being updated, words and MWEs do not have translations into the same languages. This leaves translation resources such as Panlex and Google Translate. However, after manually analysing the two resources for a range of MWEs, we decided not to use Google Translate for two reasons: (1) we consider the MWE out of context (i.e., we are working at the type level and do not consider the usage of the MWE in a particular sentence), and Google Translate tends to generate compositional translations of MWEs out of context; and (2) Google Translate provides only one translation for each component word/MWE. This left Panlex.

Panlex is an online translation database that is freely available. It contains lemmatized words and MWEs in a large variety of languages, with lemma-based (and less frequently sense-based) links between them. The database covers more than 1353 languages, and is made up of 12M lemmas and expressions. The translations are sourced from handmade electronic dictionaries, making it more accurate than translation dictionaries generated automatically, e.g. through word alignment. Usually there are several **direct translations** for a word/MWE from one language to another, as in translations which were extracted from electronic dictionaries. If there is no direct translation for a word/MWE in the database, we can translate indirectly via one or more pivot languages (**indirect translation**: Soderland et al. (2010)). For example, English *ivory tower* has direct translations in only 13 languages in Panlex, including French (*tour d'ivoire*) but not Esperanto. There is, however, a translation of *tour d'ivoire* into Esperanto (*ebura turo*), allowing us to infer an indirect translation between *ivory tower* and *ebura turo*.

4 Dataset

We evaluate our method over two datasets, as described below.

REDDY (Reddy et al., 2011): 90 English (binary) noun compounds (NCs), where the overall NC and each component word has been annotated for compositionality on a scale from 0 (non-compositional) to 5 (compositional). In order to avoid issues with polysemy, the annotators were presented with each NC in a sentential context. The authors tried to achieve a balance of compositional and non-compositional NCs: based on a threshold of 2.5, the dataset consists of 43 (48%) compositional NCs, 46 (51%) NCs with a compositional usage of the first component, and 54 (60%) NCs with a compositional usage of the second component.

BANNARD (Bannard, 2006): 160 English verb particle constructions (VPCs) were annotated for compositionality relative to each of the two component words (the verb and the particle). Each annotator was asked to annotate each of the verb and particle as `yes`, `no` or `don't know`. Based on the majority annotation, among the 160 VPCs, 122 (76%) are verb-compositional and 76 (48%) are particle-compositional.

We compute the proportion of `yes` tags to get the compositionality score. This dataset, unlike REDDY, does not include annotations for the compositionality of the whole VPC, and is also less balanced, containing more VPCs which are verb-compositional than verb-non-compositional.

[4] http://lcl.uniroma1.it/babelnet/
[5] http://www.wiktionary.org/
[6] http://translate.google.com/

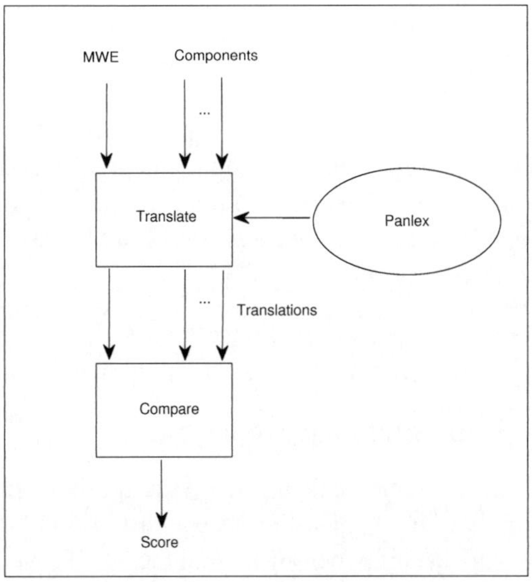

Figure 1: Schematic of our proposed method

English	Persian Translation
kick the bucket	mord
kick	zad
the	–
bucket	satl
make a decision	**tasmim** gereft
make	sakht
a	yek
decision	**tasmim**
public service	khadamaat **omumi**
public	**omumi**
service	khedmat

Table 1: English MWEs and their components with their translation in Persian. Direct matches between the translation of a MWE and its components are shown in **bold**; partial matches are underlined.

5 Method

To predict the degree of compositionality of an MWE, we require a way to measure the semantic similarity of the MWE with its components. Our hypothesis is that compositional MWEs are more likely to be word-for-word translations in a given language than non-compositional MWEs. Hence, if we can locate the translations of the components in the translation of the MWE, we can deduce that it is compositional. Our second hypothesis is that the more languages we use as the basis for determining translation similarity between the MWE and its component words, the more accurately we will be able to estimate compositionality. Thus, rather than using just one translation language, we experiment with as many languages as possible.

Figure 1 provides a schematic outline of our method. The MWE and its components are translated using Panlex. Then, we compare the translation of the MWE with the translations of its components. In order to locate the translation of each component in the MWE translation, we use string similarity measures. The score shown in Figure 1 is derived from a given language. In Section 6, we show how to combine scores across multiple languages.

As an example of our method, consider the English-to-Persian translation of *kick the bucket* as a non-compositional MWE and *make a decision* as a semi-compositional MWE (Table 1).[7] By locating the translation of *decision* (*tasmim*) in the translation of *make a decision* (*tasmim gereftan*), we can deduce that it is semi-compositional. However, we cannot locate any of the component translations in the translation of *kick the bucket*. Therefore, we conclude that it is non-compositional. Note that in this simple example, the match is word-level, but that due to the effects of morphophonology, the more likely situation is that the components don't match exactly (as we observe in the case of *khadamaat* and *khedmat* for the *public service* example), which motivates our use of string similarity measures which can capture partial matches.

We consider the following string similarity measures to compare the translations. In each case, we normalize the output value to the range $[0, 1]$, where 1 indicates identical strings and 0 indicates completely different strings. We will indicate the translation of the MWE in a particular language t as MWE^t, and the translation of a given component in

[7] Note that the Persian words are transliterated into English for ease of understanding.

language t as $component^t$.

Longest common substring (LCS): The LCS measure finds the longest common substring between two strings. For example, the LCS between `ABABC` and `BABCAB` is `BABC`. We calculate a normalized similarity value based on the length of the LCS as follows:

$$\frac{LongestCommonString(MWE^t, component^t)}{\min(len(MWE^t), len(component^t))}$$

Levenshtein (LEV1): The Levenshtein distance calculates for the number of basic edit operations required to transpose one word into the other. Edits consist of single-letter insertions, deletions or substitutions. We normalize LEV1 as follows:

$$1 - \frac{LEV1(MWE^t, component^t)}{\max(len(MWE^t), len(component^t))}$$

Levenshtein with substitution penalty (LEV2): One well-documented feature of Levenshtein distance (Baldwin, 2009) is that substitutions are in fact the combination of an addition and a deletion, and as such can be considered to be two edits. Based on this observation, we experiment with a variant of LEV1 with this penalty applied for substitutions. Similarly to LEV1, we normalize as follows:

$$1 - \frac{LEV2(MWE^t, component^t)}{len(MWE^t) + len(component^t)}$$

Smith Waterman (SW) This method is based on the Needleman-Wunsch algorithm,[8] and was developed to locally-align two protein sequences (Smith and Waterman, 1981). It finds the optimal similar regions by maximizing the number of matches and minimizing the number of gaps necessary to align the two sequences. For example, the optimal local sequence for the two sequences below is `AT--ATCC`, in which "-" indicates a gap:

Seq1: **ATGCATCC**CATGAC
Seq2: TCT**ATATCC**GT

As the example shows, it looks for the longest common string but has an in-built mechanism for including gaps in the alignment (with penalty). This characteristic of SW might be helpful in our task, because there may be morphophonological variations between the MWE and component translations (as seen above in the *public service* example). We normalize SW similarly to LCS:

$$\frac{len(alignedSequence)}{\min(len(MWE^t), len(component^t))}$$

6 Computational Model

Given the scores calculated by the aforementioned string similarity measures between the translations for a given component word and the MWE, we need some way of combining scores across component words.[9] First, we measure the compositionality of each component within the MWE (s_1 and s_2):

$$s_1 = f_1(sim_1(w_1, MWE), ..., sim_i(w_1, MWE))$$
$$s_2 = f_1(sim_1(w_2, MWE), ..., sim_i(w_2, MWE))$$

where sim is a string similarity measure, sim_i indicates that the calculation is based on translations in language i, and f_1 is a score combination function.

Then, we compute the overall compositionality of the MWE (s_3) from s_1 and s_2 using f_2:

$$s_3 = f_2(s_1, s_2)$$

Since we often have multiple translations for a given component word/MWE in Panlex, we exhaustively compute the similarity between each MWE translation and component translation, and use the highest similarity as the result of sim_i. If an instance does not have a direct/indirect translation in Panlex, we assign a default value, which is the mean of the highest and lowest annotation score (2.5 for REDDY and 0.5 for BANNARD). Note that word order is not an issue in our method, as we calculate the similarity independently for each MWE component.

In this research, we consider simple functions for f_1 such as mean, median, product, min and max. f_2

[8] The Needleman-Wunsch (NW) algorithm, was designed to align two sequences of amino-acids (Needleman and Wunsch, 1970). The algorithm looks for the sequence alignment which maximizes the similarity. As with the LEV score, NW minimizes edit distance, but also takes into account character-to-character similarity based on the relative distance between characters on the keyboard. We exclude this score, because it is highly similar to the LEV scores, and we did not obtain encouraging results using NW in our preliminary experiments.

[9] Note that in all experiments we only combine scores given by the same string similarity measure.

NC		
Language	Frequency	Family
Czech	100	Slavic
Norwegian	100	Germanic
Portuguese	100	Romance
Thai	99	Kam-thai
French	95	Romance
Chinese	94	Chinese
Dutch	93	Germanic
Romanian	91	Romance
Hindi	67	Indic
Russian	43	Slavic

Table 2: The 10 best languages for REDDY using LCS.

VPC:verb		
Language	Frequency	Family
Basque	100	Basque
Lithuanian	100	Baltic
Slovenian	100	Slavic
Hebrew	99	Semitic
Arabic	98	Semitic
Czech	95	Slavic
Slovak	92	Slavic
Latin	79	Italic
Tagalog	74	Austronesian
Polish	44	Slavic

Table 3: The 10 best languages for the verb component of BANNARD using LCS.

VPC:particle		
Language	Frequency	Family
French	100	Romance
Icelandic	100	Germanic
Thai	100	Kam-thai
Indonesian	92	Indonesian
Spanish	90	Romance
Tamil	87	Dravidian
Turkish	83	Turkic
Catalan	79	Romance
Occitan	76	Romance
Romanian	69	Romance

Table 4: The 10 best languages for the particle component of BANNARD using LCS.

was selected to be the same as f_1 in all situations, except when we use mean for f_1. Here, following Reddy et al. (2011), we experimented with weighted mean:

$$f_2(s_1, s_2) = \alpha s_1 + (1 - \alpha)s_2$$

Based on 3-fold cross validation, we chose $\alpha = 0.7$ for REDDY.[10]

Since we do not have judgements for the compositionality of the full VPC in BANNARD (we instead have separate judgements for the verb and particle), we cannot use f_2 for this dataset. Bannard et al. (2003) observed that nearly all of the verb-compositional instances were also annotated as particle-compositional by the annotators. In line with this observation, we use s_1 (based on the verb) as the compositionality score for the full VPC.

7 Language Selection

Our method is based on the translation of an MWE into many languages. In the first stage, we chose 54 languages for which relatively large corpora were available.[11] The coverage, or the number of instances which have direct/indirect translations in Panlex, varies from one language to another. In preliminary experiments, we noticed that there is a high correlation (about 0.50 for BANNARD and about 0.80 for REDDY) between the usefulness of a language and its translation coverage on MWEs. Therefore, we excluded languages with MWE translation coverage of less than 50%. Based on nested 10-fold cross validation in our experiments, we select the 10 most useful languages for each cross-validation training partition, based on the Pearson correlation between the given scores in that language and human judgements.[12] The 10 best languages are selected based only on the training set for each fold. (The languages selected for each fold will later be used to predict the compositionality of the items in the testing portion for that fold.) In Tables 2, 3

[10]We considered values of α from 0 to 1, incremented by 0.1.

[11]In future work, we intend to look at the distribution of translations of the given MWE and its components in corpora for many languages. The present method does not rely on the availability of large corpora.

[12]Note that for VPCs, we calculate the compositionality of only the verb part, because we don't have the human judgements for the whole VPC.

f_1	$sim()$	N1	N2	NC
Mean	SW	**0.541**	0.396	0.637
	LCS	0.525	**0.431**	**0.649**
	LEV1	0.405	0.200	0.523
	LEV2	0.481	0.263	0.577
Prod	SW	0.451	0.287	0.410
	LCS	0.430	0.233	0.434
	LEV1	0.299	0.128	0.311
	LEV2	0.294	0.188	0.364
Median	SW	0.443	0.334	0.544
	LCS	0.408	0.365	0.553
	LEV1	0.315	0.054	0.376
	LEV2	0.404	0.134	0.523
Min	SW	0.420	0.176	0.312
	LCS	0.347	0.225	0.307
	LEV1	0.362	0.310	0.248
	LEV2	0.386	0.345	0.338
Max	SW	0.371	0.408	0.345
	LCS	0.406	0.430	0.335
	LEV1	0.279	0.362	0.403
	LEV2	0.380	0.349	0.406

Table 5: Correlation on REDDY (NCs). N1, N2 and NC, are the first component of the noun compound, its second component, and the noun compound itself, respectively.

f_1	$sim()$	Verb	Particle
Mean	SW	0.369	**0.510**
	LCS	**0.406**	0.509
	LEV1	0.335	0.454
	LEV2	0.340	0.460
Prod	SW	0.315	0.316
	LCS	0.339	0.299
	LEV1	0.322	0.280
	LEV2	0.342	0.284
Median	SW	0.316	0.409
	LCS	0.352	0.423
	LEV1	0.295	0.387
	LEV2	0.309	0.368
Min	SW	0.262	0.210
	LCS	0.329	0.251
	LEV1	0.307	0.278
	LEV2	0.310	0.281
Max	SW	0.141	0.288
	LCS	0.268	0.299
	LEV1	0.145	0.450
	LEV2	0.170	0.398

Table 6: Correlation on BANNARD (VPC), based on the best-10 languages for the verb and particle individually

and 4, we show how often each language was selected in the top-10 languages over the combined 100 (10×10) folds of nested 10-fold cross validation, based on LCS.[13] The tables show that the selected languages were mostly consistent over the folds. The languages are a mixture of Romance, Germanic and languages from other families (based on Voegelin and Voegelin (1977)), with no standout language which performs well in all cases (indeed, no language occurs in all three tables). Additionally, there is nothing in common between the verb and the particle top-10 languages.

8 Results

As mentioned before, we perform nested 10-fold cross-validation to select the 10 best languages on the training data for each fold. The selected languages for a given fold are then used to compute s_1 and s_2 (and s_3 for NCs) for each instance in the test set for that fold. The scores are compared with human judgements using Pearson's correlation. The results are shown in Tables 5 and 6. Among the five functions we experimented with for f_1, Mean performs much more consistently than the others. Median is less prone to noise, and therefore performs better than Prod, Max and Min, but it is still worse than Mean.

For the most part, LCS and SW perform better than the other measures. There is little to separate these two methods, partly because they both look for a sequence of similar characters, unlike LEV1 and LEV2 which do not consider contiguity of match.

The results support our hypothesis that using multiple target languages rather than one, results in a more accurate prediction of MWE compositionality. Our best result using the 10 selected languages on REDDY is 0.649, as compared to the best single-language correlation of 0.497 for Portuguese. On BANNARD, the best LCS result for the verb component is 0.406, as compared to the best single-

[13]Since our later results show that LCS and SW have higher results, we only show the best languages using LCS. These largely coincide with those for SW.

language correlation of 0.350 for Lithuanian.

Reddy et al. (2011) reported a correlation of 0.714 on REDDY. Our best correlation is 0.649. Note that Reddy et al. (2011) base their method on identification of MWEs in a corpus, thus requiring MWE-specific identification. Given that this has been shown to be difficult for MWE types including English VPCs (McCarthy et al., 2003; Baldwin, 2005), the fact that our method is as competitive as this is highly encouraging, especially when you consider that it can equally be applied to different types of MWEs in other languages. Moreover, the computational processing required by methods based on distributional similarity is greater than our method, as it does not require processing a large corpus.

Finally, we experimented with combining our method ($\text{STRINGSIM}_{\text{MEAN}}$) with a reimplementation of the method of Reddy et al. (2011), based on simple averaging, as detailed in Table 7. The results are higher than both component methods and the state-of-the-art for REDDY, demonstrating the complementarity between our proposed method and methods based on distributional similarity.

In Table 8, we compare our results ($\text{STRINGSIM}_{\text{MEAN}}$) with those of Bannard et al. (2003), who interpreted the dataset as a binary classification task. The dataset used in their study is a subset of BANNARD, containing 40 VPCs, of which 29 (72%) were verb compositional and 23 (57%) were particle compositional. By applying a threshold of 0.5 over the output of our regression model, we binarize the VPCs into the compositional and non-compositional classes. According to the results shown in Table 6, LCS is a better similarity measure for this task. Our proposed method has higher results than the best results of Bannard et al. (2003), in part due to their reliance on VPC identification, and the low recall on the task, as reported in the paper. Our proposed method does not rely on a corpus or MWE identification.

9 Error Analysis

We analyse items in REDDY which have a high difference (more than 2.5) between the human annotation and our scores (using LCS and Mean). The words are *cutting edge*, *melting pot*, *gold mine* and *ivory tower*, which are non-compositional according to REDDY. After investigating their translations, we came to the conclusion that the first three MWEs have word-for-word translations in most languages. Hence, they disagree with our hypothesis that word-for-word translation is a strong indicator of compositionality. The word-for-word translations might be because of the fact that they have both compositional and non-compositional senses, or because they are calques (loan translations). However, we have tried to avoid such problems with calques by using translations into several languages.

For *ivory tower* ("a state of mind that is discussed as if it were a place")[14] we noticed that we have a direct translation into 13 languages. Other languages have indirect translations. By checking the direct translations, we noticed that, in French, the MWE is translated to *tour* and *tour d'ivoire*. A noisy (wrong) translation of *tour* "tower" resulted in wrong indirect translations for *ivory tower* and an inflated estimate of compositionality.

10 Conclusion and Future Work

In this study, we proposed a method to predict MWE compositionality based on the translation of the MWE and its component words into multiple languages. We used string similarity measures between the translations of the MWE and each of its components to predict the relative degree of compositionality. Among the four similarity measures that we experimented with, LCS and SW were found to be superior to edit distance-based methods. Our best results were found to be competitive with state-of-the-art results using vector-based approaches, and were also shown to complement state-of-the-art methods.

In future work, we are interested in investigating whether alternative ways of combining our proposed method with vector-based models can lead to further enhancements in results. These models could be especially effective when comparing translations which are roughly synonymous but not string-wise similar.

Acknowledgments

We would like to thank Timothy Baldwin, Su Nam Kim, and the anonymous reviewers for their valuable comments and suggestions.

[14]This definition is from Wordnet 3.1.

$sim()$	STRINGSIM$_{\text{MEAN}}$	STRINGSIM$_{\text{MEAN}}$ + Reddy et al.
SW	0.637	0.735
LCS	**0.649**	**0.742**
LEV1	0.523	0.724
LEV2	0.577	0.726

Table 7: Correlation after combining Reddy et al.'s method and our method with Mean for f_1 (STRINGSIM$_{\text{MEAN}}$). The correlation using Reddy et al.'s method is 0.714.

Method	Precision	Recall	F-score ($\beta = 1$)	Accuracy
Bannard et al. (2003)	0.608	0.666	0.636	0.600
STRINGSIM$_{\text{MEAN}}$	0.862	0.718	0.774	0.693

Table 8: Results for the classification task. STRINGSIM$_{\text{MEAN}}$ is our method using Mean for f_1

NICTA is funded by the Australian Government as represented by the Department of Broadband, Communications and the Digital Economy and the Australian Research Council through the ICT Centre of Excellence program.

References

Otavio Costa Acosta, Aline Villavicencio, and Viviane P Moreira. 2011. Identification and treatment of multiword expressions applied to information retrieval. In *Proceedings of the ALC Workshop on MWEs: from Parsing and Generation to the Real World (MWE 2011)*, pages 101–109.

Timothy Baldwin and Su Nam Kim. 2009. Multiword expressions. In Nitin Indurkhya and Fred J. Damerau, editors, *Handbook of Natural Language Processing*. CRC Press, Boca Raton, USA, 2nd edition.

Timothy Baldwin, Colin Bannard, Takaaki Tanaka, and Dominic Widdows. 2003. An empirical model of multiword expression decomposability. In *Proceedings of the ACL-2003 Workshop on Multiword Expressions: Analysis, Acquisition and Treatment*, pages 89–96, Sapporo, Japan.

Timothy Baldwin, Jonathan Pool, and Susan M Colowick. 2010. Panlex and lextract: Translating all words of all languages of the world. In *Proceedings of the 23rd International Conference on Computational Linguistics: Demonstrations*, pages 37–40.

Timothy Baldwin. 2005. The deep lexical acquisition of English verb-particle constructions. *Computer Speech and Language, Special Issue on Multiword Expressions*, 19(4):398–414.

Timothy Baldwin. 2009. The hare and the tortoise: Speed and reliability in translation retrieval. *Machine Translation*, 23(4):195–240.

Colin Bannard, Timothy Baldwin, and Alex Lascarides. 2003. A statistical approach to the semantics of verb-particles. In *Proceedings of the ACL 2003 workshop on Multiword expressions: analysis, acquisition and treatment-Volume 18*, pages 65–72.

Colin James Bannard. 2006. *Acquiring Phrasal Lexicons from Corpora*. Ph.D. thesis, University of Edinburgh.

Peter F. Brown, Stephen A. Della Pietra, Vincent J. Della Pietra, and Robert L. Mercer. 1993. The mathematics of statistical machine translation: Parameter estimation. *Computational Linguistics*, 19(2):263–311.

Helena Medeiros de Caseli, Carlos Ramisch, Maria das Graças Volpe Nunes, and Aline Villavicencio. 2010. Alignment-based extraction of multiword expressions. *Language Resources and Evaluation*, 44(1):59–77.

Afsaneh Fazly and Suzanne Stevenson. 2007. Distinguishing subtypes of multiword expressions using linguistically-motivated statistical measures. In *Proceedings of the ACL 2007 Workshop on A Broader Perspective on Multiword Expressions*, pages 9–16.

Afsaneh Fazly, Paul Cook, and Suzanne Stevenson. 2009. Unsupervised type and token identification of idiomatic expressions. *Computational Linguistics*, 35(1):61–103.

Su Nam Kim and Timothy Baldwin. 2007. Detecting compositionality of english verb-particle constructions using semantic similarity. In *Proceedings of the 7th Meeting of the Pacific Association for Computational Linguistics (PACLING 2007)*, pages 40–48.

Dekang Lin. 1999. Automatic identification of non-compositional phrases. In *Proceedings of the 37th annual meeting of the Association for Computational Linguistics on Computational Linguistics*, pages 317–324.

Diana McCarthy, Bill Keller, and John Carroll. 2003. Detecting a continuum of compositionality in phrasal verbs. In *Proceedings of the ACL 2003 workshop on Multiword expressions: analysis, acquisition and treatment-Volume 18*, pages 73–80.

Diana McCarthy, Sriram Venkatapathy, and Aravind K Joshi. 2007. Detecting compositionality of verb-object combinations using selectional preferences. In *Proceedings of the 2007 Joint Conference on Empirical Methods in Natural Language Processing and Computational Natural Language Learning (EMNLP-CoNLL)*, pages 369–379.

I. Dan Melamed. 1997. Automatic discovery of non-compositional compounds in parallel data. In *Proceedings of the Fifth Workshop on Very Large Corpora*. EMNLP.

Begona Villada Moirón and Jörg Tiedemann. 2006. Identifying idiomatic expressions using automatic word-alignment. In *Proceedings of the EACL 2006 Workshop on Multi-wordexpressions in a multilingual context*, pages 33–40.

Roberto Navigli and Simone Paolo Ponzetto. 2010. Babelnet: Building a very large multilingual semantic network. In *Proceedings of the 48th Annual Meeting of the Association for Computational Linguistics*, pages 216–225, Uppsala, Sweden.

Saul B Needleman and Christian D Wunsch. 1970. A general method applicable to the search for similarities in the amino acid sequence of two proteins. *Journal of molecular biology*, 48(3):443–453.

Siva Reddy, Diana McCarthy, and Suresh Manandhar. 2011. An empirical study on compositionality in compound nouns. In *Proceedings of IJCNLP*, pages 210–218.

Ivan Sag, Timothy Baldwin, Francis Bond, Ann Copestake, and Dan Flickinger. 2002. Multiword expressions: A pain in the neck for nlp. In *Proceedings of the 3rd International Conference on Intelligent Text Processing Computational Linguistics (CICLing-2002)*, pages 189–206. Springer.

Bahar Salehi, Narjes Askarian, and Afsaneh Fazly. 2012. Automatic identification of Persian light verb constructions. In *Proceedings of the 13th International Conference on Intelligent Text Processing Computational Linguistics (CICLing-2012)*, pages 201–210.

Patrick Schone and Dan Jurafsky. 2001. Is knowledge-free induction of multiword unit dictionary headwords a solved problem. In *Proceedings of the 6th Conference on Empirical Methods in Natural Language Processing (EMNLP 2001)*, pages 100–108.

TF Smith and MS Waterman. 1981. Identification of common molecular subsequences. *Molecular Biology*, 147:195–197.

Stephen Soderland, Oren Etzioni, Daniel S Weld, Kobi Reiter, Michael Skinner, Marcus Sammer, Jeff Bilmes, et al. 2010. Panlingual lexical translation via probabilistic inference. *Artificial Intelligence*, 174(9):619–637.

Sriram Venkatapathy and Aravind K Joshi. 2006. Using information about multi-word expressions for the word-alignment task. In *Proceedings of the Workshop on Multiword Expressions: Identifying and Exploiting Underlying Properties*, pages 20–27.

Charles Frederick Voegelin and Florence Marie Voegelin. 1977. *Classification and index of the world's languages*, volume 4. Elsevier Science Ltd.

Metaphor Identification as Interpretation

Ekaterina Shutova
International Computer Science Institute and
Institute for Cognitive and Brain Sciences
University of California, Berkeley
katia@berkeley.edu

Abstract

Automatic metaphor identification and interpretation in text have been traditionally considered as two separate tasks in natural language processing (NLP) and addressed individually within computational frameworks. However, cognitive evidence suggests that humans are likely to perform these two tasks simultaneously, as part of a holistic metaphor comprehension process. We present a novel method that performs metaphor identification through its interpretation, being the first one in NLP to combine the two tasks in one step. It outperforms the previous approaches to metaphor identification both in terms of accuracy and coverage, as well as providing an interpretation for each identified expression.

1 Introduction

Metaphor undoubtedly gives our expression more vividness, distinction and artistry, however, it is also an important linguistic tool that has long become part of our every-day language. Metaphors arise when one concept or domain is viewed in terms of the properties of another (Lakoff and Johnson, 1980). Consider the examples in (1) and (2).

(1) My car *drinks* gasoline. (Wilks, 1978)

(2) This policy is *strangling* business.

The *car* in (1) and *business* in (2) are viewed as *living beings* and thus they can *drink* or *be strangled* respectively. The mapping between the *car* (the target concept) and *living being* (the source concept) is systematic and results in a number of metaphorical expressions (e.g. "This oil gives your car a *second life*", "this car has is very *temperamental*" etc.) Lakoff and Johnson call such generalisations a source–target domain mapping, or *conceptual metaphor*.

The ubiquity of metaphor in language has been established in a number of corpus studies (Cameron, 2003; Martin, 2006; Steen et al., 2010; Shutova and Teufel, 2010) and the role it plays in human reasoning has been confirmed in psychological experiments (Thibodeau and Boroditsky, 2011). This makes its automatic processing an important problem for NLP and its numerous applications (such as machine translation, information extraction, opinion mining and many others). For example, the use of the metaphorical verb *strangle* in (2) reflects the speaker's negative opinion regarding the government's tight business regulations, which would be an important fact for an opinion mining system to discover (Narayanan, 1999). Other experiments (Agerri, 2008) have investigated and confirmed the role of metaphor interpretation for textual entailment resolution (RTE).

The problem of metaphor modeling is rapidly gaining interest within NLP, with a growing number of approaches exploiting statistical techniques (Mason, 2004; Gedigian et al., 2006; Shutova, 2010; Shutova et al., 2010; Turney et al., 2011; Shutova et al., 2012a). Compared to more traditional approaches based on hand-coded knowledge (Fass, 1991; Martin, 1990; Narayanan, 1997; Narayanan, 1999; Feldman and Narayanan, 2004; Barnden and Lee, 2002; Agerri et al., 2007), these more recent methods tend to have a wider coverage, as well as be more efficient, accurate and robust. However, even the statistical metaphor processing approaches so far often focused on a limited domain or a subset of

*Second Joint Conference on Lexical and Computational Semantics (*SEM), Volume 1: Proceedings of the Main Conference and the Shared Task*, pages 276–285, Atlanta, Georgia, June 13-14, 2013.

phenomena (Gedigian et al., 2006; Krishnakumaran and Zhu, 2007), and required training data (Shutova et al., 2010; Turney et al., 2011), often resulting in a limited coverage. The metaphor processing task itself has been most commonly addressed in NLP as two individual subtasks: metaphor identification and metaphor interpretation, with the systems focusing only on one of them at a time, or at best combing the two in a pipeline (Shutova et al., 2012a). Metaphor identification systems annotate metaphorical language in text, and metaphor interpretation systems discover literal meanings of the previously annotated expressions. However, cognitive evidence suggests that humans are likely to perform identification and interpretation simultaneously, as part of a holistic metaphor comprehension process (Coulson, 2008; Utsumi, 2011; Gibbs and Colston, 2012). In this paper, we also take this stance and present the first computational method that identifies metaphorical expressions in unrestricted text by means of their interpretation. Following Shutova (2010), we define metaphor interpretation as a task of finding a literal paraphrase for a metaphorically used word and introduce the concept of *symmetric reverse paraphrasing* as a criterion for metaphor identification. The main assumption behind our method is that the literal paraphrases of literally-used words should yield the original phrase when paraphrased in reverse. For example, when the expression "clean the house" is paraphrased as "tidy the house", the reverse paraphrasing of *tidy* would generate *clean*. Our expectation is that such a symmetry in paraphrasing is indicative of literal use. The metaphorically-used words are unlikely to exhibit this symmetry property when paraphrased in reverse. For example, the literal paraphrasing of the verb *stir* in "*stir* excitement" would yield "provoke excitement", but the reverse paraphrasing of *provoke* would not retrieve *stir*, indicating the non-literal use of *stir*.

We experimentally verify this hypothesis in a setting involving single-word metaphors expressed by a verb in verb-subject and verb-direct object relations. We apply the selectional preference-based metaphor paraphrasing method of Shutova (2010) to retrieve literal paraphrases of all input verbs and extend the method to perform metaphor identification. In summary, our system (1) determines the likelihood of a verb being metaphorical based on its selectional preference strength (Resnik, 1993); (2) identifies a set of literal paraphrases for verbs that may be used metaphorically using the algorithm of Shutova (2010); (3) performs reverse paraphrasing of each of the identified paraphrases, aiming to retrieve the original expression; and (4) if the original expression is retrieved then the verb is tagged as literal, otherwise it is tagged as metaphorical.

We evaluated the performance of the system using the manually annotated metaphor corpus of Shutova and Teufel (2010) in precision- and recall-oriented settings. In addition, we compared its performance to that of a baseline using selectional preference violation as an indicator of metaphor, as well as to two previous metaphor identification approaches of Shutova et al. (2010) and Turney et al. (2011).

2 Related Work

One of the first attempts to identify and interpret metaphorical expressions in text is the met* system of Fass (1991), that utilizes hand-coded knowledge and detects non-literalness via selectional preference violation. In case of a violation, the respective phrase is first tested for being metonymic using hand-coded patterns (e.g. CONTAINER-FOR-CONTENT). If this fails, the system searches the knowledge base for a relevant analogy in order to discriminate metaphorical relations from anomalous ones. The system of Krishnakumaran and Zhu (2007) uses WordNet (the hyponymy relation) and word bigram counts to predict verbal, nominal and adjectival metaphors at the sentence level. The authors discriminate between conventional metaphors (included in WordNet) and novel metaphors. Birke and Sarkar (2006) present a sentence clustering approach that employs a set of seed sentences annotated for literalness and computes similarity between the new input sentence and all of the seed sentences. The system then tags the sentence as literal or metaphorical according to the annotation in the most similar seeds, attaining an f-score of 53.8%.

The first system to discover source–target domain mappings automatically is CorMet (Mason, 2004). It does this by searching for systematic variations in domain-specific verb selectional preferences. For example, *pour* is a characteristic verb in both LAB and FINANCE domains. In the LAB domain it has a strong preference for *liquids* and in the FINANCE domain for *money*. From this the system infers the domain mapping FINANCE – LAB and the concept mapping *money – liquid*. Gedigian et al. (2006) trained a maximum entropy classifier to discriminate between literal and metaphorical use. They annotated the sentences from PropBank (Kingsbury and Palmer, 2002) containing the verbs of MOTION and CURE for metaphoricity. They used PropBank annotation (arguments and their semantic types) as features for classification and report an accuracy of 95.12% (however, against a majority baseline of 92.90%). The metaphor identification system of Shutova et al. (2010) starts from a small seed set of metaphorical expressions, learns the analogies involved in their production and extends the set of analogies by means of verb and noun clustering. As a result, the system can recognize new metaphorical expressions in unrestricted text (e.g. from the seed "*stir* excitement" it infers that "*swallow* anger" is also a metaphor), achieving a precision of 79%.

Turney et al. (2011) classify verbs and adjectives as literal or metaphorical based on their level of concreteness or abstractness in relation to a noun they appear with. They learn concreteness rankings for words automatically (starting from a set of examples) and then search for expressions where a concrete adjective or verb is used with an abstract noun (e.g. "*dark* humour" is tagged as a metaphor and "dark hair" is not). They report an accuracy of 73%.

3 Method

3.1 Selectional Preference Strength Filtering

One of the early influential ideas in the field of computational metaphor processing is that metaphor represents a violation of selectional preferences (SP) of a word in a given context (Wilks, 1975; Wilks, 1978). However, applied directly as an identification criterion, violation of SPs is also indicative of many other linguistic phenomena (e.g. metonymy), and not only metaphor, which is problematic. We modify this view and apply it to measure the potential of a word to be used metaphorically based on its selectional preference strength (SPS). The main intuition behind SPS filtering is that not all verbs have an equal potential of being a metaphor. For example, verbs such as *choose*, *remember*, *describe* or *like* do not have a strong preference for their direct objects and are equally likely to appear with many argument classes. If metaphor represents a violation of SPs, then the verbs with weak SPS are unlikely to be used metaphorically in any context. For every verb in the input text, the filter determines their likelihood of being a metaphor based on their SPS and discards the weak ones. The SPS filter is context-free, and the reverse paraphrasing method is then applied in the next steps to determine if the remaining verbs are indeed used metaphorically in the given context.

We automatically acquired selectional preference distributions for verb-subject and verb-direct object relations from the British National Corpus (BNC) (Burnard, 2007) that was parsed using the RASP parser (Briscoe et al., 2006; Andersen et al., 2008). We applied the noun clustering method of Sun and Korhonen (2009) to 2000 most frequent nouns in the BNC to obtain 200 common selectional preference classes. To quantify selectional preferences, we adopted the SPS measure of Resnik (1993). Resnik defines SPS of a verb as the difference between the posterior distribution of noun classes in a particular relation with the verb and their prior distribution in that syntactic position (regardless of the verb). He quantifies this difference using the Kullback-Leibler divergence:

$$S_R(v) = D(P(c|v)||P(c)) = \sum_c P(c|v) \log \frac{P(c|v)}{P(c)}, \quad (1)$$

where $P(c)$ is the prior probability of the noun class, $P(c|v)$ is the posterior probability of the noun class given the verb and R is the grammatical relation.

We calculated SPS for verb-subject and verb-direct object grammatical relations. The optimal selectional preference strength thresholds were set experimentally on a small heldout dataset at 0.30 for verb-subject and 0.70 for verb-direct object relations (via qualitative analysis of the data). The system excludes expressions containing the verbs with preference strength below these thresholds from the set of candidate metaphors. Examples of verbs with weak direct object SPs include e.g. *imagine, avoid, contain, dislike, make, admire, separate, remember* and the strong SPs are exhibited by e.g. *sip, hobble, roar, hoover, slam, skim, drink* etc.

3.2 Literal Paraphrasing

The verbs that can be used metaphorically according to the SPS filter are then paraphrased using the context-based literal paraphrasing method of Shutova (2010). While Shutova only used the method to paraphrase manually annotated metaphors, we extend and apply the method to paraphrasing of literally used terms and metaphor identification, eliminating the need for manual annotation of metaphorical expressions.

The system takes verbs and their context in the form of subject and direct-object relations as input. It generates a list of possible paraphrases of the verb that can occur in the same context and ranks them according to their likelihood, as derived from the corpus. It then identifies shared features of the paraphrases and the verb using the WordNet (Fellbaum, 1998) hierarchy and removes unrelated concepts. It then identifies literal paraphrases among the remaining candidates based on the verb's automatically induced selectional preferences and the properties of the context.

3.2.1 Context-based Paraphrase Ranking

Following Shutova (2010), we compute the likelihood L of a particular paraphrase of the verb v as a joint probability of the paraphrase i co-occurring with the other lexical items from its context $w_1, ..., w_N$ in syntactic relations $r_1, ..., r_N$.

$$L_i = P(i, (w_1, r_1), (w_2, r_2), ..., (w_N, r_N)). \quad (2)$$

Assuming statistical independence between the relations of the terms in a phrase, we obtain:

$$P(i, (w_1, r_1), (w_2, r_2), ..., (w_N, r_N)) = P(i) \cdot P((w_1, r_1)|i) \cdot ... \cdot P((w_N, r_N)|i). \quad (3)$$

The probabilities can be calculated using maximum likelihood estimation as $P(i) = \frac{f(i)}{\sum_k f(i_k)}$ and $P(w_n, r_n|i) = \frac{f(w_n, r_n, i)}{f(i)}$, where $f(i)$ is the frequency of the interpretation irrespective of its arguments, $\sum_k f(i_k)$ is the number of times its part of speech class is attested in the corpus and $f(w_n, r_n, i)$ is the number of times the interpretation co-occurs with context word w_n in relation r_n. By performing appropriate substitutions into (3), we obtain:

$$P(i, (w_1, r_1), (w_2, r_2), ..., (w_N, r_N)) = \frac{f(i)}{\sum_k f(i_k)} \cdot \frac{f(w_1, r_1, i)}{f(i)} \cdot ... \cdot \frac{f(w_N, r_N, i)}{f(i)} = \frac{\prod_{n=1}^{N} f(w_n, r_n, i)}{(f(i))^{N-1} \cdot \sum_k f(i_k)}. \quad (4)$$

This model is then used to rank the candidate substitutes of the verb v in the fixed context according to the data. The parameters of the model were estimated from the RASP-parsed BNC using the grammatical relations output created by Andersen et al. (2008). The goal of this model is to emphasize the paraphrases that match the context of the verb in the sentence best.

3.2.2 WordNet Filter

After obtaining the initial list of possible substitutes for the verb v, the system filters out the terms whose meanings do not share any common properties with that of the verb. This overlap of properties is identified using the hyponymy relation in WordNet. Within the initial list of paraphrases, the system selects the terms that are hypernyms of the verb v, or share a common hypernym with it. Following Shutova, we restrict the hypernym search to a depth of three levels in the taxonomy. Table 1 shows the filtered lists of paraphrases for the expressions "*stir* excitement" and "campaign *surged*". The goal of the filter is to discard unrelated paraphrases and thus ensure the meaning retention during paraphrasing. Note, however, that we define meaning retention broadly, as sharing a set of similar basic properties. Such a broad definition distinguishes our system from other WordNet-based approaches to lexical substitution (McCarthy and Navigli, 2007) and allows for a transition from metaphorical to literal language, while preserving the original meaning.

3.2.3 SP-based Re-ranking

The lists of paraphrases which were generated as described above contain some irrelevant paraphrases (e.g. "campaign lifted" for "campaign *surged*") and some metaphorically-used paraphrases (e.g. "campaign *soared*"). However, our aim is to identify literal paraphrases among the candidates. Shutova's method uses selectional preferences of the candi-

Log-likelihood	Paraphrase
Verb-DirectObject	
stir excitement:	
-14.28	create
-14.84	provoke
-15.53	make
-15.53	elicit
-15.53	arouse
-16.23	stimulate
-16.23	raise
-16.23	excite
-16.23	conjure
Subject-Verb	
campaign ***surge***:	
-13.01	run
-15.53	improve
-16.23	soar
-16.23	lift

Table 1: The list of paraphrases with the initial ranking

Association	Paraphrase
Verb-DirectObject	
stir excitement:	
0.0696	provoke
0.0245	elicit
0.0194	arouse
0.0061	conjure
0.0028	create
0.0001	stimulate
≈ 0	raise
≈ 0	make
≈ 0	excite
Subject-Verb	
campaign ***surge***:	
0.0086	improve
0.0009	run
≈ 0	soar
≈ 0	lift

Table 2: The list of paraphrases re-ranked using SPs

dates for this purpose. Candidates used metaphorically are likely to demonstrate semantic preference for the source domain, e.g. *soar* would select for *birds* or *flying devices* as its subject rather than *campaigns* (the target domain), whereas the ones used literally would have a higher preference for the target domain. This is yet another modification of Wilks' SP violation view of metaphor. Shutova (2010) has previously shown that selecting the paraphrases whose preferences the noun in the context matches best allows to filter out non-literalness, as well as unrelated terms.

As in case of the SPS filter, we automatically acquired selectional preference distributions of the verbs in the paraphrase lists (for verb-subject and verb-direct object relations) from the RASP-parsed BNC. In order to quantify how well a particular argument class fits the verb, we adopted the selectional association measure proposed by Resnik (1993). Selectional association is defined as follows:

$$A_R(v,c) = \frac{1}{S_R(v)} P(c|v) \log \frac{P(c|v)}{P(c)}, \qquad (5)$$

where $P(c)$ is the prior probability of the noun class, $P(c|v)$ is the posterior probability of the noun class given the verb and S_R is the overall selectional preference strength of the verb in the grammatical relation R.

We use selectional association as a measure of semantic fitness of the paraphrases into the context, which stands for their literalness. The paraphrases are re-ranked based on their selectional association with the noun in the context. The incorrect or metaphorical paraphrases are de-emphasized within this ranking. The new ranking is shown in Table 2. While the model in 3.2.1 selected the candidate paraphrases that match the context better than all other candidates, the SP model emphasizes the paraphrases that match this particular context better than any other context they may appear in. Shutova's experiments have shown that the paraphrase in rank 1 (i.e. the verb with which the noun in the context has the highest selectional association) represents a literal interpretation in 81% of all cases. Such a level of accuracy makes Shutova's method state-of-the-art in metaphor paraphrasing. We now apply it to the task of metaphor identification.

3.3 Reverse Paraphrasing

At the heart of our approach to metaphor identification is the concept of reverse paraphrasing. The main intuition behind it is that when literally-used words are paraphrased with their literal substitutes, the reverse literal paraphrasing of that substitute should yield the original expression as one of the candidates. This is, however, not the case for metaphor, since its literal paraphrase would yield another literal expression via literal paraphrasing. We ran the above paraphrasing method on every verb in the input text and then again on the top

Original expression	Lit. paraphrase	Reverse paraphrase
Verb-DirectObject		
stir excitement	provoke:	elicit, arouse, cause, create, stimulate, raise, make
	elicit:	provoke, arouse, see, derive, create, raise, make
buy a dress		
	get:	change, find, **buy**, purchase, take, hit, alter, ...
	purchase:	get, **buy**
Subject-Verb		
campaign ***surge***	improve:	change, turn
	run:	succeed, direct, continue, lead, last, win, extend, ...
prisoner **escape**	flee:	**escape**, run
	get:	drive, go, turn, transfer, arrive, bring, come, ...

Table 3: The list of top two literal paraphrases and their reverse paraphrases, as identified by the system

two paraphrases it produces. If this process resulted in retrieving the original expression then the latter was tagged as literal, otherwise it was tagged as metaphorical. Some examples of reverse paraphrasing results are given in Table 3. One can see from the table that when the metaphorical verb *stir* in "*stir* excitement" is paraphrased as the literal "provoke", the subsequent paraphrasing of "provoke" does not produce "stir". In contrast, when the literal expression "buy a dress" is paraphrased as "purchase", the reverse paraphrasing generates "buy" as one of the candidates, indicating the literalness of the original expression. The same is true for the metaphorical *surge* in "campaign *surged*" and the literal *escape* in "the prisoner escaped".

4 Evaluation and Discussion

4.1 Baseline

The baseline system is the implementation of the selectional preference violation view of Wilks (1978) using automatically induced SPs. Such a choice of a baseline allows us to compare our own modifications of the SP violation view to the original approach of Wilks in a computational setting, as well as evaluate the latter on real-world data. Another motivation behind this choice is that the symmetry of reverse paraphrasing can be seen as a kind of "normality" test, in a similar way as the satisfied selectional preferences are in Wilk's approach. However, we believe that the SP-based reverse paraphrasing method captures significantly more information than SP violations do and thus compare the performance of the two methods in an experimental setting.

The baseline SP classes were created as described above and the preferences were quantified using selectional association as a measure. The baseline system then classified the instances where selectional association of the verb and the noun in the phrase were below a certain threshold, as metaphorical. We determined the optimal threshold by qualitative analysis of the selectional preference distributions of 50 verbs of different frequency and SPS (through the analysis of literally and metaphorically-used arguments). The threshold was averaged over individual verbs' thresholds and equals 0.07 for direct object relations, and 0.09 for subject relations.

4.2 Evaluation Corpus

We evaluated the system and the baseline against the corpus of Shutova and Teufel (2010), that was manually annotated for metaphorical expressions. The corpus is a 14,000-word subset of the BNC, with the texts selected to retain the original balance of genre in the BNC itself. The corpus contains extracts from fiction, newspaper text, radio broadcast (transcribed speech), essays and journal articles on politics, social science and literature. Shutova and Teufel (2010) identified 241 metaphorical expressions in the corpus, out of which 164 were verbal metaphors.

We parsed the corpus using the RASP parser and extracted subject and direct object relations from its output. Among the direct object relations there were 310 literal phrases and 79 metaphorical ones; and among the subject relations 206 were literal and 67 metaphorical. This constitutes a dataset of 662 relations for the systems to classify.

4.3 Results and Discussion

The system and baseline performance was evaluated against the corpus in terms of precision and recall. Precision, P, measures the proportion of metaphorical expressions that were tagged correctly among

Relation	Bsln P	System P	Bsln R	System R
Verb-DObj	0.20	0.69	0.52	0.63
Verb-Subj	0.13	0.66	0.59	0.70
Average	0.17	0.68	0.55	0.66

Table 4: Baseline and system performance by relation

the ones that were tagged by the system. Recall, R, measures the proportion of metaphorical expressions that were identified out of all metaphorical expressions in the gold standard corpus. The system $P = 0.68$ and $R = 0.66$, whereas the baseline only attains $P = 0.17$ and $R = 0.55$. System performance by relation is shown in Table 4. The human ceiling for this task, according to the annotation experiments of Shutova and Teufel (2010) approximates to $P = 0.80$. Figure 1 shows example sentences with metaphors identified and paraphrased by the system. Table 5 provides a breakdown of the annotated instances into true / false positives and true / false negatives. As one can see from the table, the systems can accurately annotate both metaphorical and literal expressions, providing a balance between precision and recall.

The system outperforms the baseline for both verb-subject and verb-direct object constructions. Its performance is also close to the previous metaphor identification systems of Turney et al. (2011) (accuracy of 0.73) and Shutova et al. (2010) (precision of 0.79), however, the results are not directly comparable due to different experimental settings. Our method has a strong advantage over the system of Shutova et al. (2010) in terms of coverage: the latter system heavily relied on manually annotated seed metaphors which limited its applicability in unrestricted text to the set of topics covered by the seeds. As opposed to this, our method is domain-independent and can be applied to any data. Shutova et al. (2010) have not measured the recall of their system, however indicated its possible coverage limitations.

In addition, our system produces paraphrases for the identified metaphorical expressions. Since the identification is directly dependent on the quality of literal paraphrasing, the majority of the interpretations the system provided for the identified metaphors appear to be correct. However, we found a few instances where, despite the correct initial paraphrasing, the system was not able to identify the metaphor, usually in case of highly conventionalized metaphorical expressions. Overall, the most frequent system errors fall into the following categories:

FYT Gorbachev **inherited** a Soviet state which was, in a celebrated Stalinist formulation, national in form but socialist in content.
Paraphrase: Gorbachev received a Soviet state which was, in a celebrated Stalinist formulation, national in form but socialist in content.

CEK The Clinton campaign **surged** again and he easily won the Democratic nomination.
Paraphrase: The Clinton campaign improved again and he easily won the Democratic nomination.

CEK Their views **reflect** a lack of enthusiasm among the British people at large for John Major 's idea of European unity.
Paraphrase: Their views show a lack of enthusiasm among the British people at large for John Major 's idea of European unity.

J85 [..] the reasons for this superiority are never **spelled out**.
Paraphrase [..] the reasons for this superiority are never specified.

J85 Anyone who has introduced speech act theory to students will know that these technical terms are not at all easy to **grasp**.
Paraphrase: Anyone who has introduced speech act theory to students will know that these technical terms are not at all easy to understand.

G0N The man's voice **cut in** .
Paraphrase: The man's voice interrupted.

Figure 1: Metaphors tagged by the system (in bold) and their paraphrases

Errors due to incorrect parsing: The system failed to discover some of the metaphorical expressions in the corpus since their grammatical relations were missed by the parser. In addition, some of the instances were misclassified, e.g. "pounds paid to [...]" or "change was greatly *accelerated*" were labeled as subject relations. Overall, the parser missed 9 metaphorical expressions.

Errors due to incorrect paraphrasing: The most common type of error that leads to false positives is the incorrect paraphrasing (resulting in a change of meaning). This makes it nearly impossible for the system to retrieve the original term. There were also

	Positives	Negatives	Total
True	99	464	563
False	47	52	99
Total	146	516	

Table 5: System tagging statistics

cases where the system could not generate any paraphrase (usually for literal expressions, e.g. "play an anthem").

Errors due to metaphorical paraphrasing: Some of the system errors are due to metaphorical paraphrasing. For example, the metaphorical expression "*mend* marriage" was paraphrased as "*repair* marriage", which is also used metaphorically. And *repair* in return generated *mend*, when paraphrased in reverse. Errors of this type have been mainly triggered by the WordNet filter, and the fact that some metaphorical senses are included in WordNet.

Errors due to metaphor conventionality: a number of conventional metaphors were missed by the system, since the original verb was retrieved due to its conventionality. Such examples include "*impose* a decision", "*put* the issue forward", "*lead* a life". Such cases suggest that the system is better suited to identify more creative, novel metaphors.

Cases of metonymy: a few cases of general metonymy were annotated by the system as metaphorical, e.g. "shout support", which stands for "shout the words of support", and "humiliate a moment", that is likely to mean "humiliate the event of the moment". However, there were only 4 errors of this type in the data.

Baseline Errors: The output of the baseline exhibited two main types of error. The first stemmed from the conventionality of many metaphorical expressions, which resulted in their literal annotation. Conventionality leads to high selectional association for verbs with their metaphorical arguments, e.g. *embrace* has {*view, ideology, conception* etc.} class as its top ranked direct object argument with the selectional association of 0.18. The second type of error was the system selecting many language anomalies that violate selectional preferences and tagging these as metaphors. This resulted in a high number of false positives.

5 Conclusions and Future Directions

Previous research on metaphor addressed a number of its aspects using both symbolic and statistical techniques. While some of this work met with success with respect to precision in metaphor annotation, the methods often focused on a limited domain and needed manually-labeled training data. Their dependence on manually annotated training data made the systems hard to scale. As a result, many of these systems are not directly applicable to aid real-world NLP due to their limited coverage. In contrast, our method does not require any manually-labeled data, which makes it more robust and applicable to a wide range of genres. It is also the first one to perform accurate metaphor identification and interpretation in one step, as opposed to the previous systems focusing on one part of the task only. It identifies metaphor with a precision of 68% and a recall of 66%, which is a very encouraging result. We believe that this work has important implications for computational modeling of metaphor, and is relevant to a range of other semantic tasks within NLP.

Although we have so far tested our system on verb-subject and verb-object metaphors only, we believe that the described identification and paraphrasing techniques can be similarly applied to a wider range of syntactic constructions. Extending the system to deal with more parts of speech and types of phrases (e.g. nominal and adjectival metaphors) is part of our future work.

Another promising future research avenue is integrating the techniques with unsupervised paraphrasing and lexical substitution methods, using e.g. distributional similarity measures (Pucci et al., 2009; McCarthy et al., 2010) or vector space models of word meaning (Erk and Padó, 2008; Erk and Padó, 2009; De Cao and Basili, 2009; Shutova et al., 2012b). These methods could fully or partly replace the WordNet filter in the detection of similar basic features of the concepts, or add useful information to it. Fully replacing the WordNet filter by an unsupervised method would make the system more robust and more easily portable across domains and genres. This may also eliminate some of the system errors that arise from the inconsistent sense annotation and the inclusion of some metaphorical senses in WordNet.

Acknowledgments

This work was supported by the ICSI MetaNet project (grant number W911NF-12-C-0022). Many thanks to Srini Narayanan, Eve Sweetser and Jerry Feldman for their advice and feedback.

References

Rodrigo Agerri, John Barnden, Mark Lee, and Alan Wallington. 2007. Metaphor, inference and domain-independent mappings. In *Proceedings of RANLP-2007*, pages 17–23, Borovets, Bulgaria.

Rodrigo Agerri. 2008. Metaphor in textual entailment. In *Proceedings of COLING 2008*, pages 3–6, Manchester, UK.

Oistein Andersen, Julien Nioche, Ted Briscoe, and John Carroll. 2008. The BNC parsed with RASP4UIMA. In *Proceedings of LREC 2008*, pages 865–869, Marrakech, Morocco.

John Barnden and Mark Lee. 2002. An artificial intelligence approach to metaphor understanding. *Theoria et Historia Scientiarum*, 6(1):399–412.

Julia Birke and Anoop Sarkar. 2006. A clustering approach for the nearly unsupervised recognition of nonliteral language. In *In Proceedings of EACL-06*, pages 329–336.

Ted Briscoe, John Carroll, and Rebecca Watson. 2006. The second release of the rasp system. In *Proceedings of the COLING/ACL on Interactive presentation sessions*, pages 77–80.

Lou Burnard. 2007. *Reference Guide for the British National Corpus (XML Edition)*.

Lynne Cameron. 2003. *Metaphor in Educational Discourse*. Continuum, London.

Seana Coulson. 2008. Metaphor comprehension and the brain. In R.W. Gibbs, editor, *Metaphor and Thought*, Cambridge. Cambridge University Press.

Diego De Cao and Roberto Basili. 2009. Combining distributional and paradigmatic information in a lexical substitution task. In *Proceedings of EVALITA workshop, 11th Congress of Italian Association for Artificial Intelligence*.

Katrin Erk and Sebastian Padó. 2008. A structured vector space model for word meaning in context. In *Proceedings of the Conference on Empirical Methods in Natural Language Processing*, pages 897–906, Waikiki, Hawaii, USA.

Katrin Erk and Sebastian Padó. 2009. Paraphrase assessment in structured vector space: exploring parameters and datasets. In *Proceedings of the Workshop on Geometrical Models of Natural Language Semantics*, pages 57–65. Association for Computational Linguistics.

Dan Fass. 1991. met*: A method for discriminating metonymy and metaphor by computer. *Computational Linguistics*, 17(1):49–90.

Jerome Feldman and Srini Narayanan. 2004. Embodied meaning in a neural theory of language. *Brain and Language*, 89(2):385–392.

Christiane Fellbaum, editor. 1998. *WordNet: An Electronic Lexical Database (ISBN: 0-262-06197-X)*. MIT Press, first edition.

Matt Gedigian, John Bryant, Srini Narayanan, and Branimir Ciric. 2006. Catching metaphors. In *In Proceedings of the 3rd Workshop on Scalable Natural Language Understanding*, pages 41–48, New York.

Raymond W. Gibbs and Herbert L. Colston. 2012. *Interpreting Figurative Meaning*. Cambridge University Press.

Paul Kingsbury and Martha Palmer. 2002. From TreeBank to PropBank. In *Proceedings of LREC-2002*, pages 1989–1993, Gran Canaria, Canary Islands, Spain.

Saisuresh Krishnakumaran and Xiaojin Zhu. 2007. Hunting elusive metaphors using lexical resources. In *Proceedings of the Workshop on Computational Approaches to Figurative Language*, pages 13–20, Rochester, NY.

George Lakoff and Mark Johnson. 1980. *Metaphors We Live By*. University of Chicago Press, Chicago.

James Martin. 1990. *A Computational Model of Metaphor Interpretation*. Academic Press Professional, Inc., San Diego, CA, USA.

James Martin. 2006. A corpus-based analysis of context effects on metaphor comprehension. In A. Stefanowitsch and S. T. Gries, editors, *Corpus-Based Approaches to Metaphor and Metonymy*, Berlin. Mouton de Gruyter.

Zachary Mason. 2004. Cormet: a computational, corpus-based conventional metaphor extraction system. *Computational Linguistics*, 30(1):23–44.

Diana McCarthy and Roberto Navigli. 2007. Semeval-2007 task 10: English lexical substitution task. In *Proceedings of the 4th workshop on Semantic Evaluations (SemEval-2007)*, pages 48–53.

Diana McCarthy, Bill Keller, and Roberto Navigli. 2010. Getting synonym candidates from raw data in the english lexical substitution task. In *Proceedings of the 14th EURALEX International Congress*, Leeuwarden, The Netherlands.

Srini Narayanan. 1997. Knowledge-based Action Representations for Metaphor and Aspect (KARMA). Technical report, PhD thesis, University of California at Berkeley.

Srini Narayanan. 1999. Moving right along: A computational model of metaphoric reasoning about events. In *Proceedings of AAAI 99)*, pages 121–128, Orlando, Florida.

Dario Pucci, Marco Baroni, Franco Cutugno, and Alessandro Lenci. 2009. Unsupervised lexical substitution with a word space model. In *Proceedings of EVALITA workshop, 11th Congress of Italian Association for Artificial Intelligence*.

Philip Resnik. 1993. *Selection and Information: A Class-based Approach to Lexical Relationships*. Ph.D. thesis, Philadelphia, PA, USA.

Ekaterina Shutova and Simone Teufel. 2010. Metaphor corpus annotated for source - target domain mappings. In *Proceedings of LREC 2010*, pages 3255–3261, Malta.

Ekaterina Shutova, Lin Sun, and Anna Korhonen. 2010. Metaphor identification using verb and noun clustering. In *Proceedings of Coling 2010*, pages 1002–1010, Beijing, China.

Ekaterina Shutova, Simone Teufel, and Anna Korhonen. 2012a. Statistical Metaphor Processing. *Computational Linguistics*, 39(2).

Ekaterina Shutova, Tim Van de Cruys, and Anna Korhonen. 2012b. Unsupervised metaphor paraphrasing using a vector space model. In *Proceedings of COLING 2012*, Mumbai, India.

Ekaterina Shutova. 2010. Automatic metaphor interpretation as a paraphrasing task. In *Proceedings of NAACL 2010*, pages 1029–1037, Los Angeles, USA.

Gerard J. Steen, Aletta G. Dorst, J. Berenike Herrmann, Anna A. Kaal, Tina Krennmayr, and Trijntje Pasma. 2010. *A method for linguistic metaphor identification: From MIP to MIPVU*. John Benjamins, Amsterdam/Philadelphia.

Lin Sun and Anna Korhonen. 2009. Improving verb clustering with automatically acquired selectional preferences. In *Proceedings of EMNLP 2009*, pages 638–647, Singapore, August.

Paul H. Thibodeau and Lera Boroditsky. 2011. Metaphors we think with: The role of metaphor in reasoning. *PLoS ONE*, 6(2):e16782, 02.

Peter D. Turney, Yair Neuman, Dan Assaf, and Yohai Cohen. 2011. Literal and metaphorical sense identification through concrete and abstract context. In *Proceedings of the Conference on Empirical Methods in Natural Language Processing*, EMNLP '11, pages 680–690, Stroudsburg, PA, USA. Association for Computational Linguistics.

Akira Utsumi. 2011. Computational exploration of metaphor comprehension processes using a semantic space model. *Cognitive Science*, 35(2):251–296.

Yorick Wilks. 1975. A preferential pattern-seeking semantics for natural language inference. *Artificial Intelligence*, 6:53–74.

Yorick Wilks. 1978. Making preferences more active. *Artificial Intelligence*, 11(3):197–223.

Using the text to evaluate short answers for reading comprehension exercises

Andrea Horbach, Alexis Palmer and Manfred Pinkal
Department of Computational Linguistics, Saarland University, Saarbrücken, Germany
(andrea|apalmer|pinkal)@coli.uni-saarland.de

Abstract

Short answer questions for reading comprehension are a common task in foreign language learning. Automatic short answer scoring is the task of automatically assessing the semantic content of a student's answer, marking it e.g. as correct or incorrect. While previous approaches mainly focused on comparing a learner answer to some reference answer provided by the teacher, we explore the use of the underlying reading texts as additional evidence for the classification. First, we conduct a corpus study targeting the links between sentences in reading texts for learners of German and answers to reading comprehension questions based on those texts. Second, we use the reading text directly for classification, considering three different models: an answer-based classifier extended with textual features, a simple text-based classifier, and a model that combines the two according to confidence of the text-based classification. The most promising approach is the first one, results for which show that textual features improve classification accuracy. While the other two models do not improve classification accuracy, they do investigate the role of the text and suggest possibilities for developing automatic answer scoring systems with less supervision needed from instructors.

1 Introduction

Reading comprehension exercises are a common means of assessment for language teaching: students read a text in the language they are learning and are then asked to answer questions about the text. The types of questions asked of the learner may vary in their scope and in the type of answers they are designed to elicit; in this work we focus on "short answer" responses, which are generally in the range of 1–3 sentences.

The nature of the reading comprehension task is that the student is asked to show that he or she has *understood* the text at hand. Questions focus on one or more pieces of information from the text, and correct responses should contain the relevant semantic content. In the language learning context, responses classified as correct might still contain grammatical or spelling errors; the focus lies on the content rather than the form of the learner answer.

Automatic scoring of short answer responses to reading comprehension questions is in essence a textual entailment task, with the additional complication that, in order to answer a question correctly, the learner must have identified the right portion of the text. It isn't enough that a student answer is entailed by *some* part of the reading text; it must be entailed by the part of the text which is responsive to the question under discussion.

Previous approaches to automatic short answer scoring have seldom considered the reading text itself, instead comparing student answers to target answers supplied by instructors; we will refer to these as *answer-based models*. In this paper we explore the role of the text for short answer scoring, evaluating several models for considering the text in automatic scoring, and presenting results of an annotation study regarding the semantic links between reading texts and answers to reading comprehension questions.

*Second Joint Conference on Lexical and Computational Semantics (*SEM), Volume 1: Proceedings of the Main Conference and the Shared Task*, pages 286–295, Atlanta, Georgia, June 13-14, 2013.

TEXT: SCHLOSS PILLNITZ

This palace, which lies in the east of Dresden, is to me the most beautiful palace in the Dresden area. (...) One special attraction in the park is the camellia tree. In 1992, the camellia, which is more than 230 years old and 8.90 meters tall, got a new, moveable home, in which temperature, ventilation, humidity, and shade are controlled by a climate regulation computer. In the warm seasons, the house is rolled away from the tree. During the Blossom Time, from the middle of February until April, the camellia has tens of thousands of crimson red blossoms. Every year, a limited number of shoots from the Pillnitz camellia are sold during the Blossom Time, making it an especially worthwhile time to visit.

QUESTION:
A friend of yours would like to see the historic camellia tree. When should he go to Pillnitz, and why exactly at this time?

TARGET ANSWERS:

- From the middle of February until April is the Blossom Time.
- In spring the camellia has tens of thousands of crimson red blossoms.

LEARNER ANSWERS:

- `[correct]` He should go from the middle of February until April, because then the historic camellia has tens of thousands of crimson red blossoms.
- `[incorrect]` Every year, a limited number of Pillnitz camellia are sold during the Blossom Time.
- `[incorrect]` All year round against temperature and humidity are controlled by a climate regulation computer.

Figure 1: Example of reading text with question and answers (translation by authors)

These investigations are done for German language texts, questions, and answers. Figure 1 shows a (translated) sample reading text, question, set of target answers, and set of learner answers.

We show that the use of text-based features improves classification performance over purely answer-based models. We also show that a very simple text-based classifier, while it does not achieve the same performance as the answer-based classifier, does reach an accuracy of 76% for binary classification (correct/incorrect) of student answers. The implication of this for automatic scoring is that reasonable results may be achievable with much less effort on the part of instructors; namely, a classifier trained on the supervision provided by marking the region of a text relevant to a given question performs reasonably well, though not as well as one trained on full target answers.

The paper proceeds as follows: in Section 2 we discuss the task and related approaches. In Section 3, we describe our baseline model and the data set we use. In Section 4 and Section 5 we discuss our text-based models and present experiments and results.

2 Approaches to short answer scoring

In short answer scoring (SAS) the task is to automatically assign labels to individual learner answers. Those labels can either be binary, a value on some scale of points or grades, or a more fine-grained diagnosis. For example, one fine-grained set of labels (Bailey, 2008) classifies answers as (among others) correct, as missing a necessary concept or concepts, containing extra content, or as failing to answer the question. Our present study is restricted to binary classification.

Previous work on SAS, including early systems like (Leacock and Chodorow, 2003; Pulman and Sukkarieh, 2005; Sukkarieh and Pulman, 2005) is of course not only in the domain of foreign language learning. For example, Mohler et al. (2011) and Mohler and Mihalcea (2009) use semantic graph alignments and semantic similarity measures to assess student answers to computer science questions, comparing them to sample solutions provided by a teacher. Accordingly, not all SAS settings include reading or other reference texts; many involve only questions, target answers, and learner answers. Our approach is relevant for scenarios in which some sort of reference text is available.

The work we present here is strongly based on approaches towards SAS by Meurers and colleagues (Bailey and Meurers, 2008; Meurers et al., 2011a; Meurers et al., 2011b; Ziai et al., 2012). Specifically, the sentence alignment model described in Section 3 (and again discussed in Section 4) is modeled after the one used by Meurers et al. to align target answers and student answers.

Rather than using answers provided by instructors, Nielsen et al. (2008) represent target answers to science questions as a set of hand-annotated *facets*, i.e. important aspects of the answer, typically represented by a pair of words and the relation that connects them. Student answers, and consequently students' understanding of target science concepts, are then assessed by determining whether the relevant facets are addressed by the learner answers.

Evaluating short answers on the basis of associated reading texts, as we do here, is a task related to textual entailment. In the context of tutoring systems, Bethard et al. (2012) identify students' misconceptions of science concepts in essay writing using textual entailment techniques. They align students' writings to extracted science concepts in order to identify misconceptions, using a similar approach to identify the correct underlying concept.

An excellent and more detailed overview of related work can be found in Ziai et al. (2012).

To our knowledge, there is no previous work that uses reading texts as evidence for short answer scoring in the context of foreign language learning.

3 Answer-based models

In order to compare to previous work, we first implement an alignment-based model following that proposed in (Meurers et al., 2011b). We refer to this class of models as *answer-based* because they function by aligning learner answers to instructor-supplied target answers along several different dimensions, discussed below. Answers are then classified as correct or incorrect on the basis of features derived from these alignments.

Wherever possible/practical, we directly re-implement the Meurers model for German data. In this section we describe relevant aspects of the Meurers model, along with modifications and extensions in our implementation of that model.[1]

Preprocessing

We preprocess all material (learner answers, target answers, questions and reading texts) using standard NLP tools for sentence splitting and tokenization (both OpenNLP[2]), POS tagging and stemming (both Treetagger (Schmid, 1994)), NP chunking (OpenNLP), and dependency parsing (Zurich Parser (Sennrich et al., 2009)). We use an NE Tagger (Faruqui and Padó, 2010) to annotate named entities. Synonyms and semantic types are extracted from GermaNet (Hamp and Feldweg, 1997).

For keywords, which serve to give more emphasis to content words in the target answer, we extract all nouns from the target answer.

Given that we are dealing with learner language, but do not want to penalize answers for typical learner errors, spellchecking (and subsequent correction of spelling errors) is especially important for this task. Our approach is as follows: we first identify all words from the learner answers that are not accepted by a German spellchecker (aspell[3]). We then check for each word whether the word nevertheless occurs in the target answer, question or reading text. If so, we accept it as correct. Otherwise, we try to identify (using Levenshtein distance) which word from the target answer, question, or reading text is most likely to be the form intended by the student.

Prior to alignment, we remove from the answer all punctuation, stopwords (restricted to determiners and auxiliaries), and material present in the question.

Alignment

The alignment process in short answer scoring approximates determination of semantic equivalence between target answer and learner answer. During alignment, we identify matches between answer pairs on a number of linguistic levels: tokens, chunks, and dependency triples.

On the token level, we consider a number of different metrics for identity between tokens, with each

[1] Some extensions were made in order to bring performance of our re-implementation closer to the figures reported in previous work.

[2] `http://opennlp.apache.org/index.html`

[3] `http://aspell.net/`

metric associated with a certain alignment weight. After weights have been determined for all possible token pairs, the best applicable weight is used as input for a traditional marriage alignment algorithm (Gale and Shapley, 1962).

We use the following types of identity (id), weighted in the following order:

```
token id > lemma id >
spelling id > synonym & NE id >
similarity id>
NE type, semantic type & POS id
```

For synonym identity, we take a broad notion of synonymy, extracting (from GermaNet) as potential synonyms all words which are at most two levels (in either direction) away from the target word. Similarity identity is defined as two words having a GermaNet path relatedness above some threshhold. In order to have semantic type identity, two words must have a common GermaNet hypernym (from a predetermined set of relevant hypernyms). Only some closed-class words are eligible for POS identity. We treat e.g. all types of determiners as POS identical.

Unlike, for example, alignment in machine translation, in which every token pair is considered a candidate for alignment, under the Meurers model only candidates with at least one type of token identity are available for alignment. This aims to prevent completely unrelated word pairs from being considered for alignment.

In order to favor alignment of content words over alignment of function words, and in departure from the Meurers model, we use a content word multiplier for alignment weights.

Chunks can only be aligned if at least one pair of tokens within the respective chunks has been aligned, and the percentage of aligned tokens between learner and target answer chunks is used as input for the alignment process. Dependency triple pairs are aligned when they share dependency relation, head lemma, and dependent lemma.

Features and classifier

After answers have been aligned, the following features are extracted as input for the classifier: keyword overlap (percentage of aligned keywords), target token overlap (percentage of aligned target tokens), learner token overlap (percentage of aligned learner tokens), token match (percentage of token alignments that are token identical), lemma match, synonym match, type match, target triple overlap, learner triple overlap, target chunk overlap, learner chunk overlap, target bigram overlap, learner bigram overlap, target trigram overlap, learner trigram overlap, and variety of alignment (number of different token alignment types).

The n-gram features are the only new features in our re-implementation of the Meurers model, hoping to capture the influence of linear ordering of aligned tokens. These features did not in the end improve the model's performance.

For classification, we use the timbl toolkit (Daelemans et al., 2009) for k-nearest neighbors classification. We treat all features as numeric values and evaluate performance via leave-one-out cross-validation. Further details appear in Section 5.

Data

For all work reported in this paper, we use the German CREG corpus (Ott et al., 2012) of short answers to questions for reading comprehension tasks. More specifically, we use a balanced subset of the CREG corpus containing a total of 1032 learner answers. This corpus consists of 30 reading texts with an average of 5.9 questions per text. Each question is associated with one or more target answers, specified by a teacher. For each question in turn there are an average of 5.8 learner answers, each manually annotated according to both binary and fine-grained labeling schemes. When there are several target answers for a question, the best target answer for each learner answer is indicated.

4 Text-based approach

Previous approaches to this task take the instructor-supplied target answer(s) as a sort of supervision; the target answer is meant to indicate the semantic content necessary for a correct student answer. Alignment between student answer and target answer is then taken as a way of approximating semantic equivalence. The key innovation of the current study is to incorporate the reading text into the evaluation of student answers. In this section we describe and evaluate three approaches to incorporating the text. The aim is to consider the semantic relationships between target answer, learner answer, and the text itself.[4]

A target answer is in fact just one way of expressing the requisite semantic content. Teachers who create such exercises are obviously looking at the text while creating target answers, and target answers are often paraphrases of one or more sentences of the reading text. Some learner answers which are scored as incorrect by the answer-based system may in fact be variant expressions of the same semantic content as the target answer. Due to the nature of the reading comprehension task, in which students are able to view the text while answering questions, we might expect students to express things in a manner similar to the text. This is especially true for language learners, as they are likely to have a limited range of options both for lexical expression and grammatical constructions.

Along similar lines, one potential source of incorrect answers is an inability on the part of the student to correctly identify the portion of the text that is relevant to the question at hand. Our hypothesis therefore is that a learner answer which links to the same portion of the reading text as the target answer is likely to be a **correct** answer. Similarly, a learner answer which closely matches some part of the text that is *not* related to the target answer is likely to be **incorrect**.

Our text-based models investigate this hypothesis in several different ways, described in Section 4.2.

4.1 Annotation study

The CREG data includes questions, learner answers, target answers, and reading texts; associations between text and answers are not part of the annotations. We undertook an annotation project in order to have gold-standard **source sentences** for both learner and target answers. This gold-standard is then used to inform the text-based models described below.

After removing a handful of problematic questions and their associated answers, we acquired human annotations for 889 of the 1032 learner answers from the balanced subset of the CREG corpus, in addition to 294 target answers. Each answer was labeled separately by two (of three) annotators, who were given the reading text and the question and asked to identify the single best source sentence from the text. Annotators were not told whether any given instance was a target or learner answer, nor whether learner answers were correct or incorrect.

Although we expected most answers to correspond directly to a single text passage (Meurers et al., 2011b), annotators were asked to look for (and annotate appropriately) two different conditions in which more than one source sentence may be relevant. We refer to these as the repeated content condition and the distributed content condition.

In the *repeated content condition*, the same semantic content may be fully represented in more than one sentence from the original text. In such cases, we would expect the text to contain sentences that are paraphrases or near-paraphrases of one another. The *distributed content condition* occurs when the relevant semantic content spans multiple sentences, and some degree of synthesis or even inference may be required to arrive at the answer. Annotators were instructed to assume that pronouns had been resolved; in other words, a sentence should not be considered necessary semantic content simply because it contains the NP to which a pronoun in another sentence refers. For both of these multiple-sentence conditions, annotators were asked to select one single-best source sentence from among the set and also to mark the alternative source sentences.

For 31.2% of the answers annotated, one or more annotator provided more than one possible source sentence. Upon closer inspection, though, the annotations for these conditions are not very consistent. In the repeated content condition, there is very little agreement between annotators regarding when the text contains more than one full-sentence source for the answer. In the distributed content condition, sometimes annotators disagree on the primary sentence, and in many instances, one annotator identified multiple sentences and the other only one. Due to these inconsistencies, for the purpose of this study we decided to treat the multiple-sentence conditions in an underspecified fashion. When an annotator has identified either of these conditions, we convert the annotations to a single-best sentence and a set of alternatives.

The annotations were processed to automatically

[4] In future work we will also consider semantic relationships between the question and the text.

Answer type	agree	altagree	disagree	nolink
Learner answers (all)	70.3%	9.4%	16.9%	3.4%
Learner answers (correct)	75.1%	11.7%	12.7%	0.5%
Learner answers (incorrect)	65.9%	7.3%	20.7%	6.4%
Target	73.1%	8.1%	17.3%	1.4%

Table 1: Inter-annotator agreement for linking answers to source sentences in text

produce a gold-standard set of source sentence IDs, indicating the single sentence in the reading text to which each answer is most closely linked. We identify four distinct categories with respect to agreement between annotators. Agreement figures appear in Table 1.

** **agree:** In this case, both annotators linked the answer to the same source sentence, and that sentence is identified as the gold-standard link to the answer.

** **altagree:** This category covers two different situations in which the two annotators fail to agree on the single-best sentence. First, there are cases in which the best sentence selected by one annotator is a member of the set of alternatives indicated by the other. Second, in a small number of cases, both annotators agree on one member of the set of alternatives. In other words, the single sentence in the intersection of the sets of sentences identified by the two annotators is taken as the gold-standard annotation. There was no (non-**agree**) case in which that intersection contained more than one sentence.

** **disagree:** This category also includes two different types of cases. In the first, one of the two annotators failed to identify a source sentence to link with the answer. In that case, we consider the annotators to be in disagreement, and for the gold-standard we use the sentence ID provided by the one responding annotator. In the second case, the annotators disagree on the single-best sentence and there is no overlap between indicated alternative sentences. In those cases, for the gold standard we choose from the two source sentences that which appears first in the reading text.[5]

** **nolink:** For a small number of answers (n=34), both annotators found no link to the text. One example of such a case is an answer given entirely in English. For these cases, the gold standard provides no best source sentence.

If we consider both **altagree** and **nolink** to be forms of agreement, interannotator agreement is about 74% for both learner and target answers.

4.2 Text-based models

In this paper we consider two different models for incorporating the reading text into automatic short answer scoring. In the first approach, we employ a purely text-based model. The second combines either text-based features or the text-based model with the answer-based model described in Section 3. Evaluation of all three approaches appears in Section 5.

4.2.1 Simple text-based model

This model classifies student answers by comparing the source sentence most closely associated with the student answer to that associated with the target answer. If the two sentences are identical, the answer is classified as **correct**, and otherwise as **incorrect**.

We consider both the annotated best sentences (**goldlink**) and automatically-identified answer-sentence pairs (**autolink**). For automatic identification, we use the alignment model described in Section 3 to identify the best matching source sentence in the text for both learner and target answers. We use the token alignment process to align a given answer with each sentence from its respective reading text; the best-matching source sentence is that with the highest alignment weight. Chunk alignments are used only for correction of token alignments, and dependency alignments are not considered.

This model takes an extremely simple approach to answer classification, and could certainly be refined and improved. At the same time, its relatively strong

[5] This is a relatively arbitrary decision motivated by the desire to have a source sentence associated with as many answers as possible. Future work may include adjudication of annotations to reduce the noise introduced to the gold standard by this category of responses.

performance (see Table 3) suggests that the minimal level of supervision offered by teachers simply marking the sentence of a text most relevant to a given reading comprehension question may be beneficial for automatic answer scoring.

4.2.2 Combining text-based and answer-based models

In addition to the purely text-based model, we explore two ways of combining text- and answer-based models.

Textual features in the answer-based model In the first, we extract four features from the alignments between answers and source sentences and incorporate these as additional features in the answer-based model.

Features 1, 3, and 4 are each computed in two versions, using source sentences from either the annotated gold standard (**goldlink**), or the alignment model (**autolink**).

1. **SourceAgree** This boolean feature is true if both learner and target answer link to the same source sentence, and false otherwise (also if no source sentence was annotated or automatically found).

2. **SourceEntropy** For this feature we look at the two most-likely source sentences for the learner answer, as determined by automatic alignment scores. We treat the alignment weights as probabilities, normalizing so that they sum up to one. We then take the entropy between these two alignment weights as indicative of the confidence of the automatic alignment for the learner answer.

3. **AgreeEntropy** Here we weight the first feature according to the second, taking the entropy as a confidence score for the binary feature. Specifically, we value **SourceAgree** at 0.5 when the feature is true, -0.5 when false, and multiply this with $(1 - \text{entropy})$.

4. **TextAdjacency** This feature captures the distance (in number of sentences) between the source sentence linked to the learner answer and that linked to the target answer. With this feature we aim to capture the tendency of adjacent passages in a text to exhibit topical coherence (Mirkin et al., 2010).

Classifier combination In the second approach, we combine the output of the answer-based and text-based classifiers to arrive at a final classification system, allowing the text-based classifier to predominate in those cases for which it is most confident and falling back to the answer-based classifier for other cases. Confidence of the text-based classifier is determined based on entropy of the two highest-scoring alignments between learner answer and source sentence. The entropy threshhold was determined empirically to 0.5.

5 Experiments and results

This section discusses experiments on short answer scoring (binary classification) for German, in the context of reading comprehension for language learning. Specifically, we investigate the text-based models described in Section 4.2. In all cases, features and parameter settings were tuned on a development set which was extracted from the larger CREG corpus. In other words, there is no overlap between test and development data. For testing, we perform leave-one-out cross-validation on the slightly-smaller subset of the corpus which was used for annotation.

5.1 Answer-based baseline

As a baseline for our text-based models we take our implementation of the answer-based model from (Meurers et al., 2011b). As previously mentioned, our implementation diverges from theirs at some points, and we do not quite reach the performance reported for their model (accuracy of 84.6% on the balanced CREG corpus) and are far from reaching the current state of the art accuracy of 86.3%, as reported in Hahn and Meurers (2012).

Our answer-based model appears as **baseline** in Table 2. During development, the one extension to the baseline which helped most was the use of extended synonyms. This variant of the model appears in the results table with the annotation **+syn**.

model	k=5	k=15	k=30
baseline	0.817	0.820	0.822
baseline+syn	0.822	0.826	0.825
text: goldlink	0.827	0.827	0.829
text+syn:goldlink	0.830	0.835*	0.837*
text:autolink	0.837*	0.836*	0.825
text+syn:autolink	0.844*	0.836*	0.832
combined	0.810	0.819	0.816
combined+syn	0.817	0.822	0.818

Table 2: Classification accuracy for answer-based baseline (**baseline**), answer-based plus textual features (**text**), and classifier combination (**combined**). **+syn** indicates expanded synonymy features, **goldlink** indicates identifying the source sentences via annotated links, **autolink** indicates determining source sentences using the alignment model, k=number of neighbors. Results marked with * are significant compared to the best baseline model. See Section 5.2.1 for details.

	autolink	**goldlink**	**alt-set**
Accuracy	0.762	0.722	0.747
P correct	0.805	0.781	0.753
R correct	0.667	0.585	0.702
F correct	0.729	0.668	0.727
P incorrect	0.735	0.689	0.742
R incorrect	0.851	0.849	0.788
F incorrect	0.789	0.761	0.764

Table 3: Classification accuracy, precision, recall, and f-score for simple text-based classifier, under three different conditions. See Section 5.2.2 for details.

5.2 Text-based models

As described in Section 4.2, we consider three different approaches for incorporating the reading text into answer classification: use of textual features in the answer-based model, combination of separate answer-based and text-based models, and a simple text-based classifier.

5.2.1 Combining text-based and answer-based models

We explore two ways of combining text- and answer-based models.

Adding textual features to the answer-based model

We evaluate the contribution of the four new text-based features, computed in two variations: with source sentences as they are identified in the gold standard (**goldlink**) and as they are computed using the alignment model (**autolink**). We add those additional features to the two answer-based systems: the baseline (**text**) and the baseline with extended synonym set (**text+syn**). Results are presented in Table 2.

We present results for using the 5, 15, and 30 nearest neighbors for classification, as the influence of various features changes with the number of neighbors. We calculate the significance for the difference between the best baseline model (0.826) and each model which uses textual features, using a resampling test (Edgington, 1986). The results marked with a * in the Table 2 are significant at $p \leq 0.01$.

Although the impact of the textual features is clearly not as big with a stronger baseline model, we still see a clear pattern of improved accuracy. We may expect this difference to increase with more data and with additional and/or improved text-based features.

Classifier combination

Combining the two classifiers (answer-based and text-based) according to confidence levels results in decreased performance compared to the baseline. These results appear in Table 2 as **combined**.

5.2.2 Simple text-based classification

We have seen that textual features improve classification accuracy over the answer-driven model, yet this approach still requires the supervision provided by teacher-supplied target answers. In our third model, we investigate how the system performs without this degree of supervision, considering how far we can get by using *only* the text.

The simple text-based classifier, rather than taking a feature-based approach to classification, bases its decision solely on whether or not the learner and target answers link to the same source sentence. We compare three different methods for obtaining these links. The first approach (**autolink**) automatically links each answer to a source sentence from the text, based on alignments as described in Section 3. The second (**goldlink**) uses links as provided by the gold standard; in this case, learner answers without a linked sentence (e.g. **nolink** cases) are immediately classified as incorrect. The third approach (**alt-set**) exploits that fact that in many cases annotators provided alternate source sentences. Under this approach, an answer is classified as correct provided that there is a non-empty intersection between the set of possible source sentences for the learner answer and that for the target answer. For the second and third approaches, we classify as incorrect those learner answers lacking a gold-standard annotation for the corresponding target answer.

In Table 3 we present classification accuracy, precision, recall, and f-score for the three different conditions. Precision, recall, and f-score are reported separately for correct and incorrect learner answers. The 76% accuracy reached using the simple text-based classifier suggests that a system which has teachers supply source sentences instead of target answers and then automatically aligns learner answers to the text, while nowhere near comparable to the state-of-the-art supervised system, still achieves a reasonably accurate classification.

6 Conclusion

In this paper we have presented the first use of reading texts for automatic short answer scoring in the context of foreign language learning. We show that, for German, the use of simple text-based features improves classification accuracy over purely answer-based models. We plan in the future to investigate a wider range of text-based features. We have also shown that a simple classification model based only on linking answers to source sentences in the text achieves a reasonable classification accuracy. This finding has the potential to reduce the amount of teacher supervision necessary for authoring short answer exercises within automatic answer scoring systems. In addition to these findings, we have presented the results of an annotation study linking both target and learner answers to source sentences.

In the near-term future we plan to further investigate the role of the reading text for short answer scoring along three lines. First, we will address the question of the best size of text unit for alignment. In many cases, the best answers are linked not to entire sentences but to regions of sentences; in others, answers may correspond to more than one sentence. Our current approach ignores this issue. Second, we are interested in the variety of semantic relationships holding between questions, answers and texts. Along these lines, we will further investigate the sets of alternatives provided by annotators, as well as bringing in notions from work on paraphrasing and recognizing textual entailment. Finally, we are interested in moving from simple binary classification to the fine-grained level of diagnosis.

Acknowledgments

We would like to thank Erik Hahn, David Alejandro Przybilla and Jonas Sunde for carrying out the annotations. We thank the three anonymous reviewers for their helpful comments. This work was funded by the Cluster of Excellence "Multimodal Computing and Interaction" of the German Excellence Initiative and partially funded through the INTERREG IV A programme project ALLEGRO (Project No.: 67 SMLW 11137).

References

Stacey Bailey and Detmar Meurers. 2008. Diagnosing meaning errors in short answers to reading comprehension questions. In *Proceedings of the Third Workshop on Innovative Use of NLP for Building Educational Applications*, pages 107–115, Columbus, Ohio, June.

Stacey Bailey. 2008. *Content Assessment in Intelligent Computer-Aided Language Learning: Meaning Error Diagnosis for English as a Second Language*. Ph.D. thesis, The Ohio State University.

Steven Bethard, Haojie Hang, Ifeyinwa Okoye, James H. Martin, Md. Arafat Sultan, and Tamara Sumner. 2012. Identifying science concepts and student misconceptions in an interactive essay writing tutor. In *Proceedings of the Seventh Workshop on Building Educational Applications Using NLP*, pages 12–21.

Walter Daelemans, Jakub Zavrel, Ko Sloot, and Antal Van Den Bosch. 2009. TiMBL: Tilburg Memory-Based Learner, version 6.2, Reference Guide. ILK Technical Report 09-01.

Eugene S Edgington. 1986. *Randomization tests*. Marcel Dekker, Inc., New York, NY, USA.

Manaal Faruqui and Sebastian Padó. 2010. Training and evaluating a German named entity recognizer with semantic generalization. In *Proceedings of KONVENS 2010*, Saarbrücken, Germany.

David Gale and Lloyd S. Shapley. 1962. College admissions and the stability of marriage. *The American Mathematical Monthly*, 69(1):9–15.

Michael Hahn and Detmar Meurers. 2012. Evaluating the meaning of answers to reading comprehension questions: A semantics-based approach. In *Proceedings of the 7th Workshop on Innovative Use of NLP for Building Educational Applications (BEA7)*, pages 326–336, Montreal, Canada. Association for Computational Linguistics.

Birgit Hamp and Helmut Feldweg. 1997. Germanet - a lexical-semantic net for German. In *In Proceedings of ACL workshop Automatic Information Extraction and Building of Lexical Semantic Resources for NLP Applications*, pages 9–15.

Claudia Leacock and Martin Chodorow. 2003. C-rater: Automated scoring of short-answer questions. *Computers and the Humanities*, 37(4):389–405.

Detmar Meurers, Ramon Ziai, Niels Ott, and Stacey Bailey. 2011a. Integrating parallel analysis modules to evaluate the meaning of answers to reading comprehension questions. *Special Issue on Free-text Automatic Evaluation. International Journal of Continuing Engineering Education and Life-Long Learning (IJCEELL)*, 21(4):355–369.

Detmar Meurers, Ramon Ziai, Niels Ott, and Janina Kopp. 2011b. Evaluating answers to reading comprehension questions in context: Results for German and the role of information structure. In *Proceedings of the TextInfer 2011 Workshop on Textual Entailment*, pages 1–9, Edinburgh, Scottland, UK.

Shachar Mirkin, Ido Dagan, and Sebastian Padó. 2010. Assessing the role of discourse references in entailment inference. In *ACL*.

Michael Mohler and Rada Mihalcea. 2009. Text-to-text semantic similarity for automatic short answer grading. In Alex Lascarides, Claire Gardent, and Joakim Nivre, editors, *EACL*, pages 567–575.

Michael Mohler, Razvan C. Bunescu, and Rada Mihalcea. 2011. Learning to grade short answer questions using semantic similarity measures and dependency graph alignments. In Dekang Lin, Yuji Matsumoto, and Rada Mihalcea, editors, *ACL*, pages 752–762.

Rodney D. Nielsen, Wayne Ward, and James H. Martin. 2008. Learning to assess low-level conceptual understanding. In David Wilson and H. Chad Lane, editors, *FLAIRS Conference*, pages 427–432.

Niels Ott, Ramon Ziai, and Detmar Meurers. 2012. Creation and analysis of a reading comprehension exercise corpus: Towards evaluating meaning in context. In Thomas Schmidt and Kai Wörner, editors, *Multilingual Corpora and Multilingual Corpus Analysis*, Hamburg Studies in Multilingualism (HSM), pages 47–69. Benjamins, Amsterdam.

Stephen G. Pulman and Jana Z. Sukkarieh. 2005. Automatic short answer marking. In *Proceedings of the second workshop on Building Educational Applications Using NLP*, EdAppsNLP 05, pages 9–16.

Helmut Schmid. 1994. Probabilistic part-of-speech tagging using decision trees. In *Proceedings of the International Conference on New Methods in Language Processing*, Manchester, United Kingdom.

Rico Sennrich, Gerold Schneider, Martin Volk, and Martin Warin. 2009. A new hybrid dependency parser for German. In Christian Chiarcos, Richard Eckart de Castilho, and Manfred Stede, editors, *Von der Form zur Bedeutung: Texte automatisch verarbeiten ? From Form to Meaning: Processing Texts Automatically. Proceedings of the Biennial GSCL Conference 2009*, pages 115–124. Narr, Tübingen.

Jana Z. Sukkarieh and Stephen G. Pulman. 2005. Information extraction and machine learning: Automarking short free text responses to science questions. In Chee-Kit Looi, Gordon I. McCalla, Bert Bredeweg, and Joost Breuker, editors, *AIED*, volume 125 of *Frontiers in Artificial Intelligence and Applications*, pages 629–637.

Ramon Ziai, Niels Ott, and Detmar Meurers. 2012. Short answer assessment: Establishing links between research strands. In *Proceedings of the 7th Workshop on Innovative Use of NLP for Building Educational Applications (BEA7)*, Montreal, Canada.

Choosing the Right Words: Characterizing and Reducing Error of the Word Count Approach

H. Andrew Schwartz,[1] Johannes Eichstaedt,[1] Lukasz Dziurzynski,[1] Eduardo Blanco,[2] Margaret L. Kern,[1] Stephanie Ramones,[1] Martin Seligman,[1] and Lyle Ungar[1]

[1]University of Pennsylvania

[2]Lymba Corporation

hansens@seas.upenn.edu

Abstract

Social scientists are increasingly using the vast amount of text available on social media to measure variation in happiness and other psychological states. Such studies count words deemed to be indicators of happiness and track how the word frequencies change across locations or time. This *word count* approach is simple and scalable, yet often picks up false signals, as words can appear in different contexts and take on different meanings. We characterize the types of errors that occur using the word count approach, and find lexical ambiguity to be the most prevalent. We then show that one can reduce error with a simple refinement to such lexica by automatically eliminating highly ambiguous words. The resulting refined lexica improve precision as measured by human judgments of word occurrences in Facebook posts.

1 Introduction

Massive social media corpora, such as blogs, tweets, and Facebook statuses have recently peaked the interest of social scientists. Compared to traditional samples in tens or hundreds, social media sample sizes are orders of magnitude larger, often containing millions or billions of posts or queries. Such text provides potential for unobtrusive, inexpensive, and real-time measurement of psychological states (such as positive or negative affect) and aspects of subjective well-being (such as happiness and engagement). Social scientists have recently begun to use social media text in a variety of studies (Cohn et al., 2004; Kramer, 2010; Tausczik and Pennebaker, 2010; Kamvar and Harris, 2011; Dodds et al., 2011; Golder and Macy, 2011).

One of the most popular approaches to estimate psychological states is by using the *word count* method (Pennebaker et al., 2007), where one tracks the frequency of words that have been judged to be associated with a given state. Greater use of such words is taken to index the prevalence of the corresponding state. For example, the use of the word 'happy' is taken to index *positive emotion*, and 'angry' to index *negative emotion*. The most widely used tool to carry out such analysis, and the one we investigate in this paper, is Pennebaker's Linguistic Inquiry and Word Count, (*LIWC*) (Pennebaker et al., 2001; Pennebaker et al., 2007). *LIWC*, originally developed to analyze writing samples for emotion and control, has grown to include a variety of lexica for linguistic and psychosocial topics including positive and negative emotions, pronouns, money, work, and religion. The *word count* approach has high appeal to social scientists in need of a tool to approach social media, and although others have been used (see, for example (Gottschalk and Bechtel, 1998; Bollen et al., 2010), *LIWC*'s lexica are generally perceived as a "tried-and-tested" list of words (Miller, 2011).

Unfortunately, the *word count* approach has some drawbacks when used as indicators for psychological states. Words are the unit of measurement, but words can carry many different meanings depending on context. Consider the Facebook posts below containing instances of 'play', a word associated with positive emotion in *LIWC*.

*Second Joint Conference on Lexical and Computational Semantics (*SEM), Volume 1: Proceedings of the Main Conference and the Shared Task*, pages 296–305, Atlanta, Georgia, June 13-14, 2013.

1. *so everyone should come to the* ***play*** *tomorrow...*

2. *Does anyone what type of file i need to convert youtube videos to* ***play*** *on PS3???*

3. *Time to go* ***play*** *with Chalk from the Easter Bunny!*

Out of the three instances, only (3) seems to communicate positive emotion. In (1), 'play' is used as a noun rather than the expected verb, while in (2), 'play' is a verb but it is used in a sense that is not directly associated with positive emotion. (1) and (2) demonstrate how *lexical ambiguities* (i.e. multiple parts-of-speech or word senses) can affect accuracy of words in a lexicon. Additionally, even when appearing as the expected part of speech and word sense, signal from a word may change due to its context, such as being within the scope of a negation as in (4), or describing something desired as in (5).

4. *...all work no* ***play*** *:-(*

5. *i sure wish i had about 50 hours a day to* ***play*** *cod*

Our goal is to characterize the errors of the widely used *word count* approach, and show that such lexica can be significantly improved by employing an ambiguity metric to refine such lexica. Rather than work on a new method of measuring psychological states, we work within the bounds of *word count* and ask how accurate it is and whether we can improve it without sacrificing its simplicity and scalability.

We attempt to reduce the erroneous signal of the *word count* approach while maintaining legitimate signal simply by refining the lexicon. In other words, we would like to move closer to the goal in Figure 1, by eliminating words that often carry erroneous signal such as 'play', and keeping words which often carry the sought-after signal, such as 'cheerful'. The difficulty in doing this is that we do not have the data to tell us which words are most likely to carry signal (even if we had such data we would like to develop a method that could be applied to any newly created lexica). Instead we leverage part-of-speech and word sense data to help us determine which words are lexically ambiguous.

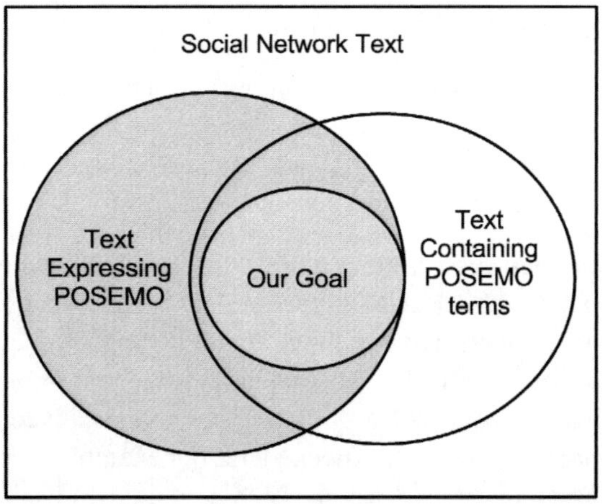

Figure 1: The relationship between text expressing positive emotion (*POSEMO*) and text containing *LIWC* terms for *POSEMO*.

Our approach of eliminating ambiguous words increases the precision at the expense of recall, a reasonable trade-off in social media where we are working with millions or even billions of word instances. Additionally, it is minimally-supervised, in that we do not require training data on human-state; instead we use existing hand-labeled corpora, such as SemCor (Miller et al., 1993), for word sense information. Not requiring training data also means our refinement is flexible; it can be applied to multiple domains and lexica, it makes few assumptions that might introduce problems of over-fitting, and it is parsimonious in that it merely improves an established approach.

This paper makes two primary contributions: (1) an analysis of the types of errors common for the *word count* approach (Section 3), and (2) a general method for refining psychosocial lexica based on the ambiguity of words (Section 4). Before describing these contributions, we discuss related work, making the case for using social media in social science and surveying some work in computational linguistics. We then evaluate both the original *LIWC* lexicon and our refinement of it against human judgments of expression of positive and negative emotions on hand-annotated Facebook posts, and show the benefit of lexicon refinement for estimating well-being over time for large aggregates of posts. Finally, we discuss the implications of our work and possible future directions.

2 Background

Compared to traditional approaches in the social sciences, large scale analysis of social media is cheap, near real-time, unobtrusive, and gives high coverage. We outline these advantages below.

Inexpensive Extracting information from sources such Facebook and Twitter is vastly cheaper than the more conventional polling done by companies such as Gallup – and by many social science researchers. Social media data does not require phone calls to be made or doors to be knocked on. For example, a representative survey asking 1,000 people by a leading polling company costs to the order of $10,000[1]. In contrast, once the software exists, social media data from tens of millions of users can be obtained and analyzed at a fraction of the cost.

Temporal Resolution Much of the attraction of social media stems from the fact that it captures a written live stream of collective thought. When Google relied on search queries to monitor health-seeking behavior to predict influenza epidemics, the reporting lag was a mere day, whereas traditional CDC surveillance systems take 1-2 weeks to publish their data (Ginsberg et al., 2009). Infrastructure based on social media and Internet use data allows reporting and analysis systems with little to no reporting lag. Additionally, traditional survey designs are typically only designed to assess psychological states at a given point in time.

Unobtrusive Estimation Traditional self-report survey approaches, even those implemented on the web, suffer from social desirability, priming, and other biases. For example, Kahneman et al. (Kahneman et al., 2006) found that the order in which questions are asked on questionnaires can determine how they are answered. By looking directly into the social worlds, many of these self-report biases can be avoided. The traces of human interactions in social media represent the goings-on in their original ecologies of meaning and signification. This approach diminishes the inferential distance between the context of the phenomena and the context of measurement – and thus decreases the room for systematic distortion of signal.

[1]Gallup, Personal correspondence.

2.1 The Word Count Approach

As previously noted, the *word count* approach is most often used by social scientists through the tool known as *Linguistic Inquiry and Word Count* or *LIWC* (Pennebaker et al., 2007). The LIWC2007 dictionary is composed of almost 4,500 words and word stems organized across one or more word categories, including 406 positive emotion words and 499 negative emotion words. When long form texts are analyzed with LIWC, the program simply returns the percentages of words belonging to the different analytical categories – the simplicity of this approach makes it popular with non-technical social scientists.

LIWC's positive and negative emotion lexica have recently begun to be used on "short form" writing in social media. For example, Golder and Macy (2011) used LIWC to study diurnal and seasonal variation in mood in a collection of 400 million Twitter messages. Kramer (2010) proposed the "Gross National Happiness" index and Kivran-Swaine and Naaman (2011) examined associations between user expressions of positive and negative emotions and the size and density of social networks. A comprehensive review can be found in Tausczik and Pennebaker (2010).

To our knowledge there is only one work which has evaluated *LIWC*'s accuracy over social media. Bantum and Owen (2009) evaluated *LIWC* on a set of posts to an Internet-based breast cancer support group. By annotating expression of emotion within this text, they were able to produce accuracy figures of *sensitivity* (much like *recall*) and *predictive validity* (*precision*). Sensitivity measured how often a word (in context) expressing positive or negative emotion was captured by *LIWC*. Predictive validity measured how often a word (in context) captured by *LIWC* as measuring positive or negative emotion was indeed expressing positive or negative emotion. While they found a recall of 0.88, the precision was only 0.31 – that is, only 31% of instances containing words indexed by *LIWC* actually conveyed the associated emotion. We contend that this is a major drawback for applying *LIWC* to social media, because while it is not important to catch every expression of emotion out of a million Tweets, it is important that when something is captured it is an accurate estimate of the true state.

2.2 Related Work in Computational Linguistics

Researchers have been exploring the use of lexica that define the subjective orientation of words for tasks such as sentiment or subjectivity analysis. A common weakly-supervised approach starts with a small set of sentiment knowledge (seed words associated with a given sentiment) and expands the words into a large lexicon (Hatzivassiloglou and McKeown, 1997; Kamps and Marx, 2002; Kim and Hovy, 2004; Kanayama and Nasukawa, 2006; Baccianella et al., 2010). We take a different approach. Rather than expanding lexica, we start with a large set of words and refine the set. The refinement increases precision at the cost of recall, which is a reasonable exchange when we are looking at millions or even billions of word instances. Standard applications of sentiment analysis, such as annotating movie reviews, may not be as inclined to skip instances, since they want to make predictions for items which have very few reviews.

Another line of work in sentiment analysis has created lexicons using supervised learning. One of the first works to do so was by Pang and colleagues (2002), who used data including author ratings of reviews, such as IMDB movie reviews. The author ratings become training data for sentiment classification. Pang et al. showed that human-created lexicons did not perform as well as lexicons based on simple word statistics over the training data. Interestingly, they found that words like 'still' were most predictive of positive movie reviews, and that punctuation marks of '!' and '?' were strong signs of negative movie reviews. Unfortunately, training data for subjective well-being or happiness is not yet available, preventing the use of such supervised learning methods. Additionally, this work seeks to experiment within the bounds of what social scientists are in fact using (with publications in high-impact venues such as Science). We thus take a different approach, and automatically improve human created lexicons.

Wiebe and Cardie (2005) generalized the task of sentiment analysis to that of discovering subjectivity such as "opinions, emotions, sentiments, speculations, evaluations, etc.". More recently, Wilson et al. (2009) contended that the context may neutralize or change the polarity of the subjective orientation of a word. It is difficult to determine where concepts of happiness such as quality of relationships or degree of achievement in life fit in with subjectivity. Thus, we do not claim to be measuring subjectivity and instead we use the general term of 'psychological state', referring to "the way something [a person] is with respect to its main attributes" (Miller, 1993).

POSEMO		NEGEMO	
term	**frequency**	**term**	**frequency**
like	774,663	hate	167,109
love	797,833	miss	158,274
good	571,687	bad	151,496
friend*	406,568	bore*	140,684
happy	384,797	shit*	114,923
LOL	370,613	hurt*	98,291
well*	284,002	craz*	94,518
great	263,113	lost	94,059
haha*	240,587	damn*	93,666
best	227,381	fuck	90,212
better	212,547	stupid*	85,587
fun	216,432	kill*	83,593
please*	174,597	hell	80,046
hope	170,998	fuckin*	79,959
thank	161,827	wrong*	70,714

Table 1: Most frequent *POSEMO* and *NEGEMO* terms in *LIWC* in the 12.7 million Facebook posts. "*" indicates a wildcard, so that "well*" matches "wellness".

To the best of our knowledge, while part-of-speech tagging and word sense disambiguation are staple tasks in the computational linguistics community, the utility of a lexical ambiguity metric has yet to be explored.

3 Annotation and Analysis of Errors from the Word Count Method

One objective of our work is to document and describe how often different types of errors occur when using the *word count* approach on social media. To do this, we first judged a sample of 1,000 instances of *LIWC* terms occurring in Facebook posts to indicate whether they contribute signal towards the associated LIWC category (i.e. positive emotion). We then took instances that were deemed to carry erroneous signal and annotated them with a label for the

category	agreement	instances	base rate
POSEMO	0.742	500	.654
NEGEMO	0.746	500	.697
TOTAL	**0.744**	**1,000**	**.676**
random	*0.343*	-	-

Table 2: Inter-annotator agreement over 1,000 instances of *LIWC* terms in Facebook posts. Base rate is the average of how often an annotator answered true.

type of signal error. This section describes the process we used in generating these annotations and the results we found.

3.1 Annotation Process

Annotating social media instances of lexica terms provides insight into how well the *word count* approach works, and also yields a "ground truth" for evaluating our lexicon refinement methods. We randomly selected for labeling a sample of 1,000 status updates containing words from a given lexicon drawn from a collection of 12.7 million Facebook status updates provided by the Cambridge myPersonality project (Kosinski and Stillwell, 2012).

We used terms from the *LIWC* positive emotion (*POSEMO*) and negative emotion (*NEGEMO*) lexica, which are the same lexica used by the works of Kramer (2010), Kivran-Swaine and Naaman (2011), and Golder and Macy (2011). Table 1 lists the most frequent *POSEMO* and *NEGEMO* terms in our Facebook sample.

As mentioned above, we did two types of annotations. First, we judged whether each given instance of a word conveyed the correct associated type of emotion. The second task took a sample of instances judged to have incorrect signal and labeled them with a reason for the error; We refer to this as *signal error type*.

For the first task, we had three human judges independently evaluate the 1,000 status update instances as to whether they were indeed correct signal. The question the judges were told to answer was "Does the word contribute to the associated psychological-state (POSEMO or NEGEMO) within the sentence it appears?". In other words, "would the sentence convey less [positive emotion or negative emotion] without this word?". Subjective feedback from the judges indicated that it was often difficult to make a decision, so we used three judges per instance. In the case of conflict between judges, the "correct" label for validation of the refined lexicon was defined to be the majority vote. A sampling of Facebook statuses demonstrates a mixed picture of relevance for the unrefined *LIWC* dictionaries:

1. *has had a very* ***good*** *day* ('good' - *POSEMO*)
2. *is so very* ***bored****.* ('bore*' - *NEGEMO*)
3. ***damn****, that octopus is good, lol* ('damn' - *NEGEMO*)
4. *thank you for his* ***number*** ('numb*' - *NEGEMO*)
5. *I got pranked sooooo* ***bad*** ('bad' - *NEGEMO*)
6. *don't be* ***afraid*** *to fail* ('afraid' - *NEGEMO*)
7. *I wish I could . . . and we could all just be* ***happy*** ('happy' - *POSEMO*)

Some posts clearly use positive or negative lexicon words such as (1) and (2). Curse words can signify negative emotion or emphasize the opposite state as in (3), which is clearly emphasizing positive emotion here. Example (5) demonstrates the word sense issue we discussed previously. Words with wildcards that expand into other words with different meanings can be particularly problematic, as the expanded word can be far more frequent – and very different in meaning – from the original word. For example, 'numb*' matches 'number' in 4.

A different problem occurs when the context of the word changes its implication for the emotional state of the writer. This can either occur through negation such as in (6) where 'afraid' signals *NEGEMO*, but is negated with 'don't' or the signal can be changed indirectly through a variety of words indicating that the writer desires (and hence lacks) the state, as in (7) where someone is wishing to be 'happy'.

Table 2 shows the agreement between annotators calculated as $\frac{\sum_i agree(A_1^{(i)}, A_2^{(i)}, A_3^{(i)})}{1,000}$, where $agree(A_1, A_2, A_3)$ was 1 when all three annotations matched and 0 otherwise. Given the average positive base rate across annotators was 0.676 the chance that all three reviewers agree according to chance (random agreement) is calculated as

category	precision	instances
POSEMO	67.9%	500
NEGEMO	72.8%	500
both	**70.4%**	**1,000**

Table 4: Accuracy of *LIWC POSEMO* and *NEGEMO* lexica over Facebook posts.

$0.676^3 + (1 - 0.676)^3 = 0.343$, the probability of all three answering yes plus the probability of all three answering no.

For the second task, we selected 100 instances judged to be incorrect signal from the first task, and labeled them according to the best reason for the mistake. This task required more linguistic expertise and was performed by a single annotator. Labels and descriptions are given in Table 3, which breaks down the cases into lexical ambiguity, direct or indirect negation, and other reasons such as the stemming issue (stem plus wildcard expanding into words indicating a different (or no) emotional state).

3.2 Analysis of Errors

Before discussing the types of errors we found when using the *word count* approach, we examine *LIWC*'s overall accuracy on our dataset. Table 4 shows the precision broken down for both the positive emotion (*POSEMO*) and the negative emotion (*NEGEMO*) lexica. We see that the precision for *NEGEMO* is slightly higher than *POSEMO*, indicating the terms in that category may be more likely to indicate their associated state.

Although the overall accuracy seems decent, one should keep in mind our subjective judgement criteria were quite tolerant, allowing any amount of contribution of the corresponding signal to be considered accurate. For example, a salutation like "Happy New Year" was judged to be a correct use of "happy" to signal POSEMO, even though it clearly does not have as strong a signal as someone saying "I feel deliriously happy".

Frequencies of signal errors are given in Table 5. The most common signal error was wrong word sense, where the word did not signal emotional state and some other sense or definition of the word was intended (e.g. "u feel like ur **living** in a music video"; corresponding to the sense "to inhabit" rather than the intended sense, "to have life; be alive" (Miller, 1993)). Other common signal errors include strict negation where the word is canceled out by a clear negative quantifier (e.g. "Don't be **afraid** to fail") and wrong part of speech where the word is signaling a different part of speech than the emotion (e.g. "**well**, we cant afford to go to NYC"). There were also various other signal error types that include stem issues where the stem matched clearly unintended words, desiring statuses where the status is commenting on wanting the emotion instead of experiencing it and other less prevalent issues such as non-English language post, memes, or clear sarcasm.

category	label	frequency
Lexical Ambiguity	Wrong POS	15
	Wrong WS	38
Signal Negation	Strict Negation	16
	Desiring	6
Other	Stem Issue	5
	Other	24

Table 5: Frequency of the signal error types.

4 Method for Refining Lexica

The idea behind our refinement method is to remove words that are likely to carry erroneous signal about the underlying state or emotion of the person writing the tweet or Facebook post.[2] We do so in an indirect fashion, without actually using training data of which posts are, in fact indicative of positive or negative emotion. Instead, we focus on reducing errors that are due to lexical ambiguity. By removing words that are often used with multiple parts of speech or multiple senses, we can tilt the balance toward precision at some cost in recall (losing some signal from the ambiguous words). This makes the *word count* approach more suitable for use in the massive corpora afforded by social media.

4.1 Lexical Ambiguity

We address lexical ambiguity at the levels of both part of speech (*POS*) and word sense. As a metric of inverse-ambiguity, we determine the probability that a random instance is the most frequent sense (*mfs*) of the most frequent part of speech (*mfp*) of

[2]Refinement tool is available at `wwbp.org`.

category	label	description	examples
Lexical Ambiguity	Wrong POS	Not a valid signal because it is the wrong POS	*so everyone should come to the* ***play*** *tomorrow...*
	Wrong WS	Not a valid signal because it is the wrong word sense (includes metaphorical senses)	*Does anyone what type of file i need to convert youtube videos to* ***play*** *on PS3???*
Signal Negation	Strict Negation	Within the scope of a negation, where there is a clear negative quantifier	*...all work* ***no play*** *:-(*
	Desiring	Within the scope of a desire / wishing for something	*i sure wish i had about 50 hours a day to* ***play*** *cod*
Other	Stem Issue	Clearly not intended to be matched with the given stem	**numb*** for *NEGEMO* matching *number*
	Other	Any other issue or difficult to classify	

Table 3: Signal error types.

the word, denoted TSP (for *top sense probability*). Given a word w, we consider all parts of speech of w ($POS(w)$) and all senses for the most frequent part of speech ($senses(mfp(w))$):

$$p_{mfp}(w) = \frac{\max\limits_{[w_{pos} \in POS(w)]} f_p(w_{pos})}{\sum\limits_{w_{pos} \in POS(w)} f_p(w_{pos})}$$

$$p_{mfs}(w) = \frac{\max\limits_{[w_{sense} \in senses(mfp(w))]} f_s(w_{sense})}{\sum\limits_{w_{sense} \in senses(mfp(w))} f_s(w_{sense})}$$

$$TSP(w) = (p_{mfp}(w) * p_{mfs}(w))^2 \quad (1)$$

Here, f_p and f_s represent the frequencies of a certain part-of-speech and a certain sense of a word, respectively. This is the squared-probability that an instance of w is the *top sense* – the most-frequent part-of-speech and the most-frequency sense of that part-of-speech. The probability is squared because both the word in the lexicon and the word occurring in context should be the *top sense* (two independent probabilities: given an instance of a word in a corpus, and another instance of the word in the lexicon, what is the probability that both are the top POS and sense?). Frequency data is provided for parts-of-speech from the Google N-Grams 2.0 (Lin et al., 2010) and for word senses from SemCor (Miller et al., 1993). This aspect of the refinement is inspired by the most frequent sense heuristic for word sense disambiguation (McCarthy et al., 2004; Yarowsky, 1993), in which the sense of a word is chosen without regard to the context, but rather is simply based on the frequencies of senses in corpora. In our case, we restrict ourselves this way in order for the application of the lexicon to remain unchanged.

For some words, we were unable to find sense frequency data. We decided to keep such terms, on the assumption that a lack in available frequency information implies that the word is not very ambiguous. Many of these terms include Web speak such as 'haha' or 'lol', which we believe can carry a strong signal for positive and negative emotion.

Lastly, since TSP is only a metric for the inverse ambiguity of a word, we must apply a threshold to determine which words to keep. We denote this threshold as θ, and the description of the refined lexicon for a category, *cat*, is below.

$$lex_\theta(cat) = \{w | w \in cat \wedge TSP(w) > \theta\}$$

4.2 Handling Stems

Some lexica, such as the *LIWC* dictionary, include word stems that are intended to match multiple forms of a word. Stems are marked by the suffix '*'. *LIWC* describes the application of stems as follows "the asterisk, then, denotes the acceptance of all letters, hyphens, or numbers following its ap-

lex	cat	prec	size
	POSEMO	67.9%	500
full	NEGEMO	72.8%	500
	both	**70.4%**	**1,000**
	POSEMO	70.9%	392
lex$_{0.10}$	NEGEMO	71.6%	423
	both	**71.3%**	**815**
	POSEMO	75.7%	239
lex$_{0.50}$	NEGEMO	78.9%	232
	both	**77.3%**	**471**
	POSEMO	72.5%	109
lex$_{0.90}$	NEGEMO	78.1%	128
	both	**75.5%**	**237**

Table 6: Precision (**prec**) and instance subset size (**size**) of refinements to the *LIWC POSEMO* and *NEGEMO* lexica with various θ thresholds $(0.10, 0.50, 0.90)$

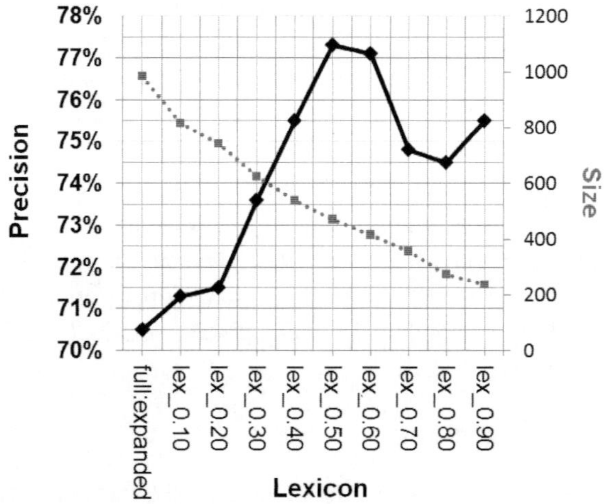

Figure 2: The relationship between precision and size when increasing the TSP threshold (θ).

pearance."[3] This presents a problem because, while the creators of such lexica obviously intended stems to match multiple forms of a word, stems also often match completely different words, such as 'numb*' matching 'number' or 'won*' matching 'won't'.

We identified how often unintended matches happen in Section 3. Finding that the stemming issues were not the biggest problem, here, we just describe how they fit into our lexical ambiguity metric, rather than describe a technique to rid the lexicon of stemming problems. One approach might be to determine how ambiguous a stem is – i.e. determine how many words, parts-of-speech, and senses a stem could be expanded into, but this ignores the fact that the dictionary creators obviously intended the stem to match multiple words. Instead, we expand stems into all words that they match and replace them into the lexica.

We base our expansion on the actual terms used in social media. We find all words matching stems among 1 million randomly selected Twitter messages posted over a 6-month period (August 2009 - February 2010), and restrict to those occurring at least 20 times. Then, each word stem in the lexicon is replaced with the expanded set of matching words.

5 Evaluation

We evaluate our refinement by comparing against human judgements of the emotion conveyed by words in individual posts. In the case of human judgements, we find that the subset of human-annotated instances matching the refined lexica are more accurate than the complete set.

In section 3 we discussed the method we used to judge instances of *LIWC POSEMO* and *NEGEMO* words as to whether they contributed the associated affect. Each of the 1,000 instances in our evaluation corpus were judged three times such that the majority was taken as truth. In order to validate our refined lexica, we find the accuracy (precision) of the subset of instances which contain the refined lexica terms.

Table 6 shows the change in precision when using the refined lexica. **size** represents the number of instances from the full evaluation corpus matching words in the refined lexica. One can see that initially precision increase as the **size** becomes smaller. This is more clearly seen in Figure 2. As discussed in the method section, our goal with the refinement is improving precision, making lexica more suitable to applications over massive social media where one can more readily afford to skip instances (i.e. smaller size) in order to achieve more accuracy. Still, removing more ambiguous words does

[3]"How it works": http://www.liwc.net/howliwcworks.php

not guarantee improved precision at capturing the intended psychological state; it is possible that that all senses of an ambiguous word do in fact carry intended signal or that the intended sense a low ambiguity word is not the most frequent.

Our maximum precision occurs with a threshold of 0.50, where things somewhat level-out. This represents approximately a 23% reduction in error, and verifies that we can increase precision through the automatic lexicon refinement based on lexical ambiguity.

6 Conclusions

Social scientists and other researchers are starting to measure psychological states such as happiness through text in Facebook and Twitter. We have shown that the widely used *word count* method, where one simply counts occurrences of positive or negative words, can often produce noisy and inaccurate estimates of expressions of psychological states. We characterized and measured the frequency of different types of errors that occur using this approach, and found that when counting words without considering context, it is lexical ambiguities (unintended parts-of-speech or word senses) which cause the most errors. We proposed a method for refining lexica by removing those words most likely to be ambiguous, and showed that we can significantly reduce error as measured by human judgements.

Acknowledgments

Support for this research was provided by the Robert Wood Johnson Foundation's Pioneer Portfolio, through a grant to Martin Seligman, "Exploring Concepts of Positive Health". We thank the reviewers for their constructive and insightful comments.

References

Stefano Baccianella, Andrea Esuli, and Fabrizio Sebastiani. 2010. Sentiwordnet 3.0: An enhanced lexical resource for sentiment analysis and opinion mining. In *Proceedings of the Seventh International Conference on Language Resources and Evaluation (LREC'10)*, Valletta, Malta, may. European Language Resources Association (ELRA).

Erin O.C. Bantum and J.E. Owen. 2009. Evaluating the validity of computerized content analysis programs for identification of emotional expression in cancer narratives. *Psychological assessment*, 21(1):79.

Johan Bollen, Huina Mao, and Xiao-Jun Zeng. 2010. Twitter mood predicts the stock market. *Computer and Information Science*, 1010:1–8.

Michael A. Cohn, M.R. Mehl, and J.W. Pennebaker. 2004. Linguistic markers of psychological change surrounding september 11, 2001. *Psychological Science*, 15(10):687.

Peter Sheridan Dodds, Kameron Decker Harris, Isabel M Kloumann, Catherine A Bliss, and Christopher M Danforth. 2011. Temporal patterns of happiness and information in a global social network: Hedonometrics and twitter. *Diversity*, page 26.

Jeremy Ginsberg, M.H. Mohebbi, R.S. Patel, L. Brammer, M.S. Smolinski, L. Brilliant, et al. 2009. Detecting influenza epidemics using search engine query data. *Nature*, 457(7232):1012–4.

Scott A. Golder and M.W. Macy. 2011. Diurnal and seasonal mood vary with work, sleep, and daylength across diverse cultures. *Science*, 333(6051):1878–1881.

Louis A. Gottschalk and RJ Bechtel. 1998. Psychiatric content analysis and diagnosis (pcad2000).

Vasileios Hatzivassiloglou and Kathleen R. McKeown. 1997. Predicting the semantic orientation of adjectives. In *Annual Meeting of the Association for Computational Linguistics*, pages 174–181.

Daniel Kahneman, A.B. Krueger, D. Schkade, N. Schwarz, and A.A. Stone. 2006. Would you be happier if you were richer? a focusing illusion. *Science*, 312(5782):1908.

Jaap Kamps and Maarten Marx. 2002. Words with attitude. In *1st International WordNet Conference*, pages 332–341, Mysore, India.

Sepandar D. Kamvar and J. Harris. 2011. We feel fine and searching the emotional web. In *Proceedings of the fourth ACM international conference on Web search and data mining*, pages 117–126. ACM.

Hiroshi Kanayama and Tetsuya Nasukawa. 2006. Fully automatic lexicon expansion for domain-oriented sentiment analysis. In *Proceedings of the 2006 Conference on Empirical Methods in Natural Language Processing*, EMNLP '06, pages 355–363, Stroudsburg, PA, USA. Association for Computational Linguistics.

Soo-Min Kim and Eduard Hovy. 2004. Determining the sentiment of opinions. In *Proceedings of the 20th international conference on Computational Linguistics*, COLING '04, Stroudsburg, PA, USA. Association for Computational Linguistics.

Funda Kivran-Swaine and M. Naaman. 2011. Network properties and social sharing of emotions in social awareness streams. In *Proceedings of the ACM 2011 conference on Computer supported cooperative work*, pages 379–382. ACM.

Michal. Kosinski and David J. Stillwell. 2012. mypersonality research wiki. mypersonality project. *http://www.mypersonality.org/wiki/.*

Adam D.I. Kramer. 2010. An unobtrusive behavioral model of gross national happiness. In *Proceedings of the 28th international conference on Human factors in computing systems*, pages 287–290. ACM.

Dekang Lin, Kenneth Church, Heng Ji, Satoshi Sekine, David Yarowsky, Shane Bergsma, Kailash Patil, Emily Pitler, Rachel Lathbury, Vikram Rao, Kapil Dalwani, and Sushant Narsale. 2010. New tools for web-scale n-grams. In *Proceedings of the Seventh International Conference on Language Resources and Evaluation (LREC'10)*, Valletta, Malta, may. European Language Resources Association (ELRA).

Diana McCarthy, Rob Koeling, Julie Weeds, and John Carroll. 2004. Finding predominant word senses in untagged text. In *Proceedings of the 42nd Meeting of the Association for Computational Linguistics (ACL'04), Main Volume*, pages 279–286, Barcelona, Spain, July.

George A. Miller, Claudia Leacock, Randee Tengi, and Ross T Bunker. 1993. A semantic concordance. In *Proceedings of the ARPA Workshop on Human Language Technology*, pages 303–308. Morgan Kaufman.

George A. Miller. 1993. Five papers on wordnet. *Technical Report, Princeton University.*

Greg Miller. 2011. Social scientists wade into the tweet stream. *Science*, 333(6051):1814–1815.

Bo Pang, Lillian Lee, and Shivakumar Vaithyanathan. 2002. Thumbs up? Sentiment classification using machine learning techniques. In *Proceedings of the 2002 Conference on Empirical Methods in Natural Language Processing (EMNLP)*, pages 79–86.

James W Pennebaker, Martha E Francis, and Roger J Booth. 2001. Linguistic inquiry and word count: Liwc 2001. *Word Journal Of The International Linguistic Association.*

James W. Pennebaker, C.K. Chung, M. Ireland, A. Gonzales, and R.J. Booth. 2007. The development and psychometric properties of liwc2007. *Austin, TX, LIWC. Net.*

Yla R. Tausczik and J.W. Pennebaker. 2010. The psychological meaning of words: Liwc and computerized text analysis methods. *Journal of Language and Social Psychology*, 29(1):24.

Janyce Wiebe and Claire Cardie. 2005. Annotating expressions of opinions and emotions in language. language resources and evaluation. In *Language Resources and Evaluation.*

Theresa Wilson, Janyce Wiebe, and Paul Hoffmann. 2009. Recognizing contextual polarity: An exploration of features for phrase-level sentiment analysis. *Computational Linguistics*, 35:399–433, September.

David Yarowsky. 1993. One sense per collocation. In *Proceedings of the workshop on Human Language Technology*, HLT '93, pages 266–271, Stroudsburg, PA, USA. Association for Computational Linguistics.

Automatically Identifying Implicit Arguments to Improve Argument Linking and Coherence Modeling

Michael Roth and **Anette Frank**
Department of Computational Linguistics
Heidelberg University, Germany
{mroth,frank}@cl.uni-heidelberg.de

Abstract

Implicit arguments are a discourse-level phenomenon that has not been extensively studied in semantic processing. One reason for this lies in the scarce amount of annotated data sets available. We argue that more data of this kind would be helpful to improve existing approaches to linking implicit arguments in discourse and to enable more in-depth studies of the phenomenon itself. In this paper, we present a range of studies that empirically validate this claim. Our contributions are threefold: we present a heuristic approach to automatically identify implicit arguments and their antecedents by exploiting comparable texts; we show how the induced data can be used as training data for improving existing argument linking models; finally, we present a novel approach to modeling local coherence that extends previous approaches by taking into account non-explicit entity references.

1 Introduction

Semantic role labeling systems traditionally process text in a sentence-by-sentence fashion, constructing local structures of semantic meaning (Palmer et al., 2010). Information relevant to these structures, however, can be non-local in natural language texts (Palmer et al., 1986; Fillmore, 1986, inter alia). In this paper, we view instances of this phenomenon, also referred to as *implicit arguments*, as elements of discourse. In a coherent discourse, each utterance focuses on a *salient* set of entities, also called "foci" (Sidner, 1979) or "centers" (Joshi and Kuhn, 1979). According to the theory of Centering (Grosz et al., 1995), the salience of an entity in a discourse is reflected by linguistic factors such as choice of referring expression and syntactic form. Both extremes of salience, i.e., contexts of referential continuity (Brown, 1983) and irrelevance, can also be reflected by the non-realization of an entity. Altough specific instances of non-realization, so-called zero anaphora, have been well-studied in discourse analysis (Sag and Hankamer, 1984; Tanenhaus and Carlson, 1990, inter alia), this phenomenon has widely been ignored in computational approaches to entity-based coherence modeling. It could, however, provide an explanation for local coherence in cases that are not covered by current models of Centering (cf. Louis and Nenkova (2010)). In this work, we propose a new model to predict whether realizing an argument contributes to local coherence in a given position in discourse. Example (1) shows a text fragment, in which argument realization is necessary in the first sentence but redundant in the second.

(1) El Salvador is now the only Latin American country which still has troops in [Iraq]. Nicaragua, Honduras and the Dominican Republic have withdrawn their troops [∅].

From a semantic processing perspective, a human reader can easily infer that "Iraq", the marked entity in the first sentence of Example (1), is also an implicit argument of the predicate "withdraw" in the second sentence. This inference step is, however, difficult to model computationally as it involves an interplay of two challenging sub-tasks: first, a semantic processor has to determine that an argument is not realized (but inferrable); and second, a suit-

*Second Joint Conference on Lexical and Computational Semantics (*SEM), Volume 1: Proceedings of the Main Conference and the Shared Task*, pages 306–316, Atlanta, Georgia, June 13-14, 2013.

able antecedent has to be found within the discourse context. For the remainder of this paper, we refer to these steps as *identifying* and *linking* implicit arguments to discourse antecedents.

As indicated by Example (1), implicit arguments are an important aspect in semantic processing, yet they are not captured in traditional semantic role labeling systems. The main reasons for this are the scarcity of annotated data, and the inherent difficulty of inferring discourse antecedents automatically.

In this paper, we propose to induce implicit arguments and discourse antecedents by exploiting complementary (explicit) information obtained from monolingual comparable texts (Section 3). We apply the empirically acquired data in argument linking (Section 4) and coherence modeling (Section 5). We conclude with a discussion on the advantages of our data set and outline directions for future work (Section 6).

2 Related work

The most prominent approach to entity-based coherence modeling nowadays is the entity grid model by Barzilay and Lapata (2005). It has originally been proposed for automatic sentence ordering but has also been applied in coherence evaluation and readability assessment (Barzilay and Lapata, 2008; Pitler and Nenkova, 2008), and story generation (McIntyre and Lapata, 2009). Based on the original model, a few extensions have been proposed: for example, Filippova and Strube (2007) and Elsner and Charniak (2011b) suggested additional features to characterize semantic relatedness between entities and features specific to single entities, respectively. Other entity-based approaches to coherence modeling include the pronoun model by Charniak and Elsner (2009) and the discourse-new model by Elsner and Charniak (2008). All of these approaches are, however, based on explicitly realized entity mentions only, ignoring references that are inferrable.

The role of implicit arguments has been studied early on in the context of semantic processing (Fillmore, 1986; Palmer et al., 1986). Yet, the phenomenon has mostly been ignored in semantic role labeling. First data sets, focusing on implicit arguments, have only recently become available: Ruppenhofer et al. (2010) organized a SemEval shared task on "linking events and participants in discourse", Gerber and Chai (2012) made available implicit argument annotations for the NomBank corpus (Meyers et al., 2008) and Moor et al. (2013) provide annotations for parts of the OntoNotes corpus (Weischedel et al., 2011). However, these resources are very limited: The annotations by Moor et al. and Gerber and Chai are restricted to 5 and 10 predicate types, respectively. The training set of the SemEval task contains only 245 resolved implicit arguments in total. As pointed out by Silberer and Frank (2012), additional training data can be heuristically created by treating anaphoric mentions as implicit arguments. Their experimental results showed that artificial training data can indeed improve results, but only when obtained from corpora with manual semantic role annotations (on the sentence level) and gold coreference chains.

3 Identifying and linking implicit arguments

The aim of this work is to automatically construct a data set of implicit arguments and their discourse antecedents. We propose an induction approach that exploits complementary information obtained from pairs of comparable texts. As a basis for this approach, we rely on several preparatory steps proposed in the literature that first identify information two documents have in common (cf. Figure 1). In particular, we align corresponding predicate-argument structures (PAS) using graph-based clustering (Roth and Frank, 2012b). We then determine co-referring entities across the texts using coreference resolution techniques on concatenated document pairs (Lee et al., 2012). These preprocessing steps are described in more detail in Section 3.1.

Given the preprocessed comparable texts and aligned PAS, we propose to heuristically identify implicit arguments and link them to their antecedents via the cross-document coreference chains. We describe the details of this approach in Section 3.2.

3.1 Data preparation

The starting point for our approach is the data set of automatically aligned predicate pairs that has been released by Roth and Frank (2012a).[1] This data

[1]cf. `http://www.cl.uni-heidelberg.de/%7Emroth/`

Sentence that comprises a PAS with an (correctly predicted) implicit argument	induced antecedent
The [$\varnothing_{A0}$] [operating$_{A3}$] **loss**, as measured by ... widened to 189 million euros ...	T-Online['s]
It was handed over to Mozambican control ... 33 years after [$\varnothing_{A0}$] **independence**.	Mozambique['s]
... [local officials $_{A0}$] failed to immediately **report** [the accident $_{A1}$] [$\varnothing_{A2}$] ...	[to] the government

Table 1: Three positive examples of automatically induced implicit argument and antecedent pairs.

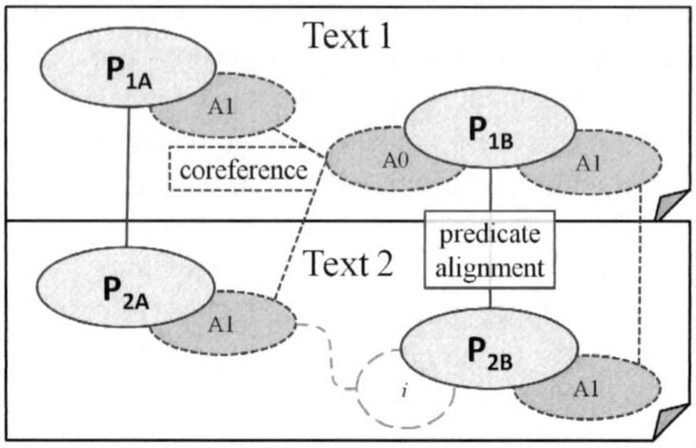

Figure 1: Illustration of the induction approach: texts consist of PAS (represented by overlapping circles); we exploit alignments between corresponding predicates across texts (marked by solid lines) and co-referring entities (marked by dotted lines) to infer implicit arguments (marked by 'i') and link antecedents (curly dashed line)

set, henceforth just **R&F data**, is a collection of 283,588 predicate pairs that have been aligned "with high precision"[2] across comparable newswire articles from the Gigaword corpus (Parker et al., 2011). To use these documents for our argument induction technique, we apply a couple of pre-processing tools on each single document and perform cross-document entity coreference on pairs of documents.

Single document pre-processing. We apply several preprocessing steps to all documents in the R&F data: we use the Stanford CoreNLP package[3] for tokenization and sentence splitting. We then apply MATE tools (Bohnet, 2010; Björkelund et al., 2010), including the integrated PropBank/NomBank-style semantic parser, to reconstruct local predicate-argument structures for aligned predicates. Finally, we resolve pronouns that occur in a PAS using the coreference resolution system by Martschat et al. (2012).

[2]The used method achieved a precision of 86.2% at a recall of 29.1% on the Roth and Frank (2012a) test set.

[3]`http://nlp.stanford.edu/software/`

Cross-document coreference. We apply cross-document coreference resolution to induce antecedents for implicit arguments. In practice, we use the Stanford Coreference System (Lee et al., 2013) and run it on pairs of texts by simply providing a single document as input, comprising of a concatenation of the two texts. To perform this step with high precision, we only use the most precise resolution sieves: "String Match", "Relaxed String Match", "Precise Constructs", "Strict Head Match [A-C]", and "Proper Head Noun Match".

3.2 Identification and linking approach

Given a pair of aligned predicates from two comparable texts, we examine the parser output to identify the arguments in each predicate-argument structure (PAS). We compare the set of realized argument positions in both structures to determine whether one PAS contains an argument position (explicit) that has not been realized in the other PAS (implicit). For each implicit argument, we identify appropriate antecedents by considering the cross-document coreference chain of its explicit counterpart. As our goal is to link arguments within discourse, we restrict candidate antecedents to mentions that occur in the same document as the implicit argument.

We apply a number of restrictions to the resulting pairs of implicit arguments and antecedents to minimize the impact of errors from preprocessing:

- The aligned PAS should consist of a different number of arguments (to minimize the impact of argument labeling errors)
- The antecedent should not be a resolved pronoun (to avoid errors resulting from incorrect pronoun resolution)
- The antecedent should not be in the same sentence as the implicit argument (to circumvent cases, in which an implicit argument is actually explicit but has not been recognized by the parser)

3.3 Resulting data set

We apply the identification and linking approach to the full R&F data set of aligned predicates. As a result, we induce a total of 701 implicit argument and antecedent pairs, each in a separate document, involving 535 different predicates. Examples are displayed in Table 1. Note that 701 implicit arguments from 283,588 pairs of predicate-argument structures seem to represent a fairly low recall. Most predicate pairs in the high precision data set of Roth and Frank (2012a) do, however, consist of identical argument positions (84.5%). In the remaining cases, in which an implicit argument can be identified (15.5%), an antecedent in discourse cannot always be found using the high precision coreference sieves. This does not mean that implicit arguments are a rare phenomenon in general. In fact, 38.9% of all manually aligned predicate pairs in Roth and Frank (2012a) involved a different number of arguments.

We manually evaluated a subset of 90 induced implicit arguments and found 80 discourse antecedents to be correct (89%). Some incorrectly linked instances still result from preprocessing errors. In Table 2, we present a range of different error types that occurred when extracting implicit arguments without any restrictions.

4 Experiment 1: Linking implicit arguments

Our first experiment assesses the utility of automatically induced implicit arguments and antecedent pairs for the task of implicit argument linking. For evaluation, we use the data sets from the SemEval 2010 task on Linking Events and their Participants in Discourse (Ruppenhofer et al., 2010, henceforth just **SemEval**). For direct comparison with previous results and heuristic acquisition techniques (cf. Section 2), we apply the implicit argument identification and linking model by Silberer and Frank (2012, henceforth **S&F**) for training and testing.

4.1 Task summary

Both the training and test sets of the SemEval task are text corpora extracted from Sherlock Holmes novels, with manual frame semantic annotations including implicit arguments. In the actual linking task ("NI-only"), labels are provided for local arguments and participating systems have to perform the following three sub-tasks: (1) identify implicit arguments (IA), (2) predict whether each IA is resolvable and, if so, (3) find an appropriate antecedent.

The task organizers provide two versions of their data sets: one based on FrameNet annotations and one based on PropBank/NomBank annotations. We found that the latter, however, only contains a subset of the implicit argument annotations from the FrameNet-based version. As all previous results in this task have been reported on the FrameNet data set, we adopt the same setting. Note that our additional training data is automatically labeled with a PropBank/NomBank-style parser. That is, we need to map our annotations to FrameNet. The organizers of the SemEval shared task provide a manual mapping dictionary for predicates in the annotated data set. We make use of this manual mapping and additionally use SemLink 1.1[4] for mapping predicates and arguments not in the dictionary.

4.2 Model details

We make use of the system by S&F to train a new model for the NI-only task. As mentioned in the previous sub-section, this task consists of three steps: In step (1), implicit arguments are identified as unfilled FrameNet core roles that are not competing with roles that are already filled; in step (2), a SVM classifier is used to predict whether implicit arguments are resolvable based on a small amount of features – semantic type of the affected Frame Element, the relative frequency of its realization type in the SemEval training corpus, and a boolean feature that indicates whether the affected sentence is in passive voice and does not contain a (deep) subject. In step (3), we apply the same features and classifier as S&F, i.e., the BayesNet implementation from Weka (Witten and Frank, 2005), to find appropriate antecedents for (predicted) resolvable arguments. S&F report that their best results were obtained when considering all entities as candidate antecedents that are syntactic constituents from the present and the past two sentences, or entities that occurred at least five times in the previous discourse ("Chains+Win" setting). In their evaluation, the latter of these two restrictions crucially depended on gold coreference chains. As the automatic coreference chains in our

[4] `http://verbs.colorado.edu/semlink/`

Sentence that comprises a PAS with an (incorrectly predicted) implicit argument	induced antecedent
(1) .. [Statistics$_*$] released [Tuesday $_{TMP}$] [$\varnothing_{A0}$] **showed** the death toll dropped ...	official statistics
(2) A [French $_{LOC*}$] [$\varnothing_{A0}$] draft **resolution** ... demands full ... compliance ...	France
(3) An earthquake ... is capable of causing .. [heavy $_{EXT}$] **damage** [$\varnothing_{A2*}$]	major

Table 2: Examples of erroneous pairs of implicit arguments and antecedents. In (1), the parser did not recognize "Statistics" as an argument of **showed**; in (2), the parser mislabeled "French" as a locative modifier; both errors lead to incorrectly identified implicit arguments. In (3), the implicit argument is correct but the wrong antecedent was identified because "major" had been mislabeled in the aligned predicate-argument structure

data are rather sparse (and noisy), we only consider syntactic constituents from the present and the past two sentences as antecedents ("SentWin" setting).

Before training and testing a new model with our own data, we perform feature selection using 10-fold cross validation. We run the feature selection on a combination of the SemEval training data and our additional data set in order to find a set of features that generalizes best across the two different corpora. We found these to be features regarding "prominence", selectional preferences ("sp_supersense"), the POS tags of entity mentions, and semantic types of argument positions ("semType_dni.entity"). Note that the S&F system does not make use of any lexicalized information. Instead, semantic features are computed based on the highest abstraction level in WordNet (Fellbaum, 1998). For detailed description of all features, see Silberer and Frank (2012).

4.3 Results

For direct comparison in the full task, both with S&F's model and other previously published results, we adopt the precision, recall and F_1 measures as defined in Ruppenhofer et al. (2010). We compare our results with those previously reported on the SemEval task (see Table 3 for a summary): Chen et al. (2010) adapted SEMAFOR, the best performing system that participated in the actual task in 2010. Tonelli and Delmonte (2011) presented a revised version of their SemEval system (Tonelli and Delmonte, 2010), which outperformed SEMAFOR in terms of recall (6%) and F_1 score (8%). The best results in terms of recall and F_1 score up to date have been reported by Laparra and Rigau (2012), with 25% and 19%, respectively. Our model outperforms their state-of-the-art system in terms of precision (21%) but at a higher cost of recall (8%). Two

	P	R	F
Chen et al. (2010)[5]	**0.25**	0.01	0.02
Tonelli and Delmonte (2011)	0.13	0.06	0.08
Laparra and Rigau (2012)	0.15	**0.25**	**0.19**
Laparra and Rigau (2013)	0.14	0.18	0.16
Gorinski et al. (2013)[6]	0.14	0.12	0.13
S&F (no additional data)	0.06	0.09	0.07
S&F (best additional data)	0.09	0.11	0.10
This paper	0.21	0.08	0.12

Table 3: Results in terms of precision (P), recall (R) and F_1 score (F) for identifying and linking implicit arguments in the SemEval test set.

influencing factors for their high recall are probably (1) their improved method for identifying (resolvable) implicit arguments, and (2) their addition of lexicalized and ontological features.

Comparison to the original results reported by S&F, whose system we use, shows that our additional data improves precision (from 6% to 21%) and F_1 score (from 7% to 12%). The loss in recall is marginal (-1%) given the size of the test set (259 resolvable cases in total). The result in precision is the second highest score reported on this task. Interestingly, the improvements are higher than those of the best training set used in the original study by Silberer and Frank (2012), even though their additional data set is three times bigger than ours and is based on manual semantic annotations. We conjecture that their low gain in precision could be a side effect triggered by two factors: on the one hand, their model crucially relies on coreference chains, which are automatically generated for the test set and hence are rather noisy. On the other hand, their heuristically created training data might not represent implicit argument instances adequately.

5 Experiment 2: Implicit arguments in coherence modeling

In our second experiment, we examine the effect of implicit arguments on local coherence, i.e., the question of how well a local argument (non-)realization fits into a given context. We approach this question as follows: first, we assemble a data set of document pairs that differ only with respect to a single realization decision (Section 5.1). Given each pair in this data set, we ask human annotators to indicate their preference for the implicit or explicit argument realization in the pre-specified context (Section 5.2). Second, we attempt to emulate the decision process computationally using a discriminative model based on discourse and entity-specific features (Section 5.3).

5.1 Data compilation

We use the induced data set (henceforth *source data*), as described in Section 3, as a starting point for composing a set of document pairs that involve implicit and explicit arguments. To make sure that each document pair in this data set only differs with respect to a single realization decision, we first create two copies of each document from the source data: one copy remains in its original form, and the other copy will be modified with respect to a single argument realization. Example (2) illustrates an example of an original and modified (marked by an asterik) sentence:

(2) [The Dalai Lama's$_{A0}$] **visit** [to France$_{A1}$] ends on Tuesday.

* [The Dalai Lama's$_{A0}$] **visit** ends on Tuesday.

Note that adding and removing arguments at random can lead to structures that are semantically implausible. Hence, we restrict this procedure to predicate-argument structures (PAS) that actually occur and are aligned across two texts, and create modifications by replacing a single argument position in one text with the corresponding argument position in the comparable text. Examples (2) and (3) show two such comparable texts. The original PAS in Example (2) contains an explicit argument that is implicit in the aligned PAS and hence removed in the modified version. Vice versa, the original text in (3) involves an implicit argument, which is made explicit in the modified version.

(3) [The Dalai Lama's$_{A0}$] **visit** coincides with the Beijing Olympics.

* [The Dalai Lama's$_{A0}$] **visit** [to France$_{A1}$] coincides with the Beijing Olympics.

We ensure that the modified structure fits into the given context grammatically by only considering PAS with identical predicate form and constituent order. We found that this restriction constrains affected arguments to be modifiers, prepositional phrases and direct objects. We argue that this is actually a desirable property because more complicated alternations could affect coherence by themselves; resulting interplays would make it difficult to distinguish between the isolated effect of argument realization itself and other effects, triggered for example by sentence order (Gordon et al., 1993).

5.2 Annotation

We set up a web experiment using the NLTK package (Belz and Kow, 2011) to collect (local) coherence ratings for implicit and explicit arguments. For this experiment, we compiled a data set of 150 document pairs. As described in Section 5.1, each text pair consists of mostly the same text, with the only difference being one argument realization.

We presented all 150 pairs to two annotators[7] and asked them to indicate their preference for one alternative over the other using a continuous slider scale. The annotators got to see the full texts, with the alternatives presented next to each other. To make texts easier to read and differences easier to spot, we collapsed all identical sentences into one column and highlighted the aligned predicate (in both texts) and the affected argument (in the explicit case). An example is shown in Figure 2. To avoid any bias in the annotation process, we shuffled the sequence of text pairs and randomly assigned the side of display (left/right) of each realization type

[5]Results as reported in Tonelli and Delmonte (2011)

[6]Results computed as an average over the scores given for both test files; rounded towards the number given for the test file that contained more instances.

[7]Both annotators are undergraduate students in Computational Linguistics.

The director of the State Administration of Coal Mine Safety has headed a team to Henan to direct the rescue efforts of a coal mine gas explosion.

The government has issued a series of regulations and measures to improve the coal mine safety **situation**.	The government has issued a series of regulations and measures to improve the safety **situation**.

Since the beginning of this year, fatal coal mine accidents in China rose 8.5 percent compared to the previous year.

Figure 2: Texts as displayed to the annotators.

(explicit/implicit). Note that instead of providing a definition of local coherence ourselves, we simply asked the annotators to rate how "natural" a realization sounds given the discourse context.

We found that annotators made use of the full rating scale, which spans from -50 to +50, with the extremes indicating either a strong preference for the text on the left hand side or the right hand side, respectively. Most ratings are, however, concentrated more towards the center of the scale (i.e., around zero). This seems to imply that the use of implicit or explicit arguments did not make a considerable difference most of the time. The first author confirmed this assumption and resolved disagreements between annotators in several group discussions. The annotators also affirmed that some cases do not read naturally when a specific argument is or is not realized at a given position in discourse. Examples (4) and (5) illustrate two cases, in which a redundant argument is realized (A4, or *destination*) or a coherence establishing argument has been omitted (A2, or *co-signer*).[8]

(4) *?* The remaining contraband was picked up at Le Havre. The containers had **arrived** [in Le Havre] from China.

(5) *?* Lt.-Gen. Mohamed Lamari (...) denied his country wanted South African weapons to fight Muslim rebels fighting the government. "We are not going to fight a flea with a hammer," Lamari told reporters after **signing** the agreement of intent [∅].

Following discussions with the annotators, we discarded all items from the final data set, for which no clear preference could be established (72%) or the annotators had different preferences (9%). We mapped all remaining items into two classes according to whether the affected argument had to be implicit (9 texts) or explicit (20 texts). All 29 uniquely classified texts are used as a small gold standard test set for evaluation.

5.3 Coherence model

We model the decision process that underlies the (non-)realization of arguments using a SVM classifier and a range of discourse features. The features can be classified into three groups: features specific to the affected predicate-argument structure (**Parg**), the (automatic) coreference chain of the affected argument (**Coref**), and the discourse context (**Disc**).

Parg includes the absolute and relative number of realized arguments; the number of modifiers in the PAS; and the total length (in words) of the PAS and the complete sentence.

Coref includes the number of previous/follow-up mentions in a fixed sentence window; the distance (in number of words/sentences) to the previous/next mention; the distribution of occurrences over the previous/succeeding two sentences;[9] and the POS of previous/follow-up mentions.

Disc includes the total number of coreference chains in the text; the occurrence of pronouns in the current sentence; lexical repetitions in the previous/follow-up sentence; the current position in discourse (begin, middle, end); and a feature indicating whether the affected argument occured in the first sentence.

Note that most of these features overlap with those successfully applied in previous work. For example, Pitler and Nenkova (2008) also use text

[8] Note that both examples are only excerpts from the affected texts. The annotators got to see the full context.

[9] This type of feature is very similar to the transition patterns in the original entity grid. The only difference is that our features are not typed with respect to the grammatical function of explicit realizations. The reason for skipping this information lies in the insignificant amount of relevant samples in our (noisy) training data.

length, sentence-to-sentence transitions, word overlap and pronoun occurrences as features for predicting readability. Our own contribution lies in the definition of PAS-specific features and the adaptation of all features to the task of predicting (non-)realization of arguments in a predicate-argument structure.

5.4 Training data

We do not make use of any manually annotated data for training. Instead, our model relies solely on the automatically induced source data, described in Section 3, for learning. We prepare this data set as follows: first, we remove all data points that also occur in the test set. Second, we split all pairs of texts into two groups – texts that contain a predicate-argument structure in which an implicit argument has been identified (IA), and their comparable counterparts that contain the aligned PAS with an explicit argument (EA). All texts are labelled according to their group. For all texts in group EA, we remove the explicit argument from the aligned PAS. This way, the feature extractor always gets to see the text and automatic annotations as if the realization decision had not been performed and can thus extract unbiased feature values for the affected entity and argument position.

5.5 Evaluation setting

The goal of this task is to correctly predict the realization type (implicit or explicit) of an argument that maximizes the coherence of the document. As a proxy for coherence, we use the naturalness ratings given by our annotators. We evaluate classification performance on the part of our test set for which clear preferences have been established. We report results in terms of precision, recall and F_1 score. We compute precision as the fraction of correct classifier decisions divided by the total number of classifications; and recall as the fraction of correct classifier decisions divided by the total number of test items. Note that precision and recall are identical when the model provides a class label for every test item. We compute F_1 as the harmonic mean between precision and recall.

For comparison with previous work, we further apply a couple of previously proposed local coherence models: the original entity grid model by Barzilay and Lapata (2005), a modified version that uses topic models (Elsner and Charniak, 2011a) and an extended version that includes entity-specific features (Elsner and Charniak, 2011b). We further apply the discourse-new model by Elsner and Charniak (2008) and the pronoun-based model by Charniak and Elsner (2009). For all of the aforementioned models, we use their respective implementation provided with the Brown Coherence Toolkit[10]. Note that the toolkit only returns one coherence score for each document. To use the toolkit for argument classification, we use two documents per data point – one that contains the affected argument explicitly and one that does not (implicit argument) – and treat the higher scoring variant as classification output. If both documents achieve the same score, we neither count the test item as correctly nor as incorrectly classified. In contrast, we apply our own model only on the document that contains the implicit argument, and use the classifier to predict whether this realization type fits into the given context or not. Note that our model has an advantage here because it is specifically designed for this task. Yet, all models compute local coherence ratings based on entity occurrences and should thus be able to predict which realization type coheres best with the given discourse context.[11]

5.6 Results

The results are summarized in Table 4. As all models provided class labels for almost all test instances, we focus our discussion on F_1 scores. The majority class in our test set is the explicit realization type, making up 20 of the 29 test items (69%).

The original entity grid model produced differing scores for the two realization types only in 26 cases. The model exhibits a strong preference for the implicit realization type: it predicts this class in 22 cases, resulting in an F_1 score of only 15%. Taking a closer look at the features of the model reveals that this an expected outcome: in its original setting, the entity grid learns realization patterns in the form of sentence to sentence transitions. Most entities are, however, only mentioned a few times in a

[10] cf. http://www.ling.ohio-state.edu/%7Emelsner/

[11] Recall that input document pairs are identical except for the affected argument position. Consequently, the resulting coherence scores only differ with respect to affected entity realizations.

	P	R	F
Entity grid models	–	–	–
Baseline entity grid	0.15**	0.14**	0.15**
Extended entity grid	0.19**	0.17**	0.18**
Topical entity grid	0.34**	0.34**	0.34**
Other models	–	–	–
Pronouns	0.43**	0.34**	0.38**
Discourse-newness	0.48**	0.48**	0.48**
This paper	–	–	–
Our (full) model	**0.90**	**0.90**	**0.90**
Simplified model	0.83	0.83	0.83
Majority class	0.69*	0.69*	0.69*

Table 4: Results in terms of precision (P), recall (R) and F_1 score for correctly predicting argument realization; results that significantly differ from our (full) model are marked with asterisks (* $p<0.1$; ** $p<0.01$)

text, which means that non-realizations make up the 'most probable' class – independently of whether they are relevant in a given context or not. The models by Charniak and Elsner (2009) and Elsner and Charniak (2011a), which are not based on an entity grid, do not suffer from this effect and achieve better results, with F_1 scores of 38% and 48%, respectively. The topical and entity-specific refinements to the entity grid model also alleviate the bias towards non-realizations, resulting in improved F_1 scores of 18% and 34%, respectively.

To counter-balance this issue altogether, we train a simplified version of our own model that only uses features that involve occurrence patterns. The main difference between this simplified model and the original entity grid model lies in the different use of training data: while entity grid models treat all non-realized items equally, our model gets to "see" actual examples of entities that are implicit. In other words, our simplified model takes into account implicit mentions of entities, not only explicit ones. The results show that this extra information has a significant ($p<0.01$, using a randomization test (Yeh, 2000)) impact on test set performance, basically raising F_1 from 15% to 83%. Using all features of our model further increases F_1 score to 90%, the highest score achieved overall.

The highest weighted features in our model include all three feature groups: for example, the number of coreferent mentions within the preceeding/following two sentences (**Coref**), the number of words already realized in the affected predicate-argument structure (**Parg**), and the total number of coreference chains in the document (**Disc**).

6 Conclusions

In this paper, we presented a novel approach to accurately induce implicit arguments and discourse antecedents from comparable texts (cf. Section 3). We demonstrated the benefit of this kind of data for linking implicit arguments and modeling local coherence. Our experiments revealed three particularly interesting results.

Firstly, a small data set of (automatically induced) implicit arguments can have a greater impact on argument linking models than a bigger data set of artificially created instances (cf. Section 4). Secondly, the use of implicit vs. explicit arguments, while being a subtle difference in most contexts, can have a clear impact on text ratings. Thirdly, our automatically created training data enables models to learn features that considerably improve prediction of locally coherent argument realizations (cf. Section 5).

For the task of implicit argument linking, more training data will be needed to further advance the state-of-the-art. Our method for inducing this kind of data, by exploiting aligned predicate-argument structures from comparable texts, has shown promising results. Future work will have to explore this direction more fully, for example, by identifying ways to induce data with higher recall. Integrating argument (non-)realization into a full model of local coherence also remains part of future work. In this paper, we presented a suitable basis for such work: a training set that contains empirical data on implicit arguments in discourse; and a feature set that models argument realization with high accuracy.

Acknowledgments

We are grateful to the Landesgraduiertenförderung Baden-Württemberg for funding within the research initiative "Coherence in language processing" at Heidelberg University. We thank our annotators and four anonymous reviewers.

References

Regina Barzilay and Mirella Lapata. 2005. Modeling local coherence: An entity-based approach. In *Proceedings of the 43rd Annual Meeting of the Association for Computational Linguistics,* Ann Arbor, Michigan, USA, 25–30 June 2005, pages 141–148.

Regina Barzilay and Mirella Lapata. 2008. Modeling local coherence: An entity-based approach. *Computational Linguistics*, 34(1):1–34.

Anja Belz and Eric Kow. 2011. Discrete vs. continuous rating scales for language evaluation in nlp. In *Proceedings of the 49th Annual Meeting of the Association for Computational Linguistics: Human Language Technologies*, pages 230–235, Portland, Oregon, USA, June.

Anders Björkelund, Bernd Bohnet, Love Hafdell, and Pierre Nugues. 2010. A high-performance syntactic and semantic dependency parser. In *Coling 2010: Demonstration Volume*, pages 33–36, Beijing, China, August. Coling 2010 Organizing Committee.

Bernd Bohnet. 2010. Top accuracy and fast dependency parsing is not a contradiction. In *Proceedings of the 23rd International Conference on Computational Linguistics (Coling 2010)*, pages 89–97, Beijing, China, August.

Cheryl Brown. 1983. Topic continuity in written english narrative. In Talmy Givon, editor, *Topic Continuity in Discourse: A Quantitative Cross-Language Study*. John Benjamins, Amsterdam, The Netherlands.

Eugene Charniak and Micha Elsner. 2009. EM works for pronoun anaphora resolution. In *Proceedings of the 12th Conference of the European Chapter of the ACL (EACL 2009)*, pages 148–156, Athens, Greece, March.

Desai Chen, Nathan Schneider, Dipanjan Das, and Noah A. Smith. 2010. SEMAFOR: Frame argument resolution with log-linear models. In *Proceedings of the 5th International Workshop on Semantic Evaluation*, pages 264–267, Uppsala, Sweden, July.

Micha Elsner and Eugene Charniak. 2008. Coreference-inspired coherence modeling. In *Proceedings of ACL-08: HLT, Short Papers*, pages 41–44, Columbus, Ohio, June.

Micha Elsner and Eugene Charniak. 2011a. Disentangling chat with local coherence models. In *Proceedings of the 49th Annual Meeting of the Association for Computational Linguistics: Human Language Technologies*, pages 1179–1189, Portland, Oregon, USA, June.

Micha Elsner and Eugene Charniak. 2011b. Extending the entity grid with entity-specific features. In *Proceedings of the 49th Annual Meeting of the Association for Computational Linguistics: Human Language Technologies*, pages 125–129, Portland, Oregon, USA, June.

Christiane Fellbaum, editor. 1998. *WordNet: An Electronic Lexical Database*. MIT Press, Cambridge, Massachusetts, USA.

Katja Filippova and Michael Strube. 2007. Extending the entity-grid coherence model to semantically related entities. In *Proceedings of the 11th European Workshop on Natural Language Generation,* Schloss Dagstuhl, Germany, 17–20 June 2007, pages 139–142.

C. J. Fillmore. 1986. Pragmatically controlled zero anaphora. In *Proceedings of the twelfth annual meeting of the Berkeley Linguistics Society*, pages 95–107.

Matthew Gerber and Joyce Chai. 2012. Semantic Role Labeling of Implicit Arguments for Nominal Predicates. *Computational Linguistics*, 38(4):755–798.

Peter C. Gordon, Barbara J. Grosz, and Laura A. Gilliom. 1993. Pronouns, names, and the centering of attention in discourse. *Cognitive Science*, 17:311–347.

Philip Gorinski, Josef Ruppenhofer, and Caroline Sporleder. 2013. Towards weakly supervised resolution of null instantiations. In *Proceedings of the 10th International Conference on Computational Semantics (IWCS 2013) – Long Papers*, pages 119–130, Potsdam, Germany, March.

Barbara J. Grosz, Aravind K. Joshi, and Scott Weinstein. 1995. Centering: A framework for modeling the local coherence of discourse. *Computational Linguistics*, 21(2):203–225.

Aravind K. Joshi and Steve Kuhn. 1979. Centered logic: The role of entity centered sentence representation in natural language inferencing. In *Proceedings of the 6th International Joint Conference on Artificial Intelligence,* Tokyo, Japan, August, pages 435–439.

Egoitz Laparra and German Rigau. 2012. Exploiting explicit annotations and semantic types for implicit argument resolution. In *Proceedings of the Sixth IEEE International Conference on Semantic Computing (ICSC 2010)*, pages 75–78, Palermo, Italy, September. IEEE Computer Society.

Egoitz Laparra and German Rigau. 2013. Sources of evidence for implicit argument resolution. In *Proceedings of the 10th International Conference on Computational Semantics (IWCS 2013) – Long Papers*, pages 155–166, Potsdam, Germany, March.

Heeyoung Lee, Marta Recasens, Angel Chang, Mihai Surdeanu, and Dan Jurafsky. 2012. Joint entity and event coreference resolution across documents. In *Proceedings of the 2012 Joint Conference on Empirical Methods in Natural Language Processing and Computational Natural Language Learning*, pages 489–500, Jeju Island, Korea, July.

Heeyoung Lee, Angel Chang, Yves Peirsman, Nathanael Chambers, Mihai Surdeanu, and Dan Jurafsky. 2013.

Deterministic coreference resolution based on entity-centric, precision-ranked rules. *Computational Linguistics*, 39(4). Accepted for publication.

Annie Louis and Ani Nenkova. 2010. Creating local coherence: An empirical assessment. In *Human Language Technologies: The 2010 Annual Conference of the North American Chapter of the Association for Computational Linguistics*, pages 313–316, Los Angeles, California, June.

Sebastian Martschat, Jie Cai, Samuel Broscheit, Éva Mújdricza-Maydt, and Michael Strube. 2012. A multigraph model for coreference resolution. In *Joint Conference on EMNLP and CoNLL - Shared Task*, pages 100–106, Jeju Island, Korea, July.

Neil McIntyre and Mirella Lapata. 2009. Learning to tell tales: A data-driven approach to story generation. In *Proceedings of the Joint Conference of the 47th Annual Meeting of the Association for Computational Linguistics and the 4th International Joint Conference on Natural Language Processing,* Singapore, 2–7 August 2009, pages 217–225.

Adam Meyers, Ruth Reeves, and Catherine Macleod. 2008. *NomBank v1.0.* Linguistic Data Consortium, Philadelphia.

Tatjana Moor, Michael Roth, and Anette Frank. 2013. Predicate-specific annotations for implicit role binding: Corpus annotation, data analysis and evaluation experiments. In *Proceedings of the 10th International Conference on Computational Semantics (IWCS 2013) – Short Papers*, pages 369–375, Potsdam, Germany, March.

Martha S. Palmer, Deborah A. Dahl, Rebecca J. Schiffman, Lynette Hirschman, Marcia Linebarger, and John Dowding. 1986. Recovering implicit information. In *Proceedings of the 24th Annual Meeting of the Association for Computational Linguistics,* New York, N.Y., 10–13 June 1986, pages 10–19.

Martha Palmer, Daniel Gildea, and Nianwen Xue. 2010. Synthesis Lectures on Human Language Technologies. Morgan & Claypool.

Robert Parker, David Graff, Jumbo Kong, Ke Chen, and Kazuaki Maeda. 2011. *English Gigaword Fifth Edition.* Linguistic Data Consortium, Philadelphia.

Emily Pitler and Ani Nenkova. 2008. Revisiting readability: A unified framework for predicting text quality. In *Proceedings of the 2008 Conference on Empirical Methods in Natural Language Processing*, pages 186–195, Honolulu, Hawaii, October.

Michael Roth and Anette Frank. 2012a. Aligning predicate argument structures in monolingual comparable texts: A new corpus for a new task. In *Proceedings of the First Joint Conference on Lexical and Computational Semantics*, pages 218–227, Montreal, Canada, June.

Michael Roth and Anette Frank. 2012b. Aligning predicates across monolingual comparable texts using graph-based clustering. In *Proceedings of the 2012 Joint Conference on Empirical Methods in Natural Language Processing and Computational Natural Language Learning*, pages 171–182, Jeju Island, Korea, July.

Josef Ruppenhofer, Caroline Sporleder, Roser Morante, Collin Baker, and Martha Palmer. 2010. SemEval-2010 Task 10: Linking Events and Their Participants in Discourse. In *Proceedings of the 5th International Workshop on Semantic Evaluations*, pages 45–50, Uppsala, Sweden, July.

Ivan A. Sag and Jorge Hankamer. 1984. Towards a Theory of Anaphoric Processing. *Linguistics and Philosophy*, 7:325–345.

Candace L. Sidner. 1979. Towards a computational theory of definite anaphora comprehension in English. Technical Report AI-Memo 537, Massachusetts Institute of Technology, AI Lab, Cambridge, Mass.

Carina Silberer and Anette Frank. 2012. Casting implicit role linking as an anaphora resolution task. In *Proceedings of the First Joint Conference on Lexical and Computational Semantics (*SEM 2012)*, pages 1–10, Montréal, Canada, 7-8 June.

Michael K. Tanenhaus and Greg N. Carlson. 1990. Comprehension of Deep and Surface Verbphrase Anaphors. *Language and Cognitive Processes*, 5(4):257–280.

Sara Tonelli and Rodolfo Delmonte. 2010. VENSES++: Adapting a deep semantic processing system to the identification of null instantiations. In *Proceedings of the 5th International Workshop on Semantic Evaluation*, pages 296–299, Uppsala, Sweden, July.

Sara Tonelli and Rodolfo Delmonte. 2011. Desperately seeking implicit arguments in text. In *Proceedings of the ACL 2011 Workshop on Relational Models of Semantics*, pages 54–62, Portland, Oregon, USA, June.

Ralph Weischedel, Martha Palmer, Mitchell Marcus, Eduard Hovy, Sameer Pradhan, Lance Ramshaw, Nianwen Xue, Ann Taylor, Jeff Kaufman, Michelle Franchini, Mohammed El-Bachouti, Robert Belvin, and Ann Houston. 2011. *OntoNotes Release 4.0.* Linguistic Data Consortium, Philadelphia.

Ian H. Witten and Eibe Frank. 2005. *Data Mining: Practical Machine Learning Tools and Techniques.* Morgan Kaufmann, San Francisco, California, USA, 2nd edition.

Alexander Yeh. 2000. More accurate tests for the statistical significance of result differences. In *Proceedings of the 18th International Conference on Computational Linguistics*, pages 947–953, Saarbrücken, Germany, August.

Bootstrapping Semantic Role Labelers from Parallel Data

Mikhail Kozhevnikov **Ivan Titov**
Saarland University, Postfach 15 11 50
66041 Saarbrücken, Germany
{mkozhevn|titov}@mmci.uni-saarland.de

Abstract

We present an approach which uses the similarity in semantic structure of bilingual parallel sentences to bootstrap a pair of semantic role labeling (SRL) models. The setting is similar to co-training, except for the intermediate model required to convert the SRL structure between the two annotation schemes used for different languages. Our approach can facilitate the construction of SRL models for resource-poor languages, while preserving the annotation schemes designed for the target language and making use of the limited resources available for it. We evaluate the model on four language pairs, English vs German, Spanish, Czech and Chinese. Consistent improvements are observed over the self-training baseline.

1 Introduction

The success of statistical modeling methods in a variety of natural language processing (NLP) tasks in the last decade depended crucially on the availability of annotated resources for their training. And while sizable resources for most standard tasks are only available for a few languages, the human effort required to achieve reasonable performance on such tasks for other languages may be significantly reduced by leveraging existing resources and the similarities between languages.

This idea has lead to the development of cross-lingual annotation projection approaches, which make use of parallel corpora (Padó and Lapata, 2009), as well as attempts to adapt models directly to other languages (McDonald et al., 2011). In this paper we consider correspondences between SRL structures in translated sentences from a different perspective. Most cross-lingual annotation projection approaches transfer the source language annotation scheme to the target language without modification, which makes it hard to combine their output with existing target language resources, as annotation schemes may vary significantly. We instead address the problem of information transfer between two *existing* annotation schemes (figure 1) for a pair of languages using an intermediate model of role correspondence (RCM). An RCM models the probability of a pair of corresponding arguments being assigned a certain pair of roles. We then use it to guide a pair of monolingual models toward compatible predictions on parallel data in order to extend the coverage and/or accuracy of one or both models.

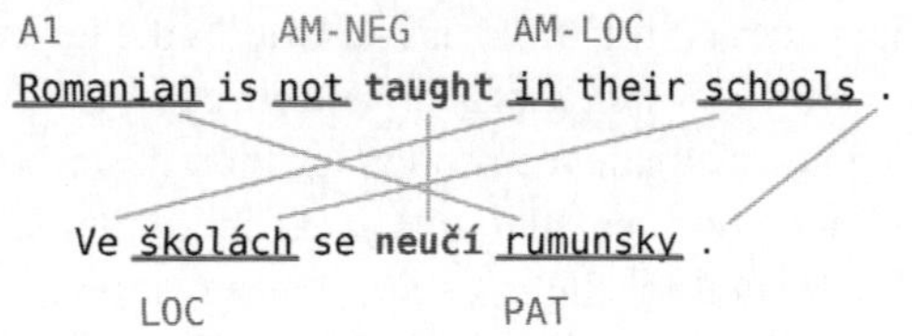

Figure 1: Role correspondence in parallel sentences, an example.

The notion of compatibility here is highly non-trivial, even for sentences translated as close to the original as possible. Zhuang and Zong (2010), for example, observe that in the English-Chinese parallel PropBank (Palmer et al., 2005b) corresponding arguments often bear different labels, even though the same inventory of semantic roles is used for both

*Second Joint Conference on Lexical and Computational Semantics (*SEM), Volume 1: Proceedings of the Main Conference and the Shared Task*, pages 317–327, Atlanta, Georgia, June 13-14, 2013. ©2013 Association for Computational Linguistics

languages and the annotation guidelines are similar. When different annotation schemes are considered, the problem is further complicated by the difference in the granularity of semantic roles used and varying notions of what is an argument and what is not.

Manually annotated training data for such a model is hard to come by. Instead, we propose an iterative procedure similar to bootstrapping, where the parameters of the RCM are initially estimated from a parallel corpus automatically annotated with semantic roles using the monolingual models independently, and then the RCM is used to refine these annotations via a joint inference procedure, serving to enforce consistency on the predictions of monolingual models on parallel sentences. The obtained annotations on the parallel corpus are expected to be of higher quality than the independent predictions of the models, so they can be used to improve the SRL models' performance and/or coverage. We evaluate this approach by augmenting the original training data with the annotations obtained on parallel data and observing the change in the model's performance. This is especially useful if one of the languages is relatively poor in resources, in which case the proposed procedure will help propagate information from the stronger model to the weaker one. Even if the two models are comparable in their predictive power, we may be able to benefit from the fact that certain semantic roles are realized less ambiguously in one language than in another. We will henceforth refer to these two alternatives as the *projection* and *symmetric* setups.

The paper is structured as follows. In the next section we present our approach and discuss the issues of role correspondence modeling, then describe the implementation and datasets used in evaluation in section 3, present the evaluation and results in section 4 and conclude with the discussion of related work in section 5.

2 Approach

We consider bootstrapping a pair of SRL models on a parallel corpus, using the correspondence between their predictions on parallel sentences to guide the learning. The models are forced toward compatible predictions, where the notion of compatibility is defined by a (statistical) role correspondence model.

Let us consider a pair of languages, α and β, and their corresponding datasets T^0_α and T^0_β, annotated with semantic roles (the upper indices here denote the iteration number). We will refer to these as the *initial* training sets. We also assume that a word-aligned parallel corpus is available for the pair of languages, which we denote P, with the predicates and their respective arguments identified on both sides.

The procedure is then as follows: we train monolingual models M^0_α and M^0_β on T^0_α and T^0_β, respectively, apply them to the two sides of the parallel corpus, resulting in a labeling P^0. We collect the semantic role co-occurrence information and train the role correspondence model C^0 on it, then proceed to the joint inference step involving M^0_α, M^0_β and C^0, resulting in a refined labeling P^1 of the parallel corpus. The two sides of the P^1 are then used to augment the initial training sets, yielding T^1_α and T^1_β, and new models M^1_β and M^1_β are trained on these. The process can then be repeated using M^1_α and M^1_β instead of the initial models.

We report the model's performance on a held-out test set, drawn from the same corpus as the corresponding initial training set.

The procedure can be seen as a form of co-training (Blum and Mitchell, 1998) of a pair of monolingual SRL models. In our case, however, the question of the models' agreement is not as trivial as in most applications of co-training, requiring a statistical model of its own (C^i).

In the low-resource (*projection*) setup our approach is also similar to self-training with weak supervision coming from the stronger model.

Note that although the approach is iterative, we have observed no significant improvements from repeating the procedure, possibly owing to the noise introduced by the errors in preprocessing. In the evaluation we run only one iteration. In the notation introduced above, the self-training baseline model (SELF) is trained on P^0_β, the joint model (JOINT) – on P^1_β and the combined model (COMB) – on T^1_β.

2.1 Modeling Role Correspondence

It is necessary to distinguish between semantic roles and their interpretation in a particular context. The former can be defined in a variety of ways, depending on the formalism used. In case of FrameNet (Baker et al., 1998), for example, the interpretation of a semantic role (frame element) is explicitly provided for each separate frame, so a frame and a frame element label together describe the semantics of an argument. PropBank (Palmer et al., 2005a) follows a mixed strategy – the labels for a relatively small set of *core roles* are numbered and their interpretations are provided separately for each predicate (although those of the first two roles, `A0` and `A1`, consistently denote what is known as Proto-Agent and Proto-Patient), while *modifiers* (Merlo and Leybold, 2001) bear labels that are interpreted consistently across all predicates. Other resources, such as Prague Dependency Treebank (Hajič et al., 2006), use a single set of semantic roles (functors), which are interpretable across different predicates.

From the standpoint of defining the semantic similarity of parallel sentences, the important implication is that we cannot assume that the corresponding arguments should bear the same label, even if the annotation schemes used are compatible (Zhuang and Zong, 2010). Nor can we write down a single mapping between the roles that will be valid across different predicates (figure 2), which motivates the need for a statistical model of semantic role correspondence.

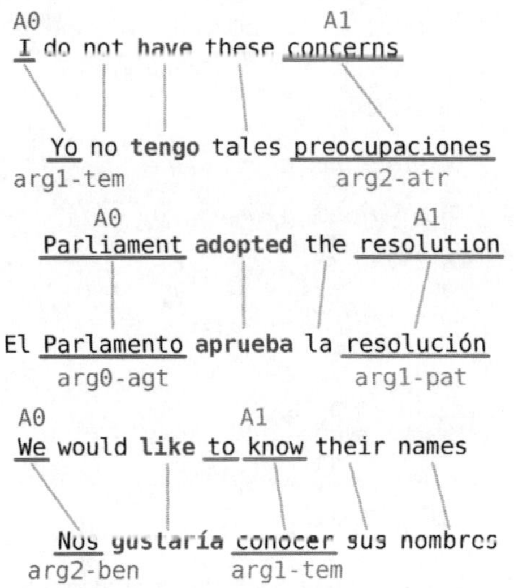

Figure 2: Predicate-specific role mapping. Note that `A0` corresponds to `art0-agt`, `art1-tem` or `art2-ben`, depending on the predicate.

We assume the existence of a one-to-one mapping between semantic roles for a given predicate pair. As the mappings are not completely independent – at least some roles have the same interpretation across different predicate pairs, – we choose to build a single model, which relies on features derived from the pair of predicates in question, rather than create a separate model for each predicate pair. The model can then make decisions specific to particular predicates or predicate pairs, where sufficient data has been observed or back off to a generic mapping where there is not enough data.

For the purpose of this study, we choose to separately model the probability of a target role, given the source one and the necessary contextual information and vice versa. These two components are referred to as *projection models* and realized as a pair of linear classifiers.

Training such a model in a conventional fashion would require a rather specific kind of dataset, namely a parallel corpus annotated with semantic roles, and assuming the availability of such data would severely limit the applicability of the approach proposed, as, to our knowledge, it is currently only available for two language pairs, namely English-Chinese (Palmer et al., 2005b) and English-Czech (Hajič et al., 2012). We instead use the automatically produced annotations on a parallel corpus, effectively enforcing consistency on the role correspondence in the monolingual models' predictions.

2.2 Joint Inference

The joint inference would have been simplest if the arguments were classified independently. This assumption is too restrictive, though, since the interdependencies between the arguments can be used to improve the accuracy of semantic role labeling (Roth and Yih, 2005).

2.2.1 Projection Setup

In the projection setup we assume that the model for one of the languages, which we will henceforth refer to as *source*, is much better informed than the one for the other language, referred to as *target*, so we only have to propagate the information one way. The scoring functions of these two models will be denoted f_s and f_t, respectively, and that of the projection model from source to target – f_{st}. Source and target sentences are denoted S_s and S_t, and aligned predicates in these sentences – p_s and p_t. The task is then to identify the target language role assignment r_t that would maximize the objective $L(r_t) = \lambda_t f_t(r_t, S_t, p_t) + \lambda_{st} f_{st}(r_t, r_s, p_s, p_t)$, where $r_s = argmax_r f_s(r_s, S_s, p_s)$ is the role assignment of the source-side arguments as predicted by the monolingual model and λ are the weights associated with the models.

The exact maximization of this objective is computationally expensive, so we resort to an approximation. We chose to use the *dual decomposition* method primarily because it fits the structure of the objective particularly well (in that it is a sum of the objectives of two independent models) and since it allows a wide range of monolingual models to be used in this setup. The only requirement here is that the monolingual model must be able to incorporate a bias toward or away from a certain prediction.

To apply this approximation, we decouple the r_t variables into r_t and r_{st} and get $L_1(r_t, r_{st}) = \lambda_t f_t(r_t, S_t, p_t) + \lambda_{st} f_{st}(r_{st}, r_s, p_s, p_t)$ under the condition that $r_t = r_{st}$. Applying the Lagrangian relaxation, we replace the hard equality constraint on r_t and r_{st} with a soft one, using slack variables δ, which results in the following objective:

$$\begin{aligned} &min_\delta max_{r_t, r_{st}} L_1'(r_t, r_{st}, \delta) = \\ &\lambda_t f_t(r_t, S_t, p_t) + \lambda_{st} f_{st}(r_{st}, r_s, p_s, p_t) + \\ &\sum_i \sum_{r \in R_t} \delta^{i,r} \left(I(r_t^i = r) - I(r_{st}^i = r) \right), \end{aligned} \tag{1}$$

where i indexes aligned argument pairs and I is an indicator function. This is equivalent to

$$\begin{aligned} &min_\delta max_{r_t, r_{st}} L_1'(r_t, r_{st}, \delta) = \\ &min_\delta \Big(max_{r_t} g_t(r_t, S_t, p_t, \delta) + \\ &max_{r_{st}} g_{st}(r_{st}, r_s, p_s, p_t, \delta) \Big), \end{aligned} \tag{2}$$

where

$$\begin{aligned} &g_t(r_t, S_t, p_t, \delta) = \\ &\lambda_t f_t(r_t, S_t, p_t) + \sum_i \sum_{r \in R_t} \delta^{i,r} I(r_t^i = r) \\ &g_{st} p(r_{st}, r_s, p_s, p_t, \delta) = \\ &\lambda_{st} f_{st}(r_{st}, r_s, p_s, p_t) - \sum_i \sum_{r \in R_t} \delta^{i,r} I(r_{st}^i = r) \end{aligned} \tag{3}$$

are the augmented objectives of the two component models, incorporating bias factors on various possible predictions.

The minimization with respect to δ is performed using a subgradient descent algorithm following Sontag et al. (2011). Whenever the method converges, it converges to the global maximum of the sum of the objectives. We found that in our case it reaches a solution within the first 1000 iterations over 99% of the time.

2.2.2 Symmetric Setup

If the models have comparable accuracy, the above inference procedure can be extended to perform projection both ways. Formulating this as a dual decomposition problem would require using three separate components, two for the monolingual models and one for the RCM, which would have to make its own predictions for the semantic roles on both sides without conditioning on the predictions of the monolingual models. This calls for a different kind of model than the one we use – a model that will rely on a (possibly simplified) feature representation of the source and target arguments to jointly predict their labels. Instead, we perform the projection setup inference procedure in both directions simultaneously, interleaving gradient descent steps and allowing the projection models to access the updated predictions of the monolingual models. This results in a block gradient descent algorithm with the following updates:

$$\begin{aligned} r_t^{n+1} &= argmax_{r_t} g_t(r_t, S_t, p_t, \delta_t^n) \\ r_s^{n+1} &= argmax_{r_t} g_s(r_s, S_s, p_s, \delta_s^n) \\ r_{st}^{n+1} &= argmax_{r_{st}} g_{st}(r_{st}, r_s^n, p_s, p_t, \delta_t^n) \\ r_{ts}^{n+1} &= argmax_{r_{ts}} g_{ts}(r_{ts}, r_t^n, p_t, p_s, \delta_s^n) \\ \forall_i \forall_{r \in R_s} \delta_s^{n+1,i,r} &= \delta_s^{n,i,r} + \\ &\gamma_s(n)(I(r_{ts}^{n,i} = r) - I(r_s^{n,i} = r)) \\ \forall_i \forall_{r \in R_t} \delta_t^{n+1,i,r} &= \delta_t^{n,i,r} + \\ &\gamma_t(n)(I(r_{st}^{n,i} = r) - I(r_t^{n,i} = r)), \end{aligned} \tag{4}$$

where $\gamma_s(n) = \gamma_t(n) = \frac{\gamma_0}{n+1}$ is the update rate function for step n, and g_s and g_{ts} are defined as in (3), but with the direction reversed.

This procedure allows us to use the same RCM implementation as in the projection setup. Moreover, the inference procedure for projection setup is a special case of this one with $\gamma_s(n)$ set to 0. The algorithm also demonstrates convergence similar to that of the projection version, although it lacks the optimality guarantees.

3 Experimental Setup

We evaluate our approach on four language pairs, namely English vs German, Spanish, Czech and Chinese, which we will denote `en-de`, `en-es`, `en-cz` and `en-zh` respectively.

3.1 Parallel Data

The parallel data for the first three language pairs is drawn from Europarl v6 (Koehn, 2005) and from MultiUN (Eisele and Chen, 2010) for English-Chinese. We applied Stanford Tokenizer for English, tokenizer scripts (Koehn, 2005) provided with the Europarl corpus to German, Spanish and Czech, and Stanford Chinese Segmenter (Chang et al., 2008) to Chinese, then performed POS-tagging, morphology tagging (where applicable) and dependency parsing using MATE-tools (Bohnet, 2010).

Word alignments were acquired using GIZA++ (Och and Ney, 2003) with its standard settings. Predicate identification on the parallel data was done using the supervised classifiers of the monolingual SRL systems, except for German, where a simple heuristic had to be used instead, as only some of the predicates are marked in the training data, which makes it hard to train a supervised classifier. Following van der Plas et al. (2011), we then retain only those sentences where all identified predicates were aligned.

In the experiments we used 50 thousand predicate pairs in each case, as increasing the amount further did not yield noticeable benefits, while increasing the running time.

3.2 Annotated Data

The CoNLL'09 (Hajič et al., 2009) datasets were used as a source of annotated data for all languages. Only verbal predicates were considered and predicted syntax was used in evaluation.

We consider subsets of the training data in order to emulate the scenario with a resource-poor language. Due to the different sources the datasets were derived from, sentences contain different proportions of annotated predicates depending on the language. The German corpus, for example, contains about 6 times fewer argument labels per sentence than the English one. We will therefore indicate the sizes of the datasets used in the number of argument labels they contain, referred to as *instances*, rather than the number of predicates or sentences. The corpus for English, for example, contains 6.2 such instances per sentence on average.

We use the 20 thousand instances of the available data as the training corpus for each language and split the rest equally between the development and the test set. The secondary ("out-of-domain") test sets are preserved as they are.

In dependency-based SRL, only heads of syntactic constituents are marked with semantic roles. The heads of corresponding arguments may or may not align, however, even if the arguments are lexically very similar, because their syntactic structure may differ. In general, one would have to identify the whole phrase for each argument and take into account the links between constituents, rather than single words (Padó and Lapata, 2005). As reconstructing the constituents from the dependency tree is non-trivial (Hwang et al., 2010), we are using a heuristic to address the most common version of this problem, i.e. a preposition or an auxiliary verb being an argument head. In such a case we also take into account any alignment links involving the head's immediate descendants.

3.3 Implementation

Our system is based on that of Björkelund et al. (2009). It is a pipeline system comprised of a set of binary or multiclass linear classifiers. Both here and in the projection model, the classifiers are trained using Liblinear (Fan et al., 2008).

We employed a uniqueness constraint on role labels (Chang et al., 2007), preventing some of them from being assigned to more than one argument in the same predicate, which appears to be more reliable in a low-resource setting we consider than the reranker the original system employed. The constraint is enforced in the monolingual model inference using a beam-search approximation with the beam size of 10. The label uniqueness information was derived from the training sets.

3.4 The Projection Model

Each projection model is realized by a single linear classifier applied to each argument pair independently. It relies on features derived from the source semantic role and source and target predicates, and predicts the semantic role for the argument in the target sentence.

The features include the source semantic role and its conjunctions with (lowercased) forms and lemmata of the source and target predicates. For example, assuming the source semantic role is `A3` and the source and target predicates are `went` and `ging` (past tense of "gehen", German), the features would be as shown in figure 3.

```
FORMPAIR=A3-went-ging
LEMMAPAIR=A3-go-gehen
FORMSRC=A3-went
FORMTGT=A3-ging
LEMMASRC=A3-go
LEMMATGT=A3-gehen
LABEL=A3
```

Figure 3: Projection model features example.

3.5 Parameters

In case of projection there are two parameters, λ_{st} and λ_t, – the weights of the component models in the objective. Only their relative values matter (except in the choice of γ_0), so we set λ_t to 1 and only tune the weight of the role correspondence model.

In the symmetric setup, the objective takes the form $L(r_t, r_s) = \lambda_t f_t(r_t, S_t, p_t) + \lambda_{st} f_{st}(r_t, r_s, p_s, p_t) + \lambda_s f_s(r_s, S_s, p_s) + \lambda_{ts} f_{ts}(r_s, r_t, p_t, p_s)$. Since we assume that the two monolingual models here have comparable performance, we do not tune their relative weights, setting both λ_s and λ_t to 1.

We also use the same weight for both projection models, $\lambda_{st} = \lambda_{ts}$, and this value plays an important role – it basically indicates how strongly we insist on the role correspondence models' correctness. If this weight is set to 0, the RCM will accept the initial predictions the monolingual models make, and if it is set to a sufficiently large value, the predictions of the monolingual models will be biased until they match the mapping suggested by the RCM. The optimal weight will therefore depend on the language pair, the sizes of the initial training sets and the RCM used. We use the value of 0.7 in all projection experiments and 0.5 in the symmetric setup, however, as excessive tuning may be undesirable in the low-resource setting.

3.6 Domains

One important factor in the understanding of the evaluation figures presented is the fact that sources of annotated and parallel data belong to different domains. The former usually contains some sort of newswire text – Wall Street Journal in case of English, Xinhua newswire, Hong Kong news and Sinorama news magazine for Chinese, etc. Parallel data, on the other hand, comes from the proceedings of European Parliament and United Nations, which are quite different. For example, the sentences in the latter domain often start with someone being addressed, either by name or by title, which can hardly be expected to occur as often in a newspaper or a magazine article.

As is well-known, the performance of many statistical tools drops significantly outside the domain they were trained on (Pradhan et al., 2008), and the preprocessing and SRL models used here are no exception, which results in relatively low quality of the initial predictions on the parallel text. The low argument identification performance, in particular, is presumably due to inaccurate dependency parses, on which it heavily relies. Several approached have been proposed to improve the accuracy of dependency parsers and other tools on out-of-domain data, but this is beyond the scope of this paper. In some cases (though seldom), sources of parallel data belonging to the same domain as the annotated training data can be obtained.

Another concern is that the performance of a model trained on automatically labeled parallel data as measured on a test set we use may not reflect the quality of these annotations. To assess the resulting model's coverage, it would be interesting to evaluate it on data outside the original domain, so we consider the out-of-domain (OOD) test sets as provided for the CoNLL Shared Task 2009 where available.

Perhaps the most interesting one of these is the German OOD test set, which is drawn from Europarl (as is the parallel data we use). It was originally annotated with syntactic dependency trees and semantic structure in the SALSA format (Burchardt et al., 2006) for Padó and Lapata (2005), and then converted into a PropBank-like form for the CoNLL Shared Task 2009 (Hajič et al., 2009). The OOD test set for English is drawn from the Brown corpus (Francis and Kucera, 1967) and the one for Czech – from a Czech translation of Wall Street Journal articles (Hajič et al., 2012).

4 Evaluation

The first question we are interested in is how the joint inference affects the quality of the automatically obtained annotations on the parallel data. To answer this, we will run the monolingual models independently and jointly, then train models on the output of these two procedures and compare their performance on a test set. Note that we do not add the initial training data at this point, so the initial model scores are provided for reference, rather than as a baseline.

4.1 Projection Setup

A small initial training set of 600 instances was used here for the target language here and the full training set (20000 instances) for the source one. λ_{st} was set to 0.7 in all experiments in this section.

	INIT	SELF	JOINT	Δ_{SELF}
en-cz*	61.11	60.68	63.01	**2.33**
en-cz	62.45	62.15	63.11	**0.96**
en-de*	66.81	63.96	67.64	**3.69**
en-de	70.40	68.34	70.13	**1.79**
en-es	64.20	64.51	66.01	**1.50**
en-zh	75.80	73.52	74.87	**1.35**
cz-en*	66.82	63.95	64.97	**1.02**
cz-en	74.92	71.60	71.90	**0.29**
de-en*	66.82	63.58	63.21	-0.37
de-en	74.93	71.31	70.72	-0.59
es-en*	66.82	63.95	64.18	0.23
es-en	74.93	71.47	72.09	**0.62**
zh-en*	66.82	64.51	63.67	-0.83
zh-en	74.93	72.26	71.24	-1.01

Table 1: Projection setup results: self-training baseline, refined model and the difference in their performance. Asterisk indicates out-of-domain test set, statistically significant improvements are highlighted in bold.

In table 1, we present the accuracy of the model trained on the output of the joint inference (JOINT) against that of the self-training baseline (SELF). The Δ_{SELF} column contains the difference between the two. Note that the SELF model is trained on the parallel data automatically annotated using monolingual SRL models (not mixed with the initial training set), since we are interested in the effect of joint inference on the quality of the annotation obtained. Where the improvement is positive and statistically significant with $p < 0.005$ according to the permutation test (Good, 2000), they are highlighted in bold.

We can see that the refined model (JOINT) outperforms the self-training baseline in most cases by a moderate, but statistically significant margin, which indicates that the joint inference does improve the quality of annotations on the parallel corpus.

The slightly higher improvement on the German OOD test set supports our hypothesis that the procedure enhances the performance of the model on parallel data, as the data for this test set is also drawn from the Europarl corpus. The improvement over the initial model (Δ_{INIT}) in this case is statistically significant with $p < 0.05$. Higher p-value may be attributed to the smaller test set size.

Figure 4 shows how the performance of the JOINT model changes with the size of the initial training set. The improvements are smaller for en-cz, en-de and en-zh, but they are also statistically significant for initial training sets of up to 2000 instances. Projection to English from other languages performs worse.

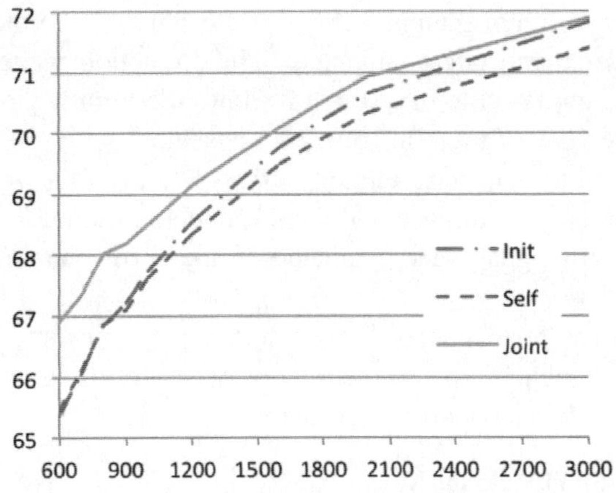

Figure 4: Projection setup, English-Spanish, model performance as a function of the size of the initial training set.

4.2 Combining

In practice, automatically obtained annotations are usually combined with the existing labeled data. For this purpose, the initial training set is replicated so as to constitute 0.3 (an empirically chosen value that appears to work well in most experiments) of the size of the automatically labeled dataset. We compare the performance of the model trained on the resulting dataset (COMB) with that of the JOINT model and the initial models. The results are presented in table 2. We omit projection from other languages to English, since the JOINT model there fails to outperform the initial model and we do not expect to benefit from adding the automatically annotated data to the initial training set in this case.

	INIT	JOINT	COMB	Δ_{JOINT}	Δ_{INIT}
en-cz*	61.11	63.01	62.98	-0.03	**1.87**
en-cz	62.45	63.11	63.30	**0.19**	**0.85**
en-de*	66.81	67.64	67.64	0.00	0.84
en-de	70.39	70.19	70.53	**0.34**	0.15
en-es	64.20	66.01	66.01	0.00	**1.81**
en-zh	75.80	74.87	75.03	0.16	-0.77

Table 2: The effect of adding automatically obtained annotation to the initial training set. Asterisk indicates out-of-domain test set, statistically significant improvements are highlighted in bold.

4.3 Symmetric Setup

In the symmetric setup evaluation, we use a slightly larger initial training set of 1400 instances for both source and target language. The projection model weight is set to 0.5. Table 3 shows the accuracy of the JOINT model and the SELF baseline.

Note that here, unlike section 4.1, the joint inference is run once and then a model is trained for each language and evaluated on the corresponding test set(s).

The results support our intuition that joint inference helps improve the quality of the resulting annotations, at least in some cases.

4.4 Oracle RCM

It would be useful to know to what extent the performance of the role correspondence model affects the quality of the output (and thus the performance of the resulting model). The RCM we use is rather simplistic, and we believe it can be substantially improved for any given language pair by incorporating prior knowledge and/or using external sources of information. In order to estimate the potential impact of such improvements, we simulate a better informed projection model, giving it access to the predictions of more accurate monolingual models on the parallel data – those trained on the full training set, rather than the initial training set used in this particular experiment. We refer to the resulting RCM as *oracle* and assess the difference it makes, compared to a regular one (table 4).

	INIT	SELF	JOINT	Δ_{SELF}
en-cz*	67.07	66.15	68.18	**2.02**
en-cz	67.56	66.42	66.72	**0.30**
en-de*	67.64	66.72	68.57	1.84
en-de	75.13	71.97	73.57	**1.60**
en-es	68.14	67.80	69.04	**1.24**
en-zh	76.28	72.96	75.22	**2.26**
cz-en*	69.37	66.45	66.22	-0.23
cz-en	77.32	74.72	75.02	**0.31**
de-en*	69.37	66.45	66.68	0.23
de-en	77.32	73.56	73.72	0.17
es-en*	69.37	66.64	66.40	-0.23
es-en	77.32	74.05	74.89	**0.84**
zh-en*	69.37	66.08	65.53	-0.56
zh-en	77.32	74.48	74.25	-0.24

Table 3: Comparing JOINT model against the self-training baseline in symmetric setup. Asterisk indicates out-of-domain test set, statistically significant improvements are highlighted in bold.

5 Related Work

There is a number of approaches to semi-supervised semantic role labeling, and most suggest that some external supervision is required for such approaches to work (He and Gildea, 2006), such as measures of syntactic and semantic similarity (Fürstenau and Lapata, 2009) or external confidence measures (Goldwasser et al., 2011). The alternative we propose is primarily motivated by the research on annotation projection (Padó and Lapata, 2009; van der Plas et al., 2011; Annesi and Basili, 2010; Naseem et al., 2012) and direct transfer (Durrett et al., 2012; Søgaard, 2011; Lopez et al., 2008; McDonald et al., 2011). The key difference of the present approach compared to annotation projection is that we assume

	INIT	SELF	JOINT	Δ_{SELF}	Δ_{INIT}
en-cz*	61.11	60.68	72.49	**11.81**	**11.38**
en-cz	62.45	62.15	70.19	**8.04**	**7.74**
en-de*	66.81	63.96	76.78	**12.82**	**9.97**
en-de	70.39	68.34	79.22	**10.88**	**8.84**
en-es	64.20	64.51	75.43	**10.92**	**11.23**
en-zh	75.80	73.52	76.75	**3.22**	**0.94**
cz-en*	66.82	63.95	70.75	**6.80**	**3.93**
cz-en	74.93	71.60	79.70	**8.10**	**4.76**
de-en*	66.82	63.58	69.46	**5.88**	**2.64**
de-en	74.93	71.31	77.34	**6.03**	**2.41**
es-en*	66.82	63.95	69.92	**5.97**	**3.10**
es-en	74.93	71.47	79.55	**8.08**	**4.62**
zh-en*	66.82	64.51	67.19	**2.68**	0.37
zh-en	74.93	72.26	76.51	**4.26**	**1.58**

Table 4: Oracle RCM performance, projection setup: initial model, self-training baseline, refined model and its improvement over the other two. Asterisk indicates out-of-domain test set, statistically significant improvements are highlighted in bold.

the availability of some amount of training data for the target language, possibly using a different inventory of semantic roles.

As mentioned previously, from the training point of view this approach can be seen as similar to co-training (Blum and Mitchell, 1998), other applications of which to NLP are too numerous to list here.

Most closely related is the joint inference in Zhuang and Zong (2010), the main difference being that it relies on a manually annotated parallel corpus, aligned on the argument level, and evaluates only the inference procedure and only on in-domain data.

Other related approaches include Kim et al. (2010), where a cross-lingual transfer of relations is performed (which basically represent parts of the predicate-argument structure considered by SRL methods), and Frermann and Bond (2012), where semantic structure matching is used to rank HPSG parses for parallel sentences.

Unsupervised semantic role labeling methods (Lang and Lapata, 2010; Lang and Lapata, 2011; Titov and Klementiev, 2012a; Lorenzo and Cerisara, 2012) present an alternative to the cross-lingual information propagation approaches such as ours, and at least one the methods in this area also makes use of parallel data (Titov and Klementiev, 2012b).

Conclusions

We have presented an approach to information transfer between SRL systems for different language pairs using parallel data. The task proves challenging due to non-trivial mapping between the role labels used in different SRL annotation schemes and the nature of parallel data – the difference in domains and the limited accuracy of the preprocessing tools. We observe consistent improvements over self-training baseline from using joint inference and the experiments suggest that improving the role correspondence model, for example using language-specific prior knowledge or external data sources, may dramatically increase the performance of the resulting system.

Acknowledgments

The authors acknowledge the support of the MMCI Cluster of Excellence and thank Alexandre Klementiev and Manfred Pinkal for valuable suggestions.

References

Paolo Annesi and Roberto Basili. 2010. Cross-lingual alignment of framenet annotations through hidden markov models. In *Proceedings of the 11th international conference on Computational Linguistics and Intelligent Text Processing*, CICLing'10, pages 12–25, Berlin, Heidelberg. Springer-Verlag.

Collin F. Baker, Charles J. Fillmore, and John B. Lowe. 1998. The Berkeley FrameNet project. In *Proceedings of the Thirty-Sixth Annual Meeting of the Association for Computational Linguistics and Seventeenth International Conference on Computational Linguistics (ACL-COLING'98)*, pages 86–90, Montreal, Canada.

Anders Björkelund, Love Hafdell, and Pierre Nugues. 2009. Multilingual semantic role labeling. In *Proceedings of the Thirteenth Conference on Computational Natural Language Learning (CoNLL 2009): Shared Task*, pages 43–48, Boulder, Colorado, June. Association for Computational Linguistics.

Avrim Blum and Tom Mitchell. 1998. Combining labeled and unlabeled data with co-training. In *Proceedings of the Workshop on Computational Learning Theory (COLT 98)*.

Bernd Bohnet. 2010. Top accuracy and fast dependency parsing is not a contradiction. In *Proceedings of the 23rd International Conference on Computational Lin-*

guistics (Coling 2010), pages 89–97, Beijing, China, August. Coling 2010 Organizing Committee.

Aljoscha Burchardt, Katrin Erk, Anette Frank, Andrea Kowalski, Sebastian Pado, and Manfred Pinkal. 2006. The SALSA corpus: a German corpus resource for lexical semantics. In *Proceedings of LREC 2006*, Genoa, Italy.

M.W. Chang, L. Ratinov, and D. Roth. 2007. Guiding semi-supervision with constraint-driven learning. *Urbana*, 51:61801.

Pi-Chuan Chang, Michel Galley, and Christopher D. Manning. 2008. Optimizing chinese word segmentation for machine translation performance. In *Proceedings of the Third Workshop on Statistical Machine Translation*, StatMT '08, pages 224–232, Stroudsburg, PA, USA. Association for Computational Linguistics.

Greg Durrett, Adam Pauls, and Dan Klein. 2012. Syntactic transfer using a bilingual lexicon. In *Proceedings of the 2012 Joint Conference on Empirical Methods in Natural Language Processing and Computational Natural Language Learning*, pages 1–11, Jeju Island, Korea, July. Association for Computational Linguistics.

Andreas Eisele and Yu Chen. 2010. MultiUN: A multilingual corpus from united nation documents. In Nicoletta Calzolari (Conference Chair), Khalid Choukri, Bente Maegaard, Joseph Mariani, Jan Odijk, Stelios Piperidis, Mike Rosner, and Daniel Tapias, editors, *Proceedings of the Seventh International Conference on Language Resources and Evaluation (LREC'10)*, Valletta, Malta, May. European Language Resources Association (ELRA).

Rong-En Fan, Kai-Wei Chang, Cho-Jui Hsieh, Xiang-Rui Wang, and Chih-Jen Lin. 2008. LIBLINEAR: A library for large linear classification. *Journal of Machine Learning Research*, 9:1871–1874.

S. Francis and H. Kucera. 1967. *Computing Analysis of Present-day American English*. Brown University Press, Providence, RI.

Lea Frermann and Francis Bond. 2012. Cross-lingual parse disambiguation based on semantic correspondence. In *Proceedings of the 50th Annual Meeting of the Association for Computational Linguistics (Volume 2: Short Papers)*, pages 125–129, Jeju Island, Korea, July. Association for Computational Linguistics.

Hagen Fürstenau and Mirella Lapata. 2009. Graph alignment for semi-supervised semantic role labeling. In *Proceedings of the 2009 Conference on Empirical Methods in Natural Language Processing*, pages 11–20, Singapore.

D. Goldwasser, R. Reichart, J. Clarke, and D. Roth. 2011. Confidence driven unsupervised semantic parsing. In *ACL*.

P. Good. 2000. *Permutation Tests: A Practical Guide to Resampling Methods for Testing Hypotheses*. Springer.

J. Hajič, J. Panevová, E. Hajičová, P. Sgall, P. Pajas, J. Štěpánek, J. Havelka, M. Mikulová, Z. Žabokrtský, and M. Ševčíková-Razímová. 2006. Prague dependency treebank 2.0. *LDC*.

Jan Hajič, Massimiliano Ciaramita, Richard Johansson, Daisuke Kawahara, Maria Antònia Martí, Lluís Màrquez, Adam Meyers, Joakim Nivre, Sebastian Padó, Jan Štěpánek, Pavel Straňák, Mihai Surdeanu, Nianwen Xue, and Yi Zhang. 2009. The CoNLL-2009 shared task: Syntactic and semantic dependencies in multiple languages. In *Proceedings of the Thirteenth Conference on Computational Natural Language Learning (CoNLL 2009): Shared Task*, pages 1–18, Boulder, Colorado.

Jan Hajič, Eva Hajičová, Jarmila Panevová, Petr Sgall, Ondřej Bojar, Silvie Cinková, Eva Fučíková, Marie Mikulová, Petr Pajas, Jan Popelka, Jiří Semecký, Jana Šindlerová, Jan Štěpánek, Josef Toman, Zdeňka Urešová, and Zdeněk Žabokrtský. 2012. Announcing prague czech-english dependency treebank 2.0. In Nicoletta Calzolari (Conference Chair), Khalid Choukri, Thierry Declerck, Mehmet Uğur Doğan, Bente Maegaard, Joseph Mariani, Jan Odijk, and Stelios Piperidis, editors, *Proceedings of the Eight International Conference on Language Resources and Evaluation (LREC'12)*, Istanbul, Turkey, May. European Language Resources Association (ELRA).

Shan He and Daniel Gildea. 2006. Self-training and co-training for semantic role labeling: Primary report. Technical report, University of Rochester.

Jena D. Hwang, Rodney D. Nielsen, and Martha Palmer. 2010. Towards a domain independent semantics: Enhancing semantic representation with construction grammar. In *Proceedings of the NAACL HLT Workshop on Extracting and Using Constructions in Computational Linguistics*, pages 1–8, Los Angeles, California, June. Association for Computational Linguistics.

Seokhwan Kim, Minwoo Jeong, Jonghoon Lee, and Gary Geunbae Lee. 2010. A cross-lingual annotation projection approach for relation detection. In *Proceedings of the 23rd International Conference on Computational Linguistics*, COLING '10, pages 564–571, Stroudsburg, PA, USA. Association for Computational Linguistics.

Philipp Koehn. 2005. Europarl: A Parallel Corpus for Statistical Machine Translation. In *Conference Proceedings: the tenth Machine Translation Summit*, pages 79–86, Phuket, Thailand. AAMT, AAMT.

Joel Lang and Mirella Lapata. 2010. Unsupervised induction of semantic roles. In *Human Language Tech-*

nologies: The 2010 Annual Conference of the North American Chapter of the Association for Computational Linguistics, pages 939–947, Los Angeles, California, June. Association for Computational Linguistics.

Joel Lang and Mirella Lapata. 2011. Unsupervised semantic role induction via split-merge clustering. In *Proc. of Annual Meeting of the Association for Computational Linguistics (ACL)*.

Adam Lopez, Daniel Zeman, Michael Nossal, Philip Resnik, and Rebecca Hwa. 2008. Cross-Language Parser Adaptation between Related Languages. In *IJCNLP-08 Workshop on NLP for Less Privileged Languages*, pages 35–42, Hyderabad, India, January.

Alejandra Lorenzo and Christophe Cerisara. 2012. Unsupervised frame based semantic role induction: application to french and english. In *Proceedings of the ACL 2012 Joint Workshop on Statistical Parsing and Semantic Processing of Morphologically Rich Languages*, pages 30–35, Jeju, Republic of Korea, July 12. Association for Computational Linguistics.

Ryan McDonald, Slav Petrov, and Keith Hall. 2011. Multi-source transfer of delexicalized dependency parsers. In *Proceedings of the Conference on Empirical Methods in Natural Language Processing*, EMNLP '11, pages 62–72, Stroudsburg, PA, USA. Association for Computational Linguistics.

Paola Merlo and Matthias Leybold. 2001. Automatic distinction of arguments and modifiers: the case of prepositional phrases. In *Proceedings of the Fifth Computational Natural Language Learning Workshop (CoNLL-2001)*, pages 121–128, Toulouse, France.

Tahira Naseem, Regina Barzilay, and Amir Globerson. 2012. Selective sharing for multilingual dependency parsing. In *Proceedings of the 50th Annual Meeting of the Association for Computational Linguistics (Volume 1: Long Papers)*, pages 629–637, Jeju Island, Korea, July. Association for Computational Linguistics.

Franz Josef Och and Hermann Ney. 2003. A systematic comparison of various statistical alignment models. *Computational Linguistics*, 29(1).

Sebastian Padó and Mirella Lapata. 2005. Cross-linguistic projection of role-semantic information. In *Proceedings of Human Language Technology Conference and Conference on Empirical Methods in Natural Language Processing*, pages 859–866, Vancouver, British Columbia, Canada.

Sebastian Padó and Mirella Lapata. 2009. Cross-lingual annotation projection for semantic roles. *Journal of Artificial Intelligence Research*, 36:307–340.

Martha Palmer, Daniel Gildea, and Paul Kingsbury. 2005a. The Proposition Bank: An annotated corpus of semantic roles. *Computational Linguistics*, 31:71–105.

Martha Palmer, Nianwen Xue, Olga Babko-Malaya, Jinying Chen, and Benjamin Snyder. 2005b. A parallel Proposition Bank II for Chinese and English. In *Proceedings of the Workshop on Frontiers in Corpus Annotations II: Pie in the Sky*, CorpusAnno '05, pages 61–67, Stroudsburg, PA, USA. Association for Computational Linguistics.

Sameer S. Pradhan, Wayne Ward, and James H. Martin. 2008. Towards robust semantic role labeling. *Computational Linguistics*, 34(2):289–310.

Dan Roth and Wen-tau Yih. 2005. Integer linear programming inference for conditional random fields. In *ICML*, pages 736–743.

Anders Søgaard. 2011. Data point selection for cross-language adaptation of dependency parsers. In *Proceedings of the 49th Annual Meeting of the Association for Computational Linguistics: Human Language Technologies: short papers - Volume 2*, HLT '11, pages 682–686, Stroudsburg, PA, USA. Association for Computational Linguistics.

David Sontag, Amir Globerson, and Tommi Jaakkola. 2011. Introduction to dual decomposition for inference. In Suvrit Sra, Sebastian Nowozin, and Stephen J. Wright, editors, *Optimization for Machine Learning*. MIT Press.

Ivan Titov and Alexandre Klementiev. 2012a. A Bayesian approach to unsupervised semantic role induction. In *Proc. of European Chapter of the Association for Computational Linguistics (EACL)*.

Ivan Titov and Alexandre Klementiev. 2012b. Crosslingual induction of semantic roles. In *Proceedings of the 50th Annual Meeting of the Association for Computational Linguistics*, Jeju Island, South Korea, July. Association for Computational Linguistics.

Lonneke van der Plas, Paola Merlo, and James Henderson. 2011. Scaling up automatic cross-lingual semantic role annotation. In *Proceedings of the 49th Annual Meeting of the Association for Computational Linguistics: Human Language Technologies: short papers - Volume 2*, HLT '11, pages 299–304, Stroudsburg, PA, USA. Association for Computational Linguistics.

Tao Zhuang and Chengqing Zong. 2010. Joint inference for bilingual semantic role labeling. In *Proceedings of the 2010 Conference on Empirical Methods in Natural Language Processing*, EMNLP '10, pages 304–314, Stroudsburg, PA, USA. Association for Computational Linguistics.

Semantic Parsing Freebase: Towards Open-domain Semantic Parsing

Qingqing Cai
Temple University
Computer and Information Sciences
qingqing.cai@temple.edu

Alexander Yates
Temple University
Computer and Information Sciences
yates@temple.edu

Abstract

Existing semantic parsing research has steadily improved accuracy on a few domains and their corresponding databases. This paper introduces FreeParser, a system that trains on one domain and one set of predicate and constant symbols, and then can parse sentences for any new domain, including sentences that refer to symbols never seen during training. FreeParser uses a domain-independent architecture to automatically identify sentences relevant to each new database symbol, which it uses to supplement its manually-annotated training data from the training domain. In cross-domain experiments involving 23 domains, FreeParser can parse sentences for which it has seen comparable unannotated sentences with an F1 of 0.71.

1 Introduction

Semantic parsing is the task of converting a sentence into a representation of its meaning, usually in a logical form grounded in the symbols of some fixed ontology or relational database (Zelle and Mooney, 1996; Zettlemoyer and Collins, 2005; Kate and Mooney, 2006). A growing body of research on semantic parsing has yielded consistent improvements in parsing accuracy. Yet existing semantic parsers have always been limited by the need for significant amounts of manually-annotated training data for each domain of discourse, or for each new database. As a result, current semantic parsers have been constrained to small domains, like answering geography questions.

In an effort to break out of these narrowly-constrained domains, we investigate semantic parsers for Freebase, an online database of user-contributed facts divided into 86 domains, including everything from architecture to zoos. Freebase is much larger than standard benchmark databases for semantic parsing; for example, it contains 300 times as many relations, and 75,000 times as many instances, as the GeoQuery database. On average, the benchmark GeoQuery dataset has 125 training sentences per relation. An equivalent dataset for Freebase would require labeling close to 40,000 training sentences, an expensive undertaking.

The size and diversity of data in Freebase forces us to consider a new task of *open-domain* semantic parsing. We introduce FreeParser, which trains on labeled examples from a select group of initial domains. It also uses the information in Freebase to automatically find unlabeled training sentences from Wikipedia for every Freebase relation. Using a self-supervised architecture, FreeParser automatically labels these sentences, and then trains a semantic parser for all of Freebase. The current restriction to Wikipedia has a downside: 44% of the test questions in our dataset contained a word that never appeared in our set of automatically-collected sentences, suggesting that significant further gains could be had by scaling to a larger corpus. However, FreeParser is able to find correct parses for 70% of the questions from new domains where it could find relevant sentences in Wikipedia, at a precision of 72%.

The next section provides background on semantic parsing for Freebase, and discusses related work. Section 3 describes the main modules of the FreeParser system. Section 4 analyzes the performance of FreeParser on an open-domain semantic parsing task. Section 5 concludes.

*Second Joint Conference on Lexical and Computational Semantics (*SEM), Volume 1: Proceedings of the Main Conference and the Shared Task*, pages 328–338, Atlanta, Georgia, June 13-14, 2013.

domain	num. queries	% of total
film	49	12
business	46	11
tv	34	8
location	32	8
award	32	8
people	30	7
medicine	25	6
organization	24	6
finance	21	5
book	21	5
et al.	89	22
total	403	100

Table 1: **Breakdown of our Freebase data set into domains.** Several questions used symbols from multiple Freebase domains, in which cases human judges selected the best domain they could for that question's category.

	Examples
1.	What are the neighborhoods in New York City? λx . $\texttt{neighborhoods}(\texttt{new\_york}, x)$
2.	How many countries use the rupee? $\texttt{count}(x)$. $\texttt{countries\_used}(\texttt{rupee}, x)$
3.	How many Peabody Award winners are there? $\texttt{count}(x)$. $\exists y$. $\texttt{award\_honor}(y) \wedge \texttt{award\_winner}(y, x) \wedge \texttt{award}(y, \texttt{peabody\_award})$

Figure 1: **Example questions with their logical forms.**

2 Background and Previous Work

2.1 Freebase Dataset

Freebase is a free, online, user-contributed, relational database (www.freebase.com) covering many different domains of knowledge. The full schema and contents are available for download.

Freebase has a number of advantages for building an open-domain semantic parser. Most obviously, it provides a much tougher test for semantic parsing than traditional benchmark databases like GeoQuery. It also provides a testbed for semantic parsing across domains. As a reference point, the GeoQuery database contains a single domain (geography), 8 relations, and 698 total instances. The "Freebase Commons" subset of Freebase, which is our focus, consists of 86 domains, an average of 25 relations per domain (total of 2134 relations), and 615,000 known instances per domain (53 million instances total). By dividing Freebase into different sub-databases according to domain, we can readily test the portability of our parser across domains, and its ability to handle relations and symbols that never occur in manually-labeled training data.

Our dataset contains 403 questions and a meaning representation for each question, written in a variant of lambda calculus[1]. We believe the dataset in itself is an important contribution to the field, as it provides a testbed for semantic parsing across multiple domains. Several examples are listed in Fig. 1, and Table 1 provides a breakdown of the domains in our data. The questions were provided by two native English speakers, one high school student and one computer science undergraduate student. Each contributor was introduced to the Freebase website, and asked to come up with English questions that they would like to have answered. No restrictions were placed on the type of questions they should produce, except that they should produce questions for multiple domains. 23 domains are represented in the data set. Inspection of the dataset indicates that most questions have relatively simple and regular syntax, compared with the more complex constructions observed in datasets like GeoQuery. Collecting more complex questions for open-domain tests is an ongoing project, but the existing dataset is already a significant challenge for current semantic parsing learning algorithms.

2.2 Challenges for a Freebase Semantic Parser

To provide a benchmark for comparison, we applied the PCCG-based semantic parser called UBL, developed by Kwiatkowski *et al.* (2010). Source code for UBL is freely available. Its authors found that it achieves results competitive with the state-of-the-art on a variety of standard semantic parsing data sets, including Geo250 English (0.85 F1). Using a fixed CCG grammar and a procedure based on unification in second-order logic, UBL learns a lexicon Λ from the training data which includes entries like:

[1]The data is available from the second author's webpage.

Example Lexical Entries

New York City $\vdash NP$: new_york
neighborhoods in $\vdash$
$S\backslash NP/NP : \lambda x \lambda y.\texttt{neighborhoods}(x, y)$

Example CCG Grammar Rules

$X/Y : f \quad Y : g \Rightarrow X : f(g)$
$Y : g \quad X\backslash Y : f \Rightarrow X : f(g)$

Using Λ, UBL selects a logical form z for a sentence S by selecting the z with the most likely parse derivations y: $h(S) = \arg\max_z \sum_y p(y, z|x; \theta, \Lambda)$. The probabilistic model is a log-linear model with features for lexical entries used in the parse, as well as indicator features for relation-argument pairs in the logical form, to capture selectional preferences. Inference (parsing) and parameter estimation are driven by standard dynamic programming algorithms (Clark and Curran, 2007; Wilks et al., 1990), using a context-free, combinatory categorial grammar that includes rules for forward application and composition.

In a standard experimental setup on our dataset, UBL provides an F1 of 0.35. We took a random split of 70% of the data for training, 30% for test. An F1 of 0.35 is significantly worse than UBL's performance on GeoQuery data (F1 of 0.85) but within the bounds of reason, given that our data has over 200 relation symbols that need to be learned using less than 300 training sentences, compared with the 8 relations and 250 sentences that make up the Geo250 English dataset.

However, UBL is not designed for open-domain semantic parsing, and after training on the training set above, it is not be able to handle questions for any of the remaining 63 domains in Freebase. In open-domain tests, it achieves an F1 of 0.0, and for most sentences, it cannot produce a parse. As one example, we created a test set from the business and finance domains, and separated the remaining domains for training. Every test example has a predicate symbol that has never been observed before in training. The F1 of 0.0 on this dataset is not a fault of UBL, but rather it shows the difficulty of the task. Porting a system across domains often results in substantial loss of accuracy for many natural language processing tasks (Huang et al., 2011), but usually the drop in accuracy is no more than 10-20%. Open-domain semantic parsing is an even starker challenge; it involves not just new natural language words in the new domains, but also new database symbols, which existing technology cannot handle.

2.3 Previous Work

Krishnamurthy and Mitchell (2012) also create a semantic parser for Freebase, covering 77 of Freebase's over 2000 relations. Like our work, their technique uses distant supervision to drive training over a collection of sentences gathered from the Web, and they do not require any manually-labeled training data. However, their technique does require manual specification of rules that construct CCG lexical entries from dependency parses. In comparison, we fully automate the process of constructing CCG lexical entries for the semantic parser by making it a learning task. We test our results on a dataset of over 400 questions covering over 200 Freebase relations, a more extensive test than the 50 questions used by Krishnamurthy and Mitchell.

Yahya *et al.* (2012) report on a system for translating natural language queries to SPARQL queries over the Yago2 (Hoffart et al., 2013) database. Yago2 consists of information extracted from Wikipedia, WordNet, and other resources using manually-defined extraction patterns. The manual extraction patterns pre-define a link between natural language terms and Yago2 relations. Our techniques automate the process of identifying matches between textual phrases and database relation symbols, in order to scale up to databases with more relations, like Freebase. A more minor difference between Yahya *et al.*'s work and ours is that their system handles SPARQL queries, which do not handle aggregation queries like argmax and count. We rely on an existing semantic parsing technology to learn the language that will translate into such aggregation queries. On the other hand, their test questions involve more conjunctions and complex semantics than ours. Developing a dataset with more complicated semantics in the queries is part of our ongoing efforts.

Goldwasser *et al.*'s self-supervised, grounded semantic parser (2011) relies on co-training between two different semantic parsing models, one being a simple machine-translation model and the other a more complex structured-prediction model. They achieve an impressive F1 of 0.66 on the benchmark GeoQuery 250 (English) dataset, compared with state-of-the-art supervised models that achieve accuracies around 0.85. Unlike semantic parsers for Freebase, Goldwasser *et al.*'s work assumes that a dataset of unlabeled geography questions already exists, for use in unsupervised training. FreeParser answers orthogonal questions: how can we automatically acquire a dataset containing the right keywords and phrases, given only the database itself, and how can we ensure that the acquired sentences are relevant to the relations in the database, without manual supervision? Also, unlike Goldwasser *et al.*'s experiments, FreeParser is tested in a significantly more challenging setting, with far more domains, relations, and entities to be learned.

Many supervised learning frameworks have been applied, including inductive logic programming (Zelle and Mooney, 1996; Thompson and Mooney, 1999; Thompson and Mooney, 2003), support vector machine-based kernel approaches (Kate et al., 2005; Kate and Mooney, 2006; Kate and Mooney, 2007), machine translation-style synchronous grammars (Wong and Mooney, 2007), and context-free grammar-based approaches like probabilistic Combinatory Categorial Grammar (Zettlemoyer and Collins, 2005; Zettlemoyer and Collins, 2007; Zettlemoyer and Collins, 2009; Kwiatkowski et al., 2010; Kwiatkowski et al., 2011; Lu et al., 2008) and discriminative reranking (Ge and Mooney, 2006; Ge and Mooney, 2009). These approaches have yielded steady improvements on standard test sets like GeoQuery, but are difficult to apply to Freebase because of their built-in assumption that relation symbols will be observed during training.

There has been a recent push towards developing techniques which reduce the annotation cost or the data complexity of the models. Models have been developed which can handle some ambiguity in terms of which logical form is the correct label for each training sentence (Chen et al., 2010; Liang et al., 2009). Another set of approaches has investigated the case where no logical forms are provided, but instead some form of feedback or response from the world is used as evidence for what the correct logical form must have been (Clarke et al., 2010; Liang et al., 2011; Artzi and Zettlemoyer, 2011). While such techniques are important, they can only reduce the annotation cost *per domain*, and annotation efforts would still be required for each new domain that contains new database symbols. The goal of the Freebase semantic parser, in contrast, is to port to all domains automatically, without any new manually-labeled data per domain.

TV domain	**program**	**actor**	**role**
cast member table	Party Down	Ryan Hansen	Kyle Bradway
Architecture domain	**structure**	**owner**	
ownership table	CN Tower	Canada Lands Co.	
Physics domain	**particle**	**sub-particle**	**number**
particle composition	Proton	Up Quark	2

Figure 2: **Example Freebase relations (tables) and instances for three domains.**

3 FreeParser

We introduce FreeParser, an automated system for converting natural language sentences into representations of their meaning, where the relation and constant symbols for the meaning representations are taken from Freebase. FreeParser's modules are described below.

Sentence Retrieval Engine: This module constructs keyword queries for sentences that are likely to express the same relationships as the ones observed in Freebase. It uses an index over a large corpus, currently a snapshot of English Wikipedia, to identify sentences that match the query. Each sentence, along with the Freebase relation r and query q that generated it, is then fed to the Auto-Labeler.

Auto-Labeler: The Auto-Labeler uses knowledge of the relation and query for a sentence to automatically generate a simple logical form for the sentence. The automatically-labeled sentences are then sent to the Assessor.

Assessor: Using a set of domain-independent features, the Assessor filters out sentences that are unsuitable for training the semantic parser. These include sentences that are too long or complex, and sentences where the label from the Auto-Labeler appears to be incorrect. The sentences that pass this filter are added to the training data for FreeParser's semantic parser.

Open-domain Regularizer: FreeParser relies on an existing semantic parser, but with a novel regularizer that helps it learn more appropriate lexical entries for domain-independent function words.

3.1 Sentence Retrieval Engine

The Sentence Retrieval Engine is FreeParser's open-domain technique for retrieving sentences from a

Input: Freebase relation r, unlabeled corpus C
Output: $Sent$, a set of sentences relevant to r

1. Initialize $Sent \leftarrow \emptyset$
2. $E \leftarrow M$ random instances from r, each projected onto two random attributes
3. $E' \leftarrow N$ pairs $(e_1, e_2) \in E$ with smallest $relation\text{-}count(e_1, e_2)$
4. **For each** $(e_1, e_2) \in E'$:
   $S2 \leftarrow \{$sentences in C containing e_1 and $e_2\}$
   $S1 \leftarrow \{$sents containing e_2, in docs with $e_1\}$
   $Sent \leftarrow Sent \cup S1 \cup S2$
5. **Return** $Sent$

Figure 3: **The Sentence Retrieval Engine algorithm**

corpus that are relevant to a particular relation in the database.

Definition *relevance*: We say that a sentence s is relevant to a relation r in Freebase if there exist database symbols $a_1, \ldots, a_k$ such that $r(a_1, \ldots, a_k)$ appears in Freebase, and $r(a_1, \ldots, a_k)$ forms part of the meaning of s, if the meaning were written in a logical form.

For example, for the `cast member` relation in the Freebase sample shown in Figure 2, the sentence

> Hansen also played Kyle Bradway on the Starz show Party Down.

would be relevant, since the sentence expresses a known instance of `cast member`.

Of course, the corpus given as input to the Sentence Retrieval Engine contains only sentences, not the logical forms required to determine relevance according to our definition. FreeParser's strategy is to generate keyword queries that list several named entities that belong to a particular relation. For instance, one query that the Sentence Retrieval Engine might generate for the `cast member` relation is "Ryan Hansen Kyle Bradway," and another might be "Kyle Bradway Party Down."

Figure 3 shows the algorithm for the Sentence Retrieval Engine. In our experiments, we create $M = 1000$ candidate entity pairs, and we select $N = 50$ for queries. We use the open-source Apache Lucene software for constructing an index over the Wikipedia corpus and retrieving relevant sentences.

We have found that selecting good queries is in fact quite tricky, and our experiments in Section 4.4 indicate how badly things can go wrong if it is not done carefully. Two important lessons stand out: First, for reasonable recall, we limit queries to just one or two names. Queries with two names (we call these 2-entity queries) are very often highly relevant, but there are not enough sentences in Wikipedia that match such queries for all relations. We therefore also include queries (which we refer to as 1-entity queries) that first identify Wikipedia articles for one name from a relation, such as articles that mention "Ryan Hansen", and then within this resulting document set, we select sentences that match a second name, such as "Party Down". The resulting sentences therefore always contain one name from the relation, and appear near (within the same document as) a second name. These sentences are noisier than sentences selected with two names, but there are far more matches of such sentences within Wikipedia.

The second lesson for sentence retrieval is that we need to select queries that are not ambiguous. For instance, "James Cameron Avatar" retrieves many sentences for the relation `directed by`. Unfortunately, this same query also produces many sentences for the relations `written by` and `won award for`. The two entities are not enough to unambiguously identify the relationship between them. To combat this problem, FreeParser scores candidate queries according to $relation\text{-}count$, the number of relations in Freebase that hold between the names in the query, and keeps the top-N least ambiguous queries, breaking ties randomly.

3.2 Auto-Labeler

The Auto-Labeler automatically generates a logical form label for every sentence in our data set. It provides a form of "distant supervision" (Bunescu and Mooney, 2007). As an example, if the sentence above were generated from the `cast member` relation using the query "Hansen Bradway", and "Hansen" and "Bradway" are names for the database symbols `Ryan Hansen` and `Kyle Bradway`, then the Auto-Labeler produces $\exists_p$`cast member(`p`,Ryan Hansen,Kyle Bradway)` as a label for the sentence. The existentially quantified p variable is necessary to supply enough arguments for the `cast member` relation.

For the general case, let s be a sentence generated from a relation r of arity n via queries involving the entities $\mathbf{e} = (e_1, \ldots, e_m)$, and let $\mathbf{a} = (a_1, \ldots, a_m)$ be the sequence of attribute indices of r such that

Input: auto-labeled sentences S for relation r
Output: $S' \subset S$, a high-quality training dataset

1. **For each** $(s, l) \in S$:
   $C[s, l] \leftarrow \textit{complexity-score}(s, l)$
2. Sort S in descending order according to C
3. $T \leftarrow$ top 100 examples from S
4. $CW \leftarrow \textit{critical-words}(T)$
5. $\textit{result} \leftarrow \emptyset$
6. **For each** $cw \in CW$:
   $S_{cw} \leftarrow$ top two $(s, l) \in (S - \textit{result})$
   such that s contains cw
   $\textit{result} \leftarrow \textit{result} \cup S_{cw}$
7. **Return** $\textit{result}$

Figure 4: **The Assessor algorithm**

e_i is a value for r's attribute a_i. The Auto-Labeler produces the following logical form for s:

$$\exists v_1, \ldots v_n \text{ s.t. } r(v_1, \ldots, v_n) \wedge$$
$$v_{a_1} = e_1 \wedge \ldots \wedge v_{a_m} = e_m$$

3.3 Assessor

Automatically retrieving training sentences from an unlabeled corpus is a noisy process. In order to improve its precision, FreeParser automatically assesses whether each sentence from the Sentence Retrieval Engine is relevant and useful for training. Its goal is to select, for each relation r, a set of sentences that are all structurally simple; that include a variety of ways of expressing r in English; and that do not include any sentences about other relations r'. The full Assessor algorithm is given in Figure 4.

The Assessor uses two sources of evidence. The first is the complexity of the sentence. After experimenting with numerous features for measuring complexity, we have found that a few types of word counts are the most helpful. Specifically, the most helpful features include: the number of words between two named entities (for two-entity queries), the number of words before the named entity that was part of the query (for one-entity queries), and the total number of non-named-entity, non-stopword words in the sentence. Our implementation uses a list of 200 common stopwords. We trained a maximum-entropy classifier over the complexity features to predict the probability that a sentence is simple enough for training. We manually labeled a small sample of 50 sentences, which were retrieved for relations not found in any of our test sentences. Sentences that truly expressed the relations in the logical form and no other relation were labeled as positive, and all others were labeled negative. The Assessor uses the probability from this classifier to rank all sentences for a relation, and selects the top 100 sentences for further processing.

Complexity statistics alone are not sufficient for selecting good training sentences. For instance, "'Being Spiderman is a dream come true,' says Andrew Garfield" is a short sentence mentioning two entities that participate in the `acted in` relation. However, none of the words in the sentence are particularly indicative of `acted in`, and if FreeParser were to use this as a training sentence, it would most likely learn a wrong lexical entry.

The Assessor additionally weeds out sentences which do not include words strongly associated with a database relation. Previous work has used statistical machine translation models like IBM Model 1 (Brown et al., 1993) as a method for initially determining which words should be associated with which database symbols. After experimenting with this and other models, as implemented in GIZA++ (Och and Ney, 2003), we have found that a simpler procedure is more effective for finding the words which are most indicative of a database relation. Taking the set T of top 100 sentences for r from the complexity ranker, we preprocess the sentences by discarding stopwords and applying stemming. We then count all the remaining word types $v \in V$ appearing in T, and rank them by frequency. We select the top K as word stems that are highly indicative of relation r; we call these word stems the *critical words* for r. For example, for the relation `date founded`, this technique produces the critical words "found," "establish," and "settl," among others. Sentences which do not contain some variant of one of these critical words are unlikely to be good training examples. To obtain a set of diverse but relevant sentences, the Assessor selects at most two sentences for each of the K critical words, taking care not to select any sentence twice. In practice we found that using more than 2 sentences per critical word has no effect on parsing accuracy, but slows the parser training procedure significantly. We tuned K on development data, and set it to $K = 7$.

Example lexical entries for "is" learned by UBL
$S\|NP : \lambda x\,.\,\mathtt{religion}(x)$
$S\|NP\|NP : \lambda x \lambda y\,.\,\mathtt{person}(x) \wedge$ $\mathtt{appearance\_type}(x, \mathtt{newscaster})$
$S\|NP\|NP : \lambda x \lambda y\,.\,\mathtt{brand}(x, y) \wedge$ $\mathtt{company\_brand\_relationship}(x)$

Table 2: **Overly-specific lexical entries for the function word "is," as learned by a state-of-the-art PCCG semantic parser on our Freebase data set.** All entries shown have significant positive weight in the learned lexicon.

3.4 Initializing the Lexicon for Learning a Semantic Parser

Existing semantic parsing technology requires some initial knowledge in order to learn a full parser. Typically, this knowledge includes lexical entries for named entities and the database symbols to which they correspond, a small number of additional entries for important function words, and a procedure for initializing the weights for learned lexical entries. For instance, UBL uses GIZA++ (Och and Ney, 2003) to initialize the weight of learned lexical entries.

FreeParser includes initial lexical entries for all named entities in our dataset, as well as 29 hand-crafted lexical entries for the words "who," "what," "when," and "where." These helped to combat the problem of learning a semantic parser from small numbers of questions and large numbers of automatically-retrieved sentences that were almost all declarative statements rather than questions. Following Kwiatkowski *et al.*, these hand-crafted lexical entries are assigned a fixed positive initial weight of 10. We found the following procedure more effective than GIZA++ for initializing the lexicon weights for learned lexical entries in practice: for each critical word and relation pair (v, r) in the sentences from the Assessor, we found a maximum likelihood estimate of $P(v|r)$, the probability of observing the critical word v, given that a sentence expresses the relation r. We then created initial learned lexical entries that pair v and r, with a weight equal to $P(v|r)$.

3.5 New Learning Component for Semantic Parsing: An Open-Domain Regularizer

Training FreeParser's semantic parsing component on the automatically-labeled sentences, as the system has been described thus far, results in disappointing performance. This is in large part because the UBL semantic parser learns highly domain-specific meanings for function words. Table 2 shows example lexical entries learned for the word "is". These types of learned meanings are the rule, not the exception, in the existing semantic parser. For single-domain tests, they pose no particular difficulties, even though intuitively they are bad representations of the meaning of a function word. For open-domain semantic parsing, however, it becomes nearly impossible to parse sentences correctly on a new domain, if the only meanings for function words include relations from training domains.

To overcome this problem, we devised a novel regularization technique to encourage the parser to learn domain-independent meanings for function words. Unlike most of FreeParser, this technique is specific to the log-linear CCG semantic parsing technique used by Kwiatkowski *et al.* However, similar mechanisms could potentially be devised for other semantic parsing frameworks. The Kwiatkowski *et al.* model includes a feature function $f_{w,l}$ for every lexical entry mapping a word w to a logical form l. Our novel regularizer $R(\cdot)$ over the parameters θ, which we call an *open-domain regularizer*, penalizes parameters for lexical entries mapping function words to any domain-specific lambda calculus expression. Formally, let F be a set of function words, and P a set of domain-specific predicates from Freebase:

$$R(\theta) = \sum_{w,l} \begin{cases} \theta_{w,l}^2 & \text{if } w \in F \wedge \exists p \in P . p \in l \\ 0 & \text{otherwise.} \end{cases}$$

In our implementation, we added all relations in Freebase that are not part of its `common` domain to P, and collected a set of 282 common English function words for F.

4 Experiments

We now test FreeParser's ability to provide semantic parses in domains where it has seen no manually-labeled training data. We also empirically analyze the design decisions for FreeParser.

4.1 Experimental Setup

All of our experiments are conducted on the Freebase dataset described in Section 2.1. To create

Q: *What is 'Big Daddy' rated?* Movie ratings are stored as special codes in Freebase, and are rarely observed 'as is' in text.
Q: *Who is the CEO of Apple?* Wikipedia regularly uses the full form 'Chief Executive Officer'; no retrieved sentence had 'CEO' together with the executive's name and company name.
Q: *When did Jack Albertson die?* Many sentences contain "$person$ died on $date$", but no retrieved sentence contained the morphological variant "(did) die."

Table 3: Example infeasible questions, and why FreeParser had difficulty finding sentences in Wikipedia that contain the relevant keywords from the question.

manually-labeled training and test sets for domain adaptation, we divide the dataset into three groups of nearly-equal size by placing similar domains together in the same group. No domain has questions in more than one group. We then perform 3-fold cross-validation across these three groups. We run FreeParser's Sentence Retrieval Engine, Auto-Labeler, and Assessor for all relations that appear in our dataset, and we include the automatically-labeled data in the training data.

4.2 Testing the Sentence Retrieval Engine

179 of the 403 questions (44%) in our dataset included critical words which could not be found using the Sentence Retrieval Engine's queries over Wikipedia. Table 3 lists example infeasible questions. One obvious improvement is to open the retrieval engine to sentences from the Web, for greater recall; this is an important task for future work. For now, this is FreeParser's biggest source of errors. However, note that without this component, the semantic parser parses none of the test data correctly.

4.3 Open-domain semantic parsing tests

We now turn to an experiment that assesses the full FreeParser system on open-domain semantic parsing. For the current experiments, we concentrate on the 224 questions (56% of the full dataset) for which all of the words (except named entities) could be found in at least one of the auto-labeled sentences returned by the Sentence Retrieval Engine. We call these 224 questions the *feasible* questions. For the remaining infeasible questions, FreeParser almost never produces a correct logical form.

Figure 5 shows FreeParser's performance on feasible questions in all test domains, as well as for each of the seven most-common test domains. FreeParser performs quite well, achieving an overall F1 of 0.71, which represents a huge improvement over the F1 of 0.0 for the supervised UBL semantic parser in a domain adaptation setting. An unsupervised parser, which uses only the initial lexical entries from FreeParser and the auto-labeled training data, achieves an F1 of 0.43. Precision and recall differences between FreeParser and these two baselines are statistically significant ($p < 0.01$) using Fisher's exact test. Including both feasible and infeasible questions, FreeParser's F1 is 0.37 because of the low recall on infeasible questions, but as more unlabeled text becomes available to FreeParser, it should have fewer and fewer infeasible questions.

4.4 Testing Critical Design Components

We tested FreeParser with different choices for key parts of the design, to measure their impact. Table 4 presents precision, recall, and F1 scores for four variations of FreeParser, where each variation is missing a critical component of the design. In the first variation, the Sentence Retrieval Engine only issues two-entity queries; it is missing the ability to issue the less-precise single-entity queries. In the second variation, the Assessor uses only the critical words to select sentences for training; it is missing the ability to rank sentences based on their complexity. In the third variation, the Assessor selects the top $2K$, or 14, sentences based on the complexity ranking; it ignores the critical words test. Finally, the last variation shows FreeParser's performance when UBL's training procedure has not been modified with the open-domain regularizer.

Deleting any one of these critical design elements substantially degrades FreeParser's performance, but the 1-entity queries appear to be the most critical design choice, followed by the critical words test and open-domain regularizer. Removing the 1-entity queries surprisingly hurts both precision and recall. The 2-entity queries do tend to retrieve better sentences on average than 1-entity queries, but because they retrieve so few, the Assessor has more difficulty selecting good critical words.

Error analysis showed that incorrect or missing

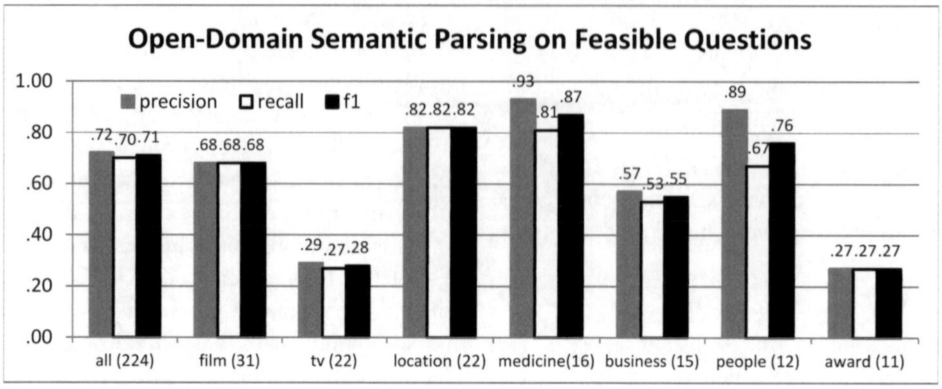

Figure 5: **FreeParser achieves an overall F1 of 0.71, in a test where every correct logical form has some element never seen in manually-labeled training data.** Results across different domains vary, but FreeParser performs well in a variety of domains. Numbers next to domain labels indicate the number of feasible test questions. Results for "all" domains are the micro-average across our three cross-validation folds.

Model	P	R	F1
−1-entity queries	.29	.29	.29
−complexity ranking	.59	.53	.56
−critical words test	.47	.41	.44
−open-domain regul.	.50	.45	.47
FreeParser	**.72**	**.70**	**.71**

Table 4: **FreeParser compared with variations that are missing critical design components.** All precision and recall differences between the full system and its variations are statistically significant ($p < 0.01$) using a two-tailed Fisher's exact test.

lexical entries for critical words were responsible for most (68%) of the 67 incorrect or missing parses for feasible test questions. Many of the incorrect entries mapped critical words like "directed" to related but incorrect predicates, like `written by`. Missing lexical entries were often because the Assessor incorrectly weeded out good auto-labeled examples. The remaining 32% of the errors were mostly due to complex syntax in the questions, or vague questions that require significant reasoning to come up with a valid interpretation.

5 Conclusion and Future Work

Most work on semantic parsing focuses on improving parser accuracy on a small number of relations in a single domain. FreeParser is an exploration of the possibility of automated semantic parsing for arbitrary domains. Among the lessons from our experience in designing FreeParser, these stand out: First, finding training sentences that cover all of the different ways a person may refer to a database element is difficult, and requires carefully constructed retrieval mechanisms for sufficient recall. Second, simple measures of sentence complexity and cooccurrence statistics are effective techniques for identifying good training sentences. And third, standard semantic parsing algorithms require modification for open-domain semantic parsing, to enforce that function words are not mapped to domain-specific logical forms. We report results that help in understanding FreeParser's current strengths and weaknesses, and that also serve as a baseline for future open-domain semantic parsers.

Significant work remains: ideally, a system would be able to incorporate relational data from multiple schemas, and could leverage much larger corpora for learning alignments. Also, FreeParser currently maps English words only to individual Freebase symbols; more sophisticated algorithms and representations are necessary for learning how to map to conjunctions, disjunctions, and more complex combinations of Freebase symbols.

Acknowledgements

This material is based upon work supported by the National Science Foundation under Grant No. IIS-1218692. We wish to thank Sophia Kohlhaas and Ragine Williams for providing data for the project.

References

Yoav Artzi and Luke Zettlemoyer. 2011. Bootstrapping Semantic Parsers from Conversations. In *Proceedings of the Conference on Empirical Methods in Natural Language Processing (EMNLP)*.

P. F. Brown, S. D. Pietra, V. J. D. Pietra, and R. L. Mercer. 1993. The mathematics of statistical machine translation: Parameter estimation. *Computational Linguistics*, 19(2):263–311.

Razvan Bunescu and Raymond Mooney. 2007. Learning to extract relations from the web using minimal supervision. In *Proceedings of the 45th Annual Meeting of the Association for Computational Linguistics (ACL-07)*.

David L. Chen, Joohyun Kim, and Raymond J. Mooney. 2010. Training a Multilingual Sportscaster: Using Perceptual Context to Learn Language. *Journal of Artificial Intelligence Research*, 37:397–435.

Stephen Clark and James R. Curran. 2007. Wide-coverage efficient statistical parsing with ccg and log-linear models. *Computational Linguistics*, 33(4):493–552.

J. Clarke, D. Goldwasser, M. Chang, and D. Roth. 2010. Driving semantic parsing from the world's response. In *Computational Natural Language Learning (CoNLL)*.

Ruifang Ge and Raymond J. Mooney. 2006. Discriminative Reranking for Semantic Parsing. In *Proceedings of the 21st International Conference on Computational Linguistics and 44th Annual Meeting of the Association for Computational Linguistics (COLING/ACL-06)*.

Ruifang Ge and Raymond J. Mooney. 2009. Learning a Compositional Semantic Parser using an Existing Syntactic Parser. In *Joint Conference of the 47th Annual Meeting of the Association for Computational Linguistics and the 4th International Joint Conference on Natural Language Processing of the Asian Federation of Natural Language Processing (ACL-IJCNLP 2009)*.

D. Goldwasser, R. Reichart, J. Clarke, and D. Roth. 2011. Confidence driven unsupervised semantic parsing. In *Association for Computational Linguistics (ACL)*.

Johannes Hoffart, Fabian M. Suchanek, Klaus Berberich, and Gerhard Weikum. 2013. YAGO2: A Spatially and Temporally Enhanced Knowledge Base from Wikipedia. *Artificial Intelligence*, 194:28–61, January.

Fei Huang, Alexander Yates, Arun Ahuja, and Doug Downey. 2011. Language Models as Representations for Weakly Supervised NLP Tasks. In *Conference on Computational Natural Language Learning (CoNLL)*.

Rohit J. Kate and Raymond J. Mooney. 2006. Using String-Kernels for Learning Semantic Parsers. In *Proceedings of the 21st International Conference on Computational Linguistics and the 44th annual meeting of the ACL*.

Rohit J. Kate and Raymond J. Mooney. 2007. Semi-Supervised Learning for Semantic Parsing using Support Vector Machines. In *Proceedings of the Human Language Technology Conference of the North American Chapter of the Association for Computational Linguistics, Short Papers (NAACL/HLT-2007)*.

Rohit J. Kate, Yuk Wah Wong, and Raymond J. Mooney. 2005. Learning to Transform Natural to Formal Languages. In *Proceedings of the Twentieth National Conference on Artificial Intelligence (AAAI-05)*.

Jayant Krishnamurthy and Tom Mitchell. 2012. Weakly Supervised Training of Semantic Parsers. In *Proceedings of the Conference on Empirical Methods in Natural Language Processing (EMNLP)*.

Tom Kwiatkowski, Luke Zettlemoyer, Sharon Goldwater, and Mark Steedman. 2010. Inducing Probabilistic CCG Grammars from Logical Form with Higher-order Unification. In *Proceedings of the Conference on Empirical Methods in Natural Language Processing (EMNLP)*.

Tom Kwiatkowski, Luke Zettlemoyer, Sharon Goldwater, and Mark Steedman. 2011. Lexical Generalization in CCG Grammar Induction for Semantic Parsing. In *Proceedings of the Conference on Empirical Methods in Natural Language Processing (EMNLP)*.

P. Liang, M. I. Jordan, and D. Klein. 2009. Learning semantic correspondences with less supervision. In *Association for Computational Linguistics and International Joint Conference on Natural Language Processing (ACL-IJCNLP)*.

P. Liang, M. I. Jordan, and D. Klein. 2011. Learning dependency-based compositional semantics. In *Association for Computational Linguistics (ACL)*.

Wei Lu, Hwee Tou Ng, Wee Sun Lee, and Luke S. Zettlemoyer. 2008. A Generative Model for Parsing Natural Language to Meaning Representations. In *Proceedings of The Conference on Empirical Methods in Natural Language Processing (EMNLP)*.

Franz Josef Och and Hermann Ney. 2003. A systematic comparison of various statistical alignment models. *Computational Linguistics*, 29(1):19–51.

C.A. Thompson and R.J. Mooney. 1999. Automatic construction of semantic lexicons for learning natural language interfaces. In *Proc. 16th National Conference on Artificial Intelligence (AAAI-99)*, pages 487–493.

Cynthia A. Thompson and Raymond J. Mooney. 2003. Acquiring Word-Meaning Mappings for Natural Language Interfaces. *Journal of Artificial Intelligence Research (JAIR)*, 18:1–44.

Y. Wilks, D. Fass, C. Guo, J. MacDonald, T. Plate, and B. Slator. 1990. *Providing Machine Tractable Dictionary Tools*. MIT Press.

Yuk Wah Wong and Raymond J. Mooney. 2007. Learning Synchronous Grammars for Semantic Parsing with Lambda Calculus. In *Proceedings of the 45th Annual Meeting of the Association for Computational Linguistics (ACL-2007)*.

Mohamed Yahya, Klaus Berberich, Shady Elbassuoni, Maya Ramanath, Volker Tresp, and Gerhard Weikum. 2012. Natural Language Questions for the Web of Data. In *Proceedings of the Conference on Empirical Methods in Natural Language Processing (EMNLP)*.

John M. Zelle and Raymond J. Mooney. 1996. Learning to Parse Database Queries using Inductive Logic Programming. In *AAAI/IAAI*, pages 1050–1055.

Luke S. Zettlemoyer and Michael Collins. 2005. Learning to Map Sentences to Logical Form: Structured Classification with Probabilistic Categorial Grammars. In *Proceedings of the Twenty First Conference on Uncertainty in Artificial Intelligence (UAI)*.

Luke S. Zettlemoyer and Michael Collins. 2007. Online Learning of Relaxed CCG Grammars for Parsing to Logical Form. In *Proceedings of the Joint Conference on Empirical Methods in Natural Language Processing and Computational Natural Language Learning (EMNLP-CoNLL)*.

Luke S. Zettlemoyer and Michael Collins. 2009. Learning Context-dependent Mappings from Sentences to Logical Form. In *Proceedings of the Joint Conference of the Association for Computational Linguistics and International Joint Conference on Natural Language Processing (ACL-IJCNLP)*.

Author Index

Association for Computational Linguistics
209 N. Eighth Street
Stroudsburg, Pennsylvania 18360

CURRAN ASSOCIATES INC
proceedings
.com